HISTORICAL DICTIONARIES
OF WAR, REVOLUTION, AND CIVIL UNREST
Edited by Jon Woronoff

1. *Afghan Wars, Revolutions, and Insurgencies*, by Ludwig W. Adamec. 1996.
2. *The United States–Mexican War*, by Edward H. Moseley and Paul C. Clark, Jr. 1997.
3. *World War I*, by Ian V. Hogg. 1998.
4. *The United States Navy*, by James M. Morris and Patricia M. Kearns. 1998.
5. *The United States Marine Corps*, by Harry A. Gailey. 1998.
6. *The Wars of the French Revolution*, by Steven T. Ross. 1998.
7. *The American Revolution*, by Terry M. Mays. 1999.
8. *The Spanish-American War*, by Brad K. Berner. 1998.
9. *The Persian Gulf War*, by Clayton R. Newell. 1998.
10. *The Holocaust*, by Jack R. Fischel. 1999.
11. *The United States Air Force and Its Antecedents*, by Michael Robert Terry. 1999.
12. *Civil Wars in Africa*, by Guy Arnold. 1999.
13. *World War II: The War Against Japan*, by Anne Sharp Wells. 1999.
14. *British and Irish Civil Wars*, by Martyn Bennett. 2000.
15. *The Cold War*, by Joseph Smith and Simon Davis. 2000.
16. *Ancient Greek Warfare*, by Iain Spence. 2002.
17. *The Vietnam War*, by Edwin E. Moïse. 2001.
18. *The Civil War*, by Terry L. Jones. 2002.
19. *The Crimean War*, by Guy Arnold. 2002.
20. *The United States Army, A Historical Dictionary*, by Clayton R. Newell. 2002.
21. *Terrorism, Second Edition*, by Sean K. Anderson and Stephen Sloan. 2002.

HISTORICAL DICTIONARIES OF RELIGIONS,
PHILOSOPHIES, AND MOVEMENTS
Edited by Jon Woronoff

31. *Zionism,* by Rafael Medoff and Chaim I. Waxman, 2000
32. *Mormonism,* 2nd ed., by Davis Bitton, 2000
33. *Kierkegaard's Philosophy,* by Julia Watkin, 2001
34. *Hegelian Philosophy,* by John W. Burbidge, 2001
35. *Lutheranism,* by Günther Gassmann in cooperation with Duane H. Larson and Mark W. Oldenburg, 2001
36. *Holiness Movement,* by William Kostlevy, 2001
37. *Islam,* by Ludwig W. Adamec, 2001
38. *Shinto,* by Stuart D. B. Picken, 2001
39. *Olympic Movement,* 2nd ed., by Ian Buchanan and Bill Mallon, 2001
40. *Slavery and Abolition,* by Martin Klein, 2001
41. *Terrorism,* 2nd ed., by Sean K. Anderson and Stephen Sloan, 2002
42. *New Religious Movements,* by George D. Chryssides, 2001

Historical Dictionary of Terrorism

Second Edition

Sean K. Anderson
Stephen Sloan

Historical Dictionaries of Religions, Philosophies, and Movements, No. 41

Historical Dictionaries of War, Revolution, and Civil Unrest, No. 21

The Scarecrow Press, Inc.
Lanham, Maryland, and London
2002

SCARECROW PRESS, INC.

Published in the United States of America
by Scarecrow Press, Inc.
4720 Boston Way, Lanham, Maryland 20706
www.scarecrowpress.com

4 Pleydell Gardens, Folkestone
Kent CT20 2DN, England

Copyright © 2002 by Sean K. Anderson and Stephen Sloan
First edition (1995) published by The Scarecrow Press, Inc.

British Library Cataloguing-in-Publication Information Available

Library of Congress Cataloging-in-Publication Data

Anderson, Sean, 1952–
    Historical dictionary of terrorism / Sean K. Anderson, Stephen Sloan.—2nd ed.
        p. cm. — (Historical dictionaries of religions, philosophies, and movements ; no.
    41 and historical dictionaries of war, revolution, and civil unrest ; no. 21)
    Includes bibliographical references.
    ISBN 0-8108-4101-0 (alk. paper)
      1. Terrorism—History—Dictionaries. 2. Terrorists—History—Dictionaries. I.
    Sloan, Stephen, 1936–. II. Title. III. Series.

HV6431 .A537 2002   2001049656
909—dc21

This book is dedicated to the memory of Lisa Evans, our research assistant in the preparation of the first edition of this work, whose bright and promising life was cut short all too soon.

Contents

Editor's Foreword

Terrorism has consistently dogged this supposedly modern and enlightened age. It has merely adopted new shapes and forms in keeping with the times. The causes have also evolved over the years, as old problems are solved and new ones created. Moreover, it has gone high tech, like everything else. Thus, as this book convincingly shows, terrorism will remain with us in the future even if, with the end of the Cold War, it again mutates and becomes more sophisticated and potentially more dangerous. So it is essential to get a better grasp of what the phenomenon consists, by whom it is practiced . . . and against whom.

That is not an easy task, not when terrorism is so widespread and diversified. Nor is it even simple to explain just what acts or groups are terrorist. Still, this new, updated, and expanded edition certainly makes the situation much clearer by tracing an amazing number of acts and groups in literally hundreds of informative entries. This edition also has many new entries on basic concepts and theory. The chronology inserts terrorism into its historical context. Of no less significance is an introduction that helps us understand the whys and wherefores. For all these reasons as well as its comprehensive and well-structured bibliography, this volume is bound to become a standard reference work.

This second edition of the *Historical Dictionary of Terrorism* was written by Sean Kendall Anderson and Stephen Sloan, each of whom specializes in different aspects of a worldwide phenomenon. Dr. Sloan had his first encounter in Indonesia in 1965-1966. During his stay an abortive coup d'état killed more than 100,000 people and was examined in his first book, *A Study in Political Violence: The Indonesian Experience*. While teaching political science at the University of Oklahoma, a post he has held since 1966, Dr. Sloan pioneered simulations of terrorist incidents and formulated counterterrorist doctrine. He worked for the public and private sectors and wrote *Simulating Terrorism* and coauthored *Responding to the Terrorist Threat, Low Intensity Conflict*, and *Corporate Aviation Security*. Sean Anderson has focused on the Middle East since returning from a stint as chief editor of the International Department of the Pars News Agency in the early 1980s. He is now associate professor of political science at Idaho State

University and has lectured and written widely on terrorism and Islamic fundamentalism. In addition to their research activities these specialists have also collaborated with federal, state, and local governments in dealing with the more practical and immediate challenges of terrorism preparedness planning. Once again in revising this work both these specialists have joined forces to research manifestations of terrorism worldwide and provide the theoretical background to understand it.

Jon Woronoff
Series Editor

Acknowledgments

The authors wish to thank those who have made the revision of this work possible. We wish to recognize the efforts of our research associates, Bobette Aken, who researched and cataloged relevant U.S. government documents and publications, and Allen F. Ross and Mike Gaylon, who researched the ever-growing on-line resources and documents. We also owe much to Justin T. Gollob for locating and cataloging materials in the general mass media. Others who contributed information, expertise, and material assistance include Ralph D. Berenger; Jessica Bremer; Judy Brinser; Elise Browning; Chad Christensen; Ambassador Edwin G. Corr; Robert C. Fritz; John George of the University of Central Oklahoma, and his associate Laird Wilcox; Donald Shane Hanson; Craig Hawkins; Greg Hoch; Geri Larsen; Leonie Morandi; Richard McNeill; Martin Murillo; John Parachini; Neal A. Pollard, President of the Terrorism Research Center; Teresa Platt; Carlos Eduardo Basso Prieto, the police editor of the newspaper *Crónica* published in Concepción, Chile; and Kevin Thompson.

We also wish to thank the librarians of Idaho State University, Nancy Anthony, Joan Juskie, and John Larry Murdock, for their services. Furthermore we wish to thank Cheryl L. Hardy for her proofreading of the text, and James Bissett, Drew Ceperley, and Randy Stamm of the Instructional Technology Resource Center at Idaho State University for their technical assistance in producing the camera-ready text of this work. Finally, we wish to thank our colleagues David Gray Adler, Craig W. Nickisch, Ralph Maughn, Corey Schou, and Delane Kritsky for their scholarly assistance.

Acronyms and Abbreviations

Note: All abbreviations used in this dictionary are included in this list, including abbreviations of names of organizations and agencies that are not terrorist groups.

AAA	Alianza Apostólica Anti-Communista, Anti-Communist Apostolic Alliance (Spanish group)
AAA	Argentine Anti-Communist Alliance
ABC	Atomic, biological, and chemical weapons
AD	Action Directe, Direct Action
ADL	Anti-Defamation League of B'nai B'rith
ADC	Arab American Anti-Discrimination Committee
AIS	Armée Islamique du Salut, Islamic Salvation Army
AISSF	All-India Sikh Students' Federation
ALA	Armenian Liberation Army
ALF	Animal Liberation Front
ALF	Arab Liberation Front (group within PLO)
AN	Avanguardia Nazionale, National Vanguard
ANAPO	National Popular Alliance
ANO	Abu Nidal Organization
ANS	Aktiongemeinschaft Nationaler Sozialisten, Action-Front of National Socialists
AOG	Army of God
APRA	American Popular Revolutionary Alliance
ARA	Armenian Revolutionary Army
ARDE	Alianza Revolucionaria Democrática, Nicaraguan Democratic Alliance
ARENA	Alianza Republicana Nacional, Republican National Alliance
ARM	Animal Rights Militia
ASALA	Armenian Secret Army for the Liberation of Armenia
ASALA-M	ASALA-Militant, extremist wing of ASALA
ASALA-RM	ASALA-Revolutionary Movement, moderate wing of ASALA

ATF	or BATF, (Bureau of) Alcohol, Tobacco, and Firearms, agency within the Department of the U.S. Treasury
AUC	Autodefensas Unidas de Colombia, Self-Defense Units of Colombia, also known as the Peasant Self-Defense Groups of Córdoba and Urabá
AUM	Aum Shinrikyo sect
AVC	Alfaro Vive Carajo Organization
AWB	Afrikaner Weerstandsbeweging, Afrikaaner Resistance Movement
AYM	Aryan Youth Movement, youth wing of WAR
BATF	Bureau of Alcohol, Tobacco, and Firearms
BKA	German Federal Office of Criminal Investigations
BLA	Black Liberation Army
BR	Brigate Rosse, Red Brigades
BSO	Black September Organization
CALN	Comandos Armados de Liberación Nacional, Armed Commandos for National Liberation
CANF	Cuban American National Foundation
CCC	Communist Combatant Cells
CERF	Frente Clara Elizabeth Ramírez, Clara Elizabeth Ramirez Front
CIA	Central Intelligence Agency
CNI	La Central Nacional de Informaciones, Chilean National Intelligence Center
CNN	Cable Network News
CNPZ	Comando Nestor Paz Zamora, Nestor Paz Zamora Commando
CON	Coordinatora Opositora Nicaragüense, Nicaraguan Opposition Coordinator
CONADEP	Comisión Nacional sobre la Desaparición de Personas, Argentine National Commission on Disappearances
CONPAZ	Coalition of Non-governmental Organizations for Peace
COVEMA	Comando de Vengadores de Mártires, Martyrs Avenging Command
C-PDL	Christian-Patriots Defense League
CPP-ML	Communist Party of the Philippines, Marxist-Leninist
CSA	The Covenant, the Sword, and the Arm of the Lord
CSAMPP	Committee for Solidarity with Arab and Mideast Political Prisoners

DEA	Drug Enforcement Agency
DFLP	Democratic Front for the Liberation of Palestine (group within PLO)
DGSE	General Directorate for State Security of the Interior Ministry (Nicaragua)
DHKP/C	Revolutionary People's Liberation Party/Front, formerly known as Dev Sol
DRFLA	Democratic Revolutionary Front for the Liberation of Arabistan
EGP	Ejército Guerrillero de los Pobres, Guerrilla Army of the Poor
ELA	Epanastatikos Laikos Agonas, Revolutionary Popular Struggle
ELF	Earth Liberation Front
ELN	Ejército de Liberación Nacional, National Liberation Army, name of a Colombian and a Bolivian group
EMETIC	Evan Mecham Eco-Terrorist International Conspiracy
EOKA	Ethniki Organosis Kyprion Agoniston, National Organization of Cypriot Fighters
EOKA-B	Ethniki Organosis Kyprion Agoniston-Beta, National Organization of Cypriot Fighters-B
EPA	Emergency Provisions Act
EPL	Ejército Popular de Liberación, Popular Liberation Army
EPR	Ejército Popular Revolucionario, Popular Revolutionary Army
ERCA	Ejército Rojo Catalán de Liberación, Red Army for the Liberation of Catalonia
ERP	Ejército Revolucionario del Pueblo, People's Revolutionary Army (member of FMLN; also name of Argentine group)
ESA	Ejército Secreto Anticommunista, Anti-Communist Secret Army
ETA	Euzkadi Ta Askatasuna, Basque Fatherland and Liberty
ETA-M	Euzkadi Ta Askatasuna-Militar, Basque Fatherland and Liberty—militant branch
ETA-PM	Euzkadi Ta Askatasuna-Politico-Militar, Basque Fatherland and Liberty—moderate branch

EZLN	Ejército de Liberación Nacional, Zapatista Army of National Liberation
FAL	Fuerzas Armadas de Liberación, Armed Forces of Liberation (member of FMLN)
FALN	Fuerzas Armadas de Liberación Nacional, Armed Forces of National Liberation
FANE	Fédération d'Action Nationale Européenne, Federation for National European Action
FAR	Fuerzas Armadas Rebeldes, Rebel Armed Forces (Guatemala)
FAR	Fuerzas Armadas Revolucionarias, Revolutionary Armed Forces (Argentina)
FARC	Fuerzas Armadas Revolucionarias de Colombia, Revolutionary Armed Forces of Colombia
FARL	Factions Armées Révolutionnaires Libanaises, Lebanese Armed Revolutionary Factions
FARN	Fuerzas Armadas de la Resistencia Nacional, Armed Forces of National Resistance (member of FMLN)
FARN	Fuerzas Armadas Revolucionarias Nicaragüenses, Nicaraguan Revolutionary Armed Forces (Contra group)
FBI	Federal Bureau of Investigation
FDN	Fuerza Democrática Nicaragüense, Nicaraguan Democratic Force
FDR	Democratic Revolutionary Front (political front of FMLN)
FIS	Front Islamique de Salut, Islamic Salvation Front
FLEC-FAC	Frente para a Libertação de Enclave de Cabinda—Forcas Armadas de Libertação, Cabinda Liberation Front—Cabinda Liberation Forces
FLN	Fuerzas de Liberación National, former name of Zapatista Army of National Liberation
FLN	Front de Libération Nationale, National Liberation Front of Algeria
FLNC	Frente de Liberación Nacional Cubana, Cuban National Liberation Front
FLNKS	*Front de Libération Nationale Kanake Socialiste,* Kanak Socialist National Liberation Front
FLQ	Front de Libération du Québec, Quebec Liberation Front
FMLN	Frente Farabundo Martí para la Liberación Nacional, Farabundo Martí National Liberation Front, or, Farabundo

	Martí Liberation Front
FNE	Faisceaux Nationalistes Européens, European National Fascists
FNLC	Front de Libération Nationale de la Corse, National Front for the Liberation of Corsica
FP-25	Forças Populares do 25 Abril, Popular Forces of 25 April
FPL	Fuerzas Populares de Liberación, People's Liberation Forces (member of FMLN)
FPM	Frente Patriótico Morazaniste, Morazanist Patriotic Front
FPMR	Frente Patriótico Manuel Rodríguez, Manuel Rodriguez Patriotic Front
FPMR-D	Frente Patriótico Manuel Rodríguez Disidentes, Manuel Rodriguez Patriotic Front—Dissident Faction
FRANCIA	Front d'Action Nouvelle Contre l'Indépendence et l'Autonomie, New Action Front Against Independence and Autonomy
FRAPH	Front Révolutionnaire pour l'Avancement et le Progrès Haitien, Revolutionary Front for the Advancement and Progress of Haiti
FRC	Fatah Revolutionary Council (Abu Nidal organization)
FRELIMO	Frente de Libertação de Moçambique, Mozambican Liberation Front
FRPL	Fuerzas Revolutionarias y Populares Lautaro, Lautaro Rebel Forces, also known as Lautaro Youth Movement
FRP-LZ	Fuerzas Revolucionarias Populares Lorenzo Zelaya, Lorenzo Zelaya Popular Revolutionary Forces
FSLN	Frente Sandinista de Liberación Nacional, Sandinista National Liberation Front
FULK	Front Uni de Libération Kanak, Kanak United Liberation Front
GAL	Grupos Antiterroristas de Liberación, Antiterrorist Liberation Groups
GBR	Grupo Bandera Roja, Red Flag Group
GIA	Groupe Islamique Armé, Armed Islamic Group
GRAPO	Grupo de Resistencia Antifascista, Primero de Octubre, October First Antifascist Resistance Group
GSG-9	Grenzschutzgruppe 9, Border Protection Group No. 9, West German antiterrorist unit of Border Patrol
HCSA	Hate Crimes Statistics Act of 1990

HRT	Hostage Rescue Team
IDF	Israeli Defense Forces
IE	Invisible Empire (Ku Klux Klan group)
IEEPA	International Emergency Economic Powers Act
IG	Islamic Group, Gama'a al Islamiya
ILO	Islamic Liberation Organization
IMRO	Inner Macedonian Revolutionary Organization
INLA	Irish National Liberation Army
IRA	Irish Republican Army
IRGC	Islamic Revolutionary Guards Corps, Sipah-i Pasdaran-i Inqilab-i Islami
IRS	Internal Revenue Service
JCAG	Justice Commandos of the Armenian Genocide
JDL	Jewish Defense League
JRA	Japanese Red Army
KDP	Kurdistan Democratic Party
KEMA	(alternate spelling GEMA) Kikuyu, Embu and Meru Association
KISAN	Kus Indian Sut Asla Nicaragua Ra, United Indigenous Peoples of Eastern Nicaragua
KKK	Ku Klux Klan
KKKK	Knights of the Ku Klux Klan (major Klan group)
KLA	Kosovo Liberation Army
LEHI	Lohamei Herut Israel, Fighters for the Freedom of Israel
LIC	Low Intensity Conflict
LPK	Levizja Poppulore e Kosoves, Popular Movement for Kosovo
LRA	The Lord's Resistance Army
LTTE	Liberation Tigers of Tamil Eelam
M-19	Movimiento 19 de Abril, April 19th Movement
M19CO	May 19th Communist Organization, also called May 19th Communist Coalition
MAGO	Muslims Against Global Oppression
MAIL	Muslims Against Illegitimate Leaders
MAPU/L	Movimiento de Acción Unitaria Popular-Lautaro, Popular Movement of United Action-Lautaro, also known as the Lautaro Youth Movement
MAS	Muerte a Secuestradores, "Death to Kidnappers" Colombian drug smugglers' anti-leftist death squad

May 1	Revolutionary Organization of May 1
May 15	Arab Organization of May 15
MBR-200	Movimiento Revolucionaria Bolivariano 200, Revolutionary Bolivarian Movement
MILF	Moro Islamic Liberation Front
MILPAS	Milicias Populares Anti-Somocistas, Popular Anti-Somocista Militia, later known as Milicias Populares Anti-Sandinistas, Popular Anti-Sandinista Militia
MIR	*Movimiento de la Izquierda Revolucionario*, Revolutionary Movement of the Left
MIR	Mujahideen-e Inqilab-e Islami, Mujahideen of the Islamic Revolution
MJL	Movimiento Juvenil Lautaro, Lautaro Youth Movement
MK	Umkhonto we Sizwe, "Spear of the Nation," military wing of African National Congress
MKO	Saziman-e Mujahideen-i Khalq-e Iran Organization, People's Mujahideen Organization of Iran
MLAPU	Marxist-Leninist Armed Propaganda Unit
MLB	Movement for the Liberation of Bahrain
MLF	Moro Liberation Front, or Moro National Liberation Front
MLN	Movimiento de Liberación Nacional, also known as the Tupamaros
MNR	Mozambique National Resistance, until 1982 the name of the current RENAMO
MPL	Cinchoneros Popular Liberation Movement
MRTA	Movimiento Revolucionario Túpac Amaru, Túpac Amaru Revolutionary Movement
MVR	Movimiento V República, Fifth Republic Movement
NAFF	New Afrikan Freedom Fighters
NAP	National Action Party
NAR	Nuclei Armati Rivoluzionari, Armed Revolutionary Nucleus
NATO	North Atlantic Treaty Organization
NBC	Nuclear, biological, and chemical weapons
NDM	Nicaraguan Democratic Movement
NLETS	National Law Enforcement Telecommunications System
NORAID	Irish Northern Aid Committee
NOV17	Epanastatiki Organosi 17 Noemvri, Revolutionary Organization of 17 November

NPA	New People's Army
NSF	National Salvation Front
NSLF	National Socialist Liberation Front
NSWPP	National Socialist White People's Party
NWLF	New World Liberation Front
OAAS	Organization for the Armed Arab Struggle
OAS	Organisation de l'Armée Secrète, Secret Army Organization
OIRA	Official Irish Republican Army
OOTW	Operations Other Than War, another term for Low Intensity Conflict
OPM/SANG	Office of the Program Manager/Saudi Arabian National Guard
ORDEN	Organización Democrática Nacional, National Democratic Organization
ORPA	Organización Revolucionaria del Pueblo en Armas, Revolutionary Organization of the People in Arms
OVPR	Organization of Volunteers for the Puerto Rican Revolution
PA	Palestinian Authority
PAGAD	People Against Gangsterism and Drugs
PALIKA	Parti de Libération Kanak, Kanak Liberation Party
PCES	Communist Party of El Salvador
PFLA	Popular Front for the Liberation of Ahwaz
PFLP	Popular Front for the Liberation of Palestine (group within PLO)
PFLP-GC	PFLP—General Command
PFLP-SC	PFLP—Special Command
PFLP-SOG	PFLP—Special Operations Group
PIJ	Islamic Jihad of Palestine
PIR-1	People's Information Relay No. 1
PIRA	Provisional Irish Republican Army
PKK	Partiya Karkaran Kurdistan, Kurdistan Workers' Party
PL	Prima Linea, Front Line group
PLA	Palestine Liberation Army
PLF	Palestine Liberation Front (group within PLO)
PLO	Palestine Liberation Organization
PNC	Palestine National Council
PNV	Basque Nationalist Party

PPC	Communist Party of Colombia
PPM	Patriotic People's Movement
PROCUP	Partido Revolucionario Obrero Campesino Unión del Pueblo, Workers and Peasants Revolutionary Party-People's Union, same as the Mexican Popular Revolutionary Army (EPR)
PRTC	Partido Revolucionario de los Trabajadores Centroamericanos, Revolutionary Party of Central American Workers (member of FMLN)
PSF	Popular Struggle Front (group within PLO)
RAF	Rote Armee Fraktion, Red Army Faction
RATF	Revolutionary Armed Task Force
RENAMO	Resistência Nacional Moçambicana, Mozambique National Resistance
RFF	Frente Ricardo Franco, Ricardo Franco Front
RGR	Red Guerrilla Resistance
RICO	Racketeering-Influenced Corrupt Organizations Act
RUF	Revolutionary United Front
RZ	Revolutionäre Zellen, Revolutionary Cells, also used for Rote Zora, Red Zora, women's group within Revolutionary Cells
SAIRI	Supreme Assembly for the Islamic Revolution in Iraq
SAS	Special Air Service, elite British antiterrorist and special operations units
SASOL	South African Coal, Gas and Oil Conversion
SDS	Students for a Democratic Society
SGPC	Shiromani Gurdwara Parbandhak Committee
SIM	"Imperialist State of Multinationals" (Red Brigade idiom for modern Italian state)
SL	Sendero Luminoso, Shining Path, Peruvian Maoist group
SLA	Symbionese Liberation Army
SPLA	Sudanese People's Liberation Army
SSC	Small Scale Contingencies, another term for Low Intensity Conflict
SSNP	Syrian Social Nationalist Party
SWAT	Special Weapons and Tactics team
TL	Terra Lliure, Free Land, Catalonian separatist group
TPLA	Turkish People's Liberation Army
TPLF	Turkish People's Liberation Front

TULF	Tamil United Liberation Front
UDA	Ulster Defence Association
UFF	Ulster Freedom Fighters
UFF	United Freedom Front
UGB	Unión de Guerreros Blancos or Unión Guerrera Blanca, White Warriors' Union
UKA	United Klans of America
UNITA	União Nacional para Independéncia Total de Angola, National Union for the Total Independence of Angola
UNL	al Qiyada al Wataniyya al Muwahhada, Unified National Leadership
UNO	Unidad Nicaragüense Opositora, Unified Nicaraguan Opposition
UP	Union Patriotico, Patriotic Union (FARC front)
URNG	Unidad Revolucionaria Nacional Guatemalteca, Guatemalan National Revolutionary Union
USIS	United States Information Service (overseas offices of United States Information Agency of U.S. Department of State)
UVF	Ulster Volunteer Force
WAR	White Aryan Resistance
WMD	Weapons of Mass Destruction
WPA	White Patriot Army
YAMATA	Yapti Tasba Masraka Aslika Takanda, Miskito Indian acronym for "United Nations of Yapti Tasba (Sacred Motherland)"
ZOG	"Zionist Occupation Government" (Neo-Nazi idiom for United States government)

Chronology

A.D. 66-70   Jewish nationalist Zealot (Sicarii) movement creates mass insurrection in Roman province of Judea, leading to Roman destruction of Jerusalem and Second Temple and mass suicide of Zealots besieged at Masada fortress.

A.D. 1090-1256   The Isma'ili Fedayeen cult of "assassins" conducts a terror campaign against the religious and political establishment of the Abbasid Islamic empire until the cult is exterminated by the Mongol invaders.

1793   May: French revolutionary Committee of Public Safety undertakes purge of real and suspected enemies of the revolution, leading to 300,000 arbitrary arrests and 17,000 executions.

1794   July: This "Great Terror" lasts until Robespierre, its original instigator, is executed himself.

1865   December 24: Ku Klux Klan is founded in Pulaski, Tennessee, by Confederate Civil War veterans.

1869:   *Catechism of the Revolutionist* written by Sergey Nechayev provides an idealized model of the political terrorist that inspires later terrorist theoreticians and practitioners.

1878 January-1881 March: Narodnaya Volya (People's Will) Russian terrorists conduct bombing campaign against Tsarist government, culminating in assassination of Tsar Alexander II on sixth attempt.

1886   May 4: In Haymarket Square, Chicago, while 180 police confronted 1,300 workers protesting for an eight-hour work day, a bomb exploded, killing eight and wounding many others. Police opened fire on the protestors triggering a riot in which at least seven were killed and about a hundred others injured.

1901 September-1902 March: An American, Ellen M. Stone, is kidnapped by the Inner Macedonian Revolutionary Organization and held for ransom of $66,000. After the U.S. government refused to pay this ransom, Stone's sponsoring organization raised and paid the required sum.

1910   October 1: During labor strike the office building of the anti-Union Los Angeles Times was dynamited and erupted into flames due to severed gas mains. At least 20 perished and another 20 were disabled due to the explosion and resulting fire.

1914   June 28: Austrian Archduke Francis Ferdinand is assassinated by Serbian terrorists in Sarajevo, Bosnia-Herzegovina. Event sets World War I in motion.

1916   July 22: A bomb set off during San Francisco's Preparedness Day kills 10 and wounds 40. Radical antiwar labor activists were blamed for the bombing due to prior antiparade pamphlet warning of "direct action."

1920   September 16: TNT bomb in parked horse-drawn wagon explodes on Wall Street across from Morgan House, killing 35 and injuring hundreds. Pro-Bolshevik or anarchist terrorists were believed responsible but were never apprehended.

1931   February 21-23: First recorded hijacking of an airplane: Rebel soldiers in Peru force two American pilots to fly them about and to drop propaganda leaflets over Lima.

1938   November 9-10: German Nazis undertake Kristallnacht terror against German Jews, smashing shop windows of Jewish-owned businesses and burning synagogues. Marks beginning of genocidal policy against Jews as part of Nazi state terror lasting until collapse of Third Reich in May 1945.

1939 January-1940 February: Irish Republican Army carries out first major bombing campaign within England proper with over 50 bombings of public places within a 13-month period.

1944   November 6: Jewish terror group Lehi assassinates Lord Moyne, the British minister for Middle Eastern affairs, in Cairo.

1946   March 11: The Fedayan-i Islam, an Iranian Islamic fundamentalist group, initiates 10-year-long assassination campaign against westernized Iranian intellectuals and political leaders by murdering Ahmad Kasravi, prominent anti-Shi'ite secularist intellectual and historian.

1946   July 22: Jewish terror group Irgun bombs British administrative headquarters located in King David Hotel, Jerusalem, killing 91 people.

1948   January 30: Mohandas K. Gandhi is killed by Hindu extremist.

1948   April 9: Jewish terror groups Irgun and Lehi massacre Arab villagers of Deir Yassin located on Jerusalem-Tel Aviv road. News of massacre creates panic among other Palestinians, who flee former mandatory Palestine at onset of first Arab-Israeli war.

1950   November 1: Puerto Rican nationalists plotting to assassinate U.S. President Harry Truman exchange gunfire with security guards at Blair House, Washington, D.C.

1952   September: Mau Mau insurgency erupts in Kenya, lasting until October 1956.

1954   March 1: Four Puerto Rican nationalists open fire on House of Representatives from visitors' gallery, wounding five representatives. All four captured by security guards.

1955   August 20: Algerian National Liberation Front (FLN) terrorists undertake wholesale slaughter of 37 European men, women, and children in Philippeville massacre.

1960   March 20: South African police massacre 69 black civil rights demonstrators in Sharpeville incident, which moves African National Congress to abandon its policy of nonviolence.

1963   September 15: The all-black Sixteenth Street Baptist Church of Birmingham, Alabama, is bombed by the United Klans of America, killing four young girls. Birmingham experienced over 50 antiblack bombings between 1947 and 1965 believed to have been the work of the United Klans of America.

1967   October 10: Ernesto Che Guevara, guerrilla leader and author of *Guerrilla Warfare*, is captured and executed by U.S.-trained Bolivian anti-insurgency forces.

1968   July 22: Popular Front for the Liberation of Palestine (PFLP) begins hijacking campaign against El Al airliners with hijacking of El Al flight from Rome to Tel Aviv, diverting it to Algeria.

1968   August 28: Guatemalan Rebel Armed Forces gunmen assassinate U.S. Ambassador John Gordon Mein in Guatemala City, the first assassination of a U.S. ambassador in the line of duty.

1969   November 4: Carlos Marighella, terrorist and author of *Manual of the Urban Guerrilla*, written in June 1969, is killed in gunfight with Brazilian police in São Paulo.

1969   December 12: The Avanguardia Nazionale, an Italian neo-Fascist group, bombs Agricultural Bank of Milan, killing 16 and wounding 90 others.

1970   July 31: Uruguayan Tupamaros kidnap and murder Daniel A. Mitrione, U.S. Agency for International Development public safety adviser.

1970   September 6-9: PFLP terrorists hijack five commercial airliners to Dawson's Field, outside Amman, Jordan, and hold 400 hostages. Three-week crisis provokes Jordanian government to expel Palestinian guerrilla groups in an armed confrontation, an event recalled by Palestinians as "Black September."

1970   October 5: Quebec Liberation Front (FLQ) terrorists kidnap James Cross, British trade commissioner to Quebec.

1970   October 10: FLQ members kidnap and murder Pierre LaPorte, Quebec Minister of Labour. Canadian government invokes War Measures Act, suspending civil liberties, in order to crack down on FLQ.

1971   March 1: U.S. Senate Office Building is bombed by Weather Underground.

1971   November 28: Jordanian Prime Minister Wasfi al Tall is assassinated by Black September assassins while in Cairo.

1972   January 30: British troops open fire on Catholic civil rights demonstrators in Londonderry, Northern Ireland, killing 13. Incident, known as "Bloody Sunday," marks renewal of IRA and sectarian violence in Northern Ireland.

1972   May 30: Three Japanese Red Army members, acting on behalf of PFLP, open fire on travelers at Israel's Lod Airport, killing 25 and wounding 76.

1972   July 21: Provisional Irish Republican Army (PIRA) conducts over 20 bombings in Belfast, killing 11 and wounding over 100, on "Bloody Friday."

1972   September 5-6: Eight Black September terrorists seize Israeli team at Munich summer Olympics after killing two team members. Eventually all hostages are murdered and all but three terrorists killed when Bavarian police open fire on terrorists moving the hostages.

1973   March 1: Eight Black September members seize Saudi Arabian embassy in Khartoum, Sudan, and murder U.S. ambassador, his chargé d'affaires, and a Belgian diplomat.

1973   March 29: Irish navy seizes cargo ship *Claudia* filled with Libyan-supplied arms and explosives being smuggled to Northern Ireland by four IRA members.

1973   September 28: Two Sa'iqa terrorists seize five Jewish hostages on Chopin Express train used to transport Soviet Jews emigrating to Israel via Austria, forcing Austria to close transit facilities for émigré Jews.

1973   December 20: Basque Fatherland and Liberty members assassinate Spanish Prime Minister Luís Carrero Blanco by exploding mined road as his automobile passes over charges.

1973   December 31: Venezuelan terrorist "Carlos" attempted assassination of Teddy Seiff, Jewish owner of British Marks and Spencer department store chain, but failed when his gun jammed.

1974   February 5: Symbionese Liberation Army abducts Patricia Hearst.

1974   April 11: PFLP terrorists attack Israeli town, Qiryat Shemona, killing 18 and wounding 16.

1974   April 13: New Peoples Army murders three U.S. Navy personnel outside Subic Bay Naval Base in Philippines.

1974   May 15: Democratic Front for the Liberation of Palestine gunmen seize school together with over 100 students and teachers as hostages in Israeli town, Ma'alot. Gunmen kill 27 students as Israeli troops try to storm building.

1974   May 17: Core group of Symbionese Liberation Army is killed in shoot-out with Los Angeles police.

1974   August 19: Cypriot right-wing nationalist EOKA-Beta gunmen stage riot at U.S. embassy in Nicosia and murder U.S. Ambassador Rodger P. Davies in revenge for perceptions of U.S. support for Turkey.

1974   September 13: Three Japanese Red Army members seize French embassy in The Hague in order to free comrade from prison. All four allowed to leave for Syria.

1974   October 6: Puerto Rican nationalist group FALN initiates mainland U.S. bombing campaign striking five New York City banks.

1974   November 9: Red Army Faction (Baader-Meinhof Gang) murders head of West German Supreme Court, Günter von Drenkmann, at his Bonn home.

1974   November 21: PIRA bombs two Birmingham pubs, killing 21 people and wounding close to 200 others.

1975   January 24: FALN bombs Fraunces Tavern in Wall Street district during lunch hour, killing four and wounding another 60.

1975   January 29: Weather Underground bombs U.S. State Department main office in Washington, D.C., causing extensive damages.

1975   February 27: June Second anarchistic leftists kidnap West German Christian Democrat leader, Peter Lorenz, who is released in exchange for five Red Army Faction prisoners.

1975   August 4: Ten Japanese Red Army (JRA) gunmen seize U.S. Consulate in Kuala Lumpur with 52 hostages, who are released in exchange for freedom of seven imprisoned JRA members in Japan.

1975   December 21-23: Venezuelan terrorist "Carlos," leading five terrorists, captures 11 oil ministers meeting at the OPEC Secretariat in Vienna, along with several other hostages, who are released in exchange for an as yet undisclosed ransom.

1975   December 23: November 17 leftists murder Athens CIA station chief Richard Welch.

1976   June 27-July 1: Hijacking of Air France Flight 139, from Tel Aviv to Paris, to Entebbe, Uganda, by PFLP and Red Army Faction members with the support of Ugandan president Idi Amin. Israeli rescue operation was carried off with great success, although four hostages lost their lives as did the Israeli commander of the rescue mission.

1976   September 10: Six Croatian nationalists hijack a TWA 727 New York-to-Chicago flight, ultimately to Paris. The hijackers demand publication of a manifesto for the release of the passengers.

1976   September 21: Former Foreign Minister Orlando Letelier of Allende government of Chile is assassinated by agents of Chilean secret police in Washington, D.C.

1977   March 9: Washington, D.C., Islamic Center and B'nai B'rith headquarters, together with 134 hostages, are seized by Muslim sectarians motivated by intra-sectarian grievances. Hostagetakers surrender after two days.

1977   May 23: South Moluccan terrorists seize passenger train near Assen, the Netherlands, and a primary school in a coordinated action. As situation with hostages on train deteriorated markedly Dutch Marines stormed both the train and the school. While the Marine units storming the train killed all six terrorists there those units that stomred the school managed to capture alive the four terrorists there.

1977   September 5: Red Army Faction (RAF) kidnaps West German businessman Hanns-Martin Schleyer, holding him hostage against release of imprisoned RAF comrades. On 18 October 1977 Schleyer is murdered.

1977   October 13-18: PFLP members hijack Lufthansa plane to Mogadishu, Somalia, demanding release of Red Army Faction members from West German jails. After pilot is murdered, West German antiterrorist commandos storm plane on October 17, killing three of four terrorists and freeing hostages. On learning of the hijackers' failure the RAF prisoners in Germany commit suicide and RAF kidnappers murder Hanns-Martin Schleyer in reprisal.

1978   March 16: Italian Red Brigades kidnap former Italian Premier Aldo Moro for release of imprisoned comrades. Moro is murdered and his body found on 9 May 1978.

1978   25 May 25: "Unabomber" Theodore J. Kaczynski begins a 17-year mail-bombing campaign directed at academics and businessmen resulting in 3 deaths and 23 maimings until his arrest on 3 April 1996 following his final bombing on 24 April 1995.

1979   August 27: IRA bombs yacht of Lord Louis Mountbatten, killing him and two others and wounding four.

1979   November 4: Iranian university students storm U.S. embassy in Tehran, with apparent blessing of Ayatollah Khomeini. They hold 53 American hostages for 444 days, resulting in severance of diplomatic relations between Iran and the United States but also ascendance of Islamic fundamentalist radicals within Iran's revolutionary regime.

1979   November 20: On first day of the year 1,400 of Hegira (Islamic) era, Sunni Muslim fundamentalists seize Masjid al Haram, Islam's holiest shrine, in Mecca, which is regained by Saudi Arabian national guards only after fierce fighting and bloodshed. Rumors of alleged U.S. involvement in the desecration of the shrine lead to riots in Pakistan in which U.S. embassy is burned and an embassy guard killed.

1980   March 24: Archbishop of El Salvador and critic of Salvadoran government, Oscar Romero y Galdames, is assassinated while saying Mass, presumably by a right-wing death squad.

1980   July 22: David Bellfield, an American follower of the Ayatollah Khomeini, murders Ali Akbar Tabataba'i, an Iranian anti-Khomeini activist, at the latter's home in a suburb of Washington, D.C.

1980   December 4: Four American church workers found murdered outside San Salvador, believed to be victims of right-wing death squads. Incident creates backlash against Salvadoran regime among U.S. public.

1981   May 13: Turkish gunman wounds Pope John Paul II in assassination attempt in St. Peter's Square. Evidence emerges of Bulgarian secret police and possible Soviet involvement in plot.

1981   October 6: Anwar Sadat assassinated by Islamic fundamentalists during review of parade commemorating October 1973 War.

1981   December 17: NATO Southern Europe Ground commander, U.S. Army General James Lee Dozier, is kidnapped by Red Brigades but is released 42 days later by Italian counterterrorist commandos.

1982   February 2: Syrian President Hafiz al-Asad orders destruction of city of Hama after its occupation by Muslim Brotherhood forces seeking to topple Syrian regime. Estimates of total deaths in this city of 180,000 ranged from 10,000 to 25,000 killed.

1982   June 3: Abu Nidal's followers wound Israeli ambassador to Britain in assassination attempt. Israel invades Lebanon in reprisal, ultimately besieging Beirut and forcing Palestine Liberation Organization (PLO) to remove its troops and offices from Lebanon.

1982   July 20: IRA bombs Royal Household Cavalry regiment in Hyde Park and also Royal Green Jacket military band at Regent's Park.

1982   August 11: May 15 Organization bombs a Tokyo to Honolulu Pan Am flight, killing a Japanese passenger and wounding 15 others. This is regarded as the first in-flight bombing of an airliner.

1982   September 16: Lebanese Phalangist troops begin two-day massacre of Palestinian refugees at Sabra and Shatila camps in revenge for assassination of Lebanese President and Phalangist leader Bashir Gemayel two days earlier in bombing by members of pro-Palestinian Syrian Social Nationalist Party.

1983   April 18: U.S. embassy in Lebanon is partially destroyed by Islamic Jihad suicide truck bomber, killing 49 people and forcing removal of U.S. embassy from West Beirut.

1983   October 9: North Korean agents detonate bomb at Martyrs's Memorial in Rangoon, Burma, killing 17 South Koreqan officials and four Burnese officials and wounding 46 others. THe bombing was intended to assassinate South Korean President Chun Doo Hwan who escaped harm.

1983   October 23: U.S. Marines temporary barracks at Beirut Airport is destroyed by Islamic Jihad suicide truck bomber, killing 241 U.S. Marines. Islamic Jihad conducted similar operation the same day against the French military headquarters, killing 56 soldiers.

1983   November 6: U.S. Senate cloakroom is bombed by Armed Resistance Unit leftist group in protest against U.S. invasion of Grenada.

1983   December 12: Suicide truck bombers of al Da'wa, a pro-Iranian Islamic fundamentalist group, attack U.S. and French embassies in Kuwait City.

1984   March 16: Beirut CIA station chief, William Buckley, is kidnapped by Islamic Jihad as part of its hostage-taking campaign against westerners in Lebanon. Buckley was later murdered, possibly in late 1985, and his remains returned only by December 1991.

1984   April 17: Libyan diplomats open fire from Libyan embassy on anti-Qaddafi protestors in St. James Square, killing British policewoman. The embassy was subsequently besieged and the diplomats were expelled from Britain while diplomatic relations between Libya and Britain were severed.

1984   June 5-6: Indian Army storms the Golden Temple, the Sikhs' holiest shrine, to end terrorist agitation directed by Sikh leaders from within sanctuary. Hundreds are killed and relations between Sikhs and Indian government reach new low.

1984   June 18: Neo-Nazi group, the Order, murders Alan Berg, a controversial Denver radio talk-show host, at his home.

1984   October 12: IRA exploded a bomb at the Brighton hotel hosting conference of top members of British Conservative government. Five died and 32 were injured but Prime Minister Margaret Thatcher escaped injury.

1984   October 31: Indian Prime Minister Indira Gandhi assassinated by two Sikh bodyguards, apparently in reprisal for her orders for June 5 attack on Golden Temple.

1985   June 14: TWA Flight 847 hijacked to Beirut by Hezbollah terrorists. Hijackers murder U.S. Navy diver, Robert Dean Stethem. Last 39 of original 145 hostages were released by June 30.

1985   June 23: Air India Flight 182 is destroyed off western coast of Ireland. Evidence suggests it was bombed, possibly by Sikh terrorists, as Dashmesh Regiment, a shadowy Sikh group, claimed credit for bombing this flight.

1985   October 1: Israeli jets strafe and bomb PLO headquarters outside Tunis in retaliation for murder by al Fatah operative of three Israeli tourists in Larnaca, Cyprus, on 25 September.

1985   October 7: *Achille Lauro* cruise ship hijacked by Palestine Liberation Front terrorists, who murder elderly Jewish American hostage, Leon Klinghoffer.

1986   December 27: Abu Nidal gunmen open fire at Rome and Vienna airports in coordinated attacks, killing 18 holiday travelers.

1986   April 5: Bombing of West Berlin LaBelle Discothèque, killing three and wounding 200 others, leads United States to bomb Libya, the suspected sponsor of the bombing, on April 15.

1986   September 6: Abu Nidal gunmen attack Istanbul synagogue, killing 21 worshipers before killing themselves.

1987   January 20: Islamic Jihad kidnaps hostage negotiator Terry Waite after media speculation links him to Iran-Contra affair.

1987   December 9: Palestinian protest over Israeli motorist's accident killing Palestinian pedestrians in Gaza Strip erupts into rioting, marking beginning of *intifada* uprising.

1988   April 5: Iranian-sponsored terrorists seeking release of comrades from Kuwaiti jails hijack Kuwait Airways Flight 422, killing two hostages and holding rest of crew and passengers captive two weeks before abandoning airplane in Algeria.

1988   April 14: Naples USO club is car bombed, killing five people. Japanese Red Army operatives acting on behalf of Libya carried out operation to mark second anniversary of U.S. raid on Libya.

1988   November 15: Palestine National Council, legislative organ of PLO, declared independent Palestinian state to exist in West Bank and Gaza Strip and accepts, in principle, Israel's right to exist within pre-1967 borders contingent on Israeli recognition of Palestinian state.

1988   December 21: Pan Am Flight 103 destroyed over Scotland by radio bomb, killing all 259 persons aboard as well as 11 villagers of Lockerbie struck by falling debris. Evidence eventually points to Libya as most probable state sponsor.

1989   February 14: Ayatollah Khomeini issues fatwa of *takfir* against British author Salman Rushdie, for the writing of *Satanic Verses*, a book regarded by many Muslims as a thinly veiled attack on the character of the Prophet Muhammad. The verdict of *takfir* anathematizes Rushdie as an apostate and enemy of Islam and authorizes any true believer to kill him on sight.

1989   July 31: U.S. Marine Lt. Colonel William R. Higgins, kidnapped on 17 February 1988 by Hezbollah elements while serving in Lebanon as truce observer, murdered by captors in reprisal for Israeli capture of Hezbollah leader Sheikh Abdulkarim Uba'id on previous day.

1989   November 16: Salvadoran soldiers murder six Jesuit priests and two maids at the José Simeón Canas University of Central America. For the first time in Salvadoran judicial history the officers involved in this death squad killing are eventually convicted for their participation.

1990   February 25: Violeta Chamorro defeats Daniel Ortega in Nicaraguan presidential elections, so ending formal Sandinista domination of Nicaragua. U.S.-supported contras begin demobilization while Nicaraguan state support for leftist insurgency in El Salvador is ended.

1990   May 30: Israeli forces thwart sea-borne attack on Tel Aviv beaches by members of Palestine Liberation Front. PLO refusal to condemn attack leads U.S. government to discontinue talks with PLO representatives.

1990   August 14: Sendero Luminoso terrorists attempt car bombing of Presidential Palace in Lima, Peru, but fail to kill or wound newly elected President Alberto Fujimori.

1990   October 12: Speaker of the Egyptian National Assembly is murdered in an assault on his motorcade, possibly by pro-Iraqi agents in retaliation for Egypt's support of Operation Desert Storm.

1991   February 7: IRA launches a mortar attack upon the British Prime Minister's residence while Prime Minister John Major and members of his cabinet were in session there. This attack resulted in no deaths or injuries.

1991   May 21: Former Indian Prime Minister Rajiv Gandhi is assassinated by Liberation Tigers of Tamil Eelam suicide bomber in southern India.

1991   August 6: Shapur Bakhtiyar, last prime minister of prerevolutionary Iranian monarchy, is assassinated by Iranian agents in Paris.

1991   August 11-December 4: All remaining six U.S. hostages held by Islamic Jihad and several other Western hostages, including Terry Waite, are released before end of year. Remains of William Buckley and Colonel William R. Higgins also surrendered and returned to United States.

1992   March 17: Islamic Jihad claims credit for car bombing of Israeli embassy in Buenos Aires, killing 20 and wounding over 200, in reprisal for Israeli killing of Hezbollah leader in air raids on Hezbollah bases.

1992   June 29: Armed Islamic Movement, believed to be the armed wing of the Islamic Salvation Front (FIS), assassinates Algerian President Muhammad Boudiaf.

1992   July 16: Sendero Luminoso begins offensive to topple Peruvian government with two massive car bomb attacks, killing 18 and wounding over 140 others in Lima.

1992   September 13: Abimael Guzman, the leader of Sendero Luminoso, is captured by Peruvian security forces along with top lieutenants during a strategy session held in Lima, Peru.

1993   January 25: Lone Pakistani gunman, Mir Aimal Kansi, opens fire on U.S. Central Intelligence Agency employees, killing two of them, at entrance of CIA compound in Washington, D.C.

1993   February 26: World Trade Center building in New York City car bombed by followers of Shaykh Omar Abdul Rahman, the exiled leader of the Egyptian fundamentalist Gama'a al Islami group. Four suspects were found guilty by a federal jury on 4 March 1994 and another two suspects later arrested and tried.

1993   September 13: Israeli-Palestinian peace agreement is signed in Washington, D.C., by Israeli Prime Minister, Yitzhak Rabin, and Palestine Liberation Organization Chairman, Yasir Arafat. Those opposed to the accord, including Palestinians affiliated with the Islamic Resistance Movement (HAMAS) or with dissident PLO factions, as well as Israeli settlers and ultra-nationalists, seek to scuttle peace settlements through terrorist attacks in following months.

1993   December 2: Pablo Escobar, fugitive head of Medellín cocaine cartel responsible for narco-terrorist bombing and kidnapping campaign against Colombian police and government officials, is shot to death by security forces in Medellín.

1994   February 25: Dr. Baruch Goldstein, a militant follower of Rabbi Meir Kahane, opened fire on Palestinian Muslims praying at the Tomb of the Patriarchs in Hebron, killing at least 29 and wounding an estimated 150. Event triggers anti-Israeli rioting in occupied territories and leads to temporary hiatus in Israeli-Palestinian negotiations on autonomy.

1994   July 18: Car-bomb explosion at the Argentine-Israel Mutual Association in Buenos Aires kills around 100 and wounds over 200.

1994   August 15: French Interior Ministry announces "Carlos" arrested in Sudan by French counterintelligence agents.

1994   December 11: Abu Sayyaf Group (ASG) bombs airliner in the Philippines, killing one Japanese citizen and wounding 10 others.

1994   December 24: Armed Islamic Group (GIA) team hijacks Air France flight in Algeria to Marseilles where, after a 54-hour siege during which three hostages were killed, all four hijackers are killed by French hostage rescue team. On December 27 GIA murders four Catholic priests in Algeria in reprisal for the killings of its own members by French rescue team.

1995   March 20: Members of Aum Shinrikyo sect release sarin nerve gas on five trains of Tokyo subway system, killing 12 persons and injuring 5,500 others.

1995   April 19: Truck bomb demolishes north section of Murrah Federal Building in Oklahoma City, killing 168 citizens and injuring hundreds more. This was the single deadliest terrorist attack ever perpetrated in the United States.

1995   June 26: Islamic Group gunmen attempt assassination of President Hosni Mubarak during visit to Ethiopia.

1995   November 4: Jewish religious extremist assassinates Israel's Prime Minister, Yitzhak Rabin, during peace rally in Tel Aviv.

1995   November 13: In Riyadh, car bomb explodes at the Office of the Program Manager/Saudi Arabian National Guard, killing four U.S. civil servants, one member of U.S. Armed Forces, and two Indian Government employees, while wounding 42 others. Three groups claimed responsibility.

1996   January 31: Truck bombing of Central Bank building in Colombo, Sri Lanka, by Liberation Tigers of Tamil Eelam kills 90 persons and wounds over 1,400 others.

1996   February 9: Irish Republican Army breaks 17-month cease-fire with bombing in Docklands area of London, killing two and wounding over 100 others.

1996   February 24-March 4: HAMAS carries out three suicide bombings, exploding two buses in Jerusalem on February 24 and March 3, and another suicide bomber detonating his device outside the Dizengoff shopping mall in Tel Aviv, in total killing 65 persons and wounding 161 others.

1996   June 25: Truck bomb explodes opposite U.S. military housing in Khobar Towers, in Dhahran, Saudi Arabia, killing 19 U.S. citizens and wounding some 500 persons.

1996   July 27: Pipe bomb explodes at Centennial Olympic Park, at the Atlanta Olympic Games, killing one man and injuring 112 others.

1996   December 17: Túpac Amaru Revolutionary Movement terrorists seize Japanese ambassador's residence in Lima, Peru, during diplomatic reception taking 500 hostages. By New Year's Day only 81 hostages remain, the others having been released. Peruvian police storm compound on 22 April 1997 freeing hostages and killing all of the terrorists.

1997   November 17: In Luxor, Egypt, members of Islamic Group shoot and knife to death 58 foreign tourists and four Egyptians at Hatshepsut Temple.

1998   August 7: Nearly simultaneous bomb attacks on U.S. embassies in Nairobi, Kenya, and Dar es Salaam, Tanzania, resulted in the deaths of 291 persons and wounding of about 5,000 in the Nairobi attack and in the deaths of 10 persons and wounding of 77 in the Dar es Salaam attack.

1999   February 17: Abdullah Ocalan, the leader of the Kurdish Workers' Party (PKK) which had waged a 14-year insurgency against Turkey, was captured in Kenya and flown back to Turkey to stand trial.

1999   November 13: Rocket attacks on U.S. and UN offices in Pakistan following Taliban refusal to hand over Osama bin Laden, suspected mastermind of August 1998 attacks on U.S. embassies in East Africa.

1999   December 13: Supporters of Taliban open fire on U.S. embassy and UN Offices in Islamabad, Pakistan, in response to U.S. and UN demands for surrender of Osama bin Laden.

1999   December 14: U.S. Customs arrest Algerian, Ahmad Rassam, trying to smuggle explosives into United States from Canada. Rassam is suspected of ties to a radical Algerian Islamic group.

1999   December 24-31: Kashmiri separatists hijack an Air India airliner with 153 passengers and crew from India to Afghanistan in the course of which one passenger is murdered. Hijackers apparently aided by Taliban.

2000   January 21: Basque Fatherland and Liberty (ETA) made two carbombings in Madrid, killing an army officer and wounding bystanders, so ending a cease-fire ETA had declared on 16 September 1998.

2000   April 23-September 10: Abu Sayyaf Group (ASG) seizes several European and American tourists, both within Philippines and also in nearby Malaysian island resorts, holding many of them for ransom and killing several before releasing remainder.

2000   June 8: November 17 assassinates British military attaché to Greece, Brig. General Stephen Saunders, as he drives to work in Athens.

2000   September 28: Outbreak of renewed Palestinian *intifada* in Gaza and West Bank in reaction to visit by Ariel Sharon to disputed holy sites in East Jerusalem.

2000   October 12: U.S.S. *Cole* badly damaged by large bomb deployed by two suicide bombers by skiff along ship during docking in harbor of Aden, Yemen. Blast kills 17 sailors and cripples ship.

2000   November 28: Japanese Red Army (JRA) leader, Fusako Shigenobu, captured in western Japan town after 31-year manhunt for her by police forces throughout the world.

2001   January 2: Trial of four defendants accused of the conspiracy to bomb the U.S. Embassies in East Africa in August 1998 begins in U.S. Federal District Court in New York.

2001   August 27: IDF forces kill PFLP leader Mustafa Zibri in reprisal for involvement in suicide bombing attacks in Israel.

2001   September 9: Al Qa'eda suicide bombers assassinate Ahmad Shah Massoud, leader of Northern Alliance in Afghanistan.

2001   September 11: Suicide bombers hijacked four American domestic flights, crashing one into World Trade Center north tower and another into the south tower, and another into the east side of the Pentagon. The fourth flight crashed following apparent struggle between hijackers and passengers. At least 4,304 persons killed at the World Trade Center and 125 killed at the Pentagon. Altogether all 19 hijackers and 238 passengers also perished in this attack.

2001   September 14: Congress approved Senate and House of Representatives Joint Resolution No. 23, an authorization for use of military force against suspected agents and state sponsors responsible for the September 11 attack on New York and Washington, D.C. Following the Taliban's refusal to hand over Qa'eda elements within Afghanistan, the United States launched Operation Enduring Freedom on 7 October 2001 against Taliban and al Qa'eda forces within Afghanistan.

2001   September 18-October 9: Anthrax-contaminated letters mailed to American Media, Inc., Senate Majority Leader, Tom Daschle, the *New York Post*, and Tom Brokaw of NBC news, and other possible targets. On 5 October AMI employee Robert Steves died of inhalation anthrax. Altogether by mid-November, 17 cases of anthrax exposure were confirmed and five persons had died from inhalation anthrax.

2001   November 9-13: Following a month of U.S. air strikes on Taliban and al Qa'eda positions, the opposition Northern Alliance forces occupy Mazar-i Sharif, Herat, and Kabul following rout of Taliban forces.

Introduction

The Subjectivity of Terrorism

The study of terrorism has been burdened by a continuing and often acrimonious debate over the definition and consequent nature and scope of terrorism. The overused platitude "one man's terrorist is another man's freedom fighter" aptly illustrates how subjectivity has obscured the identification of terrorism without which there can be no systematic study of this matter. This subjectivity stems from several related factors. At the outset, the very mention of "terrorism" evokes a fearful image of slaughter, an image that has been perpetuated and magnified through the mass media. The vision of unarmed civilians taken hostage, wounded, or murdered has seared the consciousness of a global audience. Terrorists themselves have skillfully exploited that image to force their message on a mass audience with the stereotypical picture of an armed and hooded perpetrator pointing an AK-47 or M-16 at helpless victims. This frightening imagery of terrorism in turn has often provoked an emotional response equally in the lay observer, the scholar, or the policy maker who cannot ignore their gut reactions to the threats and acts of bloodshed. All too understandably such indignation and condemnation act as impediments to a detached assessment of the causes, dynamics, and outcomes of terrorism. Blanket condemnation of terrorists as crazed killers may act as a catharsis, but it does not provide any foundation for understanding the phenomenon.

This moralistic blanket condemnation of terrorism makes it difficult to arrive at any dispassionate objectivity in understanding terrorism, and even the attempt to study terrorism without immediate condemnation of it may be viewed as tacit acceptance of what is judged to be pernicious and reprehensible. The disturbing questions of morality are carried over into the equally heated debate over the nature of terrorism in which competing interpretations of what terrorism really is also complicate the debate on terrorism.

Elements of Terrorism

Many view terrorism as, first and foremost, criminal acts that cannot be justified. Terrorist acts are accordingly viewed as assaults upon the civil order that should not be dignified by being regarded as instruments for pursuing some higher cause. Viewed in this manner, terrorism is nothing more than a form of criminal violence.

Another approach recognizes that even while terrorism may consist of criminal actions, they are nonetheless actions meant to achieve certain goals. However brutal or reprehensible terrorism may be it cannot simply be dismissed as mindless violence. Accordingly terrorism can be defined as

> a purposeful human activity directed toward the creation of a general climate of fear designed to influence in ways desired by the protagonists, other human beings, and through them some course of events.[1]

This attempt to define terrorism as purposeful action may provide, in turn, the basis for an objective analysis, for it offers a functional means for understanding the major common elements of terrorism irrespective of the differing goals of various perpetrators.

The first common element of terrorism is the use, or threat, of violence. The mere threat of violence alone is not enough, however. Ultimately there must be the use of violence, or else the threat, however ominous, will lose its credibility. There may be some disagreement on whether such violence must be physical. Do different forms of mental cruelty, for example, constitute a form of terrorism? Even while there is no consensus on the answer to this question, a second common element of terrorism helps to clarify the problem, for the use of terrorism, irrespective of its goal, involves "violent behavior designed to generate fear in the community [or individual]."[2]

The intent to generate fear is the second common element that distinguishes terrorist violence from other forms of violence. One authority aptly notes that terrorism ultimately is "a form of psychological operations."[3] This psychological component of seeking to create fear as a primary goal, whether in an individual, a community, a state, or a corporation, is essential to the concept of terrorism.

Another common element of terrorism as purposeful action is that the terrorist act is a form of communication meant to send a message of fear and intimidation not just to the immediate victim but also to a broader audience. As an often-quoted definition notes:

> Terrorism is the threat of violence and the use of fear to coerce, persuade, and gain public attention.[4]

Terrorism, then, is a form of "armed propaganda," a potent way not only to communicate but also to send a message in an age dominated by the mass media.

Types of Terrorism: The Primacy of Politics

While in practice it is not always clear whether a given terrorist act is the work of "crusaders, criminals, or crazies,"[5] since even criminals will try to disguise or justify their acts on a political basis, there is basic agreement that terrorism is a form of political violence and action. There is, however, a reluctance to append the word "political" to a terrorist act since it is feared that doing so will transform the criminal into a political actor and so confer some degree of legitimacy upon the act. Nevertheless the political content of terrorism has largely been accepted in the scholarly literature. While there are many definitions of political terrorism, Grant Wardlaw's pioneering effort tightly defines its major characteristics:

> Political terrorism is the use, or threat of use, of violence by an individual or a group, whether acting for or in opposition to established authority, when such action is designed to create extreme anxiety and/or fear-inducing effects in a target group larger than the immediate victims with the purpose of coercing that group into acceding to the political demands of the perpetrators.[6]

Starting from this base point scholars have sought to establish typologies to identify different types of terrorism as a foundation for comparative analysis. One of the most useful is the dichotomy developed by T. P. Thorton, who differentiates between "enforcement terrorism" and "agitational terror." The former is also called "terror from above," which is used by governments and authorities to maintain their control and to suppress threats to their own power. The latter is used by those who wish to replace, transform, or destroy the existing order.[7] This basic typology is exceedingly useful for it recognizes that terror is not an instrument used just by those supporting the status quo, a liberal view often used to justify violence against the state, nor is it an instrument used only to attack the civil order, a conservative view often used to condemn terrorism and to justify harsh countermeasures.

There are more elaborate typologies such as the well-known classification system by Richard Schultz, who identifies three general categories: (1) "Revolutionary Terrorism . . . the threat and/or development of extranormal forms of political violence, in varying degrees, with the object of successfully effecting a complete revolutionary change (i.e., a change of fundamental political-social processes) within the political system. Such means may be employed by revolutionary elements indigenous to a particular political system or by similar groups acting outside the geographic boundaries of the system." (2) "Sub-Revolutionary Terrorism . . . the threat and/or employment of extranormal forms of political violence, in varying degrees, with the objective of effecting various changes in the particular political system . . . The goal is to bring about certain changes in the body politic, not to abolish it in favor of a complete system change. Perhaps the broadest of the three categories, groups included here span the political spectrum from left to right . . . Such means are employed primarily by groups or movements indigenous to the particular political system, though similar elements beyond the system's geographic boundaries may also rely on such means." (3) "Establishment Terrorism . . . the threat and/or employment of extranormal forms of political violence in varying degrees, by an established political system, against both external and internal opposition. Specifically such means may be employed by an established political system against other nation-states and groups external to the particular political system, as well as internally to repress various forms of domestic opposition/unrest and/or to move the populace to comply with programs/goals of the state."[8]

Schultz's definitions, however, may be culturally bound. How one determines what constitutes "extranormal forms of political violence" may depend largely on what is "normal" for the particular culture and political tradition in which the violence takes place. What is regarded as "extranormal political violence" in the Netherlands may be viewed as normal, indeed as routine, political violence in Lebanon.

The other unexamined assumption within this typology lays in the distinction between "revolutionary" and "subrevolutionary" political violence, which appears to reflect a tendency largely unquestioned in contemporary Western political thought to link the idea of revolution connotatively with that of political development or progress, and specifically with leftist or socialistic political movements, while regarding rightist or fascist political movements as atavisms, which cannot be classified as truly "revolutionary."

In fact, right-wing authoritarian states and left-wing totalitarian states resemble each other structurally far more closely than does either type resemble Western liberal democracy while they and their state functionaries, or else state-sponsored agents and proxies, also behave very similarly. The implied claim that true revolutionary movements achieve systematic transformation while subrevolutionary ones do not actually begs the question whether the supposedly "true" revolutionary movements ever do live up to their aspirations of holistic change and transformation. Historically it seems more evident that on seizing power the new revolutionary order usually incorporates large structural elements of the systems it replaces. Thus the Bolshevik revolutionaries replaced the Tsarist Okhrana with their own Cheka that eventually became the Soviet Union's KGB, so perpetuating in a more efficient form an instrument of statist absolutism.

Moreover even "subrevolutionary" nationalistic or secessionist political movements often claim to seek the same types of social and economic transformations sought by avowedly socialist and internationalist movements. Despite these reservations Schultz's typologies, and others like it, have provided a valuable comparative framework in which to analyze terrorism in its many forms.

Impact of Technology on Changing Types of Terrorism

While the common elements described above provide lines of continuity running through terrorism's long and complex history, nonetheless a strong case can be made that technological innovation has created a new form of terrorism:

Non-Territorial Terrorism—a form of terror that is not confined to a clearly delineated geographical area.[9]

That is, as a result of a joint revolution in the 1960s with the large-scale introduction of jet aircraft into international travel and the proliferation of television, terrorists could literally strike at global targets of opportunity in a matter of hours and force their message upon a mass audience undreamed of by their most dedicated and skillful predecessors. Moreover, their objective might not be the seizure of territorial power but rather regional or even global destabilization. Faced with this challenge, authorities were forced to recognize that traditional means of prevention and control of terrorism appropriate within a specifically identifiable strife zone would not be effective against those who might be many thousands of miles away from their intended target. In reality nonterritorial terrorists had at their disposal, and used, an intercontinental delivery missile rivaling the missiles of mass destruction that, fortunately, were never employed in any general war. This was something new and invidious under the sun.

Historical Dimensions

Despite these innovations and the emphasis on contemporary terrorism as being, as one authority deemed it, "A New Mode of Conflict,"[10] terrorism actually comes from a very ancient tradition. As one author notes,

> We tend to think of political terrorism as a modern development .
> . . But the terrorizing of humans by fellow humans on political or
> political-ethnic grounds goes much further back, in many forms.
> As a missionary in Burundi sadly said about the massacre of 10,000
> Hutu tribesmen by the ruling Tutsi in 1972 . . . "This has been
> going on for centuries and will happen again."[11]

The same could be said for the tragic ethnic violence in the former republics of Yugoslavia and the disintegrated Soviet Union, the relentless attacks against the Kurds, and any other number of primordial conflicts in both industrialized and agrarian societies.

In the long history of terrorism the names of certain groups surface repeatedly; they share the tendency to use violence to promote and exercise their religious beliefs. The Zealots were religious nationalists in first-century Judea who revolted against the Roman occupation. Hidden in crowds they would stab secular officials, priests, and soldiers with their daggers (*sicarii*) and then escape by merging back into the crowds. Their actions created an environment of fear where no one was to be trusted and everyone was feared. The Zealots pioneered the techniques of pure terror that would be used by future generations of true believers.

The word "assassin" came from another religious-political group. In the 11th and 12th centuries Isma'ili Shi'ite activists in southwest Asia organized corps of assassins, known as the Fedayeen, literally the "self-sacrificers." These assassins were willing to undertake attacks against Sunni rulers in spite of the certainty of their own death or capture, as they were assured of their place in Heaven if they fell as martyrs fighting in the path of God. To counter the awe and respect these bold attacks created among the common people, apologists of the Abbasid dynasty targeted by the Isma'ilis gave out that the attackers were really "Hashshishin," those acting under the influence of hashish. This official disinformation became the source of the word "assassin." The car and truck bombers of the 1980s who blew up the U.S. Embassy in West Beirut, and later bombed the U.S. Marine barracks and French military headquarters there all within one year, reproduced in a modern setting the same tactics used by the earlier Isma'ili Fedayeen.

Other English words have come from the ancient lexicon of terrorism. The term "thug" was taken from "Thugee," the name of a secret sect in India that also employed terrorism as part of its ritual worship of Kali, the Hindu goddess of destruction.

The genesis of modern terrorism took place during the French Revolution and the reaction that followed it. Under Citizen Robespierre and his Committee of Public Safety, the "Great Terror" was directed against the real and imagined enemies of the revolution. In excess of 17,000 people were victims of this first exercise of mass state terrorism. It is sad to note how this figure pales into insignificance when compared with the statistics of the mass terrorism of modern totalitarian states, which have refined with murderous efficiency the ability to engage in genocide, whether in the gas chambers of the Third Reich or the killing fields of Kampuchea.

The resort to terrorism as an instrument of revolutionary transformation was more fully developed in Imperial Russia. In the *Catechism of the Revolutionist*, written in 1869, Sergey Nechayev provided an idealized guide that would be employed by later generations as the model of a terrorist dedicated to his or her cause to the death. As he noted in this Catechism:

> The revolutionary is a doomed man. He has no interests of his own, no affairs, no attachments, no belongings, not even a name. Everything in him is absorbed by a single thought, a single passion—the revolution. . . . The revolutionary enters into the world of the state, of class, of so-called culture, and lives in it only be-

cause he has faith in its speedy and total destruction. He is not a
revolutionary if he feels pity for anything in this world. If he is
able to, he must face the annihilation of a situation—everything
and everyone must be equally odious to him. All the worse for him
if he has family and loved ones in this world; he is no revolutionary if he can stay his hand.[12]

The antecedents of modern terrorist tactics were also developed during
this period. The Narodnaya Volya (People's Will) organization employed
dynamite in its assassination campaigns against the officials of the Tsarist
regime.

The use of terrorism as a weapon of propaganda and communication
was further developed during this period by the followers of anarchism.
The leading advocate of anarchism, Mikhail Bakunin, recognized that violence sent a potent message to both allies and enemies. This message,
through the medium of violence called "propaganda by the deed," is still
practiced today before the lens of the video camera.

The impact of technology on communications and control of information heightened the capacity of those who utilized terrorism as a form of
propaganda not only to convey a message but, more ominously, to exert
social and political control over subject populations that went far beyond
the capability of the most repressive dictators of the past. The penetration
and consequent control of all levels of political, social, and economic life
by a repressive regime led to the development of the modern totalitarian
state. The reign of terror pioneered by the French revolution was expanded
with murderous efficiency by Stalin through the massive purges and show
trials of the 1920s and 1930s and reached its zenith in the genocide attempted under the Third Reich with its concentration camps and cremato-
ria. The murderous combination of technology and attendant organizational
capabilities led to the maturation of "terrorism from above." Modern state
terrorism, which is aptly defined in what follows, had come of age:

state terrorism can be seen as a method of rule whereby some
groups of people are victimized with great brutality, and more or
less arbitrarily by the state, or state-supported actors, so that others
who have reason to identify with those murdered, will despair,
obey, or comply. Its main instruments are summary arrest and in-

carceration without trial, torture, political murder, disappearances, and concentration camps.[13]

Contemporary Terrorism

In the 1960s, "terror from below" continued as a new generation of revolutionaries attempted to overthrow what they regarded as repressive regimes. In Latin America the use of terror as part of insurgent movements was accelerated by the Cuban revolution and the attempt to export it to Central and South America. Ernesto Che Guevara perhaps best embodied the mystique that surrounded the new revolutionaries. Guevara emphasized the need to employ terror tactics in an essentially rural guerrilla war. He emphasized the importance of the foco—a small clandestine group of rebels who could ignite the fires of revolution. Guevara, however, overlooked the importance of slowly developing a foundation of support among the indigenous peasantry. His failure to rally the peasants led to his capture and death in Bolivia. In spite of Guevara's failure, his mystique would influence other real and self-styled revolutionary terrorists.

In contrast to Guevara's rural-based approach, Carlos Marighella emphasized the importance of employing terrorism in the cities as a means of dramatizing the rebels' cause and provoking the government to overreact. In turn this overreaction was supposed to antagonize the general population, either neutralizing their support for the established order or else prompting them to join the revolutionary cause. Marighella's *Manual of the Urban Guerrilla* provided a tactical guide instructing future urban terrorists on how to finance their operations through bank robberies among other things.[14] In the United States the Symbionese Liberation Army would follow Marighella's approach, even using the kidnapped Patty Hearst in their short-lived and violent history. During this period groups such as the Red Army Faction in Germany (better known to the public then as the Baader-Meinhof Gang), the Red Brigades in Italy, and the Weather Underground in the United States in reality revived and renewed the anarchistic tradition even though they conceived of themselves as bona fide internationalist socialist revolutionaries.

During the late 1960s the scope and impact of terrorism was greatly expanded, as was earlier noted, as a result of the large-scale global introduction of jet aircraft. The Popular Front for the Liberation of Palestine (PFLP) engaged in a number of highly dramatic operations in the period from 1968-1970 that would be copied by numerous terrorist groups in the following decades.

With the seizure of 53 American hostages at the U.S. Embassy in Tehran in November 1979, another chapter in modern terrorism was opened:

> the behavior of Iran, Libya, and other countries points to the development of rogue, or outlaw states, who no longer use terror [solely] as an instrument of maintaining internal control, but rather as a technique in a new diplomatic method—'armed diplomacy'—as a means of carrying out foreign policy.[15]

In the 1980s states increasingly supported various terrorist groups in pursuit of their foreign policy objectives. "State-sponsored terrorism" by the Soviet Union, the United States, Iran, Iraq, Syria, North Korea, and other governments enabled terrorists to have levels of financial, logistical, and tactical support unavailable to them in the past. The linkages between various terrorist groups and their state sponsors were hotly debated, particularly by the United States, which sought to verify the degree of Moscow's involvement with terrorists during the waning days of the Cold War. Such diverse groups as the West German Baader-Meinhof Gang, the Irish Republican Army, and the Popular Front for the Liberation of Palestine received funding from their respective state sponsors.[16] State sponsorship, particularly in the Middle East, continues to enhance the capability of various terrorist groups to pursue their objectives.

Threats of Mass Destruction and Changing Motivations

In the introduction to the first edition the authors noted, "modern terrorism is entering a very dangerous period." We were referring to the disintegration of the Soviet Union, the resurgence of ethnicity that had long been suppressed during the Cold War by the Soviet Empire, and the revival of religious fundamentalism. Our concerns particularly focused on the increased availability of chemical, biological, and nuclear weapons, or what are now called weapons of mass destruction (WMD), which could be used by a state, state-sponsored terrorists, or independent terrorist groups to pursue their objectives. While there have been threats and resorts to such weapons, they had been limited until the sarin gas attack by Aum Shinrikyo in the Tokyo subway system in March 1995. As the Oklahoma City bombing represented a new phase in terrorism to the United States, so did that attack (and a previous one by the group upon the Japanese city of Matsumoto that was less well known) by what until then had been a relatively obscure cult open the Pandora's box of mass terrorism. Until that event, Brian Jenkin's dictum that "terrorists wanted more people alive than dead" had remained essentially valid since terrorist groups sought some level of support within a targeted audience, or wanted enough intimidated survivors to recognize their cause and, if possible, to force their governments to adapt policies that would further the aims of the terrorist group. Moreover, most terrorists realized that if their acts were too provocative the public might support the government taking whatever measures were necessary to defeat them. The attacks on the World Trade Center and Pentagon of 11 September 2001 are the most deadly mass casualty attacks to date. The scale of these attacks has mobilized not only the U.S. government and public, but also a wider community of nations, to punish the perpetrators and to halt the repetition, much less the escalation, of such attacks in the futre.

The development of various cults and religious fundamentalist groups that viewed their acts to be divinely inspired, who were ultimately not concerned about achieving temporal goals, but goals in a next life, broke this implicit constraint based on concerns over public opinion. Thus, as we now start a new millennium there is good reason to believe that such groups will continue to use such mass terrorism to achieve their respective apocalyptic visions. These groups may also be joined by rogue states and regional powers that might seek to engage a stronger enemy in asymmetric warfare by indirectly supporting such groups and so achieving "plausible deniability" in pursuing their national and transnational goals.

Terrorist destructive capabilities have unfortunately not only increased in the area of weapons of mass destruction but even more conventional "rational" terrorist groups have at their disposal an increasingly sophisticated arsenal of standoff weapons that will make it increasingly difficult to place a physical defensive zone around a potential target. The implications, particularly in regards to aviation security, are very serious with the incredible availability of targets created by the rapid expansion of airline traffic and the continued growth in general aviation. The state of the terrorists' capabilities plus their increased willingness to use lethal means will in all likelihood dramatically increase in both the near and far term. It is worth reiterating that an overreaction to the WMD threat could place democratic orders on a very dangerous path of incremental repression in the name of preserving order.

Another New Terrorist Theater of Operations: The Internet

Perhaps the most glaring gap in the introduction of our first edition was the lack of any discussion of the role of the Internet in the changing face of terrorism. If it is of any comfort to both authors, we were not alone in our oversight. The incredible rise and development of the "net" and World Wide Web was only taking off when we wrote the first edition.

Certainly the Internet provides terrorists at the outset with an expanding capability to engage in what could be called "electronic unarmed propaganda." The Web page, for example, gives a terrorist group of three, 30, or 300 the ability to publish their manifesto through the anonymity of cyberspace. Perhaps even more significantly, the Internet provides the means by which various terrorist groups can maintain their security via the anonymity of cyberspace but increasingly have the ability and opportunities to coordinate operations with highly diverse groups which may share a general strategic goal of destabilizing a city, a country, or a region.

However, what is perhaps most significant is the fact that the Internet has enabled terrorists to engage in what is called "netwar." In so doing they are now evolving into new self-contained, "free-floating cells" that can engage in concerted attacks, but which may remain essentially free from the need for external support be it from state or nonstate actors. Such groups will continue to be increasingly difficult to identify, since many may be small with no track record, and also difficult to penetrate, since they are not part of a larger organization that can be placed under surveillance by technical intelligence or infiltrated by a hostile intelligence service. In the past it was understood that even the most sophisticated techniques of technical collection could not monitor the person-to-person discussion of two terrorists in a safe house in Beirut or Tokyo. It will continue to be a very daunting technological task to separate "the noise from the signal" in the cacophony of cyberspace. And if it becomes possible to do so, what will be the implications for the rights of ordinary individuals to converse over the net without fear of government eavesdropping?

Since the initial study concerns have been voiced over the development of "cyber-terrorism." The authors note that this term is too general for analysis. As was stated in the first edition, an essential element of terrorism is "the threat or use of violence." Thus, however disruptive hacking might be in regards to a database, or a banking system, it would not be regarded as terrorism unless the intended results of such disruption could or did lead to physical violence against people. Thus, disruption of a flight schedule by itself is not terrorism, but the disruption of an air traffic control system that led to second order effects of the deaths of passengers would indeed be a form of terrorism. One should emphasize that the difference between cyber-disruption and cyber-terrorism is more than a semantic exercise. Failure to recognize this difference creates a serious problem of establishing the scope of the threat.

New Players in Terrorism

Since the first edition one of the classifications of type of actor, namely, "entrepreneurial terrorists," has become increasingly important for two reasons. First, the rise of nonstate actors in international affairs is increasingly challenging the traditional domination of the state in the classic "state-centered" international order. Increasingly tied together by the Internet, a wide variety of nongovernmental organizations (NGOs) and other non-state entities are increasingly replacing or making a parallel hierarchy to the existing state order. Second, in a world where large areas of the world consist of "failed states" or the "gray area" phenomenon of ungovernable states, nonstate actors will fill the political, economic, and social vacuum of disorder for their own purposes and seek to achieve their own objectives. These entities may increasingly engage in acts of terrorism for mercenary rather than political ends. They can, and will, hire themselves out to threatened regimes, or seek to corrupt and control them, as in the case of narco-terrorists, or pursue other objectives.

Also there will continue to be those with "deep pockets" able to support their own terrorist networks to achieve their own goals. The Osama bin Laden network illustrates how dangerous entrepreneurial terrorists can use private resources for political purposes in a world where the power of independent wealth and the Internet have replaced the tradition interaction among states. The impact of such individuals might be multiplied if these included disaffected individuals who are also highly versed in computer technology and who therefore would have the capability to engage in technological terrorism in the form of information operations in which the gun or bomb is replaced by the personal computer. NGOs can use this power for both good and evil. The Seattle riots against the World Trade Organization (WTO) illustrate how disparate groups can use the Internet to coordinate themselves in seeking to achieve what may be either laudable or evil goals. Moreover, within such "electronic" movements there have always been those entrepreneurs who will use violence created by such protests for both political and violent agenda.

The development of such groups has serious implications for those governments that are seeking to combat terrorism. Just as there has been a vast increase in internal defense budgets, there will also be a massive growth of private security firms, which will increasingly compete with national governments in providing security for their citizens. We are witnessing what has elsewhere been labeled the "privatization of public violence,"[17] a trend that will challenge the state's classic monopoly over the use of force. How a national government can either cooperate with such organizations to combat terrorism, without becoming dependent on them, or else avoid becoming vulnerable to them because of a lack of governmental oversight and regulatory capabilities, will become major tests for national governments in the continuing war on terrorism.

Future Trends

The trends noted in the first edition will likely not only continue but intensify. The breakup of the Soviet Union, unleashed by the forces of nationalism so long repressed and hidden under communist rule, manifest a profound and fundamental change in the international environment: The very technology that has made the world more interconnected has also promoted the assertion of "primordial loyalties fueled by ethnicity, race, and language." If anything, these tendencies have accelerated not only as reactions to Western secular culture by various fundamentalist groups, but also by the desire of other subnational groups seeking their own identity as they react to the danger of imposed homogeneity of a mass society driven, as they see it, by a rampant consumerism and loss of basic spiritual values. In seeking their brand of nationalism these groups have already used the technology of the postindustrialized societies against them. The Zapatistas, for example, have used the Internet to dramatize their cause through the use of netwar[18] much in the way that the Black September Movement seized the world's attention through what is now called the "CNN-drome."[19] Groups using terrorism as a means of achieving their goals may increasingly combine ancient loyalties with modern technology in their quest for identity.

At the same time, this assertion of traditional loyalties demonstrates that the arbitrary borders imposed by old colonial policies are not only being eroded but destroyed. Tribes, clans, and extended families will no longer play by the rules of international affairs, which emphasized the centrality of the nation-state in international politics that were written during the great power dominance of the Congress of Vienna. In the new international arena where nonstate actors will be increasingly important, geographic and political boundaries will be replaced by psychosocial boundaries, where individuals and groups may resort to terrorism in a world marked both by increasing technological interdependence and by an increasingly contracting sense of community.

At the same time, the power of the net, and accompanying technological developments, will also continue to promote the creation of movements that are regional in scope. The power of the Internet and television will bring together widely scattered groups into coordinated actions, as seen in the demonstrations in Europe directed by the Kurdish community to protest the Turkish government's arrest and subsequent sentencing to death of Abdullah Ocalan, head of the Kurdistan Workers Party (PKK). It is not a large step to move from using the net for mobilizing transnational demonstrations to coordinating transnational terrorist operations. Moreover, while there appear to be attempts at normalizing relations between Iran and the West, particularly the United States, the thrust toward Islamic fundamentalism will probably not be impeded. Whether they are aided by the "deep pockets" of bin Laden or not, the trained Mujahideen veterans of the Afghan conflict will continue to fight and will be joined by others who will not only seek to overthrow what they view to be the feudal, apostate states of Saudi Arabia and their allies in the Gulf, but who will also direct attacks against their most profound enemy, the "Great Satan," that is, the United States. They will practice their own form of "electronic armed propaganda" by resorting to the net in addition to using the bomb, the handheld missile, and the M-16 or AK-47.

But perhaps the most ominous possibility, based on the sarin gas incident and the proliferation of cults and fundamentalist groups, is a growing likelihood of incidents of mass terrorism involving biological, chemical, or nuclear/radiological weapons. The emergence of groups lacking inner restraints in their resort to terrorism coupled with the increased availability of such weapons underscore that there are good reasons to believe that these pose real threats both in the United States and to its allies overseas. Such threats would most likely involve biological or chemical attacks, since neither processing fissionable material into a weapon nor acquiring a nuclear device are readily within the reach of such groups. Still it is easy enough to acquire nonfissionable radioactive materials that could lead to serious contamination, so the danger of a form of radiological assault on the lower end of the spectrum of mass terrorism should not be discounted.

Having noted the possible changes in motivation and tactics, for the foreseeable future the weapons of choice will still be the gun and the bomb. Their sophistication and destructive power will increase and they will probably remain the rule and not become the exception. Those who continue to practice terrorism will for the most part still be motivated by the classic demands for self-determination, striking back at what they perceive to be a repressive regime, as well as the other traditional causes that impel individuals and groups to engage in classic hostage taking, bombings, and assassinations. The majority of these will result from territorial disputes over land and increasingly over scarce resources.

While the old ideological classifications of left and right as a means of understanding the basis of terrorism will in all probability be of even less significance, as the ideological issues used by the adversaries during the Cold War diminish, this does not portend an "end of ideology" as motivations or justifications for acts and campaigns of terrorism. First, in the uneven and dangerous transition from authoritarian rule to democracy, the possibility of reaction cannot be discounted as people look back nostalgically to the "ancien régime" because their expectations of the new order to resolve their problems have been disappointed. Second, the force of fundamentalism, and particularly those religious fundamentalisms that do not separate church from state, will remain a potent force for those who employ terrorism as a weapon in their contemporary crusades. Middle Eastern ayatollahs or their American counterparts will continue to exploit religious beliefs to justify the carnage inflicted by terrorism. One should also note that the motivations for terrorism will probably become more diffuse as a wide variety of single interest groups move beyond the politics of protest and extremism into the realm of terrorism. These groups will be particularly difficult to identify since they may be small and, as noted earlier, have no track record. Finally, the convergence between criminal enterprises and terrorism will continue, especially in geographical areas where there is little or no effective government. The law of the jungle is bound to become more lethal as a new generation of criminally inspired terrorists acting under the guise of politics has more sophisticated weapons at their disposal.

Classification System Employed in the Dictionary

Because of the great diversity of terrorist groups presented in the following pages, a classification system has been provided to enable the reader not only to identify the unique features of each group but also to have the means to acquire a comparative perspective on terrorism. As is true of all classification systems, this one is arbitrary and a given group may fit into more than one category. Nevertheless, this classification scheme meets the requirement that it be sufficiently broad in scope to discern patterns that may be obscured by the outward diversity that characterizes the landscape of terrorism.

A thorough encyclopedia of terrorism will need to identify and describe other terrorist phenomena besides the various terrorist groups, such as the principal doctrines motivating such groups; biographic sketches of important theorists, tacticians, and operators; and chronologies of events associated with particular groups or movements. Properly conceived, a regular scheme of description and comparative analysis should not preclude some discussion of the distinctive political beliefs, unique organizational features, motivations, and tactics of a group.

The scheme for classifying terrorist groups presented here is derived, in part, from Richard Schultz's proposed typology of terrorism.[20] Each entry on a given group addresses two essential questions: First, "Who are they?," that is, what sort of group or actor is behind the given terrorist action(s)? Second, "What do they want?," that is, what are the long-range political goals that the group is seeking? Together these two characteristics define the overall type of each group. Once one grasps the overall type of group, one may proceed to note the peculiarities of doctrine, strategy, tactics, targets, group origins, and history and leadership that distinguish each group within a single type from others belonging to that same basic group type.

Types of Terrorist Groups

1. Identification of Actor-Type:

Following both Paul Wilkinson[21] and Richard Schultz[22] , this classification recognizes three main types of terrorist actors:

I.   State Actor are used by governments and their agencies to direct terrorism against their own people to preserve their rule. Sovereign states can also use terrorism to topple other governments or else to force them to change their politics.

Examples would include the Tonton Macoutes of the former "Papa Doc" Duvalier regime in Haiti used to terrorize political opponents of the regime. In Nicaragua under Sandinista rule the *turbas divinas* ("divine mobs") and Iran's *hezbollahi* street mobs are also examples of state-directed and controlled terror groups.

II.   Revolutionary Actors use terrorism to overthrow a regime, or to force a regime to change fundamentally how it conducts its public business, or else to establish a new state within the territory of an existing state. Although nationalist insurgents seeking to secede from an existing nation-state appear to pursue a more modest goal than those who seek an overall sociopolitical transformation within that nation-state, both nationalist secessionists and self-styled revolutionaries are seeking fundamental changes in the status quo, which is basically the essence of revolution. Radical socialism and radical nationalism may not resemble each other in substance, but if the goal that each strives to achieve is so radically different from the existing state that realizing it requires the end of the current state then each would be equally revolutionary.

An example of this can be found in the relationship of the two groups, the Revolutionary People's Liberation Party (DHKP), formerly known as Dev Sol, and the Armenian Secret Army for the Liberation of Armenia (ASALA) with respect to the existing Turkish Republic. The former would overthrow its current regime to establish a Marxist-Leninist state within the existing Turkish borders. The latter would establish a new Armenian state within the eastern one-third of the modern Turkish state's territory. Both are counted as "revolutionary" groups since each seeks an absolute transformation of the existing status quo in Turkey, one redefining the social and economic system within Turkey and the other redefining the scope of Turkish jurisdiction and sovereignty over territory and nationalities.

III.   Entrepreneurial Actors are those transnational terrorist groups that have achieved a degree of group identity, making them autonomous from any given nation-state. While Wilkinson and Schultz count ethnic nationalist terror groups as representing forms of "Sub-Revolutionary Terrorism," under the classification system used in this text they would be considered examples of revolutionary groups rather than entrepreneurial groups. In effect, entrepreneurial groups either hire themselves out for service to various regimes on a contract basis or else pursue an agenda of limited goals distinct from any nationalistic or revolutionist program. As the Abu Nidal Organization separated itself from the mainstream Palestinian nationalist movement, it has been transformed into a self-sustaining criminal organization that sells its terrorist skills to various Arab and non-Arab regimes. Criminal organizations may also maintain their own in-house terrorist capacity, as has been the case with the Colombian drug syndicates' proprietary death squads known as "the Extraditables" and MAS (Muerte a Secuestradores, "Death to Kidnappers"). Less insidious examples of entrepreneurial groups include ecological activists and animal-rights activists who pursue a terrorist version of single-interest politics cutting across several national jurisdictions. One of the most prominent examples of such a group that has embarked on a terrorist campaign is the Animal Liberation Front, which has carried out sabotage of private and public research facilities and harassment of animal researchers in the United States, Canada, and Great Britain.

The category of entrepreneurial groups often contains groups that at an earlier stage in their history would have been more readily classified as revolutionary organizations. This can be explained often by such groups' failure to achieve their original revolutionary goals coupled with their members' inability to separate themselves from the cohesive identity of the group, for which they have often sacrificed the prime years of their lives and which has absorbed so much of their energies and devotion. Such members also often have no alternative skills with which to pursue a nonterrorist livelihood and so the group continues to exist by selling its services to various buyers.

2.   Identification of Goals:

There are three main types of goals, namely: regime maintenance, regime change, and seeking limited advantage(s).

As an example of the first, state actors use repression as a means of ensuring regime survival. Likewise, revolutionary actors seek to change a political status quo. Entrepreneurial groups specialize in coercive types of terror that may be aimed only at gaining marginal, or relative, political or economic goals, e.g., hostage taking in order to exact the profits of extortion.

TYPES OF OBJECTIVES

		Repressive	Revolutionary	Limited
TYPE OF ACTOR	**State**	Tonton Macoutes	Islamic Revolutionary Guards Corps	Wrath of God
	Revolutionary	Force 17	Sendero Luminoso	Black September
	Entrepreneurial	The Extraditables	PFLP – General Command	Animal Rights Groups

Figure 1. Typology for classification of groups and group activities and functions. Examples of each are given for each typological combination. The main characteristics of actor types and of types of goals are summarized on page 21.

The generation of a typology from these two sets of characteristics, namely, types of actor and types of motivations, is illustrated in Figure 1 above along with specific examples of each possible combination of actor type and motivation type. The types found in the upper left to lower right diagonal in Figure 1 represent the most natural congruence of actor types with goal types. State actors have a primary interest in self-maintenance. The Tonton Macoutes of Haiti are a state-sponsored repressive group. Revolutionary groups generally pursue a revolutionary agenda while entrepreneurial groups will be primarily motivated by goals other than maintaining or overthrowing state systems.

Although this congruence of actor types and goals seems intuitive, it does not tell the entire story. In fact, each basic type can use terrorism in each of the three ways described earlier. While the main upper-left to lower-right diagonal contains the most favored position for each of the actor types, the off-diagonal positions are roles that such groups can occupy as situations require. Thus, although al Fatah is primarily a revolutionary group seeking the establishment of a Palestinian state, it also has a "regime maintaining" goal of keeping other Palestinians in line and punishing dissidents. Therefore, it created Force 17 as its own version of a security police and intelligence force within the Palestinian community. Following the expulsion of the PLO from Jordan, al Fatah also sought the limited goal of punishing Jordanian government and military authorities. To that limited end Fatah created the Black September Organization, which very

SUMMARY OF TYPOLOGICAL CLASSIFICATION SCHEME

I.   Types of Actor

STATE
- Acting against their own people to preserve their regime, sometimes called state repression, regime terrorism, or "state terror"
- Acting against other states to topple their governments, known also as state sponsorship of terrorism
- Acting against other states to force political changes, that is, changes in the policies of targeted governments, also called state sponsorship of terrorism

REVOLUTIONARY
- Acting to overthrow a regime to establish a new regime
- Acting to create a new state out of the territory of an existing state, e.g., nationalist insurgents
- Acting to create a fundamental change in the nation-state system, e.g., pan-nationalist or anarchistic movements

ENTREPRENEURIAL
- Acting autonomously from any existing nation-state but also from any aspirant would-be nation-state
- Operating transnationally, may hire themselves out to states or other groups
- Engaging in criminal actions but usually as a means to other political ends, e.g., bank robberies and kidnapping for ransom in order to finance operations or else to drive out some foreign presence

II.   Goals of Actors

- Regime maintenance
- Regime change
- Limited advantage (subsystem changes)

quickly expanded its list of targets to include Israel and the western nations.

The example of the "Extraditables," an extension of the Medellín drug cartel, which is essentially a criminal entrepreneurial group, shows how even entrepreneurial groups can act as protectors of a status quo or as a revolutionary group. In this case the status quo would have been the cartel's domination over much of the economic life of Colombia and over the rural communities producing the coca crop. It has also behaved in a revolutionary manner in seeking to destabilize the Colombian government through wholesale terrorism against not only the Colombian government but even against terrorist guerrilla groups that have interfered in the drug cartel's operations and profits.

State actors also can seek to produce revolutions in other nations or else use terror to achieve limited goals. Iran has sought to export its Islamic revolution to neighboring Muslim states and the very same Islamic Revolutionary Guards Corps that acts as an organ of state repression within Iran has set up training camps in Lebanon's Bekaa valley to train Hezbollah guerrillas and terrorists bent on establishing an Islamic state in Lebanon and on destroying the State of Israel. Israel meanwhile developed its own corps of quiet killers, known as the "Wrath of God," who engage in the limited pursuit of tracking down and killing Palestinians, or others, considered to be responsible for terrorist actions against Israel, such as the Black September operatives who planned and executed the Munich Olympics massacre, or else considered to be public enemies of Israel, such as Khalil al Wazir. In fact, it is this wide range of possible motives enjoyed by each of the actor types that makes state sponsorship of terrorism at all possible.

Of course, classification schemes do not accommodate all cases perfectly. There are at least two types of terrorist groups that are anomalies, namely what this dictionary describes as "anarchistic leftists" and state co-opting groups.

Augustus Norton and others have used "anarchist" or "anarchistic" as an additional classification. One can argue that anarchists, too, should fall under the heading of "revolutionary" since they also seek a revolutionary transformation of the nation-state system to a nonstate system, which also entails the overall transformation of existing regimes. While few groups today openly identify themselves as being anarchists, there is a type of revolutionary group that espouses tentatively revolutionary socialist goals while behaving for all practical purposes as if its goals were anarchistic. During the student radicalism of the late 1960s, a number of similar student groups emerged in Europe, North America, and Japan that spoke the language of the New Left but ultimately appeared to pursue terrorist violence as an end in itself rather than as a strategy to achieve revolution. In spite of their self-identification with a world socialist revolution, they amounted to little more than practicing anarchists, or perhaps even nihilists, insofar as they limited their purposes to destroying the existing capitalist states rather than building the foundations of some successor socialist state. While this type of group does form a subspecies of the revolutionary terrorist groups, it is sufficiently different from other revolutionary groups to deserve its own distinctive label of "anarchistic leftist terrorists."

The other anomalous group type are those nonstate groups that are so powerful relative to a weak, or weakened, state that they are able to penetrate the apparatus of state power and to usurp government power for their own ends. Examples of this can be found in the penetration of the Salvadoran transitional government's military and security forces in the early 1980s by privately run "death squads," or al Qa'eda's penetration and cooptation of the Taliban regime in Afghanistan prior to initiating the mass casualty attacks of 11 September 2001.

Although these cases seem anomalous, the "anarchistic leftists" are simply a variation of the revolutionary actor while the state co-opters are entrepreneurial or revolutionary actors that exploit opportunities to usurp control over a weakened state for achieving limited ends. Having established a classification scheme broad enough to encompass even these subspecies, the reader can proceed to study who and what the various terrorist groups are and what it is each is seeking.

To provide further qualitative and quantitative information regarding the various groups that will better facilitate comparison between groups the authors have provided brief tallies of the numbers of various actions attributed to each group. These tallies are also analyzed as percentages of the total numbers of actions attributed to each group. The figures used have been based largely on the statistical database appended to Edward F. Mickolus's three major chronologies spanning the period from 1968 to 1987.

Notes

1. H. H. A. Cooper. *Evaluating the Terrorist Threat: Principles and Applied Risk Assessment. Clandestine Tactics and Technology Series.* Gaithersburg, Md.: International Association of Police Chiefs, 1974, p. 4.

2. Thomas B. Thorton. "Terror as a Weapon of Political Agitation," in *Internal War*, Harry Eckstein, ed., New York: Free Press, 1964, pp. 71-91.

3. Michael T. McEwen. "Psychological Weapons Against Terrorism: The Unused Weapon," *Military Review*, 66, 1, January 1986, p. 62.

4. National Advisory Committee on Criminal Justice Standards and Goals. *Report of the Task Force on Disorders and Terrorism.* Washington, D.C.: U.S. Government Printing Office, 1976, p. 3.

5. Taken from the title of Frederick J. Hacker's *Crusaders, Criminals or Crazies: Terror and Terrorism in our Time.* New York: Bantam, 1978.

6. Grant Wardlaw. *Political Terrorism: Theory, Tactics, and Counter-Measures.* Cambridge, Mass.: Cambridge University Press, 1982, p. 16.

7. Thorton in Eckstein, ed. p. 72.

8. Richard Schultz. "Conceptualizing Political Terrorism: A Typology," in *International Terrorism: Current Research and Directions*, Alan D. Buckley and Daniel D. Olson, eds. Wayne, N.J.: Avery Publishing Group, Inc., 1980, pp. 9-15.

9. Stephen Sloan. *The Anatomy of Non-Territorial Terrorism: An Analytical Essay. Clandestine Tactics and Technology Series*, Gaithersburg, Md.: The International Association of Chiefs of Police, 1978, p. 3.

10. Brian Jenkins. *International Terrorism: A New Mode of Conflict.* Los Angeles, Calif.: Crescent Publications, 1974.

11. Albert Parry. *Terrorism: From Robespierre to Arafat.* New York: The Vanguard Press, 1976, p. xi.

12. Reprinted from M. Confino, *Daughter of a Revolutionary.* London: Alcove Press, 1974 in Walter Laqueur, ed. *The Terrorist Reader: An Historical Anthology.* New York: New American Library, 1978, pp. 68-70.

13. P. Timothy Busnell, Vladimir Shlapentokh, Christopher K. Vanderpool and Jeyaratnam, eds., *State Terror: The Case of Violent Internal Repression.* Boulder, Colo.: Westview Press, 1991, p. 31.

14. See, "Appendix: Manual of the Urban Guerrilla," in Robert Moss, *Urban Guerrilla Warfare*. London: International Institute for Strategic Studies, 1971.

15. Stephen Sloan, "International Terrorism, Conceptual Problems and Implications," *Journal of Thought: An Interdisciplinary Quarterly*, 17, 2, Summer 1982, p. 23.

16. Claire Sterling. *The Terror Network: The Secret War of International Terrorism*. New York: Holt, Rinehart and Winston, Reader's Digest Press, 1981.

17. Stephen Sloan, "Technology and Terrorism: Privatizing Public Violence," *IEEE Technology and Society Magazine*, Vol. 10, No. 2 Summer 1991.

18. David F. Ronfeldt, John Arquilla, Graham E. Fuller, and Melissa Fuller. *The Zapatista Social Netwar in Mexico*. Santa Monica, Calif.: RAND, 1998.

19. This term was originated by Lt. Col. David G. Bradford (USAF) during discussions with Stephen Sloan and others concerning terrorism.

20. Schultz, Richard. "Conceptualizing Political Terrorism: A Typology," in Alan D. Buckley and Daniel D. Olsen ed. *International Terrorism: Current Research and Future Directions*. Wayne, N.J.: Avery Publishing Group, 1980, pp. 9-14.

21. Wilkinson, Paul. *Political Terrorism*. London: Macmillan, 1974.

22. Richard Schultz., op. cit, pp. 1-11.

Reader's Note

Note on transliterations of Arabic and Persian words and names: The authors have not adopted a single, consistent phonetic transliteration of the names or words cited in this dictionary that were originally written in the Arabic script. Popular literature and journalistic usages have made most readers familiar with inexact transliterations of Arabic and Persian words and their use has completely outpaced the efforts of linguistic purists to devise a consistent, universally observed scheme of transliteration for such words. For instance, most readers are already more acquainted with Koran than with the more precise Quran, or with Hezbollah rather than Hizballah. Therefore, to make this reference volume more accessible to a wider readership, current and more common spellings have been preferred to more unfamiliar alternative spellings. Other Arabic or Persian names have been phonetically transliterated whenever a popular usage was not already current.

Users of this volume should note that cross-references in each dictionary entry are printed in boldface type.

THE DICTIONARY

-A-

ABC WARFARE AND/OR WEAPONS. Acronym for atomic, biological, and chemical weapons. *See also* WEAPONS OF MASS DESTRUCTION

ABDUL RAHMAN, SHEIKH OMAR (1938-). Islamic fundamentalist cleric and leader of the **Islamic Group**, a fundamentalist group in Egypt. Abdul Rahman together with the **Munazzamat al Jihad** defendants was accused of **assassinating** President Anwar Sadat in 1981. Abdul Rahman, who is blind, was considered an accessory due to his issuing the Islamic judicial decree of *takfir* authorizing the killing of Sadat but was acquitted. After his release, Abdul Rahman led a puritanical Islamic fundamentalist movement which aims to topple the regime of Hosni Mubarak in order to create an Islamic state. The Islamic Group has tried to accomplish this in part by attacks upon non-Muslim tourists in Egypt, particularly those visiting the archaeological remnants of pre-Islamic Egypt.

Although banned from entering the United States as a person known to be associated with terrorist groups and activities, Abdul Rahman nonetheless obtained a tourist visa in Sudan and came to New Jersey where he became the prayer leader of a small mosque in Jersey City. Following the **World Trade Center bombing** he was implicated in that conspiracy as well as in a broader conspiracy to bomb other public places in New York, including the Holland and Lincoln tunnels, and the United Nations building as well as a plot to murder U.S. Senator Alfonse d'Amato (R., N.Y.) and UN Secretary-General Boutros Boutros-Ghali. On 24 June 1993, eight of Abdul Rahman's followers were arrested in connection with this plot. Government transcripts of conversations between Abdul Rahman and his followers secretly taped by an FBI informer revealed his discussing the relative merits of various targets for this terrorist **bombing** campaign.

On 27 August 1993 Abdul Rahman was indicted in U.S. Federal District Court with leading this conspiracy to wage the bombing campaign upon the United States. The trial of Abdul Rahman, along with 11 other defendants charged with the bombing of the World Trade Center and for the conspiracy to bomb the New York landmarks, began on 10 January 1995. On 1 October 1995 Abdul Rahman was convicted of seditious conspiracy, solicitation, and conspiracy to murder Egyptian President Hosni Mubarak; solicitation to attack U.S. military installations; and conspiracy to conduct the bombing campaign against New York tunnels and landmarks. On 17 January 1996 Abdul Rahman was sentenced to life imprisonment for his role in the **Holland Tunnel bomb plot**. He is currently serving his sentence in a U.S. federal prison.

Abdul Rahman was also the spiritual mentor of El Sayyid A. Nosair who assassinated **Jewish Defense League** (JDL) founder Rabbi Meir Kahane on 5 November 1990. Nosair was convicted for the murder of Kahane on 1 October 1995.

ABU NIDAL (1935-). Sabri Khalil al Banna was born in Jaffa, Palestine, but fled with his family to Beirut in 1948. He joined **Al Fatah** after the 1967 Arab-Israeli war, adopting the nom de guerre Abu Nidal, meaning "father of the struggle." As a high-ranking member of the **Palestine Liberation Organization** (PLO), he was put in charge of its diplomatic mission in Sudan in 1970 and afterward was appointed chief PLO representative in Iraq. After the October 1973 war he grew disillusioned with the direction of the PLO under **Yasir Arafat**'s leadership and founded his own rival group, the **Fatah Revolutionary Council**, in 1974.

Abu Nidal reputedly has tried to **assassinate** Arafat on a number of occasions and therefore was put under a death sentence by the PLO. In addition to the Fatah Revolutionary Council, Abu Nidal has founded and directed other groups such as **Black June**, the Revolutionary Organization of Socialist Muslims, and the Arab Revolutionary Brigades, which may be either separate groups or merely different names for the same group. As the organizational relationship of these groups to one another is unclear, analysts tend to speak of an "Abu Nidal Organization" rather than the Fatah Revolutionary Council or its satellite groups.

Abu Nidal has enjoyed the state sponsorship of Iraq from 1974 to 1983, Syria from 1983 to 1987, Libya from 1987 to 1997, and after a brief limited cooperation with Egypt from 1997 to 1998, he returned to Iraq in December 1998 where he again enjoyed state sponsorship. After relocating his organization to Libya, Abu Nidal reportedly spent a year in Poland under the protection of the Polish security services. The notoriety of his terrorist actions has moved each of his sponsors to distance themselves from him. Although the Iraqi government, with which Abu Nidal had the longest-standing relationship, ordered his organization to leave Iraq in 1983 subsequently during the 1990-1991 Persian Gulf crisis and Operation Desert Storm, Abu Nidal's organization is believed to have carried out assassinations on behalf of Iraq against Arab officials critical of Saddam Hussein, in particular, the Speaker of the Egyptian National Assembly, killed on 12 October 1990, and also PLO official Salah Khalaf, killed on 14 January 1991.

Abu Nidal still has 200 to 300 followers, mainly in Lebanon but also found in Syria, Libya, and Iraq. From 1983 to 1997 Abu Nidal was headquartered in Libya but moved to Egypt after the Qaddafi regime began to improve its relations with the United States by cooperating to resolve the deadlock over **extraditing** the suspects in the **Pam Am Flight 103 bombing** for trial at The Hague. While in Egypt Abu Nidal cooperated with Egyptian security officials in their operations against the **Islamic Group**. In April 1998 his operatives bombed a mosque in San'a, Yemen, used by Egyptian fundamentalists and in July 1998 his operatives assassinated an Islamic Group leader, Sheikh Mohammad Salah Mottalid, at another San'a mosque. On 3 July 1998, however, Abu Nidal was confronted by a revolt of 10 of his followers who tried to wrest control of his organization from him. The Egyptian security forces put Abu Nidal under protective arrest on 5 July 1998 and proceeded to deport the 10 dissidents. News of his presence in Egypt leaked out in August 1998, much to the embarrassment of the Egyptian regime which adamantly denied his presence in Egypt. On 6 December 1998 he was allowed to leave from Cairo to Tehran, Iran, and from there he moved to Baghdad, Iraq where he apparently enjoys renewed sponsorship by the Iraqi regime.

ABU NIDAL ORGANIZATION. Name by which Western intelligence and law-enforcement agencies refer to the umbrella organization comprising the **Fatah Revolutionary Council** and other Palestinian terrorist groups all headed by Sabri Khalil al Banna (aka, **Abu Nidal**).

ABU SAYYAF GROUP (ASG). The Abu Sayyaf group is an **Islamic fundamentalist** faction that split from the **Moro Liberation Front** (MLF) in 1991, apparently due to disagreements over the MLF's negotiations with the Philippine government. Originally led by Abdulrajik Abubakar

Janjalani (d. 1998), the ASG is attempting to create an Iranian-style Islamic republic in the Mindanao and Sulu islands of the Philippine Archipelago, which are predominantly Muslim-inhabited areas.

The ASG **bombed** a light passenger plane in Manila in 1993 and was involved in the bombing of a Philippine airliner on 11 December 1994 in which one Japanese citizen was killed and 10 others were injured. The group is linked to Ramzi Ahmad Yousef and Omar Ben Mahmoud, both later convicted in the **World Trade Center bombing**. Apparently, Yousef planned the bombing of the airliner in flight as a trial run for an intended simultaneous bombing of 10 American airliners in flight. The group apparently also planned to **assassinate** Pope John Paul II during his January 1995 visit to the Philippines.

After numerous **kidnappings**, bombings, and killings directed largely against Christians, the ASG conducted its first open offensive against the predominantly Roman Catholic town of Ipil of about 50,000 people on Mindanao Island on 7 April 1995, killing dozens of inhabitants and taking several as hostages. MLF members apparently joined the ASG in this action but eventually Philippine troops pushed the insurgents back into the hills. In 1997 the ASG conducted numerous assassinations including the killing of a Roman Catholic bishop in February.

On 18 December 1998 the leader and founder of the ASG, Abdulrajik Abubakar Janjalani, was killed in a clash with Philippine troops and leadership of the group passed to Khadaffy Janjalani. On 20 March 2000 ASG took around 50 people hostage on the island of Basilan, 550 miles south of Manila, many of them schoolchildren who were later released. On 23 April 2000 the ASG took 21 persons hostage from the Malyasian island resort of Sipadan and moved to an ASG hideout on the island of Jolo. When the Philippine government refused their demands the ASG beheaded two male hostages, which led the Philippine army to attack the rebels. By 10 September 2000 about 21 hostages were released after payments of ransom reportedly numbering millions of dollars from the European Union following Libyan mediation with the rebels. After September 20 two French journalists and one American taken hostage escaped and only one Filipino was reported as remaining a hostage. The group is estimated to have about 230-250 members with ties to other Islamic extremists in South Asia and the Middle East.

ACHILLE LAURO HIJACKING. *See* PALESTINE LIBERATION FRONT.

ACTION-FRONT OF NATIONAL SOCIALISTS. The Aktion-gemeinschaft Nationaler Sozialisten (ANS) was a German **neo-Nazi** off-shoot of the defunct right-wing National Democratic Party. This group has engaged in paramilitary training and terrorist activities to over-throw the Federal Republic of Germany and restore a right-wing au-thoritarian nationalist regime. The ANS was formed in 1977 by former West German Army lieutenant Michael Kühnen, who led the group in violent attacks against foreign immigrants, Jews, and leftists. Apart from conducting this violence and vandalism, the approximately 270 ANS members were heavily involved in paramilitary training, stealing mili-tary arms, and committing robberies.

ANS leader Michael Kühnen was first arrested in late 1977 for paint-ing swastikas on shop windows in Hamburg. In 1978 an antipolice riot in Schleswig-Holstein broke out when German police tried to prevent about 120 ANS members from dedicating a plaque honoring Adolf Hitler. Michael Kühnen and 19 other ANS members were arrested then and later released. Four other ANS members were arrested in August 1978 for plotting to **bomb** the Kiel office of the Communist Federation party.

Kühnen was sentenced to four years in jail for incitement to racism and glorification of violence. In 1980 his followers in Hamburg "tried" an ANS member whom they suspected of being an informant and a homosexual, who was accordingly murdered on 28 May 1981. During Kühnen's imprisonment his lieutenant, Christian Worch, led the ANS until he, too, was arrested on bombing charges in March 1980. Kühnen was released from jail in 1982 on condition that he not employ, train, or shelter neo-Nazis. Defying the terms of his probation, he reconstituted the ANS group under the new name "Action-Front of National Social-ists/National Activists" until it was also banned in 1983.

Although Kühnen died in mid-1991, he left behind a network of similar neo-Nazi groups which relied on **cellular structures** to elude penetration and suppression by German authorities. Kühnen reputedly also masterminded the strategy of building up support for the neo-Nazi movement in Germany by exploiting widespread antiforeigner resent-ment against guest workers and immigrants fleeing Eastern European countries in the post-Communist era.

AFRICAN NATIONAL CONGRESS (ANC). The ANC, founded in 1912, is the oldest and largest black nationalist political party in South Africa and was the leading group there in the struggle against apartheid. From

1912 to 1961 the ANC was a purely political movement but, following the 20 March 1960 massacre of some 69 demonstrators by South African police in Sharpeville, it was banned by the South African government. The political apparatus of the ANC went into exile while Nelson Mandela (1918-) and other ANC leaders remaining in South Africa created the armed wing of the ANC, **Umkhonto we Sizwe**, to carry out limited violence against the South African regime to gain redress of grievances.

As Umkhonto we Sizwe has used indiscriminate **bombings** of civilian areas and has targeted white farmers as well as South African military and security forces to attain its political agenda, it could be properly classified as a terrorist group. Accordingly, the U.S. Department of Defense 1990 publication *Profiles of Terrorist Groups* listed the African National Congress among the terrorist groups operating in Africa. Other observers and institutions, viewing the ANC in the context of South African apartheid and state repression of its black and colored citizens, argued that the African National Congress should be considered a legitimate political group and were therefore reluctant to classify it as a terrorist group. Accordingly the U.S. Department of State Office for the Coordinator for Counterterrorism did not include the ANC among its listing of the major terrorist groups.

It should be noted that the legitimacy of the ends sought by the African National Congress and the heinous nature of the apartheid it fought are matters logically distinct from the questions of the legitimacy of the tactics elected by the ANC to achieve its ends and to fight apartheid. The African National Congress, like the Sinn Fein of Ireland, can be regarded as a primarily political entity, while its armed wing, like the **Irish Republican Army**, may be studied as a military phenomenon and assessed accordingly. Therefore the terrorist actions attributed to the ANC are analyzed under the heading of Umkhonto we Sizwe.

The African National Congress obtained a majority of votes for the National Assembly of the transitional South African regime on 26-29 April 1994 which in turn elected ANC leader Nelson Mandela president on 9 May 1994. The ANC again won a majority vote in the 2 June 1999 National Assembly elections and then elected Thabo Mbeki president and successor to Mandela, who chose not to run for reelection. The ANC has therefore been the governing party in South Africa since the first truly democratic elections were held in 1994.

During this period, however, the National Truth and Reconciliation Commission conducted a review of the acts of terrorism by both the former apartheid regime and the various nonstate and antistate groups, including actions by the ANC. On 29 October 1998 the Commission published findings in a 3,500-page report which revealed the extent of both the previous apartheid regime's involvement in **state terror** against opponents of the regime, including members of the ANC, as well as the ANC's own involvement in terrorism directed against its opponents both in the apartheid government and in rival opposition groups, as well as use of repression against its own members and other black South Africans. The ANC was cited for torturing and executing prisoners in its military camps in Angola, for targeting civilians as well as members of the military forces, and for failure to control the violence of its own activists. During the post-apartheid era sporadic violence has continued between supporters of the ANC and those of rival parties, such as the Zulu-based Inkatha Freedom Party.

AIR INDIA BOMBING. On 23 June 1985 Air India Flight 182, a Boeing 747 carrying 307 passengers and 22 crew members, en route from Montreal to New Delhi, disintegrated at 30,000 feet and 180 miles off the west coast of Ireland. All aboard perished, most of them naturalized Canadian citizens of Indian origin. The same day, luggage from an Air India flight originating in Vancouver, British Columbia, exploded at Tokyo's Narita Airport, killing two Japanese baggage handlers. While forensic evidence from the fragments of Flight 182 have not conclusively proven that the airplane was **bombed**, most experts familiar with these incidents concluded that Flight 182 contained a radio bomb similar to the one reconstructed from remains of the bomb that exploded at Narita airport.

The Royal Canadian Mounted Police learned that two Sikhs had checked in bags at Vancouver to be transferred to flight 182 in Montreal but neither of them later joined that flight. Credit for bombing the Air India flight was claimed in the name of the Dashmesh Regiment (*see* SIKH MILITANTS) but also by the Kashmir Liberation Army. Canadian Sikhs have angrily denied that Sikhs had any role in the incident.

AIR TRAVEL SECURITY. Airline traffic has been an attractive target for terrorist attacks since the early 1960s and with two main types of attacks: airplane **hijackings**, with or without a barricade hostage situation, and **bombings** of airliners in flight. Airline traffic has become increasingly more attractive as a target for terrorism since more Americans fly internationally than any other nationality, making up 40 percent of passengers worldwide, while a significant portion of international air traffic is routed through the United States. Other nations, particularly in Western Europe and Israel, whose nationals have been frequently targeted also have found threats to their air carriers to be a great problem.

Bombings directed at airliners are relatively cost-effective compared to bombing attacks directed at stationary structures, such as buildings or commercial installations, and tend to be nearly completely lethal to their targets. The bombs that destroyed **Air India 182, Pan Am 103,** and **UTA 772** were much smaller than the bombs used to damage the Murrah building in **Oklahoma City,** the **World Trade Center** in New York, and the **Khobar Towers** in Saudi Arabia and whereas the numbers of those killed in those attacks were exceeded by the number of those that survived, these attack in every one of the airliner bombings not one passenger or crew member survived. Also, whereas the bombings of fixed physical structures have left sufficient forensic evidence to allow possible identification of the attackers, the physical evidence of an aerial bombing tends to be strewn over greater areas or else can be lost entirely, as in the case of the Air India bombing which occurred over the open seas, making identification and detection of the perpetrators much more difficult. Unlike ground-based physical structures, it is virtually impossible to harden airplanes so that they can survive a bombing and even a minor explosion in an airplane in flight may be sufficient to ensure catastrophic failure of the plane.

In the decade of the 1960s hijacking, or "skyjacking" as it became popularly known, was the main form of terrorist attack on air traffic. After three hijackings of American airliners to Cuba in 1961, President John F. Kennedy commissioned an interagency task force with finding ways to prevent "air piracy," as hijacking became known. Most of the over 200 hijackings occurring during the 1960s, of which only 80 involved American carriers, were carried out by persons seeking political **asylum** in other nations or else criminals seeking to hijack a plane to a remote destination in order to evade capture within their own country. Few of these situations involved hostage-barricade incidents on the ground. Countermeasures taken by nations whose airlines tended to be targeted frequently included the U.S. **Sky Marshal program** begun in 1970 in which armed U.S. Marshals were allowed to fly undercover on selected flights, the use of profiling and preboarding interviews of passengers intending to flight on the Israeli El Al airline, and intensified screening of passengers and luggage carried out in British, French, and German international airports. Such programs have been publicized in order to deter would-be hijackers. In 1972 the U.S. government required X-ray screening of luggage and that passengers and others pass through metal detectors before being allowed to access the boarding areas in airports. As a result of these measures hijackings decreased from accounting for 33 percent of the terrorist acts in 1968-1969 to about 7 percent in the 1970s, to about 4 percent in the 1980s. While hijackings accounted for about 10 percent of terrorist incidents during the 1990s this was due, in part, to the fall in the absolute numbers of terrorist incidents worldwide.

The sanctions placed on nations giving hijackers sanctuary have lessened the numbers of possible destinations for would-be hijackers and the strict security measures at most airports in most developed nations have rendered hijacking more a phenomenon limited to underdeveloped nations with minimal airport security. Moreover Great Britain, France, Germany, Israel, the United States, and more recently, Peru, have developed hostage-rescue response capabilities that put hijackers intending to hold hostages on an airport runway at a distinct disadvantage.

With the denial of opportunities for hijacking most terrorism against airliners has turned to the more deadly form of the bombing of airliners. Since 1985 approximately 1,000 passengers and crew members have been killed by bombs planted on airliners. Although luggage and carry-on items can be X-rayed this does not ensure detection of all bombs. In 1986 Nizar Hindawi arranged to have a briefcase carried onto an El AL airliner in which the explosive material had been coated evenly throughout the interior of the baggage making it virtually undetectable to X-ray. Most explosive materials can be detected by neutron-activation screening devices but these are relatively expensive and do not reliably detect Semtex, a sophisticated pliable explosive developed by the former Communist Czechoslovak regime, which sold massive quantities of it to the Libyan regime of Muammar Qaddafi.

Following the Pan Am 103 bombing, President George H. Bush established a White House Commission on Aviation Safety and Security charged with evaluating weaknesses in air travel security and making recommendations for improving air travel security. Two reports were issued, the first in May 1990 and the second in September 1996. While this commission recommended increased funding for airline security by $430 million, when the Federal Aviation Re-authorization Act of 1996 (Public-Law 104-132) was signed into law by President Bill Clinton on 9 October 1996 it actually authorized $1,097 million for various anti-terrorist security measures of which $190 would go to the Federal Aviation Administration for upgrading airport security.

The following international conventions and treaties pertain to terrorist and other threats to air travel security: the 1944 Chicago Convention on International Civil Aviation, Annex 17, which set international standards for safeguarding civil aircraft; the 1963 Tokyo Convention on Offenses and Certain Other Offenses Committed on Board Aircraft; the 1970 Hague Convention for the Unlawful Seizure of Aircraft, which has become the basis for antihijacking laws passed in the United States and other nations; the 1971 Montreal Convention for the Suppression of Unlawful Acts Against the Safety of Aircraft; and the 1988 Protocol for the Suppression of Unlawful Acts of Violence at Airports Serving International Aviation, which supplements the 1971 Montreal Convention.

Following the worst hijacking incident involving the simulataneous hijacking of four U.S. passenger flights that were used in the **suicide attacks** against the **World Trade Center and Pentagon on 11 September 2001**, President George W. Bush announced on 27 September 2001 that 4,000 National Guard troops would be mobilized to assit in security at the 420 commerical airports within the United States. He also proposed plans to increased federal oversight of training, performance, and job benefits for the 28,000 workers who screen passengers and baggage. Legislation to fulfill these aims was initiated by the U.S. Congress during the following months.

ALEX BONCAYAO BRIGADE (ABB). The death squad unit of the Communist Party of the Philippines which was active since the mid-1980s. It is believed to have carried out over 100 murders, in particular the 21 April 1989 shooting of U.S. Army Colonel James Rowe while he was driving to work in Manila. This appears to be one of several **"Sparrow Squads"** which are specialized **death squads** within the **New People's Army**, the armed wing of the Communist Party of the Philippines.

ALFARO VIVE CARAJO ORGANIZATION (AVC). The Alfaro Vive Carajo ("Alfaro Lives, Damn It!") Organization was a nonstate, Ecuadoran revolutionary group that sought to overthrow "oligarchic and imperialist" institutions and to force the withdrawal of foreign interests from Ecuador. The AVC received material aid from the **M-19** group in Colombia and possibly from Nicaragua, Cuba, and Libya.

While founded in the late 1970s this group surfaced in August 1983 with the theft of the swords of the early 20th century Ecuadoran revolutionary and national hero, Eloy Alfaro. In May 1984 the group **bombed** the U.S. embassy compound in Quito. In October 1984 it then seized the Costa Rican embassy to protest the **extradition** of AVC leader Rosa Cardenas. On 16 October 1985 it seized the Mexican embassy, telexing messages to other Latin American countries condemning the severing of diplomatic relations between Ecuador and Nicaragua and denouncing U.S. support for the **contras**. In May 1986 it **kidnapped** a Constitutional Court member, who was later freed after a negotiated surrender. In April 1987 it bombed a police station in Quito.

At its height the AVC had 200 to 300 members and financed itself primarily by bank robberies. The AVC exploited its activities as a means to gain publicity for its cause, once even seizing a radio station in February 1986 to broadcast a propaganda tape celebrating its third anniversary. Due to the death of its leader in 1986 and the killings and arrests of its rank and file in 1986-1989, accomplished largely by **death squad** activity conducted by security forces, the organization lost its strength and is apparently defunct.

ALIANZA APOSTÓLICA ANTI-COMMUNISTA (AAA). The "Anticommunist Apostolic Alliance" was a Spanish state-sponsored **death squad** with the limited aims of suppressing leftism and separatism. The AAA conducted attacks on Basque separatists of the **Basque Fatherland and Liberty** group within the Basque regions of Spain and France and bombed both the Catalan Center in Madrid and the Catalonian paper *El Papus* in Barcelona in 1977. In January 1977 two AAA gunmen killed four prominent leftist lawyers in Madrid. The arrest of these gunmen led to more convictions of other AAA activists. The activities of this group ceased in the early 1980s.

ALIEN TORTS CLAIMS ACT. Also known as the Alien Tort Statute (28 U.S. Code s. 1350), this obscure section of the Judiciary Act of 1798 allows U.S. citizens or foreigners to sue foreign persons for civil damages in U.S. District Courts for personal damages suffered in violation of the law of nations or of a treaty law of the United States. In the case *Forti v. Suarez-Mason* (1987), Argentinean nationals sued retired General Carlos Guillermo Suarez-Mason, who was a principal in carrying out the Argentinean junta's **Dirty War** against suspected leftists, for damages resulting from their family members being tortured, arbitrarily detained, suffering degrading treatment, being falsely imprisoned, assaulted and raped, and for the plaintiffs' emotional distress, and for having caused the "disappearance" of the mother of one of the plaintiffs. The Northern U.S. District Court of California ruled that the plaintiffs could sue only for the causes of torture, arbitrary detention, and summary execution, as these were the only causes recognized under the "law of nations" at the time of enactment of the Alien Tort Statute. In the case of *Ortiz v. Gramajo* (1995) the Federal District Judge Douglas P. Woodlock ruled that a former Guatemalan General, Hector Gramajo, was obliged to pay a nun, Sister Ortiz, of the Ursuline Order, $7.5 million for damages due to her being kidnapped, raped, and tortured during interrogation by Guatemalan soldiers under Gramajo's command who had accused her of collaboration with leftist insurgents.

These cases are unusual since it is unlikely that the authors of the Alien Tort Statute contemplated that foreign nationals would seek redress of grievances in U.S. court for human rights abuses committed outside the United States. On the other hand human rights advocates view this as an important avenue for U.S. citizens to seek redress of grievances for damages caused by state repression abroad or for damages caused by state-sponsored terrorist groups.

ALIENATION. Among the possible psychological causes for people being attracted to political violence or terrorism is the phenomenon of alienation, meaning that the persons or group view the nation-state entity, or the political system or constitution, or particular policies or actions by the government, as illegitimate or as harmful to their own interests. The **relative deprivation theory** held that people would resort to civil protest or political violence when concrete social, economic, or political privileges were withdrawn or denied to them that they had come to expect as customary. Generally this approach tended to belittle the role of political **ideology** or of nonmaterial values as being a sufficient cause for civil unrest.

The research of Ted Gurr examined the effects of long-term and short-term political, social, and economic deprivation on civil unrest in 114 nation-states but also examined the effects of the presence of effective governmental institutions, the impact of foreign support for internal dissidents, and also the role of perceptions of state legitimacy by the people of the nation-state. Edward N. Mueller also studied the relative impact of deprivation variables and psychological variables on civil unrest in selected nations. The findings of Gurr and Mueller demonstrated that the public's perceptions of government legitimacy have an influence on levels of civil unrest independent of the effect of economic, social, or political deprivation. To the extent that individuals and groups believe that they are members of a national community and that their governmental system is just, they will be less inclined to resort to political violence to gain redress of grievances. To the extent that they view themselves as part of a separate ethnic-national community or else view the state as oppressive, they will be more inclined to participate in secessionist or revolutionary activities. These studies did not address the specific effect of alienation in causing terrorism or certain forms of terrorist behavior.

Jerrold M. Post used the notion of alienation to account for the formation of different types of terrorist groups as well as different internal organizational forms in his study "Rewarding Fire with Fire: Effects of Retaliation on Terrorist Group Dynamics," *Terrorism*, 10: 23-36,(1987). According to Post's analysis members of **anarchistic leftist terrorist** groups are persons who are alienated from their parents' value systems, including their parents' identification with the political system. By contrast the members of **ethno-nationalist terrorist** groups identified strongly with their parents' values and "the world of their fathers" but their parents are alienated from the nation-state due to their identification with a separate national identity. Because anarchistic leftists reject the hierarchy and authority of their parents they tend to choose a **cellular organization** with little hierarchical structure whereas nationalist-separatists accept hierarchy in their political front and military wings and accept subordination to authorities within their nationalist-separatist organization. In either case the alienated group has some set of alternative values to which it subscribes which provide a political **ideology** or guide to action.

ALPHA 66. Anti-Castro Cuban exile group centered in Miami, Florida, made up mainly of Cubans of African descent. Alpha 66 planned raids on Cuba and **bombings** of Cuban interests abroad but was foiled in a plan to conduct a raid on Cuba when one of its operatives, Francisco Avila Azcuy, turned out to be a double agent both for Cuban intelligence and the FBI, and provided information sufficient to convict seven members for violating the Neutrality Act. Cuban authorities claim that Alpha 66, in tandem with other anti-Castro exile groups, has been responsible for 15 bombings since 1994 when another Alpha 66 operation was foiled by U.S. authorities.

AMAL. Amal (Arabic: "Hope," also the acronym of Afwaj al Muqawama al Lubnaniya, "Lebanese Resistance Detachments") is a political and paramilitary organization representing the Shi'a of Lebanon. Although a nonstate actor, Amal has a political infrastructure and gained territorial control over large areas of West Beirut and southern Lebanon during the Lebanese civil war. After the 1978-1979 revolution in Iran, Amal enjoyed some support from the Iranian revolutionary government. After 1982, however, Iran began to form the rival **Hezbollah** militia under its sponsorship and Amal turned to Syrian sponsorship instead.

Since Amal sought to change the terms of power in Lebanon in favor of the Shi'a by setting aside the 1943 "national covenant" between Lebanon's Christians and Sunni Muslims, it may be considered a revolutionary actor. Yet it has neither sought to exclude other confessional groups from participation in Lebanese politics nor has it sought to create a full-scale Islamic state in Lebanon after the Iranian model. For these very reasons more militant Amal members deserted Amal for the splinter group **Islamic Amal**. Most of these defectors were absorbed later into Hezbollah, a Shi'ite militia created under Iranian sponsorship that sought to establish an exclusively Islamic state in Lebanon.

While Amal is indigenous to Lebanon it was founded by an Iranian clergyman, Musa Sadr, who arrived in Lebanon in 1957 and established the "Movement of the Deprived" in 1974 to help the Lebanese Shi'a gain political power. With the outbreak of civil war in 1975 Musa Sadr authorized the creation of a military branch, which properly was the organization called "Amal." The Israeli invasion of southern Lebanon in 1978 and continual Palestinian-Israeli clashes in the largely Shi'ite south of Lebanon increased the Shi'a's acceptance of Amal as representing and protecting their community. The subsequent victory of an Islamic revolution in Shi'ite Iran also bolstered the confidence of Lebanon's Shi'a and their support for Amal.

Amal's relationship with Iran's revolutionary government was initially friendly but deteriorated rapidly. With the disappearance of Imam Musa Sadr during a visit to Libya in August 1978, Amal's leadership has passed into the hands of more secular nationalistic Shi'ite politicians who had less sympathy for the ideal of creating a theocratic Islamic state in Lebanon. Also due to the enmity that had grown between the Lebanese Shi'a and Palestinian guerrillas operating in the south of Lebanon, Amal, in effect, welcomed the 1982 Israeli invasion in the naive hope that Israeli forces would shortly leave and return the south of Lebanon to Shi'ite control. Iran's diplomatic overtures to Libya also antagonized Amal members who believed that the Libyan leader Muammar Qaddafi was responsible for Imam Musa Sadr's disappearance. The falling out between the Iranian government and Amal as well as the defection from Amal of more militant fundamentalists led Iran to sponsor the creation of the Hezbollah militia, which absorbed much of the strength of Amal's following.

Amal's notoriety as a terrorist group stems largely from a mistaken association between it and the rival Hezbollah which carried out a highly visible campaign of vehicle **bombings, assassinations,** and **hostage takings** against U.S. and other Western targets in Lebanon. By late 1988 Amal had carried out 18 notable terrorist actions affecting non-Lebanese nationals, including a major bombing, a **hijacking**, and six kidnappings. By contrast Hezbollah from 1982 until late 1988 had carried out 137 noteworthy terrorist acts, including 38 bombings, 26 **kidnappings**, four hijackings, seven assassinations, and six rocket attacks. Amal's role in assuming custody of the hostages taken in the hijacking of TWA Flight 847 in 1985 likewise was secondary to that of Hezbollah in planning and carrying out the original hijacking. Following the TWA 847 incident, open warfare erupted between Hezbollah and Amal. Amal afterwards accepted Syria as its main foreign sponsor in place of Iran.

Following the ending of the Lebanese civil war in October 1990, with the defeat of **Phalangist** forces by the Syrian-backed forces of Lebanese President Elias Hrawi, Amal joined forces with Hezbollah in a campaign of harassment and attrition against Israeli forces and allied South Lebanese Army forces in the south of Lebanon. Nabih Berri mended fences with Iran to the extent that he met with Iranian Foreign Affairs Minister Kamal Kharrazi and Majlis Speaker Ali Abkar Nateq-Nouri on 15 September 1997 in Tehran, where he declared that southern

Lebanon would become "Israel's Viet Nam." On 28 August 1997 Israeli forces seeking a preemptive strike at Hezbollah and Amal positions instead became trapped in the Wadi Hujuar canyon by crossfire from Amal and Hezbollah units. When the Israeli Golani Brigade called on their artillery to give them cover to enable a retreat, the barrage instead ignited the dry scrub forest on the hillside creating a firestorm that burned three of their members to death. On 6 September 1997 when 16 members of the Israeli naval commando unit, Shayetet 13, attempted a preemptive strike at Hezbollah positions in the village of Ansariyah midway between Sidon and Tyre they were again surprised by Amal and Hezbollah units waiting in place, who had already rigged a roadside bomb to ambush the Israeli unit. Supported by units of the Lebanese Army the joint Amal-Hezbollah units killed 11 of the Israeli team in what was considered to be the worst defeat Israel had suffered in southern Lebanon since 1985.

'AMAL. The Islamic Action [= 'Amal] Organization is one of a number of Shi'ite **Islamic fundamentalist** groups within Iraq seeking to overthrow the Ba'thist government in that country. Despite the similarity between the transliteration of its Arabic name and that of the **Amal** group in Lebanon these are different organizations having no direct ties with one another. The 'Amal group was independent of the **al Da'wa** group in Iraq, which is the largest of the Shi'ite Muslim fundamentalist groups in Iraq. Both organizations have become affiliated with the umbrella group known as the Supreme Assembly for the Islamic Revolution of Iraq, created in 1982 and headquartered in Tehran, Iran.

ANANDA MARG. The Indian Hindu group, Ananda Marg ("Path of Eternal Bliss") was a nonstate mystical and religious sect devoted to the worship of Kali, the Hindu goddess of destruction. Followers of this sect undertook terrorist activities in the period 1975-1978 for the limited purpose of freeing their founder, Prabhat Ranjan Sarkar, who had been imprisoned in India for murder. This sect comprises a large number of American, Australian, and European followers both in their home countries as well as in India. These non-Indian followers had engaged in attacks on Indian diplomatic targets abroad, giving an international terrorist character to what otherwise might have been dismissed as a rather minor sectarian, domestic Indian phenomenon.

Within India on 2 January 1975, Ananda Margists killed Narayan Mishra, India's Minister of Railways, in a **bombing**, killing two and wounding 25 others. In March 1975 they attempted to kill the Chief Justice of India in a grenade attack. On 4 July 1975 the group was banned under the Indian government's declared state of emergency. Although the ban was lifted in 1977, the group carried out a series of bombings against Indian government targets in Australia. On 15 September 1977 an Australian Ananda Margist stabbed the Indian military attaché in Melbourne, and on 19 October 1977 another stabbing attempt was made in Melbourne against an Air India official. In February 1978 they bombed a conference of the Asian and Pacific Commonwealth heads of government being held at the Sydney Hilton Hotel killing two people. American members of the sect were involved in an assault against an Indian embassy official in the Philippines on 25 March 1978 and were implicated, along with two Australians, in a plot to bomb the Indian embassy in Thailand on 21 April 1978.

Since 1978 the group, numbering around 1,000 members, has largely ceased terrorist activities and operates openly in India, principally in the West Bengal region.

ANARCHISTIC LEFTIST TERRORISTS. Also known as "Fighting Communist Organizations" (FCOs). During the late 1960s the antiwar protest movement among university students in Europe, Japan, and the United States gave rise to several terrorist groups that defy ready identification as **revolutionary** or **entrepreneurial** terrorist groups. The **Red Army Faction** in West Germany, **Direct Action** group in France, the **Red Brigades** and **Prima Linea** in Italy, the **Communist Combatant Cells** in Belgium, the **Weather Underground** in the United States, and the **Japanese Red Army** all rationalized their terrorism in revolutionary leftist terms but ultimately appeared to pursue terrorist violence as an end in itself rather than as a strategy to achieve revolution. These groups could be considered "leftist" only insofar as they despised capitalism, believed in the superiority of a socialist state, and often spoke in Marxist jargon. For the most part they consisted of alienated middle-class youth who subsisted on their support groups or from the proceeds of robberies and **kidnappings**. They were also anarchistic insofar as they limited their purposes to destroying the existing capitalist states rather than building the foundations of some successor socialist state. These groups also became known in Europe as "Fighting Communist Organizations," and included, in addition to the five European groups mentioned above, the **November 17** group in Greece, the Dev Sol group in Turkey (*see* REVOLUTIONARY PEOPLE'S LIBERATION PARTY/ FRONT), the **October First Antifascist Resistance Group**, and the **Popular Forces of April 25** in Portugal.

Many of these groups envisioned themselves as vanguard groups in a world revolutionary movement and sought contacts and working relations with such groups as the **Popular Front for the Liberation of Palestine** (PFLP), which often provided them with training and experience. The Red Army Faction eventually became co-opted by the East German communist regime while the Japanese Red Army has similarly become dependent on the Libyan and Syrian regimes. These groups were characterized by a certain heady romanticism and utopianism that drew forth the scorn of more orthodox Marxist thinkers and activists, who generally criticized such groups as seeking to substitute the volunteerism of vanguard groups for patient construction of class-based revolutionary consciousness. Although the writings of Herbert Marcuse were much admired by such anarchistic leftists, he himself derided their movement as the "pubertarian struggle."

Because most of the members of these groups reject their family origins or ethnic and religious backgrounds, they are isolated from a community support system that ensured steady recruitment of younger members into their ranks and therefore the survival of these groups became doubtful. In part for the same reason ethnic and sectarian-based terrorist groups and movements have supplanted anarchistic leftist terrorist groups as the main source of antistate and international terrorist violence in the 1990s. By the mid-1990s most of these movements had ceased to operate, with the Red Brigades ceasing in 1988, Direct Action neutralized in 1987, the Communist Combatant Cells neutralized in 1985, and the Red Army Faction issuing communiqués in June and August 1992 and finally in March 1998 announcing its laying down arms.

ANGRY BRIGADE. The "Angry Brigade" was a nonstate British group of ultraleftist university students who adopted more antiauthoritarian, anarchistic ideas in the wake of the 1968 student uprising in France. Their goal of revolutionary anarchism was sought through a series of bank robberies and some 27 **bombings** in the period from 1968 to 1971, including two bomb attacks on the home of Robert Carr, British Secretary of State for Employment. Apparently the group intended these bombings as acts of **armed propaganda** but sought to avoid causing human casualties. The arrest of the so-called Stoke Newington Eight in August 1971 effectively smashed the core of the group and ended its activities.

ANIMAL LIBERATION FRONT (ALF). The ALF is a nonstate group with the limited aim of protecting "animal rights," specifically by stopping the use of animals as foodstuffs or experimental subjects and also by freeing captive animals. The ALF emerged as one of the more radical animal rights groups when founded in 1978 by Ronnie Lee in England. Its membership now includes several thousand in both Britain and the United States.

On 17 November 1984 the ALF announced that it had contaminated Mars candy bars manufactured in Southampton, England, with rat poison to protest the manufacturer's use of monkeys in tooth decay research. Around 3,000 tons of candy bars were recalled and destroyed, equivalent to a loss of sales of 15 million pounds sterling. The ALF was believed to be responsible for the **arson** of a livestock disease laboratory under construction at the University of California at Davis that caused $3.5 million in damages. On 3 April 1989 the ALF freed 1,200 experimental rabbits, frogs, and mice from a University of Arizona research lab and then torched the lab as well as the university administration building. On 6 July 1990, British police defused a **bomb** the ALF had planted in London's Regent Park.

In the United States since June 1991 the ALF has targeted facilities supporting mink fur production beginning with the arson of a mink feed storage barn at Oregon State University. In this campaign the ALF has destroyed the equivalent of 130 years of data on mink fur production. In February 1992 the ALF torched a Michigan State University researcher's office, destroying 10 years of toxicology research data even though the experiments had used animal semen samples rather than direct testing upon live animals. Although the ALF claims to adhere to a policy of nonviolence its members often stage attacks under different names, such as the "Animal Avengers," and whenever violence is threatened or done to victims the credit is taken in the name of the "Justice Department," which many observers believe is merely another name under which ALF members operate.

In the period 1977 to 1993 about 313 attacks in the United States by animal rights activists have been documented, for over half of which

ALF claimed responsibility. Of these about one half of the cases involved minor vandalism of property, one quarter involved the release of animals, while others involved threats against a person, major property damage, arson, bomb threats, firebombings, and some bomb hoaxes. The main targets have been biomedical research facilities, comprising university, federal, and private research facilities, accounting for 135 of the 313 attacks; fur retailers, 48 attacks; private homes, 43 attacks; and sellers of meat products, 33 attacks. Due to the number of such attacks and threats to property and lives involved, the FBI classified ALF as a domestic terrorist organization in 1991.

More recent ALF incidents include the following: during 1996 ALF activists raided over 22 mink farms; in January the "Justice Department" mailed 65 envelopes to hunting outfitters in British Columbia and Alberta which contained razor blades coated with rat poison; 30 March 1997 animal rights activists released 10,000 mink from a fur farm in Mount Angel, Oregon; on 4 July 1998 a United Vaccines Research Facility in Middleton, Wisconsin was attacked and 150 ferrets and mink released; on 24 October 1999 animal rights activists vandalized a research laboratory at Western Washington University in Bellingham, Washington, stealing several lab animals; in October 1999 a "Justice Department" communiqué claimed it had mailed over 80 razor blade booby-trapped devices to primate researchers after which seven of such devices showed up at primate research facilities; in November 1999 about 40 activists invaded a mink farm in South Jordan, Utah, and destroyed about 300 breeding cards and released 20 mink while the ALF attacked and vandalized the Avian Health Laboratory at the Veterinary College of Washington State University causing thousands of dollars of damage to the facility.

Other animal rights activists, such as People for the Ethical Treatment of Animals and the University Students Against Vivisection, have criticized the ALF's activities for drawing the animal rights movement into disrepute.

ANIMAL RIGHTS MILITIA (ARM). The Animal Rights Militia is a more radical British splinter group of the **Animal Liberation Front** (ALF). While having the same limited aims as its parent group of stopping the use of animals in foodstuffs and experimental research, the ARM has resorted to more violent tactics of direct attacks upon researchers rather than limiting itself to vandalism of research facilities or economic sabotage. In January 1986 the ARM planted **bombs** under two cars and at two homes of four different victims, all involved either in the commercial breeding of animals or in research involving animal subjects. Although the ARM gave prior warnings about its bombs, none of which exploded, the British government regarded this group as a grave public menace at that time.

ANTHRAX ATTACKS. Anthrax is an acute infectious disease caused by the bacterium *Bacillus anthracis* which affects livestock and humans. It has also been weaponized to serve as a **weapon of mass destruction** by the United States, Russia, and Iraq. Anthrax has been used in a terrorist attack within the United States during September-October 2001.

Weaponized anthrax is finely-milled to a particle size of five microns or less. It is also treated to neutralize static electric charges that make particles cling together, so making their dispersal more difficult. The milled anthrax is also mixed with silicate powders or bentonite to facilitate aerosol dispersal. While intestinal or subcutaneous anthrax can be fatal, the inhaltion form of anthrax is most acute if not correctly diagnosed and treated with antibiotics within 36 hours after exposure. The anthrax used in the U.S. attacks was milled to weapons grade but lacked the bentonite additive known to be used in Iraqi weapons-grade anthrax.

On October 5 Robert Steves, an employee of American Media, Inc. of Boca Raton, Florida, died of inhalation anthrax. By October 15 it was discovered that an anthrax-contaminated letter had also been mailed to U.S. Senate Majority Leader, Tom Daschle. Other targets of anthrax-contining letters included the *New York Post*, Tom Brokaw, news anchor of NBC news, and Dan Rather, news anchor of CBS News. Anthrax contamination was also found at the congressional mail sorting center, the Brentwood general mail facility, which sorts White House mail, the office of New York Governor George E. Pataki, as well as other post offices in Florida, Virginia, and Missouri. Anthrax contamination was also found at the home offices of the Pakistan daily *Jang* as well as in the mail bags of the U.S. embassy in Moscow, Russia. Altogether by mid-November, five persons had died from inhalation anthrax and 17 cases of anthrax exposure were confirmed after over 1,000 people had been tested for anthrax infection.

All of the known contaminated letters originated in Trenton, New Jersey, and three letters contained threatening messages. Although these letters were dated "Sept. 11" and contained slogans of a militant **Islamic fundamentalist** character, the FBI regarded these letters as possible decoys to disguise the work of a domestic terrorist or terrorist group not connected with the **World Trade Center and Pentagon attacks of 11 September 2001**.

On 15 October 2001 Prediednt George W. Bush requested Congress appropriate $1.5 billion to buy antibiotics to treat up to 12 million people.

ANTI-ABORTION TERRORISM. Controversy over the legalization of abortion since the U.S. Supreme Court decision in *Roe v. Wade* in 1973 has led to the creation of a large, grassroots movement of anti-abortion groups which have sought to pressure state and national politicians to take steps to curtail and even outlaw abortion in all but the most extreme circumstances. Another set of tactics has included protests and sit-ins at abortion clinics while another extreme wing of the anti-abortion movement has embarked on several forms of violence meant to intimidate abortion providers and to scare away their clients. Such acts of violence have included vandalism, **arsons**, **bombings**, assaults, and killings and may be regarded as an **entrepreneurial** form of single-issue terrorism.

During the 1980s and 1990s the federal government used various laws and court rulings to stop anti-abortion protestors from blocking access to clinics and from engaging in blatant intimidation of clients and clinic workers. Such laws include the **Racketeering-Influenced Corrupt Organizations Act** (RICO), originally passed to outlaw interstate operations of organized crime, as well as the Freedom of Access to Clinic Entrances Act (FACE) passed in late 1994, which limited the scope of protest activities near clinics. Some extremists in the pro-life movement reacted by deciding to engage in violent activities aimed not only at the clinics and clinic workers but also in some cases aimed at police and firefighters who have arrived at clinics to respond to bombings.

On 10 March 1993 Dr. David Gunn was shot to death outside his Pensacola, Florida, clinic by Michael Griffin, a Christian fundamentalist who was later convicted for murder and sentenced to life imprisonment. On 20 August 1993 Dr. George R. Tiller, owner of a clinic in Wichita, Kansas, which had been the object of unruly protests in 1991, was shot by Rachelle Shannon, an anti-abortion protestor. Shannon was later convicted for firebombing six clinics in California, Nevada, and Oregon. Tiller was not seriously injured in this attack but on 29 July 1994 Paul Hill, a former Presbyterian minister, shot to death Dr. John B. Britton along with his bodyguard, also at a clinic in Pensacola. Paul Hill, who was the first person to be tried under the FACE Act for this killing, was found guilty of murder and sentenced to death. In August 1994 Federal Marshals were sent to guard a dozen clinics, including the Pensacola clinic which immediately hired a new doctor to replace the one slain by Hill.

On 3 August 1994 the FBI began an investigation of the extreme pro-life movement which included persons such as the Rev. David C. Trosch, a Roman Catholic priest who was teaching his followers that the killing of abortion providers was "justifiable homicide," as well as Michael Bray, a former member of the **Army of God** (AOG) who had served prison time for bombing clinics in 1984, to determine whether the up-surge in anti-abortion violence was due to a criminal conspiracy. Anti-abortion violence spread to Canada where Dr. Garson Romalis, a doctor who performed abortions, was shot by a sniper in his home in Vancouver, British Columbia, on 8 November 1994. On 31 December 1994 John Salvi III attacked the Planned Parenthood Clinic in Brookline, Massa-chusetts, opening fire with a semiautomatic rifle. Because of its security arrangements no one was hurt there but Salvi proceeded to the PreTerm Clinic where he killed two attendants and wounded five persons in the waiting room. Salvi was later convicted for murder in 1996 but shortly afterwards committed suicide. By the end of 1994 death threats against abortion providers have occurred at 25 percent of the clinics through-out the United States and during 1995 threats continued while five clinics were burned in San Francisco in the period February 15 to March 2. Although the lethality of attacks was increasing the total numbers on violent incident had been falling since the FACE Act, with a total of 3,429 acts in 1993; 1,987 in 1994, 1,815 in 1995, and fewer than 400 in 1996 by September 23. By January 1996 the U.S. Justice Department continued to search for a conspiracy but anonymous officials stated that they had found no evidence of conspiracy so far.

In 1997 the most serious anti-abortion bombings to that time were claimed in the name of the Army of God in Atlanta. On 16 January 1997 there were two bombings at the Atlanta Northside Planning Services abortion clinic and another at the Otherside Lounge, a bar frequented by lesbians. The first bomb at the Northside clinic injured no one but when police and firefighters arrived a secondary bomb exploded that wounded six persons, including two FBI special agents and an agent of the Bureau of Alcohol, Tobacco, and Firearms. The intended purpose of the secondary bomb was to kill first responders. This was the first time in 30 years that bombers used a secondary device with the intention of killing or maiming first responders. The bombs at the Northside clinic were made with 10 to 20 sticks of dynamite and showed a sophistication not ordinarily seen with amateur bombmakers. Earlier in January 1997 two firebombings of clinics in Tulsa turned out to be the work of a juvenile.

The first fatality from an abortion clinic bombing occurred at the All Women Health Care Clinic of Birmingham, Alabama, on 29 January 1998 when a bomb that exploded at opening time killed a security guard who was also an off-duty police officer, Robert Sanderson, and severely injured the clinic's head nurse, Emily Lyons. In February 1998 the FBI named Eric Robert Rudolph as the main suspect in this bombing, putting him on the 10 Most Wanted List. Five sniper attacks occurred in Ontario and western New York, one killing Dr. Barnett A. Slepian of Buffalo, New York, on 23 October 1998 and the other crippling Dr. Hugh Short of Ancaster, Ontario, on 10 November 1998. Other sniper attacks occurred in Rochester, Ontario, in October 1997; Winnipeg, Manitoba, in November 1997; and the earlier attack in Vancouver in November 1994. On 6 May 1999 the FBI charged James C. Koop, a roving anti-abortion protestor, with the murder of Dr. Slepian. Koop was arrested in France on 29 March 2001 in Dinan, Brittany, and was due to be extradited to the United States.

Because of the extreme religious motivation of many of the anti-abortion extremists and the continuing controversy over the abortion issue in the United States and Canada, it is likely that lethal instances of anti-abortion terrorism will continue for the foreseeable future. The outbreak of anti-abortion violence in 1993 had the effect of raising the security costs for clinics from $3,000 to $100,000 a year with $50,000 a year being typical for clinics in metropolitan areas.

ANTICOMMUNIST SECRET ARMY. The Ejército Secreto Anticommunista (ESA) was a state-sponsored, repressive organization aimed at silencing leftist dissent and activism in Guatemala that operated largely as a death squad. The ESA emerged in 1977 during a period when the leftist guerrilla movement was reconsolidating its forces. The

ESA involved members of the Guatemalan security forces who partici-pated in assaulting and killing students at San Carlos University. The ESA published death lists of leftist intellectuals and labor leaders and forced many left-wing politicians to flee Guatemala. Also the ESA is thought to have been responsible for the **bombing** of the Soviet Tass News Agency office in Guatemala City in 1988.

ANTI-IMPERIALIST INTERNATIONAL BRIGADE. The Anti-Imperi-alist International Brigade was a nonstate, revolutionary leftist group that was a front for the **Japanese Red Army** (JRA) set up to carry out retaliatory strikes against the United States for its April 1986 bombing of Libyan targets.

ANTITERRORISM AND EFFECTIVE DEATH PENALTY ACT OF 1996. Public Law 104-132 signed by President Bill Clinton on 24 April 1996 gave federal law enforcement agencies new powers with which to counter domestic and international terrorists. It permits blocking fund-raising by groups for terrorist causes abroad. It increases the power to exclude persons affiliated with groups designated as terrorist organiza-tions from entering the United States and also limits use of **political offense exception** claims by suspected terrorists to avoid deportation or **extradition.** The act bans U.S. aid to nations that provide military assis-tance to **terrorist states.** The act also enhanced standing of U.S. citizens to sue foreign nations for terrorist acts against U.S. citizens abroad (*see* ALIEN TORTS CLAIMS ACT). The act also authorized $1 billion to be spent over a four-year period to strengthen law enforcement efforts against terrorism and also increased federal penalties for engaging in international terrorist activities within the United States.

ANTITERRORIST LIBERATION GROUPS. The Grupos Antiterroristas de Liberación (GAL) was a Spanish government-sponsored group that acted largely as an anti-Basque **death squad**, killing **Basque Father-land and Liberty** (ETA) members and other prominent Basques whether within Spain or France. Spanish police comprised much of the member-ship of this group, who in turn recruited, financed, and directly aided hit men to **assassinate** as many as 37 Basques in France during 1983-1987.

In November 1984 GAL killed a popular Basque leader, Santiago Brouad, and in September 1985 killed four Basques in France. GAL members were well-equipped killers who were provided with surprisingly good intelligence about the whereabouts of ETA members. Within France alone GAL killed over 20 ETA members and suspected sympathizers during the 1980s. In 1991 two GAL members were tried and convicted for attempted murder. In 1994 two Spanish police officers, José Amedo and Michel Domínguez, were sentenced to a total of 108 years for ordering and carrying out **kidnappings** and murders of suspected ETA members. During 1995 the Spanish Supreme Court investigated allegations that Prime Minister Felip González had authorized these secret death squad activities but by November 1996 the court ruled there was insufficient evidence to warrant his prosecution. The controversy surrounding González's alleged involvement cost his Socialist Party the parliamentary election in March 1996.

ARAB LIBERATION FRONT. The Arab Liberation Front is an Iraqi-sponsored Palestinian militia group numbering about 500 militants. While this group's purported goal was to establish an independent Palestinian state, the Iraqi government created it in 1969 mainly to extend Iraqi influence within the Palestinian movement and within Lebanon. This has brought the group into conflict with other groups in Lebanon enjoying Syrian state sponsorship, such as **Amal**. Apart from its role in Lebanon, the Front has conducted some armed raids into Israeli territory. This group helped form part of the **Rejection Front** in 1974 opposed to the peace overtures of **Palestine Liberation Organization** (PLO) Chairman **Yasir Arafat** and is led by Abdul Rahim Ahmad, one of Arafat's critics.

ARAFAT, YASIR (1929-). Given name, Abdul-Rahman Abdul-Rauf Arafat al Qudwa al Hussayni, nom de guerre, Abu Ammar, Yasir Arafat has been the head of the **al Fatah** group since the early 1960s and has been concurrently chairman of the **Palestine Liberation Organization** (PLO) since February 1969. Arafat was born in Jerusalem into a Palestinian family related to the Grand Mufti of Jerusalem who played a key role in organizing and leading Palestinians against the Israelis during the first Arab-Israeli war. Arafat studied engineering at Cairo University in the 1940s and 1950s, where he met other Palestinians such as Khalil al Wazir and Salah Khalaf, who become cofounders with Arafat of **Fatah** in 1957, originally a secret group that surfaced in 1959.

Following the defeat of the Arab states in the 1967 war Fatah undertook guerrilla warfare with Israel, and its popularity, together with that of Arafat, grew among the Palestinians, allowing Arafat and other guerrilla leaders to take over control of the PLO in 1969.

Arafat has survived a number of challenges to his preeminence in the leadership of the PLO. In 1974 leftist and pro-Syrian groups, which coexisted with Fatah within the framework of the PLO, formed a **"Rejection Front"** in protest to Arafat's willingness after the October 1973 war to adopt diplomatic initiatives on behalf of the Palestinians rather than relying an armed struggle alone. Although Fatah was responsible for the terrorist actions committed by the **Black September** group, in 1974 Arafat committed Fatah to abstaining from terrorist actions outside of the borders of former mandatory Palestine, a declaratory policy not always observed in practice as shown by the activities of the Fatah-controlled **Hawari Group** and **Force 17** group. In 1982 the Israeli army forced the PLO and Arafat out of Lebanon although both returned in 1983. In 1983 Syria instigated a revolt against Arafat among extremists within the PLO including some members of Fatah, and he was again forced to flee from Lebanon when his new base in Tripoli was besieged by PLO mutineers.

Arafat used the opportunity afforded by the *intifada* to shift the attention of PLO leaders and subgroups from their intramural quarreling to adopting a common strategy. The 19th Palestine National Council held in Algiers in November 1988 vindicated Arafat's approach with an implicit endorsement of the right of Israel to exist alongside a Palestinian state in the West Bank and the Gaza Strip and by adopting a resolution renouncing the use of terrorism outside the borders of former mandatory Palestine. While Arafat explicitly denounced the use of terrorism, he regarded subsequent armed struggle within Israel and the occupied territories as a form of insurgency rather than terrorism. With his signing of the 13 September 1993 peace accord with Israel on behalf of the PLO, Arafat has renounced such further insurgent or terrorist activity within Israel proper or the occupied territories. In 1994 both Arafat and the late Yitzhak Rabin became joint recipients of the Nobel Peace Prize for their efforts in establishing the peace settlement.

Following the Peace Accord the Palestinian Authority established its initial headquarters in the West Bank city of Jericho and opened offices in Gaza. On 20 January 1996 elections were held throughout the areas controlled by the Palestinian Authority for the 88-seat Palestine Council with Arafat's slate winning 88 percent of the vote. On 12 February 1996 Arafat was sworn in as president of the Palestinian Authority.

On 14 December 1998, in the presence of U.S. President Bill Clinton, Arafat presided over a meeting of the Palestine National Council, with 500 of its 650 members present, which voted to ratify the PLO Central Council's 10 December 1998 decision to rescind the specific clauses in the PLO Charter calling for the destruction of the State of Israel.

ARENA. The Alianza Republicana Nacional, the "Republican National Alliance," is a Salvadoran right-wing political party that formerly sponsored, or directly engaged in, repressive violence against Salvadoran leftists. On 28 March 1982 ARENA won a plurality of the seats in the Constituent Assembly elections, and its leader, Roberto D'Aubuisson (d. 1992), was elected president of that body. Due to ARENA's substantial role both in shaping the Salvadoran polity and later in winning the Salvadoran presidency, it cannot be accurately described as being either a nonstate actor or a state-sponsored actor but rather as a state-co-opting one (*see* STATE CO-OPTATION).

With the intensification of leftist guerrilla attacks in the early 1980s, right-wing **death squad** activity soared. In 1982 Roberto D'Aubuisson led a coalition of Salvadoran businessmen and rightist politicians in forming the ARENA party on whose ticket D'Aubuisson made an unsuccessful bid for the presidency in 1984. Many ARENA members, including D'Aubuisson, appear to have been directly involved in death squad activity both before and after ARENA was formed. ARENA itself was believed to have been behind the **assassinations** of political rivals both in the centrist Christian Democrat party and the leftist Democratic Revolutionary Front.

On 19 March 1989 ARENA candidate Alfredo Cristiani won the Salvadoran presidential election, which was preceded by an intensification of death squad activity, rising from an average of 21 deaths per month in 1987 to 30 deaths per month in the first three months of 1988. The rate then fell to 16 deaths per month following Cristiani's election. Since then, during the early 1990s, ARENA has largely desisted from terrorist activities, having achieved most of its political aims.

ARGENTINE ANTICOMMUNIST ALLIANCE (AAA). The AAA consisted of policemen and security forces who began in 1973 to take the law into their own hands in intimidating and killing leftist politicians, journalists, and intellectuals. The AAA may be considered a nonstate **death squad** precursor to the state-sanctioned death squad terror from

1976 to 1983 known as the **"dirty war."** The AAA would publish notices signed "AAA" listing targeted persons who were warned to leave the country. Victims included not only Argentine Communists and leftwing Peronistas but also persons of moderate political opinions whose statements or actions incurred the ire of AAA members. The AAA was the creation of Jose Lopez Riga, an astrologer who became an influential confident of Juan and Isabel Peron before Juan Peron returned to Argentina in 1973. Jose Lopez Riga, also known as "El Brujo" (the Sorcerer) due to his fascination with the occult, was an ardent rightist who saw no role for the left wing of the Peronista movement once Peron had returned to Argentina.

When several thousand **Montoneros** arrived at Ezeiza airport among an estimated one million who had turned up to greet Peron on his returned they were fired upon by armed thugs recruited by Riga with the result that 13 people perished and over 100 were wounded in the crossfire between the leftist Montoneros and rightist followers of Riga. Following the Ezeiza massacre the interim government of Dr. Hector Campora resigned on 13 July 1973 and Raul Lasitiri, who was Riga's son-in-law, assumed the interim presidency. Between this time and Peron's reelection as president on 12 October 1973, Riga organized the AAA which began to attack Montoneros, as well as prominent writers, union members, and priests whom Riga viewed as leftists. The most prominent victim of AAA was Jose Rucci, the head of the Congress of Workers on 25 September 1973, an action wrongly blamed on the Montoneros.

Jose Lopez Riga was appointed Minister of Welfare after Peron's election and the AAA operated out of the Welfare Ministry building during the brief presidency of Peron, which ended with his death on 1 July 1974, and during the brief tenure of Isabel Peron, which ended with the military coup of 24 March 1976. Riga succeeded in totally alienating the Montonero movement from Peron and during this time antigovernment terrorism both by the Montoneros and **People's Revolutionary Army** escalated to an unacceptable level. Due to pressure by the military and the remaining leftists within the Peronista movement Isabel Peron was forced to send Riga into exile in the form of an ambassadorial appointment to Spain, and after this the AAA effectively ceased to exist. Once the military dictatorship came to power it took over death squad activity in a much more conscious and brutal manner.

ARMED COMMANDOS FOR NATIONAL LIBERATION. The Comandos Armados de Liberación Nacional (CALN) was a Puerto Rican separatist group formed in 1969. CALN **bombed** five U.S. businesses in Puerto Rico on 14 November 1970 as well as bombing the San Juan consulate of the Dominican Republic on 23 November 1970. The Puerto Rican police broke up this group, but its members later reorganized themselves and joined with members of another separatist group forming in 1974 the **Armed Forces of National Liberation** (FALN).

ARMED FORCES OF LIBERATION. Fuerzas Armadas de Liberación. *See* FARABUNDO MARTÍ NATIONAL LIBERATION FRONT.

ARMED FORCES OF NATIONAL LIBERATION. The Fuerzas Armadas de Liberación Nacional (FALN) is the name of two unrelated groups:
1. Puerto Rican FALN: This group sought Puerto Rican independence through terrorist attacks in Puerto Rico and the United States. The group was formed from the merger of the remnants of the **Armed Commandos for National Liberation** (CALN) and the Armed Independence Revolutionary Movement in 1974.

   The group's first operation was to **bomb** five banks in New York City on 26 October 1974. FALN concentrated largely on bombing symbolic targets such as banks, corporation headquarters, government offices, and military installations, usually avoiding harm to life and limb. On 25 January 1975, however, FALN bombed the Fraunces Tavern, a site close to Wall Street apparently chosen for its symbolic value because George Washington bade farewell to his troops there at the conclusion of the War of Independence. Since the bomb exploded at the height of the lunch hour four diners were killed and 63 others injured, the first time a FALN bombing had caused fatalities. Afterwards FALN expanded its targets to include department stores and hotels, striking the Chicago area as well as New York and Puerto Rico. Despite a hiatus caused by the arrest of several members in April 1980, FALN continued its bombing campaign until 1983. With the capture of FALN bombing expert William Morales in June 1983 the bombing campaign on the mainland United States, totaling around 160 bombings, came to a virtual halt. The arrest of several FALN and **Macheteros** leaders in Puerto Rico on 30 August 1985 appeared to have set the group back and it has remained relatively inactive since then.

FALN differed from other Puerto Rican groups as it included among its roughly 50 members a large number of Puerto Ricans born and raised in the United States. This may explain why it was the only active Puerto Rican separatist group that regularly carried out terrorist acts on the U.S. mainland. FALN also had the distinction of being one of the few terrorist groups that ever threatened to use nuclear terrorism. In a communiqué published on 21 March 1980, FALN hinted that it would not hesitate to sabotage nuclear reactors. Such sabotage has never occurred, but FALN and other groups attacked several nonnuclear energy-related facilities in Puerto Rico, such as power pylons, substations, and even an oil refinery.

On 13 December 1998 Puerto Rico held its second referendum on the question of independence or statehood. Given five choices of statehood, independence, continued commonwealth status, or "free association" with the United States, and "none of the above," the largest share of votes at 50.2 percent went to "none of the above" with statehood winning 46.5 percent and independence winning only 2.5 percent and the free association and commonwealth options each receiving less than 1 percent. On 11 August 1999 President Bill Clinton offered clemency to 14 FALN members imprisoned for acts of terrorism contingent on their renunciation of the use of terrorism. On 7 September 1999 12 accepted the offer of clemency and were freed while two rejected the offer and remained in prison. The clemency offer drew criticism from Republican members of Congress as well as from members of law enforcement units whose members had lost life or limb from FALN attacks.

Earlier, on 6 December 1994, Claude Daniel Marks and Donna Jean Wilmott, two FALN members wanted for engineering the 1985 escape of FALN leaders from Leavenworth prison, surrendered themselves to federal authorities in Pittsburgh. Given the low vote for independence in the Puerto Rican referendum and the desperation evident among those FALN members at large who were surrendering themselves to authorities, the Clinton decision to grant clemency to the long-imprisoned FALN members may have been calculated to move the remaining FALN members at large to renounce the use of terrorism.

2. Venezuelan FALN: Younger members of the Venezuelan Communist Party, more attracted to the Cuban model of revolution, joined forces with the Venezuelan Revolutionary Movement of the Left (Movimiento Izquiereda Revolucionario, MIR), a left-wing faction of the ruling Democratic Action party, to form this Marxist guerrilla

group active in the 1960s and 1970s. With Cuban backing FALN carried out an urban terrorist campaign and also sabotaged foreign businesses and oil production facilities. FALN used **kidnapping** and **hijacking** as means to embarrass the Venezuelan government and to create publicity, at one point kidnapping the U.S. Army attaché, Colonel James Chenault, on 27 November 1963, and releasing him after the government freed several imprisoned leftists.

In 1969 after Cuba abandoned support for leftist guerrillas in Venezuela, MIR abandoned FALN to return to legality. FALN became inactive and its leader, Douglas Bravo (1933-), eventually accepted a presidential pardon in 1979.

ARMED FORCES OF NATIONAL RESISTANCE. Fuerzas Armadas de la Resistencia Nacional. *See* FARABUNDO MARTÍ NATIONAL LIBERATION FRONT.

ARMED ISLAMIC GROUP. The Groupe Islamique Armé (GIA) is a nonstate **Islamic fundamentalist** group that has sought to create an Islamic state in Algeria and took the leading role in the insurgency and civil war in Algeria 1992-2000 in the course of which well over 100,000 persons were killed. Following the 11 January 1992 Algerian army coup against President Ben Jedid, who had become resigned to an imminent victory by the Islamic fundamentalist **Islamic Salvation Front** (FIS) in the second round of national elections scheduled for 16 January 1992, the Islamic fundamentalists became divided over how to deal with the military takeover that had blocked their almost certain democratic ascent to power.

While many moderate fundamentalists favored conciliation and dialogue most of the FIS leaders favored confrontation. The **Islamic Salvation Army** (AIS) emerged from FIS cells that armed themselves to confront the regime violently. However this appears to have been in response to the emergence of the Armed Islamic Group, whose members were actually more radical Islamic extremists who had derided the electoral approach favored by the FIS. The GIA believed violent confrontation was inevitable and that armed **jihad** was the proper way to establish an Islamic state in Algeria. Most of the GIA members were "Afghans," that is, Islamic militants who had volunteered to fight with the **Mujahideen** of Afghanistan against the Soviet occupiers. Many of these were deeply influenced by their Iranian and Sudanese supporters who favored Islamic revolution and terrorism as means to establish an Islamic state. On 29 June 1992 President Boudiaf was **assassinated** by one of his own guards who appeared to have pro-Islamist sympathies. The Army generals began repression of the FIS and the GIA cells went into action beginning with primitive black powder **bombs** but progressing to the use of car bombs by late 1992.

The GIA sought to bring down the Algerian regime not simply through internal attacks on the government, its troops, and supporters but also by trying to bring international pressure on the regime. With the support of Iran and Sudan the GIA embarked on four successive strategies during 1992-1996 to pressure France and other Western governments to withhold material and moral support from the Algerian regime and to force the Algerian state to accommodate them in some externally imposed settlement in their favor. First, in August 1992 they bombed Hoari Boumedienne International Airport, near the Air France ticket counter, killing 12 and injuring about 128. This was meant to warn foreign travelers away from visiting Algeria and it also had the effect of making Algerians examine the social program of the FIS more closely and critically.

The second strategy was initiated in May 1993 when the GIA began targeting foreign or local journalists for killing. By the end of 1995 over 50 journalists had been murdered and often mutilated.

The third strategy began in August 1993 with attacks on French diplomats and citizens in Algeria. After **kidnapping** three French consular officials, when releasing the last one the GIA gave him a scrawled message to deliver: "Foreigners, leave the country. We give you one month." The implicit message was that France and other nations that supported the Algerian regime would pay with the blood of their own citizens. By December 1995 the GIA had killed over 100 foreigners, most of them French and none of them American. France retaliated with a crackdown in November 1993 arresting 88 persons known to have ties to the FIS.

The fourth strategy was to bring the war home to France. This was done dramatically with the **hijacking** of an Air France airbus A300 from Algiers on 24 December 1994, the second anniversary of the invalidated national election. The plane was flown to Marseilles where, after three passengers were murdered, the French Special Forces stormed the plane, killing all four hijackers and freeing the remaining 171 passengers. About 20 sticks of dynamite were found on board with which the hijackers had planned to explode the plane while in flight over Paris, raining plane fragments and human bodies over the French capital.

To bring the war to France more dramatically the GIA pursued a bombing campaign centered on Paris. On 25 July 1995 a bomb exploded in the Paris Metro killing seven and wounding 17. The series of bombings that followed wounded up to 150 people by October.

The killings, bombings, and massacres involved not only GIA and AIS attacks on government officials, soldiers, and police, but targeted entire villages of Algerian Muslims. It must also be noted that the Algerian government and progovernment paramilitary groups engaged in massive reprisals involving mass executions of jailed militants as well as entire villages viewed as sympathetic to the Islamists. This eight-year insurgency of 1992-2000 recalled the political violence and social division of the earlier Algerian war of independence of 1954-1962. A brief chronology of some of the more notable events follows which is more of a representative than a comprehensive and complete summary of the violence of this period.

On 27 December 1994 the GIA murdered four Roman Catholic priests in reprisal for the killing of its four hijackers, an action ordered by Abu Abdulrahman Amin, who was the purported "amir," or commander of the GIA. During 1995 the GIA exploded at least two bombs in France, wounding 31 people, and three massive car bombs in Algiers, killing 57 people and wounding more than 359 others.

In 1996 car bombs struck Algiers several times with one on February 11 killing 17 and wounding 93 and another on November 30 killing 15 and wounding 30. During December the GIA conducted mass slayings of five villages in which they slashed and hacked to death men, women, and children using knives and axes. A total of 82 civilians were killed in this grisly manner in December 1996 which the Algerian press came to call the "month of horrors."

In 1997 in the GIA carried out several mass killings of entire villages viewed as disloyal to the GIA cause. On 24 September 1997 when the Islamic Salvation Army called for a truce beginning October 1, GIA disregarded the FIS call for peace and continued its assaults, killing 11 female schoolteachers in a remote town 260 miles southwest of Algiers.

In 1998 another four massacres occurred in the period January 7-20 killing 98 total while a car bomb outside an Algiers café killed 10 and wounded 20. In July and December authorities uncovered mass graves of victims of the GIA one of which contained over 110 bodies.

By 1999 while a few isolated GIA attacks occurred Algeria was beginning to experience a return to normalcy. On April 15 Algeria elected a new president, Abdelaziz Bouteflika, who convinced some FIS leaders to agree to a national referendum to formalize an end to the civil war to be held on September 16. Over 5,000 imprisoned militants were released in July. After eight years from 1992 until 2000 of what some have called "the Second Algerian War," in which over 100,000 persons were killed, the GIA had largely ceased to operate. However, killings by other aggrieved groups or army units have continued sporadically to the present.

ARMED PROPAGANDA. Armed propaganda, or "propaganda by the deed," refers to the use of violent force not so much to achieve a tactical objective through the direct physical effects of the action, but rather to focus attention on the symbolic, political importance of the action or else to draw attention to the executing group's demands. In its earliest activities the **Basque Fatherland and Liberty** (ETA) group tended to bomb or vandalize Spanish Civil War memorials, actions of armed propaganda that had little effect on Spanish domination in the Basque provinces but ones that strongly signaled a Basque rejection of Spanish hegemony.

While campaigns of armed propaganda can be directed toward symbolic, nonliving targets, they can also be more lethal. The **Kurdish Workers' Party** (PKK) used to occupy villages in southeastern Turkey, murder scores of Turkish civilian men, women, and children, and then leave before the Turkish army could arrive on the scene. While the murder of those civilians could hardly serve any military purpose, such events would serve to portray the Turkish army as ineffective in protecting Turkish nationals, who would then be terrorized into leaving those regions claimed by the PKK terrorists as Kurdish lands. Similarly the seizure of the U.S. embassy in Tehran can be considered an act of armed propaganda meant to demonstrate the powerlessness of the United States to intervene in Iranian affairs.

Armed propaganda is by no means solely a tactic of nonstate terrorist groups. Brilliantly executed counterinsurgency actions or police raids on terrorist hideouts, orchestrated with favorable mass media coverage, could also be undertaken to produce a psychological impact on insurgent or terrorist groups far out of proportion to the physical effects of the act itself. An action such as the FBI's capture of the Lebanese hijacker Fawaz Younis on the high seas is meant not only to bring one suspected terrorist to trial, but also to serve notice to other would-be hijackers that a similar fate could await them, and so to deter them from future hijackings. Ordinarily when such tactics are being used by counterterrorist forces they are called "psychological operations."

ARMED RESISTANCE UNIT. Pseudonym for the **Revolutionary Armed Task Force**.

ARMED REVOLUTIONARY NUCLEUS. The Nuclei Armati Rivoluzionari (NAR) was an Italian right-wing terrorist group seeking to overthrow the current constitutional democracy in Italy to replace it with a Fascist-style authoritarian regime. This group appeared in December 1977 when it bombed the Rome offices of the Christian Democratic and Communist parties. In June 1980 NAR **assassinated** Roman judge Mario Amato, who had been instrumental in uncovering and convicting rightist groups violating Italy's ban on neo-Fascist groups, in particular the NAR. In the period from 1977-1981 the group perpetrated at least 25 terrorist acts, and Italian police implicated it in the 2 August 1980 **bombing** of the Bologna train station. On 2 May 1985 some 53 members of the NAR were sentenced to prison for their role in the terror campaign of 1977-1981.

In 1993 the NAR and other similar subversive right-wing groups were officially banned under the Mancino Law. In 1997 Massimo Morsello, the former NAR leader, joined together with Roberto Fiore, the former leader of the radical nationalist Terza Posizione (Third Position) group to create a new **neo-Nazi** organization, Forza Nuova (New Force), to embrace all the radical right, to the right of the National Alliance, the extreme right-wing party that escaped the Mancino ban.

ARMENIAN LIBERATION ARMY (ALA). The ALA was a nonstate Armenian guerrilla group with the revolutionary goal of restoring formerly Armenian portions of eastern Turkey to Armenian sovereignty. While this group **bombed** Turkish targets in Western Europe in the 1970s it has since sunk into obscurity.

ARMENIAN SECRET ARMY FOR THE LIBERATION OF ARMENIA (ASALA). The ASALA was a formerly Soviet-sponsored, revolutionary organization with the triple aims of regaining portions of eastern Turkey claimed as parts of historic Armenia, avenging the Armenians killed by the Ottoman forces during World War I, and forcing the Turkish government to acknowledge responsibility for the events of 1915. ASALA was a Marxist-Leninist organization that also declared its opposition to "imperialism." It is suspected that the Soviet Union sponsored ASALA as a means of pressuring Turkey to play a less accommodating role within NATO. ASALA also received aid from radical Palestinian groups with which it collaborated in Lebanon. Interestingly ASALA, an anti-American group, has committed only a few terrorist acts in the United States, one being the **bombing** of the Swiss Bank Corporation in New York on 26 May 1982, while a plot to bomb an Air Canada cargo building in Los Angeles was foiled on 30 May 1982.

ASALA was founded in 1975 and concentrated on the **assassination** and terrorization of Turkish diplomats to avenge Armenians killed in the pogroms in eastern Turkey. By 1981 it had engaged in at least 40 attacks in 11 countries. By mid-1982 ASALA had killed 24 Turkish officials and had carried out about 100 bombings, including an attack at Ankara airport in August 1982. It also attacked French targets under the name "the Orly Organization" and Swiss targets under the names "October Movement" and "June 9" to punish France and Switzerland for cracking down on ASALA agents traveling under falsified passports. The 15 July 1983 attack on Orly Airport that killed seven persons reportedly caused a split in the organization due to the disaffection of less militant members over the harm to the Armenian cause due to such "blind" acts of terrorism. One month later ASALA conducted an attack at Esenboga Airport in Ankara killing nine persons and injuring 28 while another assault in the Grand Bazaar of Istanbul killed two persons and wounded 27 others. The dissident group became known as the ASALA-Revolutionary Movement, while the main group became known as ASALA-Militant.

As its headquarters were located in Beirut, ASALA suffered some disruption, having been forced to flee due to the Israeli siege and bombardment of Beirut in the summer of 1982. ASALA bombed the French embassy in Lebanon in October 1987. It is believed that the leader of ASALA-Militant, Hagop Hagopian, was killed on 28 April 1988 by members of his own group. The head of ASALA-Revolutionary Movement is Monte Melkonian.

The power struggle within, and between, ASALA factions has led to a reduction in its terrorist acts since the mid-1980s, although ASALA members were suspected in playing a role in the September 1986 bombing campaign in Paris aimed at pressuring the French government into releasing three convicted terrorists, one of whom was an ASALA member. In the early 1980s ASALA also began using the front name of the Armenian Resistance Army. Although the ASALA claimed credit for an unsuccessful attack on a Turkish diplomat in Hungary on 20 December 1991, the group has been inactive since 1996. *See also* JUSTICE COMMANDOS OF THE ARMENIAN GENOCIDE.

ARMY OF GOD (AOG). The AOG is a nonstate terrorist group that has claimed responsibility for **bombings** against abortion clinics, a gay nightclub and which may have been involved in the **Olympic Park bombing** in Atlanta on 27 July 1996. In 1982 a group calling itself the Army of God **kidnapped** an abortion provider, Dr. Hector Zevallos and his wife, and forced him to tape an appeal to President Ronald Reagan to end legalized abortion. In 1984 a series of 10 bombings of abortion clinics occurred in the Washington, D.C. area with a sign reading "AOG" found at the front of one of the bombed clinics. Michael Bray was convicted for these bombings and after serving four years in prison he continues to be active in radical anti-abortionist activities.

Following Bray's release from prison, when four anti-abortion protestors were arrested during an Operation Rescue sit-in at the Democratic National Convention in Atlanta, one of them turned out to be Shelly Shannon, who was wanted for the attempted murder of Dr. George Tiller. A search of her home by authorities revealed the operations manual of the Army of God, which uses moral theology and casuistry to convince Christians that killing abortion providers is morally justified and which details various ways of halting abortion services, from using stink bombs made of butyric acid, to instructions for building bombs with C-4 and ammonium nitrate-fuel oil bombs.

The most serious attacks claimed in the name of "Units of the Army of God" were two bombings at the Atlanta Northside Planning Services abortion clinic on 16 January 1997 and another at the Otherside Lounge, a bar frequented by lesbians. The first bomb at the Northside clinic injured no one but when police and firefighters arrived a secondary bomb exploded that wounded six persons, including two FBI special agents and an agent of the Bureau of Alcohol, Tobacco, and Firearms. This was the first time in 30 years that bombers used a secondary device with the intention of killing or maiming first responders. On 21 February 1997 another bomb exploded at the Otherside Lounge, wounding five persons but this time the secondary device was located and deactivated without harm to life or limb. Following the Otherside bombing, letters in the name of "Units of the Army of God" claimed responsibility for the bombings and include invective against abortion providers, homosexuals, and federal law enforcement authorities. Similarities between these bombings and the previous Olympic Park bombing led investigators to consider the likelihood that all three bombings were the work of the same person or group. On 29 April 1997 an Atlanta Bombing Task Force was established comprised of FBI, BATF, and Georgia Bureau of Investigation personnel and on 9 June 1997 this investigation was merged with that of the Olympic Park bombing.

ARYAN NATIONS. The Aryan Nations is a nonstate, **revolutionary** organization dedicated to the creation of an independent, "whites-only" homeland in the Pacific northwestern states and to the overthrown of the "Zionist Occupation Government" (ZOG) of the United States. The visible corporate organ of the Aryan Nations is the Church of Jesus Christ Christian headed by Richard Butler, a minister of the **Identity Christian movement**. While Butler's church is headquartered on the Aryan Nations compound outside Hayden Lake, Idaho, in fact the Aryan Nations refers also to Butler's umbrella organization that seeks to unite disparate right-wing groups sharing **white-supremacist**, anti-Semitic, or populist **ideologies**, such as the **Ku Klux Klan** (KKK), American **neo-Nazi** groups, the **Posse Comitatus**, and the **Covenant, the Sword and the Arm of the Lord** (CSA).

The Aryan Nations achieved this coordination through conferences held at its Hayden Lake compound each year 1979-2000 and through the creation of the Aryan Nations Net, a computer bulletin board system that allows members of like-minded groups to share ideas and plans year-round. The Aryan Nations has an outreach ministry to the Aryan Brotherhood, itself a network of white supremacist prison gangs whose members are recruited into the Aryan Nations upon their release from prison.

While the visible Butler organization itself does not directly participate in terrorist actions it has given moral encouragement to such groups as the Posse Comitatus and White Aryan Resistance and has spawned terrorist splinter groups such as **the Order**. The Aryan Nations is estimated to have 150 to 500 members in about 18 states. Richard Butler denies that the Aryan Nations has any involvement in terrorism or sedition, but in 1987 two Aryan Nations members were convicted on counterfeiting charges and another convicted for a series of **bombings** in Idaho in 1986 in connection with a plot to terrorize anti-Aryan Nations residents into leaving the Coeur d'Alene area. Richard Butler was acquitted in April 1988 by the U.S. District Court in Fort Smith, Arkansas, of sedition charges arising from the links between the Aryan Nations and the Order, with the latter's involvement in armed robberies and the deprivation of Alan Berg's civil rights. Later on 19 October 1990 three other Aryan Nations members were convicted for conspiracy to bomb a Seattle gay nightclub.

At its 1990 summer conference the Aryan Nations featured John Trochman as one of its speakers, who later founded the Militia of Montana. In 1993 Carl Franklin, who had been Butler's designated successor, resigned as security chief for the Aryan Nations due to disagreements with Butler and Louis Beam, Jr., former Texas Ku Klux Klan Grand Dragon, who had been Butler's "Ambassador at Large," and is apparently in line to succeed Butler. According to the Southern Poverty Law Center, the Aryan nations grew from having branches in only three states to having branches in 15 other states from 1993 to 1994, which seems to augur further vitality in this organization despite Butler's advanced age (1918-). However on 7 September 2000 a civil lawsuit against the Aryan Nations, due to an incident in which three Aryan Nations guards manhandled a native American woman and her son, Victoria and Jason Keenan, resulted in a $6.3 million judgment against Richard Butler and the Aryan Nations for the role played by both the leader and organization in inciting the guards to malicious injury against the plaintiffs. Acting on behalf of the Keenans, the Southern Poverty Law Center was pursuing liens against the assets of the Aryan Nations, including its compound, in order to force the organization in bankruptcy, actions which have put the future of the group into doubt.

ARYAN RESISTANCE ARMY. Four men, whom law enforcement officers in Ohio had labeled the "midwestern bank bandits" for their 22 bank robberies committed before their capture in January 1996, had formed a right-wing underground cell which they called the Aryan Resistance Army. They had intended to use their robberies' proceeds to fund the violent overthrow of the U.S. government and to kill all Jews. The group had prepared a two-hour training video called "The Aryan Resistance

Army Presents: The Armed Struggle Underground" in which they tried to model themselves on the **Order** led by Mathew Roberts, who was killed in a shoot-out with the FBI in December 1984. A search of their hideout in Columbus revealed 13 pipe bombs, seven homemade grenades, assault weapons, bomb-making materials, and FBI and DEA hats and t-shirts, as well as the training video. The group was formed by Mark Thomas, a member of the **Aryan Nations** who himself took no direct part in the robberies of the group. One of the four suspects hanged himself in jail while the other three were convicted on robbery, conspiracy, and weapons charges in January 1997 and sentenced the following month.

ARSON. Much arson is simply criminal activity in which buildings are burned either for insurance fraud, personal animosity, random vandalism, or else pyromania. However arson has been used as a weapon by terrorists, whether in the form of arson of properties or else throwing firebombs at police, civilians, or property. In July 1998, after nine weeks of hunger strikes by 260 leftists in 33 Turkish prisons, in which three hunger strikers died, a wave of firebombings hit Turkish-owned businesses and centers throughout Germany. German police believed that leftist sympathizers among the two million expatriate Turks living in Germany staged these attacks to pressure the Turkish government to improve living conditions for their imprisoned comrades.

In recent years in the United States large numbers of church burnings, particularly churches with predominantly African American congregations, have raised concerns that these arsons represent **hate crimes** being perpetrated against racial minority groups, which would be a form of terrorist arson. On 10 October 1996 the United States Commission on Civil Rights stated that church burnings in the southern United States reflected an "alarming rise in racial tensions in society." A few incidents seemed to confirm this view: On 10 December 1996, two former **Ku Klux Klan** (KKK) members pled guilty to charges of having burned the Macedonia Baptist Church in South Carolina in June 1995 as well as having burned the Mount Zion African Methodist Episcopal Church in Greeleyville in June 1995.

However Deval L. Patrick, the Assistant Attorney General for Civil Rights, testified before the U.S. House Judiciary Committee on 21 May 1996 that although racism appeared to be a motive in many of the church fires there was no evidence of any organized regional or nation-wide conspiracy behind these burnings.

Since January 1995 the Bureau of Alcohol, Tobacco, and Firearms (BATF) had investigated 2,600 fires of which 47 were church burnings, 25 having burned black churches in the south. On 7 June 1996 the BATF report indicated that five black churches were burned in 1995 and 20 in 1996 out of a total of 47 church fires since 1 January 1995. Of the remainder eight fires struck Jewish Synagogues while the other 14 involved predominantly white churches. In five of the cases involving black churches seven arrests were made. Another five fires were cleared as caused by accident and not by arson. On 1 July 1999 two brothers, James and Benjamin Williams, who were arrested for the shotgun slayings of two gay men near Redding, California, were also found to have evidence that connected them with the burning of three synagogues on 18 June in Sacramento. The two brothers had literature from the white supremacist World Church of the Creator and appeared to be involved in the **white supremacy** movement.

Another case revealed an antireligious rather than racial motivation: On 21 April 1999 one man was indicted for 10 church burnings comprising all seven church burnings in Indiana and all three fires in Georgia under investigation. Jay Scott Ballinger confessed to having started up to 50 church fires in Indiana alone from 1994 to 1998. One fire he set killed a firefighter on 31 December 1998 when the burning roof of the New Salem United Methodist Church collapsed on him. Ballinger was arrested in February 1998 when he had to seek treatment for burns he had received when setting fire to a church in Brookville, Ohio, on 7 February 1998. Ballinger's motivation appeared to be rooted in a personal obsession with Satanism and the occult rather than race.

A borderline area between simple criminal arson and terrorist arson is the use of firebombs, or Molotov cocktails, by organized street gangs to intimidate, silence, or punish rival gangs or civilians who try to resist gang activities in their neighborhoods. A large-scale study of urban arson conducted by the BATF in 1996 that reviewed arson fires in Chicago, Kansas City, Los Angeles, New Haven, and Philadelphia indicated that 15 percent of all arson in those cities was related to drug trafficking and that one-quarter of these incidents were intended to injure targeted persons and not just destroy property.

ASSASSINATION. The deliberate murder or killing of political or military figures, or of ordinary civilians, for political ends, assassination is perhaps the oldest and most fundamental of the terrorist tools. The Isma'ili **Fedayeen** attacked high secular and religious authorities using corps of assassins willing to undertake attacks against Sunni rulers in which the individual assassin was certain to be killed or captured. To counter the awe and respect these bold attacks created among the common people, apologists of the Abbasid dynasty targeted by the Isma'ilis alleged that the attackers were really "Hashshishin," those acting under the influence of hashish. This term became the source of the word "assassin."

The term *assassination* has usually been restricted to the murder of high-ranking or prominent personages. Not all assassinations are necessarily instances of terrorism. Many of the assassins of prominent political figures appear to have been driven by complex psychological motives rather than acting to advance a clear-cut political motive or agenda. For instance the attempted assassination of Egyptian President Hosni Mubarak by **Islamic Group** gunmen during his 26 June 1995 visit to Ethiopia was clearly meant to advance the cause of their group by removing their main enemy. The 4 November 1995 assassination of Israeli Prime Minister Rabin by a member of the **Eyal** group was also meant to punish one considered an enemy by the religious-political tenets of this group. During the October 1994 trial of an Iraqi accused of plotting to assassinate former President George H. Bush during his visit of Kuwait City the previous year, the accused gave personal revenge as his reason for wishing to assassinate Bush whom he held responsible for the deaths of members of his family during the 1991 Gulf War. An assassination attempted for such personal reasons need not be considered a terrorist action even if the target was a prominent political figure.

ASYLUM, POLITICAL. Under the Convention Relating to the Status of Refugees (28 July 1951), and the Protocol Relating to the Status of Refugees (31 January 1967), a bona fide "refugee" is anyone who flees to another country to avoid persecution due to his or her race, religion, nationality, ethnic affiliation, or political opinion and who cannot secure legal protection from such persecution in the country from which he or she is fleeing. Such a person has the right to request political asylum in the country to which that person has fled. This **political offense exception,** which would grant such a refugee a right to remain in the country to which he or she fled and which would also protect them from deportation or **extradition** to the country of origin, may not include serious nonpolitical offenses, such as murder, assault, or participation in acts of persecution against others on account of race, religion, nationality, ethnic affiliation, or political belief. Prior criminal convictions could bar refugee status unless the offense was not recognized as criminal by the state granting asylum.

AUM SHINRIKYO (AUM). The Aum Supreme Truth group is an apocalyptic doomsday cult founded by Asahara Shoko which was responsible for the sarin gas poisoning of the Tokyo subway system on 20 March 1995 (*see* TOKYO SUBWAY GAS ATTACK). Asahara Shoko, originally named Matsumoto Chozuo, was born in February 1955 and attended a special school for the blind from which he graduated in 1975. In 1982 he was arrested for selling a counterfeit medicine which he claimed was merely officially unapproved. In 1984 he established his group, originally named Aum Shinsen No Kai and changed his name to Asahara Shoko. After going to India in 1986 to study yoga and Tantric mysticism Asahara Shoko returned to Japan in 1987 and changed the group's name to Aum Shinrikyo which received official recognition as a religion in August 1989 which gave it tax exempt status.

AUM is an eclectic synthesis of Hindu mysticism, Christian **millennialist**, and apocalyptic beliefs derived from the Book of Revelation, and prophecies taken from the writings of Nostradamus. Asahara was regarded as Christ by his followers, whom he claimed numbered about 40,000 worldwide, with 9,000 in Japan alone by the time the Tokyo subway sarin gas attack took place. Asahara claimed to have revelations of an imminent world war which would initiate Armageddon in which his group would fight and overcome the enemies of Japan, including the United States. Asahara commanded his followers to begin trying to procure nuclear, biological, and chemical weapons to be able to fight and win the coming prophesied war.

In November 1989 Tsutsumi Sakamoto, a lawyer investigating allegations of brainwashing on behalf of concerned family members of cult members, was murdered by AUM members along with his wife and infant son. Asahara and 24 of his followers ran for seats in the Japanese House of Representatives in February 1990 but none of them won any seat. The encounter with Sakamoto and this electoral failure convinced Asahara that the Japanese government was conspiring against him. A siege mentality prevailed in the group that led them to make the sarin gas attack to paralyze the national police headquarters by introducing the gas into the police offices from the subway tunnels running under that building.

Prior to the 20 March 1995 sarin gas attack on the Tokyo subway system, the AUM group had attempted on nine occasions to deploy botulinum poison via airborne dispensers against targets as varied as the Japanese Diet, the Imperial Palace complex, and the housing of U.S. military bases in Japan, without causing even one casualty. After testing the use of their homemade sarin against the Japanese city of Matsumoto on 27 June 1994, killing seven civilians and injuring 150, the sect then deployed it in the Tokyo Subway system.

Following the subway gas attack on 20 March 1995, in which 12 people died and over 5,000 were injured, Asahara was arrested on 16 May 1995, while found hiding in a cubbyhole in one of his group's properties. With the arrest of Asahara and 400 of his followers, who faced charges ranging from **kidnapping**, to illegal production of drugs and weapons, to murder, the Japanese government moved to ban the sect under the Anti-Subversive Law in December 1995. In spite of this the sect continued to recruit new members and operate in Japan and abroad in Taiwan. Although the government decision to ban the group was overturned in January 1997 on the grounds that the cult posed no further danger to society, it had lost its tax exempt status in October 1995.

On 28 March 1996 the Tokyo District Court declared Aum Shinrikyo bankrupt as a result of the expenses for the defense of Asahara and his followers on criminal charges and also from the effects of the civil lawsuits filed by those who lost family members or who had suffered disabilities from the subway sarin gas attack. In 1997 the United States declared Aum Shinrikyo a terrorist organization pursuant to the 1996 **Antiterrorism and Effective Death Penalty Act**. At the time of this writing Asahara Shoko and 104 of his followers were still being tried on several charges arising from the sarin gas attack, the murders of cult members and enemies, and other cult-related activities. In February 2000 the acting leader of the group, Fumihiro Joyu, declared that the group, which had changed its name to Aleph, was reorganizing itself. In the following months Aleph publically distanced itself from Asahara Shoko and the sarin gas attack.

AUTHORITARIAN PERSONALITY THEORY. This theory, originally proposed by Theodore W. Adorno and others, holds that attraction to right-wing **ideologies** and extremist violence is associated with a specific personality type marked by a paranoid worldview, misanthropy, and rigidity. The authoritarian personality is also held to be ethnocentric and inclined toward racism. Adorno's work, *The Authoritarian Personality*, formerly widely cited as a pioneering study of right-wing behavior and motivations, has come to be criticized lately both on theoretical and empirical grounds.

Psychological profiling and study of convicted terrorists, whether of the left or the right, has not demonstrated that political extremists generally or terrorists in particular are psychologically abnormal or that they are marked by a unique pathological personality. Second, many of the qualities that the authoritarian personality thesis held to be unique to right-wing extremists can also be observed among some left-wing extremists and terrorists, who often exhibit their own versions of paranoid thinking, authoritarian attitudes, and rigidity. To the extent that such traits are found among committed terrorists an equally plausible hypothesis would hold that such traits are not so much the cause of the behavior of these terrorists but a consequence of the clandestine lifestyle of committed terrorists on the run which requires extreme suspicion and caution as well as extreme personal and group discipline to evade arrest while still being able to conduct terrorist operations.

Another empirical objection to this study is that many right-wing extremists among the **militia movement** and other far-right groups in the United States display strong overt antiauthoritarian attitudes and have proven themselves to be flexible in adapting their organizations and tactics to changing social and political environments. While there have been other attempts to find commonalities in the profiles of members of terrorist groups, such commonalities that have been found, such as coming from a broken family background, having a juvenile arrest history, or having narcissistic attitudes, are also found among a larger population whose members do not become terrorists so that such traits are useless for explaining why some persons and not others become terrorists.

AVANGUARDIA NAZIONALE (AN). The "National Vanguard" was an Italian right-wing terrorist group founded in 1959 by **Stephano Delle Chiaie**. During the 1960s the group collaborated with other right-wing groups throughout Europe in an umbrella organization known as the "Black Orchestra." On 12 December 1969 the group bombed the Banca della Agricultura in Milan, killing 16 people and wounding 90 others, in an attempt to create a backlash against leftists whom they tried to frame as the perpetrators. The AN attempted a coup d'état on 7 December 1970 against the Italian government. The AN, along with other smaller right-wing organizations, merged with the **Black Order** after 1973.

- B -

BAADER-MEINHOF GANG. Journalistic name for the Rote Armee Fraktion, or **Red Army Faction**, founded by the German leftists Andreas Baader and Ulrike Meinhof.

BABBAR KHALSA. *See* SIKH MILITANTS.

BANDERA ROJA. The Bandera Roja, "Red Flag" group (also referred to by the initials GBR), was a Venezuelan revolutionary group, operating independently of any state sponsor, dedicated to achieving a Marxist-Leninist state in Venezuela through armed struggle. The GBR rejected assimilation into peaceful politics and broke with the Venezuelan Revolutionary Movement of the Left (Movimiento Izquiereda Revolucionario, MIR) in 1969 after Cuba abandoned support for leftist guerrillas in Venezuela. The armed wing of GBR is called the Americo Silva Front.

Like many other guerrilla groups in South America formerly sponsored by Cuba and the Soviet Union, the GBR has taken to financing its activities through **kidnapping** for ransom and extorting protection payments from wealthy individuals and firms. In 1972 the GBR began abducting wealthy businessmen for ransom, kidnapping Caracas industrialist Carlos Domínguez Chávez in a joint operation with MIR activists, and releasing him for $1 million in ransom. After GBR leaders Carlos Betancourt and Gabriel Puerta Aponte were captured in 1973, the GBR arranged for both to escape from Caracas's San Carlos Prison in January 1975, along with 21 other guerrillas, by means of a 60-meter tunnel that the GBR had dug into the prison, apparently with the cooperation of other leftist guerrillas. In March 1975 the GBR renounced all ties to leftist parties working within the constitutional order and published a death list against 20 prominent landowners.

From 1976 to 1977, the GBR conducted sporadic attacks on military convoys and temporarily captured small towns. After Betancourt was recaptured in 1977, Bandera Roja activity halted. In December 1981 the GBR hijacked three domestic flights, demanding the release of Betancourt and other prisoners but the Venezuelan government rejected those demands. In April 1982 Puerta was captured in a firefight in which 25 militants were killed.

Bandera Roja operated mainly in eastern Venezuela and along the Colombian border and has had contact with Colombia's **M-19** and **National Liberation Army** (ELN) groups. Membership in the armed wing is estimated at no more than 50.

BANNA, SABRI KHALIL AL. *See* ABU NIDAL.

BASQUE FATHERLAND AND LIBERTY. The Euzkadi Ta Askatasuna (ETA), is a nonstate Basque separatist group that has undertaken terrorist operations to win independence for Euzkadi, the Basque fatherland, consisting of the Spanish provinces of Vizcaya (Basque: Bizkaia), Alava (Arava), Guipuzcoa (Gipuzkoa), and Navarra (Nafarroa), as well as the French Basque provinces of Le LaBourg (Lapurdi), La Basse Navarre (Baxenabarra), and La Soule (Zuberoa). Due to the general antipathy of France and other European states toward the Franco regime, the French government tolerated the presence of ETA terrorists who used France as a base and sanctuary. Since the return of democracy in Spain in the mid-1970s and the appearance of signs of ETA radicalization of French Basques, France no longer tolerates ETA activities within its territory and cooperates with Spanish authorities to combat Basque terrorism.

The ETA organization enjoyed moral and material support from the **Palestine Liberation Organization** (PLO) in training camps in Lebanon, South Yemen, and Algeria. The Cuban and Sandinista Nicaraguan governments gave safe haven and training to ETA members. The ETA and **Irish Republican Army** (IRA) also were reported to cooperate with each other. The Colombian **M-19** group, and other Latin American guerrilla groups, declared their support for ETA while immigrant communities of Basques in Venezuela and elsewhere also materially contributed to ETA.

The ETA is an offshoot of the Basque Nationalist Party (PNV). In 1957 the youth movement of the PNV met in Paris with the exiled PNV leadership to persuade them to undertake armed struggle against the Franco regime. Failing in this, many of the PNV youth created the ETA on 31 July 1959. Because most of the other non-Basque anti-Franco groups were Marxist many ETA members also adopted a Marxist-Leninist ideology whereas PNV had been, and remains, solidly Catholic and nationalistic. Disagreements over the correct **ideological** interpretation of the Basque struggle have split the ETA into several factions. The two major factions are the ETA-Militar (ETA-M), which advocates unending armed struggle until full independence is won, and the ETA-Politico-Militar (ETA-PM), which laid down arms temporarily after formal autonomy was granted to a designated Basque region in January 1980.

ETA activities began in 1961 with the derailment of a train carrying Spanish Civil War veterans en route to a celebration in San Sebastian. During the 1960s ETA struck symbolic targets such as defacing Civil War monuments and symbols of Spanish domination. The murder of a Basque in 1968 by the Spanish Civil Guard led to the first **assassination** by the ETA of the security chief of Guipuzcoa, triggering severe regime repression of Basques, which in turn further radicalized many Basques. ETA actions are largely intended as **armed propaganda**, called *ekintzak*, meant to focus attention on the symbolic, strategic, and political importance of the action. The ETA has shown itself to be very selective in choosing targets and means of attacks and also to take great care in avoiding injury to noncombatants so that over 70 percent of those killed or wounded by the ETA have been members of the Spanish security forces or government.

Generally the ETA has targeted facilities to **bomb** or persons for assassination symbolizing Spanish hegemony: army and Civil Guard barracks, government buildings, Spanish military and political figures. **Kidnapping** for ransom plays a role in financing the ETA, but even then victims are chosen not simply for their potential ransom but usually have been figures of consequence who have spoken out against the ETA. Prior to most bomb attacks the ETA issued warnings to allow civilians a chance to remove themselves from the target area. Yet, as France began cooperating with Spain in 1987 in an antiterrorist crackdown aimed at Basque separatists, the ETA began a campaign of terrorization against French targets in Spain, including tourist transit and hotel facilities, which have victimized increasing numbers of civilians.

From 1961 to 1970 only three deaths resulted from ETA actions. From 1971 to 1975, the year of Franco's death, ETA caused 31 deaths. From 1976 to 1980, when limited Basque autonomy was granted, ETA caused 253 deaths. From 1981 to 1985 the figure dropped to around 190 and from 1986 to 1990 the figure fell to around 159. Each year since 1990 has witnessed in excess of 50 ETA-caused deaths. Most of the 50 victims killed by the ETA in 1991 were involved in preparatory projects for the Barcelona Olympics, the fifth centennial celebrations of Columbus's voyage, and the Seville World's Fair, since these events were used by Spanish authorities to stress Spanish social and economic progress since the Franco era. Ironically, as democratization has proceeded in Spain, ETA violence has risen, and as more autonomy has been granted to the Basque region, ETA violence has increased even further, despite the laying down of arms by ETA-PM.

Currently the ETA has a political wing, Herri Basatuna (Popular Unity) Party, which was allowed to work openly in Spanish politics. In 1986 this party won 32 percent of the parliamentary votes cast in the three Basque provinces of Navarra, Guipuzcoa, and Vizcaya. In the March 1996 elections, which followed the unsuccessful ETA assassination attempt against José María Aznar, who was the candidate leading in the national polls, this figure dipped to 12 percent but in the October 1998 election, which followed the ETA cease-fire on 16 September 1998, it had improved to 18 percent.

Figures of persons killed by ETA violence vary from source to source depending on whether the actions of certain breakaway groups, such as **Iraultza**, are counted. If only the confirmed actions of the ETA are considered from 1968-1990, the total is just over 500 deaths, but if the actions of other Basque terrorist groups are counted, the figure is in excess of 750 deaths. By the cease-fire of 16 September 1998 the deaths attributed to the ETA alone had risen to over 800.

Some more notable ETA actions are listed here: On 20 December 1973 the ETA assassinated Spanish Prime Minister Luís Carrero Blanco (1903-1973), whose limousine was blown five stories high by the detonation of an explosives-packed 25-foot-long tunnel under the pavement over which he would pass on a daily trip. On 12 September 1989 the ETA-M assassinated public prosecutor Carmen Tagle in Madrid. During 1993 the ETA carried out four major carbombings, two on 21 June in Madrid killing seven persons and wounding 22 others, and another two on 29 October in Barcelona. The ETA's plan to murder King

Juan Carlos in August 1995 was thwarted by continuing Spanish and French police anti-ETA efforts. On 19 April 1995 the ETA tried to repeat its earlier feat of mining a road with explosives to kill José María Aznar, the leader of the Popular Party, but only wounded 12 others while slightly wounding Aznar. On 10 February 1997 the ETA shot and killed Supreme Court justice, Rafael Martínez Emperador. After a government raid freed two hostages on 1 July 1997 the ETA murdered other hostages, including a city council member of Eruma, kidnapped on 10 July and found shot to death two days later, the 10th person to be murdered by the ETA in 1997. During 1998 the ETA killed six persons as opposed to the 13 killed during 1997 but by 16 September 1998 the ETA declared a cease-fire and asked for negotiations with the Spanish government. On 29 November 1999, however, ETA announced it would resume armed operations on 3 December 1999. On 21 January 2000 the ETA made two car bombings in Madrid, killing an army officer and wounding bystanders. On 22 February 2001 a car bombing intended to target Inaki Dubreuil, a Socialist councilor of the town of Ordizia, exploded in San Sebastian killing two electrical workers there. On 20 March 2001 ETA gunmen assassinated Froilan Elespe, a Socialist deputy mayor of the town of Lasarte.

The ETA members, known as *eterras,* are organized into three- to five-member cells, known as *comandos.* Most *eterras* are *legales* who may never, or only occasionally, participate in an illegal action. Most live openly but help the *ilegales*, or underground ETA activists, by material aid, communications, information gathering, and other support roles. The total number of underground activists has been estimated at 200 members, while the total numbers of *legales* is not known. *Comandos* are activated by the ETA directorate which usually is in France. Few *eterras* therefore will know who is an *eterra* outside of his own *comando*, which helps protect the ETA against police penetration should the members of one *comando* be arrested and interrogated. Spanish and French coordinated counterinsurgency measures during the 1990s have substantially weakened the ETA organization.

BEIRUT AIRPORT BOMBING. On 23 October 1983 a truck **bomb** driven by a **suicide**-volunteer demolished the building at Beirut International Airport being used as a temporary barracks, killing 241 U.S. Marines. This bombing was one in a series of anti-Western bombings, including the 18 April 1983 bombing of the U.S. embassy in West Beirut, the bombing of the French military headquarters in Beirut on the same day as the Beirut Airport bombing, and the 4 November 1983 bombing of the Israeli Defense Forces headquarters in Tyre. All these attacks used suicide drivers, were executed with great precision, and resulted in great damages and loss of life.

According to Lebanese security sources, the truck hit the airport building near a specific pillar where the planners of the bombing had determined that the explosion would do most structural damage and kill the most people. The FBI estimated that the truck bomb was the equivalent of 12,000 pounds of TNT, making it larger than any conventional bomb used in World War II. The bomb was made of a combination of TNT and hexogen, a highly sensitive and powerful explosive, packed around cylinders of gas to create an air-fuel bomb effect. The sheer cost of this bombing, the quality of intelligence about the U.S. forces needed to execute it, the technical precision needed to build the bomb, and the reluctance of any group to claim immediate responsibility for this act all pointed to state sponsorship of the bombing. **Hezbollah**, a militia under Iranian state sponsorship, on 16 February 1985 claimed responsibility in the name of **Islamic Jihad**.

On 4 October 1984, U.S. intelligence agencies identified Hezbollah as the local agent that supplied the suicide driver and Iran as the supplier of the explosives used in the attacks on the Marines and the U.S. embassy. As early as 6 November 1983, an article in the Israeli daily *Ma'ariv* had identified the Iranian Ambassador to Damascus, 'Ali Akbar Muhtashami, as having been assigned by the Iranian government to be a liaison with Syrian intelligence in directing terrorist activities through the group that eventually assumed responsibility for the bombing of the U.S. Marines barracks. This article identified Islamic Jihad as being the responsible group headquartered in Baalbak under tutelage of the **Islamic Revolutionary Guards Corps** (IRGC) of Iran.

According to a *Le Monde* report, dated 6-7 November 1983, citing an otherwise unspecified "confidential British document," the principal mastermind of the October 23 operations was one "Abu Muslih," actually 'Imad Maghniyah, the commander of the 800 or so IRGC troops in Baalbak. This report stated also that Iranian Deputy Foreign Minister Husayn Shaykhulislami, one of the leaders of those students who seized the U.S. embassy on 4 November 1979, visited Damascus twice secretly, once on 16 April 1983, and again on 19 October 1983, that is, each time a few days ahead of a bombing of a major U.S. target in Lebanon. The

Foreign Ministry of Iran and other officials and representatives of the regime have repeatedly denied any knowledge of, or involvement in, these bombings. On 20 July 1987, however, the former commander of the Islamic Revolutionary Guards Corps, Muhsin Rafiqdust, revealed in an interview to the Iranian newspaper *Risilat* that Tehran had supplied the explosives used in the bombings.

The shock of this bombing and the unpreparedness of the Reagan administration or the U.S. public to face the levels of lethal violence that had become commonplace in the Lebanese civil war led to an abrupt withdrawal of U.S. troops from Lebanon.

BELLIGERENT STATUS. When an army invading another state's territory, or else an insurgent group rebelling against the government of a nation-state, seizes effective control over a territory, excluding the military and police forces of the national government being attacked, and itself takes over the tasks of providing government and police protection to the civilians in the occupied territory, then the occupying force is said to have belligerent status. In effect when other nations officially recognize the belligerent status of an occupier this confers a recognition of that occupying power as the de facto government of that territory. Under international law the belligerent would be held to observe the same limitations on the use of its power over civilians in its jurisdiction with regard to their human rights as would any other sovereign de jure government, subject to considerations of military necessity and humanity. Foreigners traveling within the territory held by the belligerent would be considered obliged to obey the effective laws and regulations being enforced by the belligerent.

In the case of an insurgent guerrilla movement, as soon as other nations recognize its belligerent status this accords a degree of legitimacy on the insurgents, who then possess not only their own government and control over a territory and people, but also the ability to establish effective diplomatic relations with the nations who recognize their belligerent status, which grants them most of the elements needed to be recognized as a bona fide nation-state. The formal recognition of belligerent status by other national government internationalizes the conflict making it much more difficult for the government being attacked to reassert control or authority over the territory occupied by the belligerent group. During the 1979-1992 civil war in El Salvador, Mexico and other nations accorded belligerent status to the **Farabundo**

Martí Liberation Movement (FMLN) which was viewed by the United States as powerful moral support for the FMLN. During the Lebanese Civil War period of 1975-1982 when **Palestine Liberation Organization** (PLO) forces controlled portions of Beirut and other parts of Lebanon, the U.S. military forces sent to evacuate American civilians from Beirut had to contact the PLO to coordinate the evacuation of U.S. nationals from the Beirut waterfront. In spite of the U.S. declaratory policy of not recognizing, or dealing with, the PLO, this action conferred an effective belligerent status on the PLO.

BENNETT COMMITTEE. Full name, the Bennett Committee of Inquiry into Police Interrogation Procedures in Northern Ireland. After Great Britain assumed direct rule over Northern Ireland in 1974 allegations of police brutality and mistreatment of prisoners charged with terrorist offenses created controversy in the British government, particularly the numbers of convictions based on confessions uncorroborated by independent evidence which seemed to support allegations of systemic use of torture by police interrogators. These practices had also been condemned by the European Commission and Court of Human Rights. Mr. Justice Bennett was appointed by the British government to investigate these charges and to make appropriate recommendations.

The Bennett Committee report issued in 1979 led to regulations that forbade physical or verbal abuse of suspects, forbade interrogation during meals or after midnight, required interrogators to identify themselves and that the police provide the suspect a sheet outlining his rights under the law, and allowed the suspect to contact a lawyer or relative as well as to have access to a doctor, who could verify whether or not physical abuse had occurred. The Bennett guidelines allow the suspect to be incarcerated up to 48 hours before being permitted to contact relatives or a solicitor, if the police feared the phone call might be used to tip off comrades before they could act on the basis of information gleaned from the suspect. Many prisoners have complained that they have not been provided with the sheet outlining their rights or that the detectives have not identified themselves during interrogation but the Bennett report did have the effect of eliminating the more outrageous instances of coercive interrogation procedures.

BIN LADEN, OSAMA (1957-). Osama bin Laden (full Arabic name: Usama ibn Muhammad ibn Ladin) is a leading financier and organizer of an

Islamic fundamentalist terrorist network, known as **al Qa'eda** and is currently wanted by the United States as the mastermind behind the August 1998 bombings of two U.S. embassies in East Africa (*see* EAST AFRICAN U.S. EMBASSY ATTACKS) as well as the 1995 Riyadh bombing (*see* RIYADH SAUDI NATIONAL GUARD-U.S. TRAINING CENTER BOMBING) and also the September 11, 2001 attack on the World Trade Center (*see* WORLD TRADE CENTER ATTACK OF SEPTEMBER 11, 2001). He is also reputed to have ties with the group that bombed the **World Trade Center** and that plotted a terror campaign against landmark targets in New York City, and with the **Islamic Group** in Egypt that massacred foreign tourists in Luxor, in November 1997, and also to plots by Ramzi Ahmad Yousef to **bomb** U.S. airliners over the Pacific Ocean and plots to **assassinate** Pope John Paul II, Egyptian President Hosni Mubarak, and U.S. President Bill Clinton

Osama bin Laden, born in Riyadh in 1957, is one of 52 scions of Muhammad ibn Laden, a Yemeni businessman whose construction firm amassed him a personal fortune of about $5 billion. Osama bin Laden helped run part of the family business and is believed to have amassed over $250 million from his own management. Prior to receiving business management training at King Abdul Aziz University in Jeddah, bin Laden received instruction in Islamic law.

With the Soviet invasion of Afghanistan on 11 January 1979 bin Ladin quit his family business to devote himself and his fortune to helping the Afghan **Mujahideen** in their fight against the Soviets. From 1979 to 1984 he was in Pakistan funding the Afghan fighters and building shelters in Pakistan for refugees. From 1984 to 1989 he was in Afghanistan involved both in building roads and shelters for the Mujahideen and also involved in actual combat as well. He organized the Maktab al Khidamat (Services Office) that recruited devout Muslims from throughout the Arab world to come to Afghanistan to fight in the **jihad** against the Soviets. This organization had recruiting offices not only in the Muslim world but also throughout the West wherever Muslims could be recruited. One such office in Brooklyn was later used by the group that **bombed** the World Trade Center. After the Soviets left Afghanistan in 1989 the Mujahideen were urged by their Pakistani and CIA backers to attack the heavily defended city of Jalalabad. This attack proved a catastrophe for the Mujahideen whose forces suffered heavy losses. Bin Laden, who led his forces in an assault on the airport, was wounded by shrapnel and many of his Arab volunteers were killed.

Bin Laden returned to Saudi Arabia and resumed his work in the family business.

The U.S.-led deployment of forces against Iraq in 1990-1991 deeply offended bin Laden as he saw the United States as the supporter of Israel. He also viewed the policy of the Saudi regime of permitting American troops to be stationed in Arabia itself as an affront to Islam because the government of Arabia was also the "Protector of the Two Holy Places," namely the Muslim holy cities of Mecca and Medina, which are forbidden to non-Muslims to enter but which now bin Laden viewed as being under U.S. military control. At this point bin Laden not only came to view the United States as the leading enemy of Islam but also the Saudi family as traitors to Islam. He moved to Sudan in April 1991, ostensibly to undertaken his construction business there to help develop a destitute Muslim nation but by 1994 the governments of Egypt, Algeria, and Yemen were accusing him of financing and training the Islamic fundamentalist groups seeking to overthrow their regimes. The Saudi government revoked his passport and Saudi citizenship and his family has reportedly disowned him.

It is believed that bin Laden helped supply the Stinger missiles used by the Somali militias against U.S. helicopters during operations in Somalia in the autumn of 1993. Although bin Laden initially had amicable relations with the National Islamic Front ruling Sudan, by 1996 he was asked to leave the country, very likely due to pressure from Egypt, whose President, Hosni Mubarak, survived an **assassination** attempt during his 26 June 1995 visit to Ethiopia. The would-be assassins were known to have come from Sudan and now bin Laden is suspected to have been the instigator of this attack, which sunk Sudanese-Egyptian relations to such a low point that Egypt was threatening war against Sudan.

Bin Laden returned to Afghanistan although his exact movements and whereabouts from 1996 onward remain a mystery. His base outside Jalalabad, Afghanistan holds about 600 of his followers who are estimated to number around 5,000 or more in over 25 countries worldwide, including Chechnya, Algeria, Kashmir, the Philippines, Egypt, Eritrea, and elsewhere.

U.S. counterterrorism experts began to link bin Laden to anti-U.S. terrorism during their investigations of the World Trade Center bombing after finding his name and addresses of his businesses and front organizations among the documents and materials seized from the suspects. His name also came up with the arrest of Razmi Ahmad Yousef who had been staying at a safe house in Pakistan owned either by bin Laden or his brother-in-law.

In February 1996 and again in February 1998 bin Laden issued a **fatwa**, that is, an Islamic religious verdict, cosigned by himself; Ayman al-Zawahiri, the leader of the **Jihad Group** in Egypt; Abu-Yasir Rifa'i Ahmad Taha, a leader of the **Islamic Group** in Egypt; and Shaykh Mir Hamzeh, secretary of the Jamni'at-ul-Ulema of Pakistan, declaring it the religious duty of every individual Muslim to kill Americans everywhere, whether soldiers or civilians, to free the holy cities of Islam from the presence of foreign, non-Muslim troops. It should be noted that such religious decrees can only be legitimately issued by an outstanding Muslim religious authority of known sanctity, probity, and scholarship in Islamic jurisprudence. While bin Laden himself is not recognized as being such a scholar the fatwa's credibility may be said to rest on the credentials of Shaykh Mir Hamzeh, a Pakistani Sunni Muslim religious scholar.

Among the terrorist attacks that bin Laden is suspected of having directed, or otherwise having been involved in, are the following: the World Trade Center bombing of 26 February 1993 as bin Laden was the patron and protector of Razmi Ahmad Yousef who was indicted for this act on 11 March 1993; the **Riyadh bombing** of 13 November 1995 that destroyed a Saudi National Guard training center, killing four American military advisors and two Indian government advisors; the **Khobar Towers** bombing in Dhahran, Saudi Arabia, on 25 June 1996, in which a powerful truck bomb killed 19 U.S. service personnel and wounded about 300 others; the massacre of 58 foreign tourists and four Egyptians on 17 November 1997 at the Temple of Queen Hatsheput outside **Luxor**, Egypt; the U.S. embassy bombings in Nairobi, Kenya, and Dar es Salaam, Tanzania, on 7 August 1998, which killed 291 persons and wounded about 5,000 in the Nairobi attack and which killed 10 persons and wounded 77 in the Dar es Salaam attack; and the assassination attempt against Crown Prince Abdullah of Jordan in June 1993. Most recently bin Ladin is suspected of sponsoring the 12 October 2000 suicide-bombing attack on the USS *Cole* at anchor in Aden, Yemen.

Bin Laden has had close relations with the **Taliban** who took over Afghanistan. In spite of reports of estrangement between him and the Taliban, the latter have refused to accede to United Nations (UN) demands to hand over bin Laden and upon the expiration of the deadline to hand him over attackers believed to be backed by the Taliban attacked the U.S. embassy and UN offices in Islamabad, Pakistan, on 13 December 1999. Regarding bin Laden's possible relationship to Iran or other **state sponsors**, currently there is no evidence of him having had ties to any governments other than those of Pakistan and the United States, dating from before 1989, and Sudan and the current Taliban regime in Afghanistan. There is little likelihood that he has any ties to the Iranian regime.

Following the **World Trade Center and Pentagon Attacks of 11 September 2001** President George W. Bush demanded on 17 September 2001 that the Taliban hand over Osama bin Laden to U.S. authorities. Following their refusal to do so the United States initiated Operation Enduring Freedom on 7 October 2001 aimed at destroying the al Qa'eda network and the capture of bin Laden.

BLACK BRIGADES. An obscure Kuwaiti Shi'ite revolutionary group active in Iraq and Kuwait, possibly a nom de guerre of **Da'wa al Islami** or other groups enjoying Iranian **state sponsorship**. On 11 July 1985, the group attacked a restaurant in Kuwait, killing a high-ranking Kuwaiti security official.

BLACK HAND. In 1911 a splinter group broke away from the Narodna Obrana Pan-Serbian secret society in Bosnia to form the more radical Ujedinjernje ili Smrt, "Union or Death," more commonly known as the Crna Ruka, or "Black Hand" group. This group, which aimed to undermine Austrian control over Bosnia through acts of terrorism, was covertly supported by the Serbian government being led by Lieutenant-Colonel Dragutin Dmitrievich, chief of the Intelligence Department of the Serbian military and with many of its members also being Serbian military officers. They recruited from among Serbian youth in Bosnia, many of whom were smuggled into Serbia to undergo paramilitary training. The Black Hand used secret oaths and gory initiation rituals and defectors were often murdered. Gavrilo Princip, the **assassin** of Archduke Franz Ferdinand, underwent training with the Black Hand and was supplied by the Black Hand with the pistol used to murder the archduke.

BLACK JUNE. Black June was a non-PLO Palestinian group founded by **Abu Nidal**, a onetime **Fatah** member who later opposed the **Palestine**

Liberation Organization's (PLO) increasing reliance on diplomacy rather than armed struggle. Black June is an Iraqi **state-sponsored** group with the revolutionary aim of destroying Israel and establishing a Palestinian state by force of arms. Secondary objectives include the use of terrorist coercion against the PLO to punish it for retreating from the use of armed struggle as the primary means for the liberation of Palestine. The Iraqi government also used Black June as a means of maintaining its own influence over the Palestinian movement within Lebanon. Black June was one of a number of different groups founded by Abu Nidal and numbered about 500 members.

Black June took its name from June 1976 when **Phalangist** troops with Syrian backing massacred the Palestinian fighters and civilians within the besieged Tal az Za'tar refugee camp. Black June tried to kill the Syrian Foreign Minister in 1977 but missed him, killing instead a bystander, the visiting United Arab Emirates's Minister of State for Foreign Affairs. Black June has made numerous attacks on PLO representatives and offices abroad. In the period from 1978-1979 they killed Sa'id Hammami, the PLO representative in London, 'Ali Yassin, the PLO representative in Kuwait, Izzidin Qalaq, PLO representative in Paris, and **bombed** a PLO office in Istanbul in August 1978, killing four people.

Following a truce with Fatah, Black June turned to attacks on Jewish and Israeli targets. On 3 June 1982 a Black June gunman attacked and wounded Shlomo Argov, Israeli Ambassador to Great Britain, which was used to justify Israel's invasion of Lebanon a few days later. On 9 August 1982 Black June made a grenade attack on a Jewish restaurant in Paris and then opened automatic weapons fire on the restaurant and on a crowd outside a nearby synagogue, killing six and wounding 27. On 10 April 1983 Black June again struck at the PLO, killing its delegate Issam Sartawi at a meeting of the Socialist International in Portugal. *See also* FATAH REVOLUTIONARY COUNCIL.

BLACK LIBERATION ARMY (BLA). One of the two most violent left-wing nonstate, **revolutionary** groups in the United States during the 1960s, the other being the **Weather Underground**. Born out of the social unrest of the 1960s, the BLA particularly targeted law enforcement officers and was responsible for eight killings in the period from 1971-1973, including two New York City policemen on 27 January 1972. An FBI crackdown led to arrests of leading members after which the group's activities subsided. In the early 1980s remnants of the BLA merged with the Weather Underground to form the **Revolutionary Armed Task Force**, which engaged in a series of **bombings** of federal government and multinational corporation offices as well as an attempted robbery of a Brinks armored carrier in October 1981.

On 2 May 1973, when Joanne Chesimard and two other BLA members driving the New Jersey Turnpike in New Brunswick were stopped for a routine check by two New Jersey state troopers, they shot the troopers, killing one and wounding the other. Chesimard, wounded in the gunfire, was arrested when found five miles from the shooting scene. Law enforcement officials considered her the "soul" of the BLA and, although the prosecution never proved she had fired on the officers, she was convicted of murder under state law as an accessory and sentenced to prison. On 2 November 1979 she broke out of the state prison in Clinton with the help of three armed men.

In 1984 she fled to Cuba, where she was granted political **asylum** as well as living expenses. Chesimard, who changed her name to Assatur Shakar, gave an interview to a WNBC-TV reporter covering the January 1998 visit to Cuba of Pope John Paul II, in which she maintained her innocence and denounced the New Jersey court system as racist. New Jersey Governor Christine Todd Whitman denounced the interview as "an affront," raised the reward for Chesimard's capture from $25,000 to $100,000, and contacted U.S. Attorney General Janet Reno and U.S. Secretary of State Madeleine Albright to demand that the United States pressure Cuba into **extraditing** Chesimard.

BLACK ORDER. The Ordine Nero was an Italian nonstate, revolutionary Fascist group that sought to destroy the democratic government in Italy. The Black Order was the violent successor to the New Order party, which had been suppressed as a proscribed neo-Fascist organization in 1973 and was thought to have had ties to the Italian Social Movement, another neo-Fascist group.

Among its terrorist actions, in 1976 the group killed Judge Vittorio Occorsio, who had earlier helped ban the New Order. The group targeted left-wing supporters usually by indiscriminate **bombings** of public places. On 4 August 1974 the group bombed a train on the Munich-Bologna route, killing 12 people. On 2 August 1980 they bombed the Bologna railway station, killing over 80 and wounding around 200 people. Bologna was targeted apparently because of the domination of the city government by Italian Communists.

At its height the Black Order numbered around 300 followers. Following the conviction in 1978 of its leader, Pierluigi Concutelli, for the murder of Judge Occorsio the group's prominence in the far right was overtaken by that of the **Armed Revolutionary Nucleus**.

BLACK PANTHERS. The Black Panther Party was a group founded in October 1966 by Huey Newton (1942-1989) and Bobby Seale (1937-) and promoted a revolutionary black nationalism. While Panthers sought, among other things, amnesty for all black prisoners, comprehensive welfare benefits for black Americans, and exemption from military service for all black Americans, the notoriety of the group came from its drift into **revolutionary** violence. Like many other radical groups born out of the radicalism of the late 1960s, such as the **Weather Underground** and the **Red Army Faction**, the Panthers were revolutionary insofar as they sought to fight what they perceived to be a racist capitalist system but also appeared to be anarchistic insofar as they lacked a clear program for creating an alternative social order.

The appeal for "black power" drew a response from other politically disaffected young black Americans. Among those drawn into the group were Stokeley Carmichael, H. Rap Brown, and Eldridge Cleaver. By 1970 the group had around 2,000 members in some 61 cities in 26 states, mainly outside of the south. Following the 4 April 1968 **assassination** of Rev. Martin Luther King, Jr., the Panthers advocated arming themselves and conducting military training for their members. Not only were the Panthers viewed by FBI Director J. Edgar Hoover, and other public officials, as being a subversive organization, but many of the Panther leaders also had criminal records and had in some cases jumped bail. This created a situation in which armed conflict between the group and the police was unavoidable. In June 1969 a gunfight erupted between the Sacramento police and the Panthers in which 13 policemen were wounded before the Panthers fled their headquarters.

During the period 1967 to 1972 about 2,000 Panthers were arrested while 20 others were killed in shoot-outs with police, other Panthers, or rival revolutionaries. In 1969 William Lee Brett **hijacked** a plane bound for New York from San Francisco to Cuba where he was granted **asylum** and continues to live. Eldridge Cleaver (1936-1998), who had jumped bail in November 1968, went to Cuba, then to Algeria, and then to North Korea seeking refuge and support for the Panthers. In 1971 he quit the Panthers and returned to the United States in 1977 where he negotiated a plea bargain with authorities. Although he had become a member of the Nation of Islam before joining the Panthers, after his return to the United States he became an evangelical Christian and joined the Republican Party.

By mid-1970 most of the original Panther leadership had either fled the country or gone underground. H. Rap Brown was arrested in October 1971 on armed robbery charges. Bobby Seale was imprisoned for contempt of court while Huey Newton renounced armed struggle by May 1971. While two hijackings did occur in June and July of 1972 by Panthers and some sympathizers wishing to find asylum abroad, by that time the Black Panther movement had spent itself out. On 17 February 1999 Elmer Pratt, known as "Geronimo," was released from prison after the Orange Country Superior Court overturned his 1968 conviction for robbery and murder, citing the withholding of critical evidence by the prosecution at the original trial. Rap Brown, who converted to Sunni Islam upon his release from prison taking the name Jamil Abdullah Al-Amin, moved to Atlanta where he began a community service program to keep inner-city youth off of drugs and where he became the leader of the Community Mosque in the West End district in 1985. In March 2000 he became a fugitive suspect following the shooting death of one sheriff's deputy and the wounding of another who were serving an arrest warrant in connection with a traffic violation in May 1999.

While the militant image of the Panthers inspired fear in the public, in retrospect Panther violence appeared to be more sporadic and reactive than coherent tactics to foment a revolution. Nonetheless the Black Panthers were the predecessors of the **Black Liberation Army**, which in turn, together with remnants of the Weather Underground, helped form the **Revolutionary Armed Task Force** that continued a campaign of leftist revolutionary terrorism within the United States until 1986.

BLACK SEPTEMBER ORGANIZATION (BSO). The BSO was a clandestine group created by **al Fatah** in December 1971 for the limited purpose of avenging the suppression and expulsion of the **Palestine Liberation Organization** (PLO) from Jordan in the "Black September" of 1970. During that September the **Popular Front for the Liberation of Palestine** (PFLP) had **hijacked** several airplanes to Dawson's Field in Jordan and was holding about 400 Western hostages there. King Hussein ordered the Jordanian Army to rescue the hostages and, in the course of the fighting that followed, the Palestinians suffered enormous losses and their survivors were expelled to Lebanon. As Fatah held a declaratory policy of not involving itself in the domestic politics of Arab nations, yet nonetheless planned to kill King Hussein and those who shared responsibility in carrying out his orders, it was essential that Fatah be able to maintain a plausible deniability of responsibility for the BSO. In actuality the scope of targets of the BSO grew to include Israeli, U.S., and other Western targets, while their attacks rivaled those of the PFLP in ferocity and media impact. During its period of activity from 1971 to 1974, the BSO was run by Salah Khalaf (aka, Abu Iyad), one of **Yasir Arafat's** closest deputies.

On 28 November 1971 the BSO **assassinated** Jordanian Prime Minister Wasfi al Tall in Cairo. The BSO tried, but failed, several times to assassinate King Hussein. The most notorious BSO action, however, was its attack on the Israeli team at the 1972 Summer Olympics in **Munich** in which all 11 Israeli hostages and five of the eight terrorists were killed in a shoot-out with West German police in which one German was also killed. On 29 October 1972, BSO members hijacked a Lufthansa plane and forced West German authorities to release the three surviving BSO gunmen from the Munich attack in exchange for the lives of the Lufthansa hostages. On 16 September 1972 the BSO also mailed out 64 **letter bombs** to Israeli and non-Israeli Jewish targets, most of which were intercepted and deactivated, but some of which succeeded in killing Israeli diplomats, other Jews, and some postal workers. On 1 March 1973 BSO gunmen seized the Saudi Arabian embassy in Khartoum and murdered U.S. Ambassador Cleo A. Noel, Jr., the U.S. chargé d'affaires, and a Belgian chargé d'affaires.

From 1971 to 1974 the BSO carried out at least 34 noteworthy actions: 16 **bombings**, 11 assassinations, three hijackings, three **hostage seizures**, and a rocket attack upon the U.S. embassy in Beirut. On 5 September 1973 Italian police foiled a BSO plot to shoot down an El Al airplane with two SAM-7 Strela antiaircraft missiles. Israel, whose citizens and diplomats abroad had become the primary **targets** of the BSO assassination and letter-bombing campaigns, undertook covert and overt operations to quash the BSO. Israeli Wrath of God operatives began killing BSO operatives in Cyprus and Europe while the Israeli Defense Forces launched a raid on Beirut on 10 April 1973 in which they attacked the BSO headquarters, killing 17 terrorists, and destroyed the BSO letter-bomb factory.

In spite of Fatah's desire to conceal its connections with the BSO, the arrests of a BSO agent in Jordan and of another in France produced evidence linking the two organizations. Although the BSO was dissolved by Fatah in December 1974 many former BSO operatives then joined either the PFLP or else Abu Nidal's **Fatah Revolutionary Council**. The murder of Israeli diplomat Yosef Alon in December 1975 in Washington, D.C., was once believed to be the work of local proxies acting on behalf of Black September. From 1981 to 1987 about 17 actions were claimed in the name of the BSO but these were most likely the work of **Abu Nidal** operatives.

In 1996 Mohammad Oudeh, the mastermind of the Munich Olympics attack also known as Abu Daoud, was allowed by Israeli authorities to enter the West Bank to attend a PLO leadership meeting where he stayed establishing a law practice in Ramallah. After publishing his autobiography in France, in which he acknowledged his role in the Black September attack at the Munich Olympics, German authorities issued an arrest warrant for him in June 1999. Upon receiving word of this Prime Minister Binyamin Netanyahu ordered that Daoud, who was in Jordan at the time, be barred from returning to the West Bank and also canceled his VIP pass that was issued to PLO officials to permit them unhindered passage through Israeli checkpoints in the West Bank. For many Palestinians and Israelis this incident raised the question whether this action violated an understanding of amnesty implicit in the 1996 Israeli government decision to allow former PLO terrorists to return to areas under Palestinian Authority control.

BOER ATTACK FORCE. The Boere Aanvals Troepe is a South African antistate group made up of Afrikaaners disaffected with the post-apartheid regime. Among their demands are an autonomous homeland for white South Africans, government "recognition of the Christian faith," release of all "right wing political prisoners," and lower fuel prices. This group claimed responsibility for two **bombings** on Christmas Eve 1996 in a crowded shopping area of Worcester, a town 90 miles north of Cape Town, one homemade pipe bomb planted near a supermarket and another near a pharmacy, which together killed four persons, three of them children, and wounded dozens more. On 5 January 1997 another three bombings claimed by this group occurred in Rustenburg, located northwest of Johannesburg, one at a newly remodeled Mosque about 1:15 a.m., wounding two guards there. Then at 3:00 a.m. another bombing struck the Marikana Post Office about 13 miles east of Rustenburg, and another at a liquor store in Olifantsnek, a suburb of Rustenburg.

The Afrikaaner Resistance Movement (AWB) led by Eugene TerreBlanche disclaimed any knowledge of this group. Hours after the attacks in Rustenburg police arrested two white men, Christian Harmse and Pierre Jacobs, at a roadblock when explosives were discovered in their car.

BOMBINGS, BOMBERS. Bombs are among the top two weapons of choice for terrorists, the other being automatic weapons. However bombing is also used extensively for merely criminal purposes, whether for murder, revenge, **arson**, or as diversionary devices. Whether a bombing is a terrorist act or not depends on whether the bomber(s) intended to achieve some political objective with it and to use the bombing as part of their communication of demands and threat fulfillments to the society they are targeting. Since no credit is claimed for most of the bombings that occur most apparently are done for merely criminal purposes. In some of the most famous cases of serial bombers, such as George P. Metesky, the infamous "Mad Bomber" who terrorized New York City from 1940 to 1956, and Theodore Kaczynski, the **Unabomber**, who terrorized the United States from 1978 to 1995, the motives of the bomber appear to have been rooted in personal grudges but articulated and rationalized in political terms.

While there is a great variety of bombs for specialized purposes there are a few types favored by terrorists, namely, vehicle bombs, **letter/parcel bombs**, and small bombs designed to destroy airplanes in flight, which have been infrequently used but almost always with great lethality when successful. Bombs are attractive to terrorists because: first, they cause high loss of life and casualties, creating terror when civilians are being randomly targeted and which gets the desired media coverage and attention to the terrorists and their demands. Second, they usually can be deployed in such a way that the terrorist planting the device can escape injury or arrest. Finally, they are relatively easy and inexpensive to prepare. **Suicide bombings** are a special case and generally more lethal because the suicide bomber can deploy the bomb to achieve maximum lethality and usually can detonate it before others have a chance to evacuate or to disarm the bomb. Moreover, the willingness of bombers to kill themselves along with a large number of victims is itself more dramatic, more shocking and frightening to the general public, and especially problematic for law enforcement and security forces who ordinarily can count on the terrorist's will to live to deter them from attacking or else as a bargaining chip in, for example, hostage-barricade situations.

Apparently the **Narodnaya Volya** group in Tsarist Russia was the first terrorist group to employ bombing in a systematic terrorist campaign. Oddly enough, although the members of this group frankly admitted to being "terrorists" they wanted to bomb only those persons whom they viewed as major political or police functionaries of the Tsarist regime and they took great pains to avoid killing or injuring bystanders. By contrast the terrorists of the late 20th century, such as in the **World Trade Center bombing** and the **Oklahoma City bombing** cases, wanted to maximize the killing of innocent people at the scene.

BROOKLYN BOMBING PLOT. Acting on a tip from an Arabic-speaking informant, on 31 July 1997 New York police raided a Brooklyn apartment shooting two men before either of them could activate several pipe bombs amid other bomb-making materials. Two days before this raid a note had been mailed to the U.S. Department of State warning of a series of attacks unless **Sheikh Omar Abdul Rahman** and Ramzi Ahmad Yousef were released as well as Sheikh Ahmad Yassin, a **Hamas** leader jailed in Israel. At the raided apartment police found a draft of the same note.

The two men, Gazi Ibrahim Abu Mezer and Lafi Khalil, had two pipe bombs assembled, made with black powder and loaded with nails as shrapnel which each could have killed up to 25 feet away within an enclosed space. They apparently were planning to bomb the Atlantic Avenue subway station and a commuter bus and the presence of toggle switches on the bombs and lack of any timer or remote detonating device suggested that the two men were planning **suicide attacks**. The two men, both Palestinian, had entered and remained in the United States in violation of immigration law, Abu Mezer having falsely claimed Israeli persecution to seek **asylum,** and Khalil having a bogus alien registration document. Neither man was found to have any known connection to Hamas or other Islamic militant groups. Abu Mezer was convicted of conspiracy to use a **weapon of mass destruction** on 23 July 1998 while Lafi Khalil was acquitted of charges relating to the bomb plot but convicted for possession of a forged immigration document. *See also* BOMBING.

- C -

CABINDA LIBERATION FRONT-CABINDA LIBERATION FORCES (FLEC-FAC). Cabinda is the oil-rich enclave of Angola separated from the rest of the country by the territory of the Democratic Republic of Congo (the former Zaire) on both banks of the Congo River from its estuary inland. During the Angolan civil war between the forces of **UNITA** (União Nacional para Independécia Total de Angola) and those of the Angolan government, which has continued intermittently since Portugal quit its former colony in 1975, there has also been separatist violence by antigovernment forces in the Cabinda enclave who seek independence from the rest of Angola.

During 1990 the Frente para a Libertação de Enclave de Cabinda (FLEC) **kidnapped** 13 French oil workers, several Congolese workers, and two Portuguese aid workers, who were held hostage but all later released unharmed. In 1992 FLEC kidnapped three Portuguese construction workers and two French citizens, as well as attacking Chevron buses used to transport workers. In the most serious incident that year, in December FLEC murdered three Angolan employees of Chevron. In February 1993 FLEC kidnapped an officer of the United Nations Angola Verification Mission who was released unharmed three weeks later. In May 1993 FLEC and UNITA forces reportedly joined together in an attack on the Cabinda Gulf Oil Company, which is managed by Chevron International of America, and took several Portuguese workers hostage. In January 1995 FLEC took credit for a mortar attack on the Chevron administration building in Malongo. On 8 February 1997 FLEC and the Forcas Armadas de Libertação (FAC) kidnapped a Malaysian and a Filipino forest worker whom they accused of spying for the Angolan government and threatened to kill. On 23 March and 22 April 1998 FLEC-FAC kidnapped three Portuguese construction workers. On these occasions FLEC-FAC has issued warnings to all foreign companies to leave Cabinda to deprive the Angolan government of the oil revenues it needs.

CARIBBEAN REVOLUTIONARY ALLIANCE. The Caribbean Revolutionary Alliance was a leftist group seeking Guadeloupe's independence from France. On 13 March 1985, a **bomb** exploded at a restaurant at Point-à-Pitre owned by a member of France's right-wing **National Front**, killing one person and wounding 11 others.

CARLOS (1950-). Carlos "the Jackal," whose true name was Ilyich Ramírez Sánchez, was a Venezuelan-born terrorist who briefly became notorious in the mid-1970s before sinking into obscurity. Born into a middle-class but Communist family, Sánchez was named in honor of Lenin. Later he went to a Cuban youth camp and ultimately attended Patrice Lumumba University in Moscow from which he was expelled in 1971 for frivolity. Others maintain that he was really recruited as a KGB agent and that the expulsion was faked to maintain his cover.

Using the nom de guerre "Carlos," Sánchez went to Paris where he took command of a **Popular Front for the Liberation of Palestine** (PFLP) cell in the early 1970s. Sánchez is believed to have made an **assassination** attempt on 31 December 1973 against Marks and Spencer magnate Teddy Sieff who was wounded but not killed due to a malfunction of the gun. Sánchez was implicated in terrorist **bombings** of three pro-Israeli newspapers and an attempt to destroy an El Al airliner at Orly airport in 1975. Sánchez is best remembered for his role in the siege of the OPEC Secretariat in Vienna on 21 December 1975 (*see* OPEC SIEGE, VIENNA) in which he held 11 OPEC oil ministers hostage and collected a massive ransom from the governments of Iran and Saudi Arabia, reportedly over $50 million.

After that episode he dropped out of view. For some time it was speculated that he was either dead or else had become a trainer of terrorists in Libya or Syria. In 1983 a group calling itself the **Organization for the Armed Arab Struggle** surfaced, reportedly under Sánchez's leadership, which carried out a bombing of a Paris-Toulouse train, the Capitole, in March 1982, and the bombing of a train station in Marseilles in December 1983, apparently to put pressure on the French government to release his lover, Magdelena Kopp, a **Red Army Faction** (RAF) member serving a jail sentence in France on a conviction for illegal possession of firearms and explosives. After some brief activity it also subsided into obscurity.

In the 1980s Carlos settled in Damascus, Syria, where he was reunited in December 1985 with his lover, Magdelena Kopp, whom he then married. He remained in Syria under the protection of President Hafiz al Asad until December 1993 when French officials learned of his whereabouts and began to press for his **extradition**. The Syrian government, which was finding its association with terrorist groups an embarrassment, forced him to leave. Carlos apparently spent time in Yemen before deciding to move to Sudan. He was arrested by Sudanese officials on 14 August 1994 and handed over to French officials. Apparently both the governments of Syria and Sudan viewed Carlos as an anachronistic misfit and saw political advantages with the West in helping to turn him over since he was no longer a useful asset for their current political agendas.

Carlos boasted of having been responsible for killing 83 people in the 1970s and 1980s although French authorities considered him a suspect in terrorist attacks in which 15 persons were killed and over 200 wounded in France alone. For a long time the mass media wrongly associated him with the **Black September** (BSO) **Munich massacre** of the Israeli Olympic team in 1972 and he was rumored to have been linked to over 30 other major terrorist actions. Most of this was part of a myth that Carlos himself helped create but upon his arrest most terrorist experts, such as Brian Jenkins and others, stated that his significance had been greatly exaggerated and that he was often a mediocre and bungling terrorist. On 24 December 1997 he was sentenced to life imprisonment for murdering three people in 1975 and on 16 January 1999 he was cleared of a charge for a bombing in 1974. In 1999 Austria was seeking to extradite Carlos to face charges stemming from the OPEC siege.

CELLULAR ORGANIZATION. To protect themselves from penetration and also to maintain control over members, most terrorist groups opt for a cellular organization. Cells are groups of three to 10 members headed by one leader. Rudimentary terrorist organizations, such as the **Symbionese Liberation Army** (SLA), by default have a cellular structure but in the case of larger organizations, such as the **Basque Fatherland and Liberty** (ETA) group having hundreds of members, the cellular organization protects the entire organization from penetration. While the ordinary bureaucratic organization is pyramidal, hierarchical, and transparent the cellular system is better described as a circular, or "solar," system, whose links to other cells or parts of the organization remain hidden.

Within each cell the ordinary members may know one another but have no knowledge of the existence of other cells or of their members and have no link to the rest of the organization except through the cell leader. Cell leaders, in turn, may have no other link to the rest of the organization except through group leaders subordinate to a central operations committee. In the event members of one cell are captured and interrogated they can reveal only what they know of their own cell. Even that knowledge can be limited through the use of false names among the group members while the cell itself may adopt a distinctive name to mask its relationship with the parent organization.

The circumstances under which terrorists operate perhaps ensure that only those organizations having cellular structures can continue to survive for long. The **Irish Republican Army** (IRA) originally conceived of itself as being a regular army and so produced general orders, official handbooks, rules and records of courts-martial, and the hierarchical command structure of a regular army. The need of clandestinity to protect the organization from penetration by informers or the confessions of captured members forced the Irish Republican Army to adopt cellular structures.

It should be noted that many or even most cells in a terrorist organization may be merely support groups that do not directly execute terrorist activities. Their members may run businesses or operate safe houses that provide support to persons whose identities and about whose activities they may know nothing.

The "phantom cells," or autonomous leadership units, are cells which remain inactive for a long period to infiltrate a nation or an organization, but which may become active after a certain time when they have achieved access to a critical facility. Following the **World Trade Center bombing** the FBI began to suspect that Middle Eastern **Islamic fundamentalist** groups had been setting up such phantom cells within the United States to activate at some later, critical time.

Apart from cells in a networked structure there are also cases of free-floating terrorist cells which are independent entities that are fed by an environment of ideological extremism. The Symbionese Liberation Army was one such free-floating cell that fed off the currents of left-wing extremism and antiwar activism in the 1970s while Timothy McVeigh and Terry Nichols may be considered a right-wing variant of the free-floating cell who fed off the environment of antigovernment extremism and prejudice current among right-wing extremists in the 1990s.

Many **national-separatist groups** maintain parallel political front and military wing structures: The political front is a relatively transparent, hierarchical organization that can serve as a legitimate political party or interest group if conditions allow. However it has a shadow military organization, organized on a solar cellular basis, which is linked to the leaders in the political front by some "chain-network," a series of personal links so that authorities may not track the connections between the political and military wings easily. In the event the authorities crack down on the political front and arrest all known leaders the military wing can swing into action on the basis of contingency orders to retaliate for the seizure of their leaders and to pressure for their release. *See also* NETWAR; NETWORKS.

CHECHNYAN TERRORISM. Following the collapse of the Soviet Union in 1991 one of the strongest challenges to the territorial integrity of the successor Russian Federation has come from nationalist and **Islamic fundamentalist** extremists seeking independence for the Chechnyan republic within the Federation. Chechnya is one of several enclaves of non-Russian Muslim ethnicities in the Caucasus region, an area which already experienced separatist ethnic strife in the Nagorno-Karabakh war between Armenia and Azerbaijan as well as the secessionist movement among the Abkhazian Muslim minority in Georgia. A successful secession of the Chechnyan region would have grave implications for the rest of Russia, in which Muslim ethnic minorities alone number around 18 million and in which several other non-Russian minorities exist.

In 1859 the Muslim regions of the northern Caucasus, including Chechnya and Daghestan, were incorporated into the Tsarist Empire after decades of fighting and resistance. During 1944-1953 there was a mass deportation of Chechens to Central Asia ordered by Stalin due to alleged Chechen wartime collaboration with the Nazi invaders. On 6 September 1991 a retired Soviet Air Force general, Dzhukar Dudayev, led a coup against the regional government and declared Chechnya's independence. After Russia adopted its new constitution on 12 December 1993 its new government refused to recognize Chechen claims to independence. From 11 December 1994 to 27 May 1996 the Russians fought to reassert control over Chechnya but weak political and military direction led to high Russian casualties and repeated humiliations of Russian troops at the hands of Chechen militias and guerrillas. The fighting concluded with a peace agreement that allowed increased autonomy for Chechnya and an interim Russian role in security affairs but which fell short of the recognition of independence sought by Chechen nationalists and fundamentalist extremists.

During and following the disastrous Russian 20-month campaign of 1994-1996 there were a number of terrorist attacks by Chechen militias, including many on foreign contract workers, humanitarian workers, missionaries, as well as against Russians and moderate Chechens. On 14 June 1995 a Chechen rebel leader and extremist, Shamil Basaev, seized 1,000 **hostages** at a hospital in the Russian town of Budyonnovsk. After four days of fighting Russian troops retook the hospital at a cost of 150 lives but the rebels escaped with about 100 hostages. On 4 December 1995 a **bombing** of the Russian administration building in Grozny killed 11 persons and wounded more than 60. On 9 January 1996 Chechen rebels attacked a hospital in Kizlyar, Daghestan, and seized over 3,000 hostages. A week later Chechen rebel sympathizers **hijacked** a Black Sea ferry bound from Trabzon, Turkey, to Sochii, Russia, holding 165 passengers and crew hostage but releasing them shortly later.

Following the tentative peace between Russia and Chechen rebel leaders more terrorist attacks continued, with six Red Cross workers being murdered on 17 December 1996, leading to a suspension of Red Cross efforts in Chechnya. On 28 April 1997 a bomb struck a train station in Pyatigorsk, in southern Russia, killing one person and wounding 11 others, for which Chechen militants were blamed. In July 1997 British relief workers were **kidnapped** but then released by militants after over 14 months in captivity. In October 1997 Hungarian relief workers were kidnapped but then released by militants eight months later. On 3 October 1998, four British telecommunications workers installing a cellular telephone system were kidnapped by rebels and when Chechen security forces tried to rescue them all four were beheaded on December 7.

Part of the continuing violence was directed not only at foreigners working within Chechnya but also against Chechen security officials as well as attacks on Russian troops and border police in nearby Daghestan. These attacks appeared to be part of a power struggle between nationalist Chechens, who favored more conciliatory relations with Russia, and more radical fundamentalists intent on sabotaging the negotiations with Russia as well as pushing the interim Chechnyan government further in the direction of an Islamic state. Although Dudayev, who was killed by Russian missiles on 25 April 1996, and his successor as Chechen President, Aslan Maskhadov, were primarily nationalists for whom Islam was but part of the Chechen national identity, many other Chechen factions sought to create a more Islamic fundamentalist state.

One of the main rebel fighters, Shamil Basaev, acted as a virtually independent warlord and was willing to side with more extreme Islamic fundamentalists to augment his own power within Chechnya. Basaev had helped Abkhazian Muslim secessionists in Georgia in 1992-1993 and within post-1996 Chechnya he sided with fundamentalist extremists led by Khattab, a Jordanian of Chechen descent and "Afghan" veteran, who was a promoter of the Wahhabi version of Islam. On 10 June 1997 after denouncing Wahhabism in his sermon a prominent Grozny mullah, Hasanbek Yakhyayev, was murdered by an Islamic militant. On 16 July 1998 fighting broke out between Chechen security forces and Wahhabi fundamentalists in Gudermes, the second largest city in Chechnya.

Several terrorist acts appeared to have been aimed at sabotaging negotiations between Russia and more moderate Chechen leaders. On 19 March 1999 a powerful bombing in Vladikavkaz, in the Ossetia region of Russia, killed 58 and wounded 100. On 21 March 1999 Chechen President Maskhadov survived a car-bomb assassination attempt, reportedly the fifth attempt on his life, which apparently was carried out by Chechen extremists. In fact these attempts by extremists to push the Chechen government in the direction of increased Islamization were partly effective. At the same time that Russia had abolished its death penalty to comply with European Union human rights standards, Chechnya officially imposed death sentences for violations of Islamic law and televised these executions.

In the summer of 1999 matters came to a head when the Chechen Wahhabi extremists provoked attacks in Daghestan in August 1999 in an attempt to create a "Russian-free zone" or corridor under Chechen control from Chechnya to the Caspian Sea. Unlike Chechnya, in which the Chechens are the predominant nationality, neighboring Daghestan has over 30 national groups, including non-Muslim minorities, few of whom had aspirations for greater autonomy from Russia. Within three weeks Russian forces regained most of the disputed Daghestani villages and Basaev and his followers were forced to withdraw to Chechnya. On 9 and 13 September 1999 two major bombings destroyed apartment complexes in Moscow, killing over 32 in the first attack and over 76 in the second attack. In Volgodonsk, on 16 September 1999 another apartment complex bombing killed another 18. A total of five such bombings took place within Russia during September 1999 killing over 300 people, for which credit was claimed by anonymous telephone calls stating that the bombings were in retaliation for Russian air strikes in the Daghestan campaign. Some Russian sources alleged that **Osama**

bin Laden had been involved not only in support for the Chechen Wahhabis but also in backing the bombing campaign within Russia.

On 1 October 1999 Russia began what has been described as its "second Chechnyan" war ostensibly to destroy terrorist training camps and to root terrorism out of the Caucasus region. Some observers believe that the government of Boris Yeltsin was deliberately playing up Russian national feelings and resentments over the disastrous 1994-1996 war to create a mood of national unity and support for his government that would help his electoral coalition in the 19 December 1999 parliamentary elections. In fact both the alleged Chechen bombings within Russia occurring that autumn and the second offensive late in 1999 were to help Boris Yeltsin's successor, Vladimir Vladimirovitch Putin, to bolster his image as a hardline defender of Russian nationalist values prior to the presidential elections in Russia. In late December 1999 Russian troops had succeeded in occupying much of Chechnya and captured Grozny on 6 February 2000 following a two-month siege. In the Russia presidential election of 26 March 2000 Putin won a majority of 53 percent, an electoral mandate won in part by public perceptions of his effectiveness in suppressing the Chechen revolt.

The main external support for the Chechen extremists appears to come from the estimated 15,000-strong "Afghans," those Islamic veteran volunteers who came from outside Afghanistan to help the **Mujahideen** fight the Soviet occupation in that country and who have since then dispersed throughout the Muslim world seeking to promote Islamist insurgencies elsewhere, including Chechnya. However the Islamic Republic of Iran, which found itself at odds with the Sunni Wahhabi-dominated Afghans and with the Wahhabi-dominated **Taliban** regime in Afghanistan, has been strongly supportive of Russia in its attempts to contain the spread of Wahhabi-style fundamentalism in the Caucasus region. Azerbaijan, with its more secularized society and predominantly Shi'ite Muslim culture, has not shown itself inclined to support the Chechens in this conflict with Russia, nor has Georgia, which experienced its own secessionist movement among the Abkhazians.

CHICAGO CONVENTION. Same as Convention on International Civil Aviation. *See* AIR TRAVEL SECURITY.

CHRISTIAN IDENTITY. *See* IDENTITY CHRISTIANITY.

CHRISTIAN-PATRIOTS DEFENSE LEAGUE (C-PDL). The C-PDL was a nonstate group of right-wing survivalists who sought to create a **militia** and fortified encampments to preserve white, Christian Americans against a coming Communist invasion and racial war. Although the group's aims appeared to be limited by the remoteness of the imagined future holocaust insofar as the group formed part of the network of **white supremacist** and anti-Semitic groups, such as the **Aryan Nations** and **Ku Klux Klan**, it held the same revolutionary goals of resisting and destroying the United States government, or what such circles refer to as the "Zionist Occupation Government."

Despite the similarity in names, the C-PDL was not directly related to the **Identity Christianity** preacher Wesley Smith's Christian Defense League. Rather it was the brainchild of John Robert Harrell ("Johnny Bob"), a former mausoleum salesman who devoted himself to the Identity Christian message after experiencing an apocalyptic vision during an illness in 1959. Convinced that a Jewish conspiracy was leading to a Communist invasion of the United States as well as a racial war, Harrell sought to train militia to defend a "Mid-America Survival Zone." He became an associate of Robert dePugh, founder of the **Minutemen**, and became a frequent contributor to the Minutemen's tabloid *On Target*.

Harrell gave refuge to a Marine who had gone AWOL after embracing the Identity creed, and in August 1961 Federal agents overran Harrell's fortified Louisville, Illinois, estate where they found four underground two-man bunkers and stockpiles of food and ammunition. Harrell and his followers did not resist arrest, and Harrell was sentenced to four years in prison for harboring a federal fugitive and on various tax evasion charges. After DePugh was imprisoned in 1968 on a conspiracy conviction, Harrell created four organizations to fill the void left by the defunct Minutemen: the religious organization was the Christian Conservative Church of America, which teaches a synthesis of Christianity, nationalism, anti-Semitism, and anti-Communism. The political branch was the Christian-Patriots Defense League. The military branch was the Citizens Emergency Defense System, a private militia. The fundraising branch was the Paul Revere Club. One could be a member of the religious branch without having to belong to the other branches while members of the military and political branches were not required to believe in the group's Identity Christian doctrine so long as they otherwise supported its white supremacist and anti-Semitic program.

The C-PDL operated a 220-acre compound beside the Mark Twain National Forest, near Licking, Missouri; a 55-acre paramilitary training facility near Flora, Illinois; and its "Survival Base" near Smithville, West Virginia. The group hosted an annual "Freedom Festival" in Flora in which survivalist and Identity groups conducted weapons workshops and held Identity doctrine speeches and seminars. In recent years it has ceased to be active.

CHUKAKU-HA. The "Central Core" or "Nucleus Faction" was a Japanese revolutionary Marxist group that originated from a 1957 split in the Japanese Communist Party and that has sought to overturn Japan's constitutional system and monarchy. Chukaku-Ha was not only the largest faction out of the 23 factions that make up the Japanese New Left movement but also the largest militant domestic opposition group in Japan. The group's "anti-Imperialist" position was expressed in frequent protests against the U.S.-Japan Security Treaty while its rejection of the Japanese corporate state was concretely expressed in its frequent attacks on the construction of the New Tokyo International Airport and against the subway and railroad mass-transit systems.

Even though Chukaku-Ha could be considered typically leftist because of its membership in the Japanese New Left and its stated objectives and ideals, this group should also be considered anarchistic insofar as its program seemed more intent on destroying the existing Japanese corporate state rather than building an alternative socialist state. Chukaku-Ha was not known to have any foreign state sponsors. Almost all of their activities have taken place within Japan while their base membership of 3,500 members supported the 200 or so full-time activists. Among the full-time activists were members of the Kansai Revolutionary Army, the group's covert active measures group that actually carried out most of the group's terrorism.

The group relied on the use of homemade but sometimes surprisingly sophisticated incendiary **bombs**, flamethrowers, mortars, and rockets. Most of their **targets** have been property, whether the headquarters of the Japanese Liberal-Democratic Party, the national railroad system, U.S. Armed Forces facilities, the Imperial Palace grounds, or government offices. Of 41 major incidents from 1984 to 1991, about 19 involved **arson** using incendiary bombs and devices; 10 involved the use of crude mortars and rocketlike devices; eight involved assaults and beatings; two involved bombings; one act of sabotage; and one murder.

group has used mass rallies of its general membership as feints to draw police attention away from actual targets. On one occasion in the frequent clashes at the construction site of Narita airport, throngs of Chukaku-Ha members armed with Molotov cocktails rushed a police barricade and created a small riot. While police concentrated on holding back the demonstrators, the Chukaku-Ha covert operations specialists burglarized the control tower of the airport, entering through underground service corridors, and then smashed much of the computer equipment there.

Actions included the 19 September 1984 assault on the headquarters of Japan's ruling Liberal Democratic Party: A truck with a flamethrower device was driven into the side of the building and gutted six of its nine floors. Meanwhile the same group exploded a bomb near the Israeli embassy. On 25 March 1986 they launched three of their homemade rockets at the Imperial Palace and another three at the U.S. embassy. On 4 May 1986 they launched five rockets at Akasaka palace where the economic summit of the seven major industrialized powers was meeting. The rockets flew 3.5 kilometers and landed within 550 meters of their target. Because of the coincidence of this attack following the U.S. bombing raid on Libya some observers speculated a Libyan connection, but Chukaku-Ha had been engaged in a spree of rocket launching that year even before that raid, however. On 23 February 1991 they fired rockets upon U.S. Navy housing outside Yokohama. Most of these rocket attacks have caused little damage and no harm to life or limb due to the missiles' inaccuracy. Their last known attacks included a bombing of the UN Technology Center in Osaka on 7 July 1993, which caused but minor damage. On 9 July 1993 they fired four rockets at the U.S. Army base at Camp Zama during the G-7 Summit in Tokyo, none of which caused any apparent damage.

CIA HEADQUARTERS ATTACK. On 25 January 1993 a lone gunman walked up to a line of cars waiting to enter the headquarters compound of the Central Intelligence Agency (CIA) in Langley, Virginia, opened fire with an AK-47 machine gun, killing two CIA employees, a communications worker, Frank Darling, and an analyst, Lansing Bennett, and wounding two other CIA workers and one telephone repairman. The gunman, a Pakistani immigrant named Mir Aimal Kansi (1960-), apparently acted alone and was motivated by anger over U.S. influence in Pakistan, U.S. foreign policy in the Middle East, and the treatment of

Palestinians by Israel. Kansi was born into a well-to-do family in Quetta, which borders Afghanistan and which was a center for a $3 billion CIA paramilitary operation supporting the anti-Soviet **Mujahideen**. A specialized FBI counterterrorist team arrested Kansi in Pakistan on 17 June 1997 and returned him to the United States where he was tried in a Virginia state court on murder charges and sentenced to life imprisonment for the murder of Bennett. On 14 November 1997 he received the death penalty for the murder of Darling due to his having shot him twice, first in the back but then once more in the head, which the jury believed demonstrated excessive brutality. Kansi was not tried under U.S. federal antiterrorism statutes because he apparently acted alone.

Following the conviction of Kansi, gunmen in Karachi, Pakistan, opened fire killing four American workers from a Texas oil and gas company, along with their driver, in apparent retaliation for the conviction against Kansi.

CINCHONEROS POPULAR LIBERATION MOVEMENT (MPL). The Movimiento Popular de Liberación (MPL) was a state-sponsored revolutionary group seeking to overthrow the Honduran government and to oppose U.S. interests in the region. Its own **ideology** represented an eclectic blend of Marxist-Leninist and populist notions. The MPL was the armed wing of the People's Revolutionary Union, a splinter group of the Honduran Communist Party that appeared in 1980. Their informal name "Cinchoneros" is derived from the nickname of Serapio "Cinchonero" Romero, a Honduran peasant leader supposedly executed in the late 1800s.

The group's activities included **bombings** and **hostage taking**. While it largely financed itself through bank robberies and **kidnapping** for ransom, the MPL was suspected of receiving training, arms, logistical support, and funds from Cuba. Salvadoran **Farabundo Martí National Liberation Front** (FMLN) guerrillas reportedly trained Cinchonero forces within Honduras and participated with them in kidnapping operations. The **Sandinista** government allowed Cinchonero guerrillas safe haven in Nicaraguan territory and had used them as auxiliary forces in fighting the **contras**.

On 24 March 1980 five Cinchoneros **hijacked** a Honduran Airlines 737 to Managua, Nicaragua, to force the release of 15 Salvadoran leftists imprisoned in Honduras. The hijacked plane was flown to Panama before the captive passengers and crew were finally released. On 17

September 1982 they took 105 hostages at an economic conference at the Chamber of Commerce in San Pedro Sula, killing one guard and wounding two businessmen in the takeover. When their demands for the release of imprisoned comrades were not met, they traded the hostages for safe passage to Cuba. From August 1983 to March 1985 the group bombed U.S., Honduran, and Costa Rican business and airline offices in retaliation for these countries' military cooperation against the Sandinista regime in Nicaragua. On 17 July 1988 the group claimed credit for an attack in San Pedro Sula in which some U.S. servicemen were wounded. On 25 January 1989 the group killed the former head of the Honduran army, General Gustavo Álvarez Martínez.

From late 1984 onward the group appeared to withdraw into a period of reorganization. Little is known about its leadership, while its membership was estimated to consist of, at most, about 200 combatants.

CLARA ELIZABETH RAMÍREZ FRONT (CERF). The Frente Clara Elizabeth Ramírez was a splinter group that broke away in 1983 from the Popular Liberation Forces, one of the five major groups united into the **Farabundo Martí National Liberation Front** (FMLN). As such, it has essentially the same **revolutionary** objectives that the FMLN held at the time the group separated, namely, to overthrow the Salvadoran government and create a revolutionary state in El Salvador after the Nicaraguan model. Due to its defection from the FMLN front, however, it cut itself off from Cuban or Sandinista backing.

CERF consisted of 10 to 20 well-trained, urban guerrillas who succeeded in preventing infiltration by security forces. CERF concentrated on **assassinations** and targeted in particular U.S. military personnel and advisers as well as Salvadoran military and police officials. Its record was short but deadly: On 23 May 1983 CERF shot Lieutenant Commander Albert Schaufelberger (USN), deputy commander of the U.S. military advisory mission in El Salvador. On 17 November 1984 CERF assassinated the security supervisor of the U.S. embassy, who was a Salvadoran national. On 7 March 1985 CERF shot and killed Lieutenant Colonel Ricardo Cienfuegos, chief Salvadoran military spokesman, at a downtown San Salvadoran health club. On 23 March 1985 they followed up with the assassination of General José Alberto Medrano, founder of **ORDEN** and patron of extreme right-wing groups and politicians.

On 19 June 1985 the Central American Workers' Revolutionary Party, a member group of the FMLN, publicly machine-gunned off-duty U.S. Marines and other patrons sitting in a sidewalk café in the Zona Rosa district, killing four and wounding nine others. The Salvadoran government responded with intensive counterterrorist operations that, in addition to capturing the responsible culprits, crippled but did not totally destroy the CERF. Since that time, CERF has been struggling to rebuild itself through recruitment efforts among university students.

CNN SYNDROME. Sometimes shorted to "CNN-drome," refers to the Atlanta-based Cable Network News (CNN) channel which revolutionized news coverage by having 24-hour satellite and cable-fed news. This term was coined by Lt. Col. David Bradford (USAF, ret.) to identify the effect of instant coverage of provocative major news events, such as terrorist attacks, in stampeding decision-makers and the public into reactive statements and actions. Insofar as terrorists seek to exploit media coverage of their actions to pressure governments through psychological manipulation of the targeted audiences who are following the news as it unfolds, the CNN effect greatly magnifies the impact of terrorism. It also has the unfortunate effect of driving public opinion and policy making to reacting before a careful marshaling and analysis of evidence can be completed. Thus, for example, the chance remark by a person interviewed near the **Oklahoma City bombing** site that he had seen "a Middle Eastern-looking man" driving away from the scene of the bombing prompted both a flurry of false news media leads about purported Muslim or Middle Eastern terrorists and also a regrettable wave of anti-Arab and anti-Muslim bigotry and hostility among many Americans.

COLOMBIAN COCAINE CARTELS. These criminal syndicates are considered terrorist threats for at least three reasons. First, they are considered agencies of a purported **"narco-terrorism"**; second, there is a growing concern about the convergence of **organized crime** with terrorism in the post-Cold War era and these groups are the clearest examples of such a convergence; and finally, the Colombian drug cartels have carried out **entrepreneurial terrorist** actions to eliminate leftist groups which have interfered with their operations as well as to co-opt and intimidate the national government of Colombia, which has been under U.S. pressures to eradicate the cocaine and opium drug trade within its borders. Researcher Robert Filippone studied in depth the structure and mode of operations of these cartels and presented his findings in his article "The Medellín Cartel: Why We Can't Win the Drug War," *Studies in Conflict and Terrorism*. 17, 4 (October-December 1994): 323-344, some of which is summarized here.

The Medellín and Cali groups are not true "cartels" in the strict economic sense but rather two extended mob families which together supplied about 80 percent of the world's cocaine and sold about $20 billion worth per year to markets in the United States and elsewhere bringing about $2-4 billion back to Columbia each year.The Medellín group alone accounted for about 60 percent of this trade in 1987 and had about 120,000 full-time employees of whom 2,000-3,000 were stationed in the United States. Carlos Lehder Rivas, a member of one of Colombia's cocaine-exporting families, promoted the creation of an expanded cocaine market in the United States earning over $1 million in profits from one air shipment. After eliminating Cuban rivals in Miami during 1978-1979 rather than fighting among themselves the cocaine-producing families of Colombia agreed to share this market among themselves in a cartel-like arrangement. The actual organization joining these families was finalized due to the hostage-taking activities of the **M-19 leftist guerrillas** which gave them a common enemy to unite against. In December 1981 the heads of these three leading cocaine-producing families contributed $7.5 million each to establish their own security force and anti-leftist **death squad**, known as MAS, short for **"Muerte a Secuestradores,"** meaning "Death to Kidnappers." Thus the "Medellín Cartel" became in effect a powerful entrepreneurial terrorist group able to strike at targets both within Colombia and throughout the world.

Under the triumvirate of Carlos Lehder, Jorge Ochoa, and Pablo Escobar the Medellín Cartel consisted of 17 other "families" which each carried out tasks of importing coca leaf, processing and refining cocaine, and then smuggling and distribution of the finished product within the United States according to the specialties of each organization. Each "family" was made up of related family groups, as well as neighbors, childhood buddies, and long-established friends. Those involved in the actual production and distribution of cocaine were organized into **cellular groups** to protect the others. The cocaine cartels employ over one million people in the Andean nations of Colombia, Peru, and Bolivia, as well as Ecuador and Brazil. The biggest buyers of coca leaf are cartel buyers who buy up most of the crop offering the local farmers three to 15 times the legal price set by the government. About 55 percent of the coca leaf required by the cartel comes from Peru and Bolivia.

With their $2 billion a year cash flow from the United States the drug lords have been able to spend lavishly within Colombia at no hurt to their own wealth and have gained reputations as providers for poor neighborhoods, employers of unemployed (and unemployable) young men of the slums, and benefactors both of communities and churches. In its battle for legitimacy with these cartels the Colombian government has been unable or unwilling to provide many of the basic amenities and social services required by a modernizing nation. By means of this "narco-philanthropy" the cartels have co-opted parts of the state, civil society, and even the Church. This narco-philanthropy is merely one tactic in an overall strategy of **state co-optation**. There have been three parts to this strategy:

First, Murder: The Medellín cartel seemed to specialize in the use of murder and violence to further its goals. After creating its Muerte a Secuestradores (MAS) anti-leftist paramilitary force, MAS has in turn created over 180 urban "death squads" and execution squads to deal with those instances of honest and brave judges and policemen who resisted the blandishments or threats of the cartel. Often these killings have been conducted in broad daylight in front of scores of witnesses to broadcast the event as much as possible using extremely gruesome methods, such as dismemberment by power chainsaws. Apart from politically motivated **assassinations** the MAS terror forces also specialized in debt collection and lab security.

A few of the more spectacular operations of the cartels are cited here: In 1984 Justice Minister Lara Bonilla was assassinated by cartel hit-men. In 1986 the head of the Anti-Narcotics Police was killed as well as the anti-cartel editor of the Bogota daily *El Espectador*, for which a bounty of over $1 million was paid to the killer. In 1988 the FBI thwarted a cartel plan to assassinate Mayor Ed Koch of New York City and the local Drug Enforcement Agency (DEA) chief for their efforts to neutralize cartel members there.

Second, Corruption: The Cali cartel has specialized more in the use of bribery and corruption, although they also have resorted to murder when other means have failed. With the low salaries of judges, policemen, and army officers, this is the most cost-effective means of neutralizing state intervention against the cartel. Through a mixture of bribery and intimidation the cartels induced the Colombian Congress to amend its constitution to prohibit **extradition** of accused cartel members to the United States. During 1995 the United States received disturbing reports that the Cali cartel had financed Colombian President Ernesto Samper Pizano's election and had bought off the judicial system which imposed short sentences on convicted cartel members while refusing to confiscate or impound the wealth and assets created through the illicit drug trade.

Finally, State Co-Optation: The cartel has managed to penetrate the Ministry of Justice, the National Police and Anti-Narcotics Police, the Ministry of Foreign Affairs, and even has gained access to classified cable traffic of the U.S. embassy in Bogota. Often DEA agents and Colombian anti-narcotics police arrive at remote labs only to find that they have been evacuated and most cocaine removed long before their arrival thanks to the intelligence efforts of the cartels. The cartels were willing to pay informants over three times what the DEA would offer its informants while those who were suspected of being double agents faced cartel retaliation of torture and murder whereas the DEA's sanctions against treacherous informants were more constrained.

There was evidence of collusion in the early 1980s between drug traffickers and leftist guerrillas, who shared a common enemy in the Colombian government, which some have referred to as narco-terrorism. However this relationship was problematic at best, probably more on the level of mutual extortion than cooperation. By the late 1980s, the drug traffickers began attacking the leftists in earnest. On 11 October 1987 Jaime Pardo Neal, a leader of the **Revolutionary Armed Forces of Colombia** (FARC)–associated Patriotic Union (UP) Party, was killed by agents of a major drug trafficker. On 22 March 1990 traffickers also assassinated UP presidential candidate Bernardo Jaramillo Ossa at Bogotá airport and on 26 April 1990 killed **M-19** presidential candidate Carlos Pizarro León-Gómez. Ironically both candidates had opposed **extradition** of narcotics traffickers to the United States. MAS was also suspected of perpetrating the January 1989 killings of 12 members of a judicial commission investigating death squad activity in Colombia.

One of the Medellín drug cartel's terrorist organizations, the "Extraditables," was formed to pressure the Colombian government to desist from its campaign to end cocaine production and smuggling in Colombia. The group was formed in reaction to the late 1989 Colombian government crackdown on the Medellín cartel and was intended to prevent the extradition of key drug kingpins to the United States. By the end of 1989 the Extraditables had carried out 200 bombings, killing 261 and wounding over 1,200 people. On 27 November 1989, the group **bombed** in mid-flight an Avianca Airlines Boeing 727 flight, killing all 107 passengers and crew abroad reportedly just to kill five police informants on board. On 6 December 1989, a truck bomb loaded with at least one-half ton of dynamite was exploded by the group outside the Bogotá police headquarters, killing over 60 and wounding over 250 people. On 15 December 1989, however, Colombian police ambushed and killed José Gonzalo Rodríguez Gacha, the major Medellín cartel leader at the heart of the Extraditables.

On 13 June 1990 the mastermind behind the Extraditables' bombing campaign, Juan Jairo Arias Tascoon, was killed in a firefight with police while another leader, Gustavo de Jesús Gaviria, was likewise killed fighting the police on 11 August 1990. Pablo Escobar Gaviria surrendered himself to Colombian authorities on 19 June 1991 on the condition that he be allowed to build his own luxurious prison and to maintain his own bodyguard. After his escape from captivity in late July 1992 Pablo Escobar was responsible for over 60 car bombings in Bogotá during 1993 in an effort to pressure the Colombian government to relax its pressures on him. Finally on 2 December 1993 Pablo Escobar was tracked down and killed by Colombian police.

When the rival Cali cartel had filled the place formerly occupied by the Medellín cartel in the cocaine trade, it generally relied more on bribery to co-opt the Colombian government rather than using recourse to terrorism, but would still use its death squads against informants and undisciplined underlings.

During the 1990s the fortunes of the cartels slipped, due to U.S. pressure on the Colombian government to take more effective steps to shut down cartel operations, and also due to the resurgence of the Revolutionary Armed Forces of Colombia (FARC) which has resumed control over many of the regions in which coca is grown and processed. During 1995 the Colombian government of President Ernesto Samper Pizano undertook a campaign to cripple the financial, security, communications, and administrative structures of the cartel in the course of which the three Orejuela brothers, who ran the Cali cartel, were arrested. Following this decapitation of the main leadership of the cartel the distribution network within the United States reacted to the leadership vacuum by a power struggle and in-fighting which led to over 20 killings and abductions between branches of the Cali apparatus in New York City.

The Colombian government passed a **freezing of assets** and seizure law on 12 December 1996 that would enable it to confiscate the roughly $76 billion in assets of the cartels as well as 9.9 million acres of land acquired by the drug lords. Colombia amended its constitution again in December 1997 to allow once again extradition of suspected cartel drug dealers to the United States but the amendment would be applicable only to those charged with crimes committed after that date. In the meantime the FARC had made a comeback, occupying over 40 percent of Colombia and taking over much of the coca cultivation and processing themselves to fund their own **revolutionary** agenda.

On 7 September 2001 Fabio Ochoa Vasquez, the former right-hand man of Pablo Escobar, was extradited to the United States for his role in smuggling cocaine into the United States as well as involvement in the 1986 murder of a DEA informant.

COMMITTEE FOR SOLIDARITY WITH ARAB AND MIDEAST PO-LITICAL PRISONERS (CSAMPP). This was the cover name for a pro-Iranian Lebanese **cellular** group which engaged in an anti-French **bombing** campaign for the limited end of pressuring the French government to release Georges Ibrahim Abdullah, the leader of the **Lebanese Armed Revolutionary Factions** arrested in France in 1984 for his group's attacks on U.S. and Israeli diplomats. During the spring of 1986 CSAMPP unleashed a bombing campaign in Paris with each bombing incident followed by the release of a communiqué in Beirut claiming responsibility by CSAMPP. This bombing campaign proved an embarrassment to Prime Minister Jacques Chirac, whose inauguration ceremony was overshadowed by a CSAMPP bombing that killed two persons and injured 28 others. Eventually Chirac gave in, notifying CSAMPP through Hilarion Capucci, the Greek Catholic prelate with ties to the **Palestine Liberation Organization** (PLO) and Syrian government, that the French government would find a way to release Abdullah when his case came to trial or at least to impose a relatively light sentence. When this later came to light it exposed the conservative Chirac to withering criticism within France from the opposition Socialist Party and when Abdullah was convicted and sentenced the magistrates ignored the prosecutor's recommendation of a 10-year sentence imposing instead a sentence of life imprisonment.

"COMMON LAW COURTS." So-called common law courts are self-appointed pseudo-legal bodies created by members of the **Freemen** movement, itself a subgrouping within the radical right private **militia movement** and related "organic constitutionalist" and tax-protestor groups. The common law court movement appears to have originated with members of the **Posse Comitatus** tax-protestor group. Another group active in the 1980s that has since then been disbanded, the so-called Committee of the States, centered in Mariposa County, California, constituted itself as the Committee of the States provided for in the Articles of Confederation, which was little more than a standing committee of the Continental Congress empowered to make decisions as needed when the Continental Congress was not in session. It proceeded to send "constructive notices" to IRS and FBI agents, U.S. Marshals, and others, advising them to cease and desist their duties on pain of death.

The current so-called common law courts similarly hold their own proceedings and file bogus liens against members of federal law enforcement bodies and others whom they consider to be enemies. Even if these liens are bogus they still have the very real effect of ruining the credit histories of those whom they have targeted. These courts base their rulings on an eclectic and selective collection of documents, including the Bible, the Magna Carta, the Articles of Confederation, the Bill of Rights, and also whatever effective or abrogated statutes they choose to follow or those dicta of federal courts that they find useful to their cause. The **Freemen of Montana** group considered themselves to be a common law court. Although they refused to regard U.S. currency as legal tender, since it is not backed by a gold standard, they arrogated to themselves the right to forge bogus letters of credit to defraud others.

Such groups often serve lien documents and summonses on authentic-looking embossed papers so intimidating unwary victims into paying fines not legally owed to anyone. Another group promised the unsuspecting that for $300 they could file papers entitling a person to reclaim all taxes ever paid to the federal government. Members of these groups have also forged for themselves fake police identification papers and badges. Because of this practice of issuing false letters of credit and fraudulent financial instruments, the practice of filing bogus liens, as well as their connection with armed extremist groups of the far right, the FBI has classified these groups as a threat to national security.

COMMUNIST COMBATANT CELLS (CCC). The CCC was a nonstate Belgian leftist group active from 1984 to 1985 that engaged in **bombings** to protest against "the Americanization of Europe," capitalism, and the North Atlantic Treaty Organization (NATO) alliance. The CCC did not enjoy any state sponsorship but briefly formed an alliance with the **Red Army Faction** (RAF) and **Action Directe** (AD) known as the "Anti-Imperialist Armed Front" to coordinate their actions against NATO member governments. Unlike RAF and AD, however, the CCC tended to pick symbolic and strategic targets for bombings and to target property rather than human life, using the terrorist event as **"armed propaganda"** for publicizing their own specific issues or causes rather than as direct military tactics to achieve revolution. Two fire fighters were killed as an unintended result of a bombing attack in May 1985, while a security guard was wounded by a bombing in November 1985.

CCC activities consisted solely of bombings against international corporate offices, banks, and NATO facilities. Out of 14 major bombings by the CCC, six were directed against offices of large U.S. and international firms, such as Litton Data Systems (2 October 1984), Honeywell (8 October 1984), Motorola (21 November 1985), and the Bank of America (4 December 1985); six others were directed against NATO facilities, such as bombing several points along a NATO fuel pipeline (11 December 1984), a NATO support facility (15 January 1985), and the NATO Central Europe Operating Agency in Versailles, France, inflicting very minor damage (6 December 1985). The remaining two attacks were against the Belgian Employers Association building in May 1985, in which two fire fighters died, and one of the central offices of the Belgian police.

In late December police arrested Pierre Carette, the founder and leader of the CCC, along with three of his followers. These four were convicted on 14 January 1986 for the attempted murder of the security guard wounded in a series of bank bombings conducted on 5 November 1985 which effectively ended this organization.

COMPREHENSIVE TERRORISM PREVENTION ACT OF 1995. This was a legislative bill that eventually led to the **Antiterrorism and Effective Death Penalty Act of 1996**. In February 1995 President Bill

Clinton proposed the Omnibus Counterterrorism Act of 1995, an antiterrorism bill meant to address concerns raised by the **World Trade Center bombing** in 1993. One week following the **Oklahoma City bombing** the President submitted a revised version of the same bill to the Senate on 26 April 1995. In response Senators Bob Dole and Orrin Hatch introduced their own antiterrorism bill, the Comprehensive Terrorism Prevention Act, which was passed in the Senate following only four days of debate on 7 June 1995. Debate on this bill stalled in the U.S. House of Representatives, in part due to concerns raised over alleged federal abuses of power in the Branch Davidian and Ruby Ridge affairs. A final conference-bill version was approved on 19 April 1996, the first anniversary of the Oklahoma City bombing, and President Clinton signed into law the Antiterrorism and Effective Death Penalty Act on 24 April 1996.

CONFISCATION/IMPOUNDMENT OF PROPERTY. *See* FREEZING OF ASSETS/SEQUESTRATION.

CONTAGION EFFECT. Tendency for notorious acts of violence or terrorism to inspire imitations of the original act, also sometimes called "copycat" crimes by law enforcement officials. Typically an event, such as the **Oklahoma City bombing**, will be followed by numerous bomb hoaxes or small-scale **bombings** carried out by persons who viewed the media coverage of the original event. Similarly the Columbine High School killings of 20 April 1999 were followed by a number of smaller scale high school shootings and threats of massacres. In a free and democratic society it is impossible to forestall whatever "contagion effect" is caused by media coverage of a terrorist act. Although antistate terrorists often have been dealt "exemplary punishments" in undemocratic societies such as Iraq and Iran, including public execution, this seems, if anything, merely to romanticize and glorify further the figure of the antistate terrorist in the perceptions of those attracted to this activity.

Those who have proposed the **physiological model** of attraction to terrorism have noted that when susceptible individuals are exposed to graphic news coverage of terrorist events or to other scenes of violence they experience a release of adrenalin and noradrenalin, triggered by the **fight-or-flight response** which in turn triggers releases of pain-killing endorphins. For the susceptible individual this creates a feeling of power and euphoria which he or she will try to recapture by reenacting the terrorist action.

COUNTERTERRORISM. The term *counterterrorism* is often used to cover three different sets of actions to oppose terrorism. *Antiterrorism* refers to reactive or defensive measures to prevent terrorism while counterterrorism specifically refers to retaliation to punish terrorism. Generally antiterrorism involves attempts to deter or forestall terrorist actions before they can occur or be fully carried out whereas counterterrorism often involves dealing with terrorism after the fact. However there is a third possible course: acting on intelligence about an impending terrorist attack the targeted nation-state could deploy elite counterterrorist military units to strike at the terrorists and their base before they can launch their operation. These counterterrorist measures involve "terrorist preemption," meaning undertaking proactive and offensive initiatives against the terrorists or their bases to forestall planned terrorist actions. Between antiterrorism prevention and counterterrorist retaliation or preemption there are also actions and policies aimed at dealing with terrorist events in progress, which can be described as "crisis management" or as "situation (or events) management." Counterterrorism in its widest sense covers defensive antiterrorism, reactive counterterrorism, offensive preemptive counterterrorism, as well as management of continuing terrorist events. Events management can also be extended into "consequence management," namely measures taken after the terrorist event is concluded.

Two major problems face governments, private firms, and individuals who seek to develop a counterterrorism policy and strategy. First, as the incidence and scope of terrorist activities appeared to multiply rapidly in the latter part of the 20th century most government and private responses have been reactive in nature rather than proactive. Second, it has been extraordinarily difficult to create an effective unity of effort among the various agencies and groups involved in countering terrorist threats. Based on their growing experience of terrorist attacks and events as well as their experience in trying to fight terrorism, the United States and other liberal democracies have been working toward more proactive policies involving a greater unity of effort, not only among the judicial, police, military, diplomatic, and intelligence agencies that must deal with terrorists, but also a greater unity of effort among these governments whose nationals have been frequently attacked by terrorists.

On the legal and police front of counterterrorism, the United States and other liberal democracies have enacted several laws, some in fulfillment of their mutual treaty obligations, to prevent **hijackings, bombings**, attacks on diplomats or embassies, **assassinations, kidnappings** of hostages, or conspiracy to commit such actions or to support groups involved in such actions. Part of prevention on the part of various national and local police agencies has involved the use of counterterrorist simulations not only to train law enforcement and military officers how to react to a hostage crisis or bomb threat, but also to train government civilian employees, who are the likely targets of such threats, to know how to avoid such situations or else how best to survive such situations. **Target** hardening has involved new designs for federal office buildings and parking lots to make it more difficult for car bombs to be effectively used against them.

Outside the United States antiterrorist policies have included issuance of travel advisories for U.S. travelers when there is a threat assessment for a particular region or period of time. The Diplomatic Security Service of the Department of State develops threat assessments, provides security for diplomats or other personnel, and seeks to harden embassies and other diplomatic stations to protect them from bombings or other attacks. The State Department has also developed a watch list for members of known or suspected terrorist groups to prevent or to deter them from entering the United States. Diplomatic responses to acts of terrorism have included placing economic sanctions on nations known to promote terrorism or else that harbor terrorists, including promoting multilateral sanctions through the United Nations or else the **Group of Seven** nations.

Military counterterrorism efforts are limited within the United States by the Posse Comitatus Act, which prohibits the use of military force for the functions of ordinary police work within the United States, except in a few narrowly circumscribed situations. Use of the U.S. military for counterterrorism outside the United States has also been limited by Executive Order 12333 which prohibits unlawful assassination of individuals for political purposes. The qualification of "unlawful" does allow the military to strike at individuals during legitimate military operations, since this is a form of warfare against combatants permitted by the laws of war. Legitimate military operations are considered to include such things as the 15 April 1986 U.S. Air Force bombing of Libya in retaliation for the bombing of the LaBelle Discothèque in

Berlin by Libyan agents. However to be used effectively such counterterrorist operations must be used with restraint with minimal impact on innocent bystanders in order to preserve the legitimacy of the counterterrorist operation.

The United States has several special military counterterrorist response units, including the Delta Force and the Naval Special Warfare Development Group (formerly known as SEAL Team Six) which engage in regular training and terrorist simulations, and which have been effectively deployed on certain known occasions. Similarly Great Britain has its Special Air Service (SAS) counterterrorism units while Germany has its Grenzschutzgruppe-9 (GSG-9) units used in special operations against terrorists. Due to the secretive nature of the operations by such elite response teams very often their successful operations are not publicized in order not to compromise the tactics and intelligence gathering which have proven to be essential.

CONTRAS. The "contras," short for "counterrevolutionaries," were the armed groups that began fighting to overthrow the **Sandinista** (FSLN) regime that seized power in Nicaragua in 1979. Originally they were trained by Argentinean military advisers, enjoyed safe haven in Honduras and Costa Rica, and obtained private financial support from Cuban and Nicaraguan exiles. The Argentineans withdrew their advisers from Honduras in 1981 following the collapse of the military junta after their defeat in the Falklands war. Beginning in October 1982, the contras were put under U.S. sponsorship, including CIA advisers, military, and humanitarian aid. Due to an ongoing and inconclusive political debate between the Reagan administration and the U.S. Congress, U.S. military aid was cut off in 1984, resumed in 1985, but again cut off after the revelation of the Iran-Contra affair in late 1986.

To fulfill a condition for receiving future U.S. aid, on 12 June 1985 the contras united in an umbrella organization, the Unidad Nicaragüense Opositora (UNO), Unified Nicaraguan Opposition which comprised the following groups:

1. The Fuerza Democrática Nicaragüense (FDN), Nicaraguan Democratic Force, formed out of the September 15th League, the National Liberation Army, and Nicaraguan Democratic Union, the latter group originally made up of ex-Sandinistas and other opponents of the Somoza regime. This group numbered some 18,000 to 22,000 members and was led by Adolfo Calero, former head of the Nicaraguan

Conservative Party. Of the top 56 FDN leaders, about 13 were former National Guardsmen and about 26 were former Sandinistas. These forces were based in Honduras and fought in the north of Nicaragua.

2. The Fuerzas Armadas Revolucionarias Nicaragüenses (FARN), Nicaraguan Revolutionary Armed Forces, numbering 1,000 fighters led by a former Sandinista, Fernando "El Negro" Chamorro, who had fought Somoza since 1960, based in Costa Rica and fighting in the south of Nicaragua.

3. The Kus Indian Sut Asla Nicaragua Ra (KISAN), or United Indigenous Peoples of Eastern Nicaragua, an alliance of Miskito, Sumo, and Rama Indians and also English-speaking black Creoles, numbering some 4,000 fighters who fought in the northeastern region of Nicaragua.

4. The Coordinatora Opositora Nicaragüense (CON), Nicaraguan Opposition Coordinator, was not an armed group but rather the political front organization of political parties, business organizations, and trade unions in exile.

Another contra group was the Alianza Revolucionaria Democrática (ARDE), the Nicaraguan Democratic Alliance, numbering 3,000 fighters based in Costa Rica and led by Alfonso Robello Callejas, once a member of the post-Somoza junta, and Edén Pastora Gómez, former leader of the Sandino Revolutionary Front and Sandinista hero. ARDE did not join UNO largely due to the opposition of Edén Pastora to certain of UNO's leaders. Pastora quit the contra struggle in 1986. In May 1987 UNO merged with the Southern Opposition Bloc of Alfredo César to form the Nicaraguan Resistance, while KISAN was reorganized as Yapti Tasba Masraka Aslika Takanda, Miskito Indian acronym for "United Nations of Yapti Tasba [Sacred Motherland]" (YAMATA), separate from the Nicaraguan Resistance command.

Instances of terrorization of the civilian population by the contras and of mistreatment of FSLN prisoners have been documented, in itself hardly surprising given the bitterness that existed between the FSLN and their opponents and given the large proportion of contra fighters who lacked both education and the discipline of previous military training. Public debate over U.S. sponsorship of the contras focused on the questions, were such instances of terrorism part of a deliberate policy to suppress popular support for the FSLN regime rather than random cases?, and if so, did the United States aid, abet, or otherwise encourage such systematic terror? A CIA-sponsored Spanish-language training manual produced for training the contras in techniques of armed propaganda entitled *Psychological Operations in Guerrilla Warfare* has often been cited as evidence of a systematic contra terror campaign inspired by U.S. advisers. This manual was presented by the FSLN in its briefs to the International Court of Justice as evidence of U.S. support of contra terror but key cited passages were ambiguous. Quite apart from any deliberate systematic terrorization by the contras, with or without U.S. sponsorship, the record of the rank and file contras' respect for human rights remained, in the words of a former contra political officer, "depressing and testified to a lack of political discipline." (Pardo-Maurer, 55)

Another more substantial problem connected with the contras were the arrangements made by U.S. National Security Adviser Admiral John Poindexter and his aide Lt. Col. Oliver North, to sell arms to the Iranian government in order both to secure the release of U.S. hostages held in Lebanon and also to generate revenues independent of congressional approval to support the contra military effort. Apart from the issue of violating congressional restrictions on funding for the contras, there remained a question whether the Reagan administration was violating its own executive orders banning arms sales to Iran, having itself earlier certified Iran as a **state sponsor of terrorism**, and whether the arms-for-hostages arrangement violated long-standing U.S. declaratory policy barring the payment of ransom for hostages. The private supply network also had the effect of releasing Calero's FDN, which alone controlled these secret funds prior to the reorganization of UNO, from the necessity of having to reform itself, and its human rights record, to conform to the standards demanded by the U.S. Congress as conditions for its support for the contras.

Before 1982 the FSLN had dismissed the contras as a minor nuisance, but after the contras **bombed** two bridges spanning the Coco and Negro rivers on the Honduran border on 14 March 1982, the FSLN declared a state of emergency the next day. This state of emergency was not lifted until 16 January 1988. In August 1985 the contras suffered reverses in the battlefields as the FSLN army acquired Soviet Mi-24/5 helicopter gunships as well as Mi-17 troop transports. Within two years, by March 1987, the tide turned when the FSLN army lost several Mi-24 helicopters to the contras' U.S.-supplied Red-Eye antiaircraft missiles and failed to secure the Bocay region in northern Nicaragua against contra infiltration. By October 1987 the contras had severed the Rama road connecting Managua to the Atlantic coast and maintained their offensive for the rest of the year. Shortly after U.S. aid to the contras lapsed on 29 February 1988, the FSLN army invaded Honduras to capture the contras' headquarters, a move countered by President Ronald Reagan's deployment of 3,000 U.S. paratroopers to Honduras on 15 March 1988 and Congress's humanitarian aid package of $17.7 million for the contras on 31 March 1988.

Under the pressure of its Central American neighbors, the Sandinista regime finally agreed to a truce and talks with the contras. While the talks began on 23 March 1988, the FSLN negotiators temporized so that the contras would exhaust their recently received U.S. aid and lose their bargaining position. While this strategy succeeded in diminishing the fighting capability of the contras, political unrest within Nicaragua, and the continuing diplomatic pressure from neighboring Central American states, forced the FSLN to agreed to democratization. Following the U.S. presidential election of 1988 the contras were supplied with only sufficient nonlethal aid to maintain them pending the results of the elections the FSLN had agreed would be held in Nicaragua in February 1990. Following the Sandinista defeat by the election of Violeta Chamorro as president, the contras began their demobilization, which was completed on 25 June 1990.

About 20,000 former contras were settled in the northern town of Quilalí and most of the rest have been settled in the 26 counties along the northern mountainous region where their forces had been most active during the civil war. Although most contras laid down arms after the election of Violeta Chamorro as president in 1990, afterwards some rearmed themselves claiming the government had not honored promises made to them prior to their disarming themselves. Although the United States has given more than $2 billion in aid to Nicaragua, with some of it earmarked to help resettle the contras and to extend special aid to those who became handicapped in the course of the war in Central America, many former rebels were claiming in 1996 that this aid had not reached them.

COVENANT, THE SWORD, AND THE ARM OF THE LORD (CSA). The CSA was a nonstate religious-**revolutionary** group that developed out of a fundamentalist Christian commune in the Arkansas Ozarks from 1978 until 1985. The CSA was the military wing of the Church of Zarephath-Horeb, a commune founded and led by a former Disciples of

Christ minister, Jim Ellison, who eventually led his following to adopt the teachings of **Identity Christianity**, an amalgam of fundamentalist Christianity with **white supremacist**, anti-Semitic, and populist **ideologies**.

Ellison's commune, first organized outside Elijah, Missouri, from 1970 to 1976, was originally nonpolitical and intended to shelter its members through the tribulations of the apocalyptic end times, which they believed were at hand. In 1976 the commune relocated near Bull Shoals, Arkansas, and in 1978 Ellison embraced the Identity Christianity creed and affiliated his group with the **Aryan Nations**. The commune created its own militia, the "Covenant, the Sword, and the Arm of the Lord," set up an automatic-weapons shop, and ran a survivalist-commando training camp used by survivalists and members of groups affiliated with the Aryan Nations. The gun shop supplied the modified MAC-10 machine gun later used by the **Order** to kill Denver radio talk-show host Alan Berg. The commune also ran a press that marketed Identity Christianity literature.

In August 1983 CSA members firebombed both a Metropolitan Community Church in Springfield, Missouri, and a Jewish Community Center in Bloomington, Indiana. In November 1983, CSA members robbing a Texarkana pawnshop murdered the owner believing him to be Jewish. In June 1984 a CSA member, Richard W. Snell, killed a black Arkansas state highway patrolman. Later Snell was convicted for the murders of the Texarkana pawnbroker and the Arkansas highway patrolman and sentenced to death. Apparently the appointed date for his execution on 19 April 1995 was one of the reasons that Timothy McVeigh planned to bomb the Murrah Federal Building in **Oklahoma City** the very same day. Following the FBI crackdown on the Order in December 1984, the FBI captured David Tate, an Order member, en route to the CSA compound. On 23 April 1985 a combined force of FBI commandos, Missouri and Arkansas state police, and national guardsmen stormed the CSA compound. After two days of negotiations, CSA members besieged within the compound surrendered themselves along with the wanted Order members Randall Evans and Thomas Bentley. Jim Ellison was arrested and convicted on racketeering charges and also for conspiracy to manufacture, possess, and distribute illegal firearms.

When raided by the FBI Zarephath-Horeb held around 200 men, women, and children. Since 1982 the commune had gone into decline. As the commune proved unable to support itself economically, Ellison had sanctioned car thefts and robberies to make mortgage payments on the commune property. Claiming to obey special divine revelations, Ellison also began to practice polygamy taking followers' wives to be his own. These practices disgusted many members who left Ellison during the last three years of Zarephath-Horeb's existence. Convicted of racketeering and weapons violations in 1985, Ellison later became a state witness in the federal sedition trail held in Fort Smith in 1988. After serving his sentence he remarried, taking as his new wife the granddaughter of Richard G. Millar, the head of the Elohim City sect whose members also adhere to the **millennialist** and Identity Christian doctrines followed by Ellison and others in the U.S. white separatist movement.

CROATIAN NATIONAL RESISTANCE. The Croatian National Resistance was a nonstate group that sought Croatia's independence from Yugoslavia. Using the name "Croatian Freedom Fighters" this group carried out terrorist actions against Yugoslavian diplomatic and commercial targets abroad. Their most spectacular action was the September 1976 **hijacking** of a TWA Boeing 727 jet en route from New York to Chicago, which the five hijackers diverted to Newfoundland, from there to Iceland, and lastly to Paris with all of its 81 other passengers aboard. In addition the terrorists had planted a **bomb** in Grand Central Station whose location they would reveal only after authorities would publish communiqués of the group. After authorities complied and the bomb's location was revealed, one policeman, Brian J. Murray, was killed and another injured when they tried to deactivate it. The group claimed to have several such bombs which they displayed during the hijacking and which they threatened to explode if their demands were not met. In reality the devices they displayed were only Silly Putty and the only actual bomb was the one left in New York. After they learned that the bomb in New York had exploded and killed one policeman the hijackers surrendered themselves in Paris.

While the leader of the hijackers of the TWA Flight 355, Zvonko Busic and his wife Julienne Busic, were both convicted on U.S. federal charges of air piracy and murder in May 1977 and sentenced to life imprisonment, Julienne Busic was released from prison on lifelong parole in 1989 while her husband has been continuing to serve a jail sentence due to end in 2006. Following Croatia's winning of independence from Yugoslavia in 1993, Julienne Busic was appointed by President Franjo Tudjman to the diplomatic post of adviser to the Croatian Ambassador to the United States, Petar Sarcevic. This appointment of a convicted terrorist to a diplomatic post within the United States drew protests in December 1994 from the New York Patrolmen's Benevolent Association as well as from Kathlyn Murray, the widow of the police officer killed by the bomb in Grand Central station in 1976.

From 17 March 1980 to 4 July 1982, the group carried out five bombings in the United States. On 17 March 1980 the U.S. office of a Yugoslavian bank was bombed. On 3 June 1980 the home of the acting Yugoslavian ambassador was bombed. A pipe bomb also exploded at the Manhattan New York State Supreme Court on 23 January 1981, for which prior notice was given by the group. On 4 July 1982 a travel agency office was pipe bombed in Astoria, N.Y., while on the same day New York City police defused a bomb set at the Yugoslavian Airlines office. None of these incidents caused any injuries. Since the independence of Croatia this group has ceased to operate.

CUBAN AMERICAN NATIONAL FOUNDATION (CANF). The CANF was incorporated as a nonprofit lobbying group on 6 July 1981 by Jorge Mas Canosa, a leader in the anti-Castro Cuban exile community and a veteran of the failed Bay of Pigs intervention. Several of its members were implicated in a plot to **assassinate** Castro while Luis Posada Carrile, one of the closest personal associates of Canosa, publically admitted to directing a terrorist **bombing** campaign within Cuba.

Before Jorge Mas Canosa died in November 1997 from lung cancer, members of the inner circle of CANF made a deathbed promise to him that they would assassinate Castro. The plot was to shoot Castro with a long-range assault rifle as he disembarked from his plane on Margarita Island in Venezuela, the site of a regional summit meeting. On 27 October 1997 the U.S. Coast Guard boarded the cabin cruiser *Esperanza* off the coast of Puerto Rico and discovered a secret compartment containing two .50 caliber Barrett assault rifles, along with ammunition, which turned out to be registered to Jose Francisco Hernandez, who had succeeded Canosa as President of the CANF. The 46-foot-long cabin cruiser belonged to Jose Antonio Llama, a member of the CANF Board of Directors. Llama was indicted on 25 August 1998, along with the four other Cubans and one other man, for using an American motor vessel for criminal purposes, making false statements to a Customs official, smuggling weapons, and plotting to assassinate "an internationally protected person."

Meanwhile Luis Posada Carriles had been working with the Central Intelligence Agency (CIA) in efforts against Communist insurgents throughout the Carribean region until a falling out with his handlers in the 1970s. He was believed to have been responsible for the bombing of a Cubana Airlines flight from Barbados on 6 October 1976, which killed all 73 passengers including the entire Cuban national fencing team, most of whom were teenagers. During April 1997 he then directed a bombing campaign against tourist hotels in Cuba. By striking at the tourist hotels Posada hoped to diminish this source of income for the Castro regime and also to undermine the regime's apparent stability and invulnerability, since these hotels were very well guarded. During 1994-1997 a total of 16 bombings struck Cuba during the following months. Five non-Cuban amateurs recruited by Posada who carried out these attacks were arrested during the summer of 1997, two of whom were convicted of terrorism by a Cuban court and sentenced to death. In the summer of 1998 Posada gave a very detailed account to interviewers at a secret location in the Carribean of his activities against the Castro regime and freely admitted to having masterminded the terrorist bombings in Cuba but denied that the CANF played any role in it.

CUBAN NATIONAL LIBERATION FRONT. The Frente de Liberación Nacional Cubana (FLNC) was a nonstate Cuban émigré group with the revolutionary goal of overthrowing the Castro regime in Cuba. It was one of the six main anti-Castro Cuban exile groups in the United States, the others being **Alpha-66**, Brigade 2506, the **Cuban American National Foundation**, the Cuban Nationalist Movement, and **Omega-7**.

The Cuban National Liberation Front was active mainly in the late 1960s and early 1970s and engaged in assaults and **bombings** against persons or institutions perceived to be pro-Castro. The group had ceased to function by the 1980s, due to the diminished hopes among the Cuban exile community that Castro's government would ever be overthrown.

CYBER-TERRORISM. *See* INFORMATION WARFARE; NETWAR.

- D -

DAL KHALSA. *See* SIKH MILITANTS.

DASHMESH REGIMENT. *See* SIKH MILITANTS.

DA'WA, AL. The Hizb al Da'wa al Islamiyya, or Islamic Call (to faith) Party, is a Shi'ite **Islamic fundamentalist** party founded in Iraq by radical junior Shi'ite clergymen that seeks to overthrow the secular Ba'thist regime in Iraq to create an Iranian-style Islamic Republic. Iraq's population is nearly 60 percent Shi'ite while the governing Ba'thist party is predominantly Sunni. On the other hand, most of the Shi'ite religious leaders in Iraq come from families that either originated in Iran or else have intermarried with Iranian clerical families, thus undercutting the nationalistic credentials of potential Shi'ite leaders. While this party is one of the oldest radical Shi'ite political parties, having been founded in 1968-1969 at the latest, it has had to accept Iranian **state sponsorship** after having been virtually eradicated within Iraq by severe state repression.

Beginning in 1974 the Iraqi regime responded to Shi'ite unrest in the shrine cities of Karbala and Najaf by executing five Da'wa leaders and eight others in 1977 when riots broke out again. Following the Islamic revolution in Iran in 1979, the Iraqi regime put the pro-Khomeini Ayatollah Muhammad Baqir al Sadr under house arrest to deprive Iraqi Shi'ite fundamentalists of the rallying point of a charismatic leader. Shortly after the holding of an Islamic Liberation Movements conference in Tehran in early 1980, an "Islamic Liberation Movement of Iraq" proclaimed its existence in Europe and named the confined Ayatollah Baqir al Sadr as its leader.

Da'wa activists joined with other anti-Ba'thist guerrilla fighters and, with Iranian material and moral support, undertook attacks on police stations and Ba'thist party offices. On 1 April 1980 Da'wa members aided by Iranian revolutionaries attempted to **assassinate** Tariq 'Aziz, vice president of Iraq and close associate of Saddam Hussein. Reprisals included making Da'wa membership a capital offense, the expulsion of over 15,000 Shi'ites suspected of pro-Da'wa sympathies, and the summary execution of Ayatollah Baqir al Sadr and his sister sometime during the week following the assassination attempt. In what amounted to a declaration of war, **Ayatollah Khomeini** responded to the news of al

Sadr's execution by issuing a decree of *takfir* on 18 April 1980 against Saddam Hussein and the Ba'thist regime of Iraq and calling on the Iraqi Armed Forces to overthrow their Ba'thist rulers. By the end of 1980 over 500 Da'wa members were summarily executed in Iraq, although assassinations of government officials and sabotage against the Iraqi military continued even after the outbreak of the Iran-Iraq war in September 1980.

Members of the al Da'wa group have joined **Hezbollah** in Lebanon and formed cells in other Arab lands, particularly Kuwait, where they received arms and explosives through Iranian diplomatic offices. The spiritual leader of Hezbollah, Sheikh Muhammad Hussein Fadlullah, was a former member of a Lebanese branch of the al Da'wa party. At least three of those involved in the 12 December 1983 truck bombing attempts against the U.S. and French embassies in Kuwait were Da'wa members who claimed also to be **Islamic Jihad** members. On 25 May 1985 a Da'wa member attempted to assassinate the Emir of Kuwait in a **suicide bomb** attack. The **kidnapping** of U.S. hostages in Lebanon began in earnest after the conviction of the 17 perpetrators of the Kuwait City truck bombing attempts. The **hijackers** of TWA Flight 847 on 14 June 1985 and of Kuwait Airlines Flight 422 on 5 April 1988 also included release of the convicted truck bombers among their demands. During the 2 August 1990 Iraqi invasion of Kuwait, prison authorities there released the remaining 15 convicted bombers, two having completed their terms earlier. These and other Da'wa members participated in the partisan resistance against the Iraqi occupiers of Kuwait. Later Da'wa members aided by **Iranian Islamic Revolutionary Guards** attacked Iraqi troops in Basra during the later stages of the 1991 Persian Gulf War.

In Iran former Da'wa party members appeared to form the nucleus of the Supreme Assembly for the Islamic Revolution in Iraq (SAIRI), an umbrella group of Iraqi Shi'ite dissident groups formed under Iranian auspices in early July 1982 as a government-in-exile of a future Islamic republic in Iraq. SAIRI is headed by Hujjatulislam Baqir al Hakim, son of Muhsin al Hakim, a native Iraqi religious leader claimed by Da'wa members as the founder of their party. SAIRI used to form contingents of anti-Saddam Iraqi émigrés to fight alongside Iranian troops in the Iran-Iraq war and also collaborated with antiregime Kurds in the northern war fronts within Iraqi territory.

Although SAIRI attempted to unify the Da'wa and other Iraqi Shi'ite groups under its standard, the main body of the Da'wa party remained aloof and maintained its own separate organization.

DEADLY FORCE. Term used among U.S. law enforcement authorities to refer to the lawful use of force, including possible maiming or killing, required to constrain lawbreakers or persons whose actions pose a threat to the lives, liberty, or property of others. The authorization to use deadly force is subject to rules of engagement and every case of killing or maiming as a result of deadly force is subject to review to ensure that human life is not taken arbitrarily and that only the minimum force necessary is used to achieve the objectives of law enforcement. Deadly force incidents in which suspects or innocents are killed arbitrarily or unnecessarily undermine the legitimacy of law enforcement efforts and create a climate of public fear and distrust of authority which in turn undermines the basis of freedom and openness essential for a democratic society.

As examples of deadly force incidents involving avoidable and unnecessarily deaths some have cited the Philadelphia police's firebombing of the sectarian-political MOVE group's headquarters in May 1985 resulting in the deaths of six adults, whom the police had sought to arrest, as well as the deaths of five children and the destruction of 61 homes that left 250 people homeless. The siege of Randy Weaver's family at Ruby Ridge, Idaho, in August 1992, resulting in the death of his son and wife, and the siege and burning of the Branch Davidian compound in Waco, Texas, in April 1993, resulting in 84 deaths, of which four were agents of the Bureau of Alcohol, Tobacco, and Firearms (BATF) and 27 were children in the compound, are also instances of uses of deadly force which now appear to have been unnecessary and misguided.

The extreme cynicism and distrust which the last two incidents provoked hampered passage of antiterrorism legislation proposed in 1995 following the **Oklahoma City bombing** intended to allow federal authorities new authority for wiretapping, to expedite the deportation of illegal aliens suspected of terrorism, and to limit death row appeals of convicted terrorists. These cases of purported abuse of deadly force led the Department of Justice and FBI to review and revise their rules of engagement in deadly force situations to avoid repeating such incidents. These reforms are credited with the more peaceful resolution of the FBI siege of the **Freemen of Montana** Group in June 1996 and the later siege of the **"Republic of Texas"** militants in 1997.

DEATH SQUADS. Death squads are military, paramilitary, or irregular forces sponsored by a regime or political group to engage in violent repression against a population to prevent it from supporting the opponents of the regime or group. The term *death squad* is believed to have originated in Brazil in the 1960s where off-duty policemen formed "Esquadraos de Morte" to kill off criminal elements. Later these spontaneously generated vigilantes were co-opted by the Brazilian military regime to kill off dissidents.

The most frequently cited instances of death squads have been those sponsored by right-wing regimes in Central and Latin America to suppress leftists and suspected leftist sympathizers through **kidnapping**, torture, and murder. Human rights organizations particularly faulted Guatemalan security forces for campaigns of **state terror** in the 1970s and 1980s involving the use of death squads terrorizing not only leftists but also many innocents, particularly Indians in areas of rural insurgency. Among the more notorious of these groups were the **White Hand** group and the **Anticommunist Secret Army**. By the conclusion of the 29 December 1996 peace settlement between the Guatemalan government and leftist insurgents official figures stated that between 130,000 and 140,000 people had been killed but Roman Catholic human rights groups put the figure of dead closer to 150,000 while 50,000 who disappeared have not been accounted for.

El Salvador had death squad activity during the 1970s involving such groups as the rural militia **ORDEN**, which was declared disbanded in November 1979. In fact, its members appear to have entered newer death squads such as the **White Warriors' Union** and the **Maximiliano Hernández Martínez Anticommunist Brigade**. From 1979 until 1982 killings by Salvadoran death squads sometimes exceeded 800 people each month and included among their victims Archbishop Oscar Romero y Galdamez killed on 24 March 1980 and four American church workers on 4 December 1980. On 28 March 1998 the four Salvadoran exsoldiers convicted for this crime stated that they had killed the nuns on orders from their military superiors. The families of the slain nuns filed wrongful death lawsuits against the commanding officers of the four guardsmen on 12 May 1999. This death squad activity created much controversy regarding the Reagan administration's support of the Salvadoran transitional regime against the **Farabundo Martí National Liberation** (FMLN) leftist insurgency since it was clear that many of the leaders and members of such groups were themselves members of the Salvadoran military and police. By the mid-1980s, however, the murder rate had dropped to less than 100 killings per month and by late 1988 was about 16 killings per month, a figure that may be accounted for by ordinary murders rather than death squad activity.

Currently in Colombia paramilitary groups, such as the **Self-Defense Units of Colombia** (AUC), Colombia Without Rebels, and several neighborhood vigilante groups have been involved in killing suspected rebels, leftists, migrant workers, and vagrants. What Colombians refer to as "social cleansing" accounts for as many as 2,000 murders in the period 1988 to 1993. In Peru a retired Peruvian general indicated in December 1996 that the Peruvian government had revived an infamous military death squad, "La Colina," which had targeted university teachers and students suspected of supporting the **Sendero Luminoso** (SL) insurgents.

Examples of death squads can be found outside of Latin America. Many of the Ulster Protestant militias have been accused of acting as anti-Catholic death squads, such as the **Red Hand Commandos** and the **Ulster Volunteer Force**. South Africa's military Civil Cooperation Bureau was closed on 31 July 1990, following revelations that it had sponsored death squad activities. In Turkey a government scandal in December 1996 revealed that the Turkish government had been hiring members of drug dealing gangs to kill suspected dissidents as well as Kurdish clan members to provide "village guards" to kill off Kurdish separatists. Turkey had previously suffered from death squad activity between leftists and rightists that led to a military takeover in 1980 to restore order and political stability.

While death squads are usually state-sponsored groups, in cases where the state is relatively weak a marginally stronger political group or economic elite could sponsor its own death squads without having to rely on the state. Actually such was the situation in El Salvador following November 1979 when a weak transitional government was unable to control its own security personnel involved in death squads being financed and run by Salvadoran oligarchs opposed to agrarian and social reforms. Likewise the Medellín drug cartel formed its own death squad, MAS, to kill off leftist guerrillas who had been interfering in the smugglers' operations (*See* COLOMBIAN COCAINE CARTELS).

Although the term *death squad* has usually been used only to describe right-wing terror groups there are leftist regimes and groups that have sponsored their own death squads. In El Salvador the **Clara Elizabeth Ramírez Front** acted as a selective hit squad while the People's Revolutionary Army (*See* FARABUNDO MARTÍ LIBERATION FRONT) used to kidnap and murder functionaries of the Salvadoran government. In the Philippines the communist **New People's Army** (NPA) has been using death squads known as "Sparrow Squads" to murder Philippine government and military authorities as well as U.S. servicemen. The Peruvian Maoist group Sendero Luminoso has also engaged in selective and systematic murder of its opponents. In Turkey, prior to the military coup and crackdown of September 1980, right-wing death squads, such as the **Gray Wolves**, and left-wing death squads, such as Dev Sol (*See* REVOLUTIONARY PEOPLE'S LIBERATION PARTY/ FRONT) and the **Turkish People's Liberation Front**, were operating simultaneously.

Death squads seem to function best as repressive tools when their **targets** are limited to the leaders of the opposing groups. Once death squad activity becomes random, killing not only opposition followers but also the ordinarily politically uninvolved mass public, then the latter group becomes more politicized and emboldened to resist the sponsors of the death squads.

Moreover, once they cease to be sponsored by a state or party, they sometimes revert to becoming freelance **entrepreneurial** killers. Such was the case with the members of the disbanded ORDEN group in El Salvador and such is the case with Brazilian policemen today, many of whom have reverted to vigilante actions against petty criminals and homeless street children.

DELLE CHIAIE, STEPHANO. Italian neo-Fascist terrorist and founder of the **Avanguardia Nazionale**. This group carried out a **bombing** campaign from 1969 to 1973. It merged with the **Black Order**, which in turn produced the **Armed Revolutionary Nucleus** group responsible for the 2 August 1980 bombing of Bologna's main railroad station. These groups have been affiliated with each other, and with similar right-wing extremists outside of Italy, through the "Black Orchestra," originally masterminded by Delle Chiaie.

Delle Chiaie himself had fled to Spain in 1970 following an abortive right-wing coup d'état attempt in Italy in which he participated. In

Spain Delle Chiaie became active in state-sponsored **death squad** activities directed against members of the **Basque Fatherland and Liberty** group. Following Francisco Franco's death in 1976, Delle Chiaie reportedly moved to Latin America where he collaborated with the former right-wing military regimes in Argentina and Chile in their internal campaigns to suppress domestic leftists and other political opponents. Following his involvement in an abortive coup attempt in Bolivia in 1980 and the fall from power of his right-wing state sponsors in Argentina, Delle Chiaie went into hiding, having been last seen in October 1982.

DEMOCIDE. *Democide* is a term devised by political scientist Rudolph J. Rummel to encompass the various forms of mass killings of peoples by governments, usually their own sovereign state. Democide is defined as the murder of any person or people by a government, whether by **genocide**, politicide, or mass murder. Genocide is the killing of people for, among other things, their ascriptive group membership, such as race, ethnicity, religion of parents, language, or culture. Politicide is the murder of individuals or groups of people due to their politics or else for purposes of political expediency. Mass murder is the indiscriminate killing of any person or group of people by a government. Democide and each of its components can be viewed as examples of **state terrorism**, whether the killings are accomplished by regular armed forces or else by irregular militias or mercenaries. Rummel presents persuasive statistics to argue that democide, rather than warfare or nonstate terrorism, has been the leading cause of death by political violence in the 20th century. The results of Rummel's initial research were published under the title "War Isn't This Century's Biggest Killer," in the 7 July 1986 issue of *The Wall Street Journal.* Eventually Rummel determined that democide was directly responsible for over 169 million human deaths in the 20th century as opposed to only 35.6 million deaths due to the direct effects of warfare.

DEMOCRATIC FRONT FOR THE LIBERATION OF PALESTINE (DFLP). The DFLP is a Palestinian Marxist-Leninist guerrilla organization and **Palestine Liberation Organization** (PLO) member that advocates the creation of an independent Palestinian state on the West Bank and Gaza Strip. It also advocates revolutionary working-class struggle throughout the Arab world as part of an international anti-imperialist and anticapitalist revolution but has limited its own use of armed struggle or terrorism to achieving the independent Palestinian state. Formerly the DFLP was supported by Libya and South Yemen while its major sponsor was Syria; however, the DFLP lost Syrian support when it refused to join the Syrian-sponsored **National Salvation Front** in 1987. Since then the DFLP has tried to limit its dependence on any external sponsors. DFLP members have received Soviet training and Cuban aid and are believed to have had contact with the **Sandinistas.**

The DFLP was born out of a division between extreme leftists and pan-Arabists within George Habash's **Popular Front for the Liberation of Palestine** (PFLP). This factionalism escalated to armed clashes in Amman, Jordan, during February 1969 until **al Fatah** intervened, recognizing the breakaway leftists as a group separate from the PFLP. Until August 1974 the group was known as the Popular Democratic Front for the Liberation of Palestine. The DFLP members are Marxist-Leninists who reject the chauvinistic Pan-Arabism of the PFLP in favor of socialist internationalism and who also reject the use of international terrorism. The DFLP believed terrorist or guerrilla actions should be conducted only within Israel and the occupied territories, a position that Fatah adopted five years later in 1974 and that eventually was declared official PLO policy on 15 November 1988 at the 19th Palestine National Council (PNC) meeting. The DFLP also preceded Fatah in diplomatic initiatives, making contact with Israeli socialist internationalist counterparts such as the Israeli Matzpen group in 1970 but later opposed any negotiations with the former Likud government of Israel. The DFLP pioneered in 1973 the idea of the establishment of an independent Palestinian state on the West Bank and Gaza Strip that Fatah also later adopted.

During the 1970s the DFLP carried out several attacks within Israel, usually involving hostage takings or **bombings.** Their most notorious action was the 15 May 1974 assault on the Israeli town of Ma'alot in which three DFLP terrorists took 90 schoolchildren hostage to be released in exchange for freeing 23 Arab prisoners as well as Kozo Okamoto, the **Japanese Red Army** terrorist who had participated in the Lod airport massacre on 30 May 1972. When the negotiations broke down, the Israeli troops stormed the dormitory, but not before the terrorists machine-gunned the children, killing 16 outright and wounding 70 others, five of whom later died. Seven other Israelis, two of them Arabs, were also killed and 69 other Israelis were wounded in the course of this action. This massacre prompted Israeli air force retaliatory strikes against Palestinian refugee camps in southern Lebanon believed to have been the bases of the attackers. A similar attack took place in Beit She'an on 19 November 1974 in which all three attackers were killed along with four Israelis. In July 1977 and March 1979, the DFLP carried out several bombings in public markets and buses. In January 1979 a DFLP terrorist team tried to repeat a hostage taking at Ma'alot but was intercepted by a routine Israeli military patrol. Following 1982, DFLP actions within Israel consisted of grenade and small firebomb attacks throughout Israel, the West Bank, and the Gaza strip, but after 1988 DFLP actions were limited to small border raids.

The importance of the DFLP derives more from its swing votes within the PLO organization than from its declining record of terrorist activities. DFLP support was essential for Fatah to rally the votes needed to have the PNC accept UN Resolutions 242 and 338, contingent on creation of a Palestinian state in the occupied territories, in the 19th PNC meeting held during 12-15 November 1988. The deputy head of the DFLP, Yasir Abdul Rabbo, led the first PLO delegation to meet officially with U.S. diplomats following President Ronald Reagan's authorization of direct U.S.-PLO talks on 14 December 1988. In 1991 the DFLP split into two factions with the original leader, Nayef Hawatmeh, leading a faction opposed to **Yassir Arafat** and Abdul Rabbo leading the pro-Arafat faction. This split reflected a general dissatisfaction felt within the PLO over the slowness and indirection of efforts on the diplomatic front.

On 24 September 1995 the DFLP denounced the agreements reached between Israel and the Palestinian Authority on expanding Palestinian self-rule. Nayef Hawatmeh boycotted the 22 April 1996 meeting of the Palestine National Council convened in Gaza to reconsider Article 15 of the PLO Covenant, which declares it a duty "to purge the Zionist presence from Palestine." However on 8 February 1999 Israeli President Ezer Weizmann shook hands with Nayef Hawatmeh at the funeral of King Hussein of Jordan in Amman and on 22 April 1999 Yasir Arafat met with Hawatmeh in Cairo for the first time since the Oslo Accord was signed in 1993 and began talks aimed at reuniting the DPLF with the rest of the PLO.

The DFLP had about 1,000 followers in the early 1970s and perhaps as many as 2,000 on the eve of Israel's invasion of Lebanon in the summer of 1982. Currently its two factions together may have about

500 followers. In 1999 the U.S. State Department removed the DFLP from the Foreign Terrorist Organizations (FTOs) list due to its lack of activities during the preceding two years. Although no longer designated as an FTO the DFLP remains subject to restrictions on fund-raising activities and to **freezing/sesquestration** of its assets in the United States due to an Executive Order signed by President Clinton in January 1995 aimed at groups that threaten to disrupt the Middle East peace process.

DEMOCRATIC REVOLUTIONARY FRONT FOR THE LIBERATION OF ARABISTAN (DRFLA). Originally a Marxist-Leninist splinter group of the Popular Front for the Liberation of Ahwaz (PFLA), both organizations appear to have been Iraqi-sponsored groups ostensibly seeking the independence of the largely Arab-inhabited regions of Khuzistan province in southwestern Iran.

In reaction to a long-standing dispute with Iran over sovereignty of the Shatt-al-Arab estuary, the Iraqi government began in 1960 to support irredentist Arab claims to Iran's Khuzistan Province on the eastern banks of the disputed waterway by supporting the Popular Front for the Liberation of Ahwaz. With the signing of the 1975 Algiers Accord in which Iraq ceded its previous claims over the entire waterway, jurisdiction of which would be divided between the two nations, Iraqi support of the PFLA insurgency ceased.

The Democratic Revolutionary Front for the Liberation of Arabistan emerged from the remnant of the PFLA, which acquired Iraqi support once again following the Islamic revolution in Iran in 1978-1979 and the outbreak of hostilities between Iraq and Iran in September 1980. The DRFLA emerged into the limelight with its seizure of the Iranian embassy in London from 30 April 1980 to 5 May 1990 in which six terrorists held 26 hostages. Commandos of Great Britain's 22nd Special Air Service Regiment executed a daytime assault on the embassy in which five terrorists and two hostages were killed. Within Khuzistan Province, which became a major battleground between Iranian and Iraqi troops, the DRFLA played little effective role in supporting the Iraqi invasion or in harassing Iranian troops.

DEPORTATION. *See* EXTRADITION.

DEV SOL. *See* REVOLUTIONARY PEOPLE'S LIBERATION PARTY/
FRONT.

DIPLOCK COURTS. Special antiterrorism courts established in Northern
Ireland to address the problem of intimidation of juries in cases involving members of Irish nationalist or Ulster Protestant paramilitaries or
else persons charged with terrorist offenses of a "political" nature. Jury
trials seemed impractical because either the jurors would acquit defendants out of sympathy for the defendant's political cause or else out of
fear of reprisal. Lord Diplock headed a commission to review the judicial process in cases involving terrorism in Northern Ireland which issued its report in December 1972 (Cmnd. 5185) recommending the use
of a single judge to determine matters both of fact and of law.

    · Unlike those nonjury trials that were later initiated under the
"Supergrass" system in 1981, in the Diplock court trials the defendant
would enjoy the right to face and cross-examine his or her accusers.
These trials were also public and the defendant would have legal counsel and would have the right of appeal. The standard of conviction
remained guilt beyond a reasonable doubt. Defense counsels could pe-
tition the British attorney general to "certify out" cases which were
claimed not to involve terrorist offenses which then would require jury
trials. In 1995 alone 932 of 1,234 such applications were granted. Of the
418 cases not removed from Diplock courts the rate of conviction for
those who pled "not guilty" was only 40 percent. Whenever judges find
a defendant guilty in the Diplock courts they are required to provide a
written opinion to explain their reasoning which verdict can then be
appealed. In this way those charged with terrorist offenses continue to
enjoy rights of due process despite the lack of a jury.

DIPLOMATIC INVIOLABILITY. According to statistics of the Office for
Combating Terrorism of the U.S. Department of State, diplomats, their
families, and others attached to them have increasingly become favored
targets of terrorist attacks. In 1975 over 30 percent of terrorist attacks
were directed at diplomats while in 1980 this figure rose to 54 percent.
Several of these attacks have involved hostage-barricade situations,
such as the seizure of the U.S. embassy in Tehran on 4 November 1979
or the occupation of the Japanese Ambassador's residence in Lima, Peru
on 17 December 1996, while others have involved **bombings** with great
loss of life, such as the 18 April 1983 bombing of the U.S. embassy in

West Beirut and the 7 August 1999 simultaneous bombings of the U.S. embassies in Nairobi, Kenya, and Dar es Salaam, Tanzania (*See* EAST AFRICAN U.S. EMBASSY ATTACKS).

To implement the New York Convention (the UN Convention on the Prevention and Punishment of Crimes Against Internationally Protected Persons, Including Diplomatic Agents, adopted on 14 December 1973) Title 18 of the U.S. Code was amended on 8 October 1976 to make attacks upon, or threats against, diplomats within the United States a federal felony and to allow its enforcement by whatever federal, state, or local agency is needed, whether civilian or military. Following the U.S. embassy seizure in Tehran the UN Convention Against the Taking of Hostages was adopted on 17 December 1979 and ratified by the United States on 4 September 1981. The Comprehensive Crime Control Act of 1985, sections 2001 and 2002, amended chapter 55 of Title 18 to make any **kidnapping** with an international dimension involving threats against life, limb, or liberty subject to federal jurisdiction.

In essence this allowed the United States to claim the right to arrest anyone involved in taking any U.S. citizen hostage, whether or not that victim were a U.S. diplomat, whether the crime took place within or outside the borders of the United States, and allowed U.S. authorities to arrest the suspect even outside of the borders of the United States. Ordinarily the United States would try to extradite (*see* EXTRADITION) such suspects but the propensity of terrorists to seek sanctuary in nations not disposed to extraditing them to U.S. authorities made this extreme assertion of extraterritorial jurisdiction seem necessary even though it may appear to violate the sovereignty of such nations.

The other issue involves cases of diplomatic immunity in which diplomatic status is abused to shelter terrorist agents from the law or else abuse of this status by the diplomats themselves to carry out terrorist activities. Following the end of the October 1985 **hijacking** of the *Achille Lauro*, Abu Abbas and his four fellow hijackers had left Egypt on an Egyptian airliner intending to fly to some sanctuary when U.S. fighter jets forced the plane to land at the Sigonella Airbase in Sicily. Over U.S. objections the Italian authorities allowed Abu Abbas to go free on the plea that he had an Iraqi diplomatic passport. Similarly Libyan diplomats abused their status on 17 April 1984 when they opened fire on Libyan protesters in St. James's Square, London, killing one British police officer. In such cases the national government whose territory and citizens have been attacked has the option of declaring the diplomats persona non grata, requiring them to leave, or even of down-grading diplomatic ties with the other nation or subjecting it to economic boycott and sanctions.

DIRECT ACTION. Action Directe (AD) was a group of French **anarchistic leftist terrorists** active from May 1979 until February 1987. The name of the group derives from a statement made by the group outlining its anarchistic program: "[We will] wreck society through direct action by destroying its institutions and the men who serve it." AD divided itself into two wings, one specializing in international targets, which has deliberately killed and maimed persons connected with West European business or military defense, the other wing striking domestic targets but usually in such a way that human life would not be taken, by **bombing** buildings after closing hours.

An analysis of 35 noteworthy actions committed by AD from 1979 to 1987 shows that 17 of these involved bombings, killing at least five and wounding at least 58 others; eight involved **assassination** attempts, half of them successful; five involved armed attacks with automatic weapons; and the remaining five involved theft, threats, and arms smuggling.

Bombing **targets** have included the European headquarters of the World Bank (4 June 1982); the European Space Agency (2 August 1984); and the officers' club at the Rhein-Main U.S. Air Force Base, which was car bombed, killing two and wounding 19 others (8 August 1985). Successful assassinations included the killing of French General René Audran (25 January 1985); Georges Besse, chairman of Renault (17 November 1986); and an American serviceman, murdered to get his car to be used in the Rhein-Main car bombing attack.

The Rhein-Main attack is one of the few in which AD crossed borders to carry out its operations. It was also done in partnership with the **Red Army Faction** (RAF) which may account for its more calculated brutality. In February 1987, four AD leaders were arrested outside Orleans for the murder of Georges Besse. In November 1987 Max Frerot, the AD bombing expert, was also arrested. The organization appears to have been ended with these arrests.

DIRTY BOMBS. *See* WEAPONS OF MASS DESTRUCTION.

DIRTY WAR(S). Name used to describe the Argentinean military junta's campaign of **state terror** to annihilate leftist guerrillas, politicians, students, unionists, and intellectuals, which lasted from 24 March 1976 until the fall of the military junta in 1983. The junta began a massive **death squad** campaign using the police and military forces to arrest tens of thousands of Argentines who were tortured to death in prisons and their bodies dumped in river estuaries, the sea, or unmarked graves.

It is estimated that between 9,000 and 10,000 persons perished or disappeared in the junta's so-called process of national reorganization. The campaign was principally directed against leftists and enjoyed some support from middle-class, conservative Argentineans exasperated with the violence of the **Montoneros** and similar leftist terrorists. The dirty war allowed no formal process of documentation or defense of those considered enemies of the regime and was particularly directed at those not already in official custody for whom there would be no arrest record once they entered the ranks of the "disappeared." After careful review of forensic evidence, and the testimony both of surviving leftists and military officials, the Comisión Nacional sobre la Desaparición de Personas (CONADEP), the Argentine National Commission on Disappearances, determined the figure of the disappeared to be around 9,000, which accords well with the totals of lost comrades given by surviving members of the Montoneros and the **People's Revolutionary Army** (ERP).

Beginning in 1975 Argentina coordinated its efforts to crush its leftists with five other Latin American regimes confronting leftist insurgencies, namely Bolivia, Brazil, Chile, Paraguay, and Uruguay in "Operation Condor" in which each regime assisted the police of other regimes in hunting down wanted leftists in each others' jurisdictions, in effect aiding each other in each's own version of a "dirty war." General Carlos Prats Gonzales, the army commander under President Salvador Allende who resigned his commission and went into exile in Argentina rather than join the military junta, was killed in 1974 by a **bomb** placed within his car outside his home in exile in Buenos Aires. A former Chilean intelligence agent, Enrique Arancibia Clavel, was arrested in January 1996 on charges of having arranged the bombing. Similarly the former chief of Chile's military secret police, General Manuel Contreras Sepulvade, was convicted in May 1995 for the September 1976 **assassination** of Orlando Letelier, the former foreign minister of the Allende government, who was also killed by a bomb within his car outside his home in Washington, D.C. These actions can be viewed as extensions of the dirty war of Chile against its enemies beyond its national boundaries.

DISAPPEARANCES. *See* DIRTY WAR(S); GUATEMALAN NATIONAL REVOLUTIONARY UNION.

DOUKHOBORS. Also known as the "Sons of Freedom," or "Freedomites," the Doukhobors, whose name is actually Russian for "Spirit Wrestlers," are members of a Russian Christian sect who emigrated to Canada in 1899. They are a nonstate communal religious group who adhere to a radical ideal of freedom and antiauthoritarianism, rejecting both secular and religious hierarchical authority. A long-standing Doukhobor ritual meant to demonstrate the Doukhobors' radical freedom even from their material possessions has been the periodic communal burning of all their worldly goods. In the course of this ritual, participating Doukhobors would ultimately strip off their garments to burn as well until all participants were naked. Like the Amish, the Doukhobors deny the authority of the government to send their children to public schools but, unlike the pacifistic Amish, the Doukhobors have used **arson** and **bombing** of public property as means of protesting and resisting Canadian federal and provincial government intervention in their lives.

There are about 20,000 Doukhobors in Canada, of which some 2,500 are the more radical Sons of Freedom, located mainly in eastern British Columbia, who have been responsible for most Doukhobor terrorism. The first recorded protest of Doukhobors occurred in Saskatchewan in 1929 when many burned their homes in protest at the provincial government's requiring their children to attend public schools. Most of the terrorist acts by Doukhobors occurred in the period from 1961-1962, although incidents occurred as late as 1972, and consisted of burnings and bombings directed at other Doukhobors, businesses, railroads, power pylons, and government buildings. In the period from 1960-1985 Doukhobor violence accounted for 38.3 percent (130 events) of all terrorist incidents in Canada and was second only to Québécois separatism (166 events) as the largest source of political terrorism in Canada. Although some have described this violence as being religiously motivated, and therefore presumed to be nonpolitical, it is clear that the religious doctrine of independence from all external authority also implies a rather thoroughgoing political anarchism as well as legitimizing instrumental **revolutionary** violence. While Doukhobor terrorism has greatly subsided, its future demise is not a foregone conclusion.

- E -

EAST AFRICAN U.S. EMBASSY ATTACKS. On 7 August 1998 the U.S. embassies in Nairobi, Kenya, and Dar es Salaam, Tanzania, were struck by almost simultaneous truck **bombings** believed to have been carried out by members of **Osama bin Laden's** al Qa'eda group. The attack in Dar es Salaam involved a gasoline truck which exploded as it entered the embassy compound, killing 10 Tanzanians, seven of whom were embassy employees and wounding 77 others, one of whom was an American. A few minutes later at 10:30 a.m. another truck bomb in Nairobi was exploded outside the U.S. embassy. After being denied entry by a guard to the front parking lot of the embassy, which would have positioned the bomb close to the ambassador's office, the terrorists drove the truck to the rear entrance of the building where one terrorist threw a grenade at parked cars causing the guard to flee. When the bomb exploded there it killed 291 persons and wounded over 5,000. Twelve U.S. citizens were killed and six injured in this attack while the remaining casualties were mainly Kenyan citizens.

After the U.S. government obtained information implicating Osama bin Laden in the attacks the Clinton administration issued Executive Order 12947 on 20 August 1998 adding bin Laden and his key aides in the al Qa'eda organization to the list of known terrorist groups and ordering the **freezing** of their financial assets in U.S. banks and other properties. On the same day the United States launched cruise missiles at three bin Laden bases outside Khost in Afghanistan and the Al Shifa pharmaceutical plant in Sudan originally declared to have been associated with bin Laden.

On 28 August 1998 the United States issued indictments against Mohamed Rashed al-Owhali and Mohammed Saddiq Odeh on charges of conspiracy to commit terrorism, use of **weapons of mass destruction**, and 12 counts of murder for each of the U.S. citizens killed in the blast. Al-Owhali had originally been designated to be a **suicide** volunteer in the Kenyan bombing but instead fled from the truck just before it was due to explode while the other man, called "Ahmad the German," died in the blast. Al-Owhali was arrested later when trying to obtain medical help for his wounds sustained from the blast and handed over to the United States by Kenyan officials. The second suspect, Odeh, was arrested and questioned by Pakistani officials after arriving in Karachi, Pakistan, on a flight from Nairobi the day of the bombing. After three days he was returned to Kenya and detained there and handed over to U.S. officials two weeks later.

On 4 November 1998 a Federal grand jury in Manhattan returned a 238-count indictment charging Osama bin Laden for the bombings of the two embassies and conspiracy to commit other acts of terrorism against U.S. citizens abroad. The United States offered awards of $5 million each for information leading to the arrest or capture of bin Laden, or of his chief aide, Muhammad Atef. On 16 December 1998 five more suspects were named in indictments and another suspect, Mamdouh Mahmud Salim, was **extradited** from Germany to the United States on 21 December 1998. Two other suspects were arrested in the United States, one Wadih el-Hage on 19 September 1998 in Texas, and one Ali A. Mohamed, a former U.S. Army sergeant assigned to Special Forces in the period 1986-1989, arrested in California on 11 September 1998. Several other suspects were identified and arrested overseas while a few, including bin Laden and Atef, remain at large.

While this bombing drew forth the most extensive FBI investigation in its history, in which the CIA as well as Kenyan, Tanzanian, and Pakistani authorities participated, it also drew attention to the failure of selective efforts of hardening of U.S. diplomatic facilities overseas which had neglected security upgrading of the embassies in Kenya and Tanzania in favor of hardening of facilities elsewhere deemed to be at higher risk.

On 20 October 2000 Ali A. Mohamed testified that bin Laden had ordered him to surveil U.S., British, French, and Israeli targets in Nairobi including the U.S. embassy. The trial of four bombing suspects began in March 2001 and on 29 May 2001 a U.S. federal court convicted Khalfan Khamis Mahmoud, of Tanzania, and Mohamed Rashed Daoud Owhali, of Saudi Arabia, for conspiracy and murder for their roles in assembling and delivering the truck bombs used in the two attacks. The court also convicted Mohammed Saddiq Odeh, a Palestinian, and Wadih Hage, a naturalized U.S. citizen from Lebanon, for conspiring to kill Americans around the world. On 11 June 2001 al Owhali was sentenced to life imprisonment. On 18 October 2001 Mohammed Saddiq Odeh, a Jordanian al Qa'eda member, Khalfan Khamis Mohamed, and Wadih el-Hage were also sentenced to life imprisonment.

ECOTAGE. A name used by environmentalist terrorists, as well as "Eco-defense," to describe their own nonstate political violence with the limited objective of combating what they view as anti-environmental actions and policies, whether by private or public agencies. The term *ecotage*, or "monkeywrenching," is meant to emphasize that they target property rather than people, which they believe distinguishes their violence from terrorism proper. Critics of environmental extremism have used the term *environmental terrorism* to cover a wide range of groups, actions, and causes, such as Earth First! and Earth Liberation Front environmental activists, Sea Shepard and Greenpeace antiwhaling and anti-seal hunting activists, and animal rights activists such as the **Animal Liberation Front** (ALF).

Properly speaking the environmentalist terrorists are just those groups involved in monkeywrenching, or sabotage activities directed at logging, ski resort development, and the like. The agenda of the animal rights groups is not environmentalist as such: certain actions conducted by these groups, such as the release of lab animals or mink into the wild, are arguably anti-environmental insofar as certain of these animals are exotic to the environment in which they are released and may well carry diseases and parasites into the local ecosystem that would harm native species. The Sea Shepherd and Greenpeace groups represent groups bridging environmentalism and animal rights activism since they are seeking to preserve whales, dolphins, and seals but within the context of their existing habitats.

The term *monkeywrenching* gained currency with Dave Foreman's 1985 book *Ecodefense: A Field Guide to Monkeywrenching* which gives step-by-step procedures for tree-spiking (putting metal or ceramic spikes into trees to make them unprofitable as lumber), spiking devices for flattening the tires of off-road vehicles, destruction of bulldozing and logging equipment, destroying traps, trashing billboards and unoccupied cabins and condos, and tying up corporate 800 numbers with automated computer phone-ins, and the like.

Violent activism by environmentally oriented groups appears to have been increasing in response to a decline in the environmental movement's effectiveness in conventional interest group activism. According to *North American Research*, which tracks crimes against property in the United

States and Canada, there were about six instances of environmentalist sabotage of private development in 1986 whereas by 1998 there was an average of 300 such crimes a year, with much of the increase occurring the period 1995-1998. While the FBI prevented four planned acts of sabotage by the EMETIC (Evan Mecham Eco-Terrorist International Conspiracy) group in Arizona in 1989, in the period 1987-1990 environmentalist-related violence accounted for six out of the 21 officially designated domestic acts of terrorism of that period. Outside the United States the Greenpeace group attempted in July 1995 to sail the *Rainbow Warrior II* into the French nuclear testing grounds at Mururoa Atoll in the South Pacific in response to the renewed nuclear testing planned by the French government. In October 1998 environmental activists, calling themselves the "Earth Liberation Front," set fires at a Vail ski area under expansion, destroying three major buildings and damaging four chairlifts. On 21 May 2001 the University of Washington Center for Urban Horticulture research laboratory in Seattle was set ablaze while on the same day two buildings of the Jefferson Popular Farms in Clatskanie, Oregon, were also burned down. Credit for the **arson** of the Oregon tree farm was claimed by the Earth Liberation Front which alleged the nursery was engaged in genetic engineering. Environmentalist activists had also been protesting the use of genetically engineered grains in livestock feeds in the United States as well as for human consumption in developing nations.

Thus environmental activists were becoming more active not only in the United States but also in other countries.

EMERGENCY PROVISIONS ACT (EPA), NORTHERN IRELAND. In 1973 Great Britain instituted special guidelines for search, arrest, and interrogation procedures involving suspected members of the **Irish Republican Army** (IRA), and related groups, or suspected members of Protestant paramilitary groups, or others suspected of terrorist activities. The current Emergency Provisions Act allows army and police in Northern Ireland to conduct searches without warrants using the standard of "reasonable suspicion" which is less than the "probable cause" standard required by the Fourth Amendment of the U.S. Constitution. Amendments to this Act in 1987 added the "reasonable suspicion" requirement to allow judicial review of police actions whereas prior to 1987 police and army units needed only orders from their superiors to conduct searches. Under the Act suspects may be held and interrogated for a maximum of three days. The **Prevention of Terrorism Acts** allow detention and interrogation of suspects up to seven days where a stronger "probable cause" exists that the suspect is involved in terrorism. Under the EPA Northern Ireland security forces have conducted over 100,000 searches in recent years which have yielded over 10,000 illegal firearms and almost 100 tons of explosives. Some critics believe that these extensive searches have alienated more of the Catholic population in Northern Ireland and increased recruits to the IRA.

ENTEBBE HIJACKING. On 27 June 1976 Air France Flight 139 from Tel Aviv to Paris, carrying 245 passengers and 12 crew members, was **hijacked** out of Athens by seven members of the **Popular Front for the Liberation of Palestine** (PFLP) to Benghazi, Libya, where the plane was refueled. From there it flew to Entebbe Airport, Uganda, where the hijackers were aided by Ugandan troops in guarding the hostages. The hijackers demanded the release of 53 terrorists held in French, Israeli, Kenyan, Swiss, and West German jails, including Kozo Okamoto, sole surviving terrorist involved in the May 1972 Lod airport attack. Throughout the hostage seizure the Ugandan dictator, Idi Amin, fully supported the terrorists.

By 1 July 1976, the terrorists had released nearly all non-Jewish and non-Israeli hostages, leaving 103 at Entebbe. On 2 July the Israeli cabinet decided upon Operation Thunderbolt, a plan to send Israeli commandos to Entebbe to rescue the hostages. On 4 July 1976 the Israelis rescued all but four of the hostages, three having been killed by the cross fire at the rescue scene, while another passenger, Dora Bloch, age 75, was absent having been hospitalized in Kampala. The rescuers killed seven of the terrorists and about 20 Ugandan soldiers, while the Israeli officer leading the rescue, Jonathan Netanyahu, who was the brother of the future Prime Minister of Israel, Binyamin Netanyahu, was the only Israeli soldier killed in the attack. The Israelis destroyed 11 Ugandan air force MIGs to prevent any attempt to interfere with the rescue mission on its return to Israel.

Following the rescue Dora Bloch was reportedly murdered and her body burned, while Idi Amin carried out a widespread purge and executions of Ugandan officials charged with guarding Entebbe airport and the hostages.

ENTREPRENEURIAL TERRORISM. This category consists of instances of terrorism and terrorists having much more limited aims that do not fit into either category of **state terrorism** meant to preserve an existing social-political status quo or of revolutionary terrorism meant to change that status quo in part or in whole. Entrepreneurial terrorism consists of single-interest terrorist causes, such as **anti-abortion terrorism** involving attacks on clinics and doctors who provide abortion services, or such as animal rights terrorism involving vandalism and destruction of fur shops or research facilities or attacks on medical and biological sciences researchers. It can also cover such things as terrorist activities sponsored by criminal syndicates, such as the **Colombian cocaine cartels,** to pressure or co-opt the governments opposing such criminals.

The term *entrepreneurial* is used to designate this third category since very often the limited end(s) being sought are merely the profits the group can extract from either extortion or from the sale of its terrorist abilities to whatever buyer, or else a limited policy goal that the policy entrepreneurs of a specialized interest group are seeking. Sometimes a **revolutionary** group that is never able to achieve its original goals will become entrepreneurial, an example being the **Inner Macedonian Revolutionary Organization** (IMRO), which began as a nationalist society in 1900 but had degenerated to becoming a criminal for-hire hit squad by World War II.

This term, however, is also used in this dictionary to refer to terrorist groups that are essentially single-interest groups or criminal enterprises. Thus groups like the **Animal Liberation Front** or the **Ananda Marg** cult, which each sought only a very limited and specific goal, quite apart from changing or maintaining a social-political status quo, are also considered entrepreneurial insofar as they are absorbed in the marginal gain or loss of their limited ends. Another example concerns **hijacking**: Hijacking to gain passengers as hostages with which to put pressure on a government to comply with political demands could be either a revolutionary act or, if the group is a state-sponsored proxy, a state terrorist act. Hijacking a plane merely to escape to a desired country could be considered an entrepreneurial act.

ENVIRONMENTALIST TERRORISM. *See* ECOTAGE.

EOKA. The Ethniki Organosis Kyprion Agoniston (National Organization of Cypriot Fighters) was a Greek Cypriot revolutionary nationalist group dedicated to winning Cypriot independence from Great Britain and uniting Cyprus with Greece. This group also had Greek state support from 1971 to 1974. Beginning on 31 March 1955 up to 1958, EOKA conducted anti-British terrorist **bombings** and shootings throughout Cyprus. In 1958 the British granted Cyprus independence under a constitution that, however, recognized and protected the rights of the island's Turkish minority and allowed the British to maintain control over certain military bases, conditions that blocked the unification with Greece that EOKA had sought.

As the original EOKA-Alpha, disbanded in 1960, had failed to achieve reunification, it was reactivated as EOKA-Beta and tried to force the issue of unification during the period from 1971-1974 after the EOKA founder, George Grivas, returned from Greece assured of Greek military support. EOKA-Beta engaged in terrorism against the Turkish Cypriots and played a role in the 15 May 1974 coup d'état overthrowing Cypriot President Archbishop Makarios. This prompted Turkey to invade Cyprus and to impose a de facto partition of the island into Turkish and Greek zones.

Frustrated over a perceived U.S. tilt toward Turkey in these hostilities, EOKA-Beta instigated an anti-U.S. riot on 19 August 1974 at the U.S. embassy compound in Nicosia, in the course of which EOKA-Beta sharpshooters **assassinated** U.S. Ambassador Rodger P. Davies and his secretary. While six EOKA-Beta suspects were tried for these murders, only two of them were convicted, the rest having been released on legal technicalities, while the Greek Cypriot community regarded their sentences, respectively of five and seven years' imprisonment, as outrageously severe. Evidence emerged during the trial revealing that EOKA-Beta had penetrated the Greek Cypriot national guard as well as the civilian government while the lenient behavior of the Cypriot judiciary also suggested EOKA-Beta **co-optation** of the state. EOKA-Beta announced its dissolution in 1978, having failed in its goals and having lost the sponsorship of the Greek military junta that was overthrown following its failure to resist the Turkish invasion and partition of the island.

EJÉRCITO REVOLUCIONARIO DEL PUEBLO (ERP). *See* FARABUNDO MARTÍ NATIONAL LIBERATION FRONT.

ETHNIC CLEANSING. *See* ETHNO-NATIONALIST TERRORISM; GENO-CIDE.

ETHNO-NATIONALIST TERRORISM. A form of **revolutionary** terror-ism by antistate ethnic groups to achieve independence or secession, autonomy, redefinition of the existing nation-state, or unification with another state, or else a form of **state terrorism** aimed at ethnic cleansing (*see* GENOCIDE) of a disputed territory. Another term for antistate ethno-nationalists is *nationalist separatists*.

Ethno-nationalist conflicts have increased markedly during the lat-ter part of the 20th century with the end of the Cold War as various ethnic groups have sought independent nation-state status. According to findings by Ted Robert Gurr, presented in an address to the April 1994 convention of the International Studies Association, during the period 1987-1994 there have been over 50 serious ethno-political conflicts underway in which over four million people have perished and at least 26 million people been displaced. Most of these conflicts have involved civil wars, **insurgencies**, or war between states, but much of the **low-intensity conflict** associated with ethno-nationalist causes has involved terrorism either by antistate groups or else state terror against targeted minorities. The **Irish Republican Army** and the **Basque Fatherland and Liberty** groups provide examples of antistate ethno-nationalist terrorists. The anti-Hutu **genocides** conducted in Rwanda and Burundi in 1994 and the ethnic cleaning directed against Albanians that oc-curred in Kosovo in 1998-1999 provide two examples of state ethno-nationalist terrorism.

EUROPEAN CONVENTION ON THE SUPPRESSION OF TERROR-ISM. This regional convention, which came into force on 25 October 1978 seeks to reduce the use of the **political offense exception** in cases of terrorism involving planning or carrying out air piracy, attacks on diplomats or other "internationally protected persons," **kidnapping** or hostage taking, use of explosives to harm life or limb, or being an acces-sory to any of these actions. The convention allows a state to refuse **extradition**, if it has reason to believe a suspect is really being perse-cuted for his or her race, religion, nationality, ethnic affiliation, or po-litical opinion. In cases where extradition is refused Article 7 of the Convention requires that the state refusing jurisdiction must submit the case for prosecution to its own competent authorities. All members of the Council of Europe, with the exception of the Republic of Ireland, have signed this convention. Ireland has refused to sign it on the claim that it violates a right of political **asylum** implicit in Article 29 of its constitution.

EUROPEAN NATIONAL FASCISTS. The Faisceaux Nationaux Européens (FNE) was a French neo-Fascist group that sought to harass and intimidate Jews, North Africans, and black Africans to force them to leave France. This organization is the direct successor of the Fédération d'Action Nationale Européene (FANE), the Federation for National European Action, a group founded in 1966 by French Fascists and anti-Semites. In 1980 anti-Semitic violence crested in France, with 122 incidents of **arson** and violence directed against minority group members as well as 66 threats and acts of violence. In September 1980 FANE was banned by the French government for its role in promoting two violent incidents. FANE members were suspected of **bombing** the Rue Copernic synagogue in Paris on 4 October 1980, which killed four and wounded 12, but this terrorist act turned out to have been the work of Palestinian terrorists. In spite of the ban on FANE, its members immediately reconstituted themselves as the European National Fascists (FNE). FNE installed as its head Robert Petit, director of the Vichy regime's "Center for the Study of the Jewish Question."

Following the spate of anti-Semitic incidents that forced the banning of FANE, the French authorities seemed to avoid investigating the activities of FNE. French Jewish organizations and the secretary-general of the French detectives union in 1980 believed that at least 150 national policemen were members of this, and similar, neo-Fascist groups. Some sources claimed that one-third of FNE's membership was made up of policemen. If true, this would represent an example of penetration and **co-optation** of the state by a subversive terrorist organization. In recent years much of the membership of FNE has defected to Jean-Marie Le Pen's **National Front** party.

EUZKADI TA ASKATASUNA. *See* BASQUE FATHERLAND AND LIBERTY.

EXTRADITABLES. *See* COLOMBIAN COCAINE CARTELS.

EXTRADITION. Cases of extradition, exclusion, or deportation of aliens on the grounds that they have been accused of terrorist offenses is governed by international conventions and national laws to protect the rights of due process of such persons. The two main international conventions are the Convention Relating to the Status of Refugees (28 July 1951) and the Protocol Relating to the Status of Refugees (31 January 1967). These define as a "refugee" anyone who flees to another country to avoid persecution due to his or her race, religion, nationality, ethnic affiliation, or political opinion and who cannot secure legal protection from such persecution in the country from which he or she is fleeing. Under such circumstances even if the refugee has entered the signatory nation illegally that nation cannot deport the refugee back to the country from which he or she fled.

This protection from deportation to the nation of origin is incorporated in the United States Refugee Act of 1980. U.S. authorities can resort to exclusion or deportation in the case of illegal aliens whose claim of persecution is doubtful but the choice of exclusion can apply only to immigrants who are not yet legally admitted to the jurisdiction of the United States. Those immigrants who have entered the land or maritime borders of the United States but not yet reported to an Immigration and Naturalization Service (INS) inspection station can be considered subject to exclusion. The difference is that in deportation proceedings the burden of proof is on the government to prove that the alien is worthy of deportation. By contrast in exclusion proceedings the burden of proof is on the alien, with the exception being returning resident aliens, to establish his or her admissibility. In cases where the alien would face "a well grounded fear" of certain persecution for the grounds cited earlier the **political offense exception** would establish admissibility. One significant difference in the outcome of a deportation or exclusion proceeding is that if exclusion is indicated then the alien must be returned to the country of origin whereas if deportation is determined then the alien may choose to which country to go.

Prior to the 1993 **World Trade Center bombing** the U.S. State Department maintained lists of known and suspected members of foreign terrorist organizations who were to be excluded from admission to the United States. In the event that such persons actually entered the United States they often relied on their claim under the political offense exception that they would face persecution in their homelands to avoid deportation. In the wake of the convictions of the World Trade Center bombers the **Antiterrorism and Effective Death Penalty Act of 1996** and the Illegal Immigration Reform and Immigrant Responsibility Act of 1996 were passed to restrict the use of the political offense exception claim.

In some cases nations have refused to extradite persons suspected of terrorism when the country seeking extradition has a death penalty for conviction for the alleged offense while the country from which extradition is being sought subscribes to the principle that capital punishment is a violation of human rights. Under such circumstances the legal principle of *Aut Dedere, Aut Judicare*, is applicable, namely that the country refusing extradition must prosecute the person whom they refuse to extradite under the relevant antiterrorist treaties and conventions to which that country subscribes. The passage of the 1996 Antiterrorism and Effective Death Penalty Act by the United States has made it more difficult to seek extradition of suspected international terrorists from Canada and members of the European Union due to the rejection of capital punishment by those nations. Similarly the **European Convention for the Suppression of Terrorism** has allowed for more expeditious extradition of suspected terrorists by reducing the scope of the political offense exception.

EYAL. Hebrew acronym of Irgun Yehudi Lohem, "Jewish Fighting Organization," this is believed to be a splinter group of the banned Kach organization, a radical Jewish group founded by the late Rabbi Meir Kahane, also founder of the **Jewish Defense League**. The founder of Eyal is reputed to be one Avishai Raviv whom some Israeli sources believe was actually an undercover Shin Bet (General Security Services) informant. Eyal came to public attention with the **assassination** of Israeli Prime Minister Yitzhak Rabin by Yigal Amir, a member of the Eyal group, on 4 November 1995. Yigal Amir regarded Rabin as an enemy of the Jewish nation due to his role in promoting the Israeli-Palestinian peace process and rationalized his right to kill Rabin as his being a "pursuer" under Mosaic Law who was allowed to hunt down and kill one who had killed other Jews. Eyal was previously known only for having vandalized the property of Arabs in Hebron as well as threatening left-wing Israeli politicians and vandalizing their property.

A notebook seized from an Eyal activist from the Jewish settlement of Kiryat Arba, near Hebron, revealed internal instructions for Eyal members. All members were given special aliases and passwords to prevent them from revealing identities of other group members under interrogation and also to prevent infiltration of the group. According to this notebook the Eyal had four sections, an intelligence section with 15 members, a communications section with eight members, a handlers section, and a control center. Eyal members were required to practice firing handguns and an Uzi submachine gun at least twice a year as well as to receive training in first aid, navigation, sabotage, scouting, street fighting, and surveillance. Following the assassination of Count Bernadotte on 16 September 1948 by a member of **LEHI** the Israeli government issued "Law and Administration Ordinance 5708-1948: Emergency Regulations for the Prevention of Terrorism" which was written to empower the new Israeli government to outlaw LEHI and which was largely based on the British Mandatory Administration's Defence (Emergency) Regulation of 1937 meant to prosecute the Arabs during the 1936 Arab anti-Jewish riots and subsequently used to prosecute Jewish terrorists. This law has been applied in recent times to prosecute members of the Kach and Kahane Chai groups as well as members of the Eyal group.

On 11 September 1996 Yigal Amir, his brother Haggai Amir, and Dror Adani were convicted for conspiracy to assassinate Rabin and to attack Palestinian Arabs. Yigal Amir apparently formed a subgroup within Eyal which he led, and he apparently had planned to assassinate Rabin on two previous occasions, once at a Yad Vashem (Holocaust Memorial) ceremony on 22 January 1995 and the other time at the dedication of a tunnel on 11 September 1995 but was unable to do so due to the cancellation of the Prime Minister's appearance for the first ceremony and due to his inability to approach the Prime Minister on the second occasion.

- F -

FEDERATION FOR NATIONAL EUROPEAN ACTION (FÉDÉRATION D'ACTION NATIONALE EUROPÉEN). *See* EUROPEAN NATIONAL FASCISTS; NATIONAL FRONT.

FARABUNDO MARTÍ NATIONAL LIBERATION FRONT. The Frente Farabundo Martí para la Liberación Nacional (FMLN) was an umbrella group uniting several leftist guerrilla groups that sought to create a Marxist revolution within El Salvador following the **Sandinista** model

in Nicaragua. The creation of this united front of all major leftist guerrilla groups was a condition imposed by Fidel Castro for Cuban sponsorship of the Salvadoran leftist insurgents. In addition to Cuban state
sponsorship, the FMLN received arms, sanctuary, and other material
assistance from the Sandinista government of Nicaragua prior to 25
February 1990 and afterward continued to receive arms sporadically
from units of the Sandinista People's Army. The five groups joined in
the FMLN are described separately in what follows:

1. Fuerzas Populares de Liberación (The People's Liberation Forces,
   FPL) founded in 1970 was the oldest of the armed guerrilla groups.
   The FPL had its stronghold in Chalatenango province in the mountains bordering Honduras. While the FPL had 1,500 to 2,000 regular
   guerrilla fighters, it also had "urban front" guerrilla fronts that were
   responsible for much of the antigovernment terrorism in El Salvador's
   cities following 1977, including intimidation of voters during the
   March 1978 municipal elections, the machine-gun murders of 12
   prominent citizens, including Carlos Alfaro Castillo, the chancellor
   of the National University, and Rubén Alfonso Rodríguez, a former
   president of the National Congress. On 28 November 1979 the FPL
   kidnapped South African Ambassador Archibald Dunn, whom they
   later murdered. An urban front of this group was responsible for the
   first killing of an American official by an FMLN group when it **assassinated** Lt. Commander Schaufelberger, the Deputy Commander
   of the U.S. Advisory Group in El Salvador, on 25 May 1985. From
   April 1980 to November 1984 the FPL carried out seven attacks on
   U.S. targets, including three attacks on the U.S. embassy, using light
   antitank rockets and two assassinations of U.S. embassy personnel.
   Apart from its urban terrorist campaign the FPL has on occasion
   committed atrocities against civilians in rural areas, such as the massacre of 22 civilians in Santa Cruz Loma in 1985.

   This group suffered from some internal quarreling, leading to the
   murder of the second-in-command, Melinda Anaya Montes (aka
   "Commandante Anna María"), in the FMLN Managua office at the hands
   of other FPL members. This reportedly led the founder of the FPL,
   Cayetano Carpio (aka "Marcial"), to take his own life on 6 April 1983.

2. Ejército Revolucionario del Pueblo (The People's Revolutionary
   Army, ERP), founded in 1972, was the strongest FMLN guerrilla
   organization, having 2,000 combatants. This group operated largely
   in Morazán province and other areas in eastern El Salvador but had

very little involvement in political front organizations in the cities, having preferred a rural military strategy over political negotiations. Its leader, Joaquín Villalobos, was a brilliant and ruthless tactician. The ERP followed a policy of kidnapping and murdering local mayors and other functionaries of the Salvadoran government and has committed numerous atrocities against peasants suspected of collaboration with the government. As in the case of the FPL, instances of intramural terror have occurred in the ERP. The murder of ERP member Roque Dalton, a Salvadoran intellectual and world-renowned poet, at the hands of comrades within the ERP for an alleged ideological offense created much scandal within the Salvadoran left and among their sympathizers. The excessive brutality and **ideological** rigidity of the ERP under Villalobos's leadership led many observers to dub him the "Pol Pot of Central America."

While most of ERP's terrorism has been both repressive and **revolutionary**, directed internally at domestic targets, it has also struck at some international targets. On 4 February 1980 ERP gunmen attacked the Guatemalan embassy with automatic weapons fire. On 25 March 1980 the ERP bombed the International Telephone and Telegraph office in San Salvador. On 16 September 1980 the ERP fired five Chinese anti-tank rockets at the U.S. embassy, causing damage but no injuries.

3. Fuerzas Armadas de la Resistencia Nacional (The Armed Forces of National Resistance, FARN) was formed in 1975 partly in reaction to the ERP's excessive use of terrorism and brute force. By contrast the FARN concentrated not only on guerrilla operations with its 1,000 guerrillas but also on infiltrating and influencing the legal labor, students, and human rights organizations active within Salvadoran society. Virtually no major terrorist incidents have been attributed to this group. In addition to eschewing purely terrorist actions the FARN differs from other members of the FMLN in stressing Salvadoran nationalism rather than Marxism in its political platform and program.

4. Partido Revolucionario de los Trabajadores Centroamericanos (The Revolutionary Party of Central American Workers, PRTC) actually began in Costa Rica in 1976 as a regional movement but was most active in El Salvador. Its armed wing was known as the Armed Forces of Revolutionary Popular Liberation, numbering some 500 combatants.

The PRTC compensated for its small numbers by some audacious terrorist actions, including the 19 June 1985 Zona Rosa massacre in which four off-duty U.S. Marine embassy guards, two private U.S. citizens, and seven Salvadoran civilians were machine-gunned to death at a sidewalk café in the Zona Rosa district of San Salvador. The perpetrator, Nidia Díaz, was captured but freed on 24 October 1985 in exchange for the kidnapped daughter of Salvadoran president José Napoleón Duarte.

5. Fuerzas Armadas de Liberación (The Armed Forces of Liberation, FAL) was the armed wing of the Communist Party of El Salvador (PCES). While numerically small, having around 500 combatants, it was of great importance to the FMLN during the Salvadoran civil war due to its close connections with the Soviet and Cuban leadership. Its leader, Shafik Handal, served as the FMLN spokesman in the formerly Communist countries and also played a role in creating support networks in non-Communist countries, including the United States. Its urban guerrillas on 10 September 1985 kidnapped Inez Guadalupe Duarte Durán, daughter of the then Salvadoran president José Napoleón Duarte. Both she and another kidnap victim, the Civil Aviation Director Colonel Omar Napoleón Avalos, were released along with 33 kidnapped mayors and municipal officials on 24 October 1985 in a prisoner exchange between the FMLN and the Salvadoran government.

While the Salvadoran transitional regime was often criticized for its human rights abuses due its failure to suppress the operation of rightwing **death squads**, the FMLN also was guilty of human rights violations in conducting its rural insurgency and urban terrorist campaigns. By 1986 the United Nations report on human rights in El Salvador noted that the FMLN was guilty of increasing human rights violations while the Salvadoran government's record had improved substantially.

Prior to 1980 the constituent groups of the FMLN believed in the theory of prolonged popular warfare. With the Sandinista victory in Nicaragua in July 1979 the leftist guerrillas already active were encouraged to redouble their own efforts at revolution. On 15 October 1979, a reformist coup ousted the ineffective and corrupt President Carlos Humberto Romero and sought to implement badly needed social and economic reforms to forestall a Nicaraguan-style revolution in El Salvador. The leftist rebels, not to be deterred from their own goals, rejected conciliation with the new junta. The transitional government meanwhile had its own problems with rightist military and police officials who sought to preempt a leftist insurgency there by using death squads to kill off as many supporters of the guerrillas as possible.

The leftists unified their military command in November 1979 as a precondition to receiving Cuban aid. In May 1980, the Unified Revolutionary Directorate (DRU) was established in Havana to be the decision-making body for the entire FMLN. In January 1981 the FMLN attempted a "final offensive" against the major cities of El Salvador in which they were defeated by a Salvadoran army resupplied with U.S. military aid. They retreated to the rural areas, and from 1982 until 1983 their numbers of combatants grew from 2,000 to 12,000 until they were engaging the Salvadoran army in battalion-sized engagements. At the same time, the FMLN was engaged in systemic sabotage of the economic infrastructure and intimidation of the rural population.

By 1985 the Salvadoran army had improved to the point that the FMLN was forced to go back to deploying its forces in smaller groups. Following November 1986 the leadership and rank and file of the FMLN began suffering declining morale. FMLN documents captured during that period indicated there was much internal criticism of the ERP and its strategy. In July 1987 the FMLN undertook to rebuild its forces within the cities to foment a popular uprising, a move reflected in increasing incidents of urban terrorism in the following year. The FMLN tried with little success to disrupt the 19 March 1989 elections, which were held in at least 90 percent of the country. Even the Revolutionary Democratic Front (FDR), the leftist coalition of parties sympathetic to the FMLN, broke with the FMLN over the question of participating in the elections and ran a candidate in those elections.

The FMLN attempted a second "final offensive" on 16 November 1989 with no greater success. Elsewhere the changes under way in the Soviet Union and Eastern Europe began to make Cuba, the Sandinistas, and the FMLN seem anachronistic. When Violeta Chamorro was elected president of Nicaragua on 25 February 1990, ending Sandinista domination, future Nicaraguan aid was put into doubt. Negotiations resumed in May 1990 and continued in three rounds until a cease-fire was signed on 31 December 1991. During these negotiations a U.S. helicopter carrying three U.S. military advisers was shot down by FMLN forces on 2 January 1991. One crewman was critically injured and died later, but two survivors, Lt. Col. David Pickett and crew chief PFC Earnest Dawson, were murdered by the FMLN. This incident undermined international and regional moral support for the FMLN.

The FMLN and Salvadoran government agreed on 1 January 1992 to end the 12-year-long civil war in which at least 75,000 people had perished. One agreement reached on 25 September 1991 allowed the armed units of the FMLN to be incorporated under a separate command into the civilian Ministry of the Interior rather than under the Ministry of Defense, therefore allaying the guerrillas' fears for their personal security. While numerous acts of political violence have occurred since January 1992, many of these appear to be individual acts of revenge rather than part of any systematic terrorist campaign. Although the FMLN remained as an armed force until a staged incremental demilitarization was completed, it continues today essentially as a political grouping within El Salvador rather than as a guerrilla or terrorist force.

By the mid-1990s many of the former leaders of the Front had made the transition to civilian politics. In April 1995 the Front held the second-largest delegation in the Legislative Assembly of El Salvador and its deputies had offices occupying the third floor of the National Congress building, just one floor down from those of the deputies of the ruling Republican National Alliance (**ARENA**) party. Joaquín Villalobos, the former ERP guerrilla leader, organized another social democratic party independent of the FMLN grouping.

During the 16 March 1997 elections the FMLN quadrupled the number of city halls under their control, from 13 to 54 out of 210 municipal governments, and nearly doubled their share of seats in the Salvadoran congress. While ARENA kept 33.3 percent of the votes and retained control of the government, the FMLN won 32.1 percent, giving them 26 deputies to ARENA's 27 deputies in the 84-seat congress. In 1994 the FMLN won 21 seats to ARENA's 39 seat but then lost seven seats when former FMLN deputies split off to form another center-left party which then won only two seats in the 1997 election. On 10 March 1999, when President Bill Clinton addressed the Salvadoran Congress, he was warmly received both by the 26 members of the opposition FMLN party and the 27 members of the ruling ARENA party.

While most of the violence of the civil war is past there have been a few incidents of political killings which appear to be vengeance killings to settle old scores. On 20 February 1997 a machine-gun attack on an FMLN office in a region 20 miles north of San Salvador killed two

FMLN activists. Salvador Sánchez, secretary general of the FMLN, blamed these on remnants of right-wing death squads.

FARAN, AL. *See* KASHMIRI SECESSIONISTS.

FATAH, AL. Fatah, the oldest of the Palestinian guerrilla groups founded in 1957, is currently the dominant member of the **Palestine Liberation Organization** (PLO) and currently also constitutes a political party within the Palestinian Authority. The name Fatah, the Arabic word meaning "conquest," is also the reverse acronym of the name Harakat al Tahrir al Filastiniyya, meaning "Palestinian Liberation Movement." Throughout most of its existence Fatah has been led and dominated by **Yasir Arafat**.

The current goals of Fatah are to seek establishment of an independent, secular Palestinian state on any part of "historic Palestine liberated from Zionist occupation" and to preserve the PLO and the institutions of the Palestinian Authority as the sole legitimate representative and governing institutions of the Palestinian people. Prior to 1974 Fatah aimed to regain all of former mandatory Palestine but began to revise this goal gradually. In 1974 Fatah declared its intention to cease terrorism outside of Israel and the occupied territories. By 15 November 1988, Fatah had persuaded the 19th Palestine National Council (PNC) to declare its acceptance of the right of Israel to exist embodied in UN resolutions 242 and 338 in exchange for Israeli withdrawal from the lands occupied in the 1967 war. On 13 September 1993 a peace accord between the PLO and Israel was signed by PLO Chairman Yasir Arafat and Israeli Prime Minister Yitzhak Rabin, allowing mutual recognition and the eventual creation of an autonomous Palestinian government under PLO auspices within the West Bank and Gaza Strip.

Although Fatah formerly received support from both conservative and radical Arab states, it has lost the support it once enjoyed from Kuwait, Saudi Arabia, and the Persian Gulf emirates, because it openly sided with Iraq during the Gulf War of 1990-1991. While the Soviet Union and eastern bloc nations also formerly provided substantial aid, following the collapse of communist governments in those countries this source likewise has ended, leaving only China and North Korea, which continue to provide some support.

Fatah differs from other Palestinian guerrilla groups in insisting on self-determination for the Palestinian people apart from seeking the goal of Pan-Arab unity. Fatah also has sought to prevent itself, or the PLO, from becoming co-opted into the service of any Arab state. Since self-determination also implies self-initiative and independence of action, Fatah held that the Palestinians needed to undertake armed struggle themselves rather than trusting in the Arab states to deliver them.

Fatah's strong resistance against the Israeli army during the latter's March 1968 raid on the Fatah camp at Karameh, Jordan, boosted the group's prestige in the Palestinian community and encouraged enlistments of young Palestinians into Fatah's ranks. By July 1968 Fatah was admitted to the PLO in its fourth Palestine National Council meeting. At the fifth PNC meeting in February 1969, Fatah took control of the PLO and the history of the two organizations merged.

From 1969 to 1974 PLO-sponsored terrorism was carried out throughout the Middle East and non-Communist nations against Israeli, U.S., West European, and Arab targets. The government of Jordan was especially singled out for terrorists reprisal due to its crackdown and expulsion of the PLO in September 1970, following the confrontation between King Hussein and the PLO over the **Popular Front for the Liberation of Palestine's** (PFLP) **hijacking** of airplanes to Dawson's Field and holding over 400 civilian passengers as hostages. The most notorious Palestinian terrorist group during this period was Fatah's own **Black September**, which was responsible for the massacre of the Israeli athletic team at the **Munich** Summer Olympic games in 1972 as well as several other atrocities.

The 1974 renunciation of terrorism was part of a revision within Fatah of its goals from seeking the liberation of all of Palestine and replacing Israel by a secular democratic state, to the creation of a separate Arab Palestinian state on any "liberated part of Palestine." This last phrase was understood to mean the West Bank and Gaza Strip following an Israeli withdrawal from those territories. While Fatah still believed armed struggle was necessary to achieve its goals, it came to view armed struggle as not sufficient in itself without parallel initiatives on the diplomatic front. This revisionism was anathema to the more radical leftists within the PLO, who then sought to sabotage Fatah's diplomatic initiatives with their own terrorist operations and who also tried to depose Yasir Arafat from the leadership of the PLO both by political and even military means.

After September 1970, Fatah and other PLO groups regrouped in Lebanon from which they staged raids into Israeli territory. In spite of securing increased quantities of more sophisticated weapons, including rockets, tanks, and antiaircraft artillery, the PLO forces have never been able to withstand the Israeli Defense Forces in conventional combat. The large Palestinian presence in southern Lebanon and the tendency of the non-Fatah PLO groups to meddle in Lebanon's internal politics helped precipitate the Lebanese civil war in 1975. This tied up Fatah and the rest of the PLO which at various times found themselves fighting the Christian **Phalange** militia, the Shi'ite **Amal** militia, the Syrians, and occasionally even anti-Fatah Palestinians. The Camp David Accords, which excluded the PLO from any role in the peace negotiations, briefly united the PLO in its denunciations of Egypt and the United States, and opposition to the Camp David agreement became a fixed feature of Fatah rhetoric and diplomacy.

The Israeli invasion of southern Lebanon and siege of Beirut in the summer of 1982 forced the PLO to remove its forces from Lebanon and to move its administrative offices to Tunis. Although Fatah troops were moved to Tunisia, Algeria, and South Yemen, they began infiltrating Lebanon again in 1983. An anti-Arafat revolt among Fatah troops instigated by Syria forced Arafat to leave Lebanon again in 1983. Following the murder by Fatah agents of three Israeli vacationers in Larnaca, Cyprus, on 25 September 1985, the Israeli air force retaliated with a bomb and missile attack on the PLO headquarters south of Tunis in which 60 Palestinians were killed and around 100 wounded. After that event Fatah dispersed its offices and personnel across several countries. One of Fatah's original founders, Khalil al Wazir, who was Yasir Arafat's second-in-command and chief of the Fatah terrorist operations unit responsible for the Larnaca murders (*see* FORCE 17), was **assassinated** by an Israeli commando team on 16 April 1988. The Israelis have claimed that Khalil al Wazir, known also as Abu Jihad, masterminded the triggering of the *intifada* uprising in addition to being "an arch-terrorist steeped in blood." Fatah lost another of its original founders and ranking members when an assassin of **Abu Nidal's Fatah Revolutionary Council** killed Salah Khalaf along with three other PLO officials on 14 January 1991.

Following the eruption of the Palestinian *intifada* on 9 December 1987, Fatah and its opposition within the PLO set aside some of their differences. The 19th PNC meeting in Algiers on 15 November 1988 issued a declaration of independence on behalf of the Palestinians in the West Bank and Gaza Strip. In this conference the PLO formally adopted Fatah's long-standing declaratory policy renouncing terrorism outside of the occupied territories and Israel and also declared its acceptance of United Nations resolutions 242 and 338 contingent on Israel's withdrawal from the occupied territories and the establishment of a Palestinian state there. Although Yasir Arafat reiterated Fatah's and the PLO's renunciation of terrorism and recognition of Israel's right to exist before the UN General Assembly on 13 December 1988, in practice this declaration entailed no willingness to denounce terrorist acts committed in the name of the *intifada* nor subsequent attacks within Israel such as the Fatah-aligned **Palestine Liberation Front**'s raid on the beaches of Tel Aviv on 30 May 1990. Al Fatah further eroded its diplomatic leverage and international goodwill for which it had strived so long by openly siding with Iraq in its August 1990 invasion of Kuwait and its defiance of the United Nations. Despite its repeated military failures and intramural frictions with other members of the PLO, Yasir Arafat's Fatah has maintained its dominant position within the PLO and still accounts for the bulk of the members of the seven security forces that make up the police forces of the Palestinian Authority (PA).

Since the creation of the PA the Fatah group has had to contend with challenges to the PLO from the **Islamic fundamentalist** groups of **Hamas** and **Islamic Jihad in Palestine**, challenges to Arafat's compromises and negotiations with Israel within the PLO from non-Fatah groups, and finally tensions within Fatah itself. On 18 November 1994 Palestinian Authority security forces opened fire on anti-Arafat demonstrations by Hamas supporters in Gaza, the first time Palestinian police had attacked fellow Palestinians under the new PA. Fatah issued a warning to the Hamas and Islamic Jihad groups that they were "crossing the red line" with attacks on the Palestinian Authority and blamed "conspiratorial plans on behalf of foreign parties," apparently referring to Iranian sponsorship of the two Islamic fundamentalist groups. Fatah fighters made up most of the 40,000-strong Palestinian police force which was reorganized in 1995 into an internal security and intelligence force, the elite Presidential Security unit, a coast guard, and a liaison unit for joint Israeli-Palestinian patrols of the autonomous zones. Members of other anti-Fatah factions, such as the Popular Front for the Liberation of Palestine and the **Democratic Front for the Liberation of Palestine** (DPLP) have been arrested by Arafat's security forces for criticizing the 1993 Accords with Israel and the continuing negotiations with Israel over implementation of those agreements.

Following the delay in the proclamation of Palestinian statehood in May 1999 members of the Fatah Party within the Palestinian Authority and the Central Council of the PLO, such as Marwan Barghouti, were growing restive over the slow and tentative pace of the implementation of the accords. Finally in October 1999, following a serious outbreak of armed fighting between rival clans in Ramallah, Arafat ordered a crackdown on illicit sales and possession of firearms arresting even some members of his own security forces in spite of a reported promise by authorities that the weapons of Fatah members themselves would never be confiscated.

Since the revival of the *intifada* following the 28 September 2000 visit to the Temple Mount by Ariel Sharon, the Likud Party leader who susequently was elected Prime Minister, Israel has accused Fatah of instigating and orchestrating the clashes and violence that continued over several months. It should be noted that various dissident Palestinian groups that have opposed Fatah, such as Hamas and Islamic Jihad of Palestine, have played roles in instigating such violence independently of any direction from Fatah.

FATAH REVOLUTIONARY COUNCIL (FRC). Also referred to by Western intelligence and law enforcement agencies as the Abu Nidal Organization, the Fatah Revolutionary Council is a Palestinian terrorist group founded in 1974 and led by Sabri Khalil al Banna, known by his nom de guerre of **Abu Nidal**, meaning "Father of the Struggle." This group was once considered the most dangerous terrorist organization in the 1990s and was credited with over 100 major terrorist attacks killing 280 and wounding over 600 others in attacks from 1974 to 1991. The FRC is an umbrella group encompassing different groups, or at least using different names depending on the **targets**. The FRC is also known as the Arab Revolutionary Council but chooses to claim credit for its actions under the names of the Arab Revolutionary Brigades, the Revolutionary Organization of Socialist Muslims when claiming credit for attacks on British targets, **Black June** when claiming credit for attacks on Jordanian targets, the **Black September Organization**, and possibly the "Peace Conquerors." Altogether these groups number several hundred. The use of these names helps to confuse opponents about Abu Nidal and his group; for example, witness the use of the "Fatah Revolutionary Council," which has no connection with Fatah, or the use of "Black September" after 1981 when the original organization of the same name had been disbanded seven years earlier.

A former member of **Fatah**, Abu Nidal broke with both Fatah and the rest of the **Palestine Liberation Organization** (PLO) in 1974 and formed the FRC as an alternative organization. The FRC seeks a total nationalist and social revolution not only to totally destroy Israel in favor of a Palestinian state but also to rid the Palestinians of those whom Abu Nidal regards as compromisers and reactionaries, and to create a total revolution throughout the Arab world. The FRC has had a number of state sponsors, having been sponsored by Iraq from 1974 until 1983, then Syria until 1987, and then Libya from 1987 until 1997, and after a brief limited cooperation with Egypt from 1997 to 1998, the FRC returned to Iraq in December 1998 where it again has state sponsorship. Such states have eventually found that the cost in international opprobrium for aiding and abetting Abu Nidal far exceeded the benefits obtained from sponsoring such a client. Yet a greater concern for them has been the irascibility and waywardness of Abu Nidal himself, who has remained beholden to no one and is too apt to turn against his erstwhile sponsors.

Despite its radical revolutionary rhetoric, the FRC in later years appeared to be pursuing terrorism almost as an end in itself and also showed an **entrepreneurial** willingness to hire itself out without regard to the politics of its patrons. While one-third of its resources came from Arab states, the FRC has also been able to derive another third of its income from extortion and another third from a consortium of businesses throughout the world, many of which may be legitimate by themselves but all of which function as a support network for FRC operations. In many respects the FRC is becoming more like an organized crime syndicate, which may perpetuate itself even after the demise of Abu Nidal regardless of the future geopolitical complexion of the Middle East. During the 1980s the FRC amassed assets through its commercial organizations totaling about $400 million but in 1995 many of these assets were frozen by President Bill Clinton as part of an effort to prevent fund-raising within the United States by terrorist groups and front organizations for financing terrorism.

Among the more notorious acts of the FRC were the following: the attempted **assassination** of Israeli Ambassador to Great Britain, Shlomo Argov, on 3 June 1982 in the name of Black June; the 23 November 1985 **hijacking** of EgyptAir Flight 648 scheduled from Athens to Cairo instead to Malta, where the hijacker Muhammad Ali Rezaq shot two Israeli and three American passengers, dumping their bodies on the runway. When Egyptian commandoes made a rescue attempt on 24 November 1985 Rezaq escaped while 58 passengers were shot or burned to death. The 27 December 1985 massacres of travelers at the Rome and Vienna airports killed 18 people and wounded 60 others; the 6 September 1986 attack was on the Neve Shalom synagogue in Istanbul, in which two gunmen murdered and mutilated 21 people. As an example of the extreme waywardness and unpredictability of the FRC, the same group that directed a **suicide** car bomber to strike the Israeli embassy in Cyprus on 11 May 1988, in revenge for Israel's assassination of PLO official Wazir al Khalil, is itself suspected of having assassinated another PLO official, Salah Khalaf, along with three other PLO officials on 14 January 1991.

The FRC was identified as having committed 44 major terrorist acts in the period from 1980-1987, of which 11 were assassinations, seven **bombings** and one a car bombing. In addition, using the name of the "Black September Organization," it carried out 17 more actions in the period from 1981-1987, of which six were assassinations, four bombings, and one a car bombing. Using the name of the "Arab Revolutionary Brigades" it committed another 15 actions from 1982-1986, of which six were assassinations, five bombings, and one a car bombing. Under the name of the "Revolutionary Movement of Socialist Muslims" it committed another 11 actions from 1984-1985 including four bombings, three **kidnappings**, and two assassinations. Using the Black June group it committed another five actions from 1981-1986, including two assassinations and one bombing. Reports indicated that during the latter part of 1988, Abu Nidal carried out a massive purge of his organization, killing around 100 former colleagues suspected of treachery. In July 1998 Abu Nidal was nearly deposed as leader of the FRC by 10 dissidents but he survived this attempt by co-opting the protection of the Egyptian security service who placed him under protective detention while deporting the dissidents.

On 15 July 1993 an FBI arrest team caught Muhammad Ali Rezaq, the hijacker of EgyptAir Flight 648, in Lagos, Nigeria, and returned him to the United States to face trial on air piracy charges. On 17 June 1996 the trial of Rezaq began in Washington, D.C., and on 7 October 1996 he was convicted and sentenced to life in prison.

FATHERLAND AND LIBERTY. The Chilean group Patria y Libertad was organized in 1971 as an antistate group, with alleged help from the United States, to oppose the Salvadore Allende government in Chile. The leader was an attorney, Pablo Rodriguez Grez, known also as "*el jefe*." Although the allegation of funding by the Central Intelligence Agency (CIA) for this group was never substantiated, one of the most active covert operations specialists in the group was a former CIA agent, Michael Townley, who would later arrange for the murder of Orlando Letelier in 1976 as well as the murder of Bernardo Leighton, among others. At its height the group had 3,500 members and 20 of them, known as the "Guerrilleros Nacionalistas," formed a covert operations unit commanded by Guillermo Burnster Thiese and Rene Claverie Barbet. Fatherland and Liberty had around 50 specialized units with jamming equipment used to disrupt the communications of the national police and army units loyal to the Allende regime.

This group conducted **bombings** and subversive radio broadcasts. Roberto Thieme joined in May 1971 in charge of propaganda and soon became the general secretary of the organization. On 29 June 1971 they attacked the offices of the magazine *La Moneda* and occupied the Defense Ministry building, apparently with the help of Army Commander General Carlos Prats. The group is also credited with the **assassination** of Allende's closest aid, Arturo Arraya. On 12 September 1973, the day after the coup that toppled Allende, the group dissolved itself. In 1980 they were pardoned in connection with the murder of Arturo Arraya.

FATWA. Arabic term designating a ruling on a matter according to Islamic law issued by a competent specialist on Islamic law, usually known as an *'alim* ("learned man," plural: *'ulama*) or as a *mujtahid*, who is a pious Muslim and not acting in self-interest or under coercion. The fatwa can be on any matter of Islamic law, from simple and mundane matters, such as how one may determine the correct times for the obligatory prayers, to weighty matters of finance, state, and warfare. Recently the term *fatwa* has been mentioned in connection with the late **Ayatollah Khomeini**'s fatwa anathematizing Salman Rushdie and sentencing him to death, and also in connection with **Osama bin Laden**'s publication of an alleged fatwa authorizing unlimited warfare against American citizens everywhere by pious Muslims.

The specific type of fatwa issued by Khomeini against Rushdie, also called a *takfir*, pronounces a Muslim to have become an apostate, and therefore liable to the death penalty according to traditional Islamic law. Ordinarily the person who has been put under this ban can have it lifted by openly repenting of his apostasy and declaring his faith in Islam again. Militant Islamic groups in Egypt have been using fatwas of *takfirs* against opponents recently to destroy the family life of their opponents, since a Muslim wife may no longer have sexual relations with her husband once he has been put under the ban of *takfir*.

The other alleged fatwa was used to justify the declaration of a state of general *jihad* as an individual obligation upon every Muslim. Such fatwas may only be issued by a competent religious authority and in the case of jihad this would require a high-ranking Islamic authority, such as the rahbar, or Supreme Religious Leader, in Iran, or perhaps the Sheikh al Azhar in Egypt. The issuance of such an alleged fatwa by a personage as obscure as bin Laden is presumptuous and without credibility.

FEDAYEEN, alternate spelling, **FIDA'IYIN.** Arabic plural of *Fida'i*, also, *Fedayan*, Persian plural of *Fida'i* "one who offers (self-sacrifice)," that is, one who offers himself sacrificially in a holy struggle. This name has been adopted by at least four different groups in the history of terrorism.

1. The Isma'ili Fedayeen. In the 11th and 12th centuries Isma'ili Shi'ite activists in southwest Asia organized corps of **assassins** willing to undertake attacks against Sunni rulers in which the assassin was certain to be killed or captured. To counter the awe and respect these bold attacks created among the common people, apologists of the Abbasid dynasty targeted by the Isma'ilis claimed that the attackers were really "Hashshishin," those under the influence of hashish. This term became the source of the word "assassin." These Fedayeen continued to operate for over a century, using the mountainous region around Alamut in central Iran as their base of operations, until they were exterminated by the invading Mongol armies.

2. The Fedayan-i Islam. An Iranian terrorist group founded by the Shi'ite junior clergyman Navab Safavi in 1944 to kill Iranian intellectuals and politicians held to be responsible for the decline of Islam in Iran. The Fedayan began with the dramatic killing of the secularist historian Ahmad Kasravi in 1946 and then followed up with the killings of the Minister of Court Hazhir, Prime Minister Razmara, and attempted assassinations of Prime Minister 'Ala and Shah Muhammad Reza Pahlavi. The Iranian security police later smashed the Fedayan organization in 1956, executing its main members, including Navab

Safavi. As late as 1965, however, the assassination of Prime Minister Alam was carried out by a self-proclaimed member of the Fedayan. Following the 1979 revolution in Iran, survivors of the group reconstituted themselves openly as a minor Islamic political party in Iran. Members of this group appear to have been behind the attempted assassination of Iraqi Vice President Tariq 'Aziz on 1 April 1980. In November 1998 the Fedayan emerged from years of obscurity by attacking a bus with 13 American tourists in downtown Tehran with stones and iron rods, some of whom suffered minor cuts from flying glass. The Fedayan then issued a communiqué denouncing the Americans as "U.S. spies" and denouncing the government of President Muhammad Khatami for its encouragement of cultural exchanges between Americans and Iranians.

3. The Palestinian Fedayeen. With the rise in Palestinian terrorist and guerrilla attacks on Israel and Israeli targets, the term *Fedayeen* came to be used by Palestinians to designate guerrilla fighters attacking Israel without being exclusively reserved for the fighters of any single Palestinian group. The organizations that sponsor Fedayeen fighters dominate the **Palestine Liberation Organization** (PLO) and are known as *tanzimat*.

4. The Fedayan-e Khalq-e Iran. The "People's Fedayan of Iran" was a Marxist guerrilla group that split from the Iranian Communist Party in 1963. Its members were mainly university students who received guerrilla training in PLO camps in Lebanon and South Yemen. On 8 February 1971 the Fedayan tried to start a guerrilla war against the Iranian government in the forested regions around Siahkhal in Gilan Province on the Caspian Sea but were crushed by regular army troops. The survivors of the Siahkhal affair tried then to organize urban guerrilla warfare but accomplished little until the revolution of 1978-1979 gave them the opportunity to participate in street fighting and attacks on police and army barracks. Following the victory of the revolution the Fedayan's open following grew to include as many as 50,000 adherents. In the face of widespread popular support for the regime of the **Ayatollah Khomeini**, the Fedayan temporized in the mistaken expectation that the situation would ripen in favor of another revolution along Marxist lines. This temporizing cost the Fedayan the support of disaffected Iranian middle-class students and intellectuals who were attracted instead to the rival **Mujahideen-**

e Khalq, which took a more forthright stand against the clerical regime.

Internal dissent over their relationship with the clerical regime led to a split into a minority faction that advocated armed struggle with the regime and a majority faction that continued to temporize. With the crackdown on the Mujahideen in June 1981, other armed leftist groups, such as the Fedayan, were crushed as well. Many surviving Fedayan joined other leftists in an abortive guerrilla campaign in the region of Amol near the Caspian Sea in which, in a curious replay of the Siahkhal affair of the previous decade, they were again crushed on 9 November 1981 by army troops and Islamic Revolutionary Guards.

FIGHT-OR-FLIGHT RESPONSE. This is the physiological response of humans and animals to situations of danger involving a number of bodily responses preparing one either to flee or else to confront and fight the source of danger. These include: Increase in heart rate, increase in blood pressure, blood volume changes, increase in electro-conductivity of the skin due in part to increased perspiration, increased muscular tension, and changes in brain wave activity reflecting increased alertness. The cardiovascular and respiratory systems operate with greater efficiency and more sugar is released into the bloodstream in preparation for physical exertion. During fight-or-flight episodes the affected individuals often exhibit feats of strength that they ordinarily could not do or else become unaware of pain from wounds or broken bones. Often after experiencing these life-threatening situations people report that they felt curiously disconnected from their actions and that they felt as if they were observing themselves reacting but not controlling their actions in a conscious and deliberative manner. In fact in the critical moments one is acting almost by reflex and ordinarily deliberative processes appear to be suspended.

The fight-or-flight response may help to explain how individuals are attracted toward political violence and also explain some of the behavior of terrorist groups. According to the **physiological model** of terrorist **contagion** susceptible individuals experience a thrill from watching and from reenacting a violent or dangerous act. By coming out of the fight-or-flight situation safe or victorious the person then experiences a feeling of well-being and power. Similarly for many isolated **cellular groups** their best moments are found in the thick of carrying out an attack, whether a hold-up, **kidnapping**, or successful assault.

Such groups cope very poorly with prolonged periods of inactivity or routine. The implication for law enforcement and counterterrorism situation managers is that pursuing cellular groups, like the former **Symbionese Liberation Army**, with state of siege tactics, or else confronting terrorists in a hostage-barricade situation with deadlines or ponderous open assaults may prove counterproductive. In the heat of the flight-or-flight situation the terrorists react quickly, rational deliberation ceases, and they are more apt to carry out their threatened actions.

Instead of "putting the heat on" underground groups, law enforcement may be better advised to maintain a quiet vigilance in the expectation that the boredom of clandestine inactivity will lead terrorist group members to make a mistake and reveal themselves. Similarly in a hostage-barricade situation the hostage negotiators and rescue units would be better advised to maintain a quiet siege and let inactivity render the hostage takers torpid and more vulnerable to a sudden, surprise rescue attempt or else more apt to surrender themselves. An example of the former would be the rescue attempt in the **Peruvian Japanese embassy hostage crisis** and an example of the latter was the successful conclusion of the FBI siege of the **Freemen** compound in Montana. *See also* CONTAGION EFFECT; PHYSIOLOGICAL MODEL OF TERRORIST CONTAGION.

FIGHTING COMMUNIST ORGANIZATIONS (FCOs). *See* ANARCHISTIC LEFTIST TERRORISM.

FORCE 17. Name of internal security unit of **al Fatah** formed in the early 1970s, charged with providing personal security for **Yasir Arafat** and other Fatah leaders, enforcing discipline within the **Palestine Liberation Organization** (PLO) by arresting and punishing dissidents and criminals, and with undertaking active measures against non-Palestinians threatening PLO interests. Within the PLO, viewed as an extraterritorial government of the Palestinians, Force 17 acted as a tool of state repression or terror while in its operations against non-Palestinians it may be regarded simply as an extension of Fatah. Force 17 was commanded by Khalil al Wazir until he was **assassinated** by an Israeli commando team on 16 April 1988.

During the early 1970s Force 17 would regulate the behavior of Palestinian guerrillas in Lebanon to prevent abuses against Lebanese nationals that might jeopardize PLO relations with the Lebanese government. On 17 April 1978 Force 17 arrested around 100 members of **Abu Nidal's Fatah Revolutionary Council**, then backed by Iraq, in southern Lebanon to prevent them from disrupting a cease-fire with the Israeli Defense Forces. In August 1987 and May 1989 two Force 17 commanders were assassinated in feuding between Fatah loyalists and Syrian-backed dissidents.

Force 17's entry into externally directed terrorism dates from 25 September 1985, when Fatah agents seized and killed three Israelis in Larnaca, Cyprus, whom they suspected to be Mossad agents. This occasioned Israel's retaliatory air raid on the PLO headquarters in Tunis on 1 October 1985 in which 60 Palestinians were killed and 100 wounded. Afterward Force 17 claimed responsibility for several attacks occurring within Israel: on 2 February 1986, a bus **bombing** in Jerusalem that injured six people; on 17 September 1986, throwing of explosives into the El Al offices in Tel Aviv; on 14 November 1986, a stabbing death of a Yeshiva student in Jerusalem; on 28 June 1987, the bombing of a popular beach near Haifa, wounding a woman and child; and on 27 November 1987, the murder of two agents of Shin Bet, Israel's internal security service, who had their throats slashed. These actions bear close resemblance to the sorts of apparently random, spontaneous attacks occurring within Israel since the beginning of the *intifada* uprising on 9 December 1987. Israeli authorities have maintained that Khalil al Wazir was actually the mastermind behind the *intifada*.

Since the 13 September 1993 Peace Accord Force 17 is not known to have engaged in terrorist actions against Israel or other external targets. However it is believed to have engaged in numerous acts of repression directed at Palestinians. The Palestinian human rights activist Bassam Eid, speaking in London on 29 January 1997, claimed that while he was working with the Israeli human rights group, B'tselem, in 1996 he had been **kidnapped** by Force 17 members from his Jerusalem home and threatened by them. According to him arbitrary arrest and torture of Palestinian dissidents by Force 17 had left many of them too frightened to speak out against abuses of power by Yasir Arafat. On 30 June 1997 Force 17 reportedly tortured Nasser Abed Radwan to death in Gaza while he was being detained without charges. A Palestinian Authority (PA) military tribunal sentenced three of the Force 17 guards to death and the other three to prison terms from six months to five years. In March 1998 Force 17 was involved in a reported in-house purge within the PA of a Palestinian military leader suspected of involvement in a plot to depose Arafat as leader of the PLO and PA.

Under the new Palestinian Authority the current name for Force 17 is the Palestinian Authority Presidential Security Unit, which has the mission of protecting Yasir Arafat, and other PA dignitaries, as well as officiating at ceremonial functions. On 14 December 1998 when President Bill Clinton arrived at the Gaza International Airport under PA authority, he was greeted by a Force 17 honor guard playing the "Star-Spangled Banner."

FOREIGN INTELLIGENCE SURVEILLANCE ACT OF 1978. This act, which is found in U.S. Code, Title 50, Chapter 36, Sub I—Foreign Intelligence and Electronic Surveillance, and is also known as Public Law 95-511, permits electronic surveillance of individuals or groups when there is probable cause to believe that these persons or groups are providing financial aid or other material assistance on behalf of a foreign state or group furthering international terrorism.

FRANCIA. The Front d'Action Nouvelle Contre l'Indépendence et l'Autonomie (New Action Front Against Independence and Autonomy) was a nonstate group of French settlers on the island of Corsica with the limited aim of opposing the **National Front for the Liberation of Corsica** (FNLC). The group was formed in 1978 mainly of French settlers displaced from Algeria. In 1979 it conducted about 40 attacks against suspected FNLC members. In August 1980 a leader of FRANCIA, Yannick Leonelli, was arrested.

FRAPH. French acronym for Front Révolutionnaire pour l'Avancement et le Progrès Haitien, or Revolutionary Front for the Advancement and Progress of Haiti, a state-run **death squad** used to repress enemies of the military junta that overthrew President Jean-Bertrand Aristide in 1991. When the junta led by Lieutenant General Raoul Cédras seized power, it organized the FRAPH movement in 1991 as a death squad for dealing with supporters of Aristide and anyone else who would oppose their rule. FRAPH included various elements including members of the **Tonton Macoutes** of the former ruling Duvalier family.

FRAPH first gained international notice when members of this group prevented the docking in Port-au-Prince in October 1993 of the U.S.S. *Harlan*, so delaying for another year the restoration of President Aristide to power in Haiti by U.S. military intervention. When the junta faced the possibility of U.S. intervention later in 1994 it armed about 30,000 civilians to form a "volunteer" force to complement the 7,000 regular troops of the Haitian armed forces. On 28 August 1994 a close friend of Aristide, Rev. Jean-Marie Vincent, was murdered by these militia members who were also known as "attachés."

During the period of military rule from 1991 to 1994 about 5,000 people were killed, mainly by pro-junta death squads of which FRAPH was the largest and most powerful. FRAPH used machetes, firebombings, and sometimes grenades to kill individuals or demonstrators opposing the junta. In early October 1994 FRAPH attacked pro-Aristide crowds, killing demonstrators in full view of U.S. warships in the harbor of Port-au-Prince with impunity. Following the FRAPH murder of the deputy mayor of Mirebalais on 4 November 1994 death squad activity by the group appeared to cease.

Debriefing of Haitian refugees who had belonged to FRAPH revealed systematic use of murder and rape against its victims which new FRAPH members were expected to watch and later to participate in as part of their initiation. Later it was learned that the leader of FRAPH, Emmanuel "Toto" Constant, had actually been a CIA informant who continued on its payroll until the spring of 1994, long after his group had organized the October 1993 demonstrations blocking U.S. naval vessels from landing in Port-au-Prince. A review of declassified State Department and Defense Department cables revealed that U.S. defense and intelligence officials had strongly distrusted Aristide and sought to protect their informants within the FRAPH organization in the event of Aristide's return to power. Shortly after U.S. troops landed in Haiti in October 1994 they raided the FRAPH headquarters, seizing over 150,000 pages of documents which were removed to the United States and never returned to Haiti despite the demands of the Aristide government. Later Emmanuel Constant, who was found hiding in Queens, New York, was arrested on 10 May 1995 but not deported to Haiti. Following extensive revelations of human rights abuses by FRAPH the United States eventually declared FRAPH to be a terrorist organization.

FREE SOUTH MOLUCCAN YOUTH ORGANIZATION. The Free South Moluccan Youth Organization, also called the South Moluccan Suicide Commando, was a nonstate-sponsored revolutionary nationalist group that used terrorism to force the Netherlands to pressure Indonesia to restore an independent South Moluccan homeland. During the Indonesian war for independence, the South Moluccans, who had been converted to Christianity by the Dutch, fought on the side of the Netherlands on their understanding that they would afterward have their own independent state. An Indonesian victory prevented the Netherlands from fulfilling this promise and instead the South Moluccan allies of the Dutch were allowed to settle in the Netherlands as refugees. Most of the members of these groups came from a younger second generation of alienated South Moluccans who lacked any outside state sponsorship.

On 2 December 1975 some seven Moluccan youths armed with automatic pistols seized a passenger train in Beilen, taking over 70 passengers hostage and killing one passenger and the train's engineer. The train was besieged by over 1,000 Dutch Marines and police. On the fourth day of the siege the terrorists killed another passenger after the Dutch government announced its refusal of the group's demands. In the face of the government's refusal to waiver and due to the severe cold in the unheated train cars, the terrorists surrendered on 14 December. During the siege, several passengers escaped while several others were released by their captors, particularly elderly or ill passengers.

On 4 December seven other members of the same group seized the Indonesian consulate in Amsterdam, also taking as hostages several schoolchildren within a classroom in the building. Three consular employees escaped by lowering themselves from the second story, but a fourth fell to his death. By 19 December 1975 all the hostages in this siege were also released.

On 23 May 1977 another passenger train **hijacking** and hostage seizure took place in Assen in which 13 Moluccans seized a train with 85 passengers. It lasted 19 days. In addition to calls for Moluccan independence, these terrorists also demanded the freeing of their comrades who had been tried and jailed for the Beilen incident. On 11 June Dutch Marines stormed the train, killing all the terrorists as well as two passengers who had bolted when the shooting began. On the same day the Assen train was seized, four other members of the same group seized a primary school in Bovinsmilde, taking 105 children and six teachers hostage. All of the children and one sick teacher were released by 26 May. Dutch Marines stormed the school on 11 June, seizing the four terrorists and freeing the remaining teachers.

In July 1975 several Moluccans were convicted for conspiracy to **kidnap** Queen Juliana and other members of the Dutch royal family.

These incidents provoked anti-Moluccan backlashes among the Dutch population while the killings of the terrorists also aggravated the anti-Dutch sentiments among the exiled Moluccan community.

FREEMEN. Antistate right-wing U.S. domestic extremists opposed to the current monetary, banking, and taxation system who form part of the right-wing extremist movement in the United States associated with the **militia movement**. The Freemen of Montana, who were besieged by the FBI for 81 days outside the small town of Jordan, Montana, are just one of several groups scattered throughout the United States calling themselves "Freemen." Although the media called them the "Militia of Montana," these groups were not identical but had overlapping memberships. The Militia of Montana group is led by John Trochman who played no role in the Freeman siege outside Jordan, Montana.

Various Freemen also call themselves the "Preamble People," meaning the "people" mentioned within the Preamble of the U.S. Constitution who "ordained and established" the original seven articles of the Constitution. Their belief is that as the United States, as well as the various state and local governments, derived their authority and sovereignty from the people whose consent created the constitutional order and federalist system these same people could withdraw their consent to be governed by those governmental forms so resuming their primordial status as "sovereign American nationals" which includes only "white Christian men." The "preamble people" are held to be the white, Anglo-Saxon, Christian settlers of the British colonies or their descendants while the nonwhite or non-Christian U.S. citizens are merely "Fourteenth Amendment" citizens who have no prior claim to be "sovereign, natural citizens."

The Freemen hold that income taxes, requirements for drivers licenses, and Social Security documentation are legally binding on the Fourteenth Amendment citizens but not legally binding on themselves. They also assert that they may remove themselves from the jurisdiction of state and federal authorities merely by filing a declaration with the local County Clerk's Office that they are sovereign citizens. Such attempts to ignore or evade legal obligations have led Freemen into confrontation with state and federal authorities, to threats of violence, and into actual armed confrontation with law enforcement and judicial authorities. When faced with summonses to appear before state or federal courts on charges of tax evasion or bank fraud Freemen have retaliated by convening so-called **Common Law Courts** which then issue pseudo-legal documents purporting to be summonses, liens, restraining orders, and the like against county sheriffs and prosecutors as well as against federal officials. Often these proceedings threaten officials with death by hanging if they do not "cease and desist."

Most of the adherents of the Freemen movement appear to be western farmers or ranchers who have overextended themselves with borrowing to run their farms. The Freemen and **Posse Comitatus** movements were a populist reaction to the economic plight of these small farmers in which the adherents convinced themselves that they had been victimized by an unjust economic and political system. These beliefs were often reinforced by anti-Semitic prejudices to the effect that the banking system was being manipulated by Jewish groups deliberately to impoverish white, Christian, American farmers. By rejecting the monetary system as fraudulent, since it was no longer based on the gold standard, the Freemen rationalized their refusals to repay loans or to pay taxes. In a bizarre twist the Freemen rationalized that as "sovereign citizens," not only could they convene their own common-law courts to threaten officials but also that they were equally entitled to issue their own paper monetary documents to pay for trucks and farm equipment and the like.

Although on 19 May 1995 a federal grand jury had indicted Freemen leaders LeRoy Schweitzer and Daniel E. Petersen, Jr., along with 10 other Freemen, for fraudulent check and money orders, authorities did not move to arrest them immediately for fear that the armed Freemen would fight back and create another Ruby Ridge-style confrontation with likely loss of life and probable public backlash against federal officials. Following these indictments about 21 Freemen of Montana assembled themselves in a 960-acre wheat farm and sheep ranch outside of Jordan, Montana, which had been sold due to foreclosure but which they occupied and then declared to be "Justus Township."

When Schweitzer and Petersen left the ranch on 25 March 1996 they were arrested by the FBI and the remaining Freemen remained in the ranch where they were surrounded by FBI teams. The "soft siege" of this compound involved 640 FBI agents and lasted 81 days and cost about $7.5 million. On June 13 after several women and children left the compound over the course of the 81-day siege, the last 16 Freemen surrendered to officials.

Schweitzer and Petersen had been giving seminars to over 800 persons, for $100 a head, on how to manufacture fraudulent financial instruments. Schweitzer and Petersen had learned the Freemen doctrine and check-kiting techniques from Roy Schwasinger of Ft. Collins, Colorado, leader of the "We the People" group, which has popularized the Freemen movement and the Common Law Courts. Using what some Montana officials have called "paper terrorism" the Freemen would harass law enforcement and tax officials by filing phoney liens against their properties and those of their relatives which often did affect their credit ratings.

On 8 July 1998 a federal grand jury issued indictments against nine of the Freemen for banking fraud conspiracy. By March 1996 the Freemen had tried to pass 3,432 bogus checks with total face value of $15.5 billion most having been rejected but up to $1.8 million worth having been accepted in the forms of money orders, certified bankers checks, comptroller warrants, or lien drafts. On 19 November 1998 these nine members were convicted for conspiracy, bank fraud, threatening federal judges, mail fraud, wire fraud, illegal possession of firearms, and interstate transportation of stolen property. In addition members of the group had robbed ABC and NBC news crews of their cameras during attempts to interview them.

Apart from the highly publicized Montana siege other evidence of the impact of the Freeman movement has emerged with investigations in 23 states by January 1997 of over 151 persons with Freemen ties involved in similar check-kiting schemes. One of the Freeman arrested at Jordan, Russell D. Landers, was convicted in North Carolina in February 1997 on fraud and conspiracy charges.

FREEZING OF ASSETS/SEQUESTRATION. Among the law enforcement powers available to counter domestic and international terrorists there are options of civil and criminal forfeiture to seize properties, buildings, airplanes, vehicles, or weapons which have been used for criminal purposes. Ordinarily these sanctions have been used to combat drug-trafficking but in principle these could be applied to punish any form of criminal enterprise, including terrorism.

On 4 June 1993 President Bill Clinton invoked provisions of the Immigration and Nationality Act, (Section 212(f)), and the International Emergency Economic Powers Act (IEEPA), known also as Public Law No. 95-223 (1977), Title 50 U.S. Code Sections 1701-6, to strengthen sanctions against Haiti dating back to 1991, including freezing the personal assets of specially designated nationals who were acting for or on behalf of the Haitian military junta or making material contributions to that regime. On 3 December 1993 the President announced tightened economic sanctions against Libya in accordance with UN Security Council Resolution 883 of 11 November 1993, which included further a freeze on Libyan government assets held in U.S. banks.

On 23 January 1995 by Executive Order 12947 President Clinton declared a national emergency and invoked his broad powers under the IEEPA to block the assets and prohibit transactions of persons determined to have committed or present a significant risk of committing acts of violence that would disrupt the Middle East peace process, and he blocked transactions by U.S. persons with these foreign persons. Regulations implementing this Executive Order were issued on 2 February 1996 [61 Fed. Reg 3,805 (1996)]. This Executive Order blocked the assets of the **Islamic Jihad in Palestine**, **Hamas**, and **Abu Nidal** organizations, among others, as well as assets of various front groups that had been established in the United States for the purposes of gathering funds for such groups under charitable and educational pretenses.

Beyond these presidential actions the Congress and President passed the **Antiterrorism and Effective Death Penalty Act of 1996** which, in Section 302, forbade fund-raising and other material support for organizations designated as terrorist groups or found to engage in activities defined as terrorist activities under U.S. law, and Section 303 criminalizes knowingly providing, or attempting to provide, material support to a foreign terrorist group. Section 303 also requires financial institutions to freeze the funds of any person or group involved in funding those terrorist groups.

Following the **World Trade Center and Pentagon attacks of 11 September 2001** the administation of President George W. Bush froze the assets of over 60 individuals and firms beleived to have ties to terrorist groups. On 7 November 2001 the assets of the Al Barakat and al Taqwa financial networks were seized as they were beleived to have direct ties to the **al Qa'eda** network of **Osama bin Laden**, the alleged principals behind the 11 September attacks.

FRUSTRATION-AGGRESSION THEORY. Psychological theory used to explain aggressive behavior. In studies of animal behavior Ivan Pavlov induced conditioned responses in dogs to respond to a certain stimulus, namely a circle, in order to obtain food. Whenever the dog responded to the wrong stimulus, namely an ellipse, it would receive no food. Not surprisingly his experimental animals learned to distinguish between circles and ellipses. However when Pavlov began to display ambiguous stimuli, circles that were slightly flattened at opposite ends or else ellipses that were almost circular, some animals responded with whimpering and others with snarling and anger. Frustration theory predicts that an individual will respond with stress and aggression whenever there is an "interference with the occurrence of an instigated goal-response at its proper time in the behavior sequence" (Dollard et al., 1939).

Many common-sense explanations of civil unrest or political violence often rely on some version of the frustration-aggression theory. However, to be a more credible description or explanation of human behavior the theory needs to incorporate notions of expectations, a standard of comparison between an actual and preferred state of affairs, and some notions of just rewards. In this more elaborate form one moves from a crude frustration-aggression model to a **relative deprivation** model.

- G -

GAL. *See* ANTITERRORIST LIBERATION GROUPS.

GENEVA PROTOCOL OF 1925. *See* WEAPONS OF MASS DESTRUCTION.

GENOCIDE. Genocide usually refers to attempts to destroy a national, ethnic, religious, or racial group by killing off members of the group. Specific instances of genocide can either be classed as **war crimes** or else as terrorist acts depending on the identity and motives of the perpetrator. The United Nations Convention on Prevention and Punishment of the Crime of Genocide defined genocide as a punishable offense in 1946, and this became effective treaty law in 1951. According to this convention genocide includes "any of the following acts committed with intent to destroy, in whole or in part, a national, ethnic, racial or religious group, such as: a) killing members of the group; b) causing serious bodily or mental harm to members of the group; c) deliberately inflicting on the group conditions of life calculated to bring about its physical destruction in whole or in part; d) imposing measures intended to prevent births within the group; e) transferring children of the group to another group."

Generally when such actions are carried out by the military forces of a recognized **belligerent** these would be considered war crimes. When carried out by nonstate groups they would be considered terrorist acts and when carried out by a nation-state against its own subjects or citizens it would be considered a form of **state terror**. If the object of the genocide is actually to physically annihilate a group altogether then it would be considered a form of **democide**, i.e., if the group being annihilated is the direct and only ultimate target of the action which is undertaken as an end in itself rather than to send a message to other potentially targeted groups. If the object of the genocide campaign is merely to remove or exile a group inconvenient to the nationalist or territorial aspirations of the regime, or else to send a message to other groups, then such genocide would be a form of terrorism or state terror. The Nazi campaign against the Jews, which was intended to exterminate all Jews worldwide in the event of a German victory in World War II and which was undertaken with great secrecy, is an example of pure genocide as an end in itself. The Nazi liquidation of the Czech village of Lidice in retaliation for the assistance that the villagers gave to the **assassins** of the Nazi governor of occupied Bohemia was meant to warn all potential anti-Nazi partisans against collaborating with the Allies and so is an instance of terrorist genocide.

Ethnic cleansing, a term that became current in the Croatian and Bosnian wars for independence from Yugoslavia in the early 1990s, refers to a limited form of genocide aimed at driving out members of a rival ethnic group so that one's own ethnic group can lay exclusive claim to that territory. When carried out by paramilitary groups or civilians it is a form of terrorism and when carried out by regular army units, as in the attempted Yugoslavian "Operation Horseshoe" in Kosovo in late 1998 and early 1999, it could be considered a form of state terror.

GEORGE JACKSON BRIGADE. The George Jackson Brigade, active in the northwestern United States from the mid- to late 1970s, had revolutionary pretensions of being a militant left-wing organization, naming itself after a black militant killed at San Quentin prison during rioting on 21 August 1971. Its record of activities appeared more criminal and opportunistic than coherently revolutionary, consisting of several small-scale thefts and **bombings** in Oregon and Washington state.

GRAY AREA PHENOMENON. Term devised by the French sociologist of political violence, Xavier Raufer, to describe the spread of ungovernability in politically unstable nations that has led to other international problems in the post-Cold War era. Although many analysts, such as Aaron Wildavsky, Max Singer, and Francis Fukuyama, believed that the post-Cold War era would herald a slow but inevitable spread of democratization, free market economic systems, and development of a vibrant, autonomous civil society in the developing nations of the world, Raufer argued instead that the weakness of the nation-state system in many postcolonial countries, the lack of legitimacy of many of the authoritarian regimes, and the resurgence of nationalist-separatist and religious fundamentalist movements would create more instability in such states. Large areas of these states would become ungovernable "gray areas" and fall under the control of terrorist groups, criminal syndicates, or regional warlords, who would use these as bases for activities that would impact neighboring nations as well as the developed liberal democracies.

The takeover of Somalia by regional warlords, the takeover of Afghanistan by militant Muslim religious seminary students, known as **Taliban**, and the takeover of large areas of Colombia either by drug cartels or by leftist groups, such as the **Revolutionary Armed Forces of Colombia** (FARC), and the recent conflicts in Congo and Sierra Leone are examples of such gray area phenomena.

GRAY WOLVES. The Bozkurtlar formed the university student and youth wing of the National Action Party (NAP), a secular, Pan-Turkist party of the extreme right-wing of Turkish politics. Originally a student group organized in the late 1960s to oppose Marxist-Leninist students in the universities of Turkey, once the Gray Wolves were put under the direction of NAP leader Col. Alparslan Türkes in 1976 they turned into a right-wing **death squad**. By 1980 the group was reputed to have committed 694 political murders. Since Türkes became Deputy Prime Minister in a coalition government that included the NAP, the Gray Wolves may be regarded as having been a quasi-state-sponsored repressive group.

Türkes ran two commando-style training camps outside Ankara and Izmir for the Gray Wolves. The group also proselytized younger expatriate workers living in western Europe. Before being recruited by the Bulgarian secret police, Mehmet Ali Agca had once been a Gray Wolf member and had murdered a leftist Turkish newspaper editor, Abdi Ipekci, prior to his attempt to kill Pope John Paul II on 13 May 1981. With the imposition of military rule in Turkey in September 1980, the terrorist activities of the Gray Wolves were constrained with the crackdown on all paramilitary and political groups that followed. The group was estimated to have had about 26,000 members in about 80 branches. After the death of Alparslan Türkes his Nationalist Action purged the more violent members who had been part of the Gray Wolves so that the party could adopt a more moderate form of nationalism compatible with contemporary European norms.

GROUP OF SEVEN COUNTERTERRORISM COOPERATION. The Summit Seven group of major industrialized nations, namely Great Britain, Canada, France, Germany, Italy, Japan, and the United States, with the recent addition of the Russian Federation to form a Summit Eight group, has emerged as one of the major and most effective forums for addressing issues of terrorism, international organized crime and drug-trafficking, and regional issues of peace and conflict. The annual forum began as an informal gathering proposed by French President Valéry Giscard d'Estaing and met first at Rambouillet in 1975 to discuss purely economic and trade issues. Beginning in 1978 the group began to address political issues, in particular, common concerns about terrorism which initiated increased and more effective **counterterrorism** cooperation among these nations. Summit declarations concerning international terrorism and proposals for joint actions to counter such terrorism were given in Bonn in 1978, Tokyo in 1979, Venice in 1980, Ottawa in 1981, London in 1984, Tokyo in 1986, Venice in 1987, Paris in 1989, Houston in 1990, and Lyons and Paris in 1996. Following the inclusion of Russia in this forum, terrorism was dealt with, among other things, in the communiqués issued at the summits in Denver in 1997 and Birmingham in 1998. Most recently the Summit Eight group held a counterterrorism conference in Berlin on 17-18 November 1999.

The Bonn meeting declaration of 1978 announced the intentions of the seven governments "to intensify their joint efforts to combat intentional terrorism," and specifically addressed the problem of **hijacking**. The declaration indicated that these nations would impose an aviation boycott on any such nation that refused **extradition** or prosecution of hijackers or which refused to return hijacked aircraft. In the Tokyo declaration of 1986 these measures were extended to deal with all forms of terrorism affecting civil aviation.

Following the takeover of the U.S. embassy in Tehran and the seizure of its diplomats as hostages the Venice declaration of 1980 focused on attacks on diplomats and consular premises and personnel and resolved that each state would "provide to one another's diplomatic and consular missions support and assistance" in such situations. The London declaration of 1984 and the Tokyo declaration of 1986 were primarily directed toward ending the abuse of diplomatic immunities for sponsoring terrorism and were particularly directed at Libya, whose diplomats had used their office in London to shoot at protestors in 1984 and who were believed to be behind the **bombing** of the LaBelle Discothèque in Berlin in 1986. In the 1986 meeting the Summit Seven resolved to refuse to export arms to states involved in the abuse of diplomatic privileges and also to reduce the size of, or close altogether, the diplomatic offices of such nations and to deny entry into any of their states to any diplomat having been previously expelled from one of the member states for such abuses. Following the wave of bombings in France during 1996 believed to have been the work of the **Armed Islamic Group** of Algeria, the **Khobar Towers bombing** in June that year, and the mysterious explosion of TWA Flight 800 the next month, which initially was thought to have been a terrorist act, the Summit Eight group proposed concrete measures for monitoring use of the Internet by terrorist groups, and developing means to track and control the manufacture, sale, transport, and export of explosives and firearms.

In 1986 the Vice President's Task Force on Combating Terrorism stated that "the best multilateral forum for the discussion of terrorism [has been found] to be the Summit Seven." These summit meets have led to effective counterterrorist policies and actions for several reasons. First, unlike the United Nations or regional organizations, the membership includes those nations whose citizens, diplomats, and business interests have been most often targeted by terrorists and excludes any of the nations that were main sponsors of terrorism. Second, the informal format of the meetings allowed greater flexibility than was possible in such organizations as NATO or the Council of Europe, whose agenda are limited by specific mandates. Finally, each of these nations is a source of significant trade, technology, and financial resources and together they dominate a significant portion of the capital and financial resources that are desperately needed by other nations. This gives them significant economic leverage over nations that directly sponsor or tolerate terrorism as well as over the trade partners of such nations. This has enabled the Summit nations to coordinate their use of nonmilitary sanctions such as economic embargos and reduction of diplomatic privileges to great effect.

GROUPTHINK. Hypothesis developed by Janis L. Irving about critical errors in strategic decision making, namely, a mode of reasoning used by members of a cohesive and exclusive in-group in which their desire to maintain group cohesion, morale, and unanimity overrides their desire to appraise realistically alternative courses of action. The groupthink syndrome is marked by overestimations of the power, correct opinion, and moral superiority of the group; by closed-mindedness to contrary information; and intense pressures of conformity within the group.

The groupthink hypothesis can be used to explain the reasoning and strategic and tactical errors made by terrorist groups. The **cellular terrorist group** is the ultimate example of a closed in-group whose members have been indoctrinated to believe in the mission of the terrorist group and in their moral and intellectual superiority over the state or other groups whom they are opposing. The conditions of clandestine existence and of doctrinal conformity within the group provide precisely the sorts of conditions that encourage groupthink. Examples of such disastrous decisions include the **Red Brigades'** decision to murder former Italian Prime Minister Aldo Moro on 9 May 1978 and Timothy McVeigh and Terry Nicoles's decision to bomb the Murrah federal building in **Oklahoma City** on 19 April 2000. In each case the perpetrators had convinced themselves that their action would be hailed by the wider public and understood in the same terms that they had used to rationalize to themselves committing each action.

There are different psychological devices and fallacies that come into play in the groupthink syndrome. These include:

Cognitive Bolstering—The group or chief decision maker marshals all of the evidence supporting the predetermined decision but excludes any contrary evidence.

Defensive Avoidance—The group either avoids hearing or examining evidence questioning the wisdom of their decision or else by refusing to make a decision that would reverse their course of action they commit themselves to continue the same course by default.

Entrapment, or the "Sunk-Cost Syndrome"—Once the decided course of action is undertaken the group refuses to contemplate backing down, or not carrying out their threats, usually on the plea that one or more of their comrades lost their life in the action and that therefore changing their decision would mean that the comrade had died "in vain."

Stereotyping—An essential part of the groupthink syndrome is the stereotyping of the enemy as being stupid, evil, and incompetent. The terrorists in the grip of groupthink refuse to assess realistically the ability of the **targeted** state to defend itself, thwart the group's intended actions, or else even defeat them.

GUARDIANS OF THE ISLAMIC REVOLUTION. Name under which credit was taken for the 7 July 1980 **bombings** of the Rome offices of Snia-Technit Corporation and for the 2 October 1987 murder of an émigré Iranian dissident and his son in London. The group is ostensibly a pro-Iranian Shi'ite terrorist group and is believed to be responsible for the murders in 1988 of a former minister of the Shah's government and of a German banker close to the Iraqi war effort.

It is entirely possible that rather than being merely an Iranian-sponsored nonstate group that this group represents actually an extension of Iranian **state terror** and active measures beyond its borders, using Iranian intelligence and military personnel rather than an independent organization. In the case of the actual organization **Hezbollah** the group took care to prevent other persons or groups from falsely claiming credit in its nom de guerre of **Islamic Jihad** by issuing its communiqués only to certain news outlets, usually accompanied by some recent photographs of their hostages proving their identity.

In the case of a dummy organization, however, it would be easier for other groups to use that dummy organization's name without facing contradiction from that source. Thus persons claiming to be the "Guardians" claimed credit for the bombing of **Pan Am Flight 103** on 21 December 1988, which has been discounted by most experts. Curiously, persons claiming to represent Islamic Jihad also claimed credit for the 19 September 1989 bombing of a French **UTA Flight 772** over Niger in which 171 people perished. Currently it is believed both airplane **bombings** were conducted by Libyan state operatives who may have used the names of Iranian-associated organizations to divert attention from Libya's possible involvement.

GUATEMALAN NATIONAL REVOLUTIONARY UNION. The Unidad
Revolucionaria Nacional Guatemalteca (URNG) is an umbrella group
uniting the three major leftist guerrilla groups and one political party,
which formerly sought to create a Marxist revolution within Guatemala
along lines similar to the **Sandinista** model in Nicaragua, but which
now forms a left-wing political party following the 29 December 1996
peace accord that formally ended their 36-year-long insurgency against
the Guatemalan government. The three armed groups are the Guerrilla
Army of the Poor (EGP), the Rebel Armed Forces (FAR), and the Revolutionary Organization of the People in Arms (ORPA). In addition the
URNG also contained the Guatemalan Workers' Party, the Partido
Guatemalteco del Trabajo (PGT). This united front was a condition
imposed by Fidel Castro for Cuban sponsorship of the Guatemalan leftist insurgents. In addition to Cuban state sponsorship, the URNG enjoyed the use of sanctuaries in Mexico and of arms, safe haven, and
other material assistance from the Sandinista government of Nicaragua
prior to February 1990. While the three groups maintained an organizational unity, in fact, each operated in separate territories and each was
sufficiently different from its fellows to merit separate descriptions:
1. Fuerzas Armadas Rebeldes (FAR). The Rebel Armed Forces was set
   up in 1962 by junior officers who had participated in a failed coup
   attempt in 1960 against a conservative government. The FAR established itself in a rugged mountainous region in the extreme northeast of Guatemala, close to Belize. The FAR was more of a nationalistic
   than Marxist group, but forged ties with leftists to fight more effectively. The FAR conducted six major assassinations, including the
   assassination of U.S. Ambassador John Gordon Mein in August 1968,
   the first time a U.S. ambassador had been murdered in the line of
   duty. In 1969 the FAR moved some of their forces into Guatemala
   City, splitting the group's command. In March 1970 they murdered
   West German Ambassador Count Karl von Spreti. The same month
   they **kidnapped** the U.S. labor attaché, Sean Holly, who was released
   in a prisoner exchange. Guatemalan counterinsurgency efforts aided
   by the U.S. Army Special Forces pushed back the FAR, which remained inactive from 1970 to 1975.
   In 1975 FAR activity resumed in Peten province with very little
   activity in the capital until 1979. On 29 June 1983 the FAR kidnapped
   the sister of President Ríos Montt, who was released in exchange for
   imprisoned comrades. During this period the urban branch of FAR spe-

cialized in terrorist operations, concentrating on assassinations and kidnappings, while the branch in the northeast tried to fight the Guatemalan army, meanwhile sabotaging economic infrastructural projects and harassing oil exploration camps.

2. Ejército Guerrillero de los Pobres (EGP). The Guerrilla Army of the Poor was established in 1975 by a former FAR commander, César Montes, who revived the strategy of conducting simultaneous rural insurgency and urban terrorism. On 15 June 1978 an EGP truck bombing in the capital killed 17 military police, while four other bombings were directed at the Argentinean, Uruguayan, and U.S. embassies, as well as the U.S. Chamber of Commerce office. On 31 March 1982 the EGP also fired RPG-7 rocket-propelled grenades at the U.S. embassy. Rural operations were resumed in the northeast areas but also expanded to the northwestern regions bordering on Mexico while a new front was opened in a mountainous area just north of the capital. Much of the rural campaign involved burning of sugarcane fields to bankrupt the large landowners.

In a 10-year period the EGP committed 22 assassinations of prominent people, killing Colonel Elías Ramírez, a former counterinsurgency commander, the Nicaraguan ambassador in October 1978, and also the Army Chief of Staff, General David Barrios, in June 1979. EGP kidnapping victims included the Salvadoran ambassador on 29 May 1977, and the Foreign Minister of Guatemala on 31 December 1977. In October 1979 the EGP kidnapped the president's nephew, who was released only after the government placed EGP political manifestos in paid advertisements in leading Western newspapers.

César Montes initiated contacts with the FAR and the ORPA, and other antigovernment guerrillas, to promote forming a common front, which was the prelude to formation of URNG.

The EGP was responsible for at least one massacre of civilians in June 1982 when they reportedly killed 120 people in Chacalte in retaliation for their collaboration with the civilian self-defense patrols which themselves later turned into **death squads**.

3. Organización Revolucionaria del Pueblo en Armas (ORPA). The Revolutionary Organization of the People in Arms was a Guatemalan leftist guerrilla group that enjoyed Cuban sponsorship and collaborated with two other major Guatemalan rebel groups within the framework of the URNG to overthrow the Guatemalan government.

The ORPA was formed in September 1979 in Solola department and, although smaller than the Rebel Armed Forces (FAR) or the Revolutionary Army of the Poor (EGP), it gained the reputation of being the most effective of the Guatemalan groups. In 1984 the ORPA forces killed more than 120 Guatemalan army soldiers during a 10-day period. Most of ORPA's area of operations has been in the southwestern region of Guatemala, west of Guatemala City. The leader of the ORPA group was Rodrigo Asturias Amado, also called "Gaspar Ilom."

While the ORPA was particularly effective in rural guerrilla warfare, and while most terrorist actions committed by URNG forces were usually carried out by FAR forces, one terrorist incident was clearly the work of the ORPA. In November 1988, about 22 villagers were massacred by ORPA in the small town of El Aguacate. Until 1984 the ORPA had largely been successful in its own propaganda work and co-optation of the Indian peasants.

Previous Guatemalan counterinsurgency efforts had played into the URNG's hands due to the heavy-handed use of death squads and indiscriminate **state terrorization** of civilians in areas of rural insurgency. Following the 23 March 1982 coup bringing Ríos Montt to power, the Guatemalan army undertook a more effective campaign to secure the support of the peasants with the result that the URNG lost much ground. Certain of these groups, such as the ORPA, began to use the same retaliatory tactics against suspected civilian collaborators that previously had been the hallmark of Guatemala's state-sponsored right-wing death squads.

After the January 1996 election of Álvaro Arzú Irigoyen the Guatemalan government moved quickly to establish talks with the URNG aimed at ending the civil war, returning the rebels to civilian life, and resettling the hundreds of thousands of Indian peasants driven from their homes by the civil war. At that time it was estimated that 100,000 people had been killed, and that 40,000 had disappeared, presumably killed by rightists or leftists, and about one million had been displaced out of a population of 10.5 million.

On 19 October 1996 the government suspended talks with the URNG due to the revelation that the deputy commander of the Organization of the People in Arms, Rafael Valdizón Núñez ("Commander Isaias"), had ordered the kidnapping of Olga Alvarado de Novella, the 84-year-old invalid matriarch of a prominent Guatemalan family, two months earlier. The URNG disavowed Valdizón's action in late October after removing him from his command and apologized to the Alvarado family. On 4 November 1996 the URNG ordered a complete cessation of all activities of **armed propaganda** and by 10 November 1996 talks had resumed. On 11 November 1996 both sides agreed to sign a peace accord on 29 December 1996. Beginning on 4 December 1996 the government and the URNG signed three agreements aimed at ending the fighting, reducing the armed forces, and reintegrating former URNG fighters and displaced peasants back into Guatemalan civil society. On 18 December 1996 the National Assembly passed a comprehensive amnesty law which drew much criticism from human rights groups. On 29 December 1996 the principal leaders of the URNG and members of the government's Peace Commission signed the "Accord for a Firm and Lasting Peace."

By March 1997 demobilization of the Guatemalan armed forces began, which were to be reduced from 46,000 to about 40,000 soldiers who were to be redeployed along the borders of the nation. About 3,600 former rebels as well as 1,600 followers were to be resettled in eight camps around the nation. The armed groups of the URNG turned in few of their weapons, apparently out of concern that certain of the miliary forces as well as powerful landowners would not respect the peace settlement and might attack the resettled rebels and peasants.

On 25 February 1999 the Historical Clarification Commission, a truth commission set up by the United Nations as part of its effort to supervise the 1996 peace accord, presented its report which estimated that more than 200,000 people had been killed and held the Guatemalan government responsible for 90 percent of the 42,000 documented human rights violations of which 29,000 had resulted in deaths or disappearances. Copies of this report were given to representatives both of the Guatemalan government and of the URNG, which had become an official political party within Guatemala. In the 7 November 1999 congressional elections the URNG won 9 of the 113 seats in the Congress of the Republic while its presidential and vice presidential candidates, Álvaro Colom Caballeros and Vitalino Similox, won 12.3 percent in the first round of elections. As the URNG presidential candidate team placed third the URNG did not qualify for the 26 December 1999 presidential run-off election.

GUERRILLA FORCES OF LIBERATION. The Guerrilla Forces of Liberation was an obscure Puerto Rican independence group that claimed credit for a series of **bombings** that occurred in Puerto Rico on 25 May

1987, the day King Juan Carlos and Queen Sophia of Spain visited the island. Five pipe bombs exploded with minimal damage and no injuries. Three others were defused while another exploded en route to a demolition center. The caller claiming credit stated that the bombings were a protest against "colonialism." As the group was previously unknown, the "Guerrilla Forces of Liberation" may have been a nom de guerre for another known organization.

GUEVARA, ERNESTO "CHE" (1928-1967). A revolutionary, a guerrilla leader, and the close aide and friend of Fidel Castro, Che Guevara was also a theorist of revolutionary warfare who became idolized by sympathizers worldwide following his death at the hands of Bolivian counterinsurgency forces. His work *Guerrilla Warfare* advocated the use of terrorist violence to create intense fear, including the **assassination** and mutilation of local notables who refused to collaborate with the revolutionaries. Guevara left Cuba in 1965 to try to foment revolution in the Congo. In December 1966 he entered Bolivia where he tried unsuccessfully to launch a peasant revolt. On 8 October 1967 Guevara was captured and executed the next day by U.S.-trained Bolivian counterinsurgency forces. Latin American revolutionaries have since then accepted Guevara's *Guerrilla Warfare* as a basic textbook on revolutionary warfare.

In November 1995 Bolivian General Vargas Salinas revealed the location of Guevara's body, whose burial along with six bodies of Guevara's executed comrades he had overseen on 11 October 1967 at a location over which was built the airstrip of Vallegrande. After Guevara's execution his hands had been cut off by Argentine agents so that his identity could be verified by his fingerprints already in possession of the Argentine police and a death mask was also made. Both the amputated hands and death mask were later taken to Cuba by a defector, the former Interior Minister, Antonio Arguedas. Although the Bolivian government in 1967 originally wanted the remains of Guevara to become lost so that the guerrilla could not be posthumously honored, in June 1997 the Bolivian government authorized a forensics team to search the Vallegrande airstrip so that the remains of the guerrillas could be exhumed and returned to their families. On 1 July 1997 these remains were unearthed and identified and on 17 October 1997 the remains of Che Guevara were buried in a mausoleum at the Guevara monument in Santa

Clara, Cuba, in a ceremony attended by Fidel Castro, his widow Aleida March, and his children.

GUILT TRANSFER. Guilt transfer refers to the ability of terrorists to distort public debate about the terrorists' political ends and particular demands by shifting public perception of the onus of responsibility from the terrorists themselves to others, either to their victims or the governments against which the terrorist actions are being directed. Guilt transfer is also achieved when public discussion shifts from the illegality or immorality of the terrorists' actions to discussion of the supposed historical and social "root causes" that compelled the terrorists to take such actions, as if the terrorists were themselves the victims and the targeted government their tormentor for having allowed the root causes to have occurred at all.

The Maze Prison hunger strikes in Northern Ireland during 1981 provide an example of guilt transfer. Ten convicted **Irish National Liberation Army** terrorists starved themselves to death in protest over the British government's refusal to grant them a special status as political prisoners as opposed to being classified as common criminals. Once the leader of the protestors, Robert "Bobby" Sands, died of starvation on 5 May 1981, a storm of protest rose in both Great Britain and the Republic of Ireland over the British government's alleged mistreatment of these prisoners. Although these prisoners had earlier decided to engage in a "dirty protest" of refusing to shave, bathe, or wear prison clothing, while also smearing the walls and floors of their cells with their own urine and feces, these self-imposed conditions were also cited by critics of the British government as evidence of mistreatment of the prisoners. Also terrorist attacks by the **Irish Republican Army** and other Irish Republican groups intensified, including several murders of the guards of Maze Prison.

The crisis of the American hostages held captive in Lebanon during the period from 1983-1991 provides another illustration. During the earliest phase of these **kidnappings**, the U.S. public's anger was directed against the shadowy kidnappers and their sponsors. Over time, however, as the U.S. public finally acknowledged the intransigence of the kidnappers and the inability of the United States to take military steps to free the hostages, its perceptions of where the onus of responsibility lay shifted instead to the U.S. government, which was expected to "do something" even if this entailed some appeasement of the terrorists' demands.

In time, the families and friends of the hostages formed political pressure groups to force such action by the U.S. government.

In the case of the victims of terrorism, guilt transfer means that the victims come to accept the terrorists' claims that they themselves, rather than their tormentors, are responsible for their misfortune. This enables the terrorists to secure the collaboration of their victims in making political statements or revealing information and also makes the demoralized victims less likely to resist the terrorists or attempt to escape. *See also* STOCKHOLM SYNDROME.

GUSH EMUNIM. The "Bloc of the Faithful" is a Jewish fundamentalist group within Israel that seeks the forcible and permanent annexation of territories occupied by Israeli forces during the 1967 war. Founded in 1974, the Gush Emunim sought to force annexation by forming settlements on the West Bank and through inciting confrontations between Israelis and Palestinians that would force the Israeli state to expel the Arabs. On 13 September 1986 Gush Emunim members rigged explosive charges to the ignition of the car of the Palestinian mayor of Nablus, Bassam Shaka, who lost both his legs, and of Ramallah mayor, Karim Khalaf, who lost a foot. Gush Emunim activists also incited a Christian millennialist zealot from Australia to set fire to the Al Aqsa mosque, an **arson** attempt that failed. In June 1986, 12,000 members of Gush Emunim and other Jewish fundamentalist groups held demonstrations at the Temple Mount, the presumed site of the Second Temple, protesting Muslim control of the site. In clashes with Israeli police, 100 protestors were arrested.

Their **ideology** is a blend of ultranationalistic right-wing Zionism and pietistic **millennialism**, which leads them to believe that the redemption of Israel can only be accomplished once all the lands of the biblical kingdom of Israel are reincorporated into the land of Israel today. Therefore they reject all forms of peaceful accommodation with Arabs within the land of Israel. *See also* TEMPLE MOUNT OPERATION.

- H -

HARAKAT UL ANSAR. *See* KASHMIRI SECESSIONISTS.

HARAKAT UL MUJAHIDEEN. *See* KASHMIRI SECESSIONISTS.

HAMAS. Hamas, the Arabic acronym for the "Islamic Resistance Movement" (Harakat al Muqawama al Islamiyya), is a nonstate, **Islamic fundamentalist**, revolutionary Palestinian group devoted to the complete eradication of the State of Israel and creation of an Islamic Palestinian state. Although Hamas is a separate organization from the **Palestine Liberation Organization** (PLO), it coordinated with other mainline Palestinian groups in conducting the *intifada* uprising, which began in December 1987. Unlike the PLO, which has always advocated a secular Palestinian state and which, since 1988, has indicated its willingness to accept a Palestinian state with a much reduced territory in coexistence with Israel, Hamas regards the entire territory of former mandatory Palestine as an "inviolable Islamic trust" and rejects the idea of a secular state altogether.

Hamas officially announced its existence with the publication of the "Covenant of the Islamic Resistance Movement" on 18 August 1988, but in fact it is continuous with the Ikhwan al Muslimin (**Muslim Brotherhood**) branch that established itself in Palestine in 1946 and that remained active in Gaza and the West Bank after the 1948 Arab-Israeli war. Until 1984 the Ikhwan had concentrated mainly on the education of Arab youth in Gaza and the West Bank and its politics seldom strayed beyond a belief in piecemeal Islamic reformism. On 17 September 1984, however, a leader of the Palestinian Ikhwan in the Gaza Strip, Sheikh Ahmad Yasin, and four other Ikhwan members were convicted of stockpiling automatic weapons and plotting to kill 300 prominent persons. Yasin is regarded now as the spiritual mentor of Hamas. In October and November 1987, the Ikhwan sometimes collaborated and other times competed with both the PLO and the **Islamic Jihad of Palestine** in creating demonstrations in the occupied territories that precipitated the *intifada* uprising.

The **ideology** of Hamas reflects not only the traditional fundamentalism of the Ikhwan but also the more radical beliefs of the Egyptian Ikhwan leader, **Sayyid Qutb**, as well as the contemporary beliefs of the Egyptian **Munazzamat al Jihad** group that assassinated Anwar Sadat. Although predominantly Sunni in composition, there is evidence that Hamas takes inspiration from the tactical example of the **Ayatollah Khomeini**'s Islamic revolution in Iran in rejecting piecemeal reformism and in its preference for direct popular uprising over either electoral campaigning or guerrilla warfare. Their covenant defines the Palestinian struggle as being part of the Islamic religious duty of **jihad** incumbent on all Muslims under Israeli occupation. While the Hamas Covenant solemnly avows the Palestinian identity of the movement, and so disavows any right by the Arab governments to determine the fate of the Palestinians, it also places the Palestinian struggle in a Pan-Islamic context as an obligation demanding the moral and material support of all Muslims even outside of the Arab nations. Article 27 of the Hamas Covenant rejects the secular, nonconfessional platform of the PLO as reflecting the devious influences of "western missionaries, orientalists, and colonialists."

Hamas derives both its autonomy from secular Palestinian nationalists and its organizational strength from the Ikhwan's control over Muslim educational and religious foundations in the West Bank. During the period of Jordanian administration (1948-1988) the Ikhwan used the authority of the Jordanian Ministry of Religious Endowments to dominate the Arab schools and the appointments of all Friday Prayers leaders. The Ikhwan network also dominated the collection and disbursement of the religious tithes of the Muslim faithful. Over 50 percent of religious publications in the West Bank have been dominated by the Ikhwan. Following the cessation of Jordanian state support, the Ikhwan continued to draw on material support from other official and semiprivate Islamic religious organizations in Saudi Arabia and other Persian Gulf emirates. Hamas initially rebuffed Iran's attempts to sponsor it through offers of financial and tactical aid.

A number of early attacks had been carried out by individual Palestinian Hamas members, usually stabbings of individual Israelis. On 14 December 1990 two Hamas members stabbed to death three Israeli factory workers in Jaffa. Yet for a one-week period beginning 3 July 1992, Hamas clashed with followers of **Yasir Arafat**'s **Al Fatah** group in the Gaza Strip in which one child was killed and over 150 people injured. Hamas opposed Fatah's participation in the October 1991 Arab-Israeli peace talks in Madrid and feared the PLO would accept newly elected Israeli Prime Minister Yitzhak Rabin's proposal for limited Palestinian autonomy on the West Bank.

Hamas began to acquire a greater following after the September 1993 peace settlement and also with the subsequent attempts by Israel to marginalize the role of the PLO. The internal leftist opposition to Arafat within the PLO and secularized middle-class Palestinians had become increasing inactive and irrelevant while Hamas, Islamic Jihad in Palestine, and similar groups still pursued direct warfare against Israel.

Earlier in October 1992 Hamas leader Muhammad Mousa Abu Marzuk went to Iran to improve relations and get more support. In December 1992 Israel exiled 400 Hamas radicals to Lebanon where they later claimed to have learned the **suicide bombing** tactic from **Hezbollah**. Suicide bombings aimed at civilians began in earnest on 6 April 1994 in the northern town of Afula with an attack that killed nine Israelis and wounded 45 other, and another attack on 13 April 1994 in Hadera that destroyed a bus and killed six Israelis and wounded 28. Another suicide bombing on a bus on 19 October 1994 killed 21 and wounded 48 along Dizengoff street in Tel Aviv. On 24 November 1994 for the first time since the Eichmann trial an Israeli court handed down a death sentence, this time upon a Palestinian convicted for his role in training the suicide bombers who carried out these attacks. According to the leaflets left at these two **bombings** Hamas had decided to switch from purely military targets to suicide bombings against civilians in reaction to the assault on 25 February 1994 of Dr. Baruch Goldstein who massacred 29 Muslims at the Ibrahimi Mosque located at the Cave of the Patriarchs in Hebron.

Apart from these suicide bombings Hamas carried out other attacks in 1994, including a **kidnapping** on 9 October of an Israeli Defense Forces corporal killed five days later; a machine-gun attack on pedestrians in Jerusalem's Yoel Salomon Street on 10 October, killing two and wounding others; a drive-by shooting on 27 November that killed a Rabbi, Ami Olami, who was traveling near Hebron; and a suicide bombing on 25 December wounding 14 Israeli soldiers.

Hamas activities in 1995 included suicide attacks killing 21 Israelis in January, a suicide bombing on 9 April, a bus bombing on 24 July killing six Israelis and wounding 28, another bus bombing on 21 August in Jerusalem, killing five and wounding over 100, leading to an Israeli crackdown that netted 32 Hamas members allegedly connected with those bombings.

On 5 January 1996 Israeli intelligence agents **assassinated** Yahya Ayyash, alias "the Engineer," believed to have been the mastermind behind most of the suicide bombings since October 1994, by means of a booby-trapped cellular phone. Hamas retailiated with more violence throughout 1996: on 25 February two suicide bombings killed 27 and wounded 75 people in Jerusalem, on 3 March another bus bombing killed 19 in Jerusalem, on 4 March 1996 another suicide bombing in Tel Aviv's Dizengoff Center, the nation's largest shopping mall, killed 12 and wounded 126 others. After over 61 killings within nine days by suicide bombings there was an unprecedented three-way meeting of CIA officials with both Israeli and Palestinian security officials to discuss ways to stop the suicide bombing attacks. Following these attacks in fact there was a lull in Hamas activity that lasted until March 1997.

During 1997 Hamas activities included a 21 March suicide attack at a crowded Tel Aviv cafe, killing four and wounding dozens more, and two suicide bombers killing themselves and 13 others and wounding over 150 in a crowded Jerusalem market on 30 July.

On 25 September 1997 Israeli agents attempted to assassinate Khaled Meshal, a Hamas political leader, in Jordan with an injectable poison, otherwise not identified. Both Mossad agents were captured and the bungled operation caused the Benjamin Netanyahu government of Israel great embarrassment at home and a loss of leverage with Arab leaders who had previously supported the peace process. To forestall an Arab backlash Israel released Sheikh Ahmad Yasin from prison on 1 October 1997, which apparently was also part of a deal to gain the release of its two agents from Jordan. Yasin flew first to Jordan, where he was greeted by Yasir Arafat, but then flew to Gaza on 6 October where he received a hero's welcome. The release of Sheikh Yasin may also have been calculated to widen a split that had appeared in Hamas' leadership in the hope that Yasin might sanction some form of "truce" with Israel but on 22 October 1997 Sheikh Yasin delivered a fiery speech to 3,000 students of Gaza's Islamic University urging Hamas not to end its jihad against Israel. From 19 February 1998 until 25 June 1998 Sheikh Yasin toured several Arab nations, beginning with Egypt where he was supposedly seeking medical care, and then continuing to Saudi Arabia, Qatar, the United Arab Emirates, Kuwait, Yemen, Syria, Iran, and Sudan, which greatly boosted the status of Hamas in the Muslim world.

During 1998 the Palestinian Authority (PA) found itself at odds with Hamas over the 29 March 1998 death of Muhyiaddin al-Sharif, a Hamas bomb maker, whom Hamas claimed had been killed by the Palestinian Authority as part of a deal with Israel. In fact Israel had increasingly been calling on Arafat to intervene to prevent Hamas bomb attacks when it believed it had intelligence of such plans. On 29 October 1998 an Israeli army jeep blocked a Hamas suicide bomber attempting to drive a bomb-laden car into a full school bus near the Israeli Kfar Darom settlement in the Gaza Strip. The attempted attack followed the signing of the Wye River Accord due to go into effect on 2 November 1998. In response Arafat ordered a crackdown which resulted in over 300 arrests and also placed Sheikh Yasin under house arrest on 29 October 1998 who was later released on 24 December 1998. Despite Hamas threats to retaliate against the Palestinian Authority for this crackdown Hamas abstained from any attacks during the two-month house arrest of Sheikh Yasin.

During 1999 the level of Hamas violence did not exceed that of previous years and the movement showed some signs of internal division. Hamas, which is not part of the PLO, was given observer status for the 27 April 1998 meeting of the Palestinian Central Council. The four-member Hamas delegation was led by Sheikh Yasin but Hamas factions outside of Gaza distanced themselves from this meeting which was aimed at defining a Palestinian sovereignty in keeping with the Oslo Accords. During this meeting, however, Sheikh Yasin specifically attacked the Oslo Accords and urged they be abandoned. On 5 September 1999 two cars exploded almost simultaneously, one in Haifa and the other in Tiberias, killing the would-be bombers and one passerby in Haifa. Although the bombings did not produce casualties as high as previous attacks the discovery that the four bombers were all Israeli Arabs came as a shock to Israel, whose naturalized Arab citizens had remained largely uninvolved in terrorism. Later it was learned that these men had been recruited by Hamas and had intended to attack passenger buses bound for Jerusalem. On 31 August 1999 the Jordanian government of King Abdullah ordered the closure of Hamas offices in Amman as well as the arrests of four Hamas officials there, including Khalid Meshal, on the basis of evidence of their involvement in the suicide bombings within Israel, including two others attempted on September 5. Meshal and others were arrested on 22 September as they disembarked at Amman airport after returning from Iran. Jordan imprisoned Meshal but offered to release him to Hamas on condition that he immediately depart the country. As late as 1999 Hamas continued to reject this condition for his release.

On 4 March 2001 a Hamas suicide bomber carrying a duffle bag killed himself and three Israelis in a crosswalk in Netanya. On 18 May 2001 another Hamas suicide bomber detonated a belt of explosives within a crowded shopping mall in Netanya, killing five and wounding over 100 others, leading Israel to retaliate with F-16 fighter jet attacks on Palestinian security forces offices in Nablus and Ramallah. On 17 June 2001 Israeli helicopters fired missiles at a farm building in Bethlehem, killing Hamas commanders Omar Saadeh and Taha Aruj, whom the Israelis claimed were planning massive attacks on the Maccabiah Games then in progress.

With regard to organization, Hamas operates several charity networks to support schools, clinics, and orphanages in the West Bank and Gaza and its funding-raising network among Arab communities overseas has also served to mask its recruiting of resources for its armed struggle. Hamas's operational budget is estimated by Israeli intelligence at about $30 million a year, 40 percent of which comes from donors in Arab nations, 20 percent from Palestinians in the West Bank and Gaza, 10 percent from Iran, about 10 to 15 percent from donors in the United States, and the remaining 15 to 20 percent from donors in other countries.

Hamas has three sections in the West Bank and one in Gaza. The first and most open level of membership in Hamas are the Da'wa groups, which evangelize lay Muslims into Islamic activism. This group includes prayer leaders, and the 5,000 undergraduates of the Islamic university in Gaza. The second layer consists of the Youth Organization, or Jihaz al Ahdath, founded in 1988 which involves youngsters in demonstrations, rock throwing, spray-painting slogans, and distributing leaflets. When members of this group are imprisoned they undertake to evangelize other, more hardened youths into Hamas activism. In 1988 Sheikh Ahmad Yasin ordered Hamas to form the Qassam Brigades which is the armed wing and which may number no more than 100 members. Leadership is decentralized within the West Bank and Gaza with leaders of cells reporting back to a Hamas leadership that is located outside of Israel and the Palestinian territories.

The spiritual leader of Hamas is Sheikh Ahmad Yasin, a Muslim Brotherhood member who founded Hamas in 1987. Although crippled by paralysis since childhood Sheikh Yasin was considered dangerous and active by Israel which sentenced him to life imprisonment in 1989. On 1 October 1997, however, he was released and allowed to return to his home in Gaza. The lay leader was Muhammad Mousa Abu Marzuk, who was imprisoned by the United States in 1995 until released on 5 May 1997. Emad al-Alami, an engineer from Gaza stationed in Damascus, assumed control over Hamas after Marzuk's arrest but was believed not able to control all factions. Mahmoud al Zahar was the civilian political leader in Gaza, though periodically arrested by the Palestinian Authority. Another Hamas figure, Abdel-Aziz al Rantisi, eventually became another prominent political leader in Gaza. The military leader was Yahya Ayyash, killed by Israel in January 1996, and believed to have been replaced by Muhammad Dief.

Direct or indirect state support has come from Jordan, which allowed transhipment of funds from overseas sources to Hamas accounts. Hamas was allowed to operate openly in Jordan until 1999 when the new king Abdullah ordered its office there closed. Syria and Sudan allowed their territories to be used by Hamas and other Islamic militant groups as bases for training. Saudi Arabia and the various Persian Gulf states allowed charities to raise funds for Hamas while Iran gives funds directly to Hamas, and other militant groups, as well as giving these groups offices in Tehran.

HATE CRIMES. Hate crime refers to criminal conduct motivated by prejudice, particularly racial, religious, or ethnic prejudice. A criminal act motivated solely by a personal hatred of a given person would not qualify. Hate crime is legislatively defined by specific prejudices against specific protected groups, however, crimes motivated by prejudice are not unique to one group and any group can be the target of prejudice. Therefore the murder in rural Texas of James Byrd, Jr., who happened to be black, by three young white men who dragged him to his death on 7 June 1998 was a heinous murder motivated by racial prejudice which qualified as a hate crime. Similarly the killings of 12 people by Colin Ferguson on 19 December 1993, when Ferguson opened fire on a Long Island Railroad passenger train, would qualify as a hate crime since Ferguson, who was black, stated, when asked why he had shot people who were perfect strangers to him, that he hated white people.

Attempts to ban prejudice itself violate the First Amendment of the U.S. Constitution and therefore "hate speech" codes enacted on many U.S. university campuses have been ruled unconstitutional when challenged in court. "Group libel" laws were used in the 1920s and 1930s to outlaw anti-Semitism and other forms for prejudice but these were also ruled unconstitutional in U.S. courts. However Great Britain, Canada, and Germany and other nations have enacted group libel laws, which are also known as "Communal Hatred" laws, and prosecuted persons not only for violence motivated by bias but also for the simple propagation of hate mongering in itself. In the post-Civil War era in the United

States several Civil Rights Acts were enacted to punish attempts by anyone "acting under color [sic] of law, or otherwise to deprive any citizen of their civil rights under the U.S. Constitution," but did so without enumerating specific groups or prejudices, however current federal and state hate crimes statutes define enumerated prejudices, predicate offenses, and substantive offenses.

The Hate Crimes Statistics Act of 1990 (HCSA) defines certain offenses as "Predicate Crimes, " namely, murder, manslaughter, rape, aggravated assault, simple assault, intimidation, arson, and vandalism, and also identifies certain biases, namely any bias based on the race, religion, ethnicity or national origin, or sexual orientation of the victim, as sufficient ground to designate a particular predicate offense as a hate crime. If a crime incident shows evidence that the offender was motivated in part by one of the biases then it is presumed to be a hate crime. The Violent Crime Control and Law Enforcement Act of 1994 mandates enhanced sentences for convictions for predicate hate crimes. It should be noted, however, that not only is there no common definition of hate crimes among national governments, there is also no common definition among the U.S. federal and state governments and that as late as 1998 there were 12 states that did not have their own hate crime statutes. Despite much publicity about the supposed prevalance of hate crimes in the United States, they represent a small portion of total felonies recorded annually: in 1993 there were 7,587 recorded hate crimes out of a base figure of roughly 14 million felonies.

HAWARI GROUP. The Hawari Group was the special operations group of the central security and intelligence apparatus of **Yasir Arafat's al Fatah**, the core group within the **Palestine Liberation Organization** (PLO). As such it shares the revolutionary goals of its parent group and is also a nonstate actor. Hawari took its name from its leader, Colonel Hawari, a pseudonym for Abdullah Abdulhamid Labib. This group had been operating since 1985, after absorbing several former members of the Arab **May 15 Organization**, including Mohammad Rashid, believed responsible for the **bombing** of a Pan Am jet over Honolulu on 11 August 1982.

The group also operates under the names of "Martyrs of Tal al Za'atar," and "Amn Araissi." In April 1985 Hawari bombed the Rome office of the Syrian state airline and in Geneva bombed a Libyan airlines office and a Syrian diplomat's car. In June 1985 Hawari bombed the Geneva railway station. On 2 April 1986 Hawari bombed TWA Flight

840 en route from Cairo to Athens, killing four Americans. In August 1986 a Hawari terrorist team was captured in Morocco plotting to carry out attacks there in retaliation for Morocco's reception of the Israeli leader, Shimon Peres. In March 1987 French police arrested Hawari operatives and seized explosives and firearms, leading to Colonel Hawari's conviction and sentencing by a French court in absentia for bombing attacks committed in France and elsewhere during the 1980s. On 22 May 1991 Col. Hawari was killed in an automobile accident while driving from Baghdad to Amman, making the future of the group problematic.

HAYMARKET BOMBING. On 4 May 1886, while Chicago police were dispersing a crowd of labor protestors, who had assembled at Haymarket Square to protest the death of a protestor the previous day when police broke up a strike outside of the McCormick Harvester plant, anarchist radicals in the crowd threw a **bomb** at the police which exploded killing one officer instantly and fatally wounding seven others. Eight anarchists were tried and seven of them condemned to die while the eighth was sentenced to 15 years imprisonment. Four of those condemned were hanged and a fifth committed suicide. The sentences of the other two were later commuted to life imprisonment.

On 1889 a nine-foot bronze statue of a Chicago policeman was erected near the site of the riot on Randolph Street near Halstead Street as a tribute to the slain police. The statue was relocated twice until in 1957 it was moved to the northwest corner of the bridge over the Kennedy Expressway at Randolph Street. In October 1969 and again in October 1970 the statue was bombed off its pedestal, presumably by members of the **Weather Underground** or their sympathizers. Finally it was relocated in the courtyard of the Police Academy at 1300 W. Jackson Boulevard.

HEZBOLLAH. Hezbollah is the name of several groups of **Islamic fundamentalist** radicals many of which are modeled after the original Iranian Hezbollah group but some of which are unrelated to these other organizations.

1. Hezbollah in Lebanon—The original Hezbollah organization was founded by Iran in Lebanon during the summer of 1982. This state-sponsored group pursues the revolutionary goals of exporting Iran's Islamic revolution to Lebanon and creating an exclusively Islamic

state there. The militia also sought to expel Israeli forces from Lebanon and for a time opposed the older **Amal** militia. The name *Hezbollah*, meaning *Party of God*, is taken from the Koran (Surat al Mujadilah, verse 22) as a term describing the true Muslim believers. It first began to be used to identify the mass followers of the Imam **Ruhollah Khomeini** in Iran, where the name was applied to organized mobs deployed by the **Islamic Revolutionary Guards Corps** (IRGC) and the Islamic Republic Party against opponents of the Islamic Republic in Iran. Once the IRGC units arrived in Lebanon they gave the same name to the militias they organized there, as was confirmed by the confession of a Lebanese Hezbollah member arrested in Turkey on 10 April 1987.

Hezbollah was established by a contingent of 2,000 Islamic Revolutionary Guards dispatched to Lebanon in the summer of 1982, ostensibly to fight Israeli troops there. In fact, the IRGC unit remained in the Baalbak region and began organizing dissidents from Amal. Iran consistently disavowed direct control over Hezbollah, and formal leadership lay in the hands of a Lebanese "Consultative Assembly" consisting of ranking Lebanese clergymen, such as Muhammad Hussein Fadlullah, and key laymen, such as Hussein Musawi. This Consultative Assembly met only infrequently from 1983 until 1987, usually in the presence of either the military attaché of the Iranian embassy in Damascus or the Iranian chargé d'affaires in Beirut.

Using the nom de guerre "Islamic Jihad" Hezbollah conducted a very lethal terrorist campaign against U.S. diplomats and civilians, and American, French, and Israeli military contingents in Lebanon. Its **suicide bombings** using explosive-packed vehicles include the following major attacks: the 18 April 1983 bombing of the U.S. embassy in West Beirut, killing 61 persons; the 23 October 1983 bombings of the U.S. Marine camp at Beirut Airport, killing 241, and of the French contingent's headquarters, killing 74 servicemen; the 4 November 1983 bombing of the Israeli Defense Forces headquarters in Tyre, killing 30 servicemen; the 9 September 1984 attempted bombing of the U.S. embassy annex in East Beirut, killing two Americans and 21 bystanders; and the 10 March 1985 car bomb attack killing 12 Israeli soldiers near Metulla.

Hezbollah masterminded the **hijacking** of Rome-bound TWA Flight 847 on 14 June 1984 from Greece to Beirut where one U.S. serviceman found among the passengers was killed. Women and children were released after some time. The 39 remaining American men were held hostage until June 30. Amal assumed custody of these hostages from Hezbollah but refused to release them immediately until it received assurances that the United States would not retaliate against Lebanon for the hijacking. By doing this, Amal inadvertently confused the situation and ended up drawing most of the immediate blame upon itself for the hijacking, while Hezbollah obtained the main credit for obtaining the release of Shi'ite prisoners held in Israel's Atlit prison. The dissension created by this affair led to an outbreak of fighting between Hezbollah and Amal following the release of the remaining TWA 847 hostages. Syria, which had supported Hezbollah initially as a means of forcing the U.S. and French forces out of Lebanon, threw its weight behind Amal and began forcing Hezbollah units out of the Bekaa valley.

Following the withdrawal of U.S. and French multinational units from Lebanon, Hezbollah apparently switched to **kidnapping** and holding of hostages as its preferred tactic for ridding Lebanon of Western influence. In 1985 at least four Americans (not counting the TWA 847 passengers), one Swiss, two Britons, three Frenchmen, one Italian, four Soviets, and four Lebanese Jews were abducted. In 1986 some 15 foreigners were kidnapped and 10 other foreigners were taken in 1987. On 17 February 1988, U.S. Marine Lt. Col. William Higgins, seconded to United Nations peacekeeping forces in Lebanon, was kidnapped and later killed on 31 July 1989. Many of the kidnappings were followed by written messages accompanied by recent photographs of hostages to the Lebanese newspaper *Ash Shira'* claiming credit in the name of **Islamic Jihad**. Another American, CIA station chief William Buckley, was also killed in captivity by Hezbollah. Revelations about the Reagan administration's arms sales to Iran in November 1986 further highlighted Iranian control over Hezbollah and prompted Hezbollah to take Church of England envoy Terry Waite hostage on 20 January 1987 as well.

Following the cessation of U.S. arms for hostages deals Tehran found little future utility in continuing to have Hezbollah seize or hold hostages. The holding of the hostages remained the main reason for Iran's diplomatic isolation following the 1988 cease-fire in the Iran-Iraq war. The increase in U.S. influence in the Middle East as a result of the 1990-1991 Gulf War and the weakening of the position of Iran's Lebanese protégés in the face of increased Syrian support for Hezbollah's enemies in Lebanon may have forced both Iran and Hezbollah to release the remaining hostages before the end of 1991.

Predictions about the demise or eclipse of Hezbollah presuppose that the necessary condition of Iranian state sponsorship had been withdrawn. Following the death of Khomeini, however, the Iranian state had not succeeded in integrating the various clerical factions, some of which have had more influence over Hezbollah than the formal offices of the Iranian state. After the release of Western hostages in December 1991, Hezbollah again resumed car bombing attacks with the 17 March 1992 bombing of the Israeli embassy in Buenos Aires for which, once again, Islamic Jihad claimed credit. On 18 July 1994 Hezbollah operatives used an explosive-packed van to **bomb** the Argentine-Israel Mutual Aid association headquarters in Buenos Aires, Argentina, killing over 100 persons and wounding about 200. On 8 August 1994 an Argentine judge Juan José Galeano announced he had evidence linking Iranian diplomats to the bombing.

During April 1996 Hezbollah engaged in Katyusha rocket attacks from southern Lebanon into northern Israel which led to a 16-day exchange of fire in which Israel would respond to Hezbollah rocket attacks with artillery or air force bombing attacks on Hezbollah positions within Lebanon. However, on 18 April 1996 one such retaliatory attack hit a United Nations refugee center in Qana, Lebanon by mistake, killing 75 civilians. On 12 April 1996 an explosion in an East Jerusalem hotel revealed that Hezbollah had been intending to carry out a **suicide bombing** within Israel. The would-be bomber, Muhammad Hussein Miqdad, a Lebanese Hezbollah member from the village of Faroun, had flown from Zurich, Switzerland on April 4 to Tel Aviv using a forged British passport. While molding a kilo of C-4 plastic explosives into a bomb there was a premature detonation which left him blind and with his lower legs and part of one arm blown off. Although Hezbollah initially denied knowledge of him he was later exchanged along with other Hezbollah prisoners for the remains of Israeli soldiers killed by Hezbollah in southern Lebanon.

Although the Miqdad incident revealed Hezbollah was still willing to use its suicide-bomber tactics, for the most part it chose to use roadside bombs to kill Israelis and their allies in southern Lebanon. Typically a parked car or roadside monument would be packed with explosives and triggered by remote control once an Israeli patrol or convoy passed close to it. In Deir Siryan on 30 January 1997 one such bomb killed three Israeli soldiers and wounded a fourth. The escalation of attacks upon Israeli troops in southern Lebanon by Hezbollah followed its decision to cease Katyusha attacks into northern Israel, a concession that Israel and the United States won through Syria which was trying to soften its image as a sponsor of terrorist groups as well as preparing for eventual peace negotiations with Israel. However, once Hezbollah developed better skills in countering Israeli troops in southern Lebanon it resumed rocket attacks on Israel in August 1997.

Following the ending of the Lebanese civil war in October 1990, Hezbollah and Amal joined forces to harass Israeli and allied South Lebanese Army forces in the south of Lebanon. On 28 August 1997 Israeli forces intending a preemptive strike at Hezbollah and Amal positions instead became trapped in the Wadi Hujuar canyon by cross-fire from Hezbollah and Amal units. When the Israeli Golani Brigade called on their artillery to give them cover to enable a retreat the artillery barrage instead ignited the dry scrub forest on the hillside creating a firestorm that burned three of their members to death. On 6 September 1997 when 16 members of the Israeli naval commando unit, Shayetet 13, attempted a preemptive strike at Hezbollah positions in the village of Ansariyah midway between Sidon and Tyre, they were again surprised by joint Hezbollah and Amal units waiting in place, who had already rigged a roadside bomb to ambush the Israeli unit. Supported by units of the Lebanese Army the joint Amal-Hezbollah units killed 11 of the Israeli team in what was considered to be the worst defeat Israel had suffered in southern Lebanon since 1985.

On 28 February 1999 a roadside bomb set by Hezbollah killed Israeli Brig. General Erez Gerstein, the highest-ranking IDF officer to be killed in the war in Lebanon. In response the Israeli air force bombed Hezbollah strongholds in Baalbak and three other positions. On 24 June 1999 in retaliation for further Hezbollah Katyusha attacks on northern Israel the Israeli air force bombed nine targets in Lebanon, including power stations and bridges, and plunged Beirut into an electric power failure. On 16 August 1999 the Hezbollah coordinator for operations in the south of Lebanon, Ali Hassan Deeb, was **assassinated** by two roadside bombs which Hezbollah blamed on Israel.

2. Hezbollah of Bahrain—Purported Iranian-backed Islamic fundamentalist subversive group in Bahrain. During 20-22 January 1996 riots and rampaging broke out in several Shi'ite villages with three automobiles vandalized and 17 fires set. Officials arrested eight Shi'ite leaders whom they accused of provoking antigovernment riots at the instigation of a foreign power, unnamed but understood to be

Iran. On 19 February 1996 Bahraini officials stated that Shi'ite dissidents suspected of bombings in Bahrain had confessed to having been trained by Iranian-backed Hezbollah militia members in Lebanon. On 3 June 1996 Bahrain announced that it had arrested a total of 44 Bahrainis of whom 34 admitted to their connection with Hezbollah and that six suspects leading the group had been trained in Iran and had met with the supreme religious leader in Iran, Ayatollah 'Ali Khamene'i. The Interior Minister claimed that the same group had been responsible for other disturbances that had broken out in December 1994. Bahrain recalled its ambassador to Tehran.

In April 1997 U.S. forces in Bahrain were put on alert when U.S. intelligence discovered a plan by Bahraini Hezbollah members to attack the 5th Fleet Headquarters located outside Manama, which has 1,000 personnel stationed on a 20-acre complex. In addition to restricting these personnel to base, the shore leaves to visit Bahrain would be canceled for the approximately 12,000 American service personnel on duty in the Persian Gulf. This was the first time in the seven years since the 1990-1991 Gulf War that such an alert had been issued. The Bahraini Hezbollah is also suspected to have ties to Shi'ite dissidents in Saudi Arabia.

3. Hezbollah of Palestine—Obscure group of Palestinian Muslim militants who took credit for a 24 July 1995 suicide bombing of a bus near Tel Aviv claiming six lives and wounding over 30. **Hamas** claimed credit for the same bombing. Hezbollah of Palestine is not connected to the Iranian and Lebanese Shi'ite groups of the same name but is believed to have some 50 followers in Lebanon, mainly Sunni Muslims.

4. Hezbollah of Saudi Arabia—Following the 25 June 1996 **Khobar Towers bombing**, in their sweep to find the group responsible Saudi authorities cracked down on a little-known Shi'ite group in Qatif, known as Hezbollah of Arabia. Between 80 and 100 of its members were arrested and investigated. Its leader, Sheikh Jabar al-Mubarak, had been released from a Saudi prison only in 1993. Shi'ite Muslims number about one million in the oil-rich al-Hasa province of Saudi Arabia, amounting to about 15 percent of the total Saudi population. While Shi'ites are treated as second-class citizens by the strongly Sunni government and have many grievances this group is viewed by observers as very weak and disorganized and probably not ca-

pable of having carried out the attack on the Khobar Towers residence.

HIJACKING. The forcible seizure of a ship, train, automobile, or airplane usually with the threat of bodily harm to the crew and/or passengers. In the 1960s most instances of hijacking involving air carriers were cases of people seeking to escape to some other country. At that time, the United States experienced scores of hijackers attempting to divert domestic flights to Cuba. During the 1970s and 1980s, however, hijackings of airplanes were increasingly used to take the passengers as hostages with which to force the sovereign governments of the hostages to accede to the hijackers' political demands, or those of their state sponsors. By the beginning of the 1990s total airplane hijackings since 1931, the year the first aerial hijacking occurred, were in excess of 700, with a total of over 500 passengers (including the hijackers) and crew members killed by hijackers.

The problem of hijacking was compounded by the **political offense exception** doctrine, which allowed some states to grant immunity from prosecution, or from **extradition**, selectively to hijackers who claimed to be acting on political grounds or else who claimed to be political refugees seeking **asylum**. In April 1986, following the 1985 TWA Flight 847 hijacking to Beirut airport, the International Federation of Airline Pilots Associations put an embargo on Beirut Airport and threatened to embargo other countries that tolerated hijacking. After the TWA 847 hijacking the United States began to apply a 1984 antiterrorist statute to prosecute hijackers who victimized American citizens, arresting Fawaz Younis in September 1987 for his role in a 11 June 1985 hijacking of a Jordanian airliner carrying some U.S. citizens. *See* HOSTAGE-TAKING ACT.

Instances of nonaerial hijackings have included the Assen and Beilen train seizures by South Moluccan terrorists in 2 December 1975 and 23 May 1977 (*see* FREE SOUTH MOLUCCAN ORGANIZATION) and the hijacking of the *Achille Lauro* cruise ship by Palestinian terrorists on 7 October 1985 (*see* PALESTINE LIBERATION FRONT). In each of these instances, hostages were murdered by the hijackers, showing that nonaerial hijackings could be just as deadly.

In late July and early August of 1994 Cuban refugees hijacked three civilian ferry boats and one civilian vessel being used by the Cuban military to flee to the United States. In the seizure of the vessel under military command the Cuban officer was reportedly killed by the hijackers. On 28 August 1995 **Liberation Tigers of Tamil Eelam** hijacked a civilian ferry with 128 civilian passengers, the *Irish Mona*, on its India to Sri Lanka route and sank two Sri Lankan naval gunboats by handheld rockets fired from the hijacked ferry.

The most deadly air hijacking to have occurred in the 20th century was the 23 November 1996 hijacking of Ethiopian Airlines Flight 961 bound from Addis Ababa to Nairobi, Kenya. Twenty minutes after takeoff three men claiming to be Ethiopians seized control of the cockpit saying they had explosives. They demanded that the Boeing 767 be flown to Australia and, despite the pilot's plea that they did not have enough fuel to cross the Indian Ocean, the plane was forced to fly eastward anyway. Four hours after leaving Addis Ababa the pilot was able to crash the plane in the water just off the beach of Mitsamouli on the Comoro Islands. The plane broke into two pieces and 123 of the 175 passengers were killed, including the three hijackers.

The worst hijacking incident involved the simultaneous hijacking of four U.S. passenger flights that were used in the **suicide attacks** against the **World Trade Center and Pentagon on 11 September 2001**. Using crude knives and razors teams of five hijackers each used threats of violecne against passengers to force their way into the cockpits of four planes, American Airlines Flight 11 and United Airlines Flight 175 both flying from Boston to Los Angeles as well as of American Airlines Flight 77 leaving Dullas Airport and United Airlines Flight 93 flying from Newark to San Francisco, where they wrested control of the planes and flew their into their targets. One of the four hijacked places , United Airlines Flight 93, had only four hijackers and crashed outside Pittsburgh, Pennsylvania. Last minute cellular phone calls by some of the passengers revealed that when the passengers had learned the fate of the other planes they determined to overcome the hijackers to prevent their plane from being used in a similar manner. *See also* AIR TRAVEL SECURITY.

HOFFMANN MILITARY SPORTS GROUP. The Wehrsportsgruppe Hoffmann was a nonstate West German **neo-Nazi** group that engaged in paramilitary training and terrorist activities for the revolutionary aim of overthrowing the Federal Republic of Germany and restoring a right-wing nationalist authoritarian regime. The group was founded by Karl-Heinz Hoffmann (1937-) in the latter 1970s. Since West German law forbids neo-Nazi parties or organizations from operating openly, the group represented itself as a club for engaging in military war games. The Sports Group stressed paramilitary training, racist **ideology**, anticommunism, and military romanticism.

The Sports Group is linked to terrorism proper first, through the activities of its own members within Germany, and second, through its ties to Palestinian terrorist groups. Hoffmann created a student branch of his organization called the University Circle of Tübingen Students. This group used to confront and beat up leftist students, often breaking up demonstrations against the apartheid policies of South Africa. The group also baited and attacked feminists and homosexuals.

In 1976 one Sports Group member tried to **bomb** the American Forces Network station in Munich. On 19 December 1980 a Sports Group member, Uwe Behrendt, murdered a Jewish publisher in Erlangen, Shlomo Levin, as well as Levin's female friend, and fled to the Middle East where he later committed suicide in 1982. While authorities could not prove that Hoffmann ordered Behrendt to commit this murder, this incident moved the West German Federal Office for Defense of the Constitution (Bundesamt für Verfassungsschutz) to ban officially the Sports Group as a neo-Nazi group on 30 January 1980.

The most notorious incident associated with the Sports Group was the 26 September 1980 bombing of the Munich Oktoberfest, which killed at least 12 people and wounded over 217 others, including seven U.S. citizens. While it now appears that the detonation of this bomb was an accident, perhaps because the timing mechanism malfunctioned, the bomb itself was produced by the Hoffmann group and the bearer of the bomb, one Gondolf Köhler, was a Sports Group member. Hoffmann was jailed on 27 September 1980 but was released the next day for lack of evidence that he was involved in the bombing.

Hoffmann and the Sports Group were also seeking ties with Palestinian groups as an opportunity to provide training and operational experience to his cadres. In 1979 Hoffmann took 15 followers to Lebanon for training. In July 1980 Hoffmann visited Damascus to form ties with the **Palestine Liberation Organization** (PLO). Hoffmann not only left 20 more of his members in PLO camps but also struck a lucrative deal to ship used trucks and heavy equipment to the PLO. Hoffmann was again arrested in June 1981 in Frankfurt as he was ready to fly to Beirut. His followers who had undergone training in PLO camps were arrested on their return to Germany.

While the Sports Group has ceased to function as an organization, many of its members have continued to work in the neo-Nazi movement, which has continued to grow both in Germany and elsewhere, where a number of other neo-Nazi groups allow them the opportunity to continue quasi-legal or terrorist activities.

HOLLAND TUNNEL BOMB PLOT. Following the **1993 World Trade Center bombing** Sheikh Omar Abdul Rahman, the spiritual leader of the four principal conspirators in the World Trade Center bombing, was implicated in that conspiracy as well as in a broader conspiracy to bomb other public places in New York, including the Holland and Lincoln tunnels and the United Nations building, as well as a plot to murder U.S. Senator Alfonse d'Amato (R., N.Y.) and United Nations Secretary General Boutros Boutros-Ghali. In 24 June 1993 eight of Abdul Rahman's followers were arrested in connection with this plot. Government transcripts of conversations between Abdul Rahman and his followers, secretly taped by an FBI informer, revealed that Abdul Rahman had discussed the relative merits of various targets for this terrorist bombing campaign.

On 27 August 1993 Abdul Rahman was charged before a U.S. Federal judge with leading this conspiracy to carry out a bombing campaign against the United States. On 9 January 1995 the trial of Abdul Rahman along with 11 other defendants charged with the bombing of the World Trade Center and for the conspiracy to bomb the New York landmarks began. In the course of this trial it was learned that two of those charged in connection with the Holland Tunnel plot, El Sayyid Nosair and Clement Hampton-El, had been under FBI surveillance, apparently to determine what material help to the Afghan **Mujahideen** was originating among private groups in the United States. Hampton-El was also a member of another covert Muslim group, the **Jama'at ul Fuqra**. On 14 March 1995 Emad Saleh, the former FBI informer, testified that the aim of the group had been to detonate 12 bombs simultaneously against **targets** thought to be associated with Jews or Jewish institutions. On 1 October 1995 Abdul Rahman was convicted of seditious conspiracy, solicitation and conspiracy to murder Egyptian President Hosni Mubarak, solicitation to attack U.S. military installations, and conspiracy to conduct the **bombing** campaign against New York tunnels and landmarks. On 17 January 1996 Abdul Rahman was sentenced to life imprisonment for his role in the Holland Tunnel bomb plot. He is currently serving his sentence in a U.S. federal prison.

HOMELAND DEFENSE. Term used to refer to an evolving strategy of **counterterrorism** based on the analogy of counterterrorist efforts with fighting a war. As a result of the **bombings** of the **World Trade Center** and the Murrah Building, the attacks against the United States embassies in East Africa, and the bombing of the **Khobar Towers** in Saudi Arabia, the threats both of domestic and foreign terrorism have been identified as among the leading dangers to national security of liberal democracies and other nations around the world. Expanding efforts to combat terrorism now involve massive expenditures by various governments to meet present and future threats. In the United States alone spending on counterterrorism is estimated to have increased from $61.7 million to $205.3 million in the 1999 appropriations as documented in the *Congressional Quarterly, Weekly Report*, January 16, 1999, p. 151.

Within the United States homeland defense efforts have involved many initiatives including the creation of a Domestic Preparedness Program to train state and local agencies to respond to threats and actual uses of **weapons of mass destruction** (WMD) and the expanded reorganization of federal agencies to combat terrorism involving over 40 agencies ranging from the Interagency Working Group on Counterterrorism, the Federal Bureau of Investigation Counterterrorism Center and its National Infrastructure Protection Center, in addition to the already existing 16 Joint Terrorism Task Forces (JTTFs) and the Central Intelligence Agency's Counterterrorist Center (CTC). Also the role of the Department of Defense has been greatly expanded, not only regarding external threats but also domestic terrorism, and very extensive research and development programs have been undertaken which place heavy emphasis on the creation and refinement of counterterrorism technology to address the challenges of mass terrorism and also to meet the growing requirements for far better information handling. Similar initiatives are being pursued by other governments as well.

While these new initiatives are significant in the short term perhaps more significant in the long term are the fundamental constitutional issues and the changing face of civil-military relations in the United States, in particular the changing roles of the Federal Bureau of Investigation and of the Department of Defense as a result of this war against terrorism.

Legally the FBI, as an agency of the Department of Justice, is entering a gray area regarding jurisdiction. As an entity within the Department of Justice its legal mandate primarily permits it to be involved in domestic law enforcement, however, the FBI has become increasingly involved in extraterritorial operations. The focus of most FBI operations is directed to gathering evidence sufficient to secure criminal prosecution and conviction of terrorist suspects in U.S. courts of law. However, using such evidence in court runs directly counter to the ongoing need to gather and analyze intelligence on terrorists because unveiling such information will compromise the covert operatives and classified methods needed to collect it.

Similarly the Department of Defense is entering a gray area in which military resources and tactics may be used to carry out ordinary police functions. With the increasing public demands to combat terrorism, the constraints imposed by the Posse Comitatus Act upon the use of military force, which were relaxed in the war against drugs, have been further lessened to fight the war on terrorism. This expansion of the direct role of the military emphasizes a direct operational role for the military, as opposed to a supportive role on behalf of civilian law enforcement. This military involvement is likely to expand on the plea that it will be essential to counter the threats of mass terrorism or its consequences within the United States. The jurisdictional questions associated with the changing roles of the military are also mirrored in the changing role of the police and other law enforcement agencies in the United States and other nations. National and local police forces are becoming more militarized as they develop armed capabilities that can be used in more aggressive actions to protect public order and security. Whereas liberal democracies formerly distinguished clearly between domestic police enforcement, in which minimal force is used to apprehend suspects, and military actions, in which maximum force is used to destroy the enemy forces, now there is an increasing "mission blur" between the roles of the police and the military in democratic societies.

Homeland defense is not the same as civil defense, which was directed against the actions of an external enemy in a war environment, for it would involve the military in defending internal security rather than national security. Since such enforcement powers would at times be directed against its own citizens and civilian authorities this raises serious questions about changing civil/military relations in democratic societies.

Following the **World Trade Center and Pentagon Attacks of 11 September 2001,** President George W. Bush announed on 15 September 2001 his intention to establish an Office of Homeland Security which would include a Homeland Security Council patterned after the National Security Council. The members of the Homeland Defense Council would be the attorney general, and the secretaries of the Departments of Defense, the Treasury, Agriculture, and Health and Human Services, supported by about 100 staff members. President George W. Bush invited Governor Tom Ridge of Pennsylvania to become director of this office. After resigning his governorship Tom Ridge was sworn in as Director of Homeland Security on 8 October 2001. This office replaced the position held formerly by Richard Clarke, who headed the White House office created during the Clinton administration to coordinate counterterrorism efforts. In turn Richard Clarke was appointed to head a new Office of Cyber-Security. The new Office of Homeland Security seeks to coordinate the actions of the 46 federal agencies that currently enforce or implement counterterrroism policies.

HOSTAGE TAKING. *See* KIDNAPPING.

HOSTAGE-TAKING ACT. The Act for the Prevention and Punishment of the Crime of Hostage-Taking (Title 18 U.S. Code, Section 1203) was enacted on October 1984, ostensibly to implement the United Nations International Convention Against the Taking of Hostages, adopted by the General Assembly on 17 December 1979. This act makes the seizure of a U.S. national anywhere in the world a crime, as well as any hostage taking directed against the U.S. government or incident in which the hostage taker is a U.S. national. This act granted the FBI powers of extraterritorial investigation and allowed the U.S. government to prosecute an alleged hostage taker whenever handed over to U.S. authorities. The act also makes the aiding and abetting of the act, or concealing knowledge of it, or otherwise obstructing investigation of such crimes, punishable when done by private persons. This statute, and the Airplane Sabotage Act of 1984, allowed the United States to capture Fawaz Younis, who participated in the 11 June 1985 **hijacking** of a Jordanian airliner carrying some U.S. citizens, as well as the arrest and **extradition** of Mohammed Hammadei, who participated in the 14 June 1985 hijacking of TWA Flight 847, which led to the murder of one U.S. serviceman aboard and the holding hostage of 39 U.S. civilians.

HOLY TERROR. Term used by David Rapaport and Bruce Hoffman to identity a strain of postmodern terrorism accentuated by a religious, transcendental, or **millennialist** motivation. While religiously motivated terrorists are not a new phenomenon, since the Jewish **Zealots** of the first century and the Isma'ili Shi'ite **Fedayeen** Assassins of the 11th century were also terrorists motivated by a religious ideal, the phenomenon has become more prominent and more lethal in the post-Cold War era in which the resurgence of religious fundamentalist and **ethno-nationalist** militant movements coincides with the availability of terrorist weapons and tactics capable of killing or maiming large numbers of people.

Whereas the leftist revolutionary groups and nationalist-separatist groups of the last decades of the 20th century had political goals that their opponents could comprehend, if not condone, and whereas many of these groups sought some degree of political legitimacy and acceptance by their adversaries, the extremist fundamentalist groups, such as **Hamas** or the **Armed Islamic Group**, or the **millennialist** doomsday groups, such as Aum Shinrikyo, pursue goals that their opponents cannot fathom much less anticipate and prevent. Whereas previous groups appeared to prefer converting their opponents to killing them the practitioners of Holy Terror tend to demonize their opponents as the incarnation of evil whose physical annihilation becomes a holy duty. Whereas other groups appeared amenable to negotiation and material incentives most of the groups motivated by holy terror shun civil contacts with their opponents.

The phenomenon of Holy Terror has appeared not only among **Islamic fundamentalists** but also among the Jewish extremists of the Kach, Kahane Chai, and **Eyal** movements, among Christian Patriot groups and millennialist sects, as well as among nonmonotheistic groups such as the Aum Shinrikyo group in Japan or the Solar Temple group in Switzerland. As such this appears to be a widespread post-modern reaction of many religious and ethnic groups that find themselves threatened by the cosmopolitan tide of secularization that has been sweeping the world during the last few decades which will likely continue to be a source of terrorist violence well in the next century. *See also* JIHAD; MILLENNIALISM.

HUKS. The Hukbalahap (an acronym for Hukbong Bayan Laban Sa Hapon, meaning "People's Anti-Japanese Resistance Army") was a resistance army founded by the Communist Party of the Philippines in March 1942. Trained by Chinese Communist instructors sent by Mao Tse-tung and led by Luis Taroc, the Huks recruited extensively among the peasants and harassed the Japanese in guerrilla raids.

Following World War II, the Huks, who renamed their organization the Hukbong Mapagpalaya ng Bayan, "People's Liberation Army," attempted to set up a communist regime but were countered by U.S. forces. The Huks numbered around 10,000 active fighters at their height but lacked good weaponry. Consequently they relied more on terrorism than on conventional tactics, their most stunning attack being the ambush and murder of the widow of President Manuel L. Quezon in April 1949. In addition to undertaking a more thorough counterinsurgency effort, the administration of Ramon Magsaysay addressed many of the social and economic grievances of the peasant following of the Huks, who eventually disbanded in 1954.

HUSSEIN SUICIDE SQUAD. One of the pro-Iranian Shi'ite **Islamic fundamentalist** terrorist groups in Lebanon that became part of **Hezbollah**.

- I -

IDENTITY CHRISTIANITY. The Identity Christianity doctrine is a synthesis of **white supremacist** doctrine, xenophobic American populism, and a post-**millennialist** version of Anglo-Israelitism that has become a major ideological inspiration for extreme right-wing terrorist groups operating in North America.

In 1794, Englishman Richard Brothers developed the Anglo-Israelite doctrine claiming that the true Israelites were not contemporary Jews but rather the northern European nations, and especially the British, who supposedly were descended from the northern "lost" tribes of Israel deported by the Assyrians in the eighth century B.C. This doctrine was modified by some Americans to identify North America rather than Great Britain as the new promised land. The modern form of Identity Christianity that grew out of Anglo-Israelitism was first propounded during the Depression era by a nondenominational preacher, Wesley Swift, who combined it with anti-Semitism and extreme anti-Communism defined broadly enough to include socialists and most liberals. The modern doctrine asserts that nonwhites are descendants of "pre-Adamites" created only as prototypes of true humans and that Jews are the descendants of a sexual union between Eve and the tempting serpent that appeared in the Garden of Eden.

The post-millennialist component of Identity Christianity implies that the realization of God's Kingdom on earth requires the true believers (identified with white, Identity Christians) to struggle actively against the forces of darkness (identified with Jews, nonwhites, and communists). What distinguishes Identity Christianity from evangelical Christian fundamentalism proper is that most evangelicals believe in premillennialism, which asserts instead that the realization of God's Kingdom on earth will proceed according to an inscrutable divine plan that can neither be helped nor hindered by human political efforts. Also most evangelicals regard modern Jews as the true descendants of the original Israelites and regard the creation of the State of Israel as a manifestation of God's gracious intervention in history fulfilling certain Biblical prophecies. By contrast, most Identity Christians regard the existence of the State of Israel as proof of a hidden, sinister conspiracy at work in the world, which they must fight.

The Identity Christian movement seems tailormade to provide a unifying religious and political worldview for such groups as the various **Ku Klux Klan, neo-Nazi**, and right-wing survivalist groups as well as a theological justification for their propagation of racial hatred. Among those groups that are founded on variations of the Identity Christianity doctrine, or else that have adopted that doctrine, are the **Aryan Nations, the Order**, and the **Christian-Patriots Defense League**. These groups have either directly participated in terrorist actions or else have condoned such actions by their members. Such terrorism usually involves attacks on Jews and other members of minority groups or else attacks on officials of the U.S. federal government, which the Identity Christians refer to as the "Zionist Occupation Government," or simply as "ZOG." The **Covenant, the Sword and the Arm of the Lord** was another such group that ceased to exist with the arrest and recantation of its leader.

Not all white supremacists or extreme rightists necessarily profess Identity Christianity. The World Church of the Creator, run by Matt Hale, a white supremacist, and headquartered in East Peoria, Illinois, is an explicitly anti-Christian as well as anti-Jewish white supremacist group operating under cover of religion which disdains open association with Identity Christian theology. Robert dePugh, founder of the **Minutemen**, was actually an avowed atheist. The leader of the Order,

Robert Mathews, who professed Identity Christianity, was secretly a worshiper of the Norse gods. Nonetheless such leaders have cynically used Identity Christianity as a means for attracting the support of disaffected white Christians who might otherwise be uninterested in the white supremacist political message. Viewed as a religious phenomenon Identity Christianity recalls the Marcionist doctrine of the early Christian era, an anti-Semitic interpretation of the New Testament that denied the validity of the Old Testament but that was rejected as heresy by orthodox Christian theologians. Viewed simply as a political phenomenon the Identity Christian movement is the closest thing to being an indigenous American fascist **ideology** having widespread appeal among politically disenchanted white populists. *See also* MILLENNIALISM

IDENTITY POLITICS. A form of domestic politics within one nation-state in which individuals relate to each other as members of competing groups based upon ascriptive characteristics such as race, gender, religion, or sexual orientation. Often the basis of a group claim of entitlement to power, or of disenfranchisement of the power of a competing group, is some claim of historical or current unredressed group grievance. The nature of the competition is often perceived by members of the competing groups as zero-sum, that is, a gain of relative power by one group necessarily entails a loss of some power by all other groups. The rise of identity politics within the United States in the past three decades accounts for recent attempts to define **hate crimes** through legally specified classes of victims and offenders distinguished both by the victim's and accused's relative memberships in legally specified groups and by alleged bias-related motives of the accused. Within the United States identity politics has been manifest in the rise of right-wing patriot and **militia movement**-type groups as well as the revival of **white supremacist** groups in the 1980s and 1990s. Identity politics has led to similar groups and movements in other liberal democracies, such as anti-Turkish nativism in Germany by **skinheads** and **neo-Nazis**, anti-Arab nativism in France by groups such as the **National Front**, and the anti-Muslim actions of the Yugoslavian government under former President Slobodan Milosevic. Taken to its extreme identity politics may become **ethno-nationalist terrorism**.

IDEOLOGY. A system of ideas and beliefs about the nature of humanity, the nature of the world, government, and politics that helps to guide the holder of the ideology in making political choices and in the exercise of political power. An ideology plays a role similar to that of a "theory" in a scientific system or to that of a "creed" in a religious system.

The Frenchman Deshutt de Tracy invented this term in 1797 to describe the "true ideas" of political philosophy which had been "proven" in the testing grounds of the French Revolution. He and his fellow-thinkers became known as *les idéologues*. Karl Marx used the term to designate instead what he regarded as a "false consciousness" of traditional and religious beliefs used by the dominant economic class to maintain its rule and legitimacy. Rather than using *ideology* as a term to designate "false political ideas" or a system of "true political ideas" it may used in a neutral manner to refer to any system of political ideas which support each other and which simplify political analysis and decision making for the individuals and groups who adhere to the ideology. A key point is that certain essential beliefs of any ideology are irrational or nonscientific and these components of the ideology may not be amenable to rational deliberation or debate, e.g., assumptions about the moral nature of man, the inevitability of human progress, and the like. The more ideological a politically engaged person is, the more selective will be his or herperception or interpretation of events and facts.

The personal or group ideology of the political extremist or terrorist achieves a near religious or revelatory quality such that it becomes the prism through which all events, persons, and groups are evaluated. Whoever questions the ideology of the extremist group is viewed not simply as in error or disagreement with the truth but also as morally reprehensible or evil. Thus highly ideological thinking facilitates the depersonalization and demonization of perceived "enemies" which allows the political extremist or terrorist to carry out horrific acts of violence against them with little sense of remorse or sympathy. Ideological thinking tends to be stereotypical and rigid in interpretation of events. The tendency of terrorist groups to form themselves into closed, clandestine cells reinforces the tendency to **groupthink**, which is reinforced by the ideological beliefs and motivations of the group.

INFORMATION WARFARE. Information-oriented warfare is associated with low- to high-intensity conflicts part of which may involve strategic information warfare in which computer infrastructures for communications and control are directly attacked, whether by physical targeting or else by means of hacking or attacks by computer viruses. It is relatively cheap and easy for individuals or groups to shut down computer systems and cause enormous financial losses through hacking and other attacks on information systems. In many well-publicized cases, such as the "I love you" virus that afflicted information systems throughout the world, the motives of the perpetrators were neither terroristic nor done for purposes of fraud. Therefore it is easy to imagine the harm that a terrorist group could inflict if it opted to use cyber-attacks as a means of pressuring its **targeted** nation or group.

However, this cyber-warfare may not involve attacks on computers so much as using computer information systems to pursue conventional tactics. For instance during the Chechen war the original Chechnyan leader Dzhukar Dudayev was killed by a Russian missile when his position was pinpointed by means of tracing the signal of his cellular phone. Another example is how U.S. **counterterrorism** efforts have focused on identifying the bank accounts of terrorist groups and leaders and then electronically "emptying" them or else transferring a large sum from the accounts of a leader to those of a trusted subordinate to create the impression of embezzlement and to sow rancor and distrust between the key members of a terrorist cadre. During the 1990-1991 Persian Gulf War the Iraqi air defense radars were cluttered with hundreds of false signals generated by chips covertly implanted in radar equipment sold to Iraq which were activated by U.S. military codes to render the air defense systems inoperative during any U.S. air attack. Another cyber-warfare tactic is to swarm a Web site with thousands of e-mail messages with the intent of shutting the site down. During the course of the 1998-1999 Kosovo conflict, official U.S. government Web sites of the CIA, the Defense Department, and the State Department were being bombarded with as many as 30,000 cyber-attacks a day originating in Eastern Europe.

The term *cyber-terrorism* has been loosely applied to cover instances of computer-assisted embezzlement or cases of extortion in which blackmailers have forced financial institutions to pay protection money to forestall their shutting down or destroying computer operations vital to the firm, however, these are cases of nonpolitical criminality. Similarly the mere release of viruses created to destroy files and software is not terrorism since such malicious mischief is not specifically targeted at any one group nor do such actions necessarily promote a political message, which are essential elements for a criminal action to be considered a form of terrorism. If cyber-terrorism is directed to cause system failures in order to cause death and damages, e.g., by shutting down air traffic guidance systems or critical failures in emergency response systems, then the elements of targeting and lethality are present which may allow such actions to be classified as terrorism, assuming the element of a political or social motivation is also present. Counterterrorism experts believe that in the future state sponsors of terrorism or nonstate groups may find ways to conduct terrorism through information warfare. *See also* NETWAR.

INNER MACEDONIAN REVOLUTIONARY ORGANIZATION (IMRO). IMRO was a state-sponsored Macedonian revolutionary nationalist group that undertook terrorist actions to create an independent Macedonian homeland. The group enjoyed Bulgarian state support from 1901 until 1912, when Bulgaria, Greece, and Serbia divided the former Turkish possession among themselves. IMRO was later supported by Hungary and Fascist Italy until World War II.

IMRO committed one of the earliest instances of **kidnapping** and holding a U.S. citizen as a hostage for political ends. In September 1901, an American Congregationalist missionary, Ellen M. Stone, was kidnapped by IMRO and held for ransom. The Theodore Roosevelt administration considered, but rejected, the payment of the demanded ransom, which was instead provided by a $66,000 subscription raised privately by Stone's sponsoring missionary society and which was accepted by the Macedonian nationalists. Stone was freed in February 1902, while the proceeds of the ransom payment financed an abortive revolt against the Turks that was quickly crushed in August 1903.

In its later years IMRO changed from being a revolutionary terrorist group into an **entrepreneurial terrorist** organization that hired itself out to various regimes to commit **assassinations** on a contract basis.

INSURGENCY. One definition for insurgency is a struggle between a group lacking authority and the governing authorities in which the group lacking authority uses both political resources and violence to either destroy the legitimacy of the ruling group or else to change the terms by which legitimate power is held, and to establish their own alternative legitimacy (Bard E. O'Neill, 1990). Another criterion for distinguishing insurgencies from isolated guerrilla hit-and-run attacks or terrorist actions is whether the guerrillas have begun openly to control areas of land within a contested country. As such insurgency falls between the extremes of **revolution**, in which the major part of the society becomes involved in the change of regime and terrorism by individuals or groups lacking any nonterrorist complementary political program. Insurgents generally will use either conventional warfare or terrorist tactics as they perceive the situation warrants but may limit their terrorist actions as their political program requires. Insurgents may choose to **target** civilians as tactics to delegitimize the government, which may be perceived as unable or unwilling to provide civilians with security, or else to provoke the government into overreacting.

Using this definition, one may regard the **Basque Fatherland and Liberty** group as part of a Basque insurgency rather than as merely a terrorist group. The political goals of this group have directed their terrorist actions to attacking symbols of Spanish hegemony, and the Spanish security forces in particular, rather than Spanish civilians generally.

INTIFADA. The *intifada* (Arabic: "uprising, revolt") refers to the popular uprising against Israeli occupation among Palestinians on the West Bank and the Gaza Strip. This revolt began on 9 December 1987, with protests over an automobile accident in the Gaza Strip in which an Israeli motorist killed Palestinian pedestrians. While the early stages of the revolt involved youngsters taunting and throwing stones at Israeli troops, it eventually spread throughout the Palestinian population and involved organized demonstrations, civil disobedience, and boycotting of Israeli goods and services.

In spite of the apparent spontaneity of the outbreak of the *intifada*, the **Palestine Liberation Organization** and other non-PLO groups, such as **Hamas** and **Islamic Jihad of Palestine**, have coordinated most of the leading events of the *intifada*. The majority of the activities carried out in the name of the *intifada* were not terrorist acts, even while such acts as stone throwing or attacks on Israeli soldiers could arguably be viewed as political violence distinct from terrorism as such. Within the Palestinian community, however, reprisals, including murders, perpetrated against Palestinians viewed as Israeli collaborators or informers became increasingly common with groups such as the "Black Panthers" on the West Bank killing those viewed as lacking zeal for their cause. Given **al**

Fatah's governing role in the *intifada* through the Unified National Leadership (UNL), a PLO front group established to coordinate *intifada* activities, and its past record of using its covert operations and internal enforcement organ, Force-17, either within Israeli territory or against Palestinians viewed as enemies of Fatah, there is a reasonable basis for viewing the bloodletting among Palestinians as constituting a terrorist campaign.

Most internationally voiced concerns about terrorism and the *intifada* centered instead on alleged Israeli **state terror** perpetrated against Palestinian demonstrators and activists. Israeli soldiers sometimes retaliated against stone-throwing youths by breaking the arms of the offenders, while the Israeli government's bulldozing of homes of activists and deportation of selected Palestinian leaders of the *intifada* have led to denunciations of Israel both internationally and within the United States. In February 1989 the U.S. Department of State's annual report on human rights charged Israel with causing "many avoidable deaths and injuries" and with violations of Palestinians' human rights due to Israeli Defense Forces actions against Palestinian protestors.

On 28 September 2000 a "second *intifada*" broke out in protest to the visit of the Likud Party leader Ariel Sharon to the Temple Mount, a place considered sacred to Muslims as the Haram ash Sharif. This second uprising convulsed those Occupied Areas in which Israeli troops or settlements were still present. Several Israelis have been killed along with over 400 Palestinian protestors. The severity of this violence included Israeli air strikes, using rockets fired from helicopters, against Fatah offices and a collapse of peace negotiations between the Palestinian Authority under **Yasir Arafat** and the Labor government of Israeli Prime Minister Ehud Barak. In turn this may have contributed to the 6 February 2001 prime ministerial election victory of Likud candidate Ariel Sharon.

INTIHARIOUN. *See* SUICIDE BOMBERS.

IRAULTZA. Also known as the "Basque Armed Revolutionary Workers' Organization," Iraultza was a Basque separatist organization dedicated to creating an independent and Marxist Basque state. Very little is known about the origins and composition of the organization or its relation to other Basque groups.

Iraultza did not leave written communiqués so all that was known about the organization came from their telephoned messages, usually given as warnings shortly before their impending **bombing** attacks. The group opposed international investments in the Basque region. The group also opposed Spain's participation in NATO and was highly critical of the U.S. foreign policy of the Reagan administration. Despite its vocal anti-American sentiments, however, this group never struck at, or threatened, U.S. diplomatic facilities or personnel.

Iraultza used very small bombs that were usually exploded late at night to avoid injuring people. The only injury caused by an Iraultza bomb was due to a malfunction that failed to detonate the activated bomb at the right time, killing a construction worker who came across it the following day. Nonetheless, Iraultza managed to inflict more bombings against U.S. business interests than any other European terrorist group. From May 1982 to the end of 1987, there were at least 31 bombings by this group, including five attacks on the offices of the Rank Xerox firm, two attacks on a Coca-Cola bottling plant, six attacks on banks, including branches of Citibank and Bank of America, and also on a theater showing the film *Red Dawn*. French business firms have also been favorite **targets**. All of these attacks have been confined to the Basque-inhabited areas of Spain. From 1987 to 1990 little was heard of this group, which appeared never to have more than 20 members. In March and April 1991, Iraultza attempted three bombings, but three of its members were killed by a premature explosion. Apparently the group, which was never very large, disbanded after this calamity.

IRGUN. The Organization for the Defense of the People (Irgun Zvai Leumi) was a nonstate Zionist paramilitary organization dedicated to the expulsion of British forces and the Arab population from Palestine to establish a Jewish state there. The Irgun was not simply a "nonstate" organization insofar as it was an illegal group from the viewpoint of the British mandatory regime but was also outside of the infrastructure of the Jewish Agency in Palestine, which already had the Haganah (Defense Organization) as its military wing, which became, respectively, the Israeli government and Israeli army upon independence. The Irgun was founded in 1937 by David Raziel, who was killed in 1941 helping the British quell a German-inspired revolt in Iraq. He was succeeded by Menachem Begin (1913-1990).

From 1944, the Irgun and **LEHI** collaborated in attacking the British army and civil administration in Palestine. On 22 July 1946 the Irgun **bombed** the British administrative center in Palestine, located in the King David Hotel in Jerusalem, killing over 90 people, many of whom, ironically, turned out to be Jewish employees of the mandatory authority. On 9 April 1948 the Irgun attacked the Arab village of Deir Yassin located on the road connecting Jerusalem to Tel Aviv, killing all of its inhabitants except for two old women and a young girl. The news of this massacre in turn prompted many Palestinian Arabs to flee their homes when the first Arab-Israeli war broke out the following month. All told, the activities of the Irgun and LEHI caused the deaths of 373 people in Palestine. With the declaration of Israeli independence and the outbreak of war with the Arab states, most Irgun members joined the Israeli army.

IRISH NATIONAL LIBERATION ARMY (INLA). INLA is an Irish nationalist terrorist group that began as the military wing of the Irish Republican Socialist Party, itself a faction that broke with the Official IRA (*see* IRISH REPUBLICAN ARMY) in 1974. INLA aims to use armed struggle to force British troops out of Northern Ireland, to impose unification of the northern six counties with the rest of Ireland, and to overthrow the current Republic of Ireland in favor of a Marxist-Leninist revolutionary state, which would withdraw from the European Union.

INLA terrorist activities have included not only **bombings** and shootings against British and Ulster officials, security forces, Protestant loyalists, and members of Protestant militias but also internecine bloodletting with both the official and provisional wings of the IRA as well as within INLA itself. The struggles with the older IRA groups lasted from 1974 until 1977, when INLA founder Seamus Costello was murdered by unknown persons.

On 30 March 1979 INLA killed Airey Neave, a British Conservative Party parliamentarian close to Prime Minister Margaret Thatcher and a vocal critic of Irish republican terrorists, by a bomb rigged within his car, which detonated within the underground parking garage of Westminster Hall. On 17 April 1979 INLA killed four members of the Royal Ulster Constabulary with a remote-control bomb, the most severe blow ever inflicted on the Ulster police until then. INLA then proceeded with a campaign of killing Ulster prison guards as well as British and Ulster undercover operatives. From November 1979 until September

1986 INLA carried out three successful bombings and at least two other attempts. The worst of these occurred on 6 December 1982, when INLA bombed a nightclub in Ballykelly, killing 17 people (12 of them soldiers) and wounding 66 others. From January to June 1987, INLA reverted to internecine fighting killing at least 12 of its veterans before members of other republican groups negotiated a truce among the surviving INLA members.

INLA is much more openly Marxist-Leninist and more doctrinaire than the IRA. INLA has cooperated with the West German **Revolutionary Cells** and French **Direct Action** leftist groups.

During the 1994 cease-fire INLA did not declare a cease-fire, but declared rather a "no-first-strike" policy. INLA has been responsible for about 125 killings during its existence of whom 45 were members of the security forces while INLA lost approximately 20 of its own members who were killed. Finally INLA called its own cease-fire on 22 August 1998.

IRISH REPUBLICAN ARMY (IRA). The name of the IRA has been used loosely to refer to the **Irish National Liberation Army**, the Official Irish Republican Army, the Provisional Irish Republican Army, and other Irish republican or nationalist splinter groups. In reality the group known as the Provisional Irish Republican Army (PIRA) is the main body of the IRA. Historically the name was used first by James Connolly to designate the nationalist forces used in the Dublin Easter rebellion of 1916. Following the creation of the Irish Free State in 1922, the new Irish state disbanded the IRA and then proscribed it when militant nationalists opposed to the partition of Ireland refused to obey the Free State government.

The IRA began a **bombing** campaign in Great Britain during most of 1939 and the early part of 1940, striking over 50 targets in London, Manchester, Glasgow, and Birmingham. The Irish government banned the IRA in 1939, cooperating with the British in their suppression. During 1955 to 1962, the IRA unleashed a "border campaign" directed against the Royal Ulster Constabulary, which again was suppressed through official Anglo-Irish cooperation.

With the advent of the 50th anniversary of the Easter rebellion in 1967, militant Ulster Protestants increased harassment of Catholics in Northern Ireland. This prompted nationalist political organizers to form a Northern Ireland Civil Rights Association, which organized marches and protests even in Protestant neighborhoods. The IRA provided escorts for these marches but lacked sufficient arms to fend off **arson** attacks by militant Protestants against the homes and businesses of Catholics.

Disagreements within the IRA over its increasingly Marxist and political character led its effective reorganization in 1969 under the name of the Provisional Irish Republican Army, the "Provos," which maintained that their primary goal was unification of Ireland by force even against the wishes of the Protestant majority in the north, not civil rights for Catholics in a separate Northern Ireland and not some sort of socialist state, and that the primary means to achieve this goal was armed struggle rather than political negotiation. PIRA is in fact the IRA that continued the armed struggled from 1969 to 1998. By default the original organization from which the current IRA emerged became known as the Official Irish Republican Army (OIRA). OIRA and PIRA competed with each other and sometimes feuded in gun battles with each other when each was not fighting the British army or Protestant paramilitary groups. In 1972, however, OIRA officially renounced armed struggle and eventually became known as the Workers' Party, competing openly in electoral politics in both Northern Ireland and the Republic of Ireland. With the end of the OIRA the name IRA came to designate the successor PIRA group.

In reality the memberships of OIRA and the post-1972 IRA were often overlapping. In an attempt to prevent its members from using OIRA arms in IRA operations, OIRA in effect expelled its more radical nationalist members in 1974. These radicals, who believed in armed struggle, in turn, formed the Irish National Liberation Army (INLA), a group at least as violent as the IRA but possessing also the extreme Marxist-Leninist **ideology** that had come to characterize OIRA.

The pre-1972 IRA had maintained a political front known as Sinn Fein (Irish for "Ourselves Alone"). With the reactivation of the IRA in 1969, the Sinn Fein party officially disavowed any connection with the IRA, a tactic that allowed the IRA a legal front and the option of resorting to negotiations if expedient. With the emergence of PIRA a Provisional Sinn Fein came into existence alongside the Sinn Fein associated with OIRA. Once OIRA renounced armed struggle, there was no longer the need for the pretense of a separate political front, and so since 1972 the name Sinn Fein now refers only to the political front of the post-1972 IRA. INLA also had as its associated political front the Irish Republican Socialist Party. When organizers of this party found that INLA, which they had viewed as their party's military wing, was unwilling to submit itself to control by the party, they dissociated themselves from INLA, which then operated without any political front group.

Despite the historical discontinuity between the pre-1969 IRA and PIRA, most references to the IRA in public discussion and news reports deal mainly with PIRA which is therefore the de facto IRA and all other Republican or Nationalist paramilitaries are merely marginal splinter groups or factions.

The IRA is the main Irish nationalist paramilitary and terrorist organization that until April 1998 sought to reunite the six counties of Northern Ireland with the rest of Ireland into an "Irish Socialist Republic" primarily by revolutionary armed struggle rather than through political or diplomatic means. As the IRA's approximately 1,500 members were quite outnumbered by the Northern Irish police together with regular British forces and security forces in Northern Ireland, the IRA has resorted heavily to terrorism aimed at inflicting maximum casualties and has targeted civilians as well as military personnel.

The most recent period of IRA terrorism began in 1969 with covert aid, including arms, from the Irish Republic during the Fianna Fail government of Prime Minister Jack Lynch. Later Irish governments desisted from covert support and took steps to intercept arms destined for the IRA being shipped through Irish territory. Libya has provided arms and financial help intermittently, having shipped five tons of arms from Tripoli on the *Claudia*, which were seized by the Irish Navy on 28 March 1973. This shipment was followed by a shipment of 150 tons of Libyan weapons, including Czech-made Semtex explosives, aboard the *Eskund*, seized by French customs and police on 1 November 1987. Iran and Algeria also have aided the IRA. The IRA developed contacts with the **Basque Fatherland and Liberty** group as well as the **Popular Front for the Liberation of Palestine** and the **Revolutionary Cells** found in Germany. However most of the IRA's resources come from within the Irish community, through extortion and protection payments among the Irish Catholic communities in the northern six counties, bank robberies both in Northern Ireland and the Republic, and through appeals for donations from people of Catholic Irish descent living in the United States and elsewhere, often through front organizations such as NORAID (the Irish Northern Aid Organization). On 29 September 1984, the Irish

Navy seized seven tons of arms on the trawler *Marita Ann* off-loaded from a ship that had transported them from the United States.

IRA terrorism had several objectives: It was intended to raise to unacceptable levels the economic and political costs to Great Britain of maintaining troops in Northern Ireland. It sought to provoke British and Northern Irish military and police forces to violate the human and civil rights of IRA suspects or of ordinary Catholics in the hope that such abuses in turn would outrage Great Britain's domestic civil libertarians and excite international condemnation. It was meant also to mobilize forcibly into the struggle the Northern Irish Catholics over whom the IRA asserted its jurisdiction. This has entailed summary punishments against Catholics who themselves do not agree with the IRA political program or who are suspected of cooperating with Northern Irish and British authorities, by means of kneecappings, summary executions, and threats against family members. In recent years the IRA developed the tactic of using detected informers as **suicide bombers** driving car bombs into the positions of Northern Irish police and British troops. The suicide driver was usually a married man with family who was told that his family would be murdered if he did not cooperate. Such a suicide car bomber killed himself and five soldiers in an attack on a Londonderry checkpoint on 24 October 1990.

The primary targets of the IRA have been British Army troops, Northern Irish security forces, judicial officials, prison wardens and guards, and members of Ulster Protestant political parties and militias. Most attacks have been carried out in Northern Ireland with some attacks against British targets in the Irish Republic and many more attacks in England. From 1969 to 1998, according to Malcolm Sutton's research, direct killings by the IRA had reached a total of 1,802 out of a total of 3,466 persons directly killed by the conflict in Northern Ireland. All told approximately 30,000 people were maimed or received nonfatal wounds in the conflict of which about 20,000 were civilians.

A few of the more notable actions of the IRA include the following: On 21 July 1972, "Bloody Friday," the IRA conducted 22 bombings in Belfast, killing 11 and wounding about 100. During September 1973 the IRA bombed the London Stock Exchange, the House of Commons, the Bank of England, the London subway, and several shopping areas. On 21 November 1974, the IRA bombed two pubs in Birmingham, England, killing 21 and wounding around 120. On 21 July 1976 the IRA assassinated Christopher Ewart-Briggs, British Ambassador to Ireland, by destroying his vehicle with a land mine. On 27 August 1979 the IRA **assassinated** Lord Louis Mountbatten by bombing his yacht, which also killed three others with him. On 20 July 1982 the IRA set off two radio-controlled bombs in London, the first striking a passing detachment of the Queen's Household Calvary passing through Hyde Park, killing four soldiers, and the other bomb killing seven members of the Royal Green Jackets, a military band, in Regent's Park. On 17 December 1983 the IRA car bombed Harrod's department store in London, killing seven (including one American) and wounding 89 others. On 12 October 1984 the IRA bombed the hotel holding the British Conservative Party conference in Brighton, England, killing one Cabinet member and three others and wounding 32 others. Prime Minister Margaret Thatcher would have been killed if she had not moved into a different room just minutes before the bomb detonated. On 8 November 1987 the IRA bombed a Remembrance Day ceremony in Enniskillen, County Fermanagh, killing 11 people and wounding 63 others.

In 1990 the IRA began to carry out more attacks in England, including two shootings and two bombings, one of which killed Conservative Member of Parliament Ian Gow on 30 July 1990. On 7 February 1991 the IRA carried out a mortar attack against the British Prime Minister's offic e residence at No. 10 Downing Street while Prime Minister John Major was consulting there with senior members of his cabinet. During 1991 the IRA also carried out numerous bombings throughout Great Britain, including a 2,000-pound bomb that was exploded outside a police station in Northern Ireland. In addition, the IRA has conducted five major attacks on British Army bases in Europe.

The IRA terror campaign has led to unintended results that may have made its goal of unification of Ireland more remote. First, the bitterness of the terrorist war being waged by the IRA and other nationalist/republican groups, by the Ulster Protestant militias, and by the British forces has exacerbated the communal and sectarian tensions to the extent that the majority of Ulster Protestants might prefer to opt for a separate Ulster republic rather than consent to unification with the south should Great Britain decide to withdraw from Northern Ireland. Second, the terror campaign against British targets in England, and particularly the attacks on the prime minister and members of Parliament, has hardened official British attitudes toward the Irish nationalists and republicans and strengthened their resolve not to retreat from Northern Ireland. Third, the terror campaign has transformed the nationalist struggle from being a mass movement centered around civil rights to becoming an insidious war of covert operations and counterintelligence in which ordinary civilians play little active role and which has stifled open political participation.

While the original IRA conceived itself to be a true army, and organized itself accordingly with general orders and a hierarchical command structure, the current IRA was forced to adopt a **cellular structure** in the 1970s to prevent the penetration and subversion of the organization by British agents. Beginning in 1981 the British resorted to the **"supergrass"** tactic of turning a captured terrorist, facing substantial charges, into a prosecution witness with immunity from prosecution for his own crimes if he would denounce several of his erstwhile colleagues. This system used trials without juries and the uncorroborated testimony of one witness to effect scores of convictions. While many of these convictions have been overturned on appeal, the tactic sowed much distrust and internal discord within the affected republican and loyalist terrorist groups and hampered their efficiency.

Although previous IRA terrorist campaigns, such as that which erupted in the Irish civil war of 1922-1923 or the "Border Campaign" of 1956-1962, eventually spent themselves out there is one important difference between those former campaigns and the 1969-1998 conflict, which has recently ended. In the prior cases the IRA had **targeted** the government of the Republic of Ireland as well as the government of Northern Ireland with the result that authorities on both sides of the border cooperated in suppressing IRA terrorism. With the beginning of the Civil Rights campaign in 1968, a tacit accord appeared to exist between the Irish Republic and the IRA to the effect that the IRA would not target the Irish Republic so long as the Republic did not cooperate with the Northern Irish authorities in their efforts to stem nationalist republican terrorists. General Order No. 8 of the IRA official handbook, "the Green Book," prohibits IRA members from "any military action against 26 County [sic] forces under any circumstances whatsoever." Note: the IRA prefered to refer to the Republic of Ireland as the "26 Counties" as they did not recognize it as a legitimate government. Although the Irish Republic began in the mid-1970s to intercept arms shipments destined for the IRA and attempted to dissuade the Libyan government from supporting the IRA, the various Irish governments have avoided vigorous prosecution and internment of IRA activists within the Republic.

The current peace process in Northern Ireland dates back to the 15 November 1985 Anglo-Irish Accord in which the governments of Great Britain and the Republic of Ireland agreed that no change in the status of Northern Ireland would be imposed that did not agree with the wishes of the majority of the people of Northern Ireland. In January 1989 a political dialogue began between the major legal political parties in Northern Ireland, including the Social Democratic Labour Party representing Catholic citizens, which later expanded to include participation by the governments of Great Britain and the Republic of Ireland as well as the United States as a mediator in the conflict. By November 1993 Sein Fein was granted admission to these negotiations conditioned upon the cessation of IRA violence. On 31 August 1994 the IRA began a cease-fire and not long afterwards the main Ulster Protestant militias, including the **Ulster Defence Association** and **Ulster Volunteer Force** responded with cease-fires of their own. In January 1994 President Bill Clinton ordered that a visa be granted to Sein Fein leader Gerry Adams to come to Washington, D.C., to confer directly with administration officials concerning the Northern Ireland peace talks.

However, due to a lack of political progress the IRA on 9 February 1996 ended its 17-month cease-fire by bombings in the Docklands area of London, killing two and wounding over 100 others. Sein Fein was then excluded from the peace talks. On 12 June 1996 the Clinton administration appointed former U.S. Senator George Mitchell to serve as a chairman in the peace talks. Following the election of a Labour government the IRA resumed its cease-fire on 20 July 1997 and Sein Fein was readmitted to the talks. The Good Friday Accord of 10 April 1998 established the basis for a peaceful settlement of the Northern Ireland conflict. The IRA announced on 30 April 1998 that it regarded the Accords as defective but would continue to maintain its cease-fire. The IRA had been refusing to decommission its weapons because it would regard this as effective surrender but otherwise accommodated itself to engagement in the peace process that began with the Anglo-Irish Accord of 1985. However, on 22 October 2001 Gerry Adams announced in West Belfast that the IRA would disarm to comply with the Good Friday Agreement while his deputy, Martin McGuinness, made the same announcement the same day in New York. The following day the IRA announced it would proceed to dismantle its stockpiles of arms hidden in various depots. These caches include surface-to-air missiles, rocket-propelled grenades, flame-throwers, detonators, and several tons of Semtex.

Various IRA cells that have rejected their leadership's accommodation to the political settlement have pursued violence on their own, and have taken names such as the Continuity IRA, the "Real IRA" (also called the "True IRA"), and the Thirty-Two County Sovereignty Committee, but the followings and arms held by these groups are negligible. The U.S. government in 2001 designated these as Foreign Terrorist Organizations thus forbidding U.S. citizens to give material aid to such groups.

ISLAMIC AMAL. Islamic Amal is a splinter group that broke away from **Amal** proper in 1982. Islamic Amal was a nonstate group of more militant Amal militiamen who hearkened to Iran's call for Islamic revolution throughout the Middle East. They had grown disillusioned with the more secular and nationalistic leadership of Nabih Berri who had succeeded Imam Musa Sadr following the latter's disappearance in 1978.

In 1982 Hussein Musawi, a high-school teacher and member of the Amal Command Council, accused Berri of implicit collaboration with Israel during its invasion of Lebanon that summer. Musawi quit, or was expelled, from Amal but founded Islamic Amal in the vicinity of Baalbak, which had become a guerrilla training center run by Iran's **Islamic Revolutionary Guards Corps**. Musawi was implicated in the 19 July 1982 **kidnapping** of David Dodge, the president of American University in Beirut, and in the October 1983 truck **suicide bombings** of the French and U.S. multinational forces. In November 1983, Israel and France launched retaliatory air strikes on Musawi's Baalbak headquarters but without harming Musawi.

Musawi continued to speak in the name of Islamic Amal as late as 1986, but it is believed that Islamic Amal was incorporated wholesale into the framework of **Hezbollah** and that the fiction of Islamic Amal as a separate entity was kept alive as a form of disinformation to confuse Hezbollah's enemies.

ISLAMIC FRONT FOR THE LIBERATION OF BAHRAIN. This is a nonstate group of Shi'ite Bahrainis seeking to create an Islamic revolution in Bahrain under Iranian state sponsorship. The Islamic Front for the Liberation of Bahrain was founded in March 1979 by Hujjatulislam Hadi al Mudarissi, a young Bahraini clergyman who had lived in Najaf,

Iraq, as a member of **Ruhollah Khomeini**'s entourage. His brother, Muhammad Taqi al Mudarissi, founded the Islamic 'Amal Party to promote an Islamic revolution in Iraq that was eventually merged into the Supreme Assembly for the Islamic Revolution of Iraq, the Tehran-based umbrella organization of Iraqi Shi'ite revolutionaries headed by the **Al Da'wa** Party of Iraq. Mudarissi was financed by two Iranian revolutionary foundations used to front subversive adventures abroad, namely the Foundation for the Oppressed and the Liberation Movements Office.

On 13 December 1981 the security police of Bahrain and Dubai arrested a total of 60 persons, six of them students in transit to Bahrain at Dubai International Airport, on charges of illegal possession of firearms and explosives, membership in a subversive organization, plotting to overthrow the government, and collaboration with a hostile foreign power. Thirteen other persons were later arrested in areas of Bahrain outside the capital of Manama. Substantial material evidence in addition to confessions of the arrested indicated that Iran had been the main principal behind the coup plot. Among the several arms caches seized police also found complete duplicate sets of Bahraini security police uniforms, which proved to be of Iranian manufacture.

Certain of those arrested revealed that they had undergone military training in Iran. Iran vehemently denied these charges but the Gulf Cooperation Council condemned Iran for its promotion of subversive activities among the Shi'ite Muslims of the Persian Gulf emirates.

ISLAMIC FUNDAMENTALISM. Islamic fundamentalism has been identified as the main **ideological** inspiration of the **assassins** of Anwar Sadat, the **Hezbollah** militia of Lebanon, and of the Islamic Republic of Iran, which has engaged in state sponsorship of terrorism.

What non-Muslim Westerners have called "Islamic fundamentalism" Muslims prefer to call "al nihdhat al Islami," meaning "the Islamic movement," or better, "the Islamic resurgence." The term *Islamic fundamentalism* misleadingly suggests an analogy with Christian fundamentalism, which accepts a radical distinction between the "kingdom of God" and the kingdom(s) of this world. So-called fundamentalist Islam radically rejects such a separation of life into secular and religious domains, or any separation of politics and religion. The closest analogy in Western Christianity would be rather the prorevolutionary **"liberation theology"** of Latin America rather than the private pietism of mainstream American Protestant fundamentalism. Although using the term

Islamic resurgence would be less misleading, the currency of the term *Islamic fundamentalism* will likely remain a linguistic fact of life and therefore is used throughout this dictionary subject to the caveats outlined above regarding its proper meaning.

Central to Islamic fundamentalism is its insistence on reviving and comprehensively applying a unitary system of Islamic law covering all private and public affairs. This closed and comprehensive legal system stems from the Koran, an even larger body of traditions, authoritative commentaries, historic consensus, and judicial precedents. The various Islamic fundamentalist movements hold in common certain beliefs, which may be summarized as follows: The Islamic laws have comprehensive solutions for all economic, social, diplomatic, criminal, and civil problems; Islamic law is itself perfect, immutable, and organic, not to be abrogated in part or amended; the current Islamic world, with its mixture of traditional Muslim and contemporary Western laws and institutions, and its division of the historic Islamic empire into several nation-states, represents a deviation from true Islam; and, the religious duties of **jihad**, holy war, or of "enjoining the good and forbidding the evil" permit violence to rid Muslim lands of un-Islamic laws, institutions, rulers, foreign powers, and agents when other means fail.

Islamic fundamentalism is not a monolithic phenomenon but exists both in an "official" form and a "populist" form. The religious establishments within Saudi Arabia and the Persian Gulf emirates are officially fundamentalist in the sense outlined above but with the difference that they maintain that the true Islam is already being implemented in those countries. Such an Islamic fundamentalism is politically conservative and even counterrevolutionary. The opposing "populist" variety of Islamic fundamentalism comes also in two forms, namely, an *islahi* (reformist) version and a *salafi* (purist) version. Reformist fundamentalists accept the notion of incrementalist reform of corrupt Muslim societies through educational efforts and such political participation or agitation as is permitted by the local Muslim government. Examples of such fundamentalists are to be found in the various **Muslim Brotherhood** groups that have operated as political parties and social welfare organizations in Egypt, Sudan, Syria, Algeria, and other Muslim lands. The *salafi* fundamentalists reject such reformism as compromising with unbelief and insist instead on violent, revolutionary means to achieve the true Islamic state and society. An example of such fundamentalists was the Sunni group that attacked and occupied the Masjid al Haram complex in Mecca on 20 November 1979. Nonetheless, even reformist fundamentalists have shown a willingness to resort to political violence and terrorism if they are frustrated in their attempts to work peacefully within the political system. The Muslim Brotherhood in Egypt in the Nasser period, the Brotherhood in Syria under Hafiz al Asad, and, more recently, the **Islamic Salvation Front** in Algeria and **Islamic Tendency Movement** in Tunisia have all resorted to political violence when denied the chance to reform those countries through political channels.

Most "populist" fundamentalists are hostile to the West, and to the United States in particular, for three main reasons: the United States is perceived as the main backer of the State of Israel; the United States is viewed as the backer and supporter of those Muslim states that populist fundamentalists regard as apostate regimes; and the United States is the source of an attractive materialistic and individualistic culture that is incompatible with the traditional and community-centered ethos of an integral Islamic moral order. These perceived antagonisms will continue to provoke violent reactions, including terrorist attacks or threats against American citizens and U.S. interests in, or near, the Muslim world for the foreseeable future. Apart from antagonism toward the United States and the West more generally, the incompatibility of Islamic fundamentalist aspirations with the conscious secularism of many Muslim states, especially the Pan-Arabist Ba'thist Syrian and Iraqi regimes, also portends terrorism by fundamentalists against such regimes as well as reciprocal **state terror** directed by those regimes against fundamentalists.

Although Islamic fundamentalism is perhaps the only remaining transnational ideological movement that challenges Western liberal democracy following the collapse of international communism, even among the *salafi* fundamentalists there is no monolithic ideological or organizational unity. Sectarian differences between Sunni and Shi'ite fundamentalists, nationalistic differences between Arab and non-Arab nationals, and idiosyncratic antagonisms among and within groups or between individual leaders have vitiated efforts to create a cohesive Pan-Islamic movement. This was particularly evident in the case of the Iranian revolution in which the Shi'ite complexion of Iranian Islam and the historical animosity between Iranians and Arabs neutralized much of the appeal of that revolution even among fundamentalists in the Arab Sunni countries. Currently the extreme Wahhabi form of Sunni Islam practised by the **Taliban** of Afghanistan forecloses the possibility of their achieving solidarity or fraternal relations with Shi'ite fundamentalist states of movements, such as the Islamic Republic of Iran and Hezbollah. Nonetheless, given the failure of attempts to implement socialism or Western-style democracy in the various Muslim countries and the repeated failures of Arab nationalist leaders to defeat Israel or the West, Islamic fundamentalism continues to grow in its appeal within Muslim countries as an indigenous moral-ethical and populist political ideology with which to answer the political and cultural challenges of the non-Muslim world.

It should also be noted that there is another strain of populist, fundamentalist Islam that is radically nonpolitical, namely, Sufism (Arabic *Tassawuf*, or *'Irfan*) which does represent an intensely personal and experience-oriented mysticism. Although in the 19th and early 20th centuries the devotees of Sufism, known as *dervishes* or *sufis*, who formed mystical brotherhoods found throughout the Islamic world, did engage in armed rebellions against European colonialism, such as occurred in the revolt of the Sudanese Mahdi in Khartoum, during recent decades these orders have tended to be apolitical and even open critics of more politically oriented variations of Islamic fundamentalism. Therefore, as one means of counteracting the influence of fundamentalist militants within Egypt, President Hosni Mubarak has given much official support to the Sufi orders both to bolster his own Islamic credentials and also to divert pietistic tendencies among the ordinary faithful into channels that do not threaten the state.

It should be noted in any case that the vast majority of Muslims who hold what may be considered fundamentalist beliefs are not engaged in extremist politics or revolutionary violence and that most of them abhor the violence of the extremist militants.

ISLAMIC GUERRILLAS IN AMERICA. The Islamic Guerrillas in America was an obscure group of black American converts to Islam who believed in the revolutionary message of the **Ayatollah Ruhollah Khomeini**. They are believed to have been sponsored by the Islamic Republic of Iran and used to repress Iranian dissidents living in the United States.

One **assassination** and an attempted assassination have been credited to the Islamic Guerrillas. On 22 July 1980 'Ali Akbar Tabataba'i, an outspoken Iranian critic of the Khomeini regime, was shot to death in Washington, D.C., by David Belfield, a black American convert to Islam also known as Daoud Salahuddin or Daoud Muhammad. Belfield fled to Iran where he was reported, in August 1996, to have been negotiating with the FBI to return to the United States and surrender himself. On 31 July 1980, the residence of another Iranian dissident, one Shah Reis, was shot at in Los Angeles, an action also believed to have been done by the same gunman. The Islamic Guerrillas supposedly were formed and supported by a naturalized Iranian in Washington, D.C., who recruited its members mainly from black inmates of the District of Columbia prison system.

ISLAMIC GROUP (IG). The Gama'a al Islamiya is a nonstate **Islamic fundamentalist** group seeking the overthrow of the current secular regime in Egypt and its replacement by their version of an Islamic state. It claims **Sheikh Omar Abdul Rahman** as its spiritual leader and threatened retaliation against Americans and U.S. interests after he was sentenced to life imprisonment on 17 January 1996. IG has targeted tourists, Coptic Christians, and senior Egyptian officials in its attempts to topple the Hosni Mubarak regime. On 26 August 1994 IG machine-gunned a bus full of Spanish tourists near Nag Hammadi killing a 13-year-old boy. On 26 June 1995 IG gunmen opened fire on Hosni Mubarak's motorcade in Addis Ababa in which the two gunmen and two Ethiopian policemen were killed. This attack stiffened Mubarak's determination to root out all wings of the fundamentalist resistance in Egypt, not stopping just the armed militants but also the social, political, and intellectual springs of the movement.

The government repression succeeded in confining most of the IG violence to the southern provinces of Minya, Asyut, and al-Qina along the Nile. However IG responded to this internal crackdown by taking the antiregime violence outside of Egypt. In October 1995 IG **bombed** Egyptian diplomats in Croatia and **assassinated** an Egyptian diplomat in Geneva on 13 November 1995. On 19 November 1995 a **suicide bomber** drove an explosives-packed pickup truck into the Egyptian embassy in Islamabad killing 15 people and wounding 56 others. On 18 April 1996 IG gunmen machine-gunned Greek tourists at the base of the Pyramids killing 18, wounding another 12, and wounding two Egyptians. On 12 February 1997 IG attacked a Coptic Christian church in Abu Qurqas and the Christian hamlet of Nag Dawoud killing nine Copts and three others. On 18 September 1997 two IG gunmen attacked a tourist bus with machine-gun fire and gasoline bombs killing nine German tourists and one other. However, IG achieved its worst notoriety with the massacre of 58 foreign tourists and 6 Egyptians on 17 November 1997 at the Temple of Queen Hatshepsut outside Luxor, Egypt. This methodical and merciless massacre greatly shocked not only world opinion but even many Islamic militants and IG issued a statement on 8 December 1997 repudiating the actions as inconsistent with the "principles of legitimacy, humanity and politics" and declaring that it would cease and desist from attacking tourists.

In February 1996 and again in February 1998, when **Osama bin Laden** issued a **fatwa** declaring it the religious duty of every individual Muslim to kill Americans everywhere, whether soldiers or civilians, this was cosigned by Ayman al-Zawahiri, the leader of one wing of the **Munazzamat al Jihad** in Egypt and also by Abu-Yasir Rifa'i Ahmad Taha, a leader of the Islamic Group in Egypt. Evidence later seemed to link those who perpetrated the **Luxor Temple massacre** with bin Laden. In spite of having cosigned this fatwa the IG leaders disclaim any link to bin Laden.

Following the Luxor Temple massacre both Sheikh Omar Abdul Rahman and Abbud al-Zumar issued an appeal to the members of the Jihad group and members of the Islamic Group to cease violence and to work to form a "peaceful front" to confront the Egyptian government.

ISLAMIC JIHAD. The name Al Jihad al Islami, meaning "Islamic holy struggle (or war)," has been used by at least three terrorist organizations:
1. Hezbollah—The Iranian-sponsored Lebanese Shi'ite militia used the nom de guerre "Islamic Jihad," allowing its own Lebanese leaders and Iranian sponsors plausible deniability for the more heinous actions undertaken by the group, such as the *intihari* suicide (*see* SUICIDE BOMBERS), vehicle-bombing attacks, and the **kidnapping** and holding of foreigners and non-Muslim Lebanese as hostages. These actions are morally repugnant not merely to non-Muslim Westerners but also to most Lebanese Shi'ite Muslims, who regard both the kidnapping of innocents and the **suicides** committed by *intihari* bombers as violations of Islamic law. The "Open Letter of Hezbollah to the Oppressed in Lebanon and the World" published on 16 February 1985, however, identified the intihari bombers of Islamic Jihad with its own "martyrs." Subsequent statements by **Hezbollah** spiritual leader Muhammad Hussein Fadlullah and Islamic Amal leader Hussein Musawi denying knowledge of Islamic Jihad must be understood in the context of the Shi'ite practice of

taqiyah, which permits dissimulation before nonbelievers on matters affecting the physical security and survival of the Shi'ite community.

2. Munazzamat al Jihad—Also known simply as "Jihad," this was the Sunni Muslim fundamentalist group in Egypt responsible for the **assassination** of Anwar Sadat on 6 October 1981. This group was an offshoot of **Tahrir al Islami**, itself an offshoot of the **Muslim Brotherhood**. It is not directly connected with the Shi'ite militia Islamic Jihad of Lebanon (*See* MUNAZZAMAT AL JIHAD).

3. Islamic Jihad of Palestine—During the British Mandate in Palestine, the increase of Jewish settlers in the 1930s prompted an Arab backlash involving riots in Jerusalem and attacks on isolated Jewish settlements. The Arab riots were directed also against the British as protectors of the Zionist settlers. Muslim resistance to British control and Jewish settlement took the form of the guerrilla group known as Islamic Jihad formed in the 1920s by Sheikh Izzidin al Qassim who led attacks on both Jewish settlers and British mandatory authorities until he was finally killed by the British in 1936.

Islamic Jihad continued to exist underground during the remaining mandate and into the period following the creation of the State of Israel. This organization has survived by adopting a **cellular structure** and a system of identifying members by six-digit numbers rather than names. Islamic Jihad remained distinct and aloof from the branch of the Muslim Brotherhood that entered Palestine from Egypt in 1946, which was more reformist than revolutionary in its orientation. By 1984, however, evidence surfaced of collaboration between members of Islamic Jihad and the Muslim Brotherhood. By 1987 this cooperation grew to include coordination with the more secular **Palestine Liberation Organization** (PLO) in planning the protests in the occupied West bank and Gaza Strip that evolved into the *intifada*.

On 16 October 1986 two Palestinians made a grenade attack on a military swearing-in ceremony at the Wailing Wall in Jerusalem, killing one and wounding 68 others. This action was claimed by the Palestinian Islamic Jihad, although several other groups also claimed credit. On 4 February 1990 Palestinian Jihad members machine-gunned an Israeli tour bus en route to Cairo, killing 11 and wounding 17 others. On 28 May 1990 Islamic Jihad bombed a Jerusalem street, killing one and wounding nine passersby.

There has been no evidence of links between the largely Sunni Islamic Jihad organization indigenous to Palestine and the Iranian-sponsored Hezbollah Shi'ite militia of Lebanon, which also uses "Islamic Jihad" as its nom de guerre. Islamic Jihad was the only Palestinian Islamic fundamentalist group that advocated the use of armed struggle against Israel prior to the outbreak of the *intifada*. Since then, however, Islamic Jihad has fully cooperated with the PLO-dominated Unified National Leadership (UNL). By contrast, the **Hamas** movement, having grown out of the Palestinian Muslim Brotherhood, has been much more inclined to compete with, and even fight against, more secular Palestinian groups active in the *intifada*. Since the Persian Gulf War in 1991 Islamic Jihad has been drawing closer to Iran while **Hamas** remained aloof toward Iran until late 1992 when Israel expelled 400 Hamas members into Lebanon, where they were supported and trained by Iranian-backed Hezbollah elements.

Following the establishment of the Palestinian Authority, Islamic Jihad shot and killed an Israeli soldier in the Gaza Strip on 5 September 1994. On 2 November 1994 Hani Abed, the leader of the military wing of Islamic Jihad, was killed by a car bomb in the Gaza Strip in what many Palestinians believed to be a Mossad action. Then, on 11 November 1994 an Islamic Jihad suicide bomber on a bicycle blew himself up along with three Israeli soldiers and wounded 12 others. Following these attacks **Yasir Arafat** ordered a crackdown on Islamic Jihad and other Islamic militants arresting 160 members of Islamic Jihad. However, on 22 January 1995 Islamic Jihad suicide bombers struck an Israeli bus-stop killing 19 and wounding 61 others.

On 26 October 1995 Israeli agents assassinated Dr. Fathi Shiqaqi, the leader of Islamic Jihad, outside a seaside hotel on the island of Malta. In reprisal two Islamic Jihad suicide bombers blew themselves up near two Israeli buses in the Gaza Strip killing only themselves while wounding 11 Israelis. Shortly after the assassination of Israeli Prime Minister Yitzhak Rabin on 4 November the new leader of Islamic Jihad was revealed to be a former University of South Florida adjunct professor, Dr. Ramadan Abdullah Shallah. In 1991 Dr. Shallah had joined the World and Islam Studies Enterprise (WISE) established by other Palestinians in the Tampa, Florida area which in March 1992 became affiliated with the University of South Florida in an agreement to cosponsor scholarly conferences and to allow WISE members to teach Middle East studies classes for the university. On 28 May 1995 the *Tampa Tribune* published Michael

Fechter's report, "Ties to Terrorists," documenting that WISE was acting as a front organization for Islamic Jihad in Palestine, which led to an FBI investigation for alleged violations of the U.S. Neutrality Act in connection with fund-raising by WISE personnel for Islamic Jihad within the United States.

For most of 1996 Islamic Jihad remained inactive until on 3 April 1997 it claimed responsibility for two attempted suicide bombings in the Gaza Strip. On 6 November 1998 two Islamic Jihad suicide bombers blew themselves up in a car bomb detonated in a Jerusalem open air market killing both bombers and wounding 24 others. On 2 June 2001 an Islamic Jihad suicide bomber killed himself and 16 Israelis outside of a Tel Aviv nightclub and on 16 June 2001 an Islamic Jihad suicide bomber struck the railroad station in Binyamina killing two Israeli soliders.

Islamic Jihad has been a target of frequent crackdowns by the Palestinian Authority.

4. Islamic Jihad for the Liberation of Palestine—Another nom de guerre of **Hezbollah** used when three American professors, Robert Polhill, Alan Steen, and Jesse Turner, and U.S. resident, Mithileshwar Singh, were kidnapped in Beirut on 24 January 1987. Singh was released on 3 October 1988; Polhill, on 22 April 1990; Turner on 22 October 1991; and Steen on 3 December 1991.

5. Islamic Jihad in Yemen—A little known group, also called the Islamic Army of Aden-Abyan, or Aden-Abyan Islamic Jihad, attempted in the later 1990s to enforce its own version of Islamic law in the villages surrounding Aden in Yemen. It came to international attention when it began **kidnapping** foreign tourists to pressure the government of Yemen.

On 28 December 1998 Yemeni kidnappers claiming to be part of the Islamic Jihad in Yemen seized 16 foreign tourists in Abyan province and demanded the release of 10 Islamic Jihad militants and foreign recruits captured by the national police in a crackdown on the group's training camp in Abyan Province. On 29 December 1998 Yemeni security forces stormed the kidnappers' stronghold, in the course of which four of the hostages were killed. Altogether three Britons, two of them women, and one Australian male were killed in the first instance in which foreign hostages had been reported to have been killed by terrorists in Yemen. Although the Yemeni security forces claimed that they had stormed the hideout only when the rebels had proceeded to kill the hostages the surviving hostages contended that it was the assault of security forces that killed the four who were being used as human shields by the kidnappers. Three kidnappers were killed and another three wounded in the rescue attempt.

The Islamic Jihad in Yemen group had abducted four German tourists three weeks earlier who then were released after negotiations between their captors and the German government. The group also issued messages under the name of the Islamic Army of Aden-Abyan. On 5 May 1998 a Yemeni court sentenced the five members of the group for the abduction of the 16 tourists and for the deaths of the four tourists killed in the attack. Three of those convicted, Zein Abu Bakr al Mihdar, Abdullah Saleh al Junaidy, both Yemenis, and Saleh Abu Huraira, an Algerian, were sentenced to death and a fourth, Ahmed Mohammed Atif, sentenced to 20 years imprisonment. The brother of Atif, Saad Mohammed Atif, was found not guilty.

The leader of the Aden-Abyan Islamic Jihad, Zein Abu Bakr al Mihdar, who also used the nom de guerre "Abu Hassan," had previously fought alongside the Afghan **Mujahideen** in their war against the Soviet occupation in the 1980s. After returning to Yemen he fought on the side of the current President Ali Abdullah Saleh in the 1994 civil war that briefly erupted following the reunification of Yemen in 1991. Although it was initially thought that al Mihdar might have ties to **Osama bin Laden** further investigations by Western intelligence agencies revealed no connections. Searches of the rebels' camp revealed bomb-making materials, antitank rockets, and a satellite telephone. The 10 Aden-Abyan Islamic Jihad members arrested and convicted for terrorism prior to the kidnapping of the tourists included eight Muslims from Britain who had entered the country under the pretext of learning the Arabic language.

ISLAMIC JIHAD IN THE HIJAZ. Also known as "Hezbollah in the Hijaz," this group and the **Soldiers of Justice** are both Iranian state-sponsored Shi'ite groups based in Lebanon that have the revolutionary goal of overthrowing the Saudi Arabian monarchy in favor of an Iranian-style Islamic Republic. The previously unheard of Islamic Jihad in the Hijaz group claimed credit on 7 January 1989 for the murder of Salah Abdullah al Maliki, the third secretary of the Saudi Arabian embassy in Bangkok, Thailand, who was shot on 4 January 1989. Their announced motive was to avenge the death of four of its members executed on 30 September 1988.

In this announcement the group identified itself as being, in effect, an extension of Islamic Jihad, also known as **Hezbollah**, a Shi'ite militia in Lebanon composed of Lebanese, Iraqi, and Kuwaiti Shi'ites under the tutelage of the **Islamic Revolutionary Guards Corps** (IRGC) contingent in Lebanon. It is doubtful that the group has much of a grass roots organization in Saudi Arabia itself, much less in the Hijaz proper. Estimates of the Shi'ite population of Saudi Arabia range from 600,000 to 1,000,000 out of a population of perhaps six million largely Wahhabi Sunni Muslims. Most of these Shi'ites live on the shores of the Persian Gulf in the eastern province of al Hasa. Due to a conscious policy of exclusion of Shi'ites from the western province of Hijaz practiced since Ottoman times until the present, there are virtually no Shi'ites living in the Hijaz.

Antiregime violence by pro-Khomeini Shi'ites in the Hijaz has invariably been the work of Iranian or Kuwaiti Shi'ite pilgrims present in the Hijaz only for the Hajj rituals. The Islamic Republic of Iran had been engaged in agitational propaganda against the Saudi dynasty during the Hajj pilgrimages from 1979 until 31 July 1987 when Iranian-incited riots killed over 400 people in Mecca. The following day the official Islamic Republic News Agency of Iran announced that a new group, the Hezbollah of the Hijaz, had vowed vengeance against the Saudi regime for the events in Mecca. The same day, an organized mob attacked the Saudi embassy in Tehran causing the Saudi political attaché to fall from an upper story; he later died from his injuries. On 15 August 1987 a gas plant in Arabia was sabotaged. While the Iranian regime hailed this as the work of Hezbollah in the Hijaz, the Saudis maintained it was not the work of native nationals. On 26 August 1987 Hezbollah in the Hijaz announced it intended to attack U.S. and Saudi interests to force the removal of "U.S. bases" from Arabia. On 3 September 1987 the Commander of the Islamic Revolutionary Guards Corps announced that Hezbollah in the Hijaz was planning to attack U.S. and Saudi interests worldwide. Given that both the names "Hezbollah" and "Islamic Jihad" have been given to the same militia under IRGC direction within Lebanon, the role of the IRGC Commander in acting as a spokesman for Hezbollah in the Hijaz strongly indicates that the latter group was also under IRGC direction and most likely identical with the group that later identified itself as "Islamic Jihad in the Hijaz."

In 1987 four indigenous Saudi Shi'ites who set fire to the Sadaf petrochemical plant in Jubayl in al Hasa province were arrested and executed by the Saudis. On 26 April 1988 Arabia severed diplomatic relations with Iran and greatly reduced the size of the Hajj pilgrimage contingent permitted to the Iranians. On 21 September 1989 Saudi Arabia executed 16 Kuwaitis for having carried out two **bombings** on behalf of Iran in the July 1988 Hajj season, from which Iranian participation had been largely excluded. Later, on 30 September 1988, four more Saudi Shi'ites were executed for sabotage in the eastern province, which became the pretext for the murder of Maliki, the third secretary of the Saudi Arabian embassy in Thailand.

While the eastern province is far more valuable economically and far more vulnerable given the larger concentration of Shi'ites and the maritime proximity of Iran, the western province is far more valuable in the eyes of the Iranian regime as holding the two most holy cities in Islam, Mecca and Medina. Whoever rules over the Hijaz may claim the title of "Protector of the Two Holy Places," which implies a preeminence among Muslim rulers. **Ayatollah Ruhollah Khomeini** and other Shi'ite clergymen have resented Saudi possession of the Hijaz since this gives preeminence to a dynasty linked to the Wahhabi sect within Islam, which anathematized the Shi'ites as heretics and apostates and which sacked and destroyed Shi'ite shrines in Karbala, Iraq, and the Arabian Peninsula as well as killing Shi'ite pilgrims in the 19th and early 20th centuries. Therefore the implied claim that Khomeini had indigenous followers within the Hijaz could serve to boost the prestige of Iran's credentials of Islamic leadership throughout the Muslim world.

ISLAMIC LIBERATION ORGANIZATION (ILO). Name used by Sunni Muslims in Lebanon responsible for the 30 September 1985 abduction and hostage holding of four Soviet diplomats. Outside the Soviet embassy in West Beirut, armed gunmen abducted the Soviet commercial attaché and embassy second secretary at gunpoint while other gunmen abducted the cultural attaché and embassy physician on another nearby street.

A group identifying itself as the Islamic Liberation Organization contacted Agence France-Press and demanded that the Soviets pressure Syria to cease their offensive against the Sunni Muslim Tawhid group in Tripoli, which had been besieged by the Syrians for the preceding two weeks. The group sent photographs of the recently abducted Soviet diplomats and threatened to kill them if their demands were not met. On 2 October the ILO killed Arkady Katkov, the cultural attaché, who had been wounded trying to escape and whose wounds had developed gangrene. On 4 October the Soviets evacuated their embassy in response to an ILO threat to car **bomb** the premises.

The Soviets contacted Sunni and Shi'ite community leaders to intercede with the ILO. On 30 October 1985, the three remaining hostages were released, the Syrian offensive against Tripoli having been played out in the intervening four weeks.

ISLAMIC REVOLUTIONARY GUARDS CORPS (IRGC). The IRGC of the Islamic Republic of Iran is a state-run paramilitary organization charged by Article 150 of the 1979 Iranian Constitution with "defending the (Islamic) Revolution and safeguarding its achievements." Domestically, in addition to protecting the regime from possible coup attempts by the older branches of the Iranian armed forces, it has also served as an instrument of **state terror** and repression. In the war fronts of the Iran-Iraq war (1980-1988) and outside Iran, in Lebanon and the Persian Gulf, it serves a revolutionary purpose in assisting "Islamic liberation movements" to oppose conservative regimes and in attacking U.S., Israeli, and other Western interests.

The current IRGC was officially organized by decree of **Ayatollah Ruhollah Khomeini** on 5 May 1979, but had existed in rudimentary form just before the 1978-1979 revolution. Some Iranian Muslim student activists abroad had either served with **Amal** units in Lebanon or had undergone **Palestine Liberation Organization** (PLO) guerrilla training there and elsewhere. With the ransacking of police and army armories during the Iranian revolution, various Shi'ite clerics armed their bodyguards and key lay followers who thereby became *pasdars* or revolutionary guards. Given the lack of control over looted arsenals following the collapse of the Shah's government and given the presence of opportunistic armed leftist and rival Muslim groups, such as the **Mujahideen-i Khalq**, the revolutionary regime saw fit to consolidate and better control a near-chaotic security situation. At the time of the May 1979 decree, there were only around 4,000 *pasdars.*

The original *pasdars* were largely unemployed and uneducated street ruffians and the IRGC was originally intended to be a political militia with internal security duties, above all to counter any attempt at a military coup by officers in the regular armed forces having monarchist or secular nationalist sympathies. With the invasion of Iran by Iraq in September 1980, the IRGC changed into a more regular military force having a hierarchical command structure, logistical support, and heavy armaments. Also the numbers of IRGC swelled from about 25,000 at the outset of hostilities to around 350,000 as of 1986. With the intensification of intraregime rivalries between nationalists and fundamentalists, the IRGC was purged of leftist and more secularist elements until it stood solidly "in the line of the Imam" against perceived moderates such as Iranian President Bani Sadr, who was deposed in June 1981. The IRGC played an essential role in organizing the street mobs of *hezbollahis*, members of the "party of God," in a wave of regime terror against internal opponents and in collapsing the attempted insurgency of the Mujahideen-i Khalq in June 1981.

Beginning in February 1981 the IRGC was ordered by Khomeini to establish an "Islamic Liberation Movements" department. This unit established guerrilla training camps for Islamic activists from other Muslim countries outside Tehran and Qum and also dispatched IRGC units to Lebanon where training camps were established in the Bekaa valley where the Lebanese **Hezbollah** militia were organized. Officers and specialists of the regular Iranian armed forces special operations unit were induced to join the IRGC and apparently were instrumental in planning and supervising the truck **bombings** of the U.S. embassy, U.S. Marines barracks, and French military forces headquarters in Lebanon during the period from April-October 1983.

In November 1982 the Islamic Republic sought to put the "revolutionary foundations," such as the IRGC, on a more regular footing with older, more bureaucratic offices of the government by giving each foundation its own ministry. Rivalries between the IRGC and the regular armed forces have been lessened, however, mainly by the experience of shared dangers and duties during the Iran-Iraq war. The factional rivalries of fundamentalist clergymen within the Iranian regime were reflected within the IRGC, as clannish and personalist ties between *pasdars* and clerical patrons continued to be felt in spite of extensive indoctrination of recruits, purging of undesirables, and **ideological** supervision by clerical political officers. According to the research of Kenneth Katzman, however, in the post-Khomeini period the IRGC has succeeded in quelling its internal factionalism and represents the strongest single institution within the Islamic Republic today.

With the amending of the Fundamental Law of the Islamic Republic in 1989 the IRGC's top commanders were included in the composition of the National Security Council of the nation, which could be mandated by the Supreme Religious Leader to make final policy decisions with regard to military and diplomatic issues. The IRGC have been developing their own Airs Corps, which uses the former U.S. embassy as one of its training centers, a Naval Corps, as well as it own Special Operations elite "Qods" (Jerusalem) Corps. In several of the joint Armed Forces and IRGC military maneuvers and war games conducted in the period 1991-1996 reports mentioned the IRGC's "Shim-Min-Rey" Corps, these being the Persian abbreviation for "Chemical-Biological-Nuclear." During these war exercises the IRGC has conducted simulations of deployments into environments affected by WMD (*see* WEAPONS OF MASS DESTRUCTION) agents. Some U.S. military analysts believe that Iran, through the IRGC, is actively pursuing its own WMD program, although this has been denied by Iranian officials.

During much of the post-Khomeini period the IRGC have become more important as an internal security force rather than as an offensive military force, having been called upon along with the Basij Mobilization and Ghast-Harasat (proregime vigilante-volunteers) to quell a number of civil disturbances that have broken out sporadically, including a riot in protest against austerity measures in March 1995. Moreover, following the 8 August 1998 **Taliban** capture of Mazar-i Sharif in which nine Iranian diplomats were murdered by the Taliban, the IRGC along with the regular Armed Forces were mobilized and deployed along the border of Afghanistan to demonstrate Iran's readiness to undertake military actions against the Taliban regime. Thus, by the late 1990s, the IRGC had begun to evolve from being a revolutionary military into a more professional one.

ISLAMIC REVOLUTIONARY ORGANIZATION. Like the **Islamic Jihad in the Hijaz** and the **Soldiers of Justice**, this appears to be an Iranian state-sponsored Shi'ite group based in Lebanon having the revolutionary goal of overthrowing the Saudi Arabian monarchy in favor of an Iranian-style Islamic Republic. The name of this group is used to claim responsibility for acts of sabotage carried out in the eastern oil-producing province of Saudi Arabia and has been used in Iranian Arabic-language broadcasts of anti-Saudi propaganda.

ISLAMIC SALVATION ARMY. The Armée Islamique du Salut (AIS) is the armed wing of the **Islamic Salvation Front** (FIS) which took up arms against the Algerian government following the 11 January 1992 coup that forestalled the second round of parliamentary elections in which the Islamic Salvation Front had been expected to have won a majority of seats.

The AIS emerged from FIS cells that armed themselves to violently confront the regime. In part this was also a reaction to the emergence of the **Armed Islamic Group**, whose members were actually more radical Islamic extremists. At its height the AIS was believed to have numbered about 2,000 experienced fighters but in 24 September 1997 it called for a truce beginning October 1. By 6 June 1999 the head of the AIS, Madani Mezrag, announced that the group was renouncing armed struggle with the Algerian government. Although the rival Armed Islamic Group continued fighting this essentially marked the beginning of the winding-down phase of the Algerian civil conflict which claimed over 100,000 lives in the period 1992-2000 but which has not ended entirely.

ISLAMIC SALVATION FRONT. Known best by its French acronym of FIS, the Front Islamique du Salut or Jabha al Islamiyyah li-Inqadh, is a nonstate **Islamic fundamentalist** group that has sought to create an Islamic regime in Algeria under which religious and political affairs would both be governed by the Shari'ah, that is, the Islamic law. It was the main underground Islamic fundamentalist party in Algeria at the time the **National Liberation Front** (FLN) took steps toward democratization in 1989. Under Algeria's new national constitution, adopted on 23 February 1989, multiparty provincial and municipal elections were held on 12 June 1990, the first freely contested elections since Algerian independence. Led by Abbasi Madani (1931-), the Islamic Salvation Front was the first new political party to be formed under the new electoral law and gained majorities in 32 of the 48 provincial governments and in 853 of the 1,539 municipalities. In the first round of parliamentary elections held on 26 December 1991, the Islamic Salvation Front won 188 of 231 races, although 199 seats required runoff elections.

Concerned over the apparent ascendence of the fundamentalists, secular nationalists within the government and armed forces staged an internal coup on 11 January 1992, forcing the resignation of President Chadhli Benjedid. The five-member High State Council formed to govern the country canceled the runoff parliamentary elections and outlawed the Islamic Salvation Front. Shortly after Algerian President Muhammad Boudiaf, who had headed the five-member junta that had assumed power, was **assassinated** by one of his own bodyguards, on 29

June 1992 an Islamic fundamentalist insurgent group, the **Armed Islamic Group** (GIA), went into action. The Algerian government declared a 12-month state of emergency and proceeded with a crackdown on the FIS, arresting over 7,000 supporters and killing about 270 before the end of 1992. In fact the Armed Islamic Group was the creation of more extreme militants who had opposed the electoral strategy of the FIS and prepared in any case for armed insurrection.

The FIS reacted both to the emergence of the GIA and to Algerian government repression by activating its own armed wing, the **Islamic Salvation Army** (AIS) which retaliated not only with several armed attacks on Algerian officials and their security forces but also with attacks on non-Muslim residents of Algeria as well as unveiled women. Algeria had accused Iran of rendering moral and material support to the FIS during the Algerian civil conflict which raged from 1992 until 2000.

During a 22 February 1995 prison riot Algerian police killed at least 96 militants including two members of the FIS consultative assembly, Yakhlef Cherati and Belcacem Tajouri. During June 1995 FIS leader Abbasi Madani denounced the killings of civilians by GIA militants. In a move to conciliate the Muslim militants Algerian President Lamine Zeroual remanded FIS leaders Madani and Belhadj from prison to house arrest on 14 September 1996. Following the renunciation of armed struggle against the regime by the Islamic Salvation Army on 6 June 1999, the Algerian government proceeded with an amnesty program for Islamic militants who laid down their arms and decided to release Madani from house arrest, suspending the remainder of the 12-year sentence that had been imposed on him in 1991. The FIS dissolved its armed wing, the Islamic Salvation Army, in January 2000 and many armed insurgents surrendered under an amnesty program designed to promote national reconciliation, however some groups have continued to fight.

ISLAMIC TENDENCY MOVEMENT. The Nahdha (literally, "resurgence"), or Islamic Renaissance Movement, is a nonstate **Islamic fundamentalist** group that seeks to replace existing secular governments in Tunisia with an Islamic regime under which religious and political affairs would both be governed by the Islamic law. The group enjoys the support of the Sudanese government, which is dominated by the National Islamic Front affiliated with the **Muslim Brotherhood**, as well as Iran, which is providing military training for Nahdha members in **Islamic Revolutionary Guard Corps** (IRGC) camps within Sudan.

During the 1980s this group emerged among university students and middle-class Tunisians who had been moved by the success of the Islamic revolution in Iran but also had been strongly influenced by the Muslim Brotherhood, which has maintained an underground presence in Tunisia since at least the 1950s. Much of the impetus for this movement comes also in reaction to the strongly secularist policies of Habib Bourguiba, president from 1956 until he was deposed in 1987. Under Bourguiba, French was preferred over Arabic as the language of government and commerce, the European workweek and calendar system remained in effect, Islamic prayers were banned from the national radio and television service, and members of Islamic groups such as Nahdha were subjected to police harassment.

Nahdha activists undertook protests against the Tunisian tourism industry, accommodating two million Western tourists each year, as promoting the use of alcohol, libertine sex, and further erosion of Islamic values. On 15 May 1987 the Tunisian government accused Iran of promoting local fundamentalists through its diplomatic mission and of meddling in Tunisian domestic politics. Several Iranian diplomats were declared persona non grata while Nahdha spokesmen denied any ties to Iran.

Following Bourguiba's ouster in 1987 by Zayn al Abidin bin 'Ali, the new president tried to identify his government more with Islam by relaxing the restrictions enforced by his predecessor. Nahdha was invited to participate as a legal political party but was forbidden to identify itself as an Islamic party. On 22 May 1991 Tunisian security forces arrested around 300 members of Nahdha, of which 100 were members of Tunisia's armed forces, including officers of the rank of major, for plotting to establish an Islamic regime through a military coup. Tunisian police arrested members of armed Nahdha groups in December 1991 following alleged coup conspiracies in September and early December 1991.

Cooperation between Algeria and Tunisia in containing their Islamic fundamentalist movements led Algeria to expel the leader of the Nahdha movement, Rashid el Ghanoushi, who went to Sudan. Diplomatic relations between Sudan and Tunisia were all but severed in October 1991 in protest of Sudan's renewing a diplomatic passport for Rashid el Ghanoushi. Rashid el Ghanoushi was wanted in Tunisia on charges of plotting to kill Tunisia's president and overthrow the government. Although el Ghanoushi once attended a fund-raising rally for Islamic militant causes held in the United States in 1989, when he tried to attend a later conference held in the United States he was refused a visa as a known member and leader of a terrorist group.

- J -

JAMA'AT AL FUQRA. The Jama'at al Fuqra (Arabic for "Group of the Poor") is a small Sunni Muslim sect led by a Pakistani Muslim clergyman of Kashmiri origin, Sheikh Mubarak Ali Shah Gilani, who resides in Lahore, Pakistan but who has a small, devoted following in the United States, Canada, and the Caribbean area. The group also goes by the name of the "Jihad Council for North America" and also the "Muslims of the Americas," a corporation front group with its own publication, *Insight*. Members live in approximately 97 small communal cells, isolated from surrounding society and attempting to live according to the precepts of an austere form of fundamentalist Islam. Most of the members are African American converts to Sunni Islam, some of whom have been recruited from rival Muslim groups, such as the Dar ul Islam group, and who are particulary hostile to the Nation of Islam group led by Louis Farrakhan. Several Fuqra members have traveled to Pakistan, where it is believed they have undergone paramilitary training with **Kashmiri separatists** controlled by Pakistani intelligence and Fuqra is believed to have had its own training camp in Sudan. The group has a minimum of 200 active members and 2,000-3,000 supporters or marginal members. Most of its members live in autonomous cells and are peaceful but a few cells have shown unusual tendencies toward violence.

The group has gained notoriety through several sporadic attacks against Muslim and non-Muslim targets viewed as enemies of Islam. Established in the 1980s this group carried out **assassinations, arsons,** and **bombings** in the United States and plotted to attack a Hindu temple and Hindu-owned movie theater in Canada. The group has also sporadically attacked members of the Hare Krishna sect, the Nation of Islam, the **Jewish Defense League**, and Israelis. Several group members have been convicted for murder and for fraud. In 1985 an American Fuqra leader, Stephen Paster, was convicted and sentenced to 20 years imprisonment for his role in carrying out bombings in Seattle in June 1984. Paster had previously been arrested for plotting a bombing in Portland in July 1983 in the course of which the bomb exploded prematurely destroying part of his hand. Clement Rodney Hampton-El, who had fought in the **Mujahideen** forces of Gulbiddin Hikmatyar against the Soviet occupiers of Afghanistan, was investigated in connection with the **World Trade Center bombing** as well as the **Holland Tunnel bomb plot**. On 12 September 1996 Fuqra member Edward Nicholas Laurent Flinton was arrested by the FBI in Lake City, South Carolina on conspiracy charges for attacks in Colorado, including a plan to poison public water supplies, for his role in the 1 August 1984 arson of a Hare Krishna temple in Denver, and his role in the 30 January 1990 murder of Rashid Khalifa, another controversial Sunni Muslim leader.

The group appears to have had indirect support from the Pakistani government through its intelligence services which have used Kashmiri separatists and Fuqra members for attacks on Indian positions along the cease-fire line dividing the Indian from Pakistani controlled portions of Kashmir. Some group members have had contact with **Hamas** and dissident **Moro** factions in the Philippines.

JAPANESE RED ARMY (JRA). The JRA was a group of Japanese **anarchistic leftists** who intended to ignite a worldwide revolution through terrorist actions. Although the JRA formerly enjoyed foreign state sponsorship from Libya and Syria, backing from these regimes has diminished as their governments have sought to improve relations with the West and to distance themselves from the groups they formerly patronized. The JRA has maintained cooperative ties since 1971 with the North Korean regime as well as having a long-term relationship with the **Popular Front for the Liberation of Palestine** (PFLP). Although the JRA formerly maintained its center and training camp in the Syrian-controlled part of the Bekaa valley in Lebanon, Syria in February 1997 effectively ended its support for the JRA by allowing Lebanese authorities to arrest and try several of its members for passport violations and illegal entry and residence in Lebanon.

The Japanese name for this "Red Army" is Sekigun, "Japanese Red Army" being Nippon Sekigun. Since May 1986 the JRA has been using the name "Anti-Imperialist International Brigades" as either a new cover or as a nom de guerre. Often the JRA has claimed to seek the role of serving as a rallying point for similar anarchistic leftists in Japan, opposing Japanese and Western "imperialism," and establishing a People's Republic in Japan. The venues of most of its actions have been outside of Japan, however, and even when the JRA used **kidnapping** of hostages or **hijacking** to force the Japanese government to release comrades imprisoned within Japan, such compliance tended to be relatively low-visibility events. Therefore, it was unclear how the JRA terrorist program could have expected to influence public opinion within Japan.

The JRA emerged from an internal purge of the Japanese Red Army Faction in 1970-1971, leading to the murders of several members. These murders led to a police crackdown in Japan, forcing many members of the JRA Faction to flee abroad. A JRA Faction liaison with the PFLP in Lebanon, Fusako Shigenobu, invited other fugitive members to join her there where the JRA was formed. Shigenobu remained the leader of the JRA until her arrest.

From 1971 to 1991, the JRA accomplished 17 noteworthy actions and planned, or attempted, at least nine major actions that were aborted. Of the 17 successful actions, two were armed attacks using knives, samurai swords, small-arms or automatic weapons; three were hijackings; four were bombings; two were hostage seizures; and six were rocket attacks. It should be noted that hijackings and hostage seizures occurred from 1971 to 1977 involved hand-held weapons and direct contact with victims. Such tactics seemed legitimated in Japanese culture by the martial Bushido tradition emphasizing personal valor in direct confrontation and actually helped boost the prestige of the group within Japan. There was a hiatus in JRA activity from late 1977 to mid-1986 after which the JRA began relying instead on **bombings** and rocket firings in which the JRA members would be quite remote from the **target** and could escape more easily. The change in tactics helped preserve in working order an organization that, given its own remoteness from Japan, had difficulties recruiting new members. Also the JRA had been and remained a rather small group, numbering at most perhaps 25 members and currently having no more than 8 active members, whose identities have become fairly well known among police organizations throughout the world, making it more imperative for them to avoid capture.

The most notorious of the JRA actions was the massacre of 26 people at Israel's Lod Airport in 30 May 1972, carried out by three JRA gunmen on behalf of the PFLP. The sole surviving gunman, Kozo Okamoto, was imprisoned in Israel until 1985 when he was released in exchange for Israeli prisoners and allowed to fly to Libya where he was accorded a hero's welcome. On 4 August 1975 10 JRA gunmen seized the U.S. Consulate in Kuala Lumpur and held 52 hostages, threatening to kill them if seven imprisoned JRA members in Japan were not released. Only five of those JRA members released opted to leave, flying to Libya via Kuala Lumpur.

On 14 May 1986 the JRA detonated a car bomb outside of the Canadian embassy and launched rockets against the U.S. and Japanese embassies in Jakarta from a nearby hotel. Fingerprints found in the room with the launcher matched those of a known JRA member, although credit was taken in the name of the "Anti-Imperialist International Brigade." This resumption of JRA activity occurred within a month following the U.S. retaliatory raid on Libya, a circumstance that along with JRA members' choice of Libya as a sanctuary tended to suggest Libyan state-sponsorship of this group. On 9 June 1987 a similar rocket attack coupled with a car bombing was made against the U.S. and British embassies in Rome, causing but minor damage. On 14 April 1988, the second anniversary of the Libya raid, the "Jihad Brigades" claimed credit for bombing a U.S. servicemen's club in Naples in which five people were killed, but the suspects seized in connection with this bombing were also JRA members. Two days earlier Yu Kikumura, a JRA member, was arrested in New Jersey in possession of three powerful bombs. It is believed that he was supposed to bomb some U.S. military facility at the same time as the Naples bombing to mark the second anniversary of the U.S. raid. Kikumura was convicted for his role in the Naples attack and is serving a lengthy prison sentence in the United States. In January 1990 the JRA attacked the Imperial palaces in Kyoto and Tokyo simultaneously using homemade rockets.

The change in tactics from direct personal combat to the use of remotely triggered rockets and bombs has made future JRA attacks potentially much more lethal. Evidence gathered from arrests of JRA members showed that the group had an extensive support network, generous finances, and an ability to move members freely throughout the world. Despite the collapse of world communism in 1991 the JRA did not renounce its terrorist program.

In the 1990s the JRA experienced several reverses and humiliations. On 18 February 1997 Lebanese security forces arrested six JRA members in the Bekaa valley, including Kozo Okamoto. Five of them were tried in June 1997 and sentenced to jails terms of up to 10 years for illegal entry into Lebanon and passport violations. On 22 April 1997 a Japanese appeals court upheld the life sentence for JRA member Osamu Maruoka, for his role in the 1973 hijacking of a plane from Tokyo to

Abu Dubai and then to Libya, where he and his comrades blew the plane up, and also his role in the 1977 hijacking of a flight to Dhaka, Bangladesh, in which he successfully extorted the release of six jailed JRA comrades as well as $6 million from the Japanese government. When he was arrested in 1987 Maruoka indicated that the JRA had been planning to organize cells in Singapore and Manila. In March 1995 Ekita Yukiko was arrested in Romania and subsequently deported to Japan. On 14 November 1997 Tsutomu Shirosaki was convicted in U.S. federal court for the 14 May 1986 rocket attack on the U.S. embassy compound in Jakarta, Indonesia. The JRA leader, Ms. Fusako Shigenobu, was arrested in Takatsuki, Japan on 8 November 2000 following a 31-year search for her although a few other JRA members remained at large.

JEWISH DEFENSE LEAGUE (JDL). The JDL was a Jewish self-defense movement that began with the limited goals of protecting orthodox Jewish neighborhoods in New York City from depredations by young black and Puerto Rican hoodlums and to protest local instances of anti-Semitism. Eventually the JDL embraced a universal program of fighting for Jewish interests worldwide. The group was self-sustaining and lacked any support from mainstream Jewish organizations in the United States or from the State of Israel.

The JDL was founded in 1968 by Rabbi Meir Kahane, who began to organize young Jewish men as vigilantes to protect Jews and Jewish businesses in the Williamsburg and Crown Heights areas of Brooklyn and elsewhere in the New York City area. Within a year the group had graduated from vigilantism and demonstrations against alleged anti-Semites to burglarizing the files of the **Palestine Liberation Organization** (PLO) UN Mission and launching attacks on Soviet diplomatic, trade, and tourism offices and personnel. According to the FBI, the JDL was responsible for at least 37 terrorist acts in the United States in the period from 1968-1983, while the International Terrorism: Attributes of Terrorist Events (ITERATE) database developed on behalf of the United States Central Intelligence Agency by Edward F. Mickolus recorded 50 such incidents from 1968-1987, making the JDL second only to the Puerto Rican **Armed Forces of National Liberation** (FALN) as the major domestic terrorist group during that period. Nonetheless the JDL is a legally incorporated political action group and has officially disavowed responsibility for any violent actions carried out by its members. **Bombings** accounted for 78 percent of all JDL terrorist activities; shootings accounted for 16 percent; while **arson** attacks, vandalism, **kidnapping**, threats, and verbal harassment accounted for the rest.

From 1969 to 1985 the JDL targeted mainly the representatives of governments perceived to be anti-Israeli or anti-Semitic, most of which were directed against Soviet **targets**. Thus the JDL bombed the San Francisco branch of the Iranian Bank Melli on 26 January 1981 and bombed the Iraqi UN Mission on 28 April 1982 to protest the mistreatment of Jews in those two countries. The JDL once bombed the office of impresario Sol Hurok, who helped arrange performances of Soviet ballet troupes in the United States, which caused the death of one employee. For the most part, these attacks seemed intended to intimidate but not to kill their victims.

Beginning late in 1985, however, the targeting shifted to individuals suspected of being anti-Israeli or anti-Semitic, and the attack mode became much more lethal. On 11 October 1985 the Los Angeles offices of the Arab-American Anti-Discrimination Committee (ADC) was bombed, killing the ADC director Alex Odeh, who had sought to rationalize the actions of the hijackers of the *Achille Lauro* on a local newscast the previous evening. On 15 August 1985 a 61-year-old Waffen-SS veteran, Tsherim Soobzokov, was bombed at his Paterson, N.J., home and later died of his wounds. In such attacks an anonymous caller would claim the action in the name of the JDL, and afterward an official JDL spokesman would disavow the group's responsibility. In 1987 several JDL members were convicted on a variety of criminal charges, and since then there has been no record of JDL terrorist activity.

As the JDL was very much the personal creation of Rabbi Kahane, following his emigration to Israel in 1971 the group began to experience factionalism. The day immediately following the bombing murder of Alex Odeh, Kahane announced his resignation as JDL leader. Despite the national prominence of the JDL, this group had poor to acrimonious relations with more conventional Jewish political and social organizations, such as B'nai B'rith's Anti-Defamation League, which regarded the JDL as a marginal group and an embarrassment to the American Jewish community. Without the leadership of Rabbi Kahane, who was shot dead by an Egyptian fundamentalist, El Sayyid A. Nosair on 5 November 1990 in New York, the prospects for a revival of the JDL appear dim. Nosair, a follower of **Sheikh Omar Abdul Rahman** was convicted for the murder of Kahane on 1 October 1995.

While living in Israel, Kahane founded the Kach Party, an ultranationalist group favoring expulsion of the Arabs from both Israel and the occupied territories. Following his death another group, Kahane Chai (Kahane Lives), split off from the Kach group. Many former JDL members who followed Kahane's example in emigrating to Israel joined these groups, often living in settlements within the Occupied Territories. On 25 February 1994, a Kach Party member and former JDL activist, Dr. Baruch Goldstein, opened fire on Palestinian Arabs in the mosque built over the Tomb of the Patriarchs in Hebron, killing at least 29 and wounding scores more before he himself was killed. This incident led to anti-Israeli rioting throughout the occupied territories and stymied the peace negotiations underway between the PLO and Israel. On 13 March 1994 the Israeli government banned both the Kach and Kahane Chai groups in an effort to stem the furor caused by the massacre in Hebron.

JEWISH UNDERGROUND. Term used in the Israeli press to designate the many Jewish religious extremists, whether members of such groups as Kach, **Eyal**, or Kahane Chai, that form an informal terrorist network of anti-Arab Jewish religious extremists intent on killing large numbers of Arabs to sabotage the Israeli-Palestinian peace process. Many of them are concentrated in the Jewish settlement of Kiryat Arba, outside Hebron, where Arab-Jewish tensions have been tense since the 25 February 1994 killing of 29 Muslims at the Tomb of the Patriarchs by Dr. Baruch Goldstein, a Kach Party member and Kiryat Arba settler. The term was earlier used by British authorities to refer to Jewish extremists during the period of the Palestine Mandate.

JIHAD. The term *jihad* is an Arabic verbal noun derived from *jahada*, meaning "to struggle," that is, to struggle with something that is disagreeable or else against something that is wrong. While the frequently used expression "holy war" is not a literal translation, it does summarize the essential idea of jihad. The Muslim jurists give the most general definition of jihad as the Muslim believers' exerting their abilities, talents, and power in struggling in the path of God using their resources of life, property, speech, and all available instruments to make the Word of God prevail in this world. Muslim jurists distinguish between a "greater jihad," which is the struggle against the world, the flesh, and the devil in the spiritual realm, and a "lesser jihad" consisting of open physical warfare with the enemies of Islam or of the Muslims. In the course of the revival of **Islamic fundamentalism** the doctrine of jihad has been invoked to justify resistance, including terrorist actions, to combat "un-Islamic" regimes, or purported external enemies of Islam, such as Israel and the United States.

The classical doctrine of jihad did not necessarily exclude its use to spread the Islamic religion by force of arms since the classical Muslim thinkers ibn Rushd and ibn Khaldun both accepted this interpretation. Most modern jurists, however, have preferred an interpretation of jihad comparable to that of purely defensive warfare. Islamic fundamentalists, such as **Sayyid Qutb**, other members of the **Muslim Brotherhood**, and members of the **Munazzamat al Jihad** group that murdered Anwar Sadat, have maintained that the object of jihad was the full enactment of the sacred law of Islam, rather than defense or conquest as such, and that there was no reason to limit the role of jihad merely to defensive warfare.

The Muslim jurists make two other distinctions regarding jihad important to understanding its possible connection with terrorism. Ordinarily jihad is a collective, rather than a personal, obligation. If a Muslim nation undertakes jihad lawfully, the duty of waging jihad is discharged by the Muslim army and its commander on behalf of the entire Muslim community. The conditions under which this form of jihad may be lawfully initiated and exercised are remarkably similar to those governing the Judeo-Christian Just War doctrine: Jihad can be declared only by the competent religious-cum-secular authorities. Recourse to jihad is permissible only after all other diplomatic channels for redress of grievances have been exhausted. During jihad, noncombatant enemy civilians may not be attacked, killed, or taken prisoner nor may the Muslim army engage in random destruction of enemy property. Muslim soldiers and officers must observe proportionality in their defensive and retaliatory attacks. Such a definition of jihad quite rules out most of what might be considered terrorist actions.

In the case of an invasion of a Muslim land by non-Muslim forces, however, jihad ceases to be a collective obligation, becoming instead the personal obligation of every Muslim man, woman, and child, whether old or young, infirm or well. Given the disproportionate force enjoyed by the invading army over that possessed by the individual believer, upon whom waging jihad becomes religiously obligatory, a greater allowance may be extended to the individual, in effect exempting him or her from the usual limits placed on lawful warfare. Islamic fundamentalist groups like **Hezbollah** in Lebanon, **Hamas** in the occupied territories of the West Bank and Gaza Strip, or the **Islamic Group** in Egypt tend to view their nation as being occupied by an invading un-Islamic power, even in the case of a nominally Muslim government such as that of Egyptian President Hosni Mubarak. This in turn allows them to claim the right to wage jihad without the authorization of competent religious authorities and by means that may be described as terroristic.

Despite the religious technicalities that limit the correct application of the term jihad to only a few situations, the tendency of secular Pan-Arab nationalism to exploit Islamic religious symbols and sentiments whenever expedient has led Arab nationalists to misuse the term "jihad" to designate what actually have been wars on behalf of Arab national-ism rather than Islam proper. During the 1990-1991 Persian Gulf con-flict, Iraqi President Saddam Hussein tried to rally Arab support for himself by describing his war as a "jihad" against the West and Israel. Saddam Hussein, however, lacked the moral and religious credentials of an authority competent to declare jihad nor could he invoke it credibly to defend Iraq's usurpation of another Muslim land. Interestingly dur-ing the entire course of the Iran-Iraq war, the Islamic Republic of Iran never described its war with Iraq in terms of jihad but only as a *jang-i difa'i-ye muqaddis*, that is, a "war of holy defense against aggression." Shi'ite fundamentalist Muslims have been less inclined to use the term jihad than their Sunni counterparts due to their belief that jihad proper can be declared only by one of their apostolic Imams.

JUNE SECOND MOVEMENT. This group was an **anarchistic leftist** group formed in West Berlin in 1971 that sought to resist the liberal demo-cratic establishment in West Berlin through **bombings**, bank robberies, **kidnappings**, and **assassinations**. The group is named after the anniver-sary of Benno Ohnejorg's death, who was killed in a demonstration against the visiting Shah of Iran in Berlin on 2 June 1967.

The group bombed the British Yacht Club in Berlin on 2 February 1972, killing a German attendant. On 10 November 1974 members of this group shot and killed West Berlin Chief Justice Günter von Drenkmann in reprisal for the death by suicide of a June Second member in jail. On 27 February 1975 the group kidnapped the leader of the Berlin Christian Democrats, Peter Lorenz, who was released in exchange for the freeing of five anarchistic leftist terrorists who were allowed to leave for South Yemen.

The group was closely associated with the **Red Army Faction** (RAF) and after the majority of its members had been arrested by the end of the 1970s, the remainder were absorbed into the RAF group.

JUSTICE COMMANDOS OF THE ARMENIAN GENOCIDE (JCAG). The JCAG was an Armenian nationalist revolutionary organization founded in 1975 seeking to reestablish an independent Armenian state on the territory occupied by the former Republic of Armenia during World War I within eastern Turkey. It pursued this goal through attacks on Turkish diplomats and economic interests outside Turkey in the belief that Turkey bore responsibility for the slaughter of Armenians and the destruction of the Armenian Republic that occurred in 1915.

The JCAG differed from the other major Armenian terrorist group, the **Armenian Secret Army for the Liberation of Armenia** (ASALA) in two important respects: First, the JCAG was primarily nationalistic rather than Marxist-Leninist. Therefore it relied almost exclusively on private support from Armenian communities rather than state-sponsorship from countries hostile to Turkey. Second, the members of the JCAG, being very westernized nationalists, valued Western and world public opinion highly and therefore took pains to avoid harming non-Turkish nationals mindful of the potential harm such actions could render the Armenian cause. Nonetheless the JCAG conducted attacks on Turkish targets within the United States.

An analysis of 29 noteworthy actions by the JCAG in the period from 1975-1983 showed that 15 involved **assassination** of Turkish diplomats; 13 involved **bombings** and **arsons** of Turkish diplomatic, tourism, and commercial offices; while one incident represented an unfulfilled threat against Turkish targets. The JCAG terrorism within the United States took place entirely from January 1982 to May 1982: On 29 January 1982 Kemal Arikan, consul general of Turkey in Los Angeles, was shot and killed as he was driving home. On 22 March 1982 the offices of Orhan Gunduz, honorary Turkish consul general in Boston, were firebombed and he himself was shot and killed on 4 May 1982. A conspiracy to bomb the home of the honorary consul general of Turkey in Philadelphia was foiled in October 1982. Since then nothing further has been heard of the JCAG either in the United States or abroad.

Beginning in July 1983, after the name "Justice Commandos of the Armenian Genocide" had dropped from use, actions similar to those of the JCAG began to be claimed in the name of the "Armenian Revolutionary Army" (ARA). Many analysts believed that the JCAG merely changed its name to ARA and that it is essentially the same organization. While ARA made the same disclaimers as had JCAG that it intended no harm to non-Turkish bystanders in contrast to earlier JCAG operations, at least six non-Turkish nationals were killed as a result of these operations.

In fact, very little is known about the memberships of these groups, their internal structures, or their relations with possible sponsor states or with other terrorist groups. What little is known about the Armenian groups indicates that they have been involved in factional disputes and internecine fighting that has reduced their effective presence as terrorist groups since the mid-1980s.

- K -

KACH. *See* JEWISH DEFENSE LEAGUE.

KACZYNSKI, THEODORE. *See* UNABOMBER.

KANAK SOCIALIST NATIONAL LIBERATION FRONT. The Front de Libération Nationale Kanake Socialiste (FLNKS) is a coalition of several proindependence political parties representing the interests of the Kanaks, that is, the Melanesian natives of New Caledonia, as opposed to the interests of settlers of French or other origins. The FLNKS coalition includes the Union Calédonienne, the oldest and largest Kanak party; the quasi-Marxist Parti de Libération Kanak (PALIKA); the socialist Union Progressiste Melanésienne; and the Front Uni de Libération Kanak (FULK) led by Yann Celene Uregei until April 2000 and currently lad by Clarence Uregei.

The agenda of FLNKS is revolutionary since attaining the twin goals of independence for New Caledonia and sovereignty for the indigenous Kanaks, who now make up only 44 percent of the archipelago, would entail civil war with the non-Kanak majority. So far terrorist actions by members of FLNKS have been sporadic and limited in their aims, being undertaken either to draw the attention of the French government and public to Kanak aspirations or else to block specific measures believed to threaten Kanak interests.

In late October 1981 three **bombings** occurred in Paris. The first on October 25 hit Fouquet's restaurant on the Champs-Élysées; the second on October 27 destroyed a car parked at Charles de Gaulle Airport; and the final bombing struck a cinema in downtown Paris. Injuries were sustained only in the last bombing, in which three persons, including a pregnant woman, were hurt. Credit for these attacks was taken by callers claiming to represent the "Kanak Liberation Front" or the "Army for the Liberation of New Caledonia." Authorities suspected PALIKA was the responsible group.

In New Caledonia clashes and shooting incidents erupted between Kanaks and French settlers from 30 November to 6 December 1984, leaving 10 dead and four wounded. Following these incidents the head of the Union Calédonienne and chief leader of FLNKS, Jean-Marie Tjibaou, confirmed that 17 Kanaks had received paramilitary training in Libya. On 4 May 1987 FLNKS officially disavowed the pro-Libyan stand and statements of FULK leader Uregei who was in Tripoli at that time. Because pending French autonomy plans and regional elections threatened the hope of Kanak sovereignty, independence activists attacked French gendarmes on the small island of Ouvea on 24 April 1988, killing four gendarmes and holding the remaining 23 as hostages in a cave. When negotiations failed, French commandos stormed the cave on 5 May, killing 19 and capturing eight of the Kanak militants. In addition the French soldiers manhandled noncombatant islanders and tortured their Kanak prisoners, three of whom died.

Following this incident Kanak youth from the FULK party attended the Thirteenth World Festival of Youth and Students held in Pyongyang, North Korea, in July 1989, eight of whom remained behind to attend a "training camp" that may have included terrorist tactical instruction. Apart from the potential importation of terrorism into New Caledonia from outside parties, such as Libya and North Korea, intramural tensions within the Kanak community also portend political violence or terrorism, as became evident in the **assassination** of the politically moderate Kanak leader Jean-Marie Tjibaou on 5 May 1989. Tjibaou went to Ouvea to attend the anniversary commemoration of the deaths of those Kanaks killed by French commandos a year before. Because Tjibaou's accompanying deputy, Yeiwene, was viewed by the Ouvea islanders as a pro-French traitor, both Yeiwene and Tjibaou were assassinated by relatives of those killed or tortured by the French commandos. Following the Kanak separatists' failure to win a majority in the 1998 referendum on Caledonian independence the FLNKS coalition ran candidates in the 9 May 1999 election for the Congrès Territorial and won 18 out of the 54 seats. Although tensions between Kanaks separatists and settlers and among the Kanaks themselves have remained high, in recent years there have been no significant terrorist incidents.

KANSAI REVOLUTIONARY ARMY. Name of covert action group of Chukaku-Ha. *See* CHUKAKU-HA.

KANSI, MIR AIMAL. *See* CIA HEADQUARTERS ATTACK.

KASHMIRI SECESSIONISTS. Most Kasmiri secessionists have been **Islamic fundamentalists** seeking to impose Muslim control over that part of Jammu and Kashmir that has been under Indian administration since the partition of India and first Indian-Pakistani war in 1947. There are a number of groups who claim to seek this goal including the Kashmir Liberation Front, the Harakat ul Mujahideen (formerly called the Harakat al Ansar), the Harakat ul Muminim, al Hadid, and al Faran, some of which may be multiple names used by the same core of militants. It is not entirely clear whether these militants are seeking to replace Indian rule with Pakistani rule or else are seeking to create the territorial basis of a future independent Kashmir. Although the rhetoric of these groups suggests that they are seeking to create an Islamic state in Kashmir it is unlikely that their immediate goal is an independent Kashmiri state because these groups enjoy Pakistani state support in the form of money, arms, and sanctuary. India controls about 60 percent of the territory of Kashmir in which 75 percent of the population are Muslims. It is the only state in the Indian federal system that has a majority of Muslims.

The current insurgency began in 1989 with separatist militants carrying out attacks on Indian army and police along the cease-fire line, attacks on Hindus living within Kashmir, and also **kidnapping** of foreign tourists. In January 1990 the Indian government imposed direct rule over Kashmir from New Delhi and in February 1994 imposed military rule, suspending scheduled elections for six months to contain the insurgency. However on 8 August 1994 military rule was extended until elections scheduled for May 1995. In the course of five years of insurgency over 12,000 people have been killed. The insurgency was reinforced by large numbers of Islamic militant veterans of the **Mujahideen** war against the Soviets in Afghanistan who include not only Afghans but also non-Kashmiri Muslims of other nations. The rise of Hindu nationalism within India in the 1990s as well as the destruction of the Ayodhya Mosque on 6 December 1992 by Hindu militants have also been cited as causes for the increased militancy of the Kashmiri separatist movement.

Separatists of the "al Hadid" group kidnapped four Western tourists in mid-October. One American tourist escaped and Indian police freed the remaining three Britons on 1 November 1994. Unfortunately sectarian and communal divisions sharpened when a fire on 11 May 1995 destroyed the 15th century Hazratbal Mosque in Charar Sharif near Srinagar. This mosque was under siege by Indian troops who sought to arrest militants who were using it as an arms depot and command post. When a fire destroyed most of the ancient wooden buildings in the town, including the Mosque, militants claimed the Indian Army had deliberately set the blaze and desecrated the Mosque. A rash of around 150 **arsons**, including attacks on Hindu shrines, and widespread unrest caused cancellation of the May elections. This was followed on 4 July 1995 by the kidnapping of five Western tourists by "al Faran." Until this time all such kidnappings had been followed by the release of the hostages unharmed. After one of the American captives escaped, village women discovered the body and severed head of a Norwegian hostage on 13 August 1995 along with a note threatening to kill the remaining hostages unless 15 imprisoned comrades were released. In a clash between al Faran and Indian Army troops on 4 December 1995 the leader of the al Faran unit was killed and discovered to be an Afghan named Abdul Hamid Turki. After many alleged sightings of the hostages, by May 1996 the Indian Army developed intelligence indicating the remaining hostages had been killed and tried to locate their remains.

On 20 April 1996 the Harakat ul Muminim **bombed** a New Delhi market killing 17 people, including some tourists, and wounding 30 others. During the period 1995-1997 another 8,000 people were killed and in 1998 separatists began a campaign of attacking and slaying large groups of Hindu civilians in remote areas and villages, causing many of the 100,000 Hindus living in the Vale of Kashmir to flee to the largely Hindu city of Jammu. However, on 2 August 1998 separatists entered the neighboring Hindu-majority state of Himachal Pradesh and massacred 26 construction workers and wounded eight others in the town of Chamba. On 26 May 1999 the conflict escalated to the point that the Indian Air Force began bombing runs on Kashmiri separatist enclaves carved out within the Indian portion of the 1949 cease-fire line which included the strategic Tololing Peak overlooking Indian artillery positions along the line of control and also overlooking a strategic northern highway linking Indian forward positions with logistical support. Following a one-day break on 5 June 1999 the air raids resumed until the 150 remaining rebels were driven off of Tololing Peak. Following this defeat the militants resumed the tactic of hitting remote Hindu villages and slaying large numbers of Hindu civilians.

On 24 December 1999 the Harakat ul Mujahideen carried out its most audacious action with the **hijacking** of an Air India A300 Airbus from Kathmandu to Qandahar, Afghanistan. Five men believed to have originated from Pakistan hijacked the Air India Airbus bound for New Delhi and directed it instead to Pakistan, from there to the United Arab Emirates, and finally to Qandahar, Afghanistan, where they held 153 passengers and crew hostage threatening to kill them unless Harakat ul Mujahideen leader Maulana Masood Azhar, a Pakistani Muslim cleric imprisoned in India since 1994, were released along with several other militants, the body of a slain militant, and payment of a ransom of $200 million. By 31 December 1999 India agreed to the release of Azhar and two other separatist leaders who were flown to Qandahar where they and the five hijackers departed releasing the surviving hostages. One Air India passenger had been killed earlier when he disobeyed the hijackers' orders not to look at them.

The incident raised many questions about the role of Pakistan, whose government disclaimed any involvement in the incident, and also the role of the **Taliban** who, while also publically condemning the hijacking, made no apparent moves to arrest the hijackers after the incident. Also several passengers indicated that automatic weapons only appeared after their arrival in Qandahar which suggested the Taliban supplied these weapons to the hijackers. This incident has led the United States government to consider including Pakistan on the list of **state sponsors of terrorism** for its continuing support for the Harakat ul Mujahideen, a group officially designated as an international terrorist organization by the U.S. State Department.

KHMER ROUGE. Originally founded under Vietnamese sponsorship in 1951, the Khmer Communist Party was a revolutionary group that sought to create a socialist state in Cambodia following the Maoist model of guerrilla warfare and cultural revolution. The name Khmer Rouge was a coinage of Prince Sihanouk, who alternatively fought and allied himself with the Khmer Rouge led by Pol Pot. After 10 years of fighting the governments of Prince Sihanouk until 1970 and of Lon Nol until 1975, the Khmer Rouge took the capital of Phnom Penh on 17 April 1975.

In an exercise of **state terror** scarcely matched in its scope and brazenness, the Khmer Rouge initiated a reign of terror and state repression to totally destroy prerevolutionary Cambodia and to create their ideal agricultural state. The Khmer Rouge depopulated the cities of Cambodia, which they renamed Kampuchea, forcing the urban population into agricultural communes where they were enslaved and brutalized. From 1975 to 1978 the Khmer Rouge systematically overworked and starved the subject population, selectively executing the educated and killing others even for minor breaches of rules. Approximately one million people perished under this phase of Khmer rule. With the 25 December 1978 invasion of Vietnamese forces lasting until 1989, the Khmer Rouge reverted once again to being a guerrilla army, continuing to terrorize and repress Cambodians in the regions it controlled.

The North Vietnamese and Khmer Rouge remained tactical allies until the fall of the pro-U.S. Lon Nol regime in 1975. By 1978 bitter warfare erupted between the Chinese-backed Khmer Rouge and the Soviet-backed Vietnamese. In 1980 Khieu Samphan replaced Pol Pot as leader and the Khmer Rouge began to receive tacit Thai aid in the form of sanctuary within border areas of Thailand while China supplied weapons, munitions, radios, and medical equipment. The Khmer Rouge fielded about 35,000 combatants and often exerted de facto rule within Cambodian refugee camps within Thailand.

Following withdrawal of Vietnamese forces in 1989, a coalition government was established in which the Khmer Rouge was invited to participate as the price to be paid to avert the continuation of civil war. Under the UN-sponsored settlement concluded on 23 October 1991, the Khmer Rouge agreed to formally dissolve their Khmer Communist Party in December 1991 and to become coalition partners in a civilian government. In fact throughout 1992 and 1993 the Khmer Rouge continued their activities as an armed, revolutionary party and attacked the militias belonging to other coalition partners as well as firing upon members of the UN Transitional Authority in Cambodia. In 1993 the Khmer Rouge boycotted the UN-sponsored elections and resumed guerrilla warfare.

By 1995 Khmer Rouge forces were estimated at between 5,000 and 10,000 troops. Government forces continued to battle the Khmer Rouge in western regions of Cambodia, seizing the Khmer stronghold of Pailin along the Thai border in 1994 only to lose it to them again in 1995. During this time, when the People's Republic of China had ceased to support the Khmer Rouge, the remnant Khmer Rouge maintained themselves by allowing Thai loggers access to Cambodian timber for a price, through sales of precious gems mined in the region, and through extortionary taxes levied on local peasant communities.

In August 1996 high-ranking Khmer Rouge commanders defected to the Cambodian regime bringing reports of factional infighting in the group. On 16 August 1996 Ieng Sary, a former chief lieutenant of Pol Pot, denounced him on Cambodian radio as the "chief of the cruel murderers," blaming him for the **genocide** against Cambodia's people. Negotiations started between his breakaway faction of the Khmer Rouge and the Army that would allow the Khmer soldiers to be integrated into the Cambodian armed forces without reprisal. Khmer Rouge units loyal to Pol Pot started to attack those units which were defecting.

On 18 June 1997 the clandestine Khmer radio station announced that Pol Pot had been arrested by his former comrades and top lieutenants. During July 1997 the Khmer Rouge attempted to negotiate some sort of alliance with coalition government leader Prince Ranariddh and held a carefully staged show trial of Pol Pot which many observers believed to be have been organized by Pol Pot himself as a survival ploy. In reality it became known later that one of his aids, Ta Mok, had seized power from Pol Pot who had been ailing for several years. Prince Ranariddh's contacts with the remaining Khmer Rouge succeeded only in provoking coleader Hun Sen to oust Ranariddh altogether by means of a military coup and once Hun Sen assumed total power he intended to settle the civil war on his own terms.

As government troops and defected Khmer Rouge fighters began closing in on the remaining Khmer Rouge stronghold of Anlong Veng, Thai military officers in contact with the remaining Khmer leaders announced that Pol Pot had died on 15 April 1998. By then the Khmer Rouge was in disarray and many leaders and ordinary soldiers defected. The Hun Sen regime in effect granted amnesty to the Khmer defectors, including Nuon Chea and Khieu Samphan, who had been the official head of state under the Khmer Rouge, and most of the amnestied defectors were allowed to run their own community in their former stronghold of Pailin. Ta Mok and his remaining 2,000 troops remained at large in the mountainous northern region bordering Laos but represented no threat to the Cambodian government. On 5 December 1998 Ta Mok and his troops surrendered, so ending the Khmer Rouge insurgency.

The Hun Sen regime resisted UN and U.S. pressures to try Khieu Samphan, Ieng Sary, and Nuon Chea, who had been partners with Pol Pot in the killing of up to two million Cambodians, and settled on a domestic trial for Ta Mok. On 11 August 1999 the Cambodia parliament voted to allow a delay of up to three years for the trying of any former Khmer Rouge officials so staying the planned beginning of Ta Mok's trial originally scheduled for 9 September 1999.

In 1999 the U.S. State Department removed the Khmer Rouge from its list of Foreign Terrorist Organizations (FTOs) due to its ceasing to exist as a viable terrorist organization.

KHOBAR TOWERS ATTACK. On 25 June 1996 at 10:00 p.m. a truck **bomb** was exploded outside of the Khobar Towers apartment complex in Dhahran, Saudi Arabia, which was being used to house U.S. Air Force personnel of the 4404th Air Wing serving at King Abdul Aziz Air Base, killing 19 persons and wounding over 500 others. The force of the explosion, which occurred 35 yards from the apartment building, created a crater 30-feet-deep and 80-feet-wide and tore off the face of the eight-story building. Security guards on the roof of the building, which housed roughly half of the 5,000 American troops deployed in Saudi Arabia, saw the truck stop outside the security perimeter and saw the driver of the truck enter another car and speed away. Immediately the guards began to notify residents to evacuate the building when the truck exploded. The size of the bomb was much greater than the **Oklahoma City bombing**, which left a 20-feet-deep crater, and involved military-style detonators and between 3,000 to 5,000 pounds of explosives, making it more than 10 times the size of the bomb used in the November 1995 **Riyadh U.S.-Saudi National Guard training center bombing**. Investigations revealed that the truck used in the bombing had been seen on previous occasions and suspicious activities by unknown persons noted on 10 occasions from April to May 1996.

As a result of the bombing and subsequent investigations more than 4,200 of the U.S. servicemen stationed in Saudi Arabia were relocated to the Prince Sultan air base near Al Kharj located 50 miles south of Riyadh in a largely uninhabited region.

The Khobar Towers bombing was first thought to be the work of Iraqi or Iranian sponsored terrorists but evidence seemed later to point to **Osama bin Laden's** organization. Although the FBI was called in to investigate the bombing it ended its investigated on 1 November 1996 due to the lack of cooperation of Saudi officials who appeared unwilling to share information that might reveal the extent of dissent among the subjects of the kingdom. On 22 May 1998 the Interior Minister of Saudi Arabia, Prince Nayef ibn Abdul Aziz, stated that the bombing was the work of Saudi nationals and did not involve a foreign power. However as of April 2000 U.S. investigators had intelligence that indicated a Saudi group that enjoyed Iranian state-sponsorship was responsible for the bombing.

KHOMEINI, RUHALLAH MUSAWI AL (1902?-1989). Under Ayatollah Khomeini's leadership, Iran became a state sponsor of terrorism in the name of fighting the influence of the United States and Israel in both Iran and the remaining Middle East and also in the name of "exporting the Islamic revolution." Khomeini was also a leading theorist of **Islamic fundamentalism** and has had an impact on the aspirations and actions of Shi'ite, as well as Sunni, Muslims worldwide.

Khomeini's involvement in politics began in 1942 with the publication of his *Kashf al Asrar*, "The Unveiling of Secrets," in which he denounced the secularist programs of Reza Shah, who had been deposed by invading British and Soviet forces in late 1941. During 1963 Khomeini began agitation against Muhammad Reza Shah Pahlavi, the son of Reza Shah, who had begun to undertake a modernization and social reform program required by the John F. Kennedy administration as a precondition for U.S. military aid to Iran. Khomeini attacked the status of forces agreement signed between Iran and the United States required for U.S. military aid as a "capitulationist" treaty violating Iranian sovereignty. These speeches led to nationwide rioting on 5 June 1963, in which at least 300 people were killed by security forces. Khomeini was arrested and exiled to Turkey in early 1964. A year later Khomeini moved to Najaf, a Shi'ite shrine city in Iraq, where he was able to gather some of his clerical and lay followers about him and where he kept in contact with supporters within Iran through visiting Iranian pilgrims. During the period from 1964-1978 he developed a network of supporters within Iran and wrote his dissertation on Islamic government *Vilayat-i Faqih*, "The Governing Role of the Scholar of

Religious Jurisprudence," which became the guiding theory for the theocratic regime he later established in Iran.

A vituperative attack on Khomeini published by the semiofficial Iranian daily *Ittila'at* in November 1977 triggered protests in Tabriz in which police killed several demonstrators. This in turn led to a nationwide round of demonstrations linked to 40-day cycles of mourning for the "martyrs" in which all sources of opposition to the rule of the shah participated, including secular nationalists and leftists. Eventually the demonstrations developed into a national **revolution** to overthrow the shah in which Khomeini's network played a mobilizing and dominating role.

Following the collapse of the shah's government on 11 February 1979, a transitional period ensued in which liberal nationalists, leftists, and subnational secessionist groups sought to gain political advantages while Khomeini's Islamic fundamentalists sought to consolidate control over government institutions and through their own revolutionary foundations, such as the **Islamic Revolutionary Guards Corps** (IRGC). When liberal nationalists within Iran's Constituent Assembly opposed codification of the principle of Vilayat-i Faqih within Iran's new constitution, Khomeini concluded that the United States was covertly involved in this, as well as in all other, manifestations of opposition to his rule within Iran.

The admission of the ailing deposed shah to the United States for medical treatment in late October 1979 provided Khomeini and his followers with the appropriate pretext to occupy the U.S. embassy, which they regarded as "the den of espionage and fountainhead of all conspiracies," and to seize in excess of 100 hostages later reduced to 53 U.S. nationals. While the embassy seizure has been regarded as a state-sponsored act of terrorism, the group of student followers of Khomeini and the accompanying IRGC members were not actually under the control of the nominal provisional government of Iran. Given Khomeini's later designation of this action as the "second (Iranian) revolution" it could also be regarded as a vanguardist coup d'état since it caused the discredited Mehdi Bazargan provisional government to fall in favor of an Islamic Revolutionary Council more directly under the control of Khomeini. The hostage seizure and U.S. reaction to it precipitated an atmosphere of crisis within Iran, facilitating the mass mobilization of Iranian opinion around Khomeini and the consolidation of effective power in the hands of his supporters.

On 23 March 1980 Khomeini issued a general directive to the Iranian government to "export the [Islamic] revolution" to other Muslim countries. Conferences of Muslim laymen, clerics, and students from throughout the Islamic world were periodically held in Iran to rally support for Iran's revolution among foreign Muslims and to build contacts within other countries. On 5 February 1981 Khomeini decreed the creation of a Liberation Movements Department within the IRGC. The IRGC developed training bases for terrorists outside Tehran, Qum, and Mashhad, while the revolutionary Foundation for the Oppressed, comprising the domestic and overseas offices and assets of the former Pahlavi Foundation, provided a support network for groups operating abroad. In June 1981 Iran began sending IRGC units to the Bekaa valley in Lebanon where training bases for Lebanese Shi'ites were established and the pro-Iranian militia **Hezbollah** was established. On 13 December 1981 Bahrain uncovered and quashed an Iranian-sponsored plot to overthrow that country's government in favor of an Islamic republic.

During 1983 the U.S. embassy in West Beirut, the U.S. Marine encampment at Beirut International Airport, and the French and Israeli military headquarters in Lebanon were all car bombed by Hezbollah suicide volunteers (*see* SUICIDE BOMBINGS). Similar **bombings** were attempted in Kuwait against the U.S. and French embassies. Beginning also in 1983 but increasing in 1984 Hezbollah undertook a campaign of **kidnapping** U.S. nationals in Lebanon as a means of removing Western influence from that country. Many of those hostages would be released only by December 1991.

At Khomeini's insistence the Islamic Guidance Ministry of Iran on 26 May 1984 undertook a role in organizing an "independent brigade for carrying out irregular warfare in enemy territory," which included references to plans to incite anti-Saudi rioting during the Hajj pilgrimages in Mecca ceremonies. Such a riot on 31 July 1987 killed more than 400 people in Mecca.

While it has been argued that Iran undertook support of terrorism against, and subversion of, other Arab and Muslim governments in reaction to their support of Iraq during the Iran-Iraq war, such a rationalization ignores the fact that Saddam Hussein decided to invade Iran partly in reaction to Iranian agitation of Iraq's Shi'ites already underway, which included an **assassination** attempt against Iraqi Vice President Tariq 'Aziz on 1 April 1980 by Iranian agents. Likewise other Arab regimes supported Iraq because of their fear of the threat of Iranian-sponsored subversion against them.

In late 1988 Khomeini authorized the Iranian government to accept a UN-sponsored cease-fire with Iraq. This signaled no retreat from a willingness to use terrorism as an instrument of policy, however, for on 14 February 1989, Khomeini issued a fatwa of *takfir* against British author Salman Rushdie, sentencing him to death on charges of blasphemy arising from the publication of his book *Satanic Verses*. Khomeini died on 3 June 1989, having presided for more than a decade over the development of an Islamic revolutionary society within Iran but without witnessing the creation of any sister Islamic Republic outside of Iran's borders.

Khomeini's own position on terrorism remained highly ambivalent. In his *Kashf al Asrar* and *Vilayat-i Faqih*, he appeared to endorse the traditional Shi'ite view that only defensive warfare, rather than **jihad** proper, is permitted in the absence of the apostolic Twelfth Imam. In questions 2826-2834 of his jurisprudential handbook *Risalih-i Taudhih al Masa'il*, "Treatise on the Clarification of Problematic Issues," Khomeini derives the right of defensive warfare and resistance to unjust rulers not from the Koranic injunctions regarding jihad but rather from the Koranic command to "enjoin the good and prohibit the bad." On 8 August 1984, while criticizing a Radio Tehran commentary that had praised the mining of the Red Sea, Khomeini declared the hijacking of ships and airplanes, the kidnapping of passengers as hostages, and the bombing of public places in which innocents might be killed or maimed as being "against the sentiments of world opinion, against Islam, and against common sense." Nonetheless this declaration was followed by Hezbollah's hijacking of TWA Flight 847 on 14 June 1985 and by the **al Da'wa** group's hijacking of Kuwaiti Airways Flight 422 on 5 April 1988, in which both groups of hijackers were under Iranian sponsorship.

On 7 January 1988, however, Khomeini publicly adopted the position that the Islamic Republic, for reasons of state, was permitted not only to act against the decrees of the Koran but even to compel Muslim believers to do so, a position that would permit the Islamic Republic or its sponsored groups to engage in any terrorist actions they deemed to be necessary. The religious scrupulosity reflected in Khomeini's earlier writings and speeches may have simply crumbled under the pressures of running a nation-state and conducting a war. To the end of his life Khomeini never renounced the Islamic Republic's right to use terrorism. That Khomeini's successor as supreme religious leader, Ayatollah 'Ali Khamenehi, has openly reaffirmed the death sentence passed against Salman Rushdie on each of the anniversaries of its promulgation only confirmed the essential continuity of Tehran's terrorist policy in the post-Khomeini era. After the election of President Muhammad Khatami on 23 May 1997 his administration stated that it would not enforce the fatwa but also that it could not reverse the fatwa of a deceased religious authority. In November 1998 the Fifteeth of Khordad Foundation increased its bounty on Rushdie's head to $2.8 million.

KIDNAPPING. The deliberate seizure of a person, or persons, as hostages has become a major tactic of terrorists. Hostage taking can serve either purely revolutionary ends or may have **entrepreneurial** ends as well. Often, the kidnapping of a prominent person, as in the case of the **Red Brigades'** kidnapping of former Italian premier Aldo Moro, or even the seizure of relatively unknown persons who have symbolic importance, such as the diplomats and staff of the U.S. embassy in Tehran, can serve to gain the terrorists publicity and leverage for obtaining political concessions from the state or society being attacked. Often, however, terrorists seize hostages as bargaining chips to obtain the release of imprisoned colleagues or else to exact ransom, which in turn may be used to finance other terrorist or political operations of the group. **Hijacking** may be considered a special case of kidnapping since it is the seizure of hostages on air or sea carriers that gives the terrorists political leverage rather than the mere fact of seizing a transportation carrier.

Kidnapping has become a major problem in Latin America, particularly in Colombia, which has the highest rate of kidnappings in the world. By 1995 Latin America was experiencing about 6,000 kidnappings per year of which 4,000 occurred in Colombia, about 800 each in Brazil and Mexico, about 200 each in Ecuador and Venezuela, and about 100 each in Guatemala and Peru. About one half of the kidnappings in Colombia are by guerrilla groups such as the **Revolutionary Armed Forces of Colombia** (FARC) or the **National Liberation Army** (ELN). In Colombia during 1992-1995 out of 3,525 cases reported to authorities the national police rescued only about 11 percent of those kidnapped and in these cases only 70 percent of those involved have been arrested, tried, and sentenced. By way of comparison the United States experiences fewer than a dozen kidnappings for ransom each year.

KNEECAPPING. Form of torture or punishment in which the victim is shot through one or more of his or herkneecaps by a small caliber pistol. The punishment has often been used by the **Irish Republican Army** (IRA), **Prima Linea**, and other groups either as a form of assault against a targeted person, or to punish a hostage and so subdue other hostages, or to punish informers, defectors, or members of the group who violate internal rules of group discipline. Often the IRA has substituted the technique of slamming a concrete block or cinder block down on the knee with the leg being outstretched and the heel propped against something, which is quite as catastrophic but which does not require shooting. The ultimate effect is to cripple the victim in the leg on which the kneecapping is executed. In fact the IRA has devised a progression of kneecapping punishments, in which one may have only one kneecap shot, to having both shot, or one or both ankles shot as well, to having one or both elbows shot through as well. When both knees, both ankles, and both elbows are shot as part of one punishment this is referred to as a "six-pack shooting."

KOSOVO LIBERATION ARMY (KLA). The KLA emerged from the former Popular Movement for Kosovo (Levizja Poppulore e Kosoves, LPK) formed in 1982 which originally claimed to follow the radical Stalinist **ideology** of the former dictator of Albania, Enver Hoxha. In fact the group appears to have been primarily an Albanian **ethno-nationalist** groupseeking independence for the Kosovars but claimed to adhere to Enverism to gain support from the former Albanian regime. The defining moment for Kosovar militant nationalists was the 17 January 1982 **assassination** of three Kosovar militants in Germany, presumably by the Yugoslavian secret police. The Yugoslavian government, and even Serbian political dissidents in Yugoslavia, regard the KLA as a terrorist group whose members engaged in atrocities against the civilian Serbian minority in Kosovo even before fighting began in earnest there in 1998.

However neither the militant LPK nor its rival the Democratic League of Kosovo had much of a following in Kosovo until after 1989 when Serbian President Slobodan Milosevic ended the limited autonomy that Kosovo's Albanians had enjoyed. The KLA emerged from a nucleus of LPK members in late 1992 but did not carry out its first military action, an attack on some Serbian policemen, until 1995. The collapse of Albania's government in 1997 gave the KLA access to weapons from looted armories and the KLA shortly thereafter established training camps in northern Albania around Krume, Kukes, and Bajram Curri. Meanwhile the KLA built up its connections with Kosovars abroad, including a heroin-smuggling ring headquartered in Zurich, to raise funds for the KLA. Hashim Thaci (1969-) is the chief leader of the KLA, who eventually joined the Albanian delegation at the Rambouillet talks in February 1999 shortly before they ended in failure. After March 1998 when Serbian police murdered Adem Jasari, a Kosovar nationalist organizer, many Kosovars turned from supporting the Democratic League for Kosovo, whose leader Ibrahim Ragova had consistently urged non-violent resistance, to supporting the KLA which offered rural farmers and their families a chance to arm and defend themselves against an almost certain Serbian campaign of ethnic cleansing (see GENOCIDE).

After the Serbs had carried out their 1998 summer offensive against KLA units, which displaced about 200,000 Albanians, they pulled back briefly from October 1998 to February 1999, apparently as a temporizing measure while negotiations on Kosovo continued in Rambouillet, France. Returning to the areas from which Yugoslavian forces had withdrawn KLA units murdered Serbian civilians in reprisal for the deaths of Albanians the previous summer but also murdered Albanians whom they considered to be collaborators, including low-level civil servants. In spite of KLA promises to the Albanian population that they would defend them against any Serbian military offensive once Operation Horseshoe began in 1999, the KLA lacked both the needed numbers of fighters and weapons to resist the Serbs, who proceeded to expel Albanians from the regional capital Pristina and other towns, often separating and executing the men among those being deported. Most observers believe that without the NATO intervention in Kosovo the Serbian army could have effectively ended the KLA as a fighting force.

The KLA fighters and their leaders are not known to be democrats nor do they have a good relationship with the Democratic League of Kosovo. Not unlike the earlier Afghan **Mujahideen** , the KLA appear to be a guerrilla force which has enjoyed a tactical alliance with Western American and European supporters but which otherwise does not share any common political agenda with its backers. Following a demilitarization agreement between the KLA and NATO commanders in late June 1999, Hashim Thaci proceeded to purge the KLA of dissidents and executed potential rivals who might challenge his domination of the group. Under NATO prodding the KLA agreed in September 1999 to reorganize itself into a nominally civilian self-defense force, to be called the Kosovo Protection Corps, while establishing a political party to be called the Progressive Party for the Renaissance of Kosovo. Although NATO recognizes a nominal Serbian sovereignly over Kosovo, the KLA members continue to adamantly reject anything short of independence from Yugoslavia.

KU KLUX KLAN (KKK). The historic Ku Klux Klan was a **white supremacist** organization founded in 1865 by Confederate veterans of the Civil War. The name has continued to be used by a number of groups which adhere to the twin beliefs of the racial superiority of the white race and the need to safeguard that primacy by protecting its purity against desegregation, integration, and miscegenation. The distinguishing marks of the Klan were the burning cross and the hooded and white-sheeted garments of its members. Its typical tactics were nighttime raids in full regalia against blacks and others, in which they would beat, tar and feather, or lynch their victims. Altogether about 1,000 blacks are estimated to have been killed by Klansmen during the early post-Civil War period although there are no definitive statistics from that time.

For most of its history the Klan and its successor groups acted largely as a repressive group, seeking to counter the power of northerners in the south and to keep blacks socially and politically subordinate. Therefore the federal banning of the Klan in 1871 made little difference since many of the Klansmen's limited aims were achieved through the electoral laws passed by post-Reconstruction southern legislatures that effectively deprived their black citizens of civil rights. The latter-day Klan groups, however, have developed beyond having limited aims of repression to becoming right-wing revolutionary groups willing to undertake more ambitious terrorist activities, including forming alliances with **neo-Nazi** and **skinhead** groups.

The original Ku Klux Klan targeted blacks and northern agents of Reconstruction. The Klan was resurrected by a former Methodist minister, William J. Simmons, with a cross-burning ceremony attended by 16 men on Stone Mountain, Georgia, on 24 November 1915. The revived Knights of the Ku Klux Klan (KKKK) in 1920 expanded its list of enemies in 1920 to include Roman Catholics, Jews, immigrants, and, later in the 1930s, Communists as well. By adding Jews and Catholics to the list of hated groups the revived Klan was able to recruit new members outside of the traditional Old South. In part this was done on the advice of Edward Clarke and Bessie Tyler, founders of the Southern Publicity

Association, who pioneered mass-marketing techniques and grass-roots organizing with great effectiveness on behalf of the Anti-Saloon League's temperance movement as well as the Prohibitionist movement. By promoting itself as "100% American, 100% Protestant, and 100% Christian" the KKKK of William J. Simmons eventually recruited over four million members nationwide and had 500,000 women members as well.

It should be noted that during this time Klan members included some of the most respectable elements of society, including Protestant ministers, doctors, lawyers, and politicians, including Senator Hugo Black, who eventually renounced the Klan before becoming an associate justice of the U.S. Supreme Court. For many of its ordinary members the Klan represented just another exclusive social fraternity, not unlike the Masonic Lodges or Kiwanis Clubs, while its anti-Catholic and anti-Jewish sentiments were also openly held by a wider public in that period. However, the personal and political scandals of the Klan leader of Indiana, David Curtis Stephenson, who was convicted for a brutal rape in November 1925, as well as extensive newspaper reports of brutalities committed by Klan members in the South and of financial improprieties by the national organization, led to a rapid loss of followers such that by 1930 the figure had fallen to about 100,000 members. In 1944 the Internal Revenue Service levied a lien for $65,000 in unpaid back-taxes on the KKKK which led to the demise of the group.

Klan membership dwindled during the Depression and following 1944 Klan activity virtually ceased until the Supreme Court decision in *Brown v. Topeka Board of Education* ordering desegregation of public schools in 1954. Since then there has been a rise in Klan memberships and activities proportionate to the advances in the Civil Rights movement. The revival of the Klan peaked in 1981 when the various Klan organizations together possessed about 11,500 members. The use of civil lawsuits by relatives of Klan victims greatly damaged some of these organizations and reduced their freedom of action. Three major Klan organizations have accounted for most Klan activities in recent years:

1. The United Klans of America (UKA), formerly headquartered in Tuscaloosa, Alabama, was the old guard of the Klan, being the most traditional, the oldest, and one of the most active in its heyday. On 14 May 1961 about 25 UKA members wielding clubs and metal pipes beat up several "Freedom Riders" when they disembarked at the Trailways station in Birmingham. A UKA leader, Robert E.

Chambliss, also known as "Dynamite Bob," ordered the bombing of Birmingham's Sixteenth Street Baptist Church in September 1963 which killed four young black girls, an event that horrified the nation. When originally arrested and tried Chambliss was convicted only for illegal possession of explosives. Following his retrial in 1977 he was convicted for the murder of the young girls and sentenced to life imprisonment. While it once boasted the largest membership of the three Klan factions, the UKA suffered a great reverse when Beulah Donald, the mother of Michael Donald, a UKA lynching victim, successfully sued the UKA for $7 million in civil damages in 1987. This body was forced to dissolve itself as a result of that action. One of the two perpetrators of the Donald lynching, Henry Hayes, was executed on 6 June 1997, the first time a Klan member had ever been executed for the murder of a black American in the 20th century South.

2. The Knights of the Ku Klux Klan (KKKK), named after the revived Klan of 1915, was established in 1975 by former neo-Nazi David Duke. This Klan group is among the most recent and made up largely of people born after the Korean War. This organization has also proved itself most adept at using media relations and mass marketing techniques to sell its message and recruit members. Duke yielded leadership of the KKKK to Don Black in 1980. The more revolutionary nature of the younger Klan groups is illustrated by Don Black's conspiracy, thwarted in April 1981, to carry out a coup d'état on the Caribbean island of Dominica, which he had planned to turn into a Klan safe haven. Following Black's arrest and conviction, the KKKK broke into two factions. Nonetheless this group has shown great adaptability, vitality, and ability to recruit new younger members.

3. The Invisible Empire (IE) was established in 1975 as a breakaway group from the Knights of the Ku Klux Klan, which struck many Klansmen as being too overtly neo-Nazi. IE membership was open to white Roman Catholics. This organization suffered loss of membership when the founder of the IE, William Wilkinson, was exposed as an FBI informant. IE had 1,500 to 2,000 members nationwide when it was forced to file for reorganization under federal bankruptcy laws.

Besides these three groups there are almost 200 splinter groups and independent Klan organizations. In the latest phase of the third revival of the Klan (i.e., since 1954) the newer Klan groups have identified themselves closely with the **Identity Christian** movement and shown less hesitation in identifying themselves with neo-Nazi groups. These Klans have established paramilitary training camps throughout the country and certain of them have affiliated themselves with the **Aryan Nations** neo-Nazi group. Louis Ray Beam, Jr., Grand Dragon of the Texas Ku Klux Klan, became "Ambassador at Large" of the Aryan Nations and heir apparent of Aryan Nations leader Richard Butler. Another more graphic instance of the greater terrorist inclinations of younger Klan groups is shown by the role of Frazier Glenn Miller, former neo-Nazi and leader of the Carolina Knights of the Ku Klux Klan, in instigating the 3 November 1979 massacre of five leftist anti-Klan demonstrators in Greensboro, North Carolina.

Attempts to curtail Klan activities through criminal and civil lawsuits continue with a mixed record of success. Miller and members of his **White Patriot Army** were arrested in 1986 for conspiracy to murder Morris Dees, the anti-Klan activist lawyer who later encouraged Beulah Donald to sue the UKA in 1987. Miller's trial revealed also his acceptance of $200,000 of stolen funds from the **Order** terrorists. An attempt, however, to convict Louis Beam and other white supremacists associated with the Aryan Nations and Klan groups on charges of sedition and violations of civil rights laws ended in acquittal of those defendants by the Federal District Court in Fort Smith, Arkansas, in April 1988.

On 22 April 1997 the FBI thwarted a conspiracy by four members of the True Knights, a splinter Klan group, to bomb a natural gas processing plant near Boyd, Texas, and to rob an armored car.

On 10 July 1997 the FBI reopened its investigation of the 1963 bombing of the Sixteenth Street Baptist church. Although the original mastermind behind this attack, Robert E. Chambliss, had been convicted in 1977 for the murders of the four girls killed in this attack and had died in prison, new evidence had come to light that identified those other three associates of Chambliss who had until then escaped arrest and prosecution. Following a trial begun in March 2001 a second suspect, Thomas E. Blanton, Jr., was also found guilty on 1 May 2001 for his role in the 1963 bombing while on 17 July 2001 an Alabama judge ruled a third suspect in the bombing case, Bobby Frank Cherry, mentally incompetent to stand trial. The fourth suspect, Herman Cash, had already died before charges could be brought against him.

On 24 July 1998 the Macedonia Baptist Church, which had been burned by Klan members in 1995, won a judgment of $37.5 million against the Christian Knights of the Ku Klux Klan as well as a $15 million judgment against Horace King, the leader of the South Carolina-based Klan group. An earlier Federal criminal trial had sentenced the four original **arsonists** to imprisonment for up to 12 years.

On 21 August 1998 a Mississippi state jury sentenced Samuel H. Bowers to life imprisonment, the former leader of the Mississippi White Knights of the Ku Klux Klan for the 10 January 1966 murder by firebombing of Vernon Dahmer, Sr., a local activist of the National Association for the Advancement of Colored People (NAACP) who used his rural store as a place to register other black voters. Bowers was a leader of the White Knights group when it carried out the murder of three young civil rights activists on 21 June 1964, which prompted one of the largest FBI investigations in the history of the South until the bodies of the three victims were recovered six weeks later. Bowers was never charged with this crime although it is virtually certain that he ordered these killings.

KURDISTAN WORKERS' PARTY. The Partiye Kargaran-i Kurdistan (PKK) is a Marxist-Leninist Kurdish **ethno-separatist** group seeking to create a Marxist-Leninist and independent Kurdish homeland comprising the Kurdish-inhibited regions of Turkey, Iraq, and Iran. Several Kurdish leftist students who had met in a Dev Genç (Revolutionary Youth) meeting in Ankara in 1974 founded the PKK on 27 November 1978 in Diyarbakir. The PKK conducts terrorist attacks on Turkish civilians and military personnel in the region claimed as "Kurdistan." The PKK received Syrian and Soviet state support, as well as the support of the Iraq-based Kurdish Democratic Party (KDP). The PKK also draws on support of expatriate Kurdish workers in Germany to obtain needed supplies, some of whom raise funds by narcotics trafficking in Europe. During the Iran-Iraq war the Iraqi government did not prevent the PKK from setting up bases in northern Iraq but also did not prevent the Turkish air force from launching retaliatory strikes against Kurdish bases in northern Iraq.

From 1978-1980 the PKK engaged in **assassinating** local landlords, robbing banks, and setting up "people's courts" to rule the few villages they overran. During this time the PKK murdered 243 people. With the military crackdown beginning on 12 September 1980, Abdullah Ocalan, the PKK leader, fled to Syria. Shortly thereafter the Turkish military uncovered 100 rocket launchers smuggled by a PKK group from Syria.

PKK fighters using Iraqi territory as a base attacked a Turkish army unit in May 1983, killing three soldiers. On 15 August 1984, the PKK took over the villages of Eruh and Semdinli, each 200 miles apart, and held each for one hour, departing before Turkish forces could arrive. On 22 October 1986, PKK fighters attacked the NATO air base at Mardin.

Whereas the preceding incidents involved probing attacks of more symbolic than material effect, the PKK proceeded with attacks directed largely against unprotected civilians. On 20 June 1987 the PKK massacred 30 Turkish villagers in Mardin province, including 16 women and eight children. Another 30 civilians were murdered on 11 July 1987, also in Mardin province. In 1987 there were 13 similar attacks, some made in larger towns such as Diyarbakir. From August 1984 until September 1989 about 1,500 people died due to PKK violence. For the entire year of 1988, 315 people were killed, but in the first six months of 1989 alone 258 were killed, showing the steady increase in PKK activity. Once world attention began to focus on the situation of Kurdish refugees from Iraq during the 1990-1991 Gulf War, the PKK decided to step up its activities, causing the death figure to rise to 900 in 1991. On two occasions in August 1991 the PKK **kidnapped** Western tourists in southeastern Turkey but in each case released them unharmed within the year.

PKK activity has centered on Mardin, Siirt, and Hakkari provinces, a triangular area bordering Iran and Iraq, which the PKK is trying to turn into a "liberated zone." The pattern of attack is always to hit, kill scores of Turks, or attack a government or military facility, and then leave before the Turkish army can arrive. This **armed propaganda** is meant to demonstrate the impotence of Turkish rule, to terrorize Turks, and to encourage Kurds to resist the government. The PKK suffered when Iraq began to suppress the Iraqi Kurds in 1987-1988. This in turn forced the Kurdistan Democratic Party (KDP) to come to terms with Turkey to gain **asylum** for 60,000 of its own forces. These terms include discontinuing support for the PKK. The tactic of murdering Turkish civilians also alienated Turkish leftist terrorists, with the exception of Dev Sol (*see* REVOLUTIONARY PEOPLE'S LIBERATION PARTY/FRONT), that had previously supported the PKK.

After 1988 the PKK desisted from its practice of massacring civilians and concentrated instead on hitting Turkish military outposts, police stations, and government offices. Heavy-handed counterinsurgency efforts by the Turkish military have exasperated the local Kurdish population in southeastern Turkey, causing many of them to accept the legitimacy of the PKK. Beginning in 1991 the PKK began striking at Turkish military targets outside of southeastern Turkey, killing four and wounding at least 12 in Adana, Istanbul, and Izmir. Estimates of PKK membership in 1987 put its fighting strength at 1,100 and noncombatant supporters at around 3,400. By mid-1989, another estimate put the fighting strength at 5,000. By 1994 PKK strength was estimated at 20,000. Following a massive Turkish military operation in which Turkish troops pursued PKK members into Iraq the PKK offered a unilateral cease-fire but threatened **suicide bombing** attacks if the Turkish government did not reciprocate by observing the cease-fire. On 28 June 1996 a female PKK suicide bomber blew herself up, killing nine Turkish soldiers and wounding 20 others during a parade in the eastern town of Tunceil. On 13 April 1998 Turkish commandos captured a former PKK leader in northern Iraq, Semdin Sakik, who had recently defected from the PKK following disagreements with Abdullah Ocalan. On 21 May 1999 Sakik was sentenced to death for his role in killing thousands of Turks when he was the top lieutenant of Ocalan in the PKK.

On 21 October 1998 Turkey and Syria signed an accord whereby Syria pledged to cease supporting and giving sanctuary to the PKK. The PKK leader Abdullah Ocalan disappeared from view about this time, apparently fearing that he would be handed over to Turkey by Syria. Ocalan first approached Russia in November 1998 for asylum but was refused. On 16 November 1998 he arrived by air in Rome where he was placed under house arrest. Italy refused to **extradite** him to Turkey on the plea that Turkey would likely impose the death penalty but Italy also refused to grant Ocalan asylum unless he renounced terrorism. On 13 December 1998 Ocalan made a pro forma renunciation of the PKK and was released from house arrest on 16 December 1998. On 16 January 1999 Ocalan disappeared from Italy but was spirited by Greek diplomats to Nairobi, Kenya, to protect a tactical ally of the Greek government in its long-standing hostility toward Turkey. On 16 February 1999 Turkish agents captured Ocalan in Nairobi after penetrating the Greek embassy and flew him to Turkey to stand trial. PKK supporters attacked Turkish diplomatic offices abroad and also attacked the Israeli Consulate in Berlin, on the assumption that Israel had played a role in Ocalan's capture. Israeli security guards opened fire, killing three Kurds who were trying to occupy the consulate.

Ocalan's trial began on 31 May 1999 on the prison island of Imrali in the Sea of Marmara. On 23 June 1999 he was found guilty of treason and murder and sentenced to death by hanging on 29 June 1999. On 5 August 1999 the PKK announced it would heed Ocalan's call for them to leave Turkey by 1 September 1999. During the course of this trial Ocalan denied that the PKK had any role in the 1986 assassination of Swedish Prime Minister Olof Palme. He alternatively pled for his life and threatened that his followers would wreak terror on Turkey if he was executed. He did admit that his decision to begin the PKK armed struggle in 1984 had led to a civil war in which over 20,000 people died. When he was sentenced to death the court automatically appealed the sentence to the Appeals Court in Ankara while the European Union, whose members have abolished the death penalty, indicated that any execution of Ocalan would present obstacles to Turkey's future role in European integration. While this trial ended Ocalan's 14-year role as PKK leader, the future fate of the PKK remained unclear. On 25 November 1999 the Appeals Court upheld the death sentence but it remained for the Turkish Parliament to amend a 15-year-old moratorium on capital punishment before any execution could be carried out.

- L -

LAUTARO YOUTH MOVEMENT. The Lautaros were militant members of the Movimiento de Acción Unitaria Popular-Lautaro, Popular Movement of United Action-Lautaro (MAPU/L), who broke away from the original United Popular Action Movement (MAPU), an extreme leftist splinter group that itself had split off from the Chilean Christian Democratic Party in 1968. The MAPU/L formed an even more radical group which sought political change through violent revolution. The youth wing of the MAPU/L, known as the Movimiento Juvenil Lautaro, Lautaro Youth Movement (MJL), also known as the Lautaro Faction, as well as its military wing known as the Fuerzas Revolucionarias y Populares Lautaro, the Lautaro Rebel Forces (FRPL). The Chilean intelligence services referred to the three related groups as the Complejo Partidario MAPU-Lautaro. Their name "Lautaro" referred to the chief of the Mapuches Indians who died resisting the Spanish conquerors of Chile in 1550.

The Lautaros began their terrorist campaign just prior to the presidential election and transfer of power on 11 March 1989, ending the rule of General Augusto Pinochet. It included a series of attacks on police stations and Mormon churches, robberies of shops, supermarkets, banks, and truck heists. Although the Lautaros appeared to have leftist leaders and used leftist rhetoric, its following consisted largely of alienated unemployed urban youth of slum areas and may represent more of a lumpenproletariate-anarchist gathering of disaffected, pleasure-seeking ruffians than a bona fide leftist revolutionary group. Often they would steal trucks carrying food and distribute these goods in the poorer neighborhood of Santiago and Concepción.

Lautaro attacks on police often involved deceptive calls for help or diversionary attacks used to lure solitary policemen to ambushes. Lautaro members have also engaged in bank robberies and attacks on Mormon missionary posts. On 24 January 1991, Lautaros shot dead two policemen in Santiago. Following the release of a Chilean government report on the **state terror** of the Pinochet era, detailing over 2,000 slayings committed by the Chilean secret police, three police stations were **bombed** and six banks robbed. The perpetrators claimed to be leftists protesting the unwillingness of the Christian Democrat administration of President Patricio Aylwin to prosecute General Pinochet, who retained command of the Chilean armed forces following the installation of the democratically elected government on 11 March 1989, or others also responsible for the state terror.

On 15 March 1991 Lautaros shot dead Héctor Sarmiento Hidalgo, chief investigator of Concepción, who had not been involved in the human rights abuses of the Pinochet era. Their motive was revenge for the killing of an escaped Lautaro leader, Marco Ariel Antonioletti, by the investigations unit led by Sarmiento. Certain Chilean government officials believe that some of these attacks were actually instigated by Chilean right-wing agents-provocateurs seeking to create an antileftist backlash in favor of a renewed authoritarian military regime and to forestall serious investigations of human rights abuses under Pinochet. Three days following the 1 April 1991 slaying by unidentified gunmen of Senator Jaime Guzmán, a former Pinochet confidante and adviser, the Chilean government announced a 150 percent increase in spending for the national police force and a 400 percent increase in spending for the government Department of Investigations and most of the group's 60 or so members were arrested and imprisoned briefly.

On 21 October 1993 the Lautaros resumed activity with the hold-up of the Bank O'Higgins in Las Condes, Santiago, in the course of which a bank guard was killed. The Lautaro robbers were escaping in a minivan when they ran into a military police patrol at the Apumanque Mall where a shoot-out ensued in which one military policeman, three Lautaros, and three bystanders were killed. Finally in 1994 the group's leader, Guillermo Ossandón, was captured and on 4 May 1998 Ossandón and two other Lautaro leaders were sentenced to life imprisonment.

Most of their more than 600 crimes took place in the Santiago area, including 25 murders, 30 attacks on police stations and cars, 50 **kidnappings**, 42 bank robberies, 120 robberies of department stores, 190 bombings, and 100 **"armed propaganda"** actions, such as the distribution of stolen foodstuffs to the poor and the like. It is estimated that the Lautaros stole a total of 500 million pesos and caused over one billion pesos worth of damage during their activity.

LEADERLESS RESISTANCE. Strategy propounded by Louis Beam, Jr., **Aryan Nations** leader and former Texas **Ku Klux Klan** Grand Dragon leader, made at the Estes Park, Colorado, meeting of Patriot and **militia movement** members in late October 1992 convened to organize support for Randy Weaver. According to this strategy right-wing groups would organize themselves into loosely confederated, autonomous cells without a central command structure that would be armed and able to resist the federal government through numerous attacks which could not be stopped by arresting key leaders or smashing a central leadership cell. The concept is not unique to right-wing extremists and was also the inspiration for the **Revolutionary Cells** movement in Germany. This nonhierarchical pattern of organization is evident in such groups as **Hamas** and in the newly emerging form of conflict known as **netwar** involving loosely coordinated violent and propaganda actions of like-minded activists.

LEADERSHIP. The formation and perpetuation of terrorist groups usually requires having a person, or a few persons, with charismatic and/or entrepreneurial qualities that enable them to articulate those political goals, hopes, and frustrations that are held inchoate among a larger group of persons who are susceptible to the message of the leader. The quality of charismatic leadership was identified by Max Weber as an alternative source of authority both to the traditional form of authority embodied in ruling families, aristocratic or religious elites, and the legal-rational authority found in bureaucratic and legal forms in a modern liberal democracy. The charismatic leader convinces his followers that he or she has some special superhuman gifts of wisdom, intellect, moral superiority, physical strength, or beauty that give him or her the right to rebel against traditions or legal and constitutional norms.

The entrepreneurial leader is one who is able to create a "market" or "demand" for a social or political good among some group which then is motivated to achieve that goal through nonviolent or violent means. A leadership principle and corresponding hierarchical organization seem to be readily adopted by **ethno-separatist** nationalist organizations or religious resurgence movements in which patrimonial or patriarchal norms are already accepted by the followers. In **anarchistic leftist** groups, in which norms of equalitarianism and antielitism prevail among the followers, a charismatic leader may be no less necessary but faces the difficult task of leading without appearing to be domineering. While charismatic leadership may be necessary to draw together a following into an effective politically active group it is not sufficient by itself but requires also entrepreneurial leadership.

While there have been a few unusually gifted leaders having both charismatic and entrepreneurial skills, Napoleon Bonaparte and George Washington being examples, it is more typically the case that the entrepreneurial skills are found in a close lieutenant of the charismatic leader, who is often the successor in the line of leadership, or else in a small inner circle of followers. The perpetuation of a terrorist, political, or religious group requires that the charisma of the founder be somehow routinized in offices, traditions, institutions, and procedures that continue to inspire and mold the group and its agenda. If the original leaders succeed in this task then the terrorist group that is formed may well be able to continue to exist, operate, and grow even if the original leaders are captured or killed. Thus the **Red Army Faction** was able to survive the capture and suicides of Andreas Baader and Ulrike Meinhof for nearly three decades before it finally ceased its armed struggle.

LEBANESE ARMED REVOLUTIONARY FACTIONS. The Factions Armées Revolutionnaires Libanaises (FARL) formed in 1979 was a Lebanese revolutionary group seeking to create a Marxist-Leninist state in Lebanon. Although this group was one of the three groups that emerged from the breakup of the Popular Front for the Liberation of Palestine-

Special Operations Group (PFLP-SOG) upon the death of its leader, Wadi Haddad, in 1978 most of its members have been Lebanese Christians rather than Palestinians. FARL opposed the **Phalange party** as well as foreign supporters of the constitutional government of Lebanon, in particular, the United States, France, and Israel, and also sought to demonstrate its revolutionary affinity with the Palestinian cause by attacking Israeli targets outside of Lebanon. The group collaborated with the French **Direct Action** and Italian **Red Brigades** groups and was suspected of having ties with **Hezbollah**. FARL was believed to number only about 25 members and was led by George Ibrahim Abdullah (aliases: Salih al Masri, Abdul-Qadir Saadi), who joined the group after 1978.

FARL conducted at least 18 noteworthy actions from 1981 until 1987, including four **assassinations**, two assassination attempts, four separate **bombings** and one bombing campaign, two **kidnappings**, one armed attack, and four threats. On 18 January 1982 FARL shot dead the U.S. Army attaché to Paris, Lt. Col. Charles Ray. On 3 April 1982 FARL machine-gunned to death an Israeli diplomat in Paris. Later a police raid on a Direct Action hideout revealed the Sten gun used in this and other FARL attacks. On 15 February 1984 FARL claimed credit for the murder in Rome of U.S. citizen Leamon Hunt, the director of the multinational observer force in the Sinai. While the Red Brigades also claimed credit for killing Hunt, it appears that FARL collaborated with the Red Brigades in this action.

The capture of Georges Ibrahim Abdullah in 1984 led to a hiatus in FARL activities, except for the kidnapping and murder of a Frenchman in Lebanon and a series of threats against the French government if Abdullah were not released. During September 1986 FARL fulfilled some of its threats by carrying out a bombing campaign in Paris, in which **Armenian Secret Army for the Liberation of Armenia** (ASALA) and some pro-Iranian elements may have participated, killing 15 people and wounding over 150 others. Nonetheless French courts sentenced Abdullah to life imprisonment in 1987 for the murder of Lt. Col. Ray, and on other charges. Most of FARL's members returned to Lebanon that year and have been relatively inactive since then. *See also* COMMITTEE FOR SOLIDARITY WITH ARAB AND MIDDLE EASTERN POLITICAL PRISONERS (CSAMPP).

LEHI. The Fighters for the Freedom of Israel (Lohame Herut Israel), also known as the Stern Gang, was a breakaway faction from the **Irgun**, which was dedicated to the same goals of ousting both the British forces and Arab population from Palestine to establish a Jewish state there. In 1940, Irgun members differed over the tactical question of observing a truce with Great Britain for the duration of the war with Germany, which the majority of Irgun believed to be necessary but which Abraham Stern (1907-1942) and others opposed.

The dissidents left Irgun, forming LEHI in 1940 to continue terrorizing British forces in Palestine during the war. Stern and his followers included among their **targets** moderate Jews opposed to the use of terrorism, killing at least 15 Jews and even contemplating a coup against the Jewish Agency in the event of winning independence. After the death of Stern in 1942, LEHI activities stayed in a lull until 1944. That year they **assassinated** Lord Moyne, the British minister for Middle Eastern affairs, in Cairo. The same year, LEHI and Irgun began cooperating in attacking British government offices and soldiers in Palestine.

In 1945 British authorities broke up most of LEHI, deporting many members while others joined other Jewish paramilitary organizations. LEHI members joined with Irgun in the 9 April 1948 attack upon the Arab village of Deir Yassin in which over 200 villagers perished. On 17 September 1948, LEHI members murdered the Swedish Count Folke Bernadotte and the French Colonel André Serot in the belief that their work as United Nations mediators would impede the full establishment of the Jewish state. Among the leaders of LEHI was Yitzhak Shamir, who later became prime minister of Israel.

LETTER BOMBS. The development of highly powerful plastic explosives and miniaturized electrical components allow for the development of letter bombs that have been used by the **Black September Organization,** which in September 1972 mailed out 64 letter bombs to Israeli targets, as well as by the **Unabomber,** Theodore Kaczynski, and several other groups. Letter or parcel bombs have also been used for purely criminal purposes of malice, revenge, or simple murder.

Letter bombers frequently either omit a return address, or have an address unknown to the intended recipient, but more cunning mail bombers have either placed a secondary target's address as the return address or else have tried to have the packet sent with insufficient postage with the return address being that of the intended victim. Tell-tale signs of letter bombs include one of more of the following in addition to a suspicious or unknown origin for the package: excessive postage, excessive taping of corners and edges of the package or letter, signs of staining of the package or letter by oil or grease, or unusual smell. Since the Unabomber's last few attempted **bombings** in 1995 the U.S. Postal Service requires all packages above a certain weight to be sent from Post Offices rather than from parcel drop-off bins. Postal clerks have been briefed to be alert for suspicious signs and those mailing packages may be required to present identification. While this may deter mailing of letter bombs within the United States this does not immediately prevent letter or parcel bombs from being sent to the United States from abroad.

In January 1997 eight letter bombs arrived in the United States posted from Alexandria, Egypt, disguised as Christmas cards. Four were sent to the Washington, D.C., offices of *Al Hayat*, an Arabic language newspaper owned by Prince Khaled bin Sultan, a pro-Western member of the Saudi royal family, while two others were addressed to "The Parole Officer" at the federal prison in Leavenworth, where **Sheikh Omar Abdul Rahman** had been incarcerated. On 13 January 1997 four other letter bombs were sent to the London offices of *Al Hayat* one of which exploded injuring two mail handlers. All these bombs contained Semtex, a powerful plastic explosive that is ordinarily difficult to detect.

LIBERATION THEOLOGY. Liberation theology is an attempt to reinterpret the Christian gospel as a creed of social, economic, and political liberation and to reconcile it with leftist revolutionary movements. This theology has spread predominantly among the Roman Catholic clergy of Latin America, although it is also being espoused by segments of older Protestant denominations represented within the World Council of Churches and has developed advocates among Roman Catholics and nonfundamentalist Protestants outside of Latin America. Of the various clerical orders the Society of Jesus has been most intimately connected with this movement, while the missionary religious order associated with Maryknoll has also undertaken advocacy of this worldview. While liberation theology appeared to be an amalgamation of Marxism and dependency theory with Christian theology, this doctrine owed much to the Catholic concept of corporal acts of mercy, to the view of the congruity and synergism of good works with faith, and to a postmillennialist view of church history. By propounding the theology of liberation and joining forces with revolutionaries fighting social injustice many clerics believed they could harmonize the spiritual and physical struggles against evil.

In 1968 the Council of Latin American Bishops in Medellín, Colombia, passed resolutions endorsing many of the tenets of liberation theology. However, following the elevation of Pope John Paul II the Vatican took a decidedly hostile line toward liberation theology. The fortunes of liberation theology declined together with the failures of those leftist insurgency movements which liberation theologians had believed would shape the future of politics in the developing nations. However liberation theology contributed significantly to success of the **Zapatista** movement which began its insurgency on 1 January 1994. Members of the young, northern Mexican leftists who founded the Zapatista movement were able to approach the closed, suspicious Mayan Indian communities in Chiapas largely through the mediation of the Rev. Samuel Ruíz, bishop of the diocese of San Cristóbal de las Casas in the central highlands of Chiapas who was known by some as the "Red Bishop" due to his outspoken support of liberation theology. Through the introductions of Marist and Dominican priests the Zapatistas were able to recruit the Mayan Indian tribes to join their cause.

LIBERATION TIGERS OF TAMIL EELAM (LTTE). The LTTE is a Tamil **ethno-nationalist** group in Sri Lanka that seeks to create a separate state for the minority Tamils in the northern and eastern provinces of Sri Lanka, areas in which they outnumber the Sinhalese who form the majority of the Sri Lankan population. The LTTE enjoyed material and moral support from Tamil Nadu State in India but this support ended when the Indian government sent the Indian Peacekeeping Force upon official Sri Lankan request in 1987.

The LTTE engage in armed attacks on Sri Lankan security forces as well as terrorism against nonseparatist Tamils and members of rival Tamil radical groups. While the group was founded in 1972, it began its first terrorist attacks in 1975 when it claimed responsibility for killing the mayor of Jaffna. The separatist terror campaign began in earnest in 1977 with attacks directed against Tamil politicians who did not endorse the separatist cause. The LTTE's attacks on Sinhalese security forces in July 1983 sparked ethnic violence between Tamils and Sinhalese throughout the island in which at least 387 people were killed. The expulsion of the moderate Tamil United Liberation Front (TULF) from Sri Lanka's parliament for its refusal to dissociate itself from separatist goals has left the LTTE as the foremost group championing the Tamil minority.

While the TULF was founded on 14 May 1972 its youth league attracted the core of younger, more militant Tamils who founded the Tamil New Tigers as a more activist clique within the youth league. On 5 May 1976 the Tamil New Tigers reconstituted themselves separately from the TULF as the Liberation Tigers of Tamil Eelam. The LTTE set up training camps in the jungles south of the Jaffna peninsula, recruiting young Tamil refugees forced from their homes by Sinhalese rioters. The Sri Lankan government unwittingly boosted recruitment into the various Tiger organizations by its practice of inflicting indiscriminate punishment on the Tamil community for specific acts of terrorism committed by Tiger groups. As a result, the LTTE was able to put about 10,000 men under arms. Training camps were later established in Tamil Nadu State in India whose state government provided active support to the LTTE while the Indian government passively acquiesced in this quasi-state sponsorship.

Up until the early 1980s the LTTE financed itself from bank robberies in Sri Lanka. Since around 1982 the LTTE has tapped into a network of expatriate Tamil supporters not only in India but also in Europe and North America. To better finance its arms acquisitions and smuggling operations it became active in the smuggling and distribution of Afghan heroin. By 1985 the LTTE was responsible for the smuggling of 500 kilograms of heroin each year into Western Europe alone, fielding around 1,000 couriers at any given time. The LTTE's arms and drug smuggling operations brought it into contact and cooperation with the rightist **Gray Wolves** organization in Turkey as well as with Palestinian terrorist groups in Lebanon.

Approximately 25 different unrelated "Tiger" organizations have appeared since the LTTE began, but it has violently asserted its preeminence over them. This reflects the leadership style of Vellupillai Prabakharan, a low-caste youth who is the lone survivor of the original founders of the Tamil New Tigers, having killed off all his rivals within the LTTE. Prabakharan directed the LTTE to eliminate all rival Tiger groups in internecine battling from May 1986 to September 1987. By April 1989 the LTTE and the remnants of three other Tiger organizations formed an umbrella group, the Eelam National Liberation Front. While Prabakharan claims to seek a "socialist egalitarian" society in the envisioned Tamil state of Eelam, he has a marked antipathy toward Marxist **ideologues**. His ruthless liquidation of rival Tiger leaders and groups as well as of ordinary Tamils unsympathetic to the separatist cause led some observers to describe him as "implacably violent and as fascist a leader as South Asia has yet produced" (Austin and Gupta, 1988). Although Prabakharan is the leading personality among the Tamil separatists, he is not articulate and chooses to speak through a front man, Anton Balasingham.

The LTTE, unlike other Tiger groups, has not limited its attacks mainly to Sinhalese government and military targets but has directly terrorized Sinhalese civilians as well. On 3 May 1986 a **bomb** hidden aboard an Air Lanka Tristar in Colombo exploded while passengers were embarking, killing 17 and wounding 21 of the 111 who had embarked. In April 1987 the LTTE bombed the main bus terminal in Colombo, killing 106 and wounding 295 others, and carried out an ambush of four buses in the Trincomalee district, killing 107 civilians. LTTE fighters are also heedless of their own lives, often killing themselves by swallowing cyanide carried in ampules around their neck rather than allowing themselves to be captured and interrogated by Sinhalese forces.

With the failure of Sri Lankan forces to retake the Jaffna peninsula following the virtual collapse of Sri Lankan authority in the north of the island in 1987 and with the outcry of Indian public opinion against Sinhalese atrocities against Tamils, Sri Lanka agreed to allow Indian troops to land in Jaffna to restore order. The LTTE turned on its erstwhile Indian supporters and inflicted heavy casualties on Indian forces trying to capture Jaffna, killing 350 and wounding 1,100 Indian troops by 15 December 1987. These casualties amounted to seven percent of India's total forces deployed in Sri Lanka, a rate of casualties twice that sustained in the wars fought with Pakistan. The campaign also cost India the life of former Prime Minister Rajiv Gandhi, who had ordered Indian troops into Sri Lanka. On 21 May 1991, while campaigning in the south of India, Gandhi was killed by an LTTE **suicide bomber** reportedly acting on orders from Prabakharan even though Indian troops had been withdrawn in 1990.

The LTTE continued to threaten the Sri Lankan government following the withdrawal of India's 100,000 troops. On 2 March 1991 a LTTE car bomb in Colombo killed the Deputy Defense Minister of Sri Lanka along with over 50 bystanders, while another car bomb destroyed the Sri Lankan Military Operations Headquarters in June 1991. On 1 May 1993 a suicide bomber killed President Ranasinghe Premadasa while he was reviewing a May Day parade in Colombo. Although police arrested 40 Tamil suspects and indicted 18 of them on 23 September 1997 Sri

Lankan Attorney General Sarath Silva closed the case due to insufficient evidence to convict the accused.

In 1994 the newly elected government of Chandrika Kumaratunga lifted the embargo on Jaffna and offered to hold peace talks with the LTTE but on 20 September 1994 the LTTE rammed two explosives-laden fishing boats into Sri Lanka's largest warship, killing 25 sailors and the five Tamils driving the suicide boats. On 24 October 1994 one day before peace talks between the LTTE and government were due to begin the LTTE bombed an opposition election rally in Colombo killing 52 persons including the presidential candidate, Gamini Dissanayake, along with other top leaders of the United National party that had led the government until August 1994.

Although the peace talks were briefly suspended following this bombing they were resumed in late December and a truce negotiated on 3 January 1995. On 18 April 1995 the LTTE broke the cease-fire with an attack on a naval base in Tricomalee that killed 11 sailors and wounded 20 others. In June 1995 India imposed a naval blockade on Tamil-controlled coasts of Sri Lanka to prevent resupplying of LTTE's arms. In July 1995 the Sri Lankan army began a drive to recapture Jaffna and on 7 August 1995 a LTTE suicide bomber struck a government office building in Colombo killing 22 persons and wounding at least 50. On 30 August 1995 LTTE rebels **hijacked** a passenger ferry, the *Irish Mona*, and used it to launch rockets at two Sri Lankan gunships sinking both of them. On 2 December 1995 Sri Lankan troops recaptured the center of Jaffna and retook control of four-fifths of the city which had been abandoned to LTTE control five years previously. Most of the 150,000 population of Jaffna had been evacuated by the LTTE in the preceding month. On 31 January 1996 LTTE retaliated with a truck-bomb attack on the central bank in Colombo, killing 88 and wounding 1,400. By 16 May 1996 Sri Lanka's army had recaptured the last major town in the rebel-held northern region and all of the Jaffna peninsula forcing the LTTE inland. On 18 July 1996 LTTE rebels overran an army base in Mullaitivu killing all but 11 of the 1,200 soldiers garrisoned there. Two bombs exploded on a passenger train south of Colombo in Dehiwala on 24 July 1996, killing at least 64 persons and wounding more than 400. The LTTE perpetrator of the train bombing was arrested on 2 September 1996 along with two accomplices.

On 8 October 1997 the U.S. State Department added the LTTE to its list of 30 terrorist organizations barred from fund-raising in the United

States. On 15 October 1997 the LTTE exploded a powerful truck bomb in downtown Colombo killing over 18 persons and wounding over 100 others as well as damaging three five-star hotels, the old parliament building, and three office towers. This bomb was parked next to the Hilton Hotel and apparently was intended to hurt foreigners of whom 36 were wounded including seven Americans. In the past LTTE had avoided targeting foreigners but apparently changed this policy in retaliation for U.S. and other Western support for the Sri Lankan government. This bombing was followed by a two-hour gun battle between government troops and 15 to 20 Tamil Tigers in the course of which a Tamil unit threw a grenade into a Buddhist temple killing Vitharandeniye Chandrajothi, one of Sri Lanka's Buddhist religious leaders. On 5 March 1998 two bombs on a bus exploded outside a crowded Colombo train station killing at least 32 persons and wounding more than 300.

During October 1998 government troops had contained Tamil fighters in the Vanni jungles of the north but had to yield the town of Kilinochchi on the north-south highway connecting Jaffna to Colombo back to rebel control. On 29 July 1999 an LTTE suicide bomber **assassinated** a moderate Tamil leader, Neelam Tiruchelvam, a leader of the Tamil United Liberation Front, whom the LTTE had **targeted** for not supporting the separatist cause. By the end of 1999 about 60,000 people had been killed as a result of the 16 years of ethnic conflict in Sri Lanka and the LTTE continued its activity. During 2000 the LTTE retook several positions in the Jaffna peninsula and by November Prabakharan was receiving diplomats from Norway, among other nations, seeking to mediate a truce or cease-fire between the LTTE and Sri Lankan government.

LORD'S RESISTANCE ARMY (LRA). The LRA is made up of about 1,500 antistate marauders in northern Uganda opposed to President Yoweri Museveni which appears to enjoy state support from the Sudanese government in retaliation for aid given by Uganda to the **Sudanese People's Liberation Army**. While it does not seriously threaten the Ugandan government, it has terrorized the poorest region in Uganda. In April 1995 they raided the town of Gulu, killing 250 persons, destroying 1,000 homes, and **kidnapping** more than 100 children.

The group is led by Joseph Kony who uses the Ten Commandments as a pretext to topple the "ungodly" Museveni government. Kony has organized his followers into a cult that has strange prohibitions, such as not eating white chickens nor allowing bicycle riding, and adopting some Muslim practices, such as congregational prayers on Friday and forbidding pork. Kony anoints his soldiers with oil before sending them into battle claiming this will protect them from bullets. Although Kony claims that he is waging war against Uganda because Museveni allegedly dismissed all Acholi people from the police and military, most of his northern victims are of the Acholi tribe.

This group has been engaged in the terrorization of ordinary civilians in northern Uganda, beatings of foreign aid workers, and the kidnapping of perhaps as many as 8,000 children, some of whom have been impressed into this army, others having been sold into slavery or prostitution, and others having been simply raped and murdered. An Italian nun, Sister Rachele Fassera, has documented the kidnapping, rapes, and murders of Ugandan children and has also successfully negotiated for the release of many of them. The Ugandan government had failed to stop the activities of this group because its army was preoccupied with protecting its southern borders during the civil war of 1997-2000 in the Democratic Republic of Congo (formerly Zaire) as well as containing Rwandan rebels opposed to the government of Paul Kigame. However, on 2 June 1999 the Army announced it had conducted a successful operation in the north and had rescued 2,172 people, who were mainly children or teenagers.

LORENZO ZELAYA POPULAR REVOLUTIONARY FORCES. The Fuerzas Revolutionarias Populares Lorenzo Zelaya (FRP-LZ) was a Honduran guerrilla group seeking to overthrow the current Honduran government through a Marxist-Leninist revolution. It **targeted** U.S. diplomatic facilities and firms as well as those of Latin American countries whose policies supported U.S. initiatives against the **Sandinista** government of Nicaragua. FRP-LZ members claim to have received training in Nicaragua and Cuba. Most of their actions have been confined to Honduras, although they are said to have served as auxiliaries in the Sandinistas' internal war against the **contras**.

The FRP-LZ was formed in 1978 but initiated its terrorist career on 30 October 1980 with a machine-gun attack on the U.S. embassy in Tegucigalpa and a **bomb** attack against the Chilean embassy. On 23 September 1981 they ambushed five members of a U.S. military training unit and bombed the second floor of the National Assembly building. On 21 April 1982 they made another machine-gun attack on the U.S.

embassy, targeting especially the Ambassador's suite and threw bombs at the Argentinean, Chilean, and Peruvian embassies. On 28 April 1982 four FRP-LZ members **hijacked** an airplane, which the Honduran government allowed to leave for Cuba on May 1 after the passengers held hostage were released. Other targets up through 1983 included IBM and Air Florida offices, two other U.S. subsidiary companies, one Salvadoran firm, the British embassy, and the Guatemalan Consulate.

In 1983 the FRP-LZ leader, Efraín Duarte Salgado, was arrested and turned informer against his own group. FRP-LZ activities fell off after the loss of this leader, and with the arrest of two remaining leaders in 1987 the activities of the group ceased.

LOW INTENSITY CONFLICT (LIC). Term used to describe violent conflicts involving levels of violence short of conventional, all-out warfare. Many of the armed conflicts following World War II involved insurgencies, civil disturbances, and simmering border wars of attrition, which seldom included large-scale battles involving the armed forces of major **belligerents**. Apart from low intensity conflict other terms for the same phenomena include *small scale contingencies* (SSC) and *operations other than war* (OOTW). *Field Manual 7-98* of the U.S. Army describes low intensity conflict as "a political-military confrontation between contending states or groups [which is] below general war and above routine peaceful competition." In this context terrorism has often been an accompanying feature of these conflicts since it has allowed both state and nonstate actors a means of striking at nations with powerful conventional militaries with plausible denial for the responsible group.

A study of 43 internal conflicts involving Western powers in the period 1945-1983 by Max G. Manwaring, ("Insurgency and Counter-Insurgency: Toward a New Analytical Approach," *Small Wars and Insurgencies*, Volume 3, Winter 1992: 272-310) revealed that much of the success or failure of counterinsurgency actions rested not merely on material resources of the contending sides but also on the qualities of discipline of the defending forces; legitimacy of the targeted government; unity of effort by the various civilian, police, military, and governmental components of the targeted nation; and also the quality of intelligence gathered. The center of gravity of the low intensity conflict is not merely physical tactical advantages, such as control of key points on the terrain, but rather the more intangible and fragile quality of regime legitimacy. Whereas the outcome of general conventional warfare depends largely on the military and economic components of national power in low intensity conflict the political and informational components are more crucial. Terrorist actions often sought to undermine the legitimacy of **targeted** governments by provoking security forces to commit acts of indiscriminate retaliation against civilians in the territories in which insurgents operated.

LOYALIST VOLUNTEER FORCE (LVF). The LVF emerged in 1996 from a few dozen disaffected members of the **Ulster Volunteer Force** (UVF) who were opposed to the cease-fire that the UVF and other Ulster Protestant paramilitaries agreed to in 1994 and who were armed with only some rifles, machine guns, and handguns, plus a small quantity of Powergel (a commercial plastic explosive). The LVF is believed to have been responsible for the murder of Michael McGoldrick, a 31-year-old Catholic man, shot outside Lurgan on 8 July 1996. It was responsible for four killings in 1997 and nine killings in 1998 although in 1998 it was also allowed by the **Ulster Freedom Fighters** (UFF) to claim credit for their own killings in the name of the LVF, since the UFF were supposed to be observing a cease-fire at that time.

On 1-2 July 1998 the LVF set fire to 10 Catholic churches to sabotage ongoing peace negotiations between the **Irish Republican Army** (IRA) and mainline Ulster Protestant groups. The LVF also was the first Protestant paramilitary group to murder a Catholic man, Gerry Devlin, shot in a parking lot in Glengormley, since the renewal in July 1997 of the IRA's previous cease-fire. The murder also seemed to be prompted by the pending reception of Sinn Fein leader Gerry Adams at No. 10 Downing street by British Prime Minister Tony Blair planned for 11 December 1997. On 11 January 1998 the LVF also murdered Terry Enwright, the nephew by marriage of Gerry Adams, to dampen the resumption of peace talks the following day. The LVF claimed the killing was in reprisal for the murder of their leader, Billy Wright, who was shot dead by members of the **Irish National Liberation Army** (INLA) inside the Maze Prison on 27 December 1997. The LVF was responsible for eight more killings in January 1998. In spite of their fierce opposition to the cease-fires and to the peace process the LVF was the first paramilitary group to hand over its weapons to the International Commission on Decommissioning following the Good Friday Accord of 10 April 1998.

LUXOR TEMPLE MASSACRE. On 17 November 1997 the **Islamic Group** (IG,) murdered 58 foreign tourists and four Egyptians at the Temple of Hatshepsut, one of the great archaeological attractions of Egypt, capturing the world's attention because of the number of victims, the horrific accounts of the survivors, and the savagery of the assailants. Eyewitnesses described how most of the victims, trapped in the raised terrace of the temple complex's middle courtyard, were killed by six men armed with knives and automatic weapons. Many of the tourists who tried to hide in the colonnades at the rear of the courtyard were hunted down and slain. The victims included 35 Swiss and a foreign resident of Switzerland; nine Japanese, including four couples on their honeymoons; six Britons, including a young mother and her baby; four Germans, a Bulgarian, a Colombian, and a Frenchman. **Osama bin Laden** is suspected of having aided the group within the Islamic Group of Egypt which carried out this attack.

After this massacre by Islamic Group terrorists the government of President Hosni Mubarak cracked down ruthlessly on the **Muslim Brotherhood** and its **cellular** offshoots. The fundamentalist terrorist underground has suffered reverses due to its public relations reverses outside Egypt caused by this, and other, attacks on foreign tourists, and also due to its attacks on Copts within Egypt which have alienated much of the traditional Muslim establishment as well.

- M -

M-19. The "April 19th Movement" (Spanish: Movimiento 19 de Abril, M-19) was a Colombian insurgent group, enjoying occasional sponsorship from other non-Colombian terrorist groups and states, that pursued both **entrepreneurial** and revolutionary agendas. Its revolutionary goal was to lead the Colombian people in a populist revolution against the "bourgeois" establishment in Colombia and to resist U.S. "imperialism," particularly in the form of U.S. economic penetration of Colombia. The group's **ideology** represented an eclectic blend of Marxist-Leninist ideas mixed with heady doses of populism and nationalism. Its entrepreneurial activities included, first, **kidnapping** and extortion directed against foreign-affiliated companies to force them to finance M-19's projected revolution, and, second, collaboration with, and/or extortion of, Colombian drug traffickers also as a means of financing its revolution. As of late 1989, M-19 entered the Colombian electoral arena as a legal political party, the Democratic Alliance M-19 Movement (Alianza Democrática Movimiento 19 de Abril, AD/M-19), but found its candidates targeted for **assassination** by the Colombian drug cartels' leaders who sought revenge for M-19's past attacks on them.

M-19 received help from Cuba, Nicaragua, and Libya, as well as training from Argentinean **Montoneros** and Uruguayan **Tupamaros**. Cuba trained 300 M-19 guerrillas in 1980. Both Cuba and Nicaragua supplied M-19 with arms in the early 1980s. M-19 has had contacts with the Ecuadoran **Alfaro Vive Carajo** group as well as other similar groups in Costa Rica, El Salvador, Guatemala, Peru, and Venezuela. In April 1984 M-19 announced it had formed ties with the **Basque Fatherland and Liberty** (ETA) separatists. M-19 became a member of the Simón Bolívar Guerrilla Coordination board, organized under **Revolutionary Armed Forces of Colombia** (FARC) auspices in 1985, and later ran candidates in the Colombian presidential elections in May 1990.

Although its activities began with a series of bank robberies in 1973, M-19 first announced its existence on 17 January 1974, when it stole the spurs and sword of Simón Bolívar from his former villa, now a Bogotá museum. It declared itself retroactively "founded" on 19 April 1970, the date of the electoral defeat of National Popular Alliance (ANAPO) presidential candidate Rojas Pinilla. Although M-19 was formed by ANAPO activists frustrated with what they regarded as the corrupt electoral system in Colombia, the ANAPO party apparatus disavowed any connection with M-19.

The terrorist activities of M-19 commenced with the February 1976 kidnapping and murder of trade unionist José Raquel Mercado whom they accused of being a CIA agent. In the next two years M-19 would kidnap for ransom over 400 victims. For nationalistic reasons M-19 has tended to target multinational companies and executives for extortion and kidnapping, including the Colombian branches of Sears and Texaco, rather than targeting purely Colombian enterprises. Beginning in 1977 M-19 also began sabotaging petroleum production facilities. By 1979 M-19 emerged as the most active of the guerrilla groups operating in Colombia.

In 1979 to show solidarity with the **Sandinista** cause M-19 kidnapped the Nicaraguan ambassador, Barquero Montiel. In February 1980 M-19 captured 15 diplomats and 16 other hostages at the embassy of the

Dominican Republic, including the U.S. ambassador, Diego Asencio, and held them 61 days in exchange for ransom and safe passage to Cuba. In January 1981, in an unsuccessful bid to force the U.S. Summer Linguistic Institute out of Colombia, they kidnapped U.S. citizen and Institute employee Chester Bitterman whom they murdered on 7 March 1981. In April 1983 they bombed the Honduran embassy, seriously wounding the Honduran Consul. In October 1985 M-19 attempted to ambush the automobile of General Rafael Samudio Molina but failed. Likewise in December 1985 they botched an ambush set for the National Police Subdirector, General Guillermo Medino Sánchez, and again in June 1986 failed in an attempt to kill Minister of Government Jaime Castro as he was driving to his office. In May 1988 M-19 kidnapped former Conservative Party presidential candidate Álvaro Gómez Hurtado, who was released two months later after a meeting between government officials and M-19 leaders at the papal nuncio's office in Bogotá. Also on 23 March 1988 M-19 struck the U.S. embassy in Bogotá with a rocket, causing minimal damages and no injuries.

The most serious terrorist action of M-19 was the 6 November 1985 seizure of the Justice Ministry building in Bogotá in which they seized nearly 500 hostages, including members of the Supreme Court and of the Council of State. Colombian security forces attacked, killing at least 19 terrorists. In the course of this operation 11 Supreme Court Justices were killed along with 50 hostages and all of the terrorists.

The most questionable undertaking of M-19 has been its relations with Colombian drug traffickers. By 1982 evidence emerged linking Colombia drug trafficker Jaime Guillot Lara with M-19 as well as four close aides of Fidel Castro. In 1982 a Miami, Florida, U.S. Federal grand jury handed down indictments against Cuban officials for assisting Lara's smuggling operations in exchange for his providing funds and Cuban arms to M-19. Whether this was a case of M-19 extortion practiced on the drug traffickers or else a temporary tactical alliance between criminals and terrorists, in either case the relationship went sour. The drug traffickers founded their own **death squad Muerte a Secuestradores** (MAS), which was directed in particular against M-19, apparently in retaliation for M-19 having kidnapped for ransom key members of the drug rings.

M-19 had around 1,000 members and was made up of two fronts, a southern front in Putumayo Department and a western front in Caldas, Cauca, Valle de Cauca, Quinido, and Tolima Departments. These fronts were subdivided into "columns" for different municipalities. Its founders included former ANAPO Congressman Carlos Toleda Plata, who led M-19 until his capture in 1982, and Jaime Bateman Cayón, a former FARC member who remained M-19's principal military commander.

M-19 participated in the "national dialogue" between the Colombian government and other major leftist guerrilla groups and signed the truce of May 1984. By September 1989, M-19 had signed a series of accords with the Colombian government allowing it to participate legally as a political party. M-19 announced its intention to demobilize in exchange for pardons and guarantees of protection and finally surrendered its weapons to the government on 8 March 1990. Subsequently agents of drug traffickers killed M-19 presidential candidate Carlos Pizarro León-Gómez on 26 April 1990. Currently the Democratic Alliance M-19 Movement along with the Patriotic Union party of FARC have been boycotting participation in elections to the Colombian Congress. *See also* COLOMBIAN COCAINE CARTELS.

MACHETEROS. The "Machete Wielders," otherwise known as the Ejército Popular de Boricua (Popular Army of Boricua), is a Puerto Rican **ethnonationalist** separatist group that considers itself engaged in a war of independence against the United States. It is not known to have any external state sponsorship nor any known contact with other Latin American leftist insurgent groups outside Puerto Rico, although they are supported by the small Marxist-Leninist Puerto Rican Socialist Party led by José Mari Bras, who is believed to be close to Fidel Castro. Within the Puerto Rican community, however, the Macheteros have shown some coordination with another separatist group, the **Organization of Volunteers for the Puerto Rican Revolution** (OVPR), and have claimed to carry out certain terrorist actions to express solidarity with members of the **Armed Forces of National Liberation** (FALN) group imprisoned in the United States. Although the Macheteros use Marxist-Leninist jargon, the essence of their program appears to reduce to nothing more than the demand for total independence for Puerto Rico.

The Macheteros appear to be a relatively small but highly organized and carefully screened group that has eluded infiltration. It operates mainly within Puerto Rico, **targeting** primarily U.S. military facilities, U.S. military personnel, as well as the Puerto Rican police. Since 1978 the group has carried out a few very competently executed terrorist actions that can be considered **armed propaganda**. On 3 December

1979 they ambushed and machine-gunned a bus carrying U.S. Navy personnel, killing two sailors and seriously wounding 10 others. On 12 March 1980 in a similar ambush of a bus the Macheteros wounded one of the three ROTC instructors aboard. On 16 May 1982 they machine-gunned four U.S. sailors leaving a San Juan nightclub, killing one and wounding the others. On 6 November 1985 they shot and seriously wounded a U.S. Army recruiting officer as he was riding his motor scooter to work.

The most dramatic Machetero action was the sabotage of the Puerto Rican National Guard airfield at Muniz Air Base outside San Juan on 12 January 1981. Disguised in military uniforms 11 Macheteros penetrated the security fence and planted 21 bombs in 11 jet fighters, eight of which were destroyed and two of which were damaged, causing in excess of $45 million in damages. The date selected was the birth anniversary of Eugenio María de Hostes, a Puerto Rican hero in the struggle for independence from Spain. The significance of the use of "eleven" in the number of men deployed and number of planes targeted was to express solidarity for 11 FALN members being tried for terrorist activities in the United States at that time. Similarly on 28 October 1986, they planted 10 **bombs** at military bases and facilities across the island, three of which exploded destroying two recruiting facilities. This action was undertaken to protest a supposed plan to train Nicaraguan **contras** in Puerto Rico. The group has also used rocket-propelled grenades in attacks on U.S. government office buildings in San Juan.

On 16 September 1983 the Macheteros conducted an operation on the U.S. mainland, robbing the Wells Fargo armored truck terminal in Hartford, Connecticut, of $7.2 million of which only $85,000 was recovered and $2.5 million of which is known to have been transported to Cuba. While bank robberies in Puerto Rico had been a primary source of funds for the group, the evidence provided by this hold-up allowed the FBI to arrest several Macheteros leaders in Puerto Rico on 30 August 1985. In spite of this crackdown, the Macheteros were responsible for nine of the 10 terrorist attacks occurring in Puerto Rico in 1986, although seven of these attacks failed to achieve their objective.

Currently one major Macheteros leader remains at large and is still active in Puerto Rico, namely Filiberto Ojeda-Rios, who had been arrested in Puerto Rico in 1985 as one of the principals of the Wells Fargo heist but who jumped bond while awaiting trial in September 1990. In 1992 Connecticut tried and convicted him in absentia for the Wells

Fargo robbery and sentenced him to 55 years in prison. Others who were indicted in this case, including Victor Gerena, a Wells Fargo employee, remain at large. During the summer of 1998 the Macheteros made two attacks on branches of the Banco Popular, striking one with a pipe-bomb and shooting through the doors of another, as a protest against privatization policies being pursued by the Puerto Rican government. Although the group has few active members it enjoys great sympathy among the island's 3.8 million inhabitants who have shown reluctance to claim the $500,000 reward offered by the FBI for the capture of Ojeda-Rios and who have equally been unwilling to assist in revealing the whereabouts of other members of this group.

MANUEL RODRIGUEZ PATRIOTIC FRONT. The Frente Patriótico Manuel Rodríguez (FPMR) was the armed wing of the Chilean Communist Party, formed originally with the aim of overthrowing the Pinochet regime by urban guerrilla warfare, one faction of which, the FPMR-D, has continued to seek the overthrow of the post-Pinochet democratic Chilean government. The group relied on **bombings** and **assassinations** directed at Chilean government and police targets, former Pinochet regime officials, and the U.S. diplomatic and economic presence in Chile. Although the group first appeared only in 1983, it had access to impressive quantities of high-quality weapons and explosives and was very well organized. Apparently it enjoyed material assistance from Cuba and other communist states. The FPMR recruited its members from Chilean communist activists who had fled during the Pinochet period but who became actively engaged in the Nicaraguan revolution and in the later conflict in El Salvador as members of the Chilean Battalion. The leader of the Chilean Battalion, Raul Pellgrín Friedman, later became leader of the FPMR.

In the period from 1983-1985 the FPMR conducted simultaneous bombing campaigns in the eight largest cities in Chile, including higher-yield attacks on power substations, the U.S.-Chilean Cultural Institute in Valparaíso on 7 August 1984, and a car bombing outside the U.S. embassy on 19 July 1985 that killed one passerby and wounded four others and two policemen. One of the 21 bombings conducted on 29 April 1986 involved a 15-kilogram bomb detonated outside the U.S. ambassador's residence, which caused no injuries.

On 11 August 1986 Chilean security forces uncovered an arms stockpile at Corral Bay consisting in part of 338 M-16 rifles, 37 Soviet hand grenades, 315 Katyusha rockets, detonators, fuses, and 1,872 kilos of high-yield explosives, and 210,000 rounds of ammunition. A clandestine field clinic and an airstrip were also located near the arms stockpile. Twenty FPMR members were arrested in this raid. Chilean authorities claimed the arms were off-loaded from Soviet and Cuban fishing vessels and were intended for use in an offensive to be launched against the government in September 1987. On 7 September 1986, 21 FPMR gunmen attempted to kill General Augusto Pinochet with grenades and automatic weapons fire as his motorcade drove to his summer residence. Five guards were killed and another 11 were wounded while Pinochet suffered only a cut on his hand. On 10 September 1986 Chilean security forces found a 25-meter-long tunnel packed with 200 kilograms of explosives beneath a road over which General Pinochet had been due to travel the next day. During late 1986 and 1987 the FPMR conducted numerous bombings of power pylons, once plunging much of Santiago and Valparaíso into a blackout just as General Pinochet was due to make a national radio and television address. On 28 December 1989 the FPMR-D bombed the American-Chilean cultural center in Santiago to protest the U.S. invasion of Panama. On 21 March 1990 the FPMR-D wounded General Gustavo Leigh, former Air Force commander, in an assassination attempt. Leigh had been accused of overseeing **death squad** activities directed against Chilean leftists during the rule of General Augusto Pinochet.

The membership of FPMR was estimated to have between 500 and 1,000 at its height but the current FPMR-D, or "Dissident" faction, now is believed to have only 50 to 100 members. The FPMR showed a greater willingness to strike at lower-ranking policemen and ordinary soldiers than did its leading rival, the **Movement of the Revolutionary Left** (MIR) and to risk indiscriminate killing of civilians and bystanders in its bombing campaign since the FPMR used higher-yield explosives than did MIR and made greater use of car bombs. The FPMR also engaged in **kidnapping** industrialists for ransom and apparently once prepared a "people's prison" to house hostages. Unlike the MIR, the FPMR also seized radio stations several times to broadcast its own messages to the public.

Following the restoration of democratic rule in Chile in 1989 the FPMR-D has not desisted from attacks against the Chilean government and actually was the first group to launch a terrorist action with an anti-tank rocket attack on police posts in the southern towns of Los Quenes and Pichi-Pehuhuen on 21 October 1988. This created division in the Chilean Communist Party, many of whose members believed that there was no rationale for such terrorist actions in the post-Pinochet period. The group split into two factions, the FPMR Party and the FPMR-D "Dissident" group. The FPMR-D rationalized its continuation of terrorism as a protest against the reluctance of the Patricio Aylwin administration to prosecute former Pinochet regime officials for human rights abuses and adopted a new strategy for a "Patriotic National War" to demoralize and to delegitimize the Chilean Armed Forces.

The FPMR-D undertook at least six armed attacks in 1988 but whereas the first five were isolated shooting attacks the sixth attack on 21 October 1988 involved the attempted takeover of the three towns of Los Queñes, Aguas Grandes, and Pichipellaupén, which was meant to inaugurate the Patriotic National War. However, the attack was sharply repelled by Chilean army and security forces with heavy casualties to the FPMR-D. On 28 October 1988 the body of Raul Pellgrín was recovered from the Tinguiririca River. On 20 August 1989 the second leader of the FPMR-D, "Commandante Aurelio," also known as Roberto Nordenflycht Farias, was shot to death in a battle with army troops. On 3 November 1990 the FPMR-D shot at U.S. Marines from the U.S.S. *Abraham Lincoln* who were dining in a restaurant in Viña del Mar. On 5 August 1993 security police captured Mauricio Hernández Norambuena, also known as "Ramirio," who was the FPMR-D's chief of military operations. On 9 September 1993 the FPMR-D bombed two McDonalds and one Kentucky Fried Chicken restaurants. On 30 December 1996 four of the top leaders of the FPMR-D, including Mauricio Hernández Norambuena and Patricio Ortiz, escaped from the High Security Prison in Santiago by helicopter.

Another FPMR-D leader, Enrique Villaneuva, also known as "el commandante Eduardo," fled to Cuba on 16 April 1997 while Patricio Ortiz fled to Switzerland in June 1997 where he was granted political **asylum.** The other three prisoners who had escaped the Santiago prison also had made it to Cuba by July 1997. Currently the FPMR-D appears to be inactive and in 1999 the U.S. State Department removed it from its list of Foreign Terrorist Organizations (FTOs) due to the lack of activity by this group in the preceding two years.

MARIGHELLA, CARLOS (1912-1969). Brazilian terrorist and theorist of terrorism best known for his tract, the *Manual of the Urban Guerrilla* written in June 1969, which has often been called a masterpiece on terrorist strategy. Specialists in political violence and terrorism have found little originality in its discussion of terrorist tactical doctrine and have found it also to be quite devoid of any discussion of the moral dimensions of terrorist action. Nonetheless this book has been avidly read by sympathizers and other would-be terrorists who have taken Marighella's prescriptions very much to heart. For instance, Marighella wrote in the *Manual* that no Marxist revolution would succeed in the United States until white college radicals joined forces with black prison inmates. Groups such as the **Symbionese Liberation Army** and the **Revolutionary Armed Task Force** proceeded to follow this precept quite literally. Because of the popularity of this work among revolutionary leftists, many Latin American and European countries have banned its publication and distribution.

As a former Executive Committee member of the Brazilian Communist Party who had become disillusioned with the ineffectiveness of political action, Marighella embraced the notion of "violence before politics" in 1967 when he left the Brazilian Communist Party and helped found a leftist terrorist group called the National Liberation Action. He was killed in a police ambush in November 1969, and the group he helped found was smashed by Brazilian security forces within a year of his death.

MARTYRS' AVENGING GROUP. The "Martyrs' Avenging Group" was a Chilean prostate **death squad** that attacked and sometimes killed suspected leftists or other opponents of the Pinochet regime. In August 1980 about 14 persons were arrested by a group calling itself the Comando de Vengadores de Mártires, "Martyrs Avenging Command" (COVEMA), which was formed following the 15 July 1980 **assassination** of Colonel Roger Vergara, director of the Army Intelligence School, by members of the **Movement of the Revolutionary Left** (MIR). Two of those whom they captured in downtown Santiago included Guillermo Hormazábal, the director of Radio Chilena, as well as Mario Romero, the head of Radio Presidente Ibañez. Both were released but Eduardo Jara, a journalism student from Catholic University, was not so fortunate and was tortured so badly that he later died.

Another related group was the Gamma Commando which murdered the artist Hugo Riveros Gómez, a MIR member who had been detained from November 1980 to March 1981 by the Central Nacional de

Informaciones, "National Intelligence Center" (CNI). After his release he sketched from memory the faces of the agents who had interrogated him which he attempted to send to comrades abroad. After CNI agents intercepted this mail he was killed along with Oscar Polanco, another MIR member.

The Eleventh of September Commando allegedly killed four leftists in reprisal for the **Manuel Rodriguez Patriotic Front's** (FPMR) attempted assassination of General Augusto Pinochet on 7 September 1986. This Commando also assassinated Jécar Neghme, the leader in exile of the MIR, on 4 September 1989.

MARXIST-LENINIST ARMED PROPAGANDA UNIT (MLAPU). The Marxist-Leninist Armed Propaganda Unit was a nonstate group seeking to overthrow the Turkish Republic in favor of a communist state. It was founded in Paris in 1973 by leftist Turkish students and the widow of Mahir Çayan, a Turkish leftist and founder of the **Turkish People's Liberation Front** killed by Turkish security forces in 1972. The group was one of several left-wing **death squads** and terrorist groups vying with right-wing extremist counterparts in the period of escalating internal political terrorism in Turkey in the late 1970s and early 1980s. MLAPU was also considered to be the most virulently anti-American of Turkish leftist groups.

In 1979 MLAPU killed seven U.S. citizens. On 2 January 1980 they machine-gunned the manager of the El Al Airlines office in Istanbul as he was driving home. On 16 April 1980 three MLAPU gunmen killed a U.S. Navy noncommissioned officer and his taxi driver. The three gunmen were pursued by police, one being killed in pursuit and the other two captured. On 15 November 1980 two other U.S. Air Force noncommissioned officers were shot at by MLAPU gunmen. One was killed, but the other escaped injury. The two gunmen were apprehended and later executed in 1985.

With the military coup of September 1980 and imposition of martial law, MLAPU and other similar groups were ruthlessly suppressed by the military. Many of those leftists already imprisoned, including the gunmen arrested for the incidents mentioned above, were executed under the military regime.

MASS SOCIETY THEORY. Theory that seeks to explain political violence as resulting from the mobilization of large numbers of people who have been dislocated from traditional social organization by industrialization, urbanization, and rapid democratization into political militancy. The theory shares the pessimistic view articulated by Ortega y Gasset that the growing working classes and lower middle class would be easily swayed by irrational passions and fall prey to **ideological** demagogues, whether of the left or the right, and would be easily led into political extremism and violence.

The theory was articulated more coherently by William Kornhauser in his *Politics of Mass Society* which held that persons who had recently entered the industrial workforce in the large cities would be cut off from the traditional socialization of family life, village life, and church and would lack a commitment to the institutions and norms of liberal democracy at the same time that they would begin to have their own political demands. However empirical studies by Lynn Lees and Charles Tilley and others indicate that those people who are securely members of primary and secondary social groups are more likely to become actively recruited into organized political activism than those who are socially isolated (*see* SOCIAL NETWORK RECRUITMENT THEORY). The empirical studies of Sydney Verba and Norman Nie also indicate that political participation tends to be correlated more with higher rather than lower socioeconomic status so that one would expect instead that political extremism would be less likely to be found in the social underclasses of "mass society."

Another implication of mass society theory that appears to be empirically false is the notion, best articulated by Samuel P. Huntington, that institutions and organizations having modern attributes of adaptability, complexity, autonomy, and coherence would effectively channel the growing demands of increasingly politically mobilized masses into constructive engagement with civil society rather than violent confrontation. Yet if one considers such organizations as the **Irish Republican Army** (IRA), or the **Palestine Liberation Organization** (PLO), they have many of these attributes of modern political organizations but have nonetheless used their organizations to carry out campaigns of political violence and terrorism targeting the civil societies in which their followers live. In these cases it is not an inchoate mass society but rather highly closed, hierarchically organized, and ideologically motivated organizations that have been responsible for civil unrest and violence.

MAU MAU. The Mau Mau were gangs deployed by the Central Association of the Kikuyu tribesmen in Kenya originally to drive British settlers off Kikuyu lands but which became part of the overall anticolonial Kenyan independence movement. The Mau Mau were active from September 1952 to October 1956, attacking and killing British settlers as well as burning their crops, slaughtering their cattle, and destroying the huts of African tenants on British farms.

Following the first attacks the British administration declared a state of emergency in October 1952 and imprisoned Jomo Kenyatta (1897/98-1978) in 1953 as the suspected leader of the Mau Mau. By the end of 1953 over 3,000 rebels had been killed and by the end of 1956 over 10,000 rebels had been killed while less than 600 of the British security forces had been killed. The vast majority of the 2,000 civilians killed were black Africans.

The power of the Mau Mau lay not so much in their material strength, for they seldom had more than 500 firearms, but rather in the psychic hold that the Kikuyu leaders wielded over followers and supporters by means of magical oaths whose violation threatened supernatural terrors against the oath breaker. The Mau Mau obtained weapons by theft from the police while local Africans were forced to contribute funds to support the group.

The Mau Mau suffered a severe blow with the capture and defection of one key Kikuyu leader in 1954. The capture and execution of another key leader, Dedan Kimathi, in October 1956 effectively destroyed the organization. Jomo Kenyatta was released from prison in 1961 and became prime minister of Kenya upon its independence in 1963.

In July 1997 following a Kenyan police crackdown on antigovernment protestors 300 members of a Kikuyu group, known as the Kikuyu, Embu and Meru Association (KEMA), met in Thika, 30 miles north of Nairobi, and threatened to revive the Mau Mau terror to remove President Arap Moi from power. However at the Naivasha meeting of the fighters' association on 5 September 1998 other former Mau Mau members demanded that KEMA leave the opposition and join with President Moi's ruling Kenyan African National Unity party.

MAXIMILIANO HERNÁNDEZ MARTÍNEZ ANTICOMMUNIST BRIGADE. This was a quasi-state-sponsored group aimed at repressing leftists and even moderates who opposed the interests of the landowning oligarchy in El Salvador. Named for the Salvadoran military dictator who suppressed the Matanza peasant uprising of 1932, this group was one of several Salvadoran right-wing **death squads** that generally grew out of the "special units" maintained by Salvadoran security forces during the 1970s and that were used to kill off suspected "subversives." Many of the leaders and members of such groups were themselves members of the Salvadoran military and police even though such groups ceased to have legal status following the dissolution of the **ORDEN** paramilitary security force in the month after the coup of 15 October 1979. The major moving force behind the Maximiliano Hernández group was Roberto D'Aubuisson, formerly an officer of the Salvadoran intelligence agency who founded the **White Warriors' Union** death squad in 1976 and who later founded the Republican National Alliance (**ARENA**) party.

The Maximiliano Hernández Martínez group is believed responsible for the 24 March 1980 **assassination** of Archbishop Oscar Arnulfo Romero y Galdamez, an outspoken critic of the Salvadoran government. On 27 November 1980, they **kidnapped** Enrique Álvarez, head of the leftist Democratic Revolutionary Front (FDR), and four other leftist leaders whom they tortured and killed. From September to October 1983 they killed the highest ranking FDR official residing in San Salvador, 18 trade unionists, a few professors, and bombed the Jesuit residence at the Central American University. This group is also believed responsible for the killings and repression of many other less prominent leftists, centrists, human rights activists, religious activists, academics, and trade unionists.

MAY 1. The Revolutionary Organization of May 1 was a nonstate Greek leftist group that engaged in terrorism for the limited purposes of opposing "U.S. imperialism," the Turkish presence in Cyprus, and government economic austerity measures. It had no known state sponsorship but appeared to work in close concert with the **November 17** and the **Revolutionary Popular Struggle** (ELA) groups. It appears likely that both May 1 and November 17 evolved from the same core membership of ELA, which originally was formed with the revolutionary objective of overthrowing the Greek military junta. In the post-junta period November 17, and these similar groups, appeared more anarchistic in nature, lacking an overall objective but attaching themselves to revolutionary raison d'être as these happen to appear.

May 1 appeared as part of a campaign against Greek jurists to demonstrate revolutionary solidarity with **May 15** terrorist Mohammad Rashid, who was fighting **extradition** to the United States due to his role in the 11 August 1982 **bombing** of a U.S. air carrier. On 23 January 1989 the group **assassinated** a deputy public prosecutor of the Greek Supreme Court in Athens. Two other public prosecutors were killed by members of the May 1 or November 17 group, which led two Supreme Court justices to resign. While Rashid was not extradited to the U.S., he was tried in October 1991, convicted in early 1992, and sentenced to 18 years imprisonment but then released on good behavior in 1996. During the Persian Gulf War May 1 and ELA mounted five bombing attacks on U.S. and British corporate offices in Athens. In mid-July 1991, May 1 and ELA joined November 17 in communiqués to Turkish terrorist groups, urging them to step up their attacks just prior to the visit of President George H. Bush to both Greece and Turkey.

Little is known about the membership of these groups or their relations with other terrorist groups or political parties. Since their area of operations seems to be confined to Athens, it is assumed their total numbers are small (less than 100). While the **ideology** of the groups is marked by Marxist themes, there is also a very strong undercurrent of Greek nationalism and anti-Turkish sentiment, evinced in the step-up in terrorist operations whenever Greece, Turkey, and the U.S. seek to discuss the issue of Cyprus.

MAY 15. The Arab Organization of May 15, named for the anniversary of the first declaration of war by the Arab states against the newly declared State of Israel, was an obscure splinter group of the Popular Front for the Liberation of Palestine-Special Operations Group, a splinter group from the original **Popular Front for the Liberation of Palestine**. Formerly led by Abu Ibrahim, it was headquartered in Baghdad, Iraq.

May 15 carried out operations under its own name from 1978 to 1983, specializing in making sophisticated barometrically triggered **bombs** used to destroy civilian air carriers, including one Tokyo to Honolulu Pan Am flight on 11 August 1982, which exploded just before landing, killing one person. Abu Ibrahim, his aide, Mohammad Rashid, and Rashid's wife Christian "Fatima" Pinter, were indicted for the bombing of the Honolulu Pan Am flight in 1987 based on evidence that Rashid and his wife had submitted visa applications that enabled them to plant the bomb on the plane before it continued on the Japan to

Honolulu leg of its flight. While Rashid was arrested in Greece on a false passport charge the government there, after refusing to **extradite** him to the United States, tried and sentenced him to 18 years imprisonment for the airline bombing in 1992 but released him in 1996 for good behavior. Rashid was handed over to the United States in June 1998 by an undisclosed nation, presumed by some to have been Egypt, and was arraigned for trial on 3 June 1998.

In the period from 1980-1982 May 15 carried out five bomb attacks against El Al offices, the Israeli embassy in Athens, a Jewish restaurant in West Berlin, and the Mount Royal hotel in London, killing two people and wounding 15. In April 1986 May 15 bombed a TWA flight killing four people. On 15 February 1984 a **letter bomb** sent by May 15 exploded, maiming Iran's ambassador to Syria, Hujjatulislam 'Ali Akbar Muhtashami, who was intimately involved in overseeing the **Hezbollah** militia in Lebanon and whom May 15 regarded as a gratuitous meddler in intra-Arab affairs.

Very little is known about this organization. It appears that many of its members have joined other groups and that May 15 ceased to be active after 1984.

MAY 19TH COMMUNIST COALITION. The May 19th Communist Coalition was an outreach umbrella organization created as a front for the **Revolutionary Armed Task Force** (RATF), itself a merger of the remnants of the **Weather Underground** and **Black Liberation Army** (BLA). The name was taken from the common birth anniversary of Malcolm X and also of Ho Chi Minh. The organization also called itself the May 19th Communist Organization.

This front attempted to recruit other leftist revolutionaries and black prison inmates into the RATF or BLA organizations. The May 19th group also established contacts and fraternal ties with other terrorist groups, such as the **New Afrikan Freedom Fighters**, the Puerto Rican **Armed Forces of National Liberation** (FALN) separatists, and even the **Palestine Liberation Organization** (PLO). The May 19th spokesperson, Judith A. Clark, represented the organization at a conference sponsored by the PLO in Beirut in September 1981.

In recruiting black inmates, May 19th cadres represented themselves to prison authorities and prisoners as offering free legal services and counsel for indigent prisoners. Once they gained access to potential recruits they would undertake "consciousness-raising" sessions to convert them to the revolutionary cause. Outside of the prisons the group maintained a network of communications and safe houses for the RATF. The group collapsed when the FBI arrested the core members of the RATF from May 1985 to February 1986, many of whom, like Judith A. Clark, were arrested on charges stemming from their participation in RATF criminal activities.

MILITIA MOVEMENT. The "Militia Movement" is a loosely organized movement promoting the creation of nonstate armed paramilitary groups ostensibly to defend the constitution and liberty of the American people against perceived internal and external enemies. It is also a highly diverse movement which includes "patriot" groups, **common law courts**, **Freemen** or "sovereign citizens," survivalists, tax protestors, constitutionalist groups, and **Identity Christian** and **white supremacist** groups, some of whose members have proven to be engaged in criminal and sometimes politically motivated violence.

Such groups as the **Minutemen** and **Christian-Patriots Defense League** can be viewed as predecessors of the current movement which appeared to gain momentum after the Estes Park meeting of Patriot and militia group members in late October 1992 convened to organize support for Randy Weaver. In this meeting Louis Beam, Jr., a former **Ku Klux Klan** leader and current member of the **Aryan Nations**, urged that these right-wing groups organize themselves into loosely confederated, autonomous **cells** without a central command structure and that they arm themselves to be able to resist oppression by the federal government through numerous attacks which could not be stopped by arresting key leaders or smashing a central leadership cell. The militia movement gained more attention after the **Oklahoma City bombing** when it became known that Timothy McVeigh had contacted and attempted to join such groups.

Right-wing extremist groups in the United States, including those that escalate into terrorism, have two advantages that **anarchistic leftist** groups here have lacked: First, the antigovernment sentiments of these groups resonate with the distinctive antiauthoritarian and individualist tenets of the political culture of the United States. Second, there is a ready-made **ethno-nationalist** core of white males who feel estranged from the current political establishment who are ready to be recruited into the militia movement.

According to the "Militia Act of 1956" of the United States Code (Title 10, Section 311, Subtitle A, Part I, Chapter 13) all able-bodied males who are not members of the Armed Forces are part of the "unorganized militia." Title 32 of the U.S. Code section 109(c) provides for the creation of "state defense forces" that were originally created during World War I and World War II essentially as "home guard" units distinct from the regular Armed Forces and National Guard. Such units can be created and regulated by state law but many states, such as New Hampshire, specifically prohibit privately formed militias or other associations from becoming registered as state defense forces. Therefore under existing federal and state laws the self-formed militias are no more than unauthorized, autonomous, voluntary paramilitary organizations which some states have declared to be subject to their regulation or else have banned as illegal.

These militias are largely autonomous from each other and lack any hierarchical relationship, coordination, or working unity. On the other hand such militias can spin off "cells" of more committed extremist activists who may strike out on their own in the name of **"leaderless resistance."**

Several explanations have been offered for the rise of the militia movement: First, there has been a popular backlash in the western United States against environmentalism and federal management of the western public lands. Second, the existence of prior Christian Patriot, tax protestor, and white supremacist groups in the Midwest and western United States provides a cadre of like-minded persons able to create new militia groups modeled after these older organizations. Third, a rise in working class frustrations may also be at work: Blue-collar white male workers have lost 15 percent of their real income in the last two decades while women and members of ethnic minority groups have experienced relative gains. Such white males see themselves excluded and passed over by affirmative action laws and their traditional positions as heads of households weakened by laws punishing spousal abuse and favoring divorced women in matters of alimony, child custody disputes, and mandatory child support.

Thus the militia movement may also be a reaction to a growing **"identity politics"** in the United States in which women, ethnic groups, and specialized lifestyle groups seek empowerment of their own respective groups through civil advocacy and claims of past victimization. White males, who are often castigated as the victimizers of these groups, find the militia movement a readymade vehicle to pursue their own version of identity politics. Finally, one should note the voiced concerns of militia movement members that the federal raids at Ruby Ridge and Waco, and passage of the Brady gun-control bill, presage a rise in authoritarianism on the part of the federal government. While such beliefs strike nonmilitia members or supporters as bizarre and ill-founded, the popularity of these populist notions may explain much of the appeal of the militia movement for those Americans who are alienated from conventional contemporary politics in the United States.

By 31 March 1995 there were about 42 known private militia groups in existence who advertized their existence. According to testimony of Bureau of Alcohol, Tobacco and Firearms officials presented in June 1995 before the U.S. Senate Judiciary Subcommittee on Terrorism, Technology, and Government Information, paramilitary militia groups could be found in at least 40 states. According to the Southern Poverty Law Center in 1996 their number reached an all time high of 858 but declined to 523 in 1997 and then to 435 in 1998. Other researchers cited around 200 as being the maximum figure.

Certain militia groups and related groups that have engaged in terrorism are related in more detail elsewhere in this work: The **Aryan Resistance Army** sought from 1985-1995 to emulate the former **Order** while the **Phineas Priesthood** engaged in attacks on homosexuals, biracial couples, and abortion clinics from 1991 to 1996. The **Viper Militia** in 1994-1996 plotted to **bomb** federal and state government buildings in Arizona. The **Freemen** of Montana in 1995-1996 and the so-called **Republic of Texas** in 1995-1997 engaged both in "paper terrorism" involving fraudulent liens and legal harassment as well as actual violence against their neighbors and local communities.

MILLENNIALISM. Specifically, this is the belief in the establishment of a thousand-year earthly Kingdom under the rule of Christ in accordance with a literal reading of the Book of Revelation. The "Thousand Year" kingdom is inferred from verses in Revelation 20:2-7, in conjunction with other scriptures in both the Old and New Testaments. In its more general sense *millennialism* refers to any religious or secular belief in the eminent establishment of a divine or earthly utopian social order and millennialist ideas are found not only among Christians but also among Muslims, Jews, other religious groups as well as adherents of purely secular **ideologies**.

According to various postmillennialist views Christians would either have to undergo trials of persecution in the tribulation period or else Christians must themselves help build the thousand-year kingdom and resist the forces of the "Anti-Christ," a prophesied evil world ruler who would appear during the tribulation preceding the millennium. The political implication is that believers must be prepared to resist the ungodly political, social, and economic order of the tribulation period which is under God's wrath. Collaboration with, or acknowledgment of the legitimacy of, the regime of the "Anti-Christ" leads to the believer's loss of salvation and consequent eternal damnation. Those who held this belief, such as Randy and Vicki Weaver or the Branch Davidians, would naturally take such measures as seeking an isolated place in which to set up a fortified home stocked with food supplies, guns, and ammunition to last them through the tribulation period.

Jewish millennialists have taken their cues from the Book of Daniel and other apocalyptic or apocryphal writings. The first century **Zealots** were convinced that if they precipitated an all-out conflict with Rome that God would be forced to reveal His Messiah who would then crush the Roman legions and reestablish a Jewish empire similar to that of King David or Solomon. In more recent times Jewish religious extremists of the **Gush Emunim** group plotted to destroy the Al Aqsa Mosque on the Temple Mount to precipitate a similar confrontation with the Arabs that would force the revelation of the Messiah. (*See* TEMPLE MOUNT OPERATION)

Islam also has its millennialist doctrines based on obscure verses in the Koran and certain *hadith* (reported sayings) of the Prophet Muhammad. Many Muslims believe that an apocalyptic final war between good and evil, similar to the Christian millennialist belief in a final battle of Armageddon, would occur, that evil forces would desecrate the Muslim holy places, and that God would send a deliverer known as the "Mahdi," whom the Twelve Imam Shi'ites identify with their "Hidden Imam," who would slay the godless forces and restore the fortunes of the Muslims. There was also a *hadith* that stated that the Mahdi would appear at the turn of one of the centuries according to the Islamic lunar calendar. Thus it is not entirely coincidental that Iran's Islamic revolution peaked around the years 1,399-1,400 A.H. in the Hegira calendar nor that a Sunni Muslim claiming to be the Mahdi and his followers took over the Ka'ba shrine in Mecca at the exact beginning of the year 1,400 A.H. on 20 November 1978. Just as many premillennialist Christians saw the establishment of the State of Israel as one of the hopeful signs of the coming of the millennium many fundamentalist Muslims interpret the existence of the State of Israel and its possession of the Muslim shrines on the Temple Mount as signs of those evils which would precede the coming of the Mahdi.

The idea of millennialism has also been appropriated by other sectarian and secular ideologies as well. The **Aum Shinrikyo** sect believed that releasing the sarin gas in the **Tokyo Subway attack** would somehow trigger a world war that would usher in the millennial kingdom under the rule of their leader Asahara Shoko.

According to David C. Rapoport's study, "Messianic Sanctions for Terror," [*Comparative Politics,* 20, 2 (1988): 195-214] millennialist ideas have a great potential to unleash political violence because the believers usually believe that they must undertake some special act of faith to ensure the arrival of the millennium. These actions, unfortunately, tend to lead either to conflict with authorities or to political violence.

MINUTEMEN. Founded in 1961 by Robert dePugh, a Missouri manufacturer of pet and livestock vitamins and food supplements, the Minutemen were the predecessors of the **Posse Comitatus** and other right-wing extremist groups that advocated or practiced terrorism against alleged "communists and traitors." The name was taken from that of the Revolutionary War militiamen and their **ideology**, which stressed extreme anticommunism and survivalism, took on a peculiar relevance during a period when fear of international communism and of nuclear war would be greatly aggravated by the Cuban missile crisis of October 1962. The anticommunist component of the group's ideology included attacks on the Internal Revenue Service and Federal Reserve System as being anti-American conspiracies while the Minutemen's tabloid *On Target* identified 20 members of Congress investigating right-wing movements as being "communists" and made veiled threats against their lives. Following the outbreak of racial rioting in the mid-1960s, the Minutemen advocated that whites undertake guerrilla warfare training to fight minority group members in the event of racial warfare.

DePugh was imprisoned in 1968 on a conspiracy conviction arising from violations of federal firearms laws. He jumped bail in 1968 and survived in the wilderness of the Rockies and New Mexico desert until arrested in Truth or Consequences, New Mexico, in 1970. Following his release from prison in 1973 he wrote a manual on survival, *Can You*

Survive? Guidelines for Resistance to Tyranny for You and Your Family, that became widely read and admired among other right-wing survivalists.

The Minutemen actually carried out very little in the way of terrorism, but this group served as the inspiration for other groups that have since then engaged in terrorist actions. The Posse Comitatus and Arizona Patriots absorbed many of the former Minutemen and much of the Minuteman ideology. The **Christian-Patriots Defense League** fused Minuteman ideology with **Identity Christianity**. (*See also* MILITIA MOVEMENT)

MOGADISHU HIJACKING RESCUE. On 13 October 1977, some four terrorists of the **Popular Front for the Liberation of Palestine** (PFLP) **hijacked** a Lufthansa Boeing 737 flying from Majorca to Frankfurt carrying 86 passengers and five crew members. The hijackers not only had handguns and crude homemade hand grenades but also 60 pounds of plastic explosives and were demanding that the 10 main **Red Army Faction** terrorists be freed from West German jails, along with two Palestinians in Turkish jails, as well as demanding a ransom of $15 million. The hijackers had the plane fly to Rome, Cyprus, Bahrain, Dubai, Aden, and finally to Somalia.

Following the murder of the pilot in Aden by the hijackers' leader, the West German government resolved to deploy a 26-member Grenzschutzgruppe-9 unit to Mogadishu Airport to free the hostages. There, on 18 October 1977, two members of the British elite antiterrorist Special Air Services accompanied the German team and blinded the terrorists with special magnesium-flash grenades for six seconds, allowing the Germans to storm the plane successfully. Only one of the terrorists survived while the remaining hostages were rescued. On hearing the news of the rescue three of the leading imprisoned Red Army Faction prisoners committed suicide while the Red Army Faction kidnappers holding West German businessman Hanns-Martin Schleyer murdered him in reprisal for the deaths of their comrades.

In January 1978 the last survivor of the four Palestinian hijackers, Souhaila Sami Andrawes, was convicted by a Somali court to 20 years imprisonment but then released later that year and sent to Baghdad on a cargo plane. Along with her husband and six-year old-daughter, Souhaila Andrawes entered Norway from Cyprus in 1991 and obtained resident status. In October 1994 she was identified and arrested in Oslo on air piracy charges stemming from the Mogadishu hijacking and faced **extradition** to Germany in 1995.

MOLLY MAGUIRES. Nonstate group of Irish labor movement agitators who carried out a campaign of intimidation and murder against anthracite coal mine owners and operators in five counties in northeastern Pennsylvania in the period 1865-1875. They were all members of an Irish American fraternal society, the Ancient Order of Hibernians, but they took their label of "Molly Maguire" from the name of an underground group in Ireland that had resisted oppressive landlords. The members of the group, who reputedly numbered around 3,000 at their height, engaged in assaults, murders, and **arson**. Eventually the group obtained recognition as a union in 1875 and called a miners' strike, which crippled the operations of the Philadelphia, Reading, and Lehigh Valley Railroads. The president of the Reading Railroad engaged the services of the Pinkerton Agency whose agent, James McParland, infiltrated the organization. After McParland gathered sufficient evidence, 20 of the leaders of the Molly Maguires were tried and convicted for murder and then hanged in 1877, effectively ending the organization.

MONTONEROS. The Movimiento Perónista Montonero was a leftist Argentinean guerrilla group formed in 1970 to promote the populist and nationalistic policies of the exiled dictator, Juan Domingo Perón, and to facilitate his return to power. Although the group was not Marxist-Leninist it did seek a type of socialist revolution within Argentina coupled with a fight to rid Argentina of foreign economic penetration. Following Perón's return to power, once the Montoneros learned that Perón had embraced the more conservative wings of the Perónist movement they turned against him to pursue their own populist and socialist revolution.

Prior to the return of Perón the Montoneros sought and received help from Cuba. In the early 1970s they had contacts with other leftist insurgents in Latin America, such as Colombia's **M-19** group, and within Argentina they had about 10,000 supporters. Following the break with Perón they made common cause with the Cuban-backed **Armed Revolutionary Forces** (FAR) as well as with Trotskyite groups in fighting the regime.

The Montoneros began their career by **kidnapping** and murdering the former president, Pedro Aramburu, on 29 May 1970. They financed themselves through numerous kidnappings of foreign executives for ransom during 1970-1973. From May until September 1973, they became, in effect, a state-sponsored group under the Perónista Campora administration. Tensions with the more right-wing Perónist groups erupted, however, in an armed clash between the factions on 20 June 1973 at Ezeiza Airport marring the homecoming ceremony planned to honor the returning Juan Perón. In this clash with rightist Perónists, 13 people perished and over 100 were wounded. After Perón's reelection as Argentina's president in October 1973, the Montoneros grew disenchanted with his rightist policies. On 12 February 1974 several Montoneros were arrested in connection with a plot to **assassinate** Perón and his wife Isabel. On 1 May 1974 Perón broke with the Montoneros, whom he castigated in his May Day rally address as "treacherous and mercenary" elements.

Two weeks following Perón's death on 1 July 1974 the Montoneros unleashed their "popular war" against the Argentinean regime using arson, **bombings**, murder, and sabotage to try to provoke the military into a crackdown that would precipitate a popular revolution against right-wing oppression. This campaign began with the 15 July 1974 assassination of a former foreign minister. Again the group sought funds through kidnapping for ransom, netting $60 million alone in ransom for the Born brothers, sons of Argentina's wealthiest family, abducted on 19 September 1974. The government reacted to this by rigorously enforcing a law forbidding negotiations with, or payments to, terrorist groups. The rigorous enforcement of this law led the Montoneros to kill executives of Fiat, Bendix, Chrysler, Ford, General Motors, and a West German pharmaceutical firm when they could not collect extortion payments from those companies. They also tried to kill a Goodyear executive and wounded three other foreign executives by bombs delivered hidden in flower bouquets.

On 16 September 1974 they conducted 40 bombings throughout Argentina targeting U.S. firms and banks. Other attacks on U.S. targets included the 8 September 1974 bomb attack on the USIA office in Rosario; an attempted bombing of the U.S. embassy on 19 September 1974; and the kidnapping and murder of U.S. consular official John Egan on 26 February 1975. On 20 September 1976 the Montoneros set fire to the new U.S. chancery building, causing $10,000 in damages. Attacks on the Argentine government included the 1 November 1974 bombing that killed Federal Police Chief Alberto Villar, the murder of

General Jorge Cáceres Monie on 3 November 1975, and the murder of General Cesaro Cardozo on 18 June 1976. On 22 August 1975 the Montoneros bombed and sank a naval destroyer under construction, causing $70 million in damages.

The Montoneros succeeded at least in their immediate goal of provoking a violent right-wing crackdown. Ultimately, however, this crackdown led to the complete suppression of all leftist insurgent groups in the country. The Argentine military took control of all security forces and undertook its **"dirty war"** to kill all suspected leftists beginning in February 1975. By the end of 1976 1,600 Montoneros had been killed and another 500 were killed in the first half of 1977. Following the flight of Montonero founder and leader Mario Firmenich to Rome in October 1977, along with a few of his lieutenants, Montonero activities continued only sporadically in Argentina and ended in 1979 when security forces killed Horacio Mendizábal, the chief Montonero leader who had remained active underground within Argentina. Finally in December 1981, Mario Firmenich called on surviving Montoneros to cease armed struggle in favor of political action, in effect signaling the end of the Montoneros as an active guerrilla and terrorist group. Firmenich returned in June 1987 to Argentina where he was tried for the terrorist offenses of the Montoneros and sentenced to 30 years imprisonment. Firmenich received a presidential pardon on 29 December 1990, ironically along with General Jorge Videla who had conducted the "dirty war" campaign against leftist groups such as the Montoneros.

The Montoneros failed to perceive that the populist message of Juan Perón, as an eclectic hodgepodge combining leftist and rightist appeals designed to draw as broad a following as possible, could not be reduced simply to an unambiguous appeal for socialist revolution. Likewise the broad support the Montoneros received prior to the return of Perón was largely a function of public adulation of Perón, which extended to the Montoneros only insofar as they were perceived as his loyal followers. Thus when the Montoneros undertook their campaign in 1974, they overestimated the degree of popular support for themselves and their own "authentic Perónism."

MORAZANIST PATRIOTIC FRONT. The Frente Patriótico Morazanista (FPM) was a leftist guerrilla group, believed to be an arm of the outlawed Honduran Communist Party founded in 1979, that sought primarily to drive out the U.S. military and diplomatic presence from Honduras.

Whereas the **Lorenzo Zelaya** and **Cinchonero** groups had sought to create a leftist **revolution** following the Nicaraguan model in the early 1980s, the success of U.S.-trained Honduran counterinsurgency forces led many leftist survivors of those groups to conclude that the U.S. presence in Honduras would first have to be driven out before any revolution could succeed. Those groups and the FPM also enjoyed Cuban support and that of the former Sandinista government of Nicaragua. Given this Sandinista support and the use of Honduras as a staging area for **Contra** forces fighting the Nicaraguan government, the Morazanistas decided to concentrate on attacking U.S. advisers and military support personnel in Honduras.

On 8 August 1987 the FPM **bombed** a restaurant in Comayagua, north of Tegucigalpa, wounding five U.S. soldiers and six Honduran soldiers. On 17 July 1988 the FPM made a machine-gun and grenade attack on U.S. soldiers leaving a discotheque in San Pedro Sula, wounding four of the nine soldiers who were part of a joint U.S.-Honduran task force stationed at the Honduran air force base in Palmerola. In December 1988 the FPM claimed credit for bombing a Peace Corps office. In 1989 there were three other similar attacks on U.S. servicemen, including a 13 July 1989 bombing attack on nine U.S. Army military policemen outside the Lido Discotheque in the northern coastal city of La Ceiba. On 31 March 1990 three FPM snipers opened fire with automatic weapons on a U.S. Air Force bus en route from the coastal city of Tela to an inland military base, in which six soldiers were wounded. On 23 June 1991 the FPM launched an antitank rocket at the UN Observer Group office in Tegucipalga causing damages. On 4 July 1994 a bombing near a U.S. military installation killed six Hondurans and wounded 25 others. While originally a communique claimed this was done by the FPM another FPM message disclaimed responsibility.

Despite the group's effectiveness in making so many attacks and wounding so many U.S. and Honduran military personnel, it appeared to be a small group.

MORO LIBERATION FRONT (MLF). The Moro Liberation Front, or Moro National Liberation Front, was a nonstate group of Muslim revolutionaries seeking autonomy for the Muslims in the islands of Mindanao and the Sulu Archipelago, a region covering about 13 provinces in the southern Philippines. The group enjoyed the support of Libya's Muammar Qaddafi, the Chief Minister of the Malaysian state of Sabah,

Tun Mustapha, and also received assistance from Iran. While not a material sponsor, the Islamic Conference Organization, through its efforts at mediation between the MLF and Philippine government or among MLF factions, does confer moral support in backing the Moro guerrillas as an oppressed Muslim minority.

In 1972 Nur Misuari reorganized the Mindanao Independence Movement, which had been a relatively passive political group, into an **ethnonationalist** and leftist revolutionary organization. In 1973 the MLF raised 15,000 fighters and captured most of Cotabato Province. In 1974 they captured Jolo Town and nearby Notre Dame College in the Sulu Islands, which the Philippine armed forces were only able to recover after first leveling them with naval artillery and air force bombardments. The offensives of 1973 and 1974 apparently were timed to coincide with the Islamic Foreign Ministers' Conferences held in Benghazi in 1973 and then in Lahore the following year to force the Moro issue upon the agenda of these conferences and to enlist the support of the Islamic Conference. On 7 April 1975 three MLF members **hijacked** a domestic Philippine Airlines flight, releasing the passengers in Manila, but holding the plane's crew and one of the airline's executives hostage to guarantee safe passage to Libya. On arriving in Libya on 13 April 1975 they freed the hostages and were granted **asylum** by the Libyan government.

Although Nur Misuari succeeded in gaining the approbation and sympathy of the Muslim states, this in turn created a backlash within the Philippines. First, the resolve of the central government to crush the rebellion grew stronger. Second, Misuari's tactics and intransigent position alienated many Muslim supporters within the Philippines who thought the MLF would jeopardize their more attainable goals of gaining civic equality for Muslims and limited autonomy.

Misuari agreed to a 16-point accord with President Ferdinand Marcos in 1976, which established a cease-fire and provided for a referendum in April 1977 in the disputed 13 provinces. As Christians formed majorities in eight of these provinces the bid for Muslim autonomy was overwhelmingly rejected at the polls. The MLF never recovered from this moral defeat. Sporadic violations of the cease-fire occurred including the killings of Brigadier General Bautista and 34 unarmed soldiers in February 1977.

Internally the MLF splintered into factions with rivals of Misuari seeking some sort of accommodation with the Philippine government while a more radical faction, the **Abu Sayyaf Group** led by Abdulrajik Abubakar Janjalani, believed the original goals of the MLF too limited and broke away from the MLF group in 1991 intending to create an Islamic republic. Misuari continued to seek aid from Libya and later from Iran following its Islamic revolution, while the Marcos government succeeded in co-opting the local Muslim aristocracy as well as Misuari's rivals in the MLF. During the period from 1984-1986, when the central government was in some disarray due to the domestic revolution against Marcos, Misuari's followers made very limited gains in the south. Their new tactic, however, of **kidnapping** and holding foreigners as hostages alienated much of the international support they had previously enjoyed. In 1986 the new Philippine President Corazon Aquino signed a truce with the MLF, and violence substantially subsided afterward.

In April 1995 an Abu Sayyaf unit of 200 rebels attacked the city of Ipil in Mindanao, looting and setting stores on fire before retreating, having killed 52 civilians. The timing of the attack coincided with government talks with the main MLF group which Janjalani sought to sabotage. On 19 August 1996 negotiations between the government and the MLF led to a compromise to allow the MLF a role in the creation of a Southern Philippine Council for Peace and Development which would allow for limited autonomy. On 2 September 1996 President Fidel Ramos traveled to the town of Malabang in Mindanao to sign a peace accord with Nur Misuari ending the 26-year rebellion and creating a four-province Autonomous Region of Muslim Mindanao. Misuari agreed to cease secessionist claims and instead to run as a candidate of Ramos's political party for the leadership of the four-province autonomous zone. Many MLF members regarded this as a sell-out and another faction, the Moro Islamic Liberation Front (MILF), numbering 300 to 500 fighters, launched sporadic attacks against the Army around Cotabato in late November 1996. By early February 1997 the government of Fidel Ramos was holding talks with the separatist Moro Islamic Liberation Front which the Abu Sayyaf Group attempted to sabotage by its murder of a Catholic Bishop, Benjamin de Jesús, outside his cathedral in Jolo Town. The original MLF group has become less active as many of its militants have defected to the rival Abu Sayyaf and Moro Islamic Liberation Front groups.

MOUNTAIN OFFICERS. The Mountain Officers were an obscure intrastate group of Guatemalan military officers that sought the limited end of moving government policy further to the right through terrorist actions and threats. The group claimed responsibility for the **bombing** of a Mexicana Airlines office in 1988 in protest against the Mexican government's granting Guatemalan leftist guerrilla leaders safe passage and sanctuary. The right-wing group also made several death threats in spring 1988 against Mario Vinicio Cerezo Arevalo, the first democratically elected civilian President of Guatemala since 1966.

MOVEMENT FOR ISLAMIC CHANGE. *See* RIYADH SAUDI NATION GUARD-U.S. TRAINING CENTER BOMBING.

MOVEMENT FOR THE LIBERATION OF BAHRAIN (MLB). The MLB was an Iranian state-sponsored group of Bahraini Shi'ite Muslims who aimed at toppling the Al Khalifa dynasty in the Emirate of Bahrain and creating an Iranian-style Islamic Republic there. Following the abortive coup attempt of 13 December 1981 by the Iranian-sponsored Islamic Front for the Liberation of Bahrain (IFLB) that group had very limited success in trying to recruit more Bahrainis. While the IFLB turned more to contacting international human rights organizations and trying to accuse the Bahraini government of mistreatment of the arrested coup plotters, the Front had lost credibility as being an independent Islamic liberation movement.

The Movement for the Liberation of Bahrain, formed in 1983, essentially is a repackaging of the IFLB in a form more attractive for the recruitment of young Bahraini Shi'ites alienated from the current Sunni government ruling the largely Shi'ite island-state. Its record so far has not been more impressive than that of its predecessor. In February 1984 the Bahraini coast guard intercepted a large shipment of Iranian arms before it landed. In late December 1987 one oil refinery engineer who had been recruited by Iran and trained to carry out a sabotage operation at Bahrain's one oil refinery was arrested.

MOVEMENT OF THE REVOLUTIONARY LEFT. The Movimiento de la Izquierda Revolucionaria (MIR) was a Chilean leftist guerrilla group and political party sponsored by Cuba that advocated revolution to establish a Marxist state in Chile. The MIR also was given the use of radio facilities by Algeria and received more limited support from other states close to Cuba such as Angola, Mozambique, and Nicaragua during the **Sandinista** period.

Founded in 1965 by leftist students at the University of Concepción, the MIR became Castroite in 1967 and obtained Cuba's moral and material backing. The MIR benefited from an amnesty under the Popular Unity government of President Salvador Gossens Allende (1970-1973) and was allowed to operate openly. The MIR fought the military takeover the hardest of all the Chilean leftist groups even long after it became apparent that Allende was dead.

While the MIR's recourse to political violence and terrorism could be rationalized in the context of the military coup of 11 September 1973 and the subsequent violent repression of leftists in Chile, in fact its terrorist actions began as far back as 1967 when it undertook armed robberies, assaults, and murder as a part of its tactical repertoire. In spite of the wide opportunities for legal political participation under the government of Salvador Allende, the MIR continued to act outside of the sphere of Chilean legality by organizing its own militias, carrying out illegal expropriations of farms and businesses, and assaulting members of rightist or rival leftist groups. The leaders of the MIR reasoned that through such illegal acts they could compel Allende to advance beyond mere electoral politics, so forcing the establishment of a Marxist revolutionary state in Chile. In fact, Allende's reluctance to control the MIR and the far-left wing of his Popular Unity government prompted the Chilean military to undertake the coup of 11 September 1973.

At its height in 1973, the MIR numbered some 10,000 members. Estimates of the total membership of the political and military branches of the MIR put their strength between 100 and 500 members, although its leader in exile, Andrés Pascal, once claimed that the MIR had at least 3,000 active members during the 1980s. The MIR stockpiled its arms through infiltration and theft of Chilean arsenals as well as through Cuban support. In its **bombings**, the MIR used low-yield explosives generally available through thefts from mining operations. Following the killing of the MIR's original leader, Miguel Enríquez, in a shoot-out with security forces on 5 October 1974, Andrés Pascal Allende took command but was forced to flee Chile by 1976. With the killing of Miguel Enríquez the original generation of the MIR's leadership had ended.

From 1974 to 1977 the MIR was relatively inactive but in 1977 the MIR escalated its campaign with Chile largely through more bomb attacks and **assassinated** Colonel Roger Vegara, head of the Army Intelligence School on 15 July 1980. On 24 September 1981 during attempts to set up bases within Chile and to try to create a liberated zone in the Neltume, Valdivia region in southern Chile, seven MIR fighters were killed by police. On 30 August 1983 the MIR assassinated Major General Carol Urzúa Ibañez, military governor of Santiago. With the wave of dissent that shook Chile beginning in 1983, the group was reinvigorated and reestablished its political wing.

The MIR carried out several machine-gun attacks on police and security forces as well as bomb attacks on police stations during the 1980s. On 15 July 1980 the MIR's killers machine-gunned to death Lt. General Roger Vergara Campos, head of the Army Intelligence School, also killing his driver. During October and November 1983 the MIR bombed four U.S.-affiliated firms. In June 1988 the MIR bombed four banks in Santiago, causing serious damage but not harm to life or limb. The MIR tried to **target** higher-ranking functionaries of the Chilean government rather than ordinary policemen or soldiers and was careful to avoid taking the lives of civilians or bystanders. Also the MIR shunned targeting foreign nationals for assassination or **kidnapping** for ransom. Although the MIR bombed four offices of U.S.-affiliated corporations in a 10-day period spanning October and November of 1983, as well as the bank bombings in June 1988, these bombings appeared intended to create maximum material damage rather than human injuries, which were minimal. Bombing attacks were also directed at power lines, but the MIR generally abstained from using car bombings, unlike the rival **Manuel Rodríguez Patriotic Front** (FPRM).

In the late 1980s the MIR's fortunes declined in part due to tactical errors made by its original leaders which resulted in large numbers of miristas being killed or captured in the early part of the Pinochet period, and also due to a lack of finances. However the main blow to the MIR came from the decision of the International Guerrilla Directorate run by Cuba and Nicaragua to stop supporting the MIR in favor of another group, the Manuel Rodriguez Patriotic Front, which initiated its operations on 23 December 1983 with a bombing of a power station that blacked out all of Santiago. The defection of large numbers of *miristas* to this new group further debilitated the MIR.

Despite the appearance of the Manuel Rodríguez Patriotic Front in 1983 as a dynamic rival, the MIR remained the foremost underground revolutionary group within Chile as late as 1986. However by 1987 the

MIR had split into two hostile factions and experienced a severe decline in membership and activities. Many MIR activists had left Chile by 1989, while in December 1989 Brazilian police cracked a kidnapping ring run by the MIR in São Paulo used to finance its activities in Chile. On 4 September 1989 the Eleventh of September Commando (*see* MARTYRS' AVENGING GROUP) had assassinated Jécar Neghme, the leader in exile of one of the MIR factions.

By 1990 many of the *miristas* decided to end armed conflict in the post-Augusto Pinochet period and instead to become another leftist party and to work with other leftist groups in democratic electoral competition. The remaining militant *miristas* broke up into a number of factions which were effectively neutralized by security forces, one by one, from 1992 to 1995 until all violence by militant *miristas* had essentially ceased. Several *miristas* left Chile to fight with the **Túpac Amaru Revolutionary Movement** (MRTA) in Peru while others joined the **National Liberation Army** (ELN) in Colombia and others eventually joined up with the **Zapatistas** in Chiapas, Mexico. In July 1995 a militant MIR faction carried out an armed robbery of a factory in Los Angeles taking 45 million pesos but an intensive police search led to the arrest of the leader of the group, José Muñoz Alcoholado, who afterwards jumped bond and fled to Spain. Later the National Antiterrorism Directorate of Peru informed Chilean officials that Muñoz had appeared for awhile in Peru where he had joined forces with the Túpac Amaru group but later went to Colombia where he joined up with the National Liberation Army (ELN). From 1995 onward there has been no further violence actions by remaining *mirista* factions.

See also TÚPAC AMARU REVOLUTIONARY MOVEMENT.

MUERTE A SECUESTRADORES (MAS). The "Death to Kidnappers" group was a nonstate **death squad** run by Colombian drug traffickers for the limited purpose of countering and containing their main enemies, namely Colombian leftist revolutionaries, politicians, and the Colombian state. The drug traffickers' alliances with leftist rebels against the government, or with right-wing elements in the security forces against leftist revolutionaries, have been purely tactical in nature and intended by the drug traffickers at preserving their relative autonomy in a fractured and weak Colombian state.

MAS was founded in December 1981 by drug traffickers Carlos Ledher Rivas and Jorge Luís Ochoa Vásquez. The leader of the Medellín drug cartel, Pablo Escobar Gaviria (d. 1993), was also believed to be among the patrons of MAS. This group was originally directed particularly against guerrilla groups, such as **M-19**, that had been **kidnapping** drug kingpins for ransom. Eventually it became a right-wing death squad that targeted leftist politicians, students, and other activists. MAS is believed to function as an umbrella organization for a number of rightwing paramilitary groups of which 128 could be identified by 1988.

Although there has been evidence of collusion in the early 1980s between drug traffickers and leftist guerrillas, who shared at least a common enemy in the Colombian government if not a common **ideology**, such a relationship was problematic at best, probably more on the level of mutual extortion than cooperation. By the late 1980s the drug traffickers began attacking the leftists in earnest. On 11 October 1987 Jaime Pardo Neal, a leader of the Patriotic Union (UP) Party, the political front of the **Revolutionary Armed Forces of Colombia** (FARC), was killed by agents of a major drug trafficker. On 22 March 1990 traffickers also **assassinated** UP presidential candidate Bernardo Jaramillo Ossa at Bogotá airport and on 26 April 1990 killed M-19 presidential candidate Carlos Pizarro León-Gómez. Ironically both candidates had opposed **extradition** of narcotics traffickers to the United States. MAS is also suspected of perpetrating the January 1989 killings of 12 members of a judicial commission investigating death squad activity in Colombia. *See also* COLOMBIAN COCAINE CARTELS

MUJAHIDEEN. The term *mujahideen* (Arabic plural of *mujahid*, "one who engages in *jihad*—struggle for the sake of God") is both a general designation for Muslim fighters engaged in **jihad** but also has been used as the name of various Muslim political and paramilitary groups

1. Afghan Mujahideen—Following the Soviet invasion of Afghanistan in December 1979, those rebel groups that had been fighting the procommunist Kabul regime then undertook to resist and expel the Soviet troops. As they were fighting what could be viewed as a jihad to rid Afghanistan of an infidel invading army, they became generally known as Mujahideen.

The Afghan fighters actually belonged to several different groups often divided along tribal and linguistic lines. Certain of these groups were primarily **Islamic fundamentalist** in character, such as the Hizb-i Islami (Islamic Party) of Gulbiddin Hikmatyar, which received support from Iran, and the Harakat-i Inqilab-i Islami (Islamic Revolutionary

Movement) led by Muhammad Nabi Muhammadi, which received support from the Persian Gulf states. Other Afghan groups, such as the National Liberation Front and the National Islamic Front of Afghanistan, were umbrella organizations that had a more nationalistic than fundamentalist emphasis.

Following the 16 April 1992 collapse of the Najibullah Ahmadzi regime, the more nationalistic Mujahideen factions formed a new government that then began fighting the Islamic fundamentalist Mujahideen led by Gulbiddin Hikmatyar, which in turn laid repeated sieges to, and made rocket attacks upon, districts and government buildings within Kabul.

In May 1996 the factions of Gulbiddin Hikmatyar and President Burhanuddin Rabbani briefly settled their differences to allow Hikmatyar to share power as Prime Minister. In reality Hikmatyar used his own power to continue training Muslim militants in his bases for Islamic militant campaigns elsewhere. Another rival, Abdul Rasul Sayyaf, leader of the Wahhabi party, ran his own training camps for foreign Muslim militants. Due to the unwillingness of the various factions to share power in the government and also due to the lack of discipline of their followers, some of whom began to rob and rape civilians with impunity, the Afghan Mujahideen gradually lost their legitimacy and ultimately were pushed aside by the Muslim seminary students, known as **Taliban**, who wanted to institute an Islamic theocratic state on Wahhabi principles.

By 27 September 1996 the Taliban had seized control of Kabul and two-thirds of the country leaving the northern third still under Mujahideen control. On 10 October 1996 General Abdul Rashid Dostam and Ahmad Shah Massoud set aside their differences to unify their factions against the Taliban. The Taliban and their Mujahideen rivals on 17 April 1998 agreed to set up a commission of religious scholars to govern Afghanistan but this agreement, like its many predecessors, fell through and fighting resumed. Later in 1999 Ahmad Shah Massoud and General Dostam fell out weakening the remaining Mujahideen alliance in the northern part of the country still under their control. Effectively defeated by the Taliban the remaining Mujahideen in the north remained in power there thanks largely to Russian and Iranian aid. On 9 September Ahmad Shah Massoud was killed by **suicide bombers** posing as Arab journalists sent apparently by **Osama bin Laden**. It is now beleived that this **assassination** was meant to strengthen the position of the Taliban in Afghanistan prior to the **World Trade Center and Pentagon Attacks of 11 September 2001**.

2. Saziman-i Mujahideen-i Khalq-i Iran (MKO)—The "People's Mujahideen Organization of Iran" is a nonstate Iranian revolutionary group that undertook armed struggle against the shah's regime to establish an Islamic state. The Iranian Mujahideen were mainly university students who formed an offshoot group from the Iran Liberation Movement, a group led by Mehdi Bazargan, which continued to exist as a token opposition group in Iran until banned on 18 October 1992.

The Mujahideen undertook armed struggle following an abortive revolt instigated by the **Ayatollah Ruhollah Khomeini** in 1963. The group became influenced by the syncretistic quasi-Islamic, quasi-Marxist teachings of the Iranian sociologist, 'Ali Shariati, who had been directly influenced by Frantz Fanon while studying in Paris. On 13 August 1972 they killed General Taheri, the police chief of Tehran, former warden of the Komiteh Prison in which Mujahideen members had been held and tortured and who had also crushed the civilian uprising in Qum during June 1963. On 2 June 1973 they killed U.S. Air Force colonels Turner and Sheafer in Tehran, and in August 1976 they killed three U.S. technicians associated with the U.S. military aid program to Iran. In 1975, however, the group split with a more secularist wing defecting to the **Fedayan-i Khalq**.

While the group participated in the street fighting that brought down the Pahlavi monarchy in 1978-1979 Khomeini rejected their credentials as Islamic revolutionaries due to their refusal to accept his principle of leadership by the Shi'ite *ulama* (specialists of religious law) and also due to the Marxist content they had incorporated into their eclectic understanding of Islam. The Mujahideen allied themselves with the more liberal and nationalistic politicians led by President Abulhassan Bani-Sadr, who, however, was later deposed from the Iranian Presidency by Khomeini on 20 June 1981. Following Bani-Sadr's ouster, the Mujahideen carried out a terrorist campaign against the Khomeini regime. On 28 June 1981 the Islamic Republic Party headquarters was **bombed**, killing at least 72 high-ranking functionaries of the regime. A bomb that killed the next Iranian President, Muhammad Ali Rajai, and Prime Minister Muhammad Javad Bahonar on 30 August 1981 was also believed to be the work of the Mujahideen. The Islamic Republic retaliated with its own campaign of **state terror** against the Mujahideen and their known supporters. In the months that followed, the Mujahideen conducted **suicide bombing** attacks in which individuals would approach Friday Prayers leaders and then detonate explosives hidden on their bodies, killing themselves and their victim. Often a motorcycle driver and passenger team would conduct drive-by machine-gun attacks on government offices. On 8 February 1981, Musa Khiabani, the operational head of the terrorist campaign within Iran, was tracked down and killed by the **Islamic Revolutionary Guards Corps** and the Mujahideen campaign within Iran sputtered into relative insignificance.

Although the Mujahideen had hoped in June 1981 to launch their own revolution against the clerical regime, they made two miscalculations. First, being themselves mainly members of the less traditional, more Western-oriented middle classes, the Mujahideen underestimated the depth of support Khomeini enjoyed among the masses of the more traditional lower classes of society. Second, because they undertook their campaign of antiregime terror during the middle of a national war of self-defense against an Iraqi invasion, their actions were arguably treasonable in spite of whatever the political failings of the regime may have been. In fact, the Mujahideen later accepted the sponsorship of the Iraqi regime, set up bases within Iraq, and deployed their own armed units under Iraqi command against Iranian troops in the warfronts, a move that cost them whatever support they had enjoyed among Iranian nationalists within Iran. The Mujahideen leader, Masud Rajavi, who had fled Iran with Bani-Sadr in 1981, briefly rallied exiled opposition groups in a National Council of Resistance. Over time, however, the Mujahideen degenerated into a cult of personality centered on Rajavi, which enforced a rigid **ideological** conformity on its membership and alienated the support of most of its allies and sympathizers.

On 5 April 1992 five MKO members took over the offices of the Iranian UN Mission and vandalized it. No injuries occurred and the five submitted to arrest by the FBI and were charged with violations of the applicable sections of Title 18 of the U.S. Code pertaining to protection of diplomatic persons and their property. Although this event was largely ignored then in fact it was one of the most serious incidents of international terrorism that had occurred in the United States up to that date.

In April 1994 the U.S. Department of State added the MKO to its list of international terrorist groups, a move that drew a hostile reaction from 100 members of Congress who demanded that the State Department justify its designation of this group, which had been actively lobbying Congress and portraying itself as a democratic opposition to the Iranian regime. Accordingly on 31 October 1994 the U.S. Department issued a report identifying terrorist actions by the MKO, its previous history of anti-U.S. attacks, its state sponsorship by the Iraqi regime, and its pattern of internal authoritarian rule over its followers and the personality cult of Masud Rajavi. This effectively ended their long-term lobbying effort to gain U.S. backing in their campaign against the Iranian regime.

In September 1997 Iranian jets bombed two MKO bases in Iraq in response to intensified cross-border attacks by the MKO and increased bombings within Tehran and on 3 June 1998 the United States condemned two bombings carried out by the MKO in Tehran in which three persons were killed. On 23 August 1998 the MKO assassinated the former prosecutor, Asadollah Lajavardi, but the assassin was apprehended and later executed on 14 March 1999. On 13 September 1998 MKO sharp-shooters attempted to assassinate Muhsin Rafiqdust, the former Islamic Revolutionary Guards Corps commander who had been appointed by supreme religious leader Ayatollah Ali Khamene'i to head the Foundation for the War-Stricken. On 31 January 1999 MKO claimed responsibility for a mortar attack on the headquarters of the Intelligence Ministry in Tehran.

3. Mujahideen-i Inqilab-i Islami—In March 1979, seven Islamic guerrilla groups that had fought against the Pahlavi regime before and during the Islamic revolution of Iran formed themselves into one militia group, the Mujahideen of the Islamic Revolution (MIR), a nonstate group enjoying Iranian state sponsorship that assisted the Islamic Republic of Iran in both its external revolutionary agenda and its internal repression of dissent. While some of its members had once been part of the People's Mujahideen of Iran (*see* above, subheading 2), the new group steadfastly avowed its belief in the leadership of the Shi'ite clergy, in particular the leadership of Ayatollah Khomeini.

This group was instrumental in the actual takeover of the U.S. embassy on 4 November 1979. The most prominent member of the group was Behzad Nabavi, who served as one of the chief Iranian negotiators in ending the holding of the U.S. hostages and who later became Minister of Heavy Industries in the Islamic Republic. The MIR group were mainly laymen and, while they rejected the quasi-Marxism of the People's Mujahideen, they nonetheless favored the state capitalism and nationalization of basic industries and foreign trade that characterized the more radical wing of the Islamic Republic Party led by Prime Minister Hussein Musavi. The group split into factions, one aligned with the more radical hardliners of the Islamic Republic Party and others supporting the more pragmatic group led by Hujjatulislam Rafsanjani. When the infighting of the group became a scandal, Khomeini recommended that the group disband itself for the sake of revolutionary unity and accordingly on 6 October 1986 the group dissolved itself, as the Islamic Republic Party had done earlier on 2 June 1996. Upon Khomeini's death in 1989, however, the radical factions within the Islamic Republic found their own base of support shrinking and accordingly revived the MIR which functions now in effect as a radical fundamentalist political party.

MUNAZZAMAT AL JIHAD. Also known as "Tanzim al Jihad," or simply as "Jihad," this was the Sunni Muslim fundamentalist group in Egypt responsible for the **assassination** of Anwar Sadat on 6 October 1981. This group was an offshoot of **Tahrir al Islami**, itself an offshoot of the **Muslim Brotherhood**. It is not directly connected with the Shi'ite militia **Islamic Jihad** (*see* HEZBOLLAH) of Lebanon.

The Jihad group is an example of a *salafi* (purist) **Islamic fundamentalist** group, believing it imperative for Muslim societies to return to a purely Islamic state similar to the city-state of Medina in the time of the Prophet Muhammad. Unlike the Egyptian Muslim Brotherhood, salafi fundamentalists, such as Jihad, reject reformism and participation in electoral politics as a means of purifying Islamic society, as being themselves part of the un-Islamic corruptions of contemporary Muslim civilization. That leaves **jihad**, or holy war in the path of God, as the only means to restore true Islam. This group regarded Anwar Sadat as an apostate ruler due to his Westernization programs and to his role in shaping the Camp David peace accords with Israel, itself regarded by them as the absolute enemy of Islam. Therefore, as an enemy of Islam, the religious duty of jihad required them to fight and kill him. Sadat's assassins fully believed that once he was killed the majority of Egyptian Muslims would rise up and finish off the work of overthrowing what they held to be an apostate regime.

Following the assassination of Sadat by Jihad members led by Khalid Islambuli, an Egyptian Army officer and brother of Muhammad Islambuli, who was another Jihad member imprisoned earlier by the Egyptian government, Egyptian security forces arrested remnants of the assassins and other members of Jihad not directly involved. The five main principals were tried and later executed. Jihad activists in Asyut seized the local radio-TV station, several police stations, and the security forces local headquarters. Government forces retook Asyut in two days of heavy fighting, killing 188 of which 54 were government forces.

The leadership of Jihad consisted of **Sheikh Omar Abdul Rahman**, a blind doctor of Islamic religious law at Asyut University, Muhammad Abdul Salam Faraj, the group's leading theoretician and publicist, and Abbud Abdul Latif al-Zumur, a lieutenant colonel in Egyptian military intelligence. At least four percent of Jihad members arrested before Sadat's assassination turned out to be members of the military, police, or intelligence services. In December 1986 about 30 Jihad members, including two Army majors, one captain, and one lieutenant, were arrested for setting up antigovernment combat training centers. In late February 1977 over 17,000 conscripts of the Central Security Police rioted in five provinces as well as Cairo, inflicting $500 million in damages on bars, nightclubs, and luxury hotels, all of which had been **targeted** by fundamentalist radicals, and looting police arsenals of their weapons.

Following the imprisonment of Jihad leader Abbud al-Zumar, a Jihad faction called Tala'a al-Fatah (Vanguard of Victory) led by Dr. Ayman al-Zawahiri, who was in exile, appeared and claimed responsibility for the 18 August 1993 **bombing** attack that wounded Interior Minister Hassan al-Alfi and the 25 November 1993 bombing assassination attempt against Prime Minister Atef Sedky, who escaped injury although one bystander was killed and 18 others wounded. Jihad differs from the **Islamic Group** (IG) insofar as it targets mainly high-level Egyptian officials instead of policemen, Coptic Christians, and tourists and also by its extensive use of car bombs. Al-Zawahiri cosigned the February 1998 **fatwa** sponsored by **Osama bin Laden** authorizing attacks on U.S. citizens worldwide. Al-Zawahiri's group was particularly incensed at joint U.S.-Egyptian efforts to identify and to expel their followers in Great Britain, Italy, South Africa, Albania, and Azerbaijan.

Following the **Luxor Temple massacre** on 17 November 1997 both Sheikh Omar Abdul Rahman and Abbud al-Zumar issued an appeal to their Jihad followers and members of the Islamic Group to cease violence and to work to form a "peaceful front" to confront the Egyptian government.

MUNICH MASSACRE. On 5 September 1972 a group of **Black September** terrorists attacked the Israeli Munich Olympic Games team in the Olympic Village, killing two Israeli athletes outright and taking the remaining nine Israeli athletes and coaches hostage. The eight terrorists demanded the release of 234 prisoners in Israel, including Kozo Okamoto, the surviving **Japanese Red Army** member of the terrorist team that had struck Lod airport in May 1972. After 17 hours of negotiations between the terrorists and the West German government, which Israel had informed of its refusal of the terrorists' demands, the terrorists and their hostages were transferred in two helicopters to Fürstenfeldbruck airport outside Munich where, they were told, a Boeing 727 would take them to Cairo. Instead Bavarian police sharpshooters botched an attempt to kill the terrorists as they left the two helicopters. In the melee that ensued at about midnight on 6 September 1972, the terrorists shot their hostages dead and set the two helicopters on fire. Five of the terrorists died as well and their remaining wounded were captured and imprisoned. These, however, were later released in exchange for the release of a Lufthansa passenger plane seized by other Black September operatives on 29 October 1972.

The incompetence of the Bavarian police operation led West Germany to develop an elite antiterrorist squad, the Grenzschutzgruppe-9 (GSG-9), while the Israelis established the Wrath of God covert operations group that tracked down and killed those responsible for the operation.

MUSLIM BROTHERHOOD. The Ikhwan al Muslimin is a nonstate **Islamic fundamentalist** group that seeks to replace existing secular governments in the Muslim world with Islamic regimes under which religious and political affairs would both be governed by the Shari'ah, that is, the traditional canon of Islamic laws. The name is applied to several territorial organizations, e.g., the Egyptian Muslim Brotherhood, the Syrian Muslim Brotherhood, and so on, that are formally independent of one another though all are historically derived from the original Ikhwan founded in Egypt by Hassan al Banna (1906-1949) in 1928. In lands whose governments are either sympathetic or at least not hostile to the Ikhwan, the local organization tends to define its aims and methods in terms of *islah*, reformism, whereas in countries whose governments are hostile the Ikhwan tends to define its mission in Islamic revolutionary terms. Terrorism has been used by the Ikhwan only instrumentally, to achieve their agenda when electoral means or other forms of political participation have been denied to them. Although individual territorial Ikhwan organizations have sought the support of other Muslim governments, whether of religious regimes such as Saudi Arabia or of secular regimes such as Ba'thist Iraq, these amount to little more than tactical alliances with what the Ikhwan may regard as its own strategic enemies.

Hassan al Banna, a primary schoolteacher in Ismailia, founded the Ikhwan to educate young men in the values of Islam and to protect them from seduction by Western values. A brilliant organizer, Banna quickly developed the group into a nationwide network. By 1933 the headquarters were moved to Cairo, and by 1940 the Ikhwan had 500 branches. The political strength of the Ikhwan aroused the fear and jealousy of the ruling Waqf party, which threw Banna into prison briefly in 1941. In 1942 Banna ordered the formation of the secret apparatus of "spiritual messengers" skilled in the "art of death." By 1946 the Ikhwan had 5,000 branches comprising at least 500,000 members as well as 40,000 employed in its secret apparatus. Members of the Ikhwan were to be found even among the teaching faculty of Al Azhar University, which remains the most esteemed Islamic theological school in the Sunni Muslim world and from which students of 22 different Muslim countries brought back home the message of the Ikhwan and began to create new branches of the organization abroad.

During the period from 1946-1947 the Ikhwan clashed with Waqf supporters in street riots, which led to the December 1948 ban on the organization. That same month the Egyptian Prime Minister Mahmud Fahmi Naqrashi was **assassinated** by Ikhwan members. In reprisal, government agents murdered Banna in February 1949. From 1950 to 1954, the Ikhwan collaborated with the Egyptian Free Officers in overthrowing King Farouk. Conflict then broke out between the Islamic fundamentalist Ikhwan and the secular, modernizing military junta under Gamal Abdel Nasser. With the failure of the 23 October 1954 assassination attempt against Nasser, a ban on the Ikhwan and crackdown ensued in which six Ikhwan leaders were hanged and 4,000 followers arrested.

Following Nasser's death, his successor, Anwar Sadat, pardoned the remaining imprisoned Ikhwan members, allowed the return of those who had fled Egypt in 1954, and allowed limited participation of the Ikhwan in elections. Sadat hoped to co-opt the Ikhwan to bolster his image among the Egyptian public as a believing, religious president. In fact, by 1978 the Ikhwan had infiltrated and co-opted the majority of the 1,000 legal Islamic associations chartered in Egypt and had become the largest legal source of opposition to Sadat's free trade and investment policies as well as to his policy of seeking a separate peace agreement with Israel. Sadat erred also in believing that by indulging a chastised Ikhwan, he could thereby split and weaken the Islamic fundamentalist opposition.

Although the Ikhwan and the more radical, illegal Islamic fundamentalist groups, such as **Munazzamat al Jihad** and **Takfir wal Higrah**, maintained an appearance of mutual disapproval and rivalry, in fact, according to research by American University in Cairo sociologist Sa'adeddin Ibrahim, the Ikhwan functions very much as the generator of these more radical groups and as their legal front organization as circumstances require. In this light, Sadat's assassination less than a month after his 3 September 1981 crackdown on the Ikhwan appears less coincidental as does also the fact that the same radical groups that did not hesitate to murder a former Minister of Religious Affairs or Sadat himself have never attacked or killed members of the Ikhwan despite their appearance of rejecting the Ikhwan for having allowed itself to be co-opted by the same abhorred regime. By the late 1980s the Ikhwan was Egypt's leading opposition party, while the other illegal fundamentalist groups had between 70,000 and 100,000 adherents.

On 30 July 1995 the Egyptian government cracked down on 15 prominent members of the Ikhwan, including Sheikh Sayid Askar, the director of public information of Al Azhar University. Also arrested were a former Deputy Minister of Industry, Rashad Nigmeldine, three former members of the Egyptian parliament, a banker, and several public school officials. On 23 November 1995 of 80 Ikhwan members put on trial 54 were sentenced to prison for antigovernment agitation and the Muslim Brotherhood headquarters were shut down. This crackdown was a result of the Hosni Mubarak government's determination that the Ikhwan served as the front and support network for the 3,000 militants engaged in political violence against the regime. Ikhwan supporters believe that this was merely a pretext to keep the group from running candidates in the parliamentary elections scheduled for 28 November 1995.

As the Ikhwan propagated and reproduced itself in other Arab lands, it has shown remarkable adaptation to local circumstances, becoming a political party wherever electoral competition promised power, such as Egypt or pre-1963 Syria, or becoming charitable and educational societies where political competition was more constrained, such as in Jordan or the emirates of the Arabian peninsula. In Tunisia the Ikhwan renamed itself the Hizb al Islami, the Islamic Party, the direct precursor of the **Islamic Tendency Movement**. In Algeria the Ikhwan called itself the Ahl al Da'wa, People of the Call (to faith), which has created the **Islamic Salvation Front** (FIS). In the Gaza Strip and West Bank the Palestinian branch of the Ikhwan formed the Islamic Resistance Movement, known also as **Hamas**, which has played a major role in the *intifada* as well as terrorist attacks in Israel following the September 1993 peace accord.

In Syria, where the Ikhwan have been banned since the Ba'thist coup of 1963, the Ikhwan has attempted to carry out an armed insurgency with occasional major terrorist acts, which have been retaliated against by massive acts of Syrian state repression. Following the military defeat of Syria in the 1967 war with Israel, Ikhwan members from the Syrian cities of Homs, Aleppo, and Hama underwent military training in **Al Fatah** camps in Jordan, which marked the transformation of the Syrian Ikhwan from a party to a paramilitary movement. Following Syrian President Hafez al-Asad's decision in 1976 to enter the Lebanese civil war on the side of the Maronite Christian forces and against the Palestinians, the Ikhwan decided to undertake jihad against the Syrian regime. In February 1978 the Ikhwan assassinated key Ba'thist officials and attacked Rifaat al-Asad, the president's younger brother, who headed the national security forces. On 16 June 1979 the Ikhwan began to strike at police stations, Ba'thist party offices, and government and military facilities, beginning with a massacre of military cadets at the Aleppo Artillery School. The Ikhwan also began to assassinate Soviet civilian and military advisers and Sunni clergymen who supported the regime.

In April 1980 al-Asad launched a crackdown on the front organizations that supported the Ikhwan and arrested 5,000 supporters. On 25 June 1980 the Ikhwan attempted to assassinate al-Asad. In reprisal the Syrian regime summarily executed as many as 300 imprisoned Ikhwan leaders and passed a decree on 7 July 1980 making membership in, or association with, the Ikhwan a capital offense. On 11 August 1980 the regime summarily executed all 80 apartment dwellers from a complex that had harbored an Ikhwan sniper. The Ikhwan had goaded the regime into such repressive measures in the hope that the Syrian people would then rise up against regime repression, but the severity of the **state terror** had the opposite effect of quelling all open support for the Ikhwan.

The Ikhwan ceased activities for one year to reassess strategy and tactics. They published a manifesto, "The Declaration and Program of the Islamic Revolution in Syria," and sought Iranian support. Iran, which had a tactical alliance with Syria against its current wartime enemy Iraq, declined its support. The Ikhwan then turned to Iraq for support and obtained light arms and shoulder-held rockets as well as the use of Iraqi radio facilities. On 28 November 1981 a massive car **bombing** killed 64 people in downtown Damascus, an action blamed on the Ikhwan by Syria but for which the Ikhwan denied responsibility. Iraqi agents had conducted similar operations in Tehran even before the outbreak of the Iran-Iraq war. In February 1982 the Ikhwan launched its offensive in Hama in which they defeated the Syrian Third Armored Division. The Iraq-based radio called on the Syrian people to rise up and join the insurgency. Al-Asad responded by sending 12,000 soldiers who cordoned off Hama, a city of 200,000 people, and began to level it over a two-week period by tank fire, artillery, and helicopter gunship fire. The Syrian army lost 1,000 men while as many as 25,000 civilians perished.

The Syrian Ikhwan have never regained their strength since this defeat. While they had 30,000 members before the 7 July 1980 decree banning membership in the group on pain of death, their numbers fell afterward to less than 5,000.

The various Ikhwan organizations have had histories of using assassination, military attacks, and **arson** or bombing of bars, nightclubs, or hotels as means to force Muslim states to heed their agenda when they have otherwise been repressed by those governments or else denied full political participation. In the period from 1990-1991, while Muslim states such as Jordan, Algeria, and Tunisia have allowed greater scope to electoral and parliamentary processes, the Ikhwan-generated Islamic political parties have scored impressive electoral victories. In this regard one should note that political violence and terrorist actions have erupted in Algeria and Tunisia only after the secular governments there have taken steps to nullify the electoral gains of such groups. In the same period the various Ikhwan organizations have sought more coordination and mutual assistance. Following the Tunisian government's crackdown on the Islamic Tendency Movement, the government of Sudan, now dominated by Ikhwan members, gave the leader of the Tunisian group refuge. The Ikhwan-dominated Sudanese government has also allowed **Iranian Islamic Revolutionary Guards** and Lebanese **Hezbollah** to set up training bases in Sudan while the Islamic Republic of Iran has declared its support for the Ikhwan-based political parties in Algeria and Tunisia, which were denied electoral victories in 1991.

In Jordan, following the conclusion of formal peace with Israel in 1994, the Ikhwan group there undertook measures to oppose normalization of relations with Israel by drawing up a "blacklist" of about 300 Jordanians accused of "consorting with the enemy" by visiting Israel and engaging in trade, artistic exchanges, and tourism between the two nations. These persons and associated firms were to be economically boycotted by Ikhwan followers. The vocal dissent of the Ikhwan increased toward the end of King Hussein's life and the period of succession of King Abdullah during which time Jordanian officials have relaxed some of their restrictions on expressions of dissent.

- N -

NARCO-TERRORISM. Narco-terrorism refers actually to two different phenomena: first, a form of revolutionary terrorism in which insurgents or terrorists use the production of narcotics to finance their revolutionary activities or else as a means of undermining the social fabric of the United States and promote instability in the countries where they operate; second, a form of **entrepreneurial terrorism** in which the drug traffickers themselves use terrorism to keep governments, police forces, or guerrilla groups from interfering with their operations or profits.

Evidence of the entrepreneurial narco-terrorism is quite striking, with the Medellín drug cartel sponsoring the "Death to Kidnappers" group (*see* MUERTE A SECUESTRADORES) as well as the "Extraditables." These groups **assassinated** three Colombian presidential candidates and have carried out several car **bombings** and also have bombed at least one domestic Colombian airplane flight, to force the Colombian government to desist from its antidrug campaign. Evidence of guerrilla involvement with drug trafficking can be found in Colombia, Peru, and Thailand where guerrilla insurgents control areas of drug crop cultivation or smuggling.

Demonstrating that guerrillas aid and abet drug trafficking to corrupt North American society is not quite so straightforward. The simplest explanation consistent with the known facts would seem to be that guerrillas will use whatever resources are available to them, whether extortion or **kidnapping** or drug trafficking, to finance their revolutionary agenda. Similarly, certain of the Afghan **Mujahideen** groups have participated in the manufacture and smuggling of heroin derived from Afghani opium but did so without regard for their own Islamic scruples against narcotics and without regard for the ultimate markets of these drugs, which were more likely to be found in the West than in the Soviet Union. While this line of reasoning suggests that narco-terrorism by guerrilla groups need not be truly revolutionary in its intent, the terrorism researcher Rachel Ehrenfeld has documented several instances of what are purported to be narco-terrorism as a form of revolutionary terrorism meant to undermine capitalist societies. *See also* COLOMBIAN COCAINE CARTELS.

NARODNA OBRANA. *See* BLACK HAND.

NARODNAYA VOLYA. The Russian People's Will group was among the earliest self-consciously revolutionary terrorist groups of the modern era. They sought to **assassinate** high-ranking Tsarist officials to bring about a social and political revolution in Russia. This group also embraced the idea of using **suicide bombing** attacks if necessary to achieve their goals but were also very careful to avoid killing innocent bystanders unnecessarily. Narodnaya Volya theorist Gerasin Romanenko argued the moral superiority of terrorism over mass revolution on the grounds that terrorism avoided the massive bloodshed certain to accompany any mass uprising. Narodnaya Volya also argued that terrorism was impermissible in democratic countries as political activists there had nonviolent means to seek social progress or redress of social wrongs. Unlike current terrorist groups which disavow being "terrorists" but instead claim to be "freedom-fighters," and the like, the Narodnaya Volya frankly avowed that they were terrorists.

From 1878 to 1881 this group assassinated the governor-general of St. Petersburg and also the head of the internal security branch of the Tsarist secret police. The group actually made eight assassination attempts against Tsar Alexander II before finally succeeding in a ninth attempt on 1 March 1881. Shortly afterward most of the 50 or so members of the group were arrested and the principal leaders hanged in public. This ended the group although later groups assumed its name.

NATIONAL FRONT. This is the name of at least two political parties, one in Great Britain and another in France.

1. British National Front—A political party of British fascists founded in 1967 with the aims of impeding nonwhite immigration to Britain, opposing leftists and Jews, and seeking to create a racialist and corporatist state in Britain through a combination of political violence and electoral competition. From 1972 to 1977 the ranks of followers of the National Front expanded greatly due to a British backlash against a heightened increase in black Caribbean, East Indian, and African immigration from former colonial possessions. In the 1974 general election, the Front averaged 3.1 percent of the vote and by 1977 gained 5 percent of the votes in Greater London's local council elections.

The Front achieved its mobilization of racist votes partly through its strategy of holding marches through predominantly nonwhite urban districts. Youths from **skinhead** gangs would use these occasions to bait nonwhites and commit acts of vandalism. These marches also attracted radical leftist counterdemonstrators. Racial riots often broke out as well as clashes between the rightists and leftists.

While the National Front became the largest and most successful of Britain's fascist groups, personal rivalries and disagreements over the group's fundamental strategy rendered it largely ineffective. In 1979, the National Front leader Martin Webster (1943-) was convicted of inciting racial hatred, while a former Front chairman, Kenneth Matthews (1935-), was sentenced to six years in prison for attempted **arson** of a leftist newspaper office.

2. French National Front—The Front National (FN) is the leading active ultra-right party in France today with about 50,000 members. Its leader, Jean-Marie Le Pen (1929-), won 15 percent in the April 1995 presidential election. Since June 1995 the Front has held mayoralties in three cities in southern France: Orange, Marignane, and Toulon. In the June 1997 general election the Front polled 15 percent of the vote, some 3.8 million voters, but only one candidate won a seat in the National Assembly, Jean-Marie Le Chevalier from Toulon whose election, however, was declared invalid in January 1998. A pending assault and battery charge against Le Pen raised the possibility that, if he were convicted, he might be barred from running again in elections. Meanwhile there appears to be factionalism among the possible successors.

During the Party's annual convention in March 1997 it hosted representations of several extreme far-right parties from Sweden, Romania,

Serbia, and Hungary, as well as hosting representatives of far right-wing German and Italian groups. Outside of the convention meeting place over 40,000 protestors from Jewish and antiracist groups demonstrated.

NATIONAL FRONT FOR THE LIBERATION OF CORSICA (FNLC).
The Front National de Libération de la Corse, a nonstate ethno-nationalist terrorist group seeking Corsican independence from France, has been active at least since May 1976 when it began a **bombing** campaign in mainland France and in Corsica. Most of its mainland targets have been French governmental offices, banks, or tourist offices connected with Air France, while in Corsica properties belonging to non-Corsicans have been targeted as well. The FNLC conducted six bombings in Paris on 23 April 1980; four bombings in 1981, including an attack causing heavy damages upon the Palais de Justice in Paris; 100 bombings in Corsica on one night alone in August 1982; 20 bombings in Paris in 1983; and 16 bombings in 1984, hitting targets in Paris, Marseilles, and Toulon. In 1985 alone the FNLC was responsible for 96 of the 142 incidents of domestic terrorism in France.

In its bomb attacks, the FNLC has been careful to avoid human casualties, its first known casualties having been caused in 1980 after four years of operations. Following the 1 May 1986 raid by the FNLC on the Cargese Holiday Camp on Corsica, two people were killed and three wounded when the camp owner tried to defuse the bomb the FNLC had left behind. In a previous case, on 22 March 1986, masked FNLC gunmen robbing a tourist resort in southern Corsica evacuated the 20 tourists from the facilities before bombing them so that none of their victims would be hurt. On 11 December 1989 the FNLC destroyed some 40 holiday homes on Corsica under construction for French buyers.

Apart from these bombings the FNLC made one machine-gun attack on French policemen guarding the Iranian embassy on 14 May 1980, apparently in retaliation for the sentencing of seven Corsican separatists that day. On 23 April 1983 French police uncovered two FNLC arms caches and discovered an FNLC counterfeiting operation.

In Corsica during 1995 about 602 bomb attacks were carried out and about 574 in 1996 but many of these were linked to organized crime rather than the FNLC in the view of French prosecutors. On 5 October 1996 the Bordeaux City Hall was bombed and responsibility claimed by the FNLC. A dozen suspects were arrested on 24 October 1996 who were associates of François Santoni, head of the Cuncolta Naziunalista, the FNLC political front. On 9 February 1996 50 bombs were exploded on Corsica by the FNLC. On 2 February 1997 the FNLC exploded 58 bombs between 4:30-5:30 a.m. at 13 post offices, 12 tax offices, several state-run banks, chambers of commerce, two Air France offices, and an office for war veterans. Only one blast occurred in the regional capital of Ajaccio and most occurred in widely separated villages involving perhaps 120 to 150 perpetrators. None of these blasts injured anyone and the FNLC appeared to adhere to a policy of attacking property and symbolic targets but avoiding human casualties.

By 1998 the FNLC had split into at least four groups, some of which abandoned the group's anticasualty policy, and on 6 February 1998 one faction, known as Sampieru, murdered Claude Erignac, the Prefect of the island, by shooting him in the back of his head. About 40,000 of the 250,000 people of Corsica took part in marches on 11 February 1998 to protest the murder of Erignac. This event led the French government to send an elite police security squad of 85 officers to Corsica with instructions not only to crackdown on terrorism but also to clean up various forms of official corruption and private tax evasion. In late September 1999 one of the FNLC factions carried out two bombings against a power station and police station in Propriano and attempted a third bombing against customs officials which failed. No one was harmed in any of these attacks although the last one was intended to kill or main.

The FNLC is not known to have any foreign state sponsorship and little more is known about its political agenda apart from the demand of independence for Corsica.

NATIONAL LIBERATION ARMY (ELN). The Ejército de Liberación Nacional (ELN) is the name of at least two major revolutionary guerrilla groups in Latin America.

1. The Colombian National Liberation Army is a Castroite revolutionary group that enjoyed Cuban state sponsorship. Its main distinction from other Colombian guerrilla groups has been its steadfast refusal to participate in the national reconciliation negotiations ongoing between the Colombian government and other major leftist insurgent groups since March 1984 or to participate in open electoral politics. The ELN has around 5,000 members and consists of several operationally independent fronts, some of which have turned into separate factions. One of these fronts, the Frente Simón Bolívar, even-

tually came to oppose the intransigence of the main leadership of the ELN.

The ELN was established on 4 July 1964 by leftist students disillusioned with the Communist Party of Colombia (PCC) and more attracted to the Cuban Revolution. Throughout its history, ELN has had poor relations with the Communist Party of Colombia which in turn formed its own guerrilla organization, the **Revolutionary Armed Forces of Colombia** (FARC) largely to counter the ELN initiative.

Although the ELN began with Cuban material and moral support, in 1968 due to Soviet pressure on Cuba to cease support for Colombian guerrilla groups, the ELN experienced a hiatus in activity and its membership fell to around 80. In 1969 it began to finance itself through a series of **kidnappings** for ransom and by bank robberies. From 1969 until 1973 the ELN was considered the most effective of Colombia's guerrilla groups until military antiinsurgency efforts destroyed its support network in the cities. Following 1975 the ELN reemerged and by the late 1980s numbered around 500 to 1,000 combatants. From 1988 to 1995 it became the most active terrorist group in Colombia, until recently the FARC resumed their insurgency. The ELN's main area of activity has been in the eastern plains of Colombia.

Some of the ELN's more noteworthy actions include the following: On 6 October 1975 the ELN killed the inspector general of the Army, Ramón Arturo Rincón Quiñones. On 21 January 1976 they **bombed** the Spanish embassy in Bogotá. During July 1983 the ELN conducted a bombing campaign called "Operation Free Central America" in which the Salvadoran Consulate in Medellín and police stations in Aranjuez were struck. On 23 November 1983 the ELN kidnapped Dr. Jaime Betancur Cuartes, the brother of the Colombian president. This action, as well as ELN reluctance to undertake peace talks with the government, drew forth a rebuke from Fidel Castro, who persuaded the ELN to release Dr. Cuartes three weeks after his capture.

Although the ELN gained publicity from having recruited the Catholic priest Fr. Camilo Torres Restrepo, a member of a prominent Colombian family who was killed in guerrilla warfare in 1966, and although another priest, Fr. Manuel Pérez Martínez, became an ELN leader, there is no evidence that the group's secular **ideology** owes any of its inspiration to **liberation theology** whose emergence it antedates by several years. Actually the ELN has been active in **targeting** religious groups or figures of whatever denomination that they view as being politically conservative or aligned with U.S. "imperialism." In October 1987, in addition to bombing a naval facility in Barrancabermeja, the ELN bombed three Mormon churches in Boyaca. In October 1989 the ELN killed the Catholic bishop of Aracua.

The ELN has tried to destroy systematically the economic infrastructure of Colombia. In December 1986 they attacked U.S.-associated oil production facilities, destroying machinery and stealing explosives. During January to August 1987 the ELN bombed petroleum pipelines, and attacked oil exploration and drilling camps, as well as other U.S.-Colombian targets. These attacks serve the twofold purpose of protesting the foreign presence in the Colombian economy and of depriving the government of economic viability. Attacks on the petroleum-producing facilities cost the Colombian government $400 million in 1988 alone. In June 1989 an ELN bombing of the pipeline terminal in Coveñas, Sucre Department, temporarily halted oil exports from that port.

Although the ELN remained one of the most active of Colombian guerrilla groups in the late 1980s, its relative prominence was due more to the reduced activity of the other major leftist groups, which chose to take advantage of the truce of May 1984 and to participate in the open political arena until 1995 when the FARC withdrew from the political arena and resumed its operations. Currently the ELN with 5,000 fighters is second place only to the FARC which now has 15,000 fighters active.

The ELN apparently ran afoul of the new President of Venezuela, Hugo Rafael Chávez Frías, elected on 6 December 1998. Since Chávez was the former leader of the far-left Bolivarian Revolutionary Movement both the FARC and the ELN expected him to support their insurgency. In fact Chávez allowed the ELN's second-in-command, Antonio Garcia, a safe haven in Maracaibo just across the border from Colombia. However, in March 1999 the ELN erred tactically in persuading a criminal gang to hand over a Caracas businessman whom they had kidnapped. When the ELN ransomed him back to his family for several million dollars this scandalized Venezuelan public opinion and disillusioned Chávez, who threatened to use the Venezuelan military against ELN forces operating from within Venezuelan territory.

2. The Bolivian National Liberation Army was an umbrella group embracing the **Nestor Paz Zamora Commando** and other minor Bolivian leftist groups. The original Bolivian ELN was the group founded and led by **Ernesto Che Guevara** in Bolivia from November 1966 to October 1967, which was routed and destroyed by Bo-

livian troops trained by U.S. counterinsurgency advisers. Little is known of the current ELN apart from the activities of the Nestor Paz Zamora Commando. The tactics and rhetoric of the group suggest that, like the original ELN, the current one may be a foreign-directed group imported into Bolivia rather than a true domestic phenomenon. In this case the **Túpac Amaru Revolutionary Movement** appears to be the primary sponsor of the ELN. On 10 October 1990, the 23rd anniversary of the announcement of Che Guevara's death, the Nestor Paz Zamora group bombed the U.S. embassy Marine guards residence in La Paz. Numerous threats were made against the U.S. embassy through 1991 in the name of the ELN, while a fake bomb was found in an elevator in the U.S. embassy in April 1991. Following 1993 this group has remained inactive.

NATIONAL LIBERATION FRONT OF ALGERIA (FLN). The Front de Libération Nationale was an Algerian nationalist party that engaged in guerrilla warfare and terrorist attacks on the French colonial government to obtain independence for Algerian Arabs. Founded on 1 November 1954, the FLN fought both an urban guerrilla terrorist campaign in Algiers and dominated large areas outside the cities. The FLN also conducted **assassinations** of procolonial Algerian Arabs and a **bombing** campaign within France during August-September 1958. Egypt and Syria provided funds and arms while Tunisia and Morocco also provided sanctuaries and bases after those states had achieved independence in 1956.

France reacted to FLN activities with massive reprisals and systematic torture of Arab suspects, which further alienated Algerian Arabs from colonial rule. About 1,200 FLN urban guerrillas contested French control of Algiers in the "battle of Algiers" for the first eight months of 1957. The French crushed this insurrection ruthlessly, but at the cost of alienating the noncombatant Arab population. By 1958 around 87,000 Algerians, 10,000 of them noncombatants, had been killed as opposed to 8,700 French, of which 1,500 were civilians. After assuming power, President Charles de Gaulle decided in 1959 to hold negotiations with the FLN to grant Algerian Arabs self-rule and eventual independence. This prompted a strong reaction from the French settlers in Algeria and certain military officers who formed the Secret Army Organization (**OAS**), which terrorized both Arab Algerians and the French government with bombings and assassinations both in France and Algeria.

France agreed on 5 July 1962 to put Algerian independence to a referendum vote in September 1962 in which 91 percent voted for independence. The FLN became the single official state party. Internal divisions led to purges within the FLN, which adopted secularist and socialist policies. During the FLN's domination, Algeria has provided **sanctuary**, facilities, and training bases to various terrorist or insurgent groups, such as the **Basque Fatherland and Liberty** (ETA) group, the Chilean **Movement of the Revolutionary Left** (MIR), the **Quebec Liberation Front** (FLQ), and Polisario, as well as financial and moral support for the **Palestine Liberation Organization**, (PLO).

The FLN ceased to be the only legal party with the adoption of a new national constitution on 23 February 1989 allowing a multiparty system. In the first freely contested elections held in Algeria since independence, however, the FLN was defeated in provincial and municipal elections on 12 June 1990 by the **Islamic Salvation Front** (FIS), an **Islamic fundamentalist** party. In the first round of parliamentary elections on 26 December 1991, the Islamic Salvation Front won 188 seats. Remnants of the FLN within the government and armed forces staged an internal coup on 11 January 1992, forcing the resignation of President Chadhli Benjedid, and canceled the runoff parliamentary elections, so denying the fundamentalists a national electoral victory.

NATIONAL SALVATION FRONT (NSF). The NSF was a coalition of Palestinian groups opposed to the 11 February 1985 Amman accords with Jordan agreed to by **Yasir Arafat** and much of the Palestine National Council. These accords would have allowed some political solution to the Palestinian problem with less than full sovereignty or total territorial integrity of pre-1948 Palestine. The Front was formed on 25 March 1985 in Damascus with the **Popular Front for the Liberation of Palestine** (PFLP), the National Alliance, and the **Palestine Liberation Front**, and several other groups opposed to Arafat. Syria and Libya, supporters of the rejectionist elements within the **Palestine Liberation Organization** (PLO), gave their support to the NSF as an organization that could challenge Arafat's leadership and legitimacy within the Palestinian community.

From the viewpoint of Syria's President Hafez Al-Asad the presence of Syrian-sponsored groups within the NSF, such as **al Sa'iqa** and the Fatah-Provisional Command, made the NSF appear to be a potential vehicle for Syrian policy. Also the NSF served to divide and weaken the

PLO, allowing Syria to dominate Lebanon more easily. These calculations went awry with the outbreak of the "war of the camps" on 19 May 1985, when members of **Amal**, a Syrian-sponsored Shi'ite militia, clashed with Palestinian militia members guarding the PLO refugee camps. In the off-again, on-again fighting that lasted until 7 April 1987, over 2,500 people were killed.

The upshot of the war of the camps was that the NSF chose to side with **al Fatah** in defending the Palestinian camps against Amal while Amal itself was weakened. Rather than becoming a vassal of Syria, the NSF was largely dominated by the PFLP while the groups beholden to Syria within the NSF played only a marginal role.

NATIONAL SOCIALIST LIBERATION FRONT (NSLF). The NSLF has been the most violent of the U.S. **neo-Nazi** groups that advocates terrorism and armed revolution to overthrow the United States government. After the 25 August 1967 **assassination** of George Lincoln Rockwell, founder and leader of the American Nazi Party, Rockwell's successor, Matthias Koehl, changed the party name to the National Socialist White People's Party (NSWPP) and undertook other changes that angered Rockwell loyalists. Karl Hand, Jr., and other neo-Nazis who did not accept Koehl as Rockwell's successor broke away from the NSWPP in 1969 to form their own American Nazi party. The NSLF made the older American Nazi party organization the first object of its attacks but later, in the 1970s, turned its energies to attacking leftist organizations, such as the now defunct Socialist Workers' Party. The NSLF is believed responsible for a number of **bombing** attacks against leftist organizations in southern California conducted in the 1970s, including the 4 February 1975 fragmentation bomb attack on the Los Angeles headquarters of the Socialist Workers Party, causing severe injuries to all present.

The group is headquartered in Metaire, Louisiana, and recruits its members heavily from the state and federal prisons, pressure cookers which promote the sort of racial hatreds and tensions that provide both the fertile ground for neo-Nazi **ideology** and those recruits having the skills needed for an organization dedicated to the use of violence and terrorism to achieve its **white supremacist** goals.

NAXALITES. Also known as the People's War Group, the Naxalites are mainly Indian university students of middle-class origin who rejected parliamentary democracy and sought to create a Chinese-style communist revolution in India beginning with guerrilla warfare and a peasant insurgency. This name, which actually has been applied to several Maoist groups active in northern India and West Bengal in the 1960s and 1970s, is derived from the West Bengal village of Naxalbara where these leftists incited a short-lived peasant revolt in 1967. Beginning in 1969 they promoted an "annihilation campaign" directed at landlords, moneylenders, and local policemen against whom the rural peasantry had substantial grievances. When the Naxalite "Red Terror" campaign was carried into Calcutta in 1970, the Indian government responded with its own wave of repression in the period from 1970-1972. Thousands more were arrested during the state of emergency declared in 1975. Many of these were shortly released under an amnesty declared by the Janata government in 1977, which had succeeded Indira Gandhi's government. Naxalite violence resumed briefly with two **bombings** of the Soviet Trade Mission in Calcutta in April 1978; it then diminished during the 1980s, however, being restricted mainly to West Bengal and other rural regions of India.

On 31 January 1997 the Home Minister for Andhra Pradesh state, Madhava Reddy, set forth a seven-point peace proposal for the Naxalites to disarm, allowing them to continue as a political party. However, following an attempted shooting of a Naxalite leader in April 1997, the Naxalites rallied themselves and vowed to continue their armed struggle. During July 1997 the Naxalites began a campaign of threats against local elected officials in Karimnagar and neighboring districts calling on them to resign from their offices. On 9 October 1998 land mines planted by the Naxalites killed 16 policemen and wounded another 15 in the Bastar region of Madhya Pradesh.

While the Naxalite movement has often been compared with **anarchistic leftist** terrorist groups that appeared in the same period, such as the **Red Army Faction** or **Direct Action**, unlike those groups the Naxalites did succeed in mobilizing a class-based constituency of oppressed rural peasants and in instigating an insurgency that went beyond the actions merely of a vanguardist group. In this respect, the Naxalites were more comparable to the **Sendero Luminoso** of Peru, which has similarly mobilized Peruvian Indian communities, although the Naxalites apparently lacked the cohesive leadership and disciplined following that Sendero achieved. Although originally active in West Bengal police actions have reduced their presence there and the group has operated recently mainly in the forested regions straddling the central and eastern states of Madhya Pradesh, Bihar, Orissa, and Andhra Pradesh.

NBC WEAPONS. Acronym for "nuclear, biological, or chemical weapons." *See* WEAPONS OF MASS DESTRUCTION.

NECHAYEV, SERGEY G. (1847-1882). Russian revolutionary and author of the *Catechism of the Revolutionist* written in 1869, which provided the portrait of the ideal terrorist willing to sacrifice everything in devotion to the revolutionary cause. In the *Catechism*, Nechayev advocated the **assassination** of moderate political leaders so that the remaining hardliners would resort to severe repression that would in turn either alienate the public or move them to join the revolutionaries, a line of thought echoed in the writings of **Carlos Marighella** and several other revolutionary terrorists. Nechayev caused a comrade to be killed as part of an internal purge in his own circle of revolutionaries. This discredited Nechayev in the eyes of other revolutionaries while he himself was convicted for the murder and sent to prison where he died of tuberculosis.

NEO-NAZIS. Neo-Nazism is an attempt to revive, rehabilitate, or romanticize the political movement or **ideology** of the Third Reich. Neo-Nazi groups usually advocate overthrowing a constitutional democratic order in favor of a racialist, totalitarian state and rationalize the use of political violence and terrorism to achieve this goal. Two essential Nazi doctrines are, first, the belief in the superiority of an imagined Indo-European racial stock that alone is believed to have advanced human civilization, and, second, the belief in the absolute evil and malice of the Jews, viewed as the corrupters of European civilization.

A number of groups have appeared both within Germany and in other countries that idolize the memory of Adolf Hitler and seek to reproduce his racist and ultranationalistic movement in some form. Such groups are outlawed in Germany under its post-World War II constitutional law as is the display of Nazi memorials and symbols. The German Federal Office for the Defense of the Constitution (Bundesamt für Verfassungsschutz) is charged with investigating and banning groups that seek to revive Nazism. Accordingly many of them assume the guise of student clubs or sporting clubs and usually do not openly display swastikas or pictures of Adolf Hitler. In Germany such groups included the **Action-Front of National Socialists**, the National Democratic Party, and the **Hoffmann Military Sports Group**, all of which are now banned or defunct, though such groups tend to reappear under different names and guises. By 1983 there were an estimated 1,400 known neo-Nazis in West Germany of whom 850 were organized into groups.

Following the reunification of Germany in 1990 the visibility of neo-Nazism in Germany increased dramatically with a marked increase in attacks upon Eastern European immigrants and Romanian Gypsies. During August 1992 over 800 neo-Nazis converged on the Baltic port of Rostock and attacked foreign refugees with firebombs, gunfire, and clubs. German neo-Nazis engaged in 4,500 such attacks on foreigners causing 17 deaths and over 100 injured in 1992 alone. On 13 October 1995 a German court sentenced four neo-Nazis, aged from 18 to 25, to prison terms of 10 to 15 years for **arson** attacks in Solingen which killed five Turkish women in 1993. On 21 March 1996 a neo-Nazi was arrested in Recklinghausen who freely confessed to having murdered five persons including one former neo-Nazi who had become a police informer. The man, identified only as "Thomas L." from the town of Gladbeck, was known to be a member of the 400-strong Free German Workers' Party, an openly antistate neo-Nazi group, and claimed that the Norse god Odin had commanded him to kill his victims.

Gary Lauck, the Lincoln, Nebraska purveyor of Nazi literature and regalia banned in Germany, was arrested when he appeared in Denmark in March 1995 on a German warrant for anticonstitutional activities, **extradited** to Germany in September 1995, and tried and convicted in May 1996. In the course of his trial in May 1996 it was revealed that he had spoken in engagements before junior officers in the German Army on a number of occasions. In December 1997 the German Defense Minister Volker Rühe revealed that Manfred Roeder, the convicted neo-Nazi terrorist of the Deutsche Aktionsgruppen, had given lectures to soldiers and others at an officers' academy in Hamburg in 1995 during the course of which soldiers had been videotaped making the Hitler salute and denigrating Jews. Roeder had been convicted in 1982 as an accomplice in a **bomb** attack that killed two Vietnamese refugees and had been imprisoned until 1990.

According to former neo-Nazi Ingo Hasselbach, young neo-Nazis are undergoing military training in deserted former East German Army training grounds in forests outside Berlin and on the island of Rügen where they learn how to use grenade launchers and automatic weapons.

In February 1998 German police discovered a bomb-making factory in Jena, in the east German state of Thuringia, which Helmut Roewer, head of the Office for the Defense of the Constitution, said denoted a qualitative leap in the level of violence being pursued by neo-Nazi groups in the former East Germany. Electronic mailboxes and devotion to racist rock bands that play on a concert circuit known as "Blood and Honor" help to consolidate feelings of group solidarity among the **skinhead** component of the neo-Nazi underground in Germany. Several neo-Nazis have grown long hair and infiltrated leftist organizations on the orders of their leaders to gather intelligence. Neo-Nazis have also compiled "hit-lists" of 280 German leftists and liberals to be "punished." On 19 December 1998 neo-Nazis bombed the headstone of Heinz Galinsky, the Jewish leader who had survived Auschwitz, who had been buried in Charlottenburg cemetery in Berlin. On the weekend of 2-3 October 1999 neo-Nazis vandalized or overturned over 100 headstones and memorials at the Weissensee Jewish cemetery in Berlin.

In other countries neo-Fascist organizations have developed that may not openly identify with Nazism but have a similar ideology and political program and whose membership contains many neo-Nazis. In Great Britain the **National Front** is an example, while in France the **European Nationalist Fascists** (FNE) is another, whose members include former functionaries of the Vichy regime of Nazi-occupied France.

In the United States the American Nazi party of George Lincoln Rockwell was the most prominent and earliest neo-Nazi group. Its name was changed to the National Socialist White People's Party after Rockwell's **assassination** and later to the New Order. The **National Socialist Liberation Front** is a more militant group that broke away from the National Socialist White People's Party. The National Alliance of William Pierce, a Rockwell disciple, is another neo-Nazi group. The **Order**, also called the Bruder Schweigen, was a neo-Nazi group that grew out of the **Aryan Nations** movement. On 27 February 1996 a North Carolina jury convicted James N. Burmeister, a former private and paratrooper in the Army's elite 82nd Airborne Division, for the murders of a black couple in December 1995. The trial revealed that Burmeister and other enlisted men were members of neo-Nazi and skinhead groups even while serving in the armed forces. An army investigation of racism in the ranks completed in March 1995 revealed that out of 7,600 soldiers interviewed fewer than 100 belonged to **white supremacist** organizations but who were then discharged from the armed services.

Those groups that adhere to the **Identity Christianity** or **white supremacy** doctrines often share beliefs and attitudes virtually identical to those of the neo-Nazis. Such groups include the Aryan Nations, the **Christian-Patriot Defense League**, the **Covenant, the Sword and the Arm of the Lord** (CSA), the **Ku Klux Klan** (KKK,), and the **White Patriot Army**. Very often members of these organizations have been formerly members of neo-Nazi groups, or else continue to hold membership in such groups, or else will join some neo-Nazi group in preference to, or in addition to, membership in these other organizations.

Neo-Nazi groups have tried to coordinate their moves with similar groups both within the United States and elsewhere. The Order donated many of the proceeds of their armored truck robberies to a number of neo-Nazi groups and leaders in the United States. German neo-Nazi groups used to receive financial support and printed materials from American neo-Nazis, such as Gary Lauck. Neo-Nazis have also sought sponsorship from states and groups known to be hostile to Israel. Manfred Roeder, formerly a leader of the neo-Nazi Deutsche Aktionsgruppen, met once with **Yasir Arafat's** deputy, Khalil al Wazir, and even tried to solicit aid from Iran, but without success. The Hoffman Military Sports Group established a cooperative arrangement with **al Fatah**, sending Sports Group members to train in **Palestine Liberation Organization** (PLO) camps.

Another phenomenon closely tied to neo-Nazism has been the skinhead movement. Just as the original Nazis recruited many of their Stormtroopers from the hoodlums and youth gangs of Berlin and other German cities, so too neo-Nazi groups in the United States such as the White Aryan Resistance, are recruiting skinheads. Similar phenomena have been witnessed in Great Britain, where soccer club rowdies as well as skinheads would spontaneously join in **National Front** demonstrations or assaults on Asian or African immigrants, as well as in Germany where soccer clubs also will join with neo-Nazis in assaulting minority members, feminists, or homosexuals. Although Nazism, and Fascism generally, are regarded by believers in the liberal democratic tradition as discredited movements, the existence and apparent vitality of so many neo-Nazi groups throughout the Western world indicates the continuing appeal of this ideology.

Neo-Nazi activities, including violence, have continued in recent years. In February 1995 several pipe-bomb attacks against displaced Gypsies occurred in Oberwart, Austria. Anti-Gypsy attacks and murders also began occurring in Serbia beginning in late 1997. Neo-Nazi underground cells in Austria have joined forces with German neo-Nazis through computer links and continue to be active even though their leader Gottfried Küssel was jailed in 1992 under Austrian anti-Nazi statutes. Ingo Hasselbach, the organizer of the first neo-Nazi party in the former East Germany in 1987-1991, has testified that the various neo-Nazi groups in Europe are reinforced through networks with each other and with American neo-Nazis who provide much of their printed materials that are legally produced in the United States although forbidden in Germany, Austria, and other nations.

On 18 January 1997 Danish police foiled a conspiracy by seven neo-Nazis to conduct a **letter-bomb** campaign against British leftists and sports personalities married to blacks. The arrested leader of the group, Thomas Derry Nakaba, was known to be a member of the British Combat 18 neo-Nazi group, which had carried out bombings of gay bars in London. Denmark's liberal freedom of expression laws has made it a center for German neo-Nazis who send banned Nazi materials to Germany from there.

The fortunes of some neo-Nazi groups and leaders have also suffered declines in recent years. In the United States in May 1996 a federal jury forced William L. Pierce, leader of the neo-Nazi National Alliance in Hillsboro, West Virginia and author of the **Turner Diaries** to surrender $85,000 to the family of Harold Mansfield, an African-American Gulf War veteran who had been murdered in 1991 by George D. Loeb, a member of the **white supremacist** "Church of the Creator" which had ceded title of some of its properties to Pierce to avoid paying civil damages to the Mansfield family. On 17 June 1997 Eugene Terre-Blanche, the leader of South Africa's neo-Nazi Afrikaner Resistance Movement (AWB), was sentenced to six years imprisonment of beating one of his black workers in 1996. On 2 April 1998 a French court in Versailles convicted Jean-Marie Le Pen, the leader of the French **National Front** Party, for having assaulted a French Socialist politician in 1997, for which he was stripped of his civil rights for two years making him ineligible to run for the European parliament in 1999.

NESTOR PAZ ZAMORA COMMANDO. The Comando Nestor Paz Zamora (CNPZ) describes itself as a unit of a **National Liberation Army** (ELN), named after the group of the same name founded and led by **Ernesto Che Guevara** in the 1960s. The CNPZ seeks to overthrow the democratic Bolivian government in favor of a Cuban-style revolutionary Marxist state. The tactics of the group strongly suggest external aid from the **Túpac Amaru Revolutionary Movement** of Peru, itself a beneficiary of Cuban state support.

The CNPZ undertook its first action with the **kidnapping** of Jorge Lonsdale, the president of the Bolivian subsidiary of Coca-Cola, on 11 June 1990 who was held for $500,000 ransom. Lonsdale was killed on 5 December 1990 during a police raid and attempted hostage rescue. On 10 October 1990 the CNPZ bombed the U.S. embassy Marine Guard residence in La Paz, severely damaging the building. This **bombing** was accompanied by a machine-gun attack that killed one Bolivian guard and wounded another.

The CNPZ is named after a former Roman Catholic seminary student who became a leftist guerrilla after the capture and execution of Che Guevara in 1967. Nestor Paz Zamora and his group perished in 1970, reportedly of starvation and exposure while trying to fight the Bolivian army. Ironically Nestor Paz Zamora was the brother of Jaime Paz Zamora, elected president of Bolivia in 1989, who also had been a Roman Catholic seminary student and leftist opponent of the Bolivian government.

While the CNPZ is supposed to be only one group within the umbrella organization of the National Liberation Army, there is little information available about other members of that umbrella group. The CNPZ is thought to have about 100 members and may constitute the bulk of the ELN. After the murder of Jorge Lonsdale, it was learned that his killer was actually an Italian, Michael (Miguel) Northfuster, while another of the guerrillas slain in the rescue attempt turned out to be a Peruvian. The Túpac Amaru group is believed to have extended its operations into Bolivia primarily to expand its fund-raising extortionary activities there and possibly sponsors and controls the CNPZ group. Since 1993 there have been few reports of activity by the CNPZ group.

NETWAR. A form of **low-intensity conflict**, involving actions falling short of conventional warfare and often involving nonviolent as well as violent confrontation in which like-minded protagonists consisting of small groups joined together in a network organization use related doctrines, strategies, and information-age technologies to communicate, coordinate, and campaign in an inter-netted manner without one central command. The contrast is between netwar-oriented groups such as **Hamas**, Mexico's **Zapatistas**, and U.S. "Patriot" or **militia movement** groups, which consist of meshes of like-minded but independent groups, and their more traditional counterparts such as the **Palestine Liberation Organization** (PLO), Castroite groups, and the **Ku Klux Klan** (KKK). Another aspect of netwar is the use of sympathetic groups in civil society to mount "swarming" campaigns of e-mail messages, FAXes, and other communications in support of affiliated groups involved in more violent activities. As an example in a netwar campaign some animal rights activists could be involved in actual attacks on research labs or mink farms, while others would be involved in nonviolent protests in front of fur shops or butcher shops, while others would be bombarding the offices of members of Congress with letters and e-mail messages denouncing the fur industry or research involving animal subjects while yet others could be involved in trying to incapacitate the Web site of a fur industry group by bombarding them with thousands of e-mails.

Analysts distinguish between social netwar, which involves interest group activities in civil society, and criminal netwar and terrorist netwar, which represent new challenges to law enforcement and national security. *See also* INFORMATION WARFARE; ORGANIZATION OF TERRORIST GROUPS.

NETWORKS. *See* ORGANIZATION OF TERRORIST GROUPS.

NEW AFRIKAN FREEDOM FIGHTERS (NAFF). The NAFF was a leftist black American group that aimed to undertake armed revolution to create an independent black homeland within the United States. This group was an offshoot of the Republic of New Afrika, a black nationalist political group that advocated that black Americans establish their own independent black homeland in the southeastern United States.

On 18 October 1984, nine NAFF members were arrested in New York City for conspiracy to rob an armored car and to assist in the prison escape of Nathaniel Burns (aka, Donald Weems), who was convicted for his participation in the October 1981 Brinks armored car attack by the **Revolutionary Armed Task Force** (RATF). FBI investigations revealed that these NAFF members had stockpiled weapons and explosives to be used in the breakout attempt. Evidence emerged that the NAFF had broken itself up into independent cells to carry out robberies and terrorist actions while connecting themselves to front organizations for support.

The NAFF activists were based in New York City and differed from the Republic of New Afrika activists in their commitment to aid in the creation of a socialist republic in what is now South Africa. The Republic of New Afrika sought, in addition to creating an independent black homeland in North America, reparations from the U.S. government of $10,000 for each black American for past injustices. Another subgroup of the Republic of New Afrika was the New Afrikan People's Organization, which sought to create a socialist republic in the future independent homeland but which believed armed struggle was necessary to achieve this goal. Since the end of the apartheid regime and the election of Nelson Mandela as President of South Africa on 10 May 1994 the membership of this group has declined.

NEW ARMENIAN RESISTANCE. *See.* ARMENIAN SECRET ARMY FOR THE LIBERATION OF ARMENIAN; JUSTICE COMMANDOS OF THE ARMENIAN GENOCIDE.

NEW PEOPLE'S ARMY (NPA). The Communist Party of the Philippines, Marxist-Leninist (CPP-ML) founded the NPA in 1969 as its armed wing to carry out protracted armed struggle to overthrow the current constitutional government in favor of a "people's democratic state." Chinese sponsorship of the NPA ended in 1976, and following some retrenchment, the group began to grow again by 1982, financing itself through extortion and arming itself by raids on police and army units. While the NPA is the armed wing of the outlawed CPP-ML, it has established its own legal political front, the National Democratic Front, which operates openly in Manila. Since 1987 the head of the CPP-ML, Jose Maria Sison, has been residing in the Netherlands. Despite an attempted legal challenge to his political refugee status Sison continues to direct the CCP from Utrecht. Among other things in 2000 Sison filed a civil lawsuit before the U.S. Supreme Court against the estate of former President Ferdinand Marcos and was active in 2001 in the political campaign to unseat President Joseph Estrada. The NPA is estimated to have 18,000 to 20,000 members and a much larger support network.

While originally a rural guerrilla insurgency following Maoist precepts of guerrilla warfare, in recent years the NPA has involved itself increasingly in urban operations and in **entrepreneurial terrorism** in **targeting** foreign investors and contract workers for extortion or else for **kidnapping** to gain ransom. The more purely revolutionary terrorism of the group is seen in the operations of its **death squads**, called "Sparrow Squads," who murder Filipino politicians, military figures, policemen, government collaborators, and members of the news media who criticize the NPA. These actions are meant to drive foreign investment out and to provoke the government to undertake repressive measures that would discredit it with the Filipino population. Prior to the 1992 closing of Clark Air Force Base and the Subic Bay U.S. Naval facility, the Sparrows had also targeted U.S. servicemen. Within those parts of central and northern Luzon island where the NPA controls rural areas and villages as well as within the ranks of NPA members and supporters, the organization also practices its own repressive terrorism, having imprisoned, tortured, or executed some 1,000 of their own ranks in recent years.

Since 1987 there has been a marked upswing in NPA terrorism. The growth and success of the group is in part due to the neglect of the countryside and corruption experienced during the Ferdinand Marcos regime as well as the difficulties of the Cora Aquino administration in presiding over the transition to a democratic order. The marked increase in NPA terrorism since 1987 may be due to the NPA exploiting a unique historic opportunity afforded by the instability accompanying the transition from dictatorship to democracy. Such an explanation may account for increased NPA terrorism directed at others but does not so readily explain the upswing in the NPA's internal purges and disciplining of its own members. This increased internally directed terrorism may be an attempt to quell dissent within the NPA ranks over the proper goal and strategy of the NPA in the post-Marcos era.

From 1974 to 1991, the NPA conducted at least 56 noteworthy actions of which 23 were **assassinations**, eight were **bombings** or **arson**, five were kidnappings, four were armed attacks, while the remaining 16 were threats not followed by any fulfilling action. Four kidnappings were for ransom, while a kidnapping of a South Korean contractor on 10 November 1987 was undertaken to force the Philippine Army to remove units from a certain region. Certain of the bombings and arson attacks against foreign-owned farms and factories also may have been retaliation for refusal to pay extortion money.

Except for the shooting deaths of three servicemen at Subic Bay on 13 April 1974 and a few sniping and mortar attacks on the Voice of America transmitting station in the Tinang area, there had been virtually no attacks on Americans until 28 October 1987 when two U.S.

servicemen, one retired U.S. serviceman, and a Filipino retired from the U.S. armed forces were gunned down by Sparrow Squads. On 15 April 1987, the NPA had announced that it would deploy the Sparrow Squads to kill U.S. military personnel or diplomats involved in the Philippines counterinsurgency program, but none of those killed on 28 October fit that description. On 21 April 1989 Sparrows shot dead U.S. Army Colonel James Rowe while he was driving to work in Manila. On 26 September 1989 the NPA murdered two U.S. Defense Department civilian workers outside Clark Air Force Base. On 6 March 1990 an American rancher was murdered for refusing to pay the NPA extortion money. On 13 May 1990 two U.S. Air Force airmen were shot dead by NPA gunmen near Clark Air Force Base.

During 1991, the Philippine government captured over 80 ranking members of the CPP-ML and the NPA, including Romulo Kintanar, head of the NPA General Command. These arrests and the successful convictions of the murderers of Colonel Rowe set back the terrorist operations of the NPA for most of that year.

Following the withdrawal of U.S. forces from the Philippines after 1991 there was a hiatus in NPA activities and its political arm, the CPP, conducted intermittent peace talks with the government. In 1997 the NPA broke off talks with the government and began several small-scale attacks on police and army troops. In May 1997 NPA guerrillas ambushed a vehicle and killed two Filipino employees of a U.S. firm. Throughout 1998 the NPA conducted a series of attacks on rural police posts across the Philippines. In June 1999 the NPA again broke off recently resumed peace talks with the government in protest against the government concluding a Visiting Forces Agreement with the United States allowing joint U.S.-Filipino military training exercises. Although the NPA claimed it would attack only American forces on many occasions it attacked government security forces.

Despite the setbacks of the early 1990s, the NPA has shown itself to be one of the few leftist insurgencies that is still actively growing, despite the demise of communism throughout the rest of the world, and through its urban terrorism it continues to pose a significant threat to the stability of the current democratic government in the Philippines.

NEW WORLD LIBERATION FRONT (NWLF). The New World Liberation Front (NWLF) was a nonstate Californian leftist group active in the 1970s that engaged in **bombings** for the limited purpose of protesting against corporate power. The NWLF declared that it sought relief for poor people and "to demonstrate that, in unity through armed struggle, poor people can and will win." The Front later also declared its support for Puerto Rican separatists.

The Front was founded in 1973 in the San Francisco Bay area and began its career in 1974 with a series of bombings against the International Telephone and Telegraph company to protest that firm's alleged involvement in the coup toppling the Allende government in Chile. The NWLF continued its bombings with numerous attacks against other public utilities and private firms, including General Motors, Standard Oil, Pacific Gas and Electric Company, and the Union Oil Company. By 1979, the NWLF had carried out almost 100 bombings in the San Francisco Bay area.

Like many other left-wing groups, such as the United Freedom Front or Armed Resistance Unit, the NWLF tended to pick symbolic **targets** for bombings, to target property rather than human life, and to use the terrorist event as **"armed propaganda"** for specific issues or causes rather than as direct military tactics to achieve revolution. Therefore the NWLF used to give frequent press conferences through its front, the Peoples' Information Relay No. 1 (PIR-1). In September 1979, however, the two core members who founded the group quarreled, leading one to murder the other for which crime he was arrested, so ending the NWLF.

NEW WORLD OF ISLAM. This was a Muslim group made up of only black Americans seeking to create a black nationalist separate homeland in the southeastern United States. Since 1978, members of this group have been involved in bank robberies in the northeastern states, 21 of which have been staged in the New York and New Jersey metropolitan areas alone. In May 1985, the group issued a threat that its members would "execute" any police officer they encountered however the group is not known to have engaged in any activities since that time and is likely defunct.

NOVEMBER 17. The Revolutionary Organization of 17 November (Epanastatiki Organosi 17 Noemvri), named for the day in 1973 of an unsuccessful student uprising in protest to the Greek army's coup, is a nonstate Greek leftist group that engages in terrorism to force Greece out of NATO, force the U.S. military presence out of Greece, and oppose imperialism and capitalism. It has no known state sponsorship but appears to work in close concert with the **May 1** and the **Revolutionary Popular Struggle** (ELA) groups, all of which operate within the Athens area. It appears likely that both May 1 and November 17 evolved from the same core membership of ELA, which originally was formed with the revolutionary objective of overthrowing the Greek military junta. In the postjunta period, November 17, and these similar groups, appear more anarchistic in nature, no longer having one governing objective but attaching themselves to revolutionary raisons d'être as these happen to appear.

While both ELA and May 1 have **bombed** U.S. targets, November 17 differed from them in having **assassinated**, or attempting to assassinate, U.S. diplomats and Armed Forces servicemen in Greece. On 23 December 1975 November 17 assassinated CIA station chief Richard Welch. On 15 November 1983 they murdered a U.S. military attaché, Capt. George Tsantes (USN) and his driver. An assassination attempt was made against Master Sergeant Robert Judd on 3 April 1984. Judd took evasive action when he spotted two riders on a motorcycle approaching his car and was only slightly wounded. November 17 has assassinated two Greek police officials, two Greek businessmen, and has wounded one other Greek businessman. On 21 January 1988 they botched an attempted assassination of a U.S. Drug Enforcement Agency (DEA) agent outside his Athens home. An unusual circumstance in all these cases has been that November 17 hit teams all used the same pistol, making verification of November 17 shootings certain. Since 1987 they also started using plastic makeshift bazookas to fire antitank missiles stolen from a military base. On 18 January 1989 they shot and wounded a Greek Supreme Court deputy prosecutor, and on 26 September 1989 they killed a member of the Greek parliament. On 7 October 1991 they shot dead a Turkish embassy press attaché.

Beginning in April 1987 November 17 twice has tried to bomb U.S. military shuttle buses using remotely detonated bombs, injuring 18 people on 24 April 1987 and another 10 on 10 August 1987 but causing no deaths. Previously on 26 November 1985, a similar bombing had been directed at a Greek police van, in which 12 were injured and one was killed. On 5 October 1987 November 17 and ELA both claimed credit for bombing four Greek government offices. On 28 June 1988 November 17 killed the U.S. military attaché with a car bomb and likewise killed a former Greek minister of public order on 4 May 1989. On 10 June 1990, November 17 claimed credit for firing a bazooka at the

Athens Procter & Gamble office, which caused no injury. A similar rocket attack narrowly missed a Greek businessman's car on 20 November 1990. November 17 used a remote-triggered bomb to kill U.S. Air Force Sergeant Ronald Stewart as he left his apartment on 12 March 1991. On 16 July 1991 November 17 used a remote-triggered car bomb to wound the Turkish chargé d'affaires and two other Turkish embassy workers.

On 15 February 1996 an antitank missile was fired at the U.S. embassy in Athens but struck only the perimeter wall and damaged three parked cars. A group calling itself "National Struggle" claimed responsibility but it bore evidence of being another November 17 attack. On 28 May 1997 November 17 assassinated shipping magnate Constantine Paratikos in broad daylight in Athens and later issued a manifesto claiming that they had **targeted** him due to his threat to close down his shipyard which would have left 2,000 workers unemployed. During the February-April 1998 period November 17 made six rocket attacks on U.S.-owned businesses, including an attack on a Citibank office which prompted FBI Director Louis Freeh to meet with Greek officials in September to discuss ways to improve mutual **counterterrorism** efforts. On 8 June 2000 November 17 assassins on a motorbike killed the British military attaché to Greece, Brig. General Stephen Saunders, as he was driving to work on a main avenue. In a communique released later to an Athens newspaper the group claimed the murder was in retaliation for Great Britain's role in the NATO campaign against Yugoslavia during 1999.

The November 17 group is assumed to be quite small, having perhaps no more than 25 members. Nonetheless it has proved itself to be professional and highly successful in carrying out the relatively few operations it has conducted killing 24 people in 25 years. To date no November 17 member has ever been arrested and very little is known about the organization.

-O-

OAS CONVENTION. The Convention to Prevent and Punish the Acts of Terrorism Taking the Form of Crimes against Persons and Related Extortion that Are of International Significance of the Organization of American States, concluded in Washington, D.C. on 2 February 1971, was originally limited to punishing crimes against diplomats. Much of the convention has been superseded by the United Nations Convention on Internationally Protected Persons, concluded in New York on 14 December 1973, which obliges states to provide protection to diplomats within their territory, to apprehend those who attack diplomats in their territory and either **extradite** them to the nation whose diplomats have been attacked, or to try and punish them themselves. In the event that the attackers escape from the jurisdiction of the state in which the attack occurred then that state is obliged to cooperate with the intelligence and law enforcement officials of the nation whose diplomats have been attacked and to make a good faith effort to determine the whereabouts of the escaped terrorists and to provide that information to the other nation.

OCTOBER FIRST ANTIFASCIST RESISTANCE GROUP (GRAPO).

The Grupo de Resistencia Antifascista, Primero de Octubre was a communist splinter group seeking to overthrow the Spanish state in favor of a Marxist state. GRAPO opposed Spanish membership in NATO and the U.S. presence in Spain. GRAPO had no known state sponsors but once had ties with **Direct Action** and the **Red Brigades**.

GRAPO emerged in 1975 as the military component of the Communist Party of Spain—Reconstituted, an illegal splinter group with Maoist tendencies that split off of the legal Spanish Communist Party. GRAPO was the second major terrorist group in Spain, the other being **Basque Fatherland and Liberty** (ETA). GRAPO finances itself through **kidnapping** for ransom, bank robberies, and exacting extortion payments from individuals and businesses.

From 1975 to 1991 GRAPO carried out 46 noteworthy actions, which can be summarized as follows: 24 **bombings,** killing at least eight and wounding at least 46; seven **assassinations**; seven kidnappings for ransom; four hostage seizures; and four armed attacks.

Bombing attacks have **targeted** foreign businesses, mainly U.S. and French firms, Spanish government offices, and the U.S. Cultural Center in Madrid. Assassinations have killed senior Spanish military officers, the director of penal institutions, the president of the Seville Association of Businessmen, as well as Civil Guardsmen and ordinary police.

More recently GRAPO bombed the Madrid Stock Exchange, the Constitutional Court, and the Economics Ministry on 17 September 1990, wounding six people. GRAPO claimed credit for having bombed parts of the NATO oil pipeline in Spain and also claimed to have bombed a railroad line outside of Madrid. GRAPO leader Juan Carlos Delgado de Codex had been killed in a shoot-out with police in 1979, and by 1991 some 20 GRAPO activists were arrested and fewer than a dozen were suspected to be remaining at large then.

In 1985 GRAPO was one of nine major leftist European **Fighting Communist Organizations**. But by late 1992 it was one of four left, the others being the Revolutionary Organization of November 17 (*see* NOVEMBER 17), Dev Sol (*see* REVOLUTIONARY PEOPLE'S LIBERATION PARTY/FRONT), and the **Red Army Faction**, which issued a communique in August 1992 announcing it would cease its armed struggle. Since late 1992 there have been few reports of activity by GRAPO. *See also* ANARCHISTIC LEFTIST TERRORISM.

OKLAHOMA CITY BOMBING. On 19 April 1995 at 9:02 a.m. a large ammonium nitrate-fuel oil bomb in a rented van exploded outside of the Alfred B. Murrah Federal Building, killing 168 persons and wounding over 500 others, as well as destroying the building. The same day Timothy James McVeigh was arrested north of Oklahoma City on Interstate I-35 near Ponca City for driving without a rear license plate and for weapons violations. On 21 April 1995 McVeigh was charged with **bombing** the Murrah building and on 11 May 1995 Terry Lynn Nichols was charged with the same offense.

Then on 10 August 1995 both men were charged with eight counts of homicide for the several law enforcement officers killed in the blast, one count of conspiracy to use a **weapon of mass destruction** to kill persons, one count of use of a weapon of mass destruction to kill persons, and one count of malicious destruction of federal property. Nichols and McVeigh gathered the bomb-making materials and van while McVeigh alone deployed the bomb. Reports of a third person involved in the attack have never been settled conclusively.

Timothy McVeigh was a loner within the fringes of the right-wing patriot movement. An avid reader of the **Turner Diaries**, a far-right novel about racist "patriots" whose antigovernment revolt was initiated with the **bombing** of a federal building which may have provided the model for the bombing of the Murrah building, McVeigh was incensed by what he considered the criminal actions of the federal government in the siege and burning of the Branch Davidian compound in Waco, Texas, two years earlier on 19 April 1993. The date of the bombing also coincided with the execution date for Richard W. Snell, the **Covenant, the**

Sword, and the Arm of the Lord member who murdered a black Arkansas state trooper in June 1984. McVeigh had convinced himself that his outrage was shared by millions of other Americans and that his attack on the Murrah building would be hailed by many as the signal for a general right-wing revolution against the United States government. In reality, for the first two days following the bombing most news media were pursuing the false lead of a Middle Eastern connection and most Americans were greatly shocked to learn that the main suspect for the most horrific act of terrorism on U.S. soil was in fact a fellow citizen.

On 2 June 1997 Timothy McVeigh was found guilty for the bombing and sentenced to death on 14 August 1997. In early 2001 his execution date was set for 16 April 2001 however, due to legal issues surrounding misfiling of papers related to his defense, the execution date was rescheduled for June 11. Terry Nichols was convicted of conspiracy and involuntary manslaughter on 23 December 1997 and later sentenced to life imprisonment. The incident served to draw public attention to the right-wing **militia movement** and galvanized public demands for more effective legislative and executive actions to counter terrorism. It should be noted that McVeigh was never accepted into membership by the various militias he approached although he did have ties to the Elohim City group in eastern Oklahoma which had ties to the former Covenant, the Sword, and the Arm of the Lord.

OLYMPIC PARK BOMBING. The Atlanta Olympics experienced a pipe **bombing** on 27 July 1996 in the 21-acre Centennial Olympic Park that killed one person outright, wounded 111 others, and caused a foreign journalist to suffer a fatal heart attack. At 12:58 a.m. an unidentified white male with an undistinguished accent called a 911 operator warning that a bomb would explode in the park in one-half hour. Three security guards found the knapsack under a park bench and began clearing the area shortly before it exploded at 1:20 a.m.

On 9 June 1997 the Task Force investigating the Olympic Park bombing announced it was connected with two other bombings, namely the 16 January 1997 bombing of the Atlanta Northside Family Planning Services and the 21 February 1997 bombing of the Otherside Lounge, for which credit was claimed by the **Army of God**. While the Olympic Park bomb used Accurate Armsbrand smokeless gunpowder the other two bombs used dynamite. However all three bombs used Westclox-brand Baby Ben wind-up alarm clocks while also using steel plates cut from the same sheet. The plates were matched to a sheet of metal owned by a friend of Eric Robert Rudolph.

On 14 October 1998 Eric Robert Rudolph was charged with the Olympic Park bombing, as well as the two bombings claimed in the name of the Army of God. In February 1998 he had already been charged with the 29 January 1998 bombing of the New Woman All Women Health Care Clinic in Birmingham, Alabama, that killed police officer Robert Sanderson, and severely injured the clinic's head nurse, Emily Lyons. In spite of an extensive multi-state manhunt, Eric Robert Rudolph had eluded capture by mid-2001.

OMEGA-7. Omega-7 was a nonstate Cuban émigré group with the revolutionary goal of overthrowing the Castro regime in Cuba. In the period from 1968-1983, over 56 anti-Castro groups claimed credit for 155 terrorist acts. Of these, only **Alpha-66**, Brigade 2506, the **Cuban American National Foundation** (CANF), Cuban Nationalist Movement, Cuban Liberation Front, and **Omega-7** were of much consequence. Of these, only Alpha-66, Omega-7, and the Cuban American National Foundation remained active into the 1980s. From 1980 to 1982 Omega-7 carried out at least 18 major terrorist acts, which included 10 bombings or attempted **bombings**, four **arson** attacks, two attacks on firms doing business with Cuba, one car bombing, and the **assassination** of a Cuban U.N. diplomat in a drive-by shooting on 12 September 1980.

Together with other similar Cuban émigré organizations, Omega-7 sought to sabotage Cuban governmental economic interests and diplomatic offices abroad, to intimidate private businesses having trade with Cuba, to attack Cubans in the United States considered to be "Communist sympathizers" as well as non-Cuban sympathizers of the Castro regime, and to discourage the tourist trade from patronizing Cuba. The longer-range goal was to raise and train an émigré Cuban army to overthrow the Castro regime. In 1978 Omega-7 twice firebombed the Cuban mission to the United Nations. On 25 March 1980 they planted a car bomb under the car of the Cuban ambassador to the United Nations, which was disarmed.

Omega-7 used the émigré Cuban community in the United States as a base of support, sometimes extorting contributions from the émigrés. By 1981, when many other major Cuban exile groups had resigned themselves to the prospect of Castro remaining in power, the Cuban émigré community lost interest in the cause of Omega-7. Omega-7 then resorted to drug smuggling and trafficking to finance itself. The increasingly criminal character of the group alienated members of the Cuban community and created internal dissension within Omega-7. In 1982, six key leaders were arrested, and in July 1983, the group's founder and leader, Eduardo Arocena, was arrested. During his arraignment his role as an FBI informant within his own organization was revealed, which effectively destroyed the organization.

OPEC SIEGE, VIENNA. On 21 December 1975 five terrorists led by Ilyich Ramírez Sánchez, also called **"Carlos,"** attacked the Secretariate office of the Organization of Petroleum Exporting Countries (OPEC) in Vienna, killing one secretariat worker and two guards and then taking 11 oil ministers and about 60 others hostage. Although the attackers called themselves "the Arab Revolution," the group consisted largely of German members of the **Red Army Faction** and the Venezuelan Carlos. The terrorists demanded $5 million in ransom and may have received as much as $50 million from Iran and Saudi Arabia.

After 36 hours of negotiations, the Austrian government allowed the terrorists and 42 of their hostages to leave Austria on a DC-9 that landed first in Algeria, where a wounded West German terrorist was taken off the plane, then to Libya where their ransom money was off-loaded and transferred to a South Yemenese bank, and then back to Algeria where the terrorists surrendered and the hostages were released.

Apparently the motive of the terrorists was primarily extortion. Carlos disappeared from public view but was ultimately arrested in Sudan and handed over to France where he was convicted and imprisoned for crimes committed there. In late 1999 Austria was beginning **extradition** proceedings against Carlos to try him on charges related to the OPEC siege. Another principal in the OPEC siege, Hans-Joachim Klein, who was shot in the stomach and recovered, later renounced terrorism in 1978 and the following year published an autobiographical book on terrorism, *Return to Humanity*, in which he criticized what he came to view as the perversions and errors of terrorism. Hans-Joachim Klein, who had been sought by German and Austrian police to stand trial for his role in the **kidnappings** and killings in the OPEC siege, was arrested in the Norman village of Ste.-Honorine-la-Guillaume in early September 1998.

ORDEN. Short for "Organización Democrática Nacional," ORDEN was a state-sponsored right-wing Salvadoran **death squad** and was originally founded in 1968 as a state-sponsored rural militia organized by General José Alberto Medrano. Recruits in the Army Reserve made up most of the ORDEN ranks and were trained by the National Guard. Units of the militia were established in all villages until by 1978 it had around 100,000 members. Within 10 years it had degenerated into a death squad, killing not only leftist guerrillas, but also union organizers, political moderates, religious workers, and human rights activists. ORDEN particularly **targeted** members of the Christian Democratic Party and politically moderate rural mayors. Guerrillas of the People's Liberation Forces, which in 1980 formed an antigovernment leftist guerrilla front known as the **Farabundo Martí Liberation Front** (FMLN), undertook an insurgency in 1978 during which they began to kill known members of ORDEN.

In November 1979, following the coup that overthrew President Carlos Humberto Romero, ORDEN was officially disbanded. In spite of this, many members of El Salvador's military and security forces continued to collaborate with members of the banned organization, and rightist death squad activities increased and grew more brutal until January 1981 when the defeat of the FMLN's "final offensive" brought a subsidence in the cycles of violence. The violence was directed not simply at FMLN guerrillas but also at government workers seeking to implement agrarian land reforms.

Although ORDEN itself officially ceased to exist, it supplied recruits to the **"White Warriors' Union"** founded in 1977 by a protégé of Medrano, Roberto D'Aubuisson, who later led the rightist Republican National Alliance Party (**ARENA**), also suspected of sponsoring death squad activities. On 23 March 1985, General Medrano was killed by **assassins** belonging to the **Clara Elizabeth Ramírez Front**, a renegade FMLN splinter group.

ORDER. The Order was a nonstate U.S. white supremacist paramilitary group with the aim of overthrowing the United States government, which they called the "Zionist Occupation Government" (ZOG). The Order was among a number of white racist groups affiliated with the **Aryan Nations** led by Richard Butler, himself a minister of the **Identity Christianity** movement. The group was headquartered in Metaline Falls, Washington, and numbered around 24 known members. The Order was also known among its members as the "Bruder Schweigen," while it identified its territorial domain around the Metaline Falls area as the "White American Bastion."

The Order was founded in 1983 by Robert Mathews (1953-1984), a right-wing enthusiast and organizer, who patterned the group on a fictional group of the same name found in the *Turner Diaries*, a novel about an apocalyptic race war in a future America. The group sought to finance the various right-wing organizations associated with the Aryan Nations by counterfeiting operations and robberies of banks and armored trucks. A series of successful holdups culminated in the 19 July 1984 holdup of a Brinks armored car outside Ukiah, California, netting around $3.6 million, the largest heist of a Brinks transport until then. The Order had also embarked on a scheme of **assassinating** those whom it believed to be influential within the "ZOG." They had considered, but dismissed, the idea of conducting a **suicide attack** to kill the Baron de Rothschild, who was to visit Seattle, and settled instead on killing a controversial and acerbic Jewish radio talk-show host in Denver, Alan Berg, who had insulted **white supremacists** on his program. Berg was murdered by the Order at his home on 18 June 1984. Other Order activities included a robbery on 16 March 1984 of a Continental armored car in Seattle, another Continental armored car robbery coupled with the diversionary **bombing** of a pornographic film theater in Seattle on 23 April 1984, and the bombing of the Ahavath Israel synagogue in Boise, Idaho, on 29 April 1984.

Robert Mathews was killed in a shoot-out with the FBI on Whidbey Island in Washington state on 8 December 1984. Most of the remaining Order members were eventually arrested and tried in the Seattle U.S. District Court on racketeering and conspiracy charges arising from the robberies and on civil rights violation charges connected with the murder of Alan Berg. While evidence from this trial clearly connected the Order with the Aryan Nations and other white supremacist groups, a subsequent trial of leaders of these other white supremacist groups on sedition and conspiracy charges before a federal court in Fort Smith, Arkansas, held February-April 1988 failed to obtain any convictions.

The Order did not totally perish with Mathews for a successor organization, the "Bruder Schweigen Strike Force II," emerged among Aryan Nations members in Hayden Lake, Idaho, whose members were involved in counterfeiting and six bombings during 1987. On 6 May 1987 and 7 August 1987 they bombed two businesses and later that August murdered Kenneth Shray whom they suspected of being a federal informant.

On 16 September 1987 they bombed the home of Fr. William Wassmuth of St. Pius X Catholic Church, who had been active in opposing the Aryan Nations and kindred racist groups. On 29 September 1987 they set off four bombs in Coeur d'Alene, including the federal building and three businesses, to divert attention from their intended heist of a bank and the Idaho National Guard Armory in Post Falls. However, they were captured in their attempt to raid the Armory and all five were arrested and later convicted, one for the murder of Shray and the others on **Racketeering-Influenced Corrupt Organizations** (RICO) charges.

ORGANISATION DE L'ARMÉE SECRÈTE (OAS). The "Secret Army Organization" was an intrastate terrorist group formed by French colonists and French military officers opposed to French President Charles de Gaulle's negotiations with the **National Liberation Front** (FLN) leading to Algerian independence. Led by four French generals, French troops and settlers opposing independence initially attempted a coup d'état in Algiers on 22 April 1961 which succeeded in seizing the city but collapsed on 26 April when other French troops remained loyal to the government. The disgruntled settlers and military officers then formed the OAS and embarked on a campaign of terror both in France and Algeria against Algerian Arabs and Frenchmen favoring independence. The initial aim was to sabotage the negotiations and force a crackdown on the Algerian Arabs. Failing in this, their aim became instead to exact vengeance upon de Gaulle.

The OAS began using plastic explosives in a massive **bombing** campaign. On 13 May 1961 one bombing in Paris wounded 10. On 16 June 1961 a bombing against the home of the French ambassador to the United States wounded five. In the period from 22-25 January 1962 three bombings occurred, one at the Foreign Ministry in Paris killing one person and wounding 13 others. Following the negotiated ceasefire a car bombing on 2 May 1962 killed 62 Arabs in Algiers. This led to a wave of anti-French terrorism in Algeria, forcing many European residents to flee that country.

On 22 August 1962 the OAS made an **assassination** attempt against de Gaulle and others who had negotiated Algerian independence. The mayor of the French town of Evian, which had hosted the independence talks, was killed in a bombing. From March 1963-August 1965, the OAS made at least another eight assassination attempts against de Gaulle, while at least three other plots were quashed in the planning stages. The

French government responded with a crackdown, eventually imprisoning around 4,000 OAS activists.

ORGANIZATION FOR THE ARMED ARAB STRUGGLE (OAAS). The OAAS was a group founded and run by the Venezuelan Ilyich Ramírez Sánchez, better known as **"Carlos,"** and accordingly the group was known also as the "Carlos Apparat." While the group generally carried out actions in support of Arab revolutionary causes, it appeared to be primarily an **entrepreneurial** rather than an **ideological** group, that is, it worked for Arab regimes or groups on a contract basis. It could also be viewed as entrepreneurial since it helped to aggrandize the reputation or myth of Carlos, its founder, as a master terrorist. This group was very small and was supported by Libya and Syria.

Carlos was a leader within the Popular Front for the Liberation of Palestine-Special Operations Group (PFLP-SOG) and directed the 21 December 1975 **OPEC Secretariat seizure** in Vienna in which several oil ministers were seized for ransom. Following this action Carlos dropped from public view. He was believed to have become a contractual consultant to various Arab regimes and Middle Eastern terrorist groups, particularly the three groups that emerged from the breakup of the PFLP-SOG in 1978, namely, the **May 15 Organization**, the **Lebanese Armed Revolutionary Factions**, and the PFLP-Special Command.

The OAAS emerged in 1983 with a series of attacks on French targets both in Lebanon and in Europe, including an August 1983 **bombing** of the French Cultural Center in West Berlin, two bombings in December 1983 of railroad facilities in France, and a January 1984 bombing of another French Cultural Center in Tripoli, Lebanon. Following this last bombing, no further actions were claimed in the name of the OAAS.

Carlos was arrested by French agents in Sudan on 15 August 1994 and later tried and convicted for the killing of a French policeman and three others in France.

ORGANIZATION OF TERRORIST GROUPS. Terrorist groups organize themselves in various ways according to their **ideology** or mode of operation. These forms include, **cellular** groups, whether single groups or part of a "solar" network, or "phantom cell" networks, which are also sometimes called "autonomous leadership units." Network structures included highly hierarchical political front organizations with a parallel military wing, as well as "chain" networks, and a more amorphous "**netwar**" network structure. *See also* CELLULAR ORGANIZATION; NETWAR.

ORGANIZATION OF THE OPPRESSED ON EARTH. One of several noms de guerre of the Lebanese Shi'ite Muslim group, **Hezbollah,** which is an **Islamic fundamentalist** revolutionary organization under Iranian state sponsorship. Hezbollah employed this name in the 14 June 1985 **hijacking** of TWA 847 in which U.S. Navy diver Robert Dean Stethem was murdered. This name was also used in taking credit for the 17 February 1988 **kidnapping** and subsequent 31 July 1989 killing of U.S. Marines Corps Lt. Col. William R. Higgins, commander of the United Nations Truce Supervisory Observer Group in Lebanon.

ORGANIZATION OF VOLUNTEERS FOR THE PUERTO RICAN REVOLUTION (OVPR). The OVPR was a Puerto Rican "political-military" group dedicated to winning independence through armed revolution. This group was closely associated with the **Macheteros,** having conducted its first operation jointly with them in a 3 December 1979 ambush and machine-gun attack upon a U.S. Navy shuttle bus, killing two sailors and seriously wounding 10 others. Also on 25 January 1985 they shared credit with the Macheteros in a rocket-grenade attack on a U.S. courthouse in San Juan. On 6 November 1985 they shot and seriously wounded a U.S. Army recruiting officer as he was riding his motor scooter to work.

In April 1986 OVPR terrorists murdered a former undercover agent of the Puerto Rican police, Alejandro González Maleve, and vowed to murder nine other policemen who were implicated in the killing of young Puerto Rican separatists. The OVPR has also made other **bombing** attacks within Puerto Rico but has largely been inactive from the late 1980s.

ORGANIZED CRIME AND CRIMINAL SYNDICATES. During the post-Cold War era organized crime and terrorism appear to occupy the same "**gray areas**" within transitional states and in the changing international nation-state order. Some observers claim that there is an increasing convergence, or synthesis, of criminal enterprises and terrorist organizations while others claim that the two activities remain separate but are increasing their tactical and even strategic coordination. Other analysts claim that while terrorist and criminal organizations share many common features and similar tactics, that their ultimate objectives are both different and ultimately incompatible so that any joint actions between them will be infrequent and exceptional rather than part of a developing **netwar** of coordinated or converged terrorist and criminal activities.

The apparent convergence or coordination of terrorism and organized crime activities has been cited in such events as the contacts and coordination between leftist terrorist movements in Colombia and Peru and narcotics traffickers, or in the open warfare of the Pablo Escobar group in the Medellin cartel against the Colombian government, or the murder campaign of the Italian mafia against crusading antimob magistrates, police, and informants, or in the use of a city-wide **bombing** campaign by a Bombay drug-smuggling ring, the Memon family, which killed over 250 people in Bombay on 12 March 1993.

Both criminal syndicates and terrorist organizations are clandestine and employ similar **cellular** and networking organizations to elude detection and arrest. Both are willing to employ violence to achieve their ends, often not so much through the direct effects of their attacks on the immediate victims but also through the demonstration effect on a larger audience. Both often are fighting the same state structures or international law enforcement efforts and so share common enemies. Criminal syndicates often used terrorist tactics to eliminate rivals, intimidate the public, and to coerce or co-opt the police and state officials while terrorist groups are developing their own skills in extortion schemes, money laundering, and drug trafficking to finance their causes. Finally it should be recognized that these disparate groups are beginning to resemble each other more in adopting flatter networking organizations and use of similar information technologies simply because doing so is a rational adaptation to the changing technology and global economy of the post-Cold War era which would continue to occur even without any contact between these two groups.

There are some cases in which an originally terrorist group with a political, social, or religious agenda ultimately has been transformed into an apolitical criminal group whose terrorist skills are let out for hire to the highest bidder, regardless of their political complexion. The **Irish Republican Army** (IRA) has become astute at running protection rackets in Northern Ireland and in video and CD piracy and wholesale smuggling operations, such that even if the IRA renounces political violence many of its cells and operatives will likely continue to operate as criminal enterprises for the foreseeable future. In Colombia the **Revolutionary Armed Forces of Colombia** (FARC) and their rivals the **National Liberation Army** (ELN) have both become deeply involved in narcotics trafficking as well as in professional **kidnapping** for ransom.

However in spite of these examples the majority of criminal syndicates and most terrorist groups differ fundamentally in their ultimate objectives and in their relationship to the nation-state system and world economic system. Criminal syndicates exist to make money and they use violence only when necessary to protect their profit-making enterprises. By contrast most terrorist organizations have a political, social, or religious ideal that they seek and they define themselves and their revolutionary politics through the use of violence, which they prefer to negotiation, ordinary politics, or tactics of co-optation or corruption. They engage in profit-making activities only as a temporary means to their ultimate political, social, or transcendent religious ideals. Therefore neither convergence nor long-range coordinations of organized crime and terrorism appear likely.

- P -

PALESTINE LIBERATION FRONT (PLF). The PLF refers to three groups that originally were one PLF group that had split from the **Popular Front for the Liberation of Palestine-General Command**. Like the PFLP-GC, the PLF factions sought the total destruction of Israel and establishment of a Palestinian state in its place by armed struggle. They also conducted infiltration operations into Israel to carry out terrorist actions and try to **kidnap** Israeli hostages to exchange them for imprisoned Arabs. Also these groups, like the PFLP-GC, showed resourcefulness in devising new ways to infiltrate Israel, having tried to use hot-air balloons in addition to hang gliders. As the PLF formed in 1976 was anti-Syrian, it found a natural sponsor in Iraq. Iraq, Libya, and Syria each back one of the three PLF fronts today while **al Fatah** supports the Abu Abbas faction also supported by Iraq.

The original PLF was founded in 1961 by Ahmad Jibril, which coordinated itself with Fatah in 1965. In December 1967 this group, along with the Arab Nationalist Movement and the "Heroes of the Return" group formed the **Popular Front for the Liberation of Palestine** (PFLP) headed by Dr. George Habash. Disgusted by the PFLP's preoccupation with ideological matters, Ahmad Jibril formed his own splinter group, the PFLP-General Command. The current PLF broke away from the PFLP-GC in 1977 due to dissent over Ahmad Jibril's support for Syria's intervention in Lebanon. The new PLF was recognized by **Yasir Arafat**, Chairman of the **Palestine Liberation Organization** (PLO) as a new PLO member in April 1977 as well as being recognized by the Rejection Front as one of its own members. In 1981 the group obtained seats on the Palestine National Council while its founder, Muhammad Abu Abbas, gained a seat on the PLO Executive Committee in 1984.

The PLF has been marked by acrimony with its parent group and among its own members. Fighting broke out between PLF and PFLP-GC members in the Sidon refugee camps in February 1978. In August 1978 the apartment building containing the PLF headquarters was blown up, killing at least 100 residents, an action likely done by the PFLP-GC. In late 1983 the PLF split when founder Muhammad Abu Abbas decided the group was growing too subservient to Syria. He and his followers left for Tunis to align themselves closer with Arafat's al Fatah. The PLF faction left in Damascus was headed by Tal'at Yaqub but itself split when Abdal Fatah Ghanim tried unsuccessfully to seize power over the PLF in January 1984. The Yaqub faction remained in Damascus while Ghanim and his followers established their rival PLF office in Libya. After Yaqub died in November 1988 the remnant of his faction merged with the Abu Abbas group in November 1989. Following the *Achille Lauro* fiasco of 7 October 1985, for which Abu Abbas and his followers were responsible, the Tunisian government asked the Abu Abbas group to leave. This group moved to Baghdad, Iraq but relocated to Lebanon following the Oslo Accords of 1993. Prior to the breakup of the PLF it numbered no more than 250 members, and currently this faction is estimated to have a few hundred followers mainly in Tunisia and Lebanon.

A summary of the more significant PLF actions follows: Seven major actions in the period 1978-1983 all involved attempts to take hostages and all but one involved attempts to infiltrate Israel. Only three of the six infiltration attempts succeeded while in only one case did the terrorists succeed in seizing hostages, but in no case did they win the release of any Arab prisoners. In April 1979 four PLF members landed on a beach near Nahariyah, Israel, on a mission to seize hostages. Three Israeli civilians were killed by the terrorists, two of whom were killed and the other two captured.

On 7 October 1985 Abu Abbas and four PLF members hijacked the *Achille Lauro*, an Italian cruise ship in Egyptian waters. In reality the five had been intending to infiltrate Israel where the ship was due to dock, but when a cabin steward discovered the five cleaning their weapons, they then decided to hijack the ship and use the passengers as hostages. In the course of the **hijacking**, they murdered an elderly Jewish American, Leon Klinghoffer, who was an invalid, and threw his body, wheelchair and all, into the sea. Eventually the hijackers negotiated with the Egyptian government for safe passage in return for the lives of the remaining hostages. Although U.S. fighter planes forced the Egyptian airplane to land at a NATO air base in Signolla, Sicily, the Italians claimed jurisdiction over the five terrorists and released Abu Abbas who possessed an Iraqi diplomatic passport. The other four were tried and convicted by Italian courts on charges arising from the hijacking, and Abu Abbas was also convicted in absentia. Nonetheless the U.S. military action forcing a civilian plane to land and attempted arrest of the terrorists outside U.S. territory, the Egyptians' allowing the terrorists safe passage, and the Italians allowing Abu Abbas to escape, all occasioned mutual acrimony between the United States and its allies. It also underscored the need for international cooperation to address the challenge of international terrorism.

On 30 May 1990 members of the Abu Abbas faction of the PLF, with Libyan support, made a seaborne attack on Tel Aviv beaches that was quashed by the Israeli Defense Forces. Four of the PLF terrorists were killed and 12 captured. This raid occurred in the 18th month of talks between the United States and the PLO. While **Yasir Arafat** disavowed any PLO connection with the raid, he also would not publicly condemn the raid nor expel Abu Abbas from the PLO Executive Committee. This in turn prompted a suspension by the United States of its dialogue with the PLO at that time. In the past, rejectionist groups such as the PFLP, the PFLP-GC, and the PLF had regularly defied Fatah and sought to sabotage its efforts at diplomacy by staging such raids, and this may have been the intended aim behind this raid as well. In 1991, however, Abu Abbas resigned his membership in the PLO Executive Committee.

On 22 April 1996 Abu Abbas, who is still wanted by the United States for his role in the *Achille Lauro* hijacking, attended the Palestine National Council meeting held in Gaza. During his attendance at this meeting Abu Abbas repeatedly stated to reporters that the *Achille Lauro* affair "was a mistake and it led to other mistakes." He claimed that his men did not know Leon Klinghoffer was Jewish or American but had killed him "because he started to incite the passengers against them." By early August 1997 the Palestine Liberation Organization had agreed to settle a civil lawsuit brought against it by the Klinghoffer family. The PLO pleaded unsuccessfully that as a sovereign state it could not be sued and Judge Stanton ordered Yasir Arafat to give a deposition. Instead the PLO moved to settle the dispute out of court and to pay the surviving Klinghoffer daughters an undisclosed sum.

PALESTINE LIBERATION ORGANIZATION (PLO). The PLO is the umbrella organization comprising the major Palestinian political and guerrilla groups that defines itself, and is recognized by all Arab governments, as being "the sole, legitimate representative of the Palestinian people."

When founded in 1964 its nominal leader, Ahmad al Shuqairy, had declared that the purpose of the PLO was "to drive the Jews into the sea." Currently the PLO asserts that it seeks an independent Palestinian homeland on any liberated part of "historic Palestine" and will recognize the right of the State of Israel to exist in exchange for that homeland. In either case, it is a revolutionary irredentist and nationalistic group that has, until recently, used terrorism and armed struggle as a means to achieve an independent Palestinian national state. While some constituent members of the PLO, such as the **Popular Front for the Liberation of Palestine** (PFLP) and other groups, have listed a Pan-Arab revolutionary movement, or a Marxist-Leninist revolution, or even a world revolutionary movement as among the goals of the Palestinians, such views are often idiosyncratic to these groups rather than representative of the PLO as a whole. **Al Fatah**, which has maintained the largest share of seats on the PLO Executive Committee, has not linked the issue of Palestinian national rights to the goal of Pan-Arab unity or to a specific social-economic order or program.

The original PLO was a creation of the Arab League founded on 28 May 1964, when the first Palestine National Council met. Its complete subservience to the Arab states at that time was reflected in the fact that its National Charter made no mention of seeking to create an independent Palestinian state. Members of Fatah, the oldest Palestinian guerrilla group, basically ignored the PLO at that time, regarding it as irrelevant to their own preparations for armed struggle against Israel. Following the 1967 war that discredited the Arab regimes sponsoring the PLO, Fatah and other similar guerrilla groups entered the PLO and seized control in February 1969 when the head of Fatah, **Yasir Arafat**, was elected Chairman of the PLO Executive Committee.

While the PLO since then has been willing to accept material aid from the various Arab states, it has jealously guarded its own claims of legitimacy apart from any other regime and of independence in decision making, on several occasions defying the wishes of several of its sponsors. These quarrels led to the PLO's expulsion from Jordan in 1970 and once again in 1986, its partial expulsion from Lebanon in 1982, and the denial of use of Syrian territory for launching raids into Israel from 1983 onward. Beginning in 1982 Tunisia hosted the administrative offices and personnel of the PLO but required Abu Abbas's **Palestine Liberation Front** to leave Tunisia following the October 1985 scandal of the *Achille Lauro* **hijacking**. Following the September 1993 Peace Accord the PLO relocated its headquarters to Jericho and then later to Gaza City.

The Arab League recognized the PLO as sole representative of the Palestinians in 1974, therefore denying Jordan any right to negotiate unilaterally with Israel over the fate of the West Bank. In 1976 the Arab League accepted the PLO as a full member. While the PLO received contributions from member states of the Arab League, it has also relied on taxes levied upon the Palestinian diaspora. The various constituent member organizations of the PLO have each cultivated their own sponsors and resources as well. While the PLO has received contributions and other material assistance from various Arab states, this does not necessarily imply influence over the PLO by individual states. Saudi Arabia and the Persian Gulf emirates have distrusted the revolutionary and secular program of the PLO and have viewed Palestinians living within their borders as potential fifth columnists. For such regimes, contributions to the PLO were no doubt partly expressions of support for Pan-Arab ideals but may also have been viewed as protection money against possible Palestinian terrorism or revolutionary activity within their borders. Following the Gulf War of 1990-1991 many of these regimes curtailed contributions to the PLO after it openly sided with Iraq in its invasion of Kuwait.

The original PLO had as its military wing the Palestine Liberation Army (PLA), which consisted of Palestinian contingents under Egyptian, Syrian, and Jordanian command. These were trained to fight conventional warfare rather than guerrilla or terrorist operations and in practice answered to the orders of their host countries rather than to the PLO. When it became apparent after 1967 that the independent guerrilla groups were attracting large numbers of recruits, the PLA developed its own guerrilla unit, the Popular Liberation Forces, which lapsed into obscurity in a few years.

Following the takeover of the PLO by Fatah and other guerrilla groups, the PLA continued to remain under the nominal command of the PLO, while the PLO has relied more on the forces of its constituent guerrilla groups to carry out terrorist attacks or insurgent warfare against Israel or against other foes of the hour. Fatah guerrilla operations began after 1 January 1965. From 1969 to 1974 PLO-sponsored terrorism was carried out throughout the Middle East and non-Communist nations against Israeli, U.S., West European, and Arab **targets**, the government of Jordan having been targeted after September 1970. The most notorious Palestinian terrorist group during this period was **Black September**, which was responsible for the **Munich massacre** of the Israeli athletic team at the Summer Olympic games in 1972.

Beginning in 1974 Fatah declared its renunciation of terrorism outside of the borders of former mandatory Palestine, a declaratory policy not always followed by Fatah-sponsored groups, such as the **Hawari group** or **Force 17**. This renunciation was part of a revision within Fatah of its goals from a liberation of the whole of Palestine, in which Israel would be replaced by a secular democratic state, to the creation of a separate Arab Palestinian state on any liberated part of Palestine, which was understood to mean the West Bank and Gaza Strip following an Israeli withdrawal from those territories. While Fatah still believed armed struggle was necessary to achieve its goals, it came to view armed struggle as insufficient if not joined with initiatives on a diplomatic front. This revisionism was anathema to the more radical leftist groups within the PLO, such as the Popular Front for the Liberation of Palestine, which in turn sponsored the creation of a **Rejection Front** of like-minded PLO members whose members boycotted the PLO Executive Committee from 1974 to 1978 while retaining their seats within the Palestine National Council. A practical consequence of this internal division was that the PFLP and other Rejection Front members stepped up their terrorist attacks on Israel and on targets outside Israel to discredit Fatah's claim to speak for the PLO and to sabotage whatever diplomatic initiatives Fatah might seek.

Fatah's diplomatic initiatives paid off in 1974 with the seventh Arab League summit meeting in Rabat, Morocco, declaring the PLO to be the sole, legitimate representative of the Palestinians, followed that same year by the United Nations General Assembly declaring the PLO also to be the Palestinians' representative and granting the PLO observer status in the General Assembly. The Rejection Front's approach in winning national rights for the Palestinians was put to the test with the outbreak of the Lebanese civil war in 1975 and Syrian intervention from 1976 onward, in which certain Syrian-sponsored Palestinian groups fought against Fatah. The conflict split the Popular Front for the Liberation of Palestine-General Command (PFLP-GC), a Rejection Front member, whose factions actually fought each other. Despite a Fatah ban on attacks against Israeli targets within the southern "security zone" declared by Israel, anti-Fatah groups continued their operations there. When another anti-Fatah group, **Black June**, attempted to **assassinate** Israel's ambassador to London in 1982, this occasioned Israel's invasion of Lebanon and siege of Beirut, which culminated in the expulsion of the PLO administrative apparatus from Lebanon and most of its fighters as well. Seeking to block the return of Fatah fighters, after 1983 Syria further incited Palestinian forces against each other and encouraged division even within Fatah. This resulted in the emergence of a splinter group under the leadership of Abu Musa, a former deputy commander of Fatah, that fought alongside Syrian troops against Fatah loyalists. The rift between the Fatah loyalists and anti-Arafat factions was narrowed when Syria began backing the Shi'ite **Amal** militia's campaign against the Palestinian refugee camps when both sides largely drew together to fend off Amal's fighters.

While the PFLP and like-minded groups agreed with certain of the grievances and criticisms of Arafat expressed by the Abu Musa faction, they grew more anxious for the integrity of the PLO and its independence from the control of Arab governments. The outbreak of the Palestinian *intifada* on the West Bank and Gaza Strip changed the focus of terrorist or insurgent activity from outside to within the borders of mandatory Palestine. On 15 November 1988, the 18th Palestine National Council declared an independent Palestinian state in the occupied territories and tied PLO acceptance of United Nations Resolutions 242 and 338 to Israeli withdrawal from the occupied territories. The PLO as a whole formally adopted Fatah's long-standing declaratory policy of abstaining from terrorism outside the occupied territories and Israel, making cessation of terrorism within those areas dependent also on an Israeli withdrawal from the occupied territories. Following 14 December 1988 the United States engaged in a diplomatic dialogue with the PLO, which was discontinued following a Palestine Liberation Front raid on a Tel Aviv beach on 30 May 1990.

With the 13 September 1993 peace accord concluded with Israel, the PLO has in principle renounced further insurgent or terrorist activity within Israel proper or the occupied territories.

The PLO has developed legislative, executive, and quasi-judicial and police functions very much along the lines of a government-in-exile. The Palestine National Council (PNC) is the highest decision-making body, having met in 22 sessions attended by delegates representing the various guerrilla groups, the Palestinian "popular organizations," as well as a number of independents who represent geographic locations. This Council determines overall policy and elects members of the PLO Executive Committee, a 15-member group that actually runs the PLO from day to day, headed by the Chairman of the PLO Executive Committee. In 1973 the PLO Executive Committee created a PLO Central Council to serve as a sounding board of policy during the long periods between PNC sessions. This device has allowed groups such as George Habash's PFLP the opportunity to be consulted on policy matters even while they were grandstanding their differences with Fatah and Yasir Arafat by boycotting sessions of the Executive Committee. The Palestine Armed Struggle Command is a PLO military police used to patrol the refugee camps and to control guerrillas.

The PLO has developed a social welfare bureaucracy, a collection of archives, a research center, and the rudiments of a foreign service. With this governmental infrastructure, the recognition by other nations of the Palestinians as a national community, and the capacity to maintain diplomatic relations, all the PLO has lacked for making a full claim to statehood is an independent territory to govern. With Israel's ceding control of Gaza, Jericho, and other portions of the West Bank to the Palestinian Authority there is a de facto Palestinian state even though it was not officially declared in May 1999 as Yassir Arafat had originally intended to do.

The guerrilla organizations, known as *tanzimat,* play roles similar to political parties in a parliamentary system. The dominant group since 1969 has remained Fatah, which may be considered the nationalist right-wing of the PLO. The groups Black September and Force 17 were Fatah subgroups created to carry out covert operations and do not have independent status in the PLO. The second most influential group is George Habash's Popular Front for the Liberation of Palestine, which represents the Pan-Arabist Marxist-Leninist left wing of the PLO. The central position is held by the **Democratic Front for the Liberation of Palestine** (DFLP). **Al Sa'iqa** is the second oldest guerrilla group within the PLO and has usually followed al Fatah's lead, although it is also highly influenced by Syria's sponsorship. The **Arab Liberation Front** (ALF) is more partial toward the PFLP and is highly influenced by its Iraqi sponsorship. The **Palestine Liberation Front** (PLF) has alternated between supporting the PFLP and Fatah and is currently very much influenced by Iraq. The **Popular Struggle Front** had quit the PLO in 1974 because of disagreement with Fatah's policies but rejoined it in 1991. It is highly influenced by Syria. The Palestine Communist Party entered the PLO in 1982 on a par with the *tanzimat*, despite lacking an armed wing, because of its ability to mobilize mass action in the West Bank due to its deeply rooted political infrastructure there.

Fatah is estimated to have 6,000 to 8,000 members; the PFLP about 800 to 1,000 members; the DFLP about 500 members; al Sa'iqa about 2,000 members; ALF about 500 members; PLF about 50 members; and PSF about 300 members.

Abu Nidal's **Fatah Revolutionary Council** has never been part of the PLO or Fatah even though **Abu Nidal** was a member of Fatah until 1974. Abu Nidal was once under a death sentence by the PLO for having **assassinated** PLO officials and having tried to assassinate Yasir Arafat. The PFLP-General Command of Ahmad Jibril was expelled from the PLO in 1983. The PFLP Special Operations Group was a breakaway group of the PFLP and has been defunct since the death of its leader in 1978. The **Lebanese Armed Revolutionary Factions** (FARL), the **May 15 Organization**, and the **PFLP-Special Command** were all offshoots of the PFLP-Special Operations Group and have never been part of the PLO. The Islamic Resistance Movement, also known as **Hamas**, is an offshoot of the **Muslim Brotherhood** and, like the **Islamic Jihad of Palestine** group, has never been a part of the PLO. It should be noted, however, that individual members of these latter organizations may have overlapping memberships in PLO groups.

Since the signing of the September 1993 Oslo Accord the PLO has come to dominate the Palestinian Authority (PA) established to administer the autonomous areas of Gaza and West Bank created with Israeli's withdrawals over time. On 20 January 1996 elections were held for the 88-seat Palestinian Legislative Council and for President of the Palestinian Authority in which Fatah won 66 of the 88 Council seats and Arafat won 88 percent of the vote to Samiha Khalil's nine percent. Under the Oslo Accord electoral provisions the members of this Council would be automatically considered members of the Palestine National Council. On 12 February 1996 Arafat was sworn in as President of the PA interim government. On 22 April 1996 the Palestine National Council convened in Gaza for its 21st meeting, for the first time on Palestinian soil since 1966, with 558 delegates representing Palestinians both in the diaspora and within the lands either under the Palestinian Authority or still under Israeli control.

The 21st PNC voted on 24 April 1996 by 504-54, with 14 abstentions, to annul anything in the PLO Charter calling for the destruction of the State of Israel. This PNC meeting was attended by PFLP leader George Habash and DFLP leader Nayef Hawatmeh, both critics of the Oslo Accord, and also by Muhammad Abbas, also know as "Abu Abbas," leader of the PLF, and by Muhammad Daoud Odeh who led the Black September assault on the Israeli Olympic team in the 1972 Summer **Munich** Olympics. The PFLP-General Command, Hamas, and Islamic Jihad in Palestine were not members of the PNC and not represented. However, following the Wye River Accord the PLO Central Council met on 10 December 1998 to vote to abrogate Articles 9, 15, 19, and 22 of the PLO Charter which in essence require armed struggle to destroy the State of Israel as the basis for Palestinian statehood. The PNC had to reconvene in December 1998 to endorse by open vote this abrogation of these articles, which was done on 14 December 1998 by show of hands in the presence of President Bill Clinton.

PAN AM FLIGHT 103 BOMBING. On 21 December 1988 Pan Am Flight 103, a Boeing 747 flying from London to New York, exploded at about 30,000 feet over Scotland. All 259 aboard perished, while 11 people in the Scottish village of Lockerbie were killed by the falling debris of the aircraft. Reconstruction of the bomb from the debris that was scattered over a large area of southwestern Scotland revealed the use of a bomb made with Semtex explosive concealed in a Toshiba radio-cassette player identical to bombs manufactured by the **Popular Front for the Liberation of Palestine-General Command** (PFLP-GC) group of Ahmad Jibril that had been seized by West German police in a raid on a PFLP-GC cell on 26 October 1989. Knowing from this the type of timing device used in the bomb, investigators determined that the bomb had been intended to explode once the airplane was over the Atlantic Ocean. A delay in departure of 25 minutes at London's Heathrow Airport caused the plane to explode instead over land, which made reconstructing the bomb and identification of its source possible. Forensic analysis of the luggage in which the bomb was placed revealed that the bomb had been loaded into the plane in Frankfurt and that the original source of the luggage was Malta.

While investigators had been certain that the bomb was manufactured by the PFLP-GC, an **entrepreneurial** terrorist group having ties with Iran, Libya, and Syria, this alone did not establish directly that the same group had itself planted the bomb nor did it reveal which state had sponsored the **bombing**. Originally credit for the bombing was claimed by telephone in the name of the **"Guardians of the Islamic Revolution,"** causing suspicion to center on Iran, which was seen as having a sufficient motive in avenging the deaths of 290 passengers and crew killed when the U.S.S. *Vincennes* shot down Iran Air Flight 655 on 3 July 1988 by mistake. The Maltese origin of the luggage, however, also suggested Libyan sponsorship.

Following further investigations, the United States issued indictments on 14 November 1991 against two Libyan officials, charging the Libyan government with sponsorship of the bombing. In its April 1992 report on global terrorism, the U.S. State Department published evidence linking the Libyan regime with the bombing while **Muammar Qaddafi** at first refused to **extradite** the two officials named in those indictments. The refusal of Libya to extradite the two men, namely intelligence official Abdel Basset Megrahi and the diplomat Al-Amin Khalifa Fahimah, as well as Libya's refusal to cooperate in the investigation of the **UTA Flight 772 bombing** led to imposition of UN Security Council Resolution 731 on 21 January 1992 condemning Libyan intransigence and also Resolution 748 on 31 March 1992 imposing an air traffic embargo on Libya, a ban on arms sales and other military aid to Libya, and limiting Libya's diplomatic ties with other nations if Libya did not comply by April 15. On 30 April 1992 Qaddafi announced that he would not hand over the suspects. By 11 November 1993 the UN Security Council tightened the economic sanctions on Libya which, by

Qaddafi's own admission, had caused losses to Libya of $23.5 billion by mid-1997.

Economic isolation together with falling oil prices led to 600 percent inflation in the period 1997-1999 and severe shortages of basic goods. Libya had announced that it would hand over the two suspects for trial before the World Court in the Netherlands, however, both the United States and Great Britain rejected this on the grounds that either a Scottish or American court should have jurisdiction given that the bombing occurred within Scottish territory and killed several residents of Lockerbie and given that it was a U.S. air carrier and that the majority of victims had been U.S. citizens.

During 1998 both Great Britain and the United States came to accept the condition of holding the trial for the two Libyan suspects before the World Court at The Hague on the condition that they be tried by a panel of three Scottish judges under Scottish law and that the suspects be liable to imprisonment in Scotland should they be found guilty, conditions that Qaddafi rejected. Finally on 19 March 1999, after South African President Nelson Mandela had met and conferred with Qaddafi, Libya announced to the United Nations that it would hand over the two suspects for trial in the Netherlands.

On 5 April 1999 the two suspects were flown to Utrecht to be held at a stockade at Camp Zeist, an old NATO air base which would be treated as Scottish territory for the duration of their trial, which satisfied U.S. and British demands that Scotland have jurisdiction over the accused. Shortly after their arrival at Camp Zeist aboard an Italian 707 with UN markings, Scottish police formally charged the two men with conspiracy, murder, and violation of the Air Security Act of 1982. Their trial began on 3 May 2000. On 31 January 2001 the three judges ruled that the diplomat Fahimah was not guilty but unanimously found Al Megrahi guilty. Fahimah returned to Libya the next day. Al Megrahi would remain imprisoned at Camp Zeist while his appeal process began that would move the case to a five-judge panel in Scotland.

PATRIOTIC PEOPLE'S MOVEMENT (PPM). The PPM was a left-wing Sinhalese organization whose terrorist activities had the limited aim of sabotaging the 1987 Indian-Sri Lankan military accord. Activities included intimidation against Sri Lankan supporters of the agreement that allowed Indian troops into Sri Lanka to quell the Tamil separatist groups. A PPM campaign of threats against voters during the 1988 presidential elections may well have brought about the electoral victory of Ranasinghe Premadasa.

PEOPLE AGAINST GANGS AND DRUGS (PAGAD). PAGAD is a South African group, composed mainly of Muslims of East Indian, Malay, and some ethnic African origins, who seek the limited aim of fighting drug traffickers in the Cape Town's Cape Flats area. Following the end of the apartheid regime in April 1994, South Africa experienced soaring crime rates. PAGAD began its activities in 1995 when its members staged public marches on the homes of suspected drug dealers. This was followed in 1996 with lynchings of suspected drug dealers and pornography vendors but none of its members were charged for those offenses.

PAGAD is not identical with Qibla, a small radical Islamic group led by Achmad Cassiem who, inspired by Iran's **Ayatollah Ruhollah Khomeini** founded Qibla in the 1980s to establish an Islamic state in South Africa. However, the memberships of PAGAD and Qibla tend to overlap. Although PAGAD has a much larger following than the 250 or so adherents of Qibla, it appears that Qibla has succeeded in co-opting PAGAD to its own anti-Western stances and has taken over much of the leadership of PAGAD. Consequently the mass media tends to treat the two groups as if they were one group. The U.S. Department of State believes that both groups have ties to Islamic extremists in the Middle East.

About 50 gunmen are associated with PAGAD and both Qibla and PAGAD operate mainly in the region of Cape Town. Qibla routinely criticizes U.S. policies toward the Muslim world and used radio state station 786 to promote its own message and to mobilize Muslims. PAGAD is suspected of conducting 170 **bombings** and 18 other violent acts in 1998 alone. Qibla and PAGAD are suspected of having conducted the 15 August 1998 bombing of the Planet Hollywood lounge and dance hall. They often use the front names Muslims Against Global Oppression (MAGO) and Muslims Against Illegitimate Leaders (MAIL) in their anti-Western campaigns. Qibla organized protests against the state visits of President Bill Clinton and British Prime Minister Tony Blair in 1999. In early 1999 the South African government issued emergency antiterrorist legislation strikingly similar to that of the antiterrorist legislation of the apartheid regime directed specifically at Islamic radical groups such as these.

PEOPLE'S REVOLUTIONARY ARMY (ERP). The Ejército Revolucionario del Pueblo was the armed wing of the Workers Revolutionary Army of Argentina, a Trotskyite political party. This group sought to launch a social revolution in the 1970s to overthrow the military regime in Argentina. Although doctrinally Trotskyite the ERP went to Cuba in the late 1970s to establish links with the Castroite regime as many of their cadre had ties to **Ernesto "Che" Guevara** dating back to the early 1960s. During that time the ERP also collaborated with leftist Perónist groups and had some contact also with the **Sandinistas**.

As part of their short-term tactics the ERP sought to embarrass and stymie the Argentine military regime, to force foreign investors to bear the costs of the revolution through **kidnapping** and extortion, and to win popular support by forcing foreign firms to engage in highly publicized distributions of goods and services to the urban poor in exchange for the lives of their local executives whom the ERP held hostage. In these actions they imitated the **Tupamaros** of Uruguay, and some analysts believe many Tupamaros had made their way into the ERP following their suppression in Uruguay.

During the 1970s the ERP became the most effective and boldest Latin American guerrilla group, in large part due to the charismatic leadership of Roberto Santucho. The ERP organized itself into cells to carry out urban terrorist operations and viewed itself as the "army of the masses." Beginning in 1970 the ERP was mainly active in the urban areas of Buenos Aires, Cordoba, Santa Fe, and Tucuman. By 1975 it had expanded its operations from purely urban terrorism to include rural guerrilla operations spread throughout many of Argentina's provinces. By October 1977, however, the ERP had been eradicated from all areas except metropolitan Buenos Aires.

A brief history of ERP operations follows: Founded in 1969, the ERP initiated its career by a series of bank robberies in Rosario during 1970. During 1972 the ERP discovered the more lucrative expedient of kidnapping foreign businessmen for ransom while targeting members of the military government for **assassination**. On 10 April 1972 the ERP killed both General Juan Carlos Sánchez in Rosario and also Dr. Oberdan Sallustro, president of the Argentine branch of Fiat, whom they had kidnapped two weeks before. On 30 April 1972 the ERP assassinated Rear Admiral Hermes Quijada.

In the two years following 1973 the ERP changed its tactics from urban terrorism to carrying out open military assaults upon various garrisons and small towns to build up their material strength and to begin creating an ERP-controlled zone in the mountainous areas. These attacks culminated in the 23 December 1975 attack upon the barracks and armory of Monte Chingolo. On 19 July 1976 the leader of the ERP, Roberto Santucho, was killed in Buenos Aires along with his deputy commander, after which the fortunes of the group declined. Within a year the insurgency had been smashed.

Remnants went into exile and formed a leftist hit team for hire calling themselves "Red Action." On 17 September 1980 seven members of Red Action assassinated the exiled Nicaraguan dictator Anastasio Somoza Debayle along with members of his entourage as they drove through Asunción, Paraguay. Red Action was foiled in a kidnapping attempt in Mexico in 1981 and several of its members were captured.

PERUVIAN JAPANESE EMBASSY HOSTAGE CRISIS. On 17 December 1996 about 14 guerrillas of the **Túpac Amaru Revolutionary Movement** (MRTA) stormed the residence of the Japanese ambassador in Lima, Peru just as a reception honoring the birthday of Emperor Akihito began, seizing about 490 guests hostage, among them the mother, sister, and brother of President Alberto Fujimori; the head of the Supreme Court; the Peruvian Ministers of Agriculture and Foreign Affairs; six members of the Peruvian Congress, the ambassadors of Austria, Brazil, Bolivia, Cuba, Japan, South Korea, and Venezuela; as well as six U.S. embassy officials. Some MRTA members entered disguised as delivery personnel bringing in crates of champagne while others blasted a hole in the wall of the compound and entered from a nearby home. The rebels threatened to kill their hostages if 400 of their jailed comrades were not released. The MRTA were being led by their top leader, Néstor Cerpa Cartolini. Several persons escaped before the MRTA could secure their perimeter while the bodyguard assigned to Fujimori's family bolted past his captors when they opened the residence door to receive some Red Cross officials. Fujimori's relatives were among the first persons to be released by the captors.

This raid came as a great shock because the MRTA had seemed to have faded into insignificance beside the **Sendero Luminoso** insurgency, which President Fujimori had successfully contained. Among the 400 MRTA prisoners whose release was being sought by the hostage takers was Víctor Polay Campos, the founder of the MRTA who was captured in 1989.

The MRTA captors began releasing captives, 38 on 21 December and 225 on 23 December, until only 74 hostages remained by 23 January 1997. On 12 January 1997 the Peruvian government announced it was setting up a negotiating commission. In fact the FBI and Peruvian **counterterrorism** agents were using the deliveries of Red Cross food, beds, and other supplies, as well as the "negotiators" both to buy time and to gather intelligence on the hostage takers. By the end of January two more hostages had been released bringing down to 72 the total number left in the hands of the MRTA.

On 3 March 1997 President Fujimori, who had paid a sudden visit to Fidel Castro in Cuba, announced that the MRTA captors would be allowed to leave for **asylum** in Cuba. However the captors grew nervous as it became evident to all that the government forces were tunneling beneath the residence compound, and talks between captors and negotiators would start and stop fitfully throughout March. At 3:30 p.m. on 22 April 1997, as the women captors were watching televison and several of their male comrades were playing soccer in the living room, about 150 counterterrorist Peruvian troops initiated their rescue action by exploding a charge set under the living room, killing the eight soccer players and giving the rescue team access to the residence. Néstor Cerpa was shot to death as he was racing up the stairs preparing to slay the hostages. Those remaining terrorists who were not killed in the initial assault were summarily executed and only two soldiers and one hostage, namely the former Supreme Court Justice Carlos Giusti Acuña, were killed as a result of the raid.

With this successful raid and the killing of the top leader of the MRTA the organization was largely destroyed with fewer than 100 cadres remaining at large. *See also* TÚPAC AMARU REVOLUTIONARY MOVEMENT.

PHALANGE. The Lebanese Phalangist Party, also known by its Arabic name as the Kata'ib, was a right-wing Lebanese militia with the aims of preserving the dominant political and social position of Maronite Christians within Lebanon, repressing other confessional or political groups that might challenge Maronite supremacy, and preserving the independence and territorial integrity of Lebanon from Syrian, Palestinian, or other claims. The Phalange was organized in the 1930s as an imitation of other Phalangist groups in Spain and Italy, which were Fascist paramilitary political parties. By the 1970s the relative growth of the non-

Maronite groups in Lebanon and the transformation of southern Lebanon into a bastion for **al Fatah** guerrillas made Maronite supremacy in Lebanese politics untenable and led to the outbreak of civil war on 13 April 1975. Unable to match the combined strength of the Palestinian and non-Maronite forces, the Phalangists invited the Syrians to intervene, which occurred on 1 June 1976. Syria since then has shifted its sponsorship to other groups, such as the Shi'ite and Druze militias, and back again to the Phalange in an effort to maintain Syrian dominance in Lebanon.

The Phalangists have been supported by the United States as a group that has been generally pro-Western and also by Israel since the enmity between the Phalange and the **Palestine Liberation Organization** (PLO) disposes the Phalange to act as a tactical ally of Israel. Following the Israeli invasion of Lebanon and siege of Beirut, the Phalangists undertook a two-day-long massacre of the Palestinian inhabitants of the Shatila and Sabra refugee camps on 16 September 1982 to avenge the **bombing** attack that killed their leader, Bashir Gemayel, two days earlier. At least 800 people perished, most of them unarmed civilians.

In 1989 most of the parliamentary deputies of Lebanon gathered in Taif, Saudi Arabia, to work out a compromise to end the Lebanese civil war. The agreement that was concluded allowed a de facto partition of Lebanon, with Maronite Christians being allowed control over their enclave east and northeast of Beirut, and the election of a Maronite as President. Although Elias Hrawi, a Phalangist, was elected President, the commander of the Phalangist force, General Michel Aoun (1935-), refused to accept the partition plan. On October 1990, while Israel was too preoccupied with the Persian Gulf crisis to come to the aid of its Lebanese ally, President Hrawi called on Syria to deploy its forces in a massive attack on Aoun's headquarters in which over 800 of his troops were killed and he himself fled. While the Phalangists continued to exist as a political party both their political and military influence has markedly declined following this event.

PHINEAS PRIESTHOOD. A **white supremacist** extremist antistate group that violently opposed racially mixed marriages and also "sexual immorality," in particular, homosexuality and abortion. The group took their name from the biblical account of how Phinehas, the son of the High Priest Aaron, stopped a plague inflicted on the Israelites as a divine punishment for their intermarriage with the idolatrous Midianites by killing the chief offender among the Israelites along with his Midianite wife, for which Phinehas and his descendants were rewarded with the high priesthood in perpetuity: "And when Phinehas, the son of Eleazar, the son of Aaron the priest, saw it, he rose up from among the congregation, and took a javelin in his hand; And he went after the man of Israel into the tent, and thrust both of them through, the man of Israel, and the woman through her belly. So the plague was stayed from the children of Israel. And those that died in the plague were twenty and four thousand. And the LORD spake unto Moses, saying, Phinehas, the son of Eleazar, the son of Aaron the priest, hath turned my wrath away from the children of Israel, while he was zealous for my sake among them, that I consumed not the children of Israel in my jealousy. Wherefore say, behold I give unto him my covenant of peace; And he shall have it, and his seed after him, *even* the covenant of an everlasting priesthood, because he was zealous for his God, and made an atonement for the children of Israel." Num. 25:7-13, AV.

In reality it is not known whether there is a network of related Phineas Priesthood groups or whether the name is simply used by a number of phantom cell groups to confuse authorities. However in 1991, after six men made an **arson** attack on a gay book and video store in Shelby, North Carolina, in which four patrons were burned alive along with the bookstore owner, credit for the attack was claimed in the name of the Phineas Priesthood.

In the period April-October 1996 a gang of four men calling themselves the "Phineas Priesthood" conducted two bank robberies in Spokane, Washington, and **bombed** the Spokane City Hall, a local newspaper, and Planned Parenthood clinic but without causing injuries to anyone. Three men, Verne J. Merrill, Charles Barbee, and Robert Berry, were identified and arrested on 8 October 1996 after a foiled bank robbery attempt near Portland, Oregon. After a mistrial on 2 April 1997 the three were eventually convicted in Federal District Court in Spokane on 24 July 1997 on charges of conspiracy, illegal possession of hand grenades, and interstate transportation of stolen vehicles. A fourth suspect in the Planned Parenthood bombing, Brian Ratigan, was tried and convicted separately later. On 21 May 1999 the Ninth Circuit Federal Appeals Court upheld the convictions of all four men.

PHYSIOLOGICAL (STIMULUS-REINFORCEMENT) MODEL OF TERRORISM. A psychological model explaining recruitment into terrorism as well as terrorist **contagion** using a physiological model of individual-level response to terrorist stimuli which seeks also to take account of social experiences and the upbringing of those attracted to terrorism. Kent L. Oots and Thomas C. Wiegele, in their article "Terrorist and Victim: Psychiatric and Physiological Approaches from a Social Science Perspective," [*Terrorism: An International Journal*, 8:1 (1986: 1-32)] noted four factors that together may account for any psychological satisfactions associated with perpetrating terror:

Biological Predisposition: Being male and being relatively young (17-22 years) seem to be frequent attributes of most terrorists. *Individual Psychological Background:* In their reviews of the psychiatric and criminological literature Oots and Wiegele noted that terrorists frequently come from single-parent homes or have had frequent run-ins with the law as juveniles, as well as having certain narcissistic personality traits, such as unrealistically high self-esteem and a low regard for the intelligence or feelings of others. *Political Cause or Pretext:* All terrorists claim that their acts of violence are justified as being in the service of a higher political or moral cause. *Reinforcement:* The terrorist act gives relief to the hormonal stresses of the terrorist. The aggression and anxiety produced by high testosterone levels produces increased levels of the **fight-or-flight response** neurohormones norepinephrine and epinephrine. Engaging in violence (or flight) produces "release" from these stresses by triggering release of endorphins—naturally occurring morphine-analogue painkillers—which create a natural "high" or euphoria. With repetition these feelings of release and exhilaration from committing terrorist acts are reinforced, becoming stronger and more pleasant.

This model, if correct, leads to some sobering implications: There is no way to predict exactly which individuals out of the population of susceptible, young, narcissist males will turn into terrorists. Since politics is largely used as a pretext to act out physiologically and psychologically driven rages there is no guarantee that terrorism would cease even if all political and social "root causes" for grievances were addressed and resolved. Finally, there is no way in a free and democratic society to forestall the "contagion effect" caused by media attention to the terrorist act.

PISHMERGA. A Kurdish word meaning "(one who puts himself) in front of death," *pishmerga* is a generic term used to refer to Kurdish guerrilla fighters among the **Kurdish Workers' Party** (PKK), Kurdish Democratic Party, and other Kurdish armed groups, whether of leftist or nationalistic complexion. Like the Arabic term *Fida'i* (plural, *Fida'iyin*; also spelled, *Fedayeen*) meaning "one who offers (self-) sacrifice," the term has been so generally appropriated by various and often opposing Kurdish groups that, by itself, it gives little clear identification of which group a particular *pishmerga* may represent.

POLITICAL OFFENSE EXCEPTION. Legal doctrine that allows nations to refuse requests for **extradition** in cases in which the person being sought for extradition is being persecuted for his or her race, religion, nationality, ethnic affiliation, or political opinion and who cannot secure legal protection from such persecution in the country from which he or she is fleeing. Such a person has the right to request political **asylum** in the country to which she or he has fled. The "political offense exception" which would grant such a refugee a right to remain in the country to which he or she fled, and protect them from deportation or extradition to the country of origin, may not include serious nonpolitical offenses, such as murder, assault, or participation in acts of persecution against others on account of race, religion, nationality, ethnic affiliation, or political belief.

POLITICAL REFUGEE STATUS. *See* ASYLUM.

POPULAR FORCES OF 25 APRIL (FP-25). The Forças Populares do 25 Abril was a Portuguese communist terrorist group formed in 1980 dedicated to overthrowing the current Portuguese government in favor of some sort of revolutionary Marxist state. It also opposed Portugal's participation in NATO and was anti-American. The group was not known to have any ties with sponsoring states or other terrorist groups, although it has been speculated that FP-25 had collaborated with **Basque Fatherland and Liberty** (ETA) and the **Red Army Faction** (RAF) and that it had received some support from Libya. The name refers to the 25 April 1975 military coup that ended the former right-wing regime. FP-25 also used the names "Autonomous Revolutionary Groups" and the "Armed Revolutionary Organization."

FP-25 incidents in 1980-1986 included 26 **bombings**, including firebombings, five armed attacks involving mortars and antitank rockets, and four **assassinations**, while the other five were miscellaneous actions such as a prison breakout, a **kidnapping**, some robberies, and the like.

On 28 October 1984 FP-25 tried to fire two antitank rockets at the U.S. embassy but failed due to a malfunction in the launching mechanism. On 25 November 1984 the ninth anniversary of the failed communist coup attempt, they fired four mortar rounds at the U.S. embassy, hitting two vehicles. On 9 December 1984 they fired four mortar rounds at NATO's Iberian Atlantic Command headquarters outside Lisbon, damaging some buildings and one car. On 28 January 1985 they fired three mortar rounds at six NATO ships at anchor in Lisbon harbor, failing to hit any of them.

During 1984 the Portuguese counterterrorism units arrested 56 members. In July 1985, however, the key prosecution witness, a defecting FP-25 member, was murdered before he could testify, and in September 1985, 10 imprisoned members managed to escape. In the following year, the group made another attempt to bomb the U.S. embassy and to bombard the NATO Iberian Atlantic Command with mortars but without success. In September 1986 the group calling itself the "Armed Revolutionary Organization" appeared, which authorities believed to be the FP-25 group under a new name. According to U.S. State Department analyst, Dennis Pluchinsky, FP-25 probably ceased to exist in 1987 and was certainly defunct by 1992.

POPULAR FRONT FOR THE LIBERATION OF PALESTINE (PFLP). Founded on 11 December 1967, the PFLP has been the main rival of **al Fatah** within the **Palestinian Liberation Organization** (PLO). Led by Dr. George Habash until 29 April 2000 when he resigned in favor of Mustafa Zubari, the PFLP stressed Pan-Arabism, considering the Palestinian struggle as only one part of a broader revolution against both imperialism and reactionary politics within the Arab world. The organization has between 800 and 1,000 members and operated in Lebanon, Israel, and the occupied territories, the remaining Middle East, and Europe. It received most of its funds and weapons from Libya and Syria.

The PFLP was a self-proclaimed Marxist organization and, unlike Fatah, did not restrain itself from intervening in the politics of Arab host countries. PFLP intrigues and challenges to the Jordanian regime led eventually to the ouster of the PLO from Jordanian territory beginning in September 1970. Once the PLO relocated its forces in Lebanon, the PFLP alliance with leftist militias in Lebanon against the right-wing

Phalange helped precipitate the Lebanese civil war in 1975, dragging the entire PLO into the conflict. While Fatah tried since 1974 to limit its terrorist attacks to Israeli targets within the borders of former mandatory Palestine, and to avoid involving itself in extraneous politics or revolutionary movements, by contrast the PFLP tried to carry out joint operations with revolutionary leftist terrorist groups in Europe and elsewhere, among them the **Japanese Red Army**, the **Red Army Faction**, the **Revolutionary Cells**, and the Nicaraguan **Sandinistas**. Due to its own commitment to a secular Arab nationalism, the PFLP eschewed support for **Islamic fundamentalist** movements generally and disowned any identification of the Palestinian struggle with notions of a religious **jihad**.

The PFLP has opposed Fatah for the latter's increasing emphasis on diplomacy rather than armed struggle and also opposed Fatah's willingness to settle for a "mini-state" in Gaza and the West Bank rather than the whole of former mandatory Palestine. In 1974 the PFLP established the **Rejection Front** to oppose the participation of the PLO in any negotiated settlement. The **PFLP-General Command**, the **Arab Liberation Front**, the **Palestine Liberation Front**, and the **Popular Struggle Front** all joined this opposition group. Opposition to the Camp David Accords drew these groups back closer to Fatah, and the PFLP rejoined the PLO executive committee in 1981 after having boycotted it. Upset over a Fatah-sponsored accommodation reached between the PLO and King Hussein of Jordan in 1985, the PFLP set up the **National Salvation Front** (NSF) composed of other groups opposed to Fatah's diplomatic approach. The PFLP broke ranks with the NSF, however, to rejoin the mainstream PLO in the 18th Palestine National Council meeting in Algiers in 1987. The PFLP finally acceded to Fatah's diplomatic approach and renunciation of terrorism outside the occupied territories and Israel in the 19th Palestine National Council meeting held on 12-15 November 1988 in Algiers.

From 1968 until 1987 the PFLP engaged in at least 81 major actions, including 38 **bombings**, one of them an aerial bombing, and five attempted bombings; 10 **hijackings** and one failed attempt; 11 armed attacks, including one maritime rocket attack and a dinghy landing attempt scuttled by the Israeli navy; nine **kidnapping** or hostage situations; three **assassinations** and one attempted assassination; and three threats. The actual record is confused by the tendency of PFLP splinter groups, like Wadi Haddad's PFLP-Special Operations Group and the Arab Nationalist Youth Organization, to claim their actions in the name of the PFLP. Among the PFLP's more notorious actions were the following: On 6 September 1970 the PFLP simultaneously hijacked three airliners to Dawson's Field, north of Amman, Jordan, in which over 400 passengers and crew were held hostage for three weeks to force the release of imprisoned terrorists elsewhere. While this operation was a terrorist tour de force, it also backfired since it completely exasperated King Hussein who dispatched his armed forces to rescue the hostages and expel the Palestinians. On 30 May 1972, acting at the behest of the PFLP three Japanese Red Army members carried out a massacre at Lod Airport, killing 28 people and wounding 76 others. On 27 June 1976 the PFLP together with members of the Red Army Faction hijacked an Air France Tel Aviv-to-Paris flight to Entebbe, Uganda, where 240 passengers were held hostage until rescued by Israeli commandos on 1 July 1976 (see ENTEBBE HIJACKING). Likewise PFLP and Red Army Faction terrorists hijacked a Lufthansa plane to Mogadishu, Somalia, on 13 October 1977 to force the German government to release several imprisoned RAF terrorists held in Germany, but these hijackers also were foiled on 18 October 1977 by West German GSG-9 commandos.

The brutality of these operations, which were directed very deliberately at innocent civilians, drew forth so much international condemnation and caused such embarrassment to the backers of the PFLP that by the end of the 1970s the PFLP came around to the Fatah proposition that terrorist actions should be confined to Israeli **targets** within the boundaries of Israel and the occupied territories. Dr. George Habash was formerly highly esteemed throughout the Palestinian community and was considered a figure of integrity as well as the outstanding representative of the more radical Pan-Arabist position within the PLO. Therefore his decision to acquiesce in, or else to resist, the PLO's renunciation of terrorism outside Israel and the occupied territories carried great weight and had far-reaching consequences. His resignation in favor of Mustafa Zibri, whom Israel allowed to return to the West Bank after 32-years exile in Damascus, was considered by observers to indicate the PFLP's repudiation of violence. However, on 27 August 2001 Zibri was killed by an Israeli helicopter rocket attack on his office. According to the IDF Zibri had been involved since 28 September 2001 in directing terrorist bombings in Jerusalem and other parts of Israel. On 17 October 2001 the PFLP retaliated by assassinating Rechavam Zeevi, Minister of Tourism in the Sharon government. Presently Abdul Rahim Maluah appears to be in line of succession as the leader of the PFLP.

POPULAR FRONT FOR THE LIBERATION OF PALESTINE-GEN- ERAL COMMAND (PFLP-GC). The PFLP-GC led by Ahmad Jibril split away from the **Popular Front for the Liberation of Palestine** (PFLP) in October 1968 when Jibril became disenchanted with PFLP leader George Habash's preoccupation with ideological issues. While this group seeks the total destruction of Israel and establishment of a Palestinian state in its place, its leader appears quite ready to hire out the services of the group on an **entrepreneurial** basis without regard for the politics of his patrons. The group joined the **Rejection Front** in 1974 but was expelled from it in 1977. It was also expelled from the **Palestine Liberation Organization** (PLO) in 1983 and has remained opposed to the PLO, although it ceased direct attacks on the PLO after 1990. From 1983-1989 it was sponsored by Libya and Syria. After being ordered out of Libya in 1989 it lately has sought Iranian sponsorship.

The Palestinian Ahmad Jibril was a former captain in the Syrian Army and head of the original **Arab Liberation Front**, which had helped to form the PFLP in 1967. While agreeing with Habash's principle of pursuing armed struggle and rejecting negotiated settlement of the Arab- Israeli conflict, Jibril has always been more interested in perfecting the mechanics of armed attacks. Because of its wayward tendency to pro- mote factionalism within the PLO, this group was excluded from the PLO in 1983. Although the PFLP-GC has excellent operational capa- bilities and an impressive record of actions for so small a group (about 500 members) it has become a marginal actor within the politics of the Palestinian resistance. Internal dissension led to the splitting off of an anti-Syrian faction, the (second) **Palestine Liberation Front**, in 1976.

The PFLP-GC imparts good commando training and uses some so- phisticated and exotic hardware, such as SA-7 antiaircraft missiles, heavy artillery, ultralight aircraft, and hang gliders. It has carried out numerous cross-border assaults as well as operations in Israel's declared "security zone" in southern Lebanon. Commandos are prepared for "suicide" missions in which they are ready to kill themselves rather than be cap- tured. In November 1987 a PFLP-GC member infiltrated Israel by cross- ing the security zone in a powered hang glider and succeeded in killing six Israeli soldiers and wounding seven others before being killed.

A favorite tactic of this group has been to seize Israeli civilians or soldiers as hostages to force the release of Arab prisoners by Israel. On 11 April 1974 three PFLP-GC members seized an apartment building in

Kiryat Shemona, demanding the release of 100 Arab prisoners by Israel. The three killed 18 hostages and wounded 16 before killing themselves by setting off explosive charges wrapped around their belts when Israeli soldiers stormed the building. In the case of four Israeli soldiers captured in Lebanon, the PFLP-GC was able to negotiate their exchange for Arab prisoners, once in March 1979, exchanging one Israeli Defense Forces (IDF) soldier held one year for 76 Arab prisoners and again in May 1985, exchanging three IDF soldiers held since September 1982 for 1,150 Arab prisoners.

On 26 October 1988 West German police raided a PFLP-GC cell in Frankfurt arresting 14 members and seizing a number of weapons, Semtex explosives, and bomb detonators. Evidence obtained there linked one of those captured, Hafiz Qassim Dalkamoni, who was also a member of the PFLP-GC Central Committee, with two **bombings** of U.S. troop trains in Germany in 1987 and 1988. Following the 21 December 1988 aerial bombing of **Pan Am Flight 103** over Lockerbie, Scotland, the PFLP-GC came under suspicion as having been the agent responsible for the action when it was learned that the bomb that destroyed Pan Am 103 was very similar to those assembled by this one PFLP-GC cell. While the bomb may have been assembled by the PFLP-GC, this alone did not mean the group itself planted the bomb on the doomed airplane, and suspicion for that act was later shifted instead to Libyan state agencies.

POPULAR FRONT FOR THE LIBERATION OF PALESTINE-SPECIAL COMMAND (PFLP-SC). One of three splinter groups that emerged from the Special Operations Group of the Popular Front for the Liberation of Palestine (PFLP-SOG), which fell apart after the death of its leader, Wadi Haddad, in 1978. The other two groups were the now defunct **May 15** group and the **Lebanese Armed Revolutionary Factions** (FARL). All three groups were critical of the diplomatic approach taken by more moderate Palestinian groups since 1982.

Formed in 1979, the PFLP-SC operated mainly in western Europe and the Middle East, claiming credit for various brutal terrorist attacks. In April 1985 the PFLP-SC bombed a restaurant in Torrejón, Spain, killing 18 Spanish civilians. This group has enjoyed Libyan and Syrian state support and was believed to have ties with the **Armenian Secret Army for the Liberation of Armenia** (ASALA), Abu Nidal's **Fatah Revolutionary Council**, and FARL. The size of the group was estimated at about 50 members but following 1985 it became defunct.

POPULAR LIBERATION ARMY (EPL). The Ejército Popular de Liberación (EPL) was a Maoist revolutionary group that sought to overthrow the Colombian state through prolonged popular warfare. The EPL was a rural guerrilla movement founded in 1967 as the armed wing of the Communist Party of Colombia-Marxist-Leninist, a Maoist political splinter group that broke away from the pro-Moscow Communist Party of Colombia (PCC) in July 1965. Although the EPL claimed to look to Peking for leadership, sponsorship by the People's Republic of China was more in the form of moral than material support, including propaganda leaflets printed in China. During the post-Mao Tse-tung era, the EPL continued to espouse the Maoist line, which secured it a loyal following among a small circle of leftist intellectuals and academics.

The numbers of EPL guerrillas have been variously estimated at 350 or as high as 600 to 800 members. The EPL operated four fronts in the Antioquía, Cordoba, and Risaralda departments. The deaths of key leaders in the 1970s led to internal dissent resulting in an unstable strategic approach and consequent tactical weakness. An example of this instability can be seen in the EPL's equivocation in choosing to abide by the May 1984 government-sponsored truce, which it did not sign. This understanding abruptly ended when the leader of the EPL, Ernesto Rojas, was killed in 1985.

During the late 1970s the EPL engaged in sabotage, bank robberies, **kidnappings**, and **bombings**. Many of its military clashes had been with members of the **Revolutionary Armed Forces of Colombia** (FARC), the armed wing of the pro-Moscow PCC. In December 1982 the EPL kidnapped a Colombian land magnate for a $2 million ransom. In March 1984 they killed eight peasants accused of being army informants as well as killing the mayor of a small town in northwestern Colombia. In November 1985 the EPL ended its tacit compliance with the May 1984 cease-fire by attacking a town in northeastern Colombia in which four people were killed. In December 1985 the EPL kidnapped two U.S. citizens working for Bechtel Corporation, one of whom died in captivity the following May while the other was later released. In June 1986 the EPL bombed the Colombian-Soviet Friendship Institute in Medellín as retaliation for attacks by FARC against EPL forces. The same month the EPL also bombed the residence of the Honduran consul in Medellín who was seriously wounded.

In early 1987 the EPL turned the Uraba region into one of its more active theaters in Colombia and maintained an urban support infrastructure in Bogotá, Cali, Convención, Medellín, Pereira, Popayan, and Tierra Alta. But by 1990 the EPL entered a cease-fire and began dialogue with government mediators. In July 1991 the ELP demobilized following peace negotiations with the government and become a political party, Esperanza, Paz y Libertad (Hope, Peace and Freedom). However a dissident faction broke off and continued armed struggle. During 1994 there were 31 kidnappings attributed to this dissident EPL. During 1997 this dissident EPL faction kidnapped 12 mayors for ransom.

POPULAR MOVEMENT OF UNITED ACTION-LAUTARO. *See* LAUTARO YOUTH MOVEMENT.

POPULAR RESISTANCE FRONT. The Frente de la Resistencia Popular was an Argentine leftist group responsible for the 23 January 1989 attack upon the Third Mechanized Infantry Regiment base at La Trablada in the southwestern outskirts of Buenos Aires. The group was composed of remnants of the **People's Revolutionary Army** (ERP) led by Enrique Haroldo Gorriarán Merlo (1942-) the second in command of the ERP. Gorriarán was among the ERP remnants who formed the Red Action **assassination** squad that murdered Anastasio Somoza in Paraguay in September 1980.

The group, numbering some 69 men and women, crashed the gates of the base, seized several recruits as hostages, took over six buildings, and fought a group of officers for three hours until police, along with army tank and artillery units, attacked the base, retaking it after 24 hours of fighting. In all, 28 attackers, nine soldiers, and two policemen were killed. About 14 persons surrendered, four of whom were soldiers who had been held hostage. During the fighting Gorriarán escaped. This incident greatly shocked the Argentine public, who believed that the leftist groups had been wiped out during the **"dirty war"** of the military junta of General Videla.

On 1 February 1989 the Popular Resistance Front published a communiqué in an Uruguayan leftist paper claiming responsibility and stating that its motive was to deter a military plot to launch a coup d'état against the government of President Raul Alfonsín. The communiqué identified the group as being composed of members of the All for the

Fatherland Movement, founded in 1988, composed of remnants of the ERP under Gorriarán's leadership.

On 28 October 1995 Gorriarán was arrested in Mexico City and **extradited** to Argentina where he arrived at El Palomar military base on 29 October 1995. Although a general amnesty had been issued by Argentine President Carlos Saúl Menem in 1989 this applied only to crimes committed by either the leftist insurgents or the army during the course of the "dirty war" which ended in 1983 and would not apply to Gorriarán's assault on the Third Infantry regiment base in La Trablada on 23 January 1989.

POPULAR REVOLUTIONARY ARMY (EPR). The Ejército Popular Revolucionario is a revolutionary leftist nonstate group which seeks to overthrow the current Mexican state in favor of a Marxist-Leninist regime. This group was formed in May 1994 from about 14 extreme leftist groups centered around the former Partido Revolucionario Obrero Campesino Unión del Pueblo (PROCUP), Workers and Peasants Revolutionary Party-People's Union, which was formed by radical university students in the Mexican states of Oaxaca and Guerrero in the 1970s and which **bombed** multinational firms in Mexico in 1991 including Citibank, Nissan, Sony, and IBM. PROCUP followed a very doctrinaire Marxist-Leninist line, insisting on the need for armed struggle over electoral tactics and it also gained an insidious reputation for murdering leftists whom it viewed as compromisers or revisionists. In 1994 PROCUP **kidnapped** Alfredo Harp Helu, president of Mexico's largest bank, whom they released after his family paid them a $30 million ransom. The leader of PROCUP, who is assumed to also lead the EPR, is Felipe Martínez Soriano, the former rector of the state university in Oaxaca, who was imprisoned for the murders of two newspaper security guards by his followers.

The EPR appeared in the town of Coyuca de Benítez in Guerrero State, located on the Pacific coast, on 28 July 1996 when 50 armed and uniformed ERP members interrupted a memorial service commemorating the anniversary of a massacre of peasant organizers the previous year to read their own manifesto calling for the overthrow of the Mexican government. After the Mexican government publically belittled the group as insignificant the EPR ambushed a Mexican Army transport on 16 July 1996 near Tixla, Guerrero State. After the Mexican government suggested that the EPR were merely regional discontents lacking any national base of support or scope of action the EPR held a clandestine news conference on 7 August 1996 in the Sierra Madre Oriental mountains somewhere in the states of Veracruz or Tamaulipas located on the Gulf of Mexico. Then on 28 August 1996 the EPR executed simultaneous military operations throughout the states of Chiapas, Guerrero, Mexico, and Oaxaca, killing 13 soldiers or police and wounding 23 others. On 30 August 1996 the EPR also struck a military convoy in Michoacán state, which is located in central Mexico some distance from the former attacks. Not only did these attacks demonstrate that the group was large, well organized, and able to carry out operations over an extensive area but the timing also upstaged the State of the Nation speech due to be delivered on the first day of September by President Ernesto Zedillo, whom the EPR had called upon to resign.

The EPR differs from the **Zapatista** movement in that it seeks a broader change in the Mexican political system rather than seeking more specific and limited redress of grievances; it is more heavily armed, better financed, and its members better trained and indoctrinated. Both the leaders of the EPR and the Zapatistas claim there is no connection between the two groups and while the EPR commanders claim that they respect the Zapatista movement they also disagree with its decision to revert to nonviolent means to seek piecemeal solutions to their demands. Also whereas the Zapatistas recruited entire Indian villages but had a very decentralized networked form of organization based on community consensus, the EPR followed the more classical **cellular organization** in which about 12 men undergo military training and political indoctrination but never see leaders other than their cell commander.

POPULAR STRUGGLE FRONT (PSF). The PSF, also called the Palestine Popular Struggle Front, is a Palestinian terrorist group that broke away from the **Palestine Liberation Organization** (PLO) in 1974 but later rejoined it in 1991. The PSF joined the **Rejection Front** in 1975 and the **National Salvation Front** in 1985 to oppose an accord reached between the PLO and King Hussein of Jordan regarding a possible future settlement of the Arab-Israeli conflict. In common with other members of the Rejection Front, the PSF rejected any accommodation with Israel in forming a Palestinian homeland out of the occupied territories, vowing instead total destruction of Israel and, until recently, opposing the PLO. The PSF is based in Damascus, Syria, with most of its forces in the

Bekaa valley of Lebanon and is believed to be under Syrian sponsorship while also enjoying Libyan support.

On 28 June 1975 the PSF **kidnapped** U.S. Army Colonel Ernest R. Morgan in Beirut, Lebanon. The PSF passed him to the **Popular Front for the Liberation of Palestine-General Command** (PFLP-GC), another Rejection Front member. Eventually the PLO, which regarded the kidnapping as an unnecessary and dangerous provocation to the United States, pressured the PFLP-GC to release Col. Morgan. The PSF also has carried out guerrilla attacks within Israel, **bombing** the Ain Fashha resort in May 1975, bombing a tourist bus in Jerusalem in March 1979, and carrying out a rocket attack against the northern Israeli town of Metullah. This latter attack occasioned an Israeli Air Force bombing raid against PSF bases near Bar Ilyas in the Bekaa valley and in Shamlan near Beirut.

The PSF numbers around 300 members and has been led by Dr. Samir Ghosheh since 1974. On 30 October 1984 six PSF members trying to infiltrate Israel from Lebanon were killed by the Israeli Defense Forces. On 30 August 1988 a four-member team dispatched to seize hostages in Israel were intercepted by South Lebanese Army forces who killed two of the PSF members and took the other two captive. Another attempt by a PSF squad to infiltrate Israel in December 1989 failed when their boat capsized and they drowned. In addition to documented attacks the group has made some claims for other attacks on Israel that have never been confirmed. Since 1989 the group has been relatively inactive.

POSSE COMITATUS. Posse Comitatus (Latin for "power of the county") is a nonstate, revolutionary antitax protest group in the United States. The group openly advocates the limited ends of eliminating state and federal individual income taxes, abolition of the power of judicial review by the federal judiciary, abolition of the Federal Reserve System, and the restoration of the gold standard. Closer scrutiny of the organization reveals a more revolutionary agenda of replacing the current federalist system, which the group considers to be "communist and unconstitutional," with supremacy of government at the county level. These goals proceed from an eccentric interpretation of the Posse Comitatus Act of 1878 and a belief in the superiority of the "organic Constitution" consisting only of those Articles and Amendments in force prior to the Civil War. The group's **ideology** views the current monetary, fiscal, and banking systems to be part of an anti-Christian conspiracy to defraud and enslave ordinary white Christians. Although the Posse Comitatus is not an **Identity Christian** or **neo-Nazi** movement, its views are congruent with the anti-Semitic and **white supremacist** beliefs held by Identity Christian and other right-wing extremist groups with which Posse Comitatus has established operational cooperation.

Posse Comitatus was formed by former neo-Nazi Henry Lamont Beach in 1969 from remnants of the **Minutemen** organization, which had fallen apart following the conviction of its founder Robert dePugh on federal firearms violations. During the 1970s Posse chapters spread throughout every state, instructing members in stratagems to avoid paying taxes legally as well as more questionable methods such as resorting to unrecorded barter transactions. Posse members also used to file harassment suits against Internal Revenue Service (IRS) officials and law enforcement officers to obstruct these officials from performing their duties. Posse also tried to create unchartered barter-and-bullion based "banks" for its members as an alternative to the existing banking system.

Following the crackdown initiated under the IRS Illegal Tax Protestor Program begun in 1980, Posse tactics grew more violent. In May 1983 Gordon Kahl, a North Dakota farmer and Posse member already once jailed on conviction for tax resistance, killed two federal marshals who sought to serve subpoenas on him. On 3 June 1983 Kahl died in a shoot-out with state and federal agents in an Arkansas cabin. On 20 August 1986 a pipe bomb intended for U.S. Federal District Court Judge Paul Benson was intercepted in Fargo, North Dakota. Benson had sentenced Kahl and other Posse members previously for tax resistance.

The Posse has produced at least one major splinter group, namely the Arizona Patriots. Members of this group were indicted in December 1986 of plotting to **bomb** the western regional office of the IRS in Ogden, Utah, using a vehicle packed with explosives; to bomb several **targets** in Los Angeles including the FBI office, the Simon Wiesenthal Center, and two offices of the **Jewish Defense League** as well as a synagogue in Phoenix.

Due to their distrust of the federal government Posse members have taken pains to avoid creating "paper trails" and have kept outsiders ignorant of the structure and leadership of their organization. Members avoid the use of standard identification cards, such as drivers licenses and Social Security cards. By the mid-1980s membership was variously estimated between 1,000 and 3,000 nationwide, but Wisconsin Posse leaders claimed to have over 2,000 members in their chapter alone. The Posse finds a major portion of potential recruits from midwestern farmers who have suffered as a result of unfavorable market conditions and bank foreclosures on mortgaged farms. One Louis Harris poll commissioned by the B'nai B'rith Anti-Defamation League of rural residents of Iowa and Nebraska in February 1986 found that 25 percent of this sample of midwesterners followed the activities of Posse Comitatus even if they were not openly affiliated with it and essentially accepted its core beliefs.

The heyday of Posse Comitatus activity appears to have been during the farming crisis of the 1980s. Several Posse members have joined other similar movements, including either the **"Common Law Courts"** or the **militia movement** and a few have surfaced in various schemes to defraud creditors, whether banks or the IRS. James Wickstrom, who is both a Posse leader in Michigan and an Identity Christian minister, was tried in 1991 for attempting to distribute counterfeit currency during a 1988 **Aryan Nations** event. Terry Nichols, later convicted for his role in the **Oklahoma City bombing**, attempted to pay credit card bills using bogus financial instruments issued by the Wisconsin Posse Comitatus affiliate, the Family Farm Preservation society.

PREVENTION OF TERRORISM ACTS. Originally passed by the British parliament after the **Irish Republican Army** (IRA) expanded its **bombing** campaign from Northern Ireland to England in 1974, these acts made the withholding of information about terrorism from police or military authorities a crime unless the person having such information could claim duress or other "reasonable excuse." British authorities used these Acts to force family members and acquaintances of suspects to give information to the security forces about the suspects and their whereabouts. However these statutes do not give the police authority to force defense lawyers or investigative reporters into revealing confidential information. Once the IRA began using car bombs the acts were then amended in 1987 to require victims of car jacking or auto theft also to report the theft immediately lest the stolen car or truck be used for a car bombing. These Acts also allowed the police to detain suspects for up to seven days for questioning, where there was a more probable cause rather than the mere "reasonable suspicion" requirement of the Emergency Provisions Act. Also it allowed British authorities to ban suspected individuals from the British mainland.

PRIMA LINEA (PL). The "Front Line" group were Italian leftist terrorists active from November 1976 until 1981, second only to the **Red Brigades** as a major terrorist threat. Like the Red Brigades or the **Red Army Faction**, they rationalized their terrorism in revolutionary leftist terms but appeared to pursue terrorist violence as an end in itself rather than as a strategy to achieve revolution. While they did not appear to have state sponsorship, the group did collaborate with **Direct Action** and the Red Brigades.

In **ideology** and organization, PL greatly resembled the Red Brigades perhaps because one of its leaders, Corrado Alunni, was also a leading Red Brigades figure. PL differed from the Red Brigades, however, in maintaining open contacts with the Italian left rather than going underground. Its initial act was an attack against the Fiat plant in Turin on 29 November 1976. By the end of 1978 PL had carried out 25 operations. In January 1979 PL murdered Milan Assistant Attorney General, Emilio Alessandrini. Like the Red Brigades, PL also specialized in **"kneecapping,"** as it did in the case of the Italian manager of the Chemical Bank of New York in Milan who was shot four times in the legs on 11 May 1978, and also to 10 hostages in the Turin School of Industrial Management on 11 December 1979. After 1980 PL began concentrating more on **assassinations**, particularly judges and jurors who had convicted leftist terrorists.

The group originated in Turin and spread to Florence, Milan, and Naples. Due to the police crackdown following the **kidnapping** and murder of former prime minister Aldo Moro in early 1978 at the hands of the Red Brigades, Italian police were able to identify about 165 members of PL who were largely apprehended by October 1982, so ending the organization.

PROVISIONAL IRISH REPUBLICAN ARMY (PIRA). Name adopted by modern **Irish Republican Army** (IRA) group that split from the "Official" RA in December 1969. Once the older Official IRA declared its cease-fire in the summer of 1972 the Provisional IRA group became the de facto IRA and this name is used to designate that group from 1972 onward.

-Q-

QADDAFI, MUAMMAR (1942-). Leader of the coup d'état that overthrew King Idris of Libya on 1 September 1969, Colonel Muammar Qaddafi has been the president of the Libyan Arab Republic, also called by Qaddafi the Libyan People's Arab Socialist Jamahariyyah. Qaddafi is of Bedouin extraction and is a devout Muslim.

As a youth he greatly admired Egyptian leader Gamal Abdel Nasser and so Qaddafi's pronounced anti-Western sentiments appear to spring from his ardent Pan-Arabism and hatred of Israel. Accordingly he ordered the U.S. military forces out of Libya in 1970, canceled the British-Libyan military accord in 1972, nationalized U.S. oil companies' holdings in Libya, and played an instrumental role within the Organization of Petroleum Exporting Countries (OPEC) in raising producer oil prices. Qaddafi's involvement with sponsorship of terrorist groups began in the same period with aid to **Black September** in its attack on the Saudi Arabian embassy in Khartoum on 1 March 1973 and in its attack on the Athens airport on 5 August 1973. Libya also supported the terrorists responsible for the OPEC Secretariat siege in December 1975, allowing them to unload their ransoms in Libya and later permitting them **sanctuary** there. The Venezuelan terrorist Ilyich Ramírez Sánchez, also called **"Carlos,"** who led the **OPEC siege**, disappeared from public view at that time until his capture in 1994.

In 1975 Qaddafi broke off relations with the **Palestine Liberation Organization** (PLO) and began to back the renegade **Fatah Revolutionary Council** led by **Abu Nidal**. Consequently Qaddafi is suspected of complicity in the 23 November 1985 **hijacking** of an EgyptAir airline to Luqua airport in Malta and the massacre of holiday travelers at Rome and Vienna airports on 27 December 1985.

Qaddafi clashed with the United States over the question of Libyan claims to sovereignty over the Gulf of Sidra. U.S. naval exercises in those waters led to confrontations between Libyan and U.S. forces in March 1986. The United States held Libya responsible for the 5 April 1986 **bombing** of the La Belle discothèque in West Berlin, a favorite nightclub of U.S. servicemen. In retaliation, the U.S. Air Force conducted bombing raids on Benghazi and Tripoli, striking one of Qaddafi's residences and apparently killing one of his foster children. Qaddafi became uncharacteristically reticent after this incident. This did not portend any renunciation of terrorism, however. On 14 April 1988 the

"Jihad Brigades," a unit of the **Japanese Red Army** acting under Libyan sponsorship, carried out a retaliatory bombing against a USO club in Naples, killing five patrons. On 14 November 1991 the United States issued indictments against Libyan officials, charging the Libyan government with sponsorship of the bombing of **Pan Am Flight 103** on 21 December 1988, and the U.S. State Department published evidence in its April 1992 report on global terrorism linking the Qaddafi regime with the bombing. On 30 April 1992 Qaddafi announced he would refuse to **extradite** the two officials named in those indictments. However, on 5 April 1999 both suspects were finally handed over, through United Nations mediators, to Scottish police in Camp Zeist in the Netherlands and their trial began on 3 May 2000.

Both Great Britain and the United States have also had concerns over Libyan **state terrorism** against anti-Qaddafi Libyans living as permanent residents or students in those countries. During 1980 Libyan agents murdered at least 10 anti-Qaddafi dissidents in Great Britain and Western Europe. Later such agents also tried to hire **assassins** to kill dissidents within the United States. On 17 April 1984, during anti-Qaddafi demonstrations outside the Libyan embassy in St. James Square, London, members of the Libyan "People's Bureau" opened fired with automatic weapons on the crowds outside, wounding 11 Libyan protestors and killing a young British policewoman. Both Britain and the United States have retaliated for such incidents by expelling the Libyan diplomats involved in such behavior.

The economic sanctions imposed on Libya in April 1992 under UN Security Council Resolution 748, which were tightened on 11 November 1993, inflicted over $23.5 billion in damages on Libya's economy and led to shortages of basic goods and inflation rates of 600 percent or more. The decade of economic sanctions and increasing unpopularity at home forced Qaddafi to curtail the adventurism of his regime outside Libya and to try to come to terms with the United States, Britain, and other nations he had previously challenged and confronted. The **Islamic fundamentalist** insurgency in Algeria may also have led Qaddafi to seek a tactical accommodation with the West for Qaddafi was an inveterate foe of the **Muslim Brotherhood** and similar movements and cooperated strongly with Algerian and French authorities to counter the activities of the **Armed Islamic Group** and **Islamic Salvation Front**.

By 1997 Qaddafi had forced Abu Nidal to leave Libya and by 1999 he had closed down the camps of hard-line Palestinian factions and had given the British files on the **Irish Republican Army** (IRA) as well as promising to help British police investigate the fatal shooting of a British policewoman that occurred outside the Libyan People's Bureau in London in 1984. Qaddafi also assisted France in identifying and bringing to trial those Libyan agents responsible for the **UTA Flight 772 bombing** that occurred in September 1989. Qaddafi's cooperation in handing over the two suspects wanted for the bombing of Pan Am Flight 103 resulted in the lifting of the UN sanctions on 5 April 1999. Many Arab diplomats have stated that Qaddafi has become a more mature and responsible leader and appears to have given up much of his previous involvement in state sponsorship of terrorism.

QA'EDA, AL-. Alternative spelling, Al Qa'ida (Arabic for "the base"), is name of organization, or network of organizations, sponsored by **Osama bin Laden**, which is a revolutionary, antistate group with the goal of restoring a pan-Islamic state according to Sunni Muslim precepts and fighting those regarded as enemies of true Islam. The various goals of this group are reflected in the multitude of names which it uses, such as the Islamic Army for the Liberation of the Holy Places, the Group for the Protection of the Holy Sites, the World Islamic Front for Jihad against Jews and Crusaders, among others. Bin Laden created this organization originally in 1990 to recruit Arab and other Sunni Muslims to fight against the Soviets in Afghanistan and to maintain some functional unity among those veterans and allied groups who share a common **Islamic fundamentalist** political program and belief in the legitimacy of violent means to achieve that program.

This group is influenced largely by the Wahhabi interpretation of the Hanbali Sunni school of law which makes it also extremely hostile to Shi'ism generally, which is viewed as heretical and un-Islamic. Accordingly the members of this group or network shun contact or cooperation with Iran or its affiliated Shi'ite groups, such as **Hezbollah**. Al Qa'eda is closely affiliated with the **Islamic Group** of Egypt, the **Munazzamat al Jihad**, and the various **Kashmiri Muslim secessionists**. Due to bin Laden's involvement in the **East African U.S. embassy bombings** of August 1998 and evidence that the group plotted several acts of terror in the Philippines in 1995, including a plot to **assassinate** Pope John Paul II and President Bill Clinton, as well as a plot to bomb 12 U.S. trans-Pacific flights in 1995, this group has been added to the official list of foreign terrorist organizations maintained by the U.S.

State Department. The group is also thought to have been responsible for attacks on U.S. troops in Somalia in 1993 as well as **bombings** directed against U.S. troops in transit through Yemen in August 1992. Most recently the group was identified as the principal behind the 11 September 2001 attacks upon the World Trade Center and the Pentagon. *See also* BIN LADEN; EAST AFRICAN U.S. EMBASSY BOMBINGS; AND WORLD TRADE CENER AND PENTAGON ATTACKS OF 11 SEPTEMBER 2001.

QIBLA. *See* PEOPLE AGAINST GANGS AND DRUGS.

QUEBEC LIBERATION FRONT. The Front de Libération du Québec (FLQ) was a French Canadian group seeking independence for the province of Quebec from the rest of Canada along with creation of a socialist regime there. From 1962 to 1980 the FLQ was the single largest source of political violence in Canada, accounting for 50 percent (= 166 incidents) of all domestic terrorism in Canada, most of which occurred before 1972. Most incidents involved **bombings** of Canadian federal buildings, and firebombings of Canadian police stations, businesses in Quebec owned by American and Canadian Anglophones, and military installations, but eventually progressing to **kidnapping** and murder. The group enjoyed moral and limited material support from Cuba and Algeria.

The FLQ was founded in February 1963 by three Quebec separatists disgruntled with existing separatist organizations. On 21 June 1970 the group botched an attempt to kidnap the U.S. consul general in Montreal. On 5 October 1970 they kidnapped James Cross, the British trade commissioner in Canada, whom they released on 3 December 1970. On 10 October 1970 they kidnapped Pierre LaPorte, Quebec's minister of labor. The Canadian government imposed the War Measures Act on 16 October 1970, suspending ordinary civil liberties and allowing police and military forces extraordinary powers to apprehend around 500 suspects and to conduct searches without warrants. The kidnappers murdered LaPorte on 17 October 1970, and his body was found the following day in the trunk of a car. The four kidnappers eventually negotiated safe passage to Cuba in exchange for the life of James Cross.

The murder of LaPorte greatly shocked English-speaking Canadian and Québécois public opinion and created a backlash against the FLQ even in Quebec. The outrage against the FLQ was heightened by the separatist Parti Québécois's impressive gains in recent elections, having secured 23 percent of the provincial election votes in 1970, which made the recourse to terrorism seem pointless and counterproductive. The War Measures Act expired in January 1971, but ordinary police powers resulted in a dozen arrests of key FLQ members that year. FLQ theoretician Pierre Vallières (1938-1998) surfaced in December 1971, publicly repudiating the FLQ and calling on FLQ members to desist from terrorism. The FLQ was dormant from then until the electoral victory of the Parti Québécois in provincial elections in 1976 by which time most former FLQ members had opted to seek separatism through the Parti Québécois. From 1963 to 1971, when the bombings stopped, the FLQ had killed about nine persons, and carried out almost 200 bombings, as well as numerous bank robberies and the two political kidnappings.

Following the narrow defeat on 30 October 1995 of the Parti Québécois-sponsored provincial referendum on secession from Canada, the former convicted FLQ bomber, Raymond Villeneuve, formed a new group, the Quebec National Liberation Movement (Mouvement de Libération Nationale du Québec), urging French-speaking Québécois to use harassment, and other forms of intimidation or violence, to drive English speakers from the province so that French speakers could achieve independence by whatever means possible.

QUTB, SAYYID (1903-1966). Egyptian Muslim theologian, social thinker and activist, and leader within the **Muslim Brotherhood**, Sayyid Qutb exercised a cardinal influence on the development of **Islamic fundamentalism** through his writings and directly influenced the theory and practice of such fundamentalist groups as the various branches of the **Muslim Brotherhood**, the **Munazzamat al Jihad** group, and others who have used Qutb's reinterpretation of the doctrine of *jihad* to justify terrorist actions against "apostate" Muslim governments and rulers as well as against perceived external enemies of Islam.

In his seminal work *Ma'alim fi al Tariq* (Milestones) Qutb advanced the argument that since the main object of jihad was enforcing full enactment of the traditional code of Islamic law, rather than defense of Muslim lands or conquest of non-Muslims as such, there was no reason for Muslims to abstain from initiating military force to advance Islam in the world. Qutb's works also demonized Westernizing and secular nationalist Muslim political leaders as agents of a revived *jahiliyyah* (pre-Islamic heathenism) who therefore were to be counted among those enemies of Islam who could be lawfully attacked at will by true believers. The Munazzamat al Jihad group incorporated Qutb's thoughts into their doctrine and enacted them with the **assassination** of **Anwar Sadat** on 6 October 1981.

Sayyid Qutb joined the Muslim Brotherhood in 1951 but was imprisoned in 1954 due to a crackdown on the Brotherhood following an unsuccessful assassination plot against Gamal Abdel Nasser. Qutb was released in the 1960s but was directly implicated in another assassination plot against Nasser in 1965 and executed the following year.

- R -

RACKETEERING-INFLUENCED CORRUPT ORGANIZATIONS (RICO) ACT OF 1970. The federal Racketeering Influenced and Corrupt Organizations statute, Title 18 U.S. Code 1963(a), was originally passed as part of the 1970 Organized Crime Control Act to address organized crime, but since then has been amended several times to make it applicable to anti-abortion violence, inner-city youth gangs, and domestic terrorism. RICO statutes were used in 1987 to convict Joseph Murray and Robert Anderson, two members of the **Irish Republican Army** (IRA), who were involved in smuggling drugs into the United States to finance IRA activities. Members of the Bruder Schweigen Strike Force II (**Order**) were convicted on RICO charges for **bombings** carried out in northern Idaho in 1987. During the period 1982-1989 over 40 percent of the charges against 1,363 terrorists tried in the United States were based on federal antiracketeering (30.2 percent) or RICO statutes (9.3 percent).

RATIONAL-CHOICE THEORY. Theory of political and social behavior that regards individuals as the main unit of analysis for understanding political behavior and their tastes, preferences, and desires as the fundamental motivators of collective actions which are followed by individuals as the most cost-effective means of gaining their desired ends.

Empirical studies of ordinary political and social behavior do not support rational-choice theorists' belief that one can eliminate cultural, **ideological**, or religious beliefs from a cogent explanation of human behavior. However in the analysis and explanation of terrorist events, groups, and motivations, rational-choice theory seems particularly barren. While terrorism appears to have paid off as a political strategy for certain groups, such as the **Irish Republican Army** (IRA) and **Palestine Liberation Organization** (PLO), which have moved from pariah status to partners in negotiations with the very states that once anathematized them, there are scores of other groups whose actions failed to achieve success and whose tactics and behavior cannot be understood in terms of rational-choice. Moreover this approach cannot easily explain the actions of **suicide bombers** or the tactics of **Holy Terror** in which individuals sacrifice themselves to achieve a transcendental ideal which outsiders cannot fathom.

RED ARMY FACTION (RAF). The RAF, formerly known as the "Baader-Meinhof Gang," was a group of German **anarchistic leftist terrorists** active from 11 May 1972 until 20 April 1998. The RAF was of several such groups also known as **"Fighting Communist Organizations."** While the RAF did not originally appear to have state sponsorship, evidence found in East German government files following the reunification of Germany showed that in the preceding 10 years the German Democratic Republic provided logistical support, **sanctuary**, and training to the RAF. In the period from 15-30 June 1990 East German police arrested 10 fugitive RAF members who had been given **asylum** by the former Communist regime. Even in the formative Baader-Meinhof period, however, the group was clearly dependent on the **Popular Front for the Liberation of Palestine** (PFLP) for initial training, which itself received Soviet and other Eastern Bloc assistance. The RAF did collaborate with **Direct Action** and the **Communist Combatant Cells**, both now defunct, and later appeared to collaborate with the **October First Antifascist Resistance Group** (GRAPO).

This group was formed out of the student unrest and leftist activism of 1968 when Andreas Baader (1943-1977), imprisoned in 1968 for firebombing a Frankfurt department store, escaped on 14 May 1970 with the help of Ulrike Meinhof (1934-1976), a left-wing journalist. Together with another comrade they went to the Middle East where they underwent terrorist training in camps run by the PFLP. On their return they engaged in shootings, **bombings**, and **kidnappings** before being arrested in 1972. The continued terrorist activities of the rest of the Baader-Meinhof Gang were directed to freeing their imprisoned comrades. On the night of 8 May 1976 Ulrike Meinhof committed suicide by hanging herself and a year later Andreas Baader also killed himself.

Since that time the surviving group has called itself the Red Army Faction.

On 27 June 1976 RAF members together with members of the PFLP **hijacked** an Air France Paris-to-Tel Aviv flight to Entebbe, Uganda, where 240 passengers were held hostage until rescued by Israeli commandos on 1 July 1976, an operation in which all seven hijackers were killed along with approximately 20 Ugandan soldiers (*see* ENTEBBE HIJACKING). PFLP terrorists hijacked a Lufthansa plane to Mogadishu, Somalia, on 13 October 1977, to force the German government to release imprisoned comrades. When the hijackers were foiled on 17 October 1977 by West German GSG-9 commandos, several of the imprisoned RAF members committed suicide.

The RAF committed 53 noteworthy actions 1972 to 1991, over half of which involved bombings; while about a quarter involved **assassinations** or armed attacks. Only one notable instance of hostage taking is noted, namely the kidnapping of Hanns-Martin Schleyer on 5 September 1977, and two hijackings, namely the 27 June 1976 Entebbe hijacking and the 13 October 1977 Lufthansa hijacking to Mogadishu, in which the RAF played a minor role.

Bombing targets have included a U.S. Officers' Club in Frankfurt (11 May 1972), an attempted bombing assassination of NATO Commander Gen. Alexander Haig (25 June 1979), U.S. Air Force headquarters in Ramstein (31 August 1981), and the Rhein-Main Air Force Base car-bombing attack carried out jointly with Direct Action (8 August 1985). Assassinations have included the killing of German Supreme Court President Günter von Drenkmann (9 November 1974); German Federal Prosecutor Siegfried Buback (7 April 1977); Deutsche Bank Chairman Alfred Herrhausen (30 November 1989); an attempt on Interior Ministry State Secretary Hans Neusel (27 July 1990); and Detlev Rohwedder, a West German businessman involved in the liquidation and sale of former East German state enterprises (1 April 1991).

The RAF was the oldest of the anarchistic, leftist terrorist groups which sought to destroy the capitalist state without any strategy to help build a successor socialist state. The collapse of international communism and the repeated failures of the RAF to build effective alliances with similar groups outside Germany led to what Dennis Pluchinsky described as "strategic confusion" and "**ideological** burn-out." The Gulf War briefly breathed zeal back into the remaining militants who, on 13 February 1991, assaulted the U.S. embassy in Bonn with 250 rounds of small-arms fire in protest against Operation Desert Storm. There remained little reason for them to carry on the armed struggle except, perhaps, to free their remaining imprisoned comrades. But the initiative of Justice Minister Klaus Kinkel to release those RAF prisoners who by now were either nearing the ends of their sentences or else simply too old or too debilitated to engage in terrorism, effectively removed this motive for continued struggle for the RAF members remaining at large.

A long communique was issued by the "Commando" of the RAF dated 10 April 1992, the first half consisting of a self-criticism of the strategy of the group and the second half containing a "conditional unilateral cease-fire." Follow-up communiques of 29 June 1992 and a 58-page document issued in August 1992 reiterated the cease-fire and outlined reasons why the group decided it would no longer engage in antistate terror. Yet on 27 March 1993 RAF members bombed and destroyed the new women's prison under construction in Wieterstadt. On 27 June 1993 German police arrested RAF member Brigit Hogefeld and shot Wolfgang Grams to death while he was resisting arrest. On 16 September 1999 Austrian police in Austria shot and killed Horst Ludwig Meyer, a suspected RAF member near Vienna. Meyer was one of five suspected members of the RAF at large and not yet accounted for.

Although this group was estimated to have had only 10 to 20 actual fighters at large at any given time, it succeeded in creating a support network of hundreds of Germans, many of whom were well-educated professionals. The RAF had also succeeded in perpetuating itself through two generations of leadership, which gave it a longevity that few other anarchistic leftist terrorist groups achieved. However, on 20 April 1998 a final memorandum sent to Reuters confirmed that the remaining members of the group had dissolved their organization and that they and their cause had now "become history."

RED ARMY FOR THE LIBERATION OF CATALONIA. The Ejército Rojo Catalán de Liberación (ERCA) is believed to be a Marxist-Leninist offshoot of the **Terra Lliure** Catalan separatist movement. As such it shares with Terra Lliure the goal of reconstituting an independent Catalan homeland in Catalonia, which would embrace also the Spanish provinces of Valencia and the Balearic Isles as well as the French province of Roussillon.

During 1987 ERCA **bombed** several U.S. targets in Barcelona. On May 13 the General Electric office was bombed, causing no injuries. On

October 14 the U.S. Consulate General was bombed, injuring eight Spaniards. On December 26 a youth lobbed two grenades of Danish manufacture into a USO club, killing one U.S. serviceman and wounding five other servicemen as well as three bystanders.

RED BRIGADES. The Brigate Rosse (BR) was a group of Italian **anarchistic leftist terrorists** founded in 1970 and active from 18 April 1974 until 23 April 1988. The BR adopted a political and military organization: The national structure was made up of a Strategic Directorate and Executive Committee under which there was a Column Command. The "columns" were modeled after the Italian Partisans of World War II and each column was responsible for specific areas, usually one per major city, and each was to be self-sufficient and compartmentalized, with a six-member directorate and four-member "brigades" which conducted political organizing among workers, students, and low-income neighborhoods. To handle specialized problems each column had "fronts," such as a "logistical front" to find a safe house, procure fake I.D.s, and carry out bank hold-ups, a "counter-revolution front" to spy on the police, and a "prison front" to maintain contacts with imprisoned comrades and help them escape. The organization had permanent militants, which included all who were wanted by the police and had gone underground but which also included those militants who were not yet known to the police and who often continued to hold ordinary jobs. The "occasional militants" were those who lived a normal life but served as a support network for the permanent militants.

The BR operated by "campaigns" that consisted of concentrated and coordinated actions to achieve goals set by the Strategic Directorate: columns and fronts would decide on appropriate **targets** and tactics and, after conducting surveillance and careful planning, would carry out those attacks. Highly complex "central actions," such as the **kidnapping** of Aldo Moro, involved recruiting a group of 10 highly experienced militants who ordinarily came from the more specialized fronts but some of whom came from the simple brigades. While the central action was taking place other columns would distract the police with scores of other tactical actions, including **arsons, kneecappings**, and even **assassinations**. While the BR did not appear to have state sponsorship it had contacts in the mid-1970s with Uruguayan **Tupamaros**, later collaborated with **Direct Action** and the **Red Army Faction**, and cultivated links with Palestinian terrorist groups, in particular the **Lebanese**

Armed Revolutionary Factions (FARL). After the collapse of the BR in Italy it appeared that some fugitive BR members joined forces with the **October First Antifascist Resistance Group** (GRAPO).

The BR viewed itself as the vanguard for a proletarian party that would spontaneously appear once the group had paved the way by destroying the "SIM," the Italian acronym for "Imperialist State of Multinationals," and by raising the revolutionary consciousness of the working classes through acts of **armed propaganda**. Founded in 1970 the BR struck at the Italian state through assassination and kneecappings of judges, prosecutors, and jurors and also through attacks on the Christian Democratic Party. About 75 percent of the BR's attacks, however, were directed at businesses, with threats of arson, kidnapping, kneecapping, or murder if protection money was not paid. The BR seldom made use of **bombing**, except on 3 May 1979 in attacking the Christian Democrat Party headquarters in Rome although it used firebombs to initiate arsons.

During the period from 1974-1988, there were at least 50 noteworthy attacks committed by the BR, 47 assassinations, 19 cases of kneecapping of victims, and 13 kidnappings. Four kidnap ransoms alone netted the BR around $6 million. Like the Red Army Faction, the BR undertook many of their kidnapping and attacks on behalf of imprisoned comrades, either to pressure the judicial system to release them or else to take revenge on jurists and police involved in their capture and convictions. The waves of assassinations of jurists eventually caused Italian magistrates to go on strike in July 1980 in protest over their lack of security. During 1978-1980, called by Italians the "years of lead," hardly a day went by without an armed attack, political murder, kidnapping, or other terrorist actions due to the Brigades, similar leftist groups and imitators, as well as Italian neo-Fascists.

Three events stand out in the history of the Brigades: Inspired by the Red Army Faction's kidnapping of Hanns-Martin Schleyer, the BR kidnapped the head of the Christian Democrat Party and former prime minister, Aldo Moro, on 16 March 1978, killing five of his bodyguards. Moro was killed 55 days later. While the BR viewed this as a great victory Italian society at large viewed it with revulsion and the Italian government empowered its security forces to suspend certain civil liberties to crack down on the Brigades and similar groups. On 17 December 1981, the BR kidnapped Brigadier General James Dozier, U.S. Army, in Verona, who was rescued by Italian counterterrorist police in Padua on 28 January 1982. The decision to kidnap a senior NATO officer had been inspired partly through a desire to show solidarity with the **Palestine Liberation Organization** (PLO) by striking at an "imperialist" target. The BR connection with Palestinian terrorists was more obvious when they assassinated an American, Leamon Hunt, the director of the multinational observer team charged with overseeing the peace accord between Egypt and Israel on 15 February 1984, apparently with weapons provided by Lebanese Armed Revolutionary Factions (FARL) agents. Following this murder, the BR carried out another three assassinations of prominent persons as well as an attempted assassination. In the first week of September 1989 Italian police arrested several brigadists after which BR activity appeared to cease.

By 1989 about 1,300 BR members had been imprisoned. By 1994 about 400 remained in jail and by 1997 only 181. On 21 November 1997 Greek police in Athens arrested Enrico Bianco, one of the BR members once thought to have been responsible for the kidnapping and killing of Aldo Moro. Although he had been cleared of those charges in January 1981 Italy sought his **extradition** on other criminal charges. On 7 October 1998 Renato Curcio, the founder of the Red Brigades and the last major BR figure to remain in prison, was freed after serving 24 years of a 30-year sentence. However, on 20 May 1999 unknown assailants in Rome shot and killed Massimo D'Antona, a senior advisor of Italy's Labor Minister, and later responsibility for the murder was claimed in the name of the Red Brigades. Since D'Antona was a member of the Democrats of the Left party, which supported the NATO bombing campaign against Yugoslavia meant to force the Serbian Army out of Kosovo, Italian observers speculated that the action may have been the work of Yugoslavian agents. Many of the former BR members, including Adriana Faranda, who had served 14 years in jail for her role in the Moro assassination, stated that they believed the cycle of armed revolutionary violence in Italy was over and doubted that any original BR members were involved in this attack.

RED GUERRILLA RESISTANCE (RGR). The RGR was a nonstate U.S. leftist group that engaged in bombings during the mid-1980s for the limited purpose of protesting U.S. and Israeli "imperialism," militarism, and South African apartheid. All of the **bombings** carried out in the name of this group occurred in New York City. On 5 April 1984 the RGR bombed the Israeli Aircraft Industries plant. On 26 September 1984, the group bombed the South African Consulate. On 23 February 1985 it bombed the New York City Police Benevolent Association offices. Some analysts believe that the Red Guerrilla Resistance was another nom de guerre of the **May 19 Communist Coalition**.

RED HAND COMMANDOS. The Red Hand Commandos were an Ulster Protestant terrorist militia established in 1972 by John McKeague after his expulsion from the **Ulster Defence Association** (UDA). This group and the **Ulster Volunteer Force** (UVF), with which it worked in tandem, functioned as anti-Catholic **death squads** in the Belfast area and were banned by the British government in 1973. In April 1975 the Commandos **bombed** a pub in a Catholic district killing six. The Red Hand Commandos were also suspected in the 17 May 1974 bombings of downtown Dublin and Monaghan, killing 30 and wounding 151.

McKeague was unsuccessfully prosecuted under the Stormont parliament's Incitement to Religious Hatred Law. Shortly after his acquittal in January 1982, McKeague was killed by militants of the **Irish National Liberation Army** (INLA). Most recently the group is known to have killed six people in the period 1992-1995 and is believed to have been associated with another group, the Loyalist Retaliation and Defence Group, which terrorized shopkeepers who sold the pro-Republican *An Phoblacht* (Republican News), killing two of them in 1991.

RED HAND DEFENDERS (RHD). The RHD is a small Ulster Protestant Loyalist group that came into existence in 1998 and is believed to consist of members of the **Loyalist Volunteer Force**, the **Ulster Defence Association**, and the **Ulster Freedom Fighters** who opposed the Good Friday agreement of 10 April 1998. The RHD first appeared when it claimed responsibility for the 7 September 1998 **bombing** that killed a Royal Ulster Constabulary officer, Frankie O'Reilly. A further action was the shooting death of a Catholic man, Brian Service, on 31 October 1998, the timing of which appeared to have been intended to stall faltering peace talks and to sabotage the cease-fire being observed by the **Irish Republican Army** (IRA) and major Ulster militia groups. The RHD also claimed responsibility for the murder of Rosemary Nelson, a Catholic human rights lawyer, killed by a car bomb in Lurgan on 15 March 1998. The group has used homemade pipe bombs but also has access to grenades and handguns. It appeared at the same time as the

Orange Volunteers and many observers believed that the membership of these two groups overlapped.

REJECTION FRONT. In 1974 the **Popular Front for the Liberation of Palestine** (PFLP) established the Front Rejecting Capitulationist Solutions to oppose the participation of the **Palestine Liberation Organization** (PLO) in any negotiated settlement of the Arab-Israeli conflict. The **PFLP-General Command**, the **Arab Liberation Front**, the **Palestine Liberation Front**, and the **Popular Struggle Front** also joined this opposition group. Given the acquiescence of the PFLP and several of these other groups with the resolutions of the 19th meeting of the Palestine National Council on 15 November 1988, recognizing UN resolutions 242 and 338 as the basis for a Middle East settlement, the Rejection Front must be regarded as defunct.

RELATIVE DEPRIVATION THEORY. Theory that ordinary crime or political violence is directly or indirectly motivated by economic factors. If true this theory could also conceivably explain terrorism as a special case of political violence or unrest. Ted Robert Gurr investigated the impact of relative deprivation on civil unrest in a study, "A Causal Model of Civil Strife: A Comparative Analysis Using New Indices," [*American Political Science Review*, (4 Dec. 1968), 62: 1104-1124.] This study, which analyzed statistically cases of civil unrest found in 114 nation-states, showed that it was not so much worsening economic conditions that led to **revolution** but rather perceptions of worsening economic conditions that set the stage for unrest. Even if economic conditions were improving, when perceptions of economic deprivation were joined to perceptions of government illegitimacy civil strife would follow. To explain civil unrest the idea of relative deprivation had to embrace not only economic deprivation but also social and political deprivation as well. Gurr also found that including the variable of political agitation by revolutionary groups enjoying foreign support in his statistical model almost doubled the amount of civil unrest it explained. These results appear to demonstrate that relative deprivation is neither sufficient nor necessary to explain political violence much less terrorism. Profiles of terrorist groups show rather that terrorists often come from backgrounds with higher rather than lower socioeconomic status and usually higher than average education. Social and political deprivation, rather than purely economic deprivation, may facilitate political unrest but terrorism proper requires the mobilizing force of **ideology** to transform inchoate disaffection into organized political violence.

RENAMO (MNR). The Mozambique National Resistance (Resistência Nacional Moçambicana) was a Mozambican insurgent group formerly sponsored by Rhodesia and South Africa which eventually became an ordinary political party in 1994. Members of this group are largely anti-Marxist Mozambicans, both native Africans and Portuguese colonials, as well as disaffected former FRELIMO (Mozambican Liberation Front) members who were seeking to change the regime. The South African sponsors of RENAMO viewed it primarily as a means of pressuring Mozambique to stop giving **sanctuary** and support to the **Umkhonto we Sizwe** guerrillas fighting South Africa, who were associated with the **African National Congress** (ANC).

When Mozambique was granted independence by Portugal on 25 June 1975 the new Marxist government began giving aid and sanctuary to Zimbabwe African National Union (ZANU) guerrillas fighting the Ian Smith regime. Rhodesia countered by sponsoring the creation of the MNR in 1976, which recruited both native African and Portuguese colonial Mozambicans to attack the anti-Rhodesian guerrillas in their bases within Mozambique. Beginning in 1978 the MNR began attacking the economic infrastructure of Mozambique as well as seeking to destabilize the FRELIMO regime. After the transition of power in 1980 that created the new state of Zimbabwe from the former colony of Rhodesia, the MNR found a new sponsor in South Africa that also wished to pressure Mozambique to stop supporting the ANC-backed guerrillas. In 1982 the MNR changed its name to RENAMO and spread its area of operations into Zimbabwe, Malawi, and Zambia. From having started with a few thousand in 1976, RENAMO expanded to in excess of 20,000 guerrillas by the end of the 1980s. It enjoyed safe haven in South Africa as well as logistical support but neighboring states, such as Malawi, Tanzania, and Zimbabwe, countered by stationing some of their troops within Mozambique.

RENAMO's campaign was marked by calculated, consistent, and extreme brutality directed toward noncombatants. An analysis of 47 noteworthy incidents from 1979 to 1987 showed that 51 percent involved **kidnappings,** 15 percent involved **assassinations**, and four percent involved **bombings**. The remaining 30 percent involved armed attacks and sabotage operations. Kidnappings generally involved foreign nationals, such as aid and development workers, relief workers, and missionaries, some of whom were killed in captivity or died of disease or malnutrition, and four of whom disappeared. African nationals of Mozambique and neighboring lands have also been, in effect, enslaved by RENAMO for use as human porters. In August 1979 the MNR murdered five Soviet advisers and in June 1982 murdered a Portuguese engineer. On 14 October 1983 RENAMO derailed a train and then murdered dozens of passengers. In July 1987 RENAMO carried out a massacre at Homoine, killing over 400 civilians. RENAMO also engaged in mutilation of its victims.

By 1990, as the South African government gradually came to terms with the ANC, its support for RENAMO came to an end. RENAMO had meanwhile built up a support network in Europe and elsewhere among private individuals and groups. During 1991 negotiations between RENAMO and the Mozambican government were underway and hostilities there had been partly suspended. Although a RENAMO leader, Afonso Marceta Dhlakama, and Mozambique's President Joaquim Alberto Chissano signed a cease-fire in Rome in October 1992, sporadic fighting continued between RENAMO and government forces until the elections of 27-28 October 1994 in which Chissano was elected president by 53 percent of the vote while RENAMO leader Dhlakama won 33 percent. In the 250-seat Assembly of the Republic FRELIMO won 129 seats while RENAMO won 112, and the smaller Democratic Union won nine seats. Despite a disclaimer that RENAMO might reject the election results if it did not win, RENAMO acquiesced to become the opposition to a FRELIMO-led government.

RENDITION. Sending a suspect to a nation where the suspect is wanted on criminal charges or merely for investigation, whether by legal means or extralegal. Rendition covers all forms of **extradition**, deportation, or return of a suspect by national authorities apart from a formal extradition procedure, as well as illegal actions such as **kidnapping** and transporting a suspect back to the nation seeking that person. In the case of the rendition of Ilyich Ramírez Sánchez, also known as **"Carlos,"** the Sudanese authorities agreed to allow French agents to arrest Carlos and return him to France for trial without the formal-legal extradition procedure. The FBI used a 1984 antiterrorism statute to arrest Fawaz Younis, a suspected hijacker, in September 1987 but did so without relying on the cooperation of Lebanese authorities. Younis was lured out to a yacht off the Lebanese coast where he was arrested by FBI agents and then transported to a U.S. naval vessel and brought back to the United States for trial.

Cases of rendition in which the country seeking the suspect asserts extraterritorial jurisdiction and bypasses reliance on local authorities are controversial because they violate the territorial sovereignty of the nation from which the suspect is taken and are probably only justifiable where the local government has given **sanctuary** to terrorists or else has been incapable of asserting effective authority over its territory. Most cases of rendition involve the extradition process or some other form of cooperation with the local authorities.

"REPUBLIC OF TEXAS." Group of antistate residents in Fort Davis, Texas, who claimed that the State of Texas was illegally annexed by the United States and who declared their own "Republic of Texas" in 1997. Led by Richard L. McClaren, this group of at most two dozen, was headquartered in a trailer home and an abandoned fire station 15 miles outside of Ft. Davis in the Davis Mountains. Like the **Freemen** of Montana they also declared themselves independent of the United States after running afoul of authorities by creating bogus financial instruments and filing bogus liens to harass Texas and federal authorities and whomever they deemed to be their enemies.

On 27 April 1997 McClaren ordered the seizure of Joe Rowe and Margaret Ann Rowe, against whom McClaren had ligitated unsuccessfully, after the local Sheriff's Department had arrested one of his followers, Robert J. Scheidt, on trespassing and firearms charge. Up to 300 Texas Public Safety officers and FBI agents besieged the McClaren compound. On 3 May 1997 McClaren and all but two of his followers, who escaped into the Davis Mountains, surrendered to authorities. On 31 October 1997 McClaren and his chief lieutenant, Robert Otto, were found guilty in State District Court for organized criminal activity and the abduction of Joe and Margaret Ann Rowe and on 4 November 1997 McClaren was sentenced to 99 years imprisonment and Otto to 50 years.

RESURGENCE MOVEMENTS. Also called "Revitalization Movements," these are attempts by a group to recover its cultural, political, or social identity through either nonpolitical, political, violent, or nonviolent means. The various **ethno-nationalist** political and military movements,

identity politics within a nation-state, and fundamentalist religious movements, such as **Islamic fundamentalism** as well as Protestant Christian revivalism associated also with **millennialism,** are all examples of resurgence movements. Resurgence movements have variously succeeded or failed in preserving a community and its way of life. The **Ku Klux Klan** and **militia movements** are examples of movements seeking to restore pre-Civil War norms of **white supremacy**, state-centered federalism, and antiforeigner nativism. The various Sikh and Kurdish militant nationalist movements seek to create new nation-states based on their respective religious or ethnic communities.

REVOLUTION. A transformation of the political system of a society in which the majority of the people in the affected society withdraw their recognition of the legitimacy of the prerevolutionary political system in favor of the system that replaces it. Revolution differs from a coup d'état insofar as a coup need only replace the main personalities governing the state without otherwise changing the state system. Revolutions usually involve some political violence, even in those using nonviolent civil disobedience, since even then the protagonists of the regime usually will violently resist being overthrown.

Several theories of revolution have been proposed, ranging from the historical-materialist thesis of Karl Marx and his followers to the theory that revolutions are the result of **ideological** movements among the intellectual elites who have grown alienated from the political order. It should be noted that since most theories of revolution attempt to explain social movements that encompass a significant portion, if not majority, of the people of a nation-state or colony, whereas terrorist activities and insurgency usually involve smaller groups, that theories of revolution do not satisfactorily address the phenomenon of terrorism.

Throughout this dictionary, groups are described as having revolutionary goals even if their aim is secession or independence for a nationalist homeland rather than the political transformation of the entire society or economic-social order. In the case of the **Irish Republican Army** (IRA) their goals included the unification of the northern and southern counties of Ireland and total separation of a united Ireland from Great Britain. The IRA intended to destroy the legitimacy of the Northern Irish government but also to cause the British to acquiesce in the redefinition of the British state as well. Similarly the transformation of an authoritarian and bureaucratic Iranian state under the shah to a theocratic state under the rule of Shi'ite clergymen must also be counted as a revolution even if such a transformation does not meet historicist expectations of some linear scheme of tentative progress. There is no a priori reason to designate only leftist groups as being "revolutionary" while designating all rightist groups as "counterrevolutionary." *See also* ALIENATION; RELATIVE DEPRIVATION THEORY.

REVOLUTIONARY ARMED FORCES OF COLOMBIA. The Fuerzas Armadas Revolutionarias de Colombia (FARC) is a nonstate guerrilla group dedicated to creating a Marxist-Leninist revolution in Colombia. FARC is considered to be the best equipped, best trained, and most effective guerrilla group in South America. Its main areas of operations have been the rural areas of the departments of Antioquía, Tolima, Magdalena, Boyaca, Caqueta, Huila, Cauca, Santander, Valle del Cauca, Cundinamarca, and Meta. Its headquarters are located in La Uribe in Meta department.

FARC's origins go back to 1958 when Colombian Communist Party (PCC) Central Committee member Manuel Marulanda Velez and Rigoberto Losada (d. 1992) founded FARC as an independent guerrilla group. In 1966 the PCC adopted FARC as its military wing. This move was taken in reaction to the creation of the Castroite **National Liberation Army** (ELN) in 1964. In the period from 1966-1968, FARC numbered some 500 combatants. The normalization of relations between the Soviet Union and Colombia weakened FARC, which could no longer count on external aid.

Its members have been drawn mainly from the middle-class intelligentsia. FARC has undercut its appeal by its tactic of **kidnapping**, and killing peasants who do not cooperate with it. During the early 1970s FARC began financing itself through kidnapping for ransom of foreign nationals and wealthy Colombians and through extortion of foreign-affiliated businesses. During this resurgence FARC organized itself into operationally independent units known as "fronts," having five fronts by 1978, which increased to 27 fronts by 1987 and to 40 fronts by 1988. One of these fronts, the **Ricardo Franco Front**, broke with the main body of FARC in March 1984 over the question of seeking a negotiated settlement with the government and became an independent terrorist organization.

The group has attacked both Colombian domestic and U.S.-affiliated targets. In February 1977 they kidnapped a U.S. Peace Corps volunteer in La Macrena who was released three years later only after payment of a $250,000 ransom. In August 1980 they kidnapped a U.S. banana grower in central Colombia, who was released three months later after payment of a $125,000 ransom. In April and August 1983 two U.S. citizens residing in La Meta department were also kidnapped and released only on payments of ransom.

In May 1984, FARC, along with the **Popular Liberation Army** (EPL) and **M-19**, signed a cease-fire with the Colombian government that did not require members of these groups to surrender their weapons. Various FARC fronts, as well as the Ricardo Franco Front, continued terrorist killings, extortionism, and kidnappings, as well as attacking military units:

During February 1985 eight U.S. businesses were bombed in Medellín, including IBM, General Telephone and Electronics, Union Carbide, and Xerox. In the course of these nighttime **bombings**, one person was killed and another wounded. The Medellín bombings may have been the work of the Ricardo Franco Front, which did not feel obligated to follow other FARC fronts in honoring the truce. In August 1985 FARC reportedly kidnapped four engineers and 30 workers of a construction company in Huila department following the firm's refusal to submit to a $80,000 extortion demand. In November 1986 a mass grave was discovered in Turbo containing the remains of about a hundred men, women, and children thought to have been killed by FARC. In December 1987 50 FARC members attacked Gaitania using automatic weapons, grenades, and antitank rockets, killing two policemen and wounding five.

While some have seen this continuation of violence by FARC fronts as evidence of duplicity on the part of FARC, another explanation equally consistent with these facts is that the decentralized command structure of FARC and the continuing violence among government troops, drug traffickers, and leftist groups created a situation in which hostilities and settling of old scores were likely to continue.

In late 1985 FARC established the Simón Bolívar Guerrilla Coordination board, an umbrella organization for all leftist insurgents in Colombia that succeeded the National Guerrilla Coordination group from which FARC had been excluded. In 1985 it also created the Patriotic Union (UP) as a political front organization.

FARC has had a problematic relationship with Colombian cocaine traffickers. FARC's protection of traffickers' interests in exchange for cash can be understood as another form of extortion, especially since drug traffickers later began to sponsor their own terrorist attacks not only against the Colombian government but also against leftist politicians associated with FARC through its Simón Bolívar Guerrilla Coordination board front: On 11 October 1987 UP member and former presidential candidate Jaime Pardo Neal was killed by agents of José Gonzalo Rodríguez Gacha, a major drug trafficker. On 22 March 1990 traffickers also **assassinated** UP presidential candidate Bernardo Jaramillo Ossa at Bogotá airport.

Although FARC accepted in principle the "national dialogue" it found that its UP candidates were murdered by the **death squads** of vengeful **Colombian cocaine cartels** which resented FARC's previous **kidnappings** of their members and extortion in the name of revolutionary taxes. By November 1991 the Simon Bolivar Guerrilla Coordination ended the dialogue to resume terrorist attacks. With the Colombian government's preoccupation with recapturing Medellín cartel leader Pablo Escobar terrorist attacks by FARC and other leftist groups left Colombia with the highest number of terrorist incidents of any nation in 1992. In March 1993 FARC kidnapped three American missionaries from Panama and in the fall of 1993 FARC and the rival ELN set aside their rivalry to cooperate in a month-long offensive against the government. In July 1994 FARC assassinated a high-ranking Colombian army general and intensified its campaign of kidnapping Colombian and foreigners for ransom. During 1995 the number of leftist-related terrorist acts nearly doubled to 76 from 41 the previous year. In 1995 FARC assassinated Alvaro Gomez Hurtado, head of the Conservative Party.

Around 1995 FARC resumed its insurgency in earnest. In the period 1986-1995 FARC had bombed oil pipelines 346 times spilling over 1.2 million barrels of crude oil, roughly five times the spillage caused in the Exxon Valdez oil spill. FARC was extorting about $140 million from oil companies a year and stepped up its attacks on oil pipelines in 1995-1996.

FARC's deadliest offensive in over 10 years started on 30 August 1996 and by 31 December 1999 it was in effective control of over 50 percent of Colombia and enjoyed recognition as a **belligerent** by the Venezuelan government. By 1996 the membership had grown from 5,500 to over 7,000 and carried its operations into neighboring countries such as Panama, Venezuela, and Ecuador. The increase in FARC's activity and the inability of the Colombia government to contain it led President Andrés Pastrana to invite FARC to renewed peace talks in 1998. FARC only agreed on the condition that the government surrender control to it over five central departments roughly the size of Switzerland. Although the government met this demand FARC leaders failed to meet with President Pastrana for the scheduled peace talks within this autonomous zone on 7 January 1999. By the end of 1999 FARC forces were estimated to be in the 9,000-12,000 range.

REVOLUTIONARY ARMED TASK FORCE (RATF). The RATF was a nonstate U.S. leftist terrorist group that sought to force changes in U.S. foreign policy through **armed propaganda** and "consciousness-raising" of the U.S. public. Sometime in 1979, or shortly thereafter, remnants of the once exclusively black **Black Liberation Army** (BLA) merged with the mainly white **Weather Underground** to form the Revolutionary Armed Task Force. This new group attempted in turn to create an outreach umbrella organization, known as the **May 19 Communist Coalition**, for recruiting other leftists or black prison inmates into the RATF or BLA organizations. The May 19 group established contact and fraternal ties with other revolutionary or nationalistic groups, such as the **New Afrikan Freedom Fighters**, the Puerto Rican **Armed Forces of National Liberation** (FALN) separatists, and even the **Palestine Liberation Organization** (PLO). The RATF financed itself through bank robberies while its **bombing** campaign targeted offices of corporations doing business with South Africa, such as IBM, as well as U.S. federal government offices. The group used a number of aliases, such as the Revolutionary Fighting Group, the Armed Resistance Unit, the Red Guerrilla Resistance, and the United Freedom Fighters—not to be confused with the United Freedom Front.

From its robberies conducted from 1979 to 1981, the RATF netted around $1 million. Members of one RATF cell that was raided in May 1985 had carried out since 1982 at least 16 bombings in the New York and Washington, D.C., areas (including the November 1983 bombing of the U.S. Senate) and, at the time the cell was raided, had been planning 12 more bombings of federal facilities in or near Washington, D.C., including the U.S. Naval Academy and the Old Executive Office Building.

A summary of the more noteworthy terrorist actions of the RATF follows: On 20 October 1981 the RATF tried to rob a Brinks armored car outside Nyack, New York, but succeeded only in killing one Brinks guard and two policemen. During December 1981 RATF bombed the South African Airways freight offices at John F. Kennedy Airport and an IBM office in Harrison, New York. In January 1984 the "Revolutionary Fighting Group" bombed the New York FBI office. On 6 November 1983 the "Armed Resistance Unit" bombed the cloakroom of the U.S. Senate, which the group stated was retaliation for the U.S. invasion of Grenada the preceding month.

The arrest of several key members of the RATF destroyed the effectiveness of the remaining organization and greatly demoralized other leftist terrorist groups. In the abortive Brinks robbery attempt, the police captured five of the terrorists, including Kathy Boudin, a Weather Underground terrorist on the FBI's most wanted list for over 10 years. In May 1985 the FBI arrested Marilyn Jean Buck, a member of the cell responsible for the bombing of the U.S. Senate. By February 1986 the FBI had arrested all but one of the 35 people responsible for the Brinks holdup attempt. With the capture of these persons, authorities also seized papers, including detailed plans and forged travel documents, that exposed the internal workings of the organization; its ties to other leftist, ethnic, or nationalist groups; and revealing the identities of its core membership of 50 people. These raids essentially ended the career of the Revolutionary Armed Task Force.

REVOLUTIONARY BOLIVARIAN MOVEMENT. The MBR-200 Movement consisted of junior officers in the Venezuelan army who were leftists and who took part in a failed coup attempt on 4 February 1992 against former president Carlos Andres Perez. Led by Lt. Col. Hugo Rafael Chávez Frías, who was pardoned and released from prison on 26 March 1994, the movement involved 10 other officers and at least 80 enlisted men who were arrested, but several other officers had fled into Ecuador and Peru. Upon being freed, Chavez said that the "Bolivarian Revolutionary Movement is going to take to the streets, to take political power in Venezuela," and added that "this military generation . . . is going to show Venezuelan politicians how to lead a people toward the rescue of its destiny." Although Chávez ostensibly rejected electoral politics he regularly placed close behind President Rafael Caldera in opinion polls ranking respected political leaders. However, in early March 1995 the Venezuelan government arrested Frías and other members of the MBR-200 charging them with conspiracy to overthrow the government. Subsequently on 6 December 1998 Hugo Rafael Chávez

Frías, as leader of the Fifth Republic Movement (MVR), was elected President of Venezuela with 57 percent of the vote.

REVOLUTIONARY CELLS. The Revolutionäre Zellen (RZ) was a group of German **anarchistic leftist terrorists** active from 12 June 1974 until the late 1980s. The RZ generally held itself aloof from the **Red Army Faction** and from groups like the **Red Brigades** or **Direct Action**. There was some evidence of contact with the **Popular Front for the Liberation of Palestine** (PFLP) and the **Irish National Liberation Army** (INLA) but no firm evidence of direct foreign state sponsorship.

While the RZ sprang from the same social grouping of disgruntled leftist university students and shared the same desire to smash capitalist society as did the RAF, it differed in rejecting the elitism inherent in the RAF's approach with its vision of itself as the revolutionary vanguard and its authoritarian control over its members. By contrast, the RZ sought to bring down capitalist society by multiplying cells of militants who would continually engage in small-scale vandalism and harassment locally. The reasoning was that a multitude of cells would be harder for the state to target than one conspicuous armed group while the cumulative effect of *Spaßguerilla*, (literally, "prank-guerilla actions") or small-scale terrorism, would prove no less deadly to the state. By advocating these radical anarchistic ideas in their journal *Revolutionäre Zorn* (Revolutionary Wrath), the RZ hoped to generate a wider generalized state of autonomous antiauthoritarian violence among disaffected individuals outside the ranks of the RZ. Apart from this different operational approach, RZ, like RAF, appeared to pursue terrorist violence as an end in itself rather than as a coherent strategy to produce a new social and political system.

From 12 June 1974 until 1987, there were at least 50 noteworthy incidents for which the RZ were responsible, including 38 **bombings**, usually directed at NATO military bases or commercial offices, but usually with minimal injuries; nine involved hoaxes, threats, or vicious pranks; seven **arsons** or firebombings; three **kneecappings**; and one murder although it appeared that the intent had been to kneecap rather than to kill their victim. This last case involved the shooting death of Heinz Karry, economics minister of Hesse, on 11 May 1981. Other kneecapping incidents took place on 28 October 1986 and 6 February 1987, both occurring in Berlin and in government offices. The overall pattern is one of low-intensity and generally nonlethal violence and harassment. RZ members also engaged in telephone harassment of victims and have resorted to pranks such as mailing victims packages containing human feces or a pig's head. Following 1987 RZ targets shifted to nuclear power plants involving sabotage of equipment at sites under construction and severing of power lines from existing plants. The RZ also vandalized the offices of German immigration authorities for alleged racism against foreigners and **asylum** seekers. RZ members have also participated in attacks on offices of firms involved in genetic engineering.

Actually such a statistical approach can only give a qualitative sampling of the RZ violence rather than a precise quantitative measure, for the RZ did not necessarily seek credit for every action its members committed and it is also not possible to distinguish between violence committed by the RZ itself from similar violence committed by emulators. Since 1980, West Germany has experienced roughly 200 petty bombings and acts of arson each year, which fit the RZ pattern. By 1987 the RZ was credited by West German police with having caused over 200 million deutsche marks of damage. Estimates of the membership in the early 1980s held that there were 50 to 100 cells with together some 300 to 500 members. As early as 1978, the German Federal Office of Criminal Investigations (BKA) rated the RZ as "currently the strongest terrorist formation." By April 1995 RZ sympathizers claimed the RZ had been responsible for at least 200 attacks since the group began. With the demise of the **June 2nd Movement** in the early 1980s and the disbanding of the **Red Army Faction** in 1998, only the Revolutionary Cells remained of the three major anarchistic leftist terrorist groups which had not formerly disbanded. On 9 June 1989 Ingrid Strobl, a Revolutionary Cells member, was convicted for terrorist offenses and sentenced to five years in prison.

It should be noted that after 1987 a women's wing of the Revolutionary Cells was formed, called Rote Zora, "Red Zora," which continued to operate independently of the rest of the RZ and which also uses the initials "RZ." Since the late 1980s members of Red Zora remained active, firebombing 10 department stores of the Adler chain due to its alleged exploitation of women textile workers in South Korea, as well as other acts of vandalism. Red Zora differs from the rest of the RZ cells by stressing a more militantly profeminist agenda.

REVOLUTIONARY PEOPLE'S LIBERATION PARTY/FRONT. The Devrimçi Halk Kurtulus Cephesi (DHKP/C), which until 1994 was better known as Dev Sol, short for Devrimçi Sol, or Revolutionary Left, of Turkey is a Marxist-Leninist group seeking to unite the Turkish proletariat to carry out a socialist revolution. This group has acted largely as a leftist **death squad**, attacking Turkish rightists from 1978 to 1983 and striking at retired Turkish security officials as well as U.S. and other nationals of NATO countries from the late 1980s to the present. The group is not known to have had foreign state sponsorship, although it is believed to have had contact with radical Palestinian groups as well as with Greek leftist terrorists and the **Kurdish Workers' Party** (PKK).

Dev Sol emerged in 1978 as a splinter group from Dev Yol (Revolutionary Road), which itself split from the **Turkish People's Liberation Army** in 1975. Dev Sol engaged in numerous murders of rightist politicians, writers, and students. Following the Turkish military coup and crackdown in September 1980, many members of the group were arrested or killed in clashes with security forces. On 2 October 1980 Dev Sol **bombed** U.S. Army buildings in Izmir, causing minor damages. Two days later an unoccupied U.S. Air Force staff sergeant's car was firebombed by Dev Sol. On 24 May 1981 a Turkish Airlines DC-9 with 112 passengers and seven crew members was **hijacked** by four Dev Sol members from Istanbul to Bulgaria where eventually the terrorists were overpowered by the passengers and captured. On 5 November 1982 the Turkish tourism office in Amsterdam was seized by 10 Dev Sol members who took two hostages for three hours until Dutch police rushed and overpowered the terrorists.

During 1983 to 1989 the group disappeared from view due to the severe repression of leftist terrorists within Turkey in that period. Unlike many other Turkish leftist groups, however, Dev Sol has made a comeback. During 1990-1991 they killed at least four active and retired Turkish generals and some 30 police officers. Beginning in 1991 they resumed attacks on Western businessmen and military personnel within Turkey. During 1991 Dev Sol murdered two American contractors and one British businessman in Turkey, attempted to murder one U.S. Air Force officer in his home in Izmir, and conducted over 30 bombings of Western diplomatic, commercial, and cultural **targets** in Turkey. In April and July of 1992 Dev Sol launched rockets at the U.S. Consulate in Istanbul and also tried to murder an American administrator of a religious hospital with a car bomb in July 1992.

The group suffered both from severe police retaliation, with raids on several of its safe houses, and from internal factionalism and splintering. The remaining active terrorist splinter group renamed itself the Revolutionary People's Liberation Party/Front and inaugurated a new campaign in January 1996 by **assassinating** the prominent Turkish businessman, Ozdemir Sabanci, in what was thought to be his high security business office building in Istanbul. During 1997 DHKP/C conducted three attacks using light antiarmor weapons, on 16 June firing on but missing the Turkish National Police headquarters, on 14 July hitting the Harbiye Officers' Club but without causing significant damage, and on 16 September with another attack on the Turkish National police headquarters but again without effect due to the failure of the rocket to explode on impact.

Most of Dev Sol's and DHKP/C's activities have occurred in the environs of Istanbul, Ankara, Izmir, and Adana. The group numbers a few dozen armed militants and several hundred supporters who also maintain a support network among Turkish expatriates in Europe.

REVOLUTIONARY POPULAR STRUGGLE. The Greek Epanastatikos Laikos Agonas (ELA) was a shadowy leftist terrorist group formed in 1973 to oppose the former military junta in Greece. Actual terrorist activities began only in the postjunta period in which it has sought the limited aims of forcing Greece out of NATO and removal of U.S. troops from Greece.

During its existence the ELA has engaged in **bombings** causing property damage but no human casualties so far. From 1975 to 1987 the ELA bombed at least eight U.S. **targets**, usually military targets of little strategic value, such as NCO clubs or commissaries, or U.S. diplomatic properties, such as the U.S. Information Agency office in Athens, or offices of private American firms, such as the American Express office in Athens. In October 1987 ELA members had a shootout with Greek police in which one terrorist was killed and two others arrested. The Greek police believed the ELA had connections with the **November 17** group and appeared to work in tandem with the **May 1** group. While the ELA often declared its solidarity with other groups, little is known about either its own members or its connections with other leftist terrorist groups.

REVOLUTIONARY UNITED FRONT (RUF). The RUF is an antistate revolutionary group seeking to overthrow the current government of Sierra Leone which has pursued remarkably vicious tactics, such as mutilation, rape, and burning alive of its victims and which has not distinguished between civilian and military targets. The group has been active since 1991, led by former army corporal Foday Sankoh, and sought to overthrow the former president, Joseph Saidu Momoh, who was the weak leader of a corrupt one-party state, and which continues to fight against the new government of President Ahmed Tejan Kabbah, elected on 15 March 1996. Although Sierra Leone has great mineral wealth of metal ores it has been in a state of economic collapse which may account for the RUF's ability to recruit thousands to its ranks. The RUF does not have a coherent **ideology** or alternative program of government but appeals mainly to populist resentments of rural Sierra Leoneans against the elites of Freetown. The signature act of RUF is cutting off the hands of civilian victims and telling them then to go to ask for new ones from President Kabbah. This is a reference to Kabbah's election campaign promise to Sierra Leoneans to "lend them a hand" toward economic recovery.

Although the rebels offer little in the way of political or economic solutions for Sierra Leone's problems they have had remarkable military success and were rumored to have enjoyed covert support from Liberia's president Charles Taylor, which he denied. In January 1999 the RUF captured Freetown but was driven out a few weeks later by a Nigerian-led military coalition of other West African nations. On 17 May 2000 Sankoh was arrested in Freetown by elite British troops assigned to the UN peacekeeping forces there. The RUF forces are dispersed in the hills but have not been definitively crushed.

REX CINEMA ARSON AND MASSACRE. On 2 August 1978 the Rex Cinema theater of Abadan, Iran, was set ablaze during a showing of an evening film resulting in over 300 deaths, which until that time was one of the worst terrorist incidents in the modern history of Iran and of the Middle East generally. This event occurred during the early stages of the Iranian revolution when **Islamic fundamentalists** had been regularly carrying out **arson** attacks against movie theaters believed to offer features offensive to Islamic sentiments. When previous arsons of this kind had taken place, however, the arsonists would order the theater to be cleared or would strike when the theater was already emptied after hours.

The shah's regime, quite naturally, blamed the arson on its fundamentalist opponents. Islamic fundamentalists accused the monarchical regime of having staged the arson to discredit the fundamentalists. The evidence supporting the view that fundamentalists were responsible is increased by the circumstance that the film showing occurred on the anniversary of the martyrdom of Imam 'Ali, an anniversary in the Islamic religious calendar on which devout Shi'ites regard indulgence even in ordinarily innocent pleasures to be blasphemous. Investigations into the event after the **revolution** were inconclusive in determining the identities and motives of the perpetrators.

RICARDO FRANCO FRONT (RFF). The Frente Ricardo Franco is a Colombian revolutionary guerrilla group not enjoying any state sponsorship. Formerly it was a front of the **Revolutionary Armed Forces of Colombia** (FARC) but severed its ties with the main body of FARC in 1984 due to its members' disagreement with FARC signing the March 1984 peace accord with the Colombian government. The RFF has the same original goals as FARC, namely, creating a Marxist-Leninist revolution in Colombia. It has, however, the additional goals of undercutting FARC's attempts to gain political advantages from the 1984 agreement and to sabotage the national reconciliation process. Sporadic clashes have occurred between the RFF and FARC forces ever since the schism occurred.

The Ricardo Franco Front has the strongest anti-U.S. stance of all leftist groups in Colombia and, during 1984-1985, it repeatedly **targeted** U.S. diplomatic and commercial facilities. To embarrass FARC and to sabotage the government's reconciliation scheme, the RFF undertook joint actions in 1985 with the **National Liberation Army** (ELN), the one major group rejecting the truce proposals and procedures, as well as with **M-19** guerrillas.

In May 1984, the RFF **bombed** a Honduran airlines office, killing two and wounding 11 people, and also bombed a U.S. diplomatic office. In January 1985 RFF bombed the Colombian Labor Ministry and the following month conducted eight bombings against U.S. companies in Medellín, killing one person and wounding another. Deploying 150 guerrillas, RFF tried to occupy the upper-class suburb of Cuba near Bogotá in spring 1985, attempting 26 bombings throughout the city. In

June 1985 the RFF kidnapped an official of the State Oil Company for a $105,000 ransom but killed him only five days later. In September 1985 the RFF fought for 10 days alongside M-19 guerrillas, afterward consolidating their joint positions in Tolima Department. During the same month the RFF made numerous attacks against the U.S. embassy, other diplomatic missions, and also offices of multinational corporations and, in one case, used two small children to plant a bomb at the gates of the U.S. embassy, which was deactivated without harm to life or limb.

In December 1985 an internal purge within the RFF led to the mass executions and burials of around 100 RFF dissidents. Colombian security forces discovered and revealed these graves, which led other major leftist groups, such as M-19, to break off relations with the RFF. Since being thus publicly discredited, the Ricardo Franco Front has ceased to conduct effective guerrilla operations and apparently has declined from being a political-military group to little more than a criminal gang. Its current membership is estimated at little more than 100.

RICIN. Among the most deadly known natural poisons, ricin is a complex albumin protein polymer derived from castor beans (*Ricinus communis*) which is difficult to synthesize. With the lowest published lethal concentration (LDLo) of 300 micrograms per kilogram of body weight a mere 27 milligrams of ricin can kill an adult male of average body weight (180 lbs.) Contrary to lurid press reports that claim ricin is "5,000 to 6,000 times more lethal than potassium cyanide," or that ricin poisoning is 100 percent lethal, in reality ricin is only about 10 times as poisonous as potassium cyanide while most cases of ricin poisoning in castor oil mills, caused by inhalation of air-borne ricin particles, have been successfully treated.

Ricin acquired its notoriety in 1978 when the Bulgarian secret police used an air-gun propelled ricin pellet to murder a defector, Georgi Markov, who was working for Radio Free Europe in London. On 28 February 1995, Douglas Allen Baker and LeRoy Charles Wheeler, two members of a right-wing militia group, the Minnesota Patriots Council, were convicted of trying to use ricin to murder a Deputy U.S. Marshal and a sheriff. On 20 December 1995 another man, Thomas Leis Lavy, was arrested on charges of conspiracy to use a **weapon of mass destruction** following an unsuccessful attempt to smuggle 130 grams of ricin across the Canadian border when returning to his native Arkansas from Alaska. *See also* WEAPONS OF MASS DESTRUCTION.

RIYADH SAUDI NATIONAL GUARD-U.S. TRAINING CENTER BOMB-ING. On 13 November 1995 two powerful **bombs** detonated one after the other at the U.S. military training center in the center of Riyadh, Saudi Arabia, known as the Office of the Program Manager/Saudi Arabian National Guard (OPM/SANG), killing four U.S. federal civilian employees, one U.S. service person, and two employees of the Indian government. Three groups claimed credit for this attack, including a so-called Movement for Islamic Change. About 60 other persons were wounded in this attack.

The primary bomb had consisted of between 150 and 225 pounds of high explosives set in a van parked in front of the OPM/SANG office. A secondary bomb exploded nearby. This was the first terrorist attack on a U.S. military installation in Saudi Arabia although terrorists had attacked the U.S. embassy in Riyadh and the U.S. Consulate in Jeddah during the June 1967 Arab-Israeli war.

On 22 April 1996 four Saudi nationals confessed on television to the bombing and stated that they had undergone training in Afghanistan and had been prepared to carry out similar actions to force U.S. troops out of the Arabian Peninsula. Later all were executed by beheading on 30 May 1996. U.S. authorities came to suspect that these militants were connected with **Osama bin Laden** and his network.

RODERIGO FRANCO COMMAND. The Roderigo Franco Command is a Peruvian **death squad** linked to the right-wing of the American Popular Revolutionary Alliance (APRA) party. The Command emerged after 1987 when the Aprista politician Roderigo Franco was murdered by **Sendero Luminoso** and was originally intended for use against Senderistas. The scope of its attacks broadened to include a defense attorney representing Senderistas, murdered on 28 July 1988, and eventually included even conservative critics of APRA. During November 1988 the Command carried out **bombings** and threats in Lima, including an attack on two journalists, one of whom died.

RUKN(S) OR EL RUKN(S). El Rukn (Arabic: "the pillar") was a Chicago-based criminal gang, a strictly **entrepreneurial terrorist** group, founded in 1968 by Jeff Fort. It was originally known as the "Blackstone Rangers" but merged with the rival Eastside Disciples. After it adopted the name "El Rukn" it succeeded in representing itself as a community service organization to federal agencies which they defrauded of $972,000 in community development grant funds. Although gang members affected Muslim names and referred to some of their meeting places as "temples," there is no evidence that the group was ever a bona fide Islamic group or sect, and it is believed to have affected the pretense of being a religious organization to mask its drug-trafficking and extortionary activities. Members of this gang have provided bodyguard services to Louis Farrakhan as well as martial arts training to members of Farrakhan's Nation of Islam, a black nationalist Islamic sect, which is also based in Chicago.

In 1986 El Rukn contacted a Libyan representative in the United States and obtained Libyan agreement in principle to sponsor terrorist actions by El Rukn in the United States in exchange for Libyan financial rewards. This plot was uncovered by FBI agents in August 1986 when police raids of a Rukn meeting place uncovered automatic weapons, pistols, hand grenades, and an M-72 rocket launcher. Wiretaps revealed that El Rukn members offered to carry out **bombings** of U.S. government offices and to shoot down a domestic commercial airliner near Chicago's O'Hare Airport on behalf of Libya in exchange for $2.5 million. In November 1987 five El Rukn members were convicted on weapons violations and conspiracy charges. None of the testimony in this trial revealed any **ideological** or sectarian sympathies between El Rukn and the Libyan regime. This is the first known instance of a domestic terrorist group allowing itself to be recruited by a foreign state sponsor of terrorism to attack **targets** within the United States.

The leader of El Rukn, Jeff Fort, was serving a sentence in a Texas prison for cocaine trafficking charges during the time of El Rukn contacts with Libya. The active membership of El Rukn was estimated to be about 250, however, with most of its leaders having been convicted and imprisoned on various criminal charges the gang is essentially defunct. On 9 March 1995 El Rukn member Melvin Edward Mays, who had been on the FBI's Top Ten Fugitive list, was arrested by the FBI's Chicago Joint Terrorism Task Force in connection with the El Rukn conspiracy to commit terrorist acts on behalf of the Libyan government.

- S -

SA'IQA, AL. Al Sa'iqa (Arabic: "Thunderbolt") is a Syrian state-sponsored Palestinian splinter group and militia with the revolutionary objective of destroying Israel to create a Palestinian state. The group was created in 1968 to allow Syria more influence over the Palestinian movement. While Sa'iqa has declared itself to be a member of the **Rejection Front** within the **Palestine Liberation Organization** (PLO), other Palestinian groups have recognized that Sa'iqa's positions directly reflect those of the Syrian government.

Sa'iqa numbers around 2,000 members, and its operations unit bears the name "Eagles of the Palestinian Revolution." This group has operated as a pro-Syrian militia during the Lebanese civil war. In the "Chopin Express" affair, Sa'iqa took three Jewish hostages in Vienna in September 1973 and forced Austrian Chancellor Bruno Kreisky to close down a transit facility for Soviet Jews emigrating to Israel. In response to the 1979 Camp David negotiations between Israel and Egypt, Sa'iqa was directed to occupy the Egyptian embassy in Ankara in July 1979. In this attack two guards were killed and 20 hostages held. Sa'iqa also struck at the northern city of Tiberias within Israel and **bombed** Jewish students in two attacks in Paris.

Sa'iqa lacks both an original political program and broad popular support among the Palestinians, largely due to its siding with Lebanese Christians against fellow Palestinians during the siege of the Tel al-Zat'ar refugee camp during January to August in 1976. Its future would apparently depend on the foreign policy options that the Syrian regime will choose to pursue in the wake of the loss of Soviet military aid essential to Syria's role as a player in the Arab-Israeli conflict.

SAM MELVILLE-JONATHAN JACKSON UNIT. This was a nonstate U.S. leftist group that conducted **bombing** attacks in Massachusetts during the late 1970s. The name of the original group was taken from Sam Melville, a white leftist killed in the Attica Prison uprising in 1971, and from Jonathan Jackson, a black radical killed in a shoot-out with California police in 1970.

With the arrests of five **United Freedom Front** terrorists in November 1984 and two more in April 1985, it was learned that the United Freedom Front was essentially the same organization as the earlier Sam Melville-Jonathan Jackson Unit. The tactics of each used bombing attacks on properties either of U.S. military organizations or else of defense-related industries and were designed to draw public attention to their protests against specific U.S. foreign or military policies rather than to seek **revolution** as such.

SANCTUARY. Grant of **asylum** to a person or group whether bona fide refugees or else political activists or terrorists enjoying the protection of a sponsoring state. Also used to describe remote or inaccessible regions used by a terrorist or insurgent group either as a base of operations or else a place of refuge from pursuit. In the Middle Ages Christian churches and monasteries were regarded as **sanctuaries** in which civil officials had no jurisdiction and in many Latin American nations university campuses have similarly been regarded as areas in which leftist opponents of the government could recruit and organize themselves without fear of police intervention.

SANDINISTAS. The Frente Sandinista de Liberación Nacional (FSLN) is a Marxist-Leninist political party that overthrew the dictatorship of Anastasio Somoza Debayle in 1979 and attempted to create a Marxist-Leninist state in Nicaragua from 1979 to 1990. Before its rise to power the FSLN maintained ties with the **Popular Front for the Liberation of Palestine** (PFLP) and afterward established close ties with Libya and Iran, both known to have been state sponsors of terrorism. The FSLN enjoyed the support of Cuba and also Costa Rica prior to gaining power. Following the revolution the United States became the foremost donor of financial aid to Nicaragua until mid-1981 when it became apparent that the Sandinistas had become involved in supporting the communist insurgency in El Salvador. Afterward the Soviet Union and Cuba remained the primary sponsors of the FSLN, while Libya also lent military aid.

The National Liberation Front was founded on 23 July 1960 in Honduras by Carlos Fonseca, Silvio Mayorga, and Tomás Borge Martínez. The name "Sandinista" was added to the name in 1962 to honor Augusto César Sandino, the nationalist general who had fought the U.S. Marines in the 1920s before being killed in 1934 by National Guard chief Anastasio Somoza García, who later became dictator and was succeeded by his son. The FSLN made sporadic attempts at starting a rural insurgency in the 1960s and early 1970s without much success. On 27 December 1974 13 FSLN members intending to take U.S. ambassador Turner

Shelton hostage crashed a Christmas party given in his honor only to find he had left. Nonetheless they seized 25 hostages including the Nicaraguan Foreign Minister as well as several businessmen and cronies of Anastasio Somoza Debayle. Negotiations through Archbishop Miguel Obando y Bravo gained the release of the hostages in exchange for safe passage to Cuba, $1 million in cash, and the release of 14 imprisoned Sandinistas.

Disagreements among the Sandinistas in 1975-1977 led to their breakup into three factions, one led by Jaime Wheelock Roman, another led by Tomás Borge, and another led by the Ortega brothers. The Ortegas' insurrectional strategy, involving the use of spectacular acts of **armed propaganda** to spur broad-based urban insurrections, was to succeed in 1977-1979 in overthrowing Somoza. On 10 January 1978 unknown **assassins** shot and killed Pedro Joaquín Chamorro, editor of *La Prensa* and longtime Somoza critic. This sparked off massive demonstrations against Somoza, who was believed responsible for Chamorro's killing. In this atmosphere the FSLN insurrectionists were able to win support from Nicaraguan liberals, social democrats, and small businessmen. On 22 August 1978 Edén Pastora Gómez led 24 other FSLN commandos in storming the Nicaraguan Chamber of Deputies and seizing 1,500 hostages who were released in exchange for safe passage to Panama, the release of 59 prisoners, including Tomás Borge, $500,000 ransom, and the broadcast of a call to insurrection in the name of the FSLN. In the abortive insurrection that followed, during September 1978 fewer than 1,500 FSLN guerrillas fought 14,000 National Guardsmen and about 5,000 people were killed and 16,000 wounded, most of whom were civilians.

As Fidel Castro required vanguard unification as a condition for Cuban aid, accordingly on 7 March 1979 the three FSLN factions were united under a Combined National Directorate (DNC) composed of nine members, three from each faction. Apart from Cuban support, the FSLN received arms and political support from Venezuela, Panama, and Costa Rica, which not only allowed the FSLN **sanctuary** and staging areas in its territory but also helped to create Radio Sandino through which the FSLN coordinated the broad-based popular uprising. A combination of rioting in the cities, labor and business strikes, and FSLN attacks on an increasingly demoralized National Guard led to Somoza's resignation and flight from the country on 17 July 1979 and the takeover of Managua by the FSLN on 19 July 1979.

During the 1960s and early 1970s members of the FSLN collaborated with guerrilla and terrorist groups outside of Nicaragua, particularly the Guatemalan Rebel Armed Forces with whom FSLN cadres fought in Guatemala from July to October 1966. In September 1970 two FSLN members took part in separate **hijackings** led by the PFLP, one of which led to the capture of Leila Khalid when the hijackers were foiled while the other succeeded in taking a British BOAC (British Overseas Airways Corporation) plane to Dawson's Field in Jordan. On 21 October 1970 Carlos Aguero hijacked a Costa Rican plane and held four United Fruit officials hostage to gain the release of imprisoned Sandinistas. Apart from the attempt to **kidnap** the U.S. ambassador, the FSLN also **bombed** the U.S. military mission in Managua on 11 April 1977.

Up until 1979 the FSLN committed 64 noteworthy actions, of which 31 were armed attacks initiated by the FSLN; 15 were robberies of banks and businesses; six were **assassinations**; five were hijackings, of which two were unsuccessful; two were bombings; and two were major hostage-taking incidents, namely the "Christmas Party" raid and the seizure of the Chamber of Deputies. Two instances of **arson** occurred as well as one bazooka attack against Anastasio Somoza's private bunker. Except for the robberies and hijackings, the FSLN appeared to **target** principally National Guard units and functionaries of the Somoza regime and otherwise avoided random killings of civilians. The two hostage takings resulted in the deaths of 15 guards and military policemen but only one civilian death.

Following the victory of the **revolution**, the FSLN created the party-controlled Sandinista Popular Army to form the core of the new armed forces. The police were similarly restructured to become instruments of party rule, and block watch committees known as Sandinista Defense Committees were created. Under Tomás Borge, the Ministry of the Interior, by mid-1985 had at least 186 Cuban advisers and instructors as well as 15 advisers and technicians from East Germany, Bulgaria, North Korea, and the Soviet Union, who proceeded to create a state intelligence and security organization typical of communist societies.

The General Directorate for State Security (DGSE) of the Interior Ministry also would mobilize members of the Sandinista "mass organizations," namely, Sandinista youth groups, women's groups, and office workers, into mobs that became known as the **turbas divinas**.

Nicaraguan human rights groups and high-level Sandinista defectors have testified that from 1979-1981 the DGSE was responsible for at least 114 summary executions of political opponents. The Nicaraguan Permanent Commission on Human Rights, which had amply documented human rights abuses under Somoza, counted 785 cases of disappearances of persons arrested by Sandinista authorities from July 1979 to September 1980. The FSLN adopted a heavy-handed relocation policy toward the Miskito, Sumo, and Rama Indians of the Atlantic coastal area. Thousands fled to Honduras where many Indian men joined the **contras** and eventually formed their own contra command. Within the cities the FSLN persecuted some small religious groups, such as Jehovah's Witnesses, Mormons, and Pentecostals, as well as Roman Catholic priests suspected of being antiregime.

Immediately after seizing power, the FSLN became a state sponsor, along with Cuba, of the **Farabundo Martí National Liberation Front** (FMLN) of El Salvador. On 2 January 1981, during the Salvadoran rebels' "final offensive," CIA aerial surveillance revealed direct FSLN logistical support for the transshipment of U.S.-made arms captured in Vietnam to Cuba, from Cuba to Nicaragua, and there to the Salvadoran rebels. On 9 March 1981 a presidential finding authorized CIA covert action to interdict the arms shipments, which led to U.S. support for the contras. On 1 April 1981 the United States ended foreign aid to Nicaragua, which had received at least $118 million in U.S. aid since the overthrow of Somoza. The FSLN support for the FMLN in the latter's effort to destroy the transitional government of El Salvador gave the Ronald Reagan administration the leverage needed to persuade a skeptical U.S. Congress to support the contras against the FSLN. Throughout the FSLN period, Nicaragua continued to be a transshipment point for Cuban and Soviet aid to the FMLN but also was used as a safe haven for the FMLN, which maintained many of its offices in Managua.

The FSLN also gave moral and material support to the **Túpac Amaru Revolutionary Movement** of Peru, the **Cinchoneros** Popular Liberation Movement, and the **Lorenzo Zelaya Popular Revolutionary Forces** of Honduras, the **Basque Fatherland and Liberty (ETA)** movement, the **Guatemalan National Revolutionary Union**, the **M-19** group of Colombia, and the **Movement of the Revolutionary Left** of Chile. The FSLN also gave safe haven to fugitives of the Italian **Red Brigades** and the **Red Army Faction**, as well as refuge to remnants of the Uruguayan **Tupamaros** and Argentinean **Montoneros**. The presence of Montoneros there in turn led Argentina to send military advisers and aid to help organize the contras in Honduras.

On 17 September 1980 the exiled Nicaraguan dictator Anastasio Somoza Debayle was murdered along with members of his entourage as they drove through Asunción, Paraguay. His assassins were members of an Argentinean group, the **People's Revolutionary Army**, which had long-standing relations with the Sandinistas even prior to their gaining power.

Nicaragua undertook training and outfitting of Marxist rebels also in Honduras and Costa Rica quite soon after taking power. The Honduran police raided a safe house of the **Morazanist** Front for the Liberation of Honduras in Tegucigalpa on 27 November 1981 and captured documents indicating the formation of the terrorist group under FSLN direction and that it had received funds and explosives from Nicaraguan authorities. During July-August 1982 the main power station in Tegucigalpa was sabotaged and several U.S.-affiliated businesses bombed. A Salvadoran arrested in this case indicated the explosives had been supplied by the Nicaraguans along with arms for Honduran rebels. On 27 July 1982 Costa Rica declared three Nicaraguan diplomats persona non grata for their role in supplying explosives and instructions to a Colombian terrorist responsible for the 3 July 1982 bombing of the Honduran National Airlines.

In an address to the Sandinista Trade Union on 13 December 1987 Daniel Ortega stated that in the event the FSLN ever lost an election it would turn over the government, but not effective power, to whomever won. Although the Sandinistas lost the 25 February 1990 election to Violetta Chamorro, the FSLN retained the Sandinista Popular Army under its own command and sporadically continued to transfer arms to the FMLN guerrillas prior to the end of the insurgency in El Salvador.

During the presidency of Violeta Chamorro the Sandinistas carried out many terrorist actions. From April 1995 to January 1996 at least eight Roman Catholic churches were bombed by Sandinistas opposed to the pending 7 February 1996 visit of Pope John Paul II whom the Sandinistas had jeered on his previous visit in 1983. Many people believe that Pope John Paul II played an instrumental role in helping bring about the collapse of Communism in Eastern Europe and the Soviet Union which in turn weakened the leftist insurgencies in Central America and helped force the Sandinistas to relinquish their monopoly of power in 1990. Protests by Sandinista and leftist student groups continued up to the Pope's visit which, however, ceased during the visit itself which was concluded without incident.

During the presidential election year of 1996 gunmen wearing the red and black FSLN army uniforms fired upon Arnoldo Alemán, the presidential candidate of the right-wing Liberal Alliance party. While missing Alemán they hit and killed his bodyguard. During the 20 October elections Alemán won 51 percent of the votes while the Sandinista candidate José Daniel Ortega Saavedra won 38 percent. During May 1993 and March 1997 huge arms caches were discovered in Nicaragua but apparently were supplies left over from the Central America conflict of the 1980s and were not intended for subversion within Nicaragua nor connected with FSLN disagreements with the Alemán administration. During March 1998 the Sandinistas suffered from the scandalous revelation of Daniel Ortega's sexual abuse of his stepdaughter.

SELF-DEFENSE, RIGHT OF. Justification cited by the United States, and other nations, for launching military retaliation upon nations known to sponsor terrorists action or against the bases of suspected terrorist groups. Although nations that subscribe to the United Nations Charter renounce the right to initiate warfare, under Article 51 they retain the right to use military force to defend themselves against foreign military attacks, to repel invasions, or to defend other signatory nations that are being attacked by an aggressor. The United States invoked this doctrine to justify its military attacks on Libya on 15 April 1986 in retaliation for the **bombing** of a West Berlin discothèque on 5 April 1986. This doctrine was also invoked to justify the 20 August 1998 U.S. retaliation against the bases in Afghanistan used by **Osama bin Laden** following the 7 August 1998 bombings of U.S. embassies by bin Laden's followers.

SELF-DEFENSE UNITS OF COLOMBIA. The Autodefensas Unidas de Colombia (AUC), which is also known as the Peasant Self-Defense Groups of Córdoba and Urabá, is a right-wing paramilitary **death squad** which seeks to counter militarily the leftist insurgents of the **Revolutionary Armed Forces of Colombia** (FARC) and **National Liberation Army** (ELN) and also to stymie Colombian government efforts to revive a national peace dialogue with the leftists which effectively ended in 1994. Although it claims to have thousands of members, the AUC has perhaps 800 men led by Carlos Castaño (1965-), who is from a landowning family in Pereira in Antioquía department. Castaño reportedly was close to Pablo Escobar and is accused of involvement in the cocaine trade.

The AUC is credited with pushing the leftists out of three of Colombia's departments but largely engages in summary executions of persons suspected of having helped the leftists. AUC raids often involved public hangings, decapitations, or quarterings of the bodies of their victims. The group began its death squad activities in earnest in 1996. In the first nine months of 1996 about 19,688 homicides were reported in Colombia of which 2,492 were politically motivated. About 59 percent of these political murders are the work of the AUC and similar groups, while leftist rebels account for 34 percent, and the remainder being the work of the police and military. On 25 November 1996 the Human Rights Watch/America group released a report alleging U.S. support for the creation of so-called self-defense forces or antileftist paramilitaries, a tactic also used in Guatemala and in Peru, who engage in death squad attacks on leftist forces and their civilian supporters. Castaño allegedly is a graduate of the School of the Americas in Fort Benning, Georgia, which human rights activists claim had instructed military officers of Latin American nations in inhumane or illegal techniques of suppressing insurgents.

In July 1997 the AUC killed 30 peasants at Mariripán in Meta department while on 4 May 1998 the AUC ransacked the town of Puerto Alvira also in Meta department killing at least 21 people. On 17 May 1998 the AUC struck the Atlantic coast town of Barrancabermaja killing 11 persons and abducting 39 others presumed to have been killed. Clashes between FARC and AUC over control of the Urabá corridor joining Colombia and Panama, which is essential for control of the flow of drugs, occurred in June 1998 making 700 people homeless. The AUC has maintained control of this region since 1996 and the FARC failed to displace them.

On 16 February 1999 the AUC **assassinated** Jaime Hurtado, head of Ecuador's Popular Democratic Movement, a Marxist party, on the steps of the Ecuadoran Congress building in Quito. In a March interview with the Bogotá newspaper *El Tiempo*, Castaño said he ordered the killing of Hurtado because the Ecuadoran was allegedly the biggest supplier of arms to FARC. Castaño then said he would also extend the conflict into Venezuela due to the apparent closeness of President Hugo Chávez with FARC guerrillas. In May 1999 the AUC claimed to have dispatched 2,000 fighters to the border of the San Vicente del Caguán region which the Colombian government effectively ceded to FARC control in late 1998 in an attempt to sway the rebels to enter negotiations.

Both the ELN and the AUC have also demanded to be admitted as equals with FARC in any such negotiations. In response FARC tried a second offensive in June 1999 to overrun Castaño's headquarters in Córdoba which again failed. On 13 August 1999 the AUC assassinated Jaime Garzón, Colombia's most popular humorist and radio-show entertainer who was a close friend of President Andrés Pastrana and who was appointed by him to participate in the planned negotiations with FARC. Garzón had previously mediated with the ELN for the release of hostages and was considered too close to the leftists by the AUC.

As of 5 October 2001 the U.S. State Department added the AUC to its list of Foreign Terrorist Organizations (FTOs).

SENDERO LUMINOSO (SL). The "Shining Path" was a Maoist guerrilla movement that sought to create a total Marxist-Leninist revolution within Peru and an ethnic Indian state by the year 2000. It differed from other leftist insurgencies in Latin America in neither having accepted assistance from other leftist Latin American states, such as Cuba or Nicaragua under the **Sandinistas,** nor associating itself fraternally with Marxist regimes or movements elsewhere. In part this was due to the extremely dogmatic and authoritarian nature of the Senderista leadership, which precluded much collaboration with other leftist groups. While there was some evidence of former limited contacts with the Colombian **M-19** and the now defunct **Alfaro Vive Carajo** group of Ecuador, the Sendero Luminoso was preeminently a homegrown, inward-looking, and highly xenophobic phenomenon. It attacked Soviet, Cuban, Chinese, and North Korean targets along with U.S. and other Western **targets**.

The SL was also the most brutal and violent of the recent leftist insurgencies in Latin America and made the most effective use of terrorism as part of its overall strategy. Insofar as Sendero Luminoso once established de facto control over its "liberated zones" in the interior Andean plateau and used terror to maintain control over the subject population, it may be said to have used terror to achieve quasi-state repression as well as its revolutionary goals.

The Sendero Luminoso was founded in 1969 by Manuel Rubén Abimael Guzman Reynoso, also known as "Comrade Gonzalo," who was regarded by his followers and himself as the "fourth sword of revolution" after Marx, Lenin, and Mao Tse-tung. Guzman was a philosophy teacher at Huamanga University, primarily a teachers' training college, in the interior city of Ayachuco. After Guzman became personnel director of the university in 1971, he systematically built up a faculty who supported his own version of revolutionary Marxism. Also responsible for the first-year course of teachers' instruction, Guzman and his fellow faculty indoctrinated the student teachers who in turn have indoctrinated an entire generation of schoolchildren in remote towns and villages throughout the Andean interior of Peru. Guzman is said to have remarked that it made more sense to educate children into revolutionary Marxism than to indoctrinate adults since children did not need to be politically reeducated. Guzman carried out his program of recruitment, indoctrination, and outreach into the rural communities for 10 years before the SL embarked on actual **revolution**.

Guzman exercised a highly personalistic and charismatic control over his followers, who accepted "Comrade Gonzalo's" word as law and obeyed his promptings without equivocation. Dissenters within the SL were summarily expelled or executed. Guzman and the other Senderista leaders showed little inclination to collaborate with other leftists much less to enter into any dialogue with the regime they fought.

Apart from its highly dogmatic Marxist component, SL doctrine also incorporated within itself an Indian, nativist component that fed off the resentments of the Indian and mixed-blood Peruvian population, who had been largely excluded from political participation and deprived of basic benefits by the Peruvian ruling elites. Originally the SL was known as the "Revolutionary Student Front for the Shining Path of Mariátegui," the reference being to José Carlos Mariátegui, one of the founders of the Peruvian Communist Party. Mariátegui had claimed in his writings that Peruvian socialism had to be built on the communalism of the pre-Colombian Peruvian Inca Indian civilizations and attributed most of the social injustices in Peru to the European-imposed feudal and capitalist culture. While many leftist groups elsewhere in Latin America have usually treated the Indian communities with disdain, the SL pioneered an extensive outreach to the native communities in which SL activists would learn Quechua and other Indian tongues, and go to live among the Indians to gain their trust.

The SL began its terrorist campaign on 17 May 1980 just as democratic rule was being restored to Peru, attacking polling places in the villages around Ayacucho. By the end of 1970, the SL had conducted between 300 and 400 operations and, until June 1986, averaged between 30 and 40 operations per month. It had about 5,000 well-armed militants but avoided direct engagements with the Peruvian military. In its terrorist activities, the SL relied on five-member cells, at least one member of which was always a woman. The SL financed itself through robberies, extortion, and a "war tax" levied on coca producers and smugglers in the "liberated zones."

In its rural campaign, SL activists typically would move into a village and hold mock trials of local officials or landowners who would then be executed in some gruesome manner and their mutilated remains left exposed as a lesson to others. Five-member councils ruled the villages and administered summary justice. In areas where peasants were once terrorized by Colombian smugglers and coca buyers, the SL intervened to promote a measure of equity on behalf of the coca-growing peasants and also to extort "war taxes" from the coca buyers. Economic infrastructure and investment projects promoted by the Peruvian government were bombed, a favorite target being the power pylons that supplied the major cities.

While the SL originally conducted only rural operations on the theory that "encirclement of the cities" would consummate a successful rural guerrilla war, it began a parallel campaign in the cities prompted by the appearance of a rival urban guerrilla organization, the **Túpac Amaru Revolutionary Movement**, in 1984. In its urban campaign the SL also sought out high-visibility targets, specializing in the **assassination** of members of the prominent American Popular Revolutionary Alliance Party or of high-ranking members of the counterinsurgency forces. On 14 August 1990 the SL drove a car **bomb** into the presidential palace in Lima, exploding it and causing extensive damage to the building, although the newly elected President Alberto Fujimori was unhurt. Afterwards, when the SL decreed a strike in Lima on 14 February 1992, Maria Elena Moyano, the deputy mayor of the Villa El Salvador district and outspoken critic of the Senderistas, defied the ban by organizing a peace march. The next day she was murdered by Senderistas and her body blown up with dynamite. On 16 July 1992, marking the end of the first 100 days of Fujimori's emergency rule, SL exploded two car bombs in Lima's wealthiest district, killing 18 and wounding 140 others, while around 100 SL fighters struck police stations throughout Lima. The SL has not hesitated to attack and kill foreign aid workers, diplomats, priests, missionaries, and family members of targeted victims.

Around 30,000 people perished and $22 billion in damages and lost revenues were suffered due to the SL insurgency. Since overcoming its setback in the urban campaign caused by the penetration of its Lima cells in 1986, the SL showed increasing organizational sophistication, relying more on front organizations called "generated organisms" to penetrate and co-opt other leftist groups and to gather more potential recruits. It set up legal aid and educational institutions in the slums surrounding Lima and used the newspaper *El Diario* as its unofficial mouthpiece.

Originally the ineptitude of the Peruvian counterinsurgency program helped to boost recruitment into the SL due to the military's tendency to exact retaliation upon Indians and "mixed bloods" generally when it could not find the actual SL perpetrators of an action. Beginning in the mid-1980s the Peruvian military began to rethink its intelligence requirements and started to have some success in penetrating the Senderista organization. By November 1989 the Peruvian military recaptured the Upper Huallaga Valley. On assuming office in 1991 President Fujimori made the insurgency the top priority of his administration, and on 13 September 1992 Peruvian security forces captured Guzman and his top lieutenants during a strategy-planning session in Lima.

The Shining Path was an enigma. It emerged just after the leftist military regime of General Juan Velasco Alvarado had completed Peru's most extensive land reform and at the very time Peruvian democracy had been restored, a time when some Peruvian leftists had begun to despair of armed revolution. The success of the SL in destroying Peru's fragile economy may well have contributed to the collapse of the presidency of the once highly popular Alan García. Its threat to the state prompted the assumption of unconstitutional powers by President Fujimori on 8 April 1992. During a time when communism was collapsing in the Soviet Union and eastern Europe and revolutionary Marxism apparently discredited, the Shining Path began to attract support from die-hard leftists throughout the world just as previous generations of revolutionary leftists used to embrace the **Sandinista** revolution or the Cuban revolution. International support groups known as "Peru People's Movements" sprung up in Europe while Maoist groups, such as the Communist Party of Turkey-Marxist Leninist and the Revolutionary Communist Party, U.S.A., embraced the Shining Path movement, together forming a Revolutionary Internationalist Movement that included other pro-Senderista Maoist parties in Germany, Sweden, France, Switzerland, and Mexico. These ties were actively cultivated by Senderista representatives living abroad who claimed political refugee status. Senderista activities have straddled the border with Bolivia while pro-Senderista factions appeared in Ecuador, Colombia, Argentina, and Chile.

The capture of Abimael Guzman on 13 September 1992 curtailed the SL's prospects within Peru as well as limiting the development of any international Senderista movement, although many observers believed that the SL had developed sufficient resources to survive even the loss of its charismatic leader. In fact after Guzman recanted in prison and called on the SL to lay down its arms the movement's leadership was assumed by Óscar Ramírez Durán, also known as Feliciano, who continued to direct the movement even after the remaining Central Committee had been captured. During November 1994 the SL bombed two branches of the country's largest bank as well as the air force officers' club in Lima but no one was hurt.

In 1990 there were an estimated 6,000 to 8,000 active SL members and about 25,000 sympathizers but by March 1995 there were estimated to be about 2,000 active members and 5,000 to 10,000 sympathizers. Following the 1992 capture of Guzman the Fujimori government offered **amnesty** to SL members which was accepted by 5,000 former SL guerrillas. In March 1995 the remaining SL members carried out a renewed terror campaign to disrupt the 9 April 1995 presidential elections, striking not only targets in Lima, including detonating a one-pound dynamite bomb outside the U.S. embassy and similar bombs outside the Chilean and Argentine embassies, police stations, and power stations, but also attacks in the Huallaga valley, their former stronghold, where 20 people were killed, and attacks on the town of Huánuco. Apart from the SL's desire to disrupt the elections another reason for the increased SL activity in the hinterland was due to a withdrawal of counter-insurgency forces from there during a border dispute with Ecuador which, however, had been resolved by 1995 allowing the redeployment of forces to the Huallaga valley to respond to the SL revival. Finally in July 1999 Óscar Ramírez Durán, the remaining SL leader, was captured by an army patrol in the jungles of Huancayo to the east of Lima, which may now mark the final demise of the movement. However with the recent departure of Fujimori from the presidency it is possible that SL remnants may try to stage a comeback.

SIKH MILITANTS. A number of different Sikh religious extremist and separatists groups appeared in the 1980s which had a common goal of creating an independent Sikh homeland in the Punjab region to be known as Khalistan. The more prominent of these groups included the following:

1. Babbar Khalsa—Babbar Khalsa was a small Sikh terrorist group originally formed for the limited purpose of avenging the deaths of Sikh fundamentalist followers of Sant Jarnail Bhindranwale who were killed on 13 April 1978 by Nirankari Sikhs when the latter had been attacked by Bhindranwale's followers as "heretics." The moving figure of the group was Bibi Amarjit Kaur, a widow of one of those slain, who became embittered toward Bhindranwale and refused to cooperate with him. The group otherwise embraced the same goals held by Bhindranwale of creating an independent Sikh homeland of Khalistan and **assassinating** perceived enemies of Khalistan among both Sikhs and non-Sikhs.

   The group consisted of only a few scores of youths operating out of the sanctuary of the Golden Temple complex in Amritsar prior to its destruction by the Indian Army in its raid of 5 June 1984. Bibi Amarjit Kaur, along with 400 other Sikh activists, surrendered in the course of the Indian Army attack. Following the death of Bhindranwale in the course of this attack, he achieved the status of a Sikh martyr, and Babbar Khalsa activists maintained that Bibi Amarjit Kaur and Bhindranwale had buried their differences in the face of the Indian Army siege of the Golden Temple. Some Sikh terrorist actions in India, Canada, and Germany have been claimed in the name of Babbar Khalsa, though very little is known of the actual membership of this group.

2. Dal Khalsa—The Dal Khalsa was a Sikh political-religious group that sought the creation of an independent state of Khalistan as a Sikh homeland out of the current Punjab State in India and certain adjacent Punjabi-speaking areas. This group resorted to terrorism to radicalize Sikh opinion, to gain public attention to its demands, and also to avenge certain alleged wrongs committed against Sikhs or the Sikh religion. Oddly enough this group, which seeks to carve a state of Khalistan out of the Union of India, originally had covert support from the ruling Congress Party which had intended to draw enough votes away from the moderate Sikh Akali Dal party in order to enable the Congress Party to win elections in Punjab State. Currently it is believed to have state support from Pakistan even though

the irredentist claims for Khalistan would encompass the Punjab districts of Pakistan as well.

In Sikh history the original Dal Khalsa, literally "the army of the Pure," was an assemblage of Sikh clans (*misl*) who all submitted to the command of a common leader for accomplishing some limited purpose, originally to battle the Mughals. The modern Dal Khalsa began as the result of an intramural sectarian quarrel among the Sikhs. On 13 April 1978, several Nirankari Sikhs held a religious gathering in the Sikh holy city of Amritsar. A prominent Sikh religious leader, Sant Jarnail Singh Bhindranwale (1947-1984), who anathematized the Nirankari Sikhs as heretics, led a demonstration to break up the Nirankari gathering. Thirteen of Bhindranwale's followers armed with swords were shot dead by the Nirankaris. Bhindranwale turned his attention to taking vengeance on the Nirankaris and on the moderate Sikh and Hindu politicians who protected them. This disaffection led him later to endorse the idea of an independent Khalistan.

In August 1978 several Sikh political youth groups, disaffected with the ineffectiveness of the moderate Akali Dal party in securing Punjabi interests against the central government, formed a group assuming the historically charged name of Dal Khalsa. Their proclaimed goal was to preserve the purity of Sikhism from Nirankari influence, which in practical terms meant opposing those who tolerated the Nirankaris (i.e., the Akali Dal). In the elections to the Shiromani Gurdwara Parbandhak Committee (SGPC), that is, the high Sikh council that oversees management of the Sikh shrines, Bhindranwale backed Dal Khalsa while the Congress party leaders encouraged both Bhindranwale and Dal Khalsa in the hope of weakening the Akali Dal party.

The idea of Khalistan came to the fore later on 16 June 1980, when a National Council of Khalistan announced its formation. On 13 March 1981 the Dal Khalsa endorsed the idea of Khalistan to upstage the more hesitant Akali Dal. That year witnessed a rise in communal tensions between Sikhs and Hindus when the head of the All India Sikh Students' Federation (AISSF), who was closely connected to Bhindranwale, demanded special laws to protect the sanctity of Amritsar. Bhindranwale led a demonstration on 31 May 1981 that clashed with police, leading to several deaths. The subsequent murder on 9 September 1981 of a Hindu publisher, whose paper heaped scorn on the idea of Khalistan and who happened to be an enemy of Bhindranwale, led to the latter's arrest on 20 September 1981 on suspicion of murder.

On 29 September 1981 five Dal Khalsa members **hijacked** an Indian Airlines Boeing 737, flying from Delhi to Srinagar with 111 passengers and six crew, to Lahore, Pakistan, where they released 66 passengers but held the rest pending the release of Bhindranwale and the creation of Khalistan. The hijackers were overcome by Pakistani soldiers on 30 September 1981. Bhindranwale was released from custody on 15 October 1981 but not before many shootings, **bombings**, and attacks between Hindus and Sikhs in Punjab took place. Bad federal relations between Indira Gandhi's government and the Punjab government added to these sectarian and communal tensions. Due to the role played by Dal Khalsa in instigating anti-Hindu violence in Punjabi cities the organization was banned on 1 May 1982, while the head of AISSF was arrested on 19 July 1982.

Beginning 20 July 1982 Bhindranwale joined other Sikh leaders in the Golden Temple of Amritsar to make a "peaceful agitation" to seek redress of Sikh grievances. While Bhindranwale remained within the temple sanctuary outside the effective reach of the law his followers, presumably with his blessing, began a campaign of terrorism against religiously lax Sikhs, political opponents, and Hindus living in Punjab. Two hijackings were attempted while an assassination attempt was made against the Chief Minister of Punjab. On 25 April 1983 Deputy Chief Inspector of Police Atvar Singh Atwal, who had visited the Golden Temple purportedly to worship, was shot dead as soon as he left its premises. The Indian government held Bhindranwale and his followers responsible for this and the massive outbreaks of sectarian violence, which Dal Khalsa often instigated. Bhindranwale moved into the innermost sanctum of the Golden Temple, the Akal Takht, on 15 December 1983, and on the following day the Indian government issued a warrant for his arrest. On 5 June 1984 the Indian Army began Operation Blue Star in the course of which they overran the Golden Temple complex and destroyed the Akal Takht with tank fire. All told, about 700 troops perished along with 5,000 civilians, among them Bhindranwale.

Following the desecration of the Golden Temple, Sikh extremists began killing not only Indian government officials known to have participated in formulating or executing Operation Blue Star but also moderate Sikhs willing to settle for anything less than an independent Khalistan. On 10 August 1986 Dal Khalsa claimed credit for the assassination of General A. S. Vaidya, who was the Chief of the Indian Army Staff during Operation Blue Star. In June 1987 Dal Khalsa members killed at least 12 people in two attacks in the village of Udhwuk. Indira Gandhi was herself assassinated by her Sikh bodyguards on 31 October 1984 although their action was not connected with any of the Sikh militant groups.

The Dal Khalsa remains under a ban, and its presumed leader, Gurbachan Singh Manochahal, has a reward on his head. The organization is estimated to have ranged between 500 and 1,000 member supporters and has carried out its activities largely within India. The AISSF, with 40,000 members, was banned in March 1984, but the ban was lifted one year later.

3. Dashmesh Regiment—The Tenth Regiment is reputed to be a Sikh militant group that aims to establish an independent nation-state of Khalistan as a homeland for the Sikhs in present-day Punjab and adjoining Punjabi-speaking areas. This group has been credited with the assassinations of prominent persons, even other Sikhs, who have criticized the cause of Khalistan. Groups using this and other names have also terrorized Hindus living in, or traveling within, their designated area of Khalistan and have engaged in at least one bombing of a commercial air carrier. The name "Dashmesh" means "tenth," referring to the tenth Guru of the Sikhs, Guru Gobind Singh, who transformed the Sikhs into a warrior society.

Knowledge about the origins, composition, and leadership of the Dashmesh regiment is fragmentary and conjectural. Unlike the Dal Khalsa or the All India Sikh Students' Federation (AISSF), this group has no history prior to the onset of secessionist troubles in Punjab, and some observers within India have concluded that it is a phantom group, a name being used to hide the culpability of those actually responsible for terrorist actions or to throw outsiders off their scent.

Supposedly the group was founded in 1984 with the blessing of Sant Jarnail Singh Bhindranwale, a Sikh fundamentalist leader who became closely identified with the Khalistan idea (*see* above, 2. DAL KHALSA): As Bhindranwale was also closely associated with the banned Dal Khalsa and AISSF, groups it is likely that if the Dashmesh Regiment exists, it has drawn its leaders and members from these groups or from the immediate circle of Bhindranwale's followers.

On 28 March 1984 the Regiment claimed credit for the shooting death of Harbans Singh Manchanda, a pro-Congress overseer of the New Delhi Sikh temple. A letter purportedly written by the Dashmesh Regiment addressed to the *Indian Express* in April 1984 threatened to assassinate Indira Gandhi. On 14 April 1984 Sikh extremists attempted to burn down at least 34 railroad stations, actions credited to the Regiment. The Regiment also claimed credit for the shooting death of Ramesh Chander on 12 May 1984, editor of the *Hind Samacher* newspaper and son of an enemy of Bhindranwale who had also been assassinated on 9 September 1981.

In the years following the Indian Army's assault on the Golden Temple during June 1984, in which Bhindranwale was killed and the Akal Takht (the Golden Temple's holy of holies) destroyed, a number of murders, massacres, and pillagings have been perpetrated both by Sikhs against Hindus and by Hindus against Sikhs. By the Punjab Home Department's estimates, in 1985 there were 61 deaths due to such terrorism; in 1985 there were 520 such deaths; 1987 witnessed 1,199 deaths; and 1988 witnessed 1,964 deaths. The Dashmesh Regiment claimed credit for at least five major incidents following the attack on the Golden Temple, including an assassination attempt on Rajiv Gandhi on 2 October 1986. But the identities of parties responsible for other terrorist actions have been masked by their use of noms de guerre, e.g., on 30 November 1986 Sikh gunmen stopped a bus and shot dead 24 Hindu passengers. This was repeated on 7 July 1987 with two buses, killing 38 and wounding 32 in one, and killing 4 and wounding 32 in the other bus. Although this action was claimed in the name of the "Khalistan Commando Force" the perpetrators turned out to be AISSF members. Similarly the Regiment may turn out to be in fact an extension of Dal Khalsa, AISSF, or other Sikh groups.

Most of these actions have been confined to India, mainly to the Punjab and nearby Haryana state. However the Dashmesh Regiment claimed responsibility for two major terrorist actions outside India, namely the premature explosion of a bomb intended to be loaded onto an Air India Boeing 747 at Tokyo's Narita Airport and the bombing on 23 June 1985 of an Air India Boeing 747 carrying 329 people from Toronto, Canada, to London (*see* AIR INDIA BOMBING). Wreckage of this plane found off the coast of Ireland indicated it may have been bombed. It should be noted that the Kashmir Liberation Army also claimed credit for these events. In 1985 the FBI foiled a Sikh extremist plot to assassinate Indira Gandhi during her visit to the United States as well as another plot to assassinate the Chief Minister of Haryana State during his visit to New Orleans.

These international terrorist events appear to be anomalies. Although militant Sikh separatists have had ample opportunity to strike at Indian targets outside India, such as diplomatic or government-managed commercial offices abroad, Sikh militants abroad have largely limited themselves to making demonstrations outside Indian embassies and consulates. It appears likely that Sikh militants realize such actions would alienate world opinion from the cause of Khalistan and would compromise the position of the diaspora of Sikh merchant communities living abroad who form a valuable support network.

Since mid-1992 terrorist activities by the various Sikh militant groups have declined by 95 percent since the all-time high of terrorist-related killings of 3,000 in 1991. This is credited largely to more effective Indian Army, paramilitary, and police actions as well as due to disenchantment among ordinary Punjabis with the excesses of the Sikh militants. During 1997 there were 25 bombings throughout New Delhi, mainly in older marketplaces and buses, which killed 25 persons and wounded around 200. Although a previously unknown Sikh group, the Saheed Khalsa Force, claimed responsibility, this also coincided with a period of rising tensions between India and Pakistan over the unresolved status of Kashmir and India was accusing Pakistan of complicity in many of the bombings that occurred during 1997.

SKINHEADS. Skinheads are young white males usually organized in gangs who, among other things, shave their heads, wear "Doc Marten" steel-toed boots, and listen to punk music bands playing violent and oftentimes racist lyrics. Like many other youth phenomena, skinheads grew more by imitation than conscious propagation, originating in Great Britain in the 1960s and spreading by the 1980s to continental Europe, North America, Australia, and New Zealand. While not all skinheads are necessarily racist, most skinhead gangs have engaged in harassment and sporadic violence aimed at Asiatics, blacks, Hispanics, homosexuals, and Jews.

Viewed in isolation, most incidents of skinhead violence could be classified as **entrepreneurial**, being aimed at the perpetrators' gratification from bullying minority scapegoats or at the gains of petty robberies. Yet insofar as the skinhead gangs have been increasingly courted by, and drawn into, the **white supremacist** and **neo-Nazi** movements, such violence has increasingly taken on the motivations and tactics of right-wing revolutionary terrorism.

Tom Metzger, the former Grand Dragon of the California branch of the Knights of the **Ku Klux Klan**, left the Klan in 1980 to form a neo-Nazi group called the White Aryan Resistance (WAR), based in San Diego. His son, John Metzger, headed the group's youth auxiliary known as the Aryan Youth Movement (AYM). The younger Metzger displaced a local skinhead leader in San Diego in May 1987 and began to co-opt other skinhead gangs nationwide through AYM chapters established on 20 U.S. college campuses. Following the November 1988 murder of an Ethiopian in Portland, Oregon, who was beaten to death by skinheads wielding baseball bats, the victim's family filed a civil lawsuit against the Metzgers and WAR for having encouraged the skinhead youths in question to commit racial violence.

Allied with AYM is the neo-Nazi "American Front," which controls many Skinheads in the San Francisco Bay area. In June 1985, CASH, the "Chicago Area Skinheads," participated in a local neo-Nazi group's demonstration and had contact with Robert Miles, a former Ku Klux Klan leader and currently a leading proponent of **Identity Christianity**.

During the decade of the 1990s the numbers of skinheads nationwide remained around 2,500-3,500 with gangs active in at least 40 states. Numbers of gangs and memberships of individual gangs fluctuate greatly due to the mobility and lack of permanent residences for most skinheads. Moreover, as police pressure has increased against them, many skinheads have started to grow their hair out again, making their identification more difficult. With their induction into white supremacist political terrorism, skinheads are now recruiting youngsters more actively. The appeal of the skinhead movement is not confined to youngsters from depressed economic backgrounds, since many come from middle-class, and even affluent, homes. Rather a more striking commonality among skinheads is a broken home with absent father, which has also been commonly observed among the members of black urban gangs.

On 27 June 1995 the Anti-Defamation League of B'nai B'rith released a report, *The Skinhead International: A Worldwide Survey of Neo-Nazi Skinheads*, that claimed that the skinhead movement embraced 70,000 people in over 30 nations. By 2000 the same organization found that the overall numbers of skinheads worldwide had not increased but that the skinhead movement had spread to a total of 33 countries. The report found that while the various skinhead groups are not linked by an overt organizational structure the predominant number of them share a preference for neo-Nazi ideology and subscribe to neo-Nazi literature they called "skinzines." Although the Southern Poverty Law Center (SPLC) documented that Ku Klux Klan groups had declined from 186 to 140 in the period 1995-1996 it also spotted a rise in racist skinhead groups from 30 to 37 in the same period. By 2000 the SPLC estimated there were 40 racist skinhead groups in the United States. A number of incidents seems to support the fear that the skinhead movement will pose a significant risk of violence and domestic terror. In 1996 German skinheads numbered 6,400, an increase of 200 over the previous year according to figures issued by Germany's Office for the Defense of the Constitution.

Among the many acts committed by skinheads some have stood out: On 23 July 1994 eight German skinheads rioted at the Buchenwald concentration camp memorial chanting Nazi slogans, stoning visitors, and threatening to burn alive a memorial supervisor. Three of these youths were sentenced to short or suspended jail sentences in October 1994. On 10 May 1995 French police arrested five skinheads in connection with the murder of a Moroccan whom they threw into the Seine river where he drowned in the course of a May Day **National Front** march in Paris. On 3 March 1995 two skinhead brothers, Bryan and David Freeman, were charged for the slaying of their parents and younger brother in Salisbury Township, Pennsylvania. In Denver, Colorado in November 1997 skinheads murdered a police officer, Bruce Vanderjagt, and other skinheads two weeks later shot a West African to death at a downtown bus stop. On 4 July 1998 two antiracist skinheads, Lin Newborn and Daniel Shersty, were found slain outside Las Vegas, apparently by members of rival racist skinhead groups.

SKY MARSHAL PROGRAM. Program begun in 1970 that allows armed U.S. Marshals to fly undercover on selected flights in order to be able to counter **hijackers** attempting to seize aircraft in flight. Following the **World Trade Center and Pentagon Attacks of 11 September 2001** the U.S. government began to take steps to increase the numbers of Sky Marshals as one of several measures to deter further hijackings as well as to restore public confidence in the safety of air travel. *See also* AIR TRAVEL SECURITY.

SOCIAL NETWORK RECRUITMENT THEORY. One explanation for the **contagion** of terrorism and recruitment of ordinary people into political extremism or violence was offered by Charles Tilley, in which community ties explain why previously politically indifferent individuals will become mobilized into collective action. In studies of right-wing extremist groups in Idaho and neighboring Rocky Mountain Basin states, sociologist James Aho found that the most frequent reason given for joining such groups was a previous tie of family kinship, personal friendship or romance, or acquaintance from school or workplace. Individuals who had been indifferent or moderate in their political views would join the extremist organization to maintain a social tie and then gradually came to absorb the indoctrination of the group. This theory suggests that groups whose members go "underground" and cut off ties to family and former friends will have greater difficulty recruiting new members to sustain the organization than groups which continue to exist openly. The theory may also explain why **ethno-nationalist** groups, which are rooted in families and organic communities, have been growing while more clandestine groups have been declining.

SOLDIERS OF JUSTICE. An Iranian state-sponsored Shi'ite group based in Lebanon that has the revolutionary goal of overthrowing the Saudi Arabian monarchy in favor of an Iranian-style Islamic Republic. The group is based in Lebanon and is composed of Shi'ite Muslims from Lebanon and Saudi Arabia. The group is thought to have been formed under the tutelage of the Iranian **Islamic Revolutionary Guards Corps** contingent present in that country.

In December 1988 Soldiers of Justice gunmen wounded an official at the Saudi Arabian embassy in Karachi, Pakistan. They claimed credit for killing a Saudi diplomat in Bangkok, Thailand, on 4 January 1989, an action also claimed by the **Islamic Jihad in the Hijaz** organization. The Islamic Republic of Iran had been engaged in agitational propaganda against the Saudi dynasty during the Hajj pilgrimages from 1979 until 31 July 1987 when rioting killed 400 people in Mecca. On 26 April 1988 Saudi Arabia severed diplomatic relations with Iran and greatly reduced the size of the Hajj pilgrimage contingent permitted to the Iranians.

One explanation for the appearance and activities of the Soldiers of Justice is that such groups were being sponsored by hard-liners within Iran opposed to the apparent conciliatory foreign policy of the Rafsanjani government toward conservative Arab regimes in the period following the death of **Ayatollah Ruhollah Khomeini**. Such terrorist actions would be intended to sabotage any rapprochement between Iran and Saudi Arabia.

SOUTH AFRICAN STATE, AND ANTISTATE, TERRORISM. In 1996 the transitional South African government created an independent Truth and Reconciliation Commission, chaired by Archbishop Desmond Tutu and including 16 others, to bring to light the various cases of terrorism that had occurred from the early 1960s, when the **African National Congress** (ANC) began armed struggle and the South African state intensified its police repression of antiapartheid activists, until 1994. The scope of the Truth and Reconciliation Commission included both antistate terrorism by opponents of the former regime as well as state terror perpetrated by the former South African regime and its allies. The terms of the Commission allowed anyone who volunteered testimony, even of a self-incriminating nature, immunity from prosecution provided that the testimony was complete and truthful. Later in the work of the Commission there would be controversies whether or not remorse or contrition had to be presented in cases of self-incrimination for immunity to be granted. Such immunity was in fact withheld from the officer who confessed to the torture and murder of ANC activist Steven Biko when it became apparent that the officer felt no remorse over his role in this killing.

Once the Commission issued its 3,500-page report on 30 October 1999 the findings placed most of the blame for the disappearances and murders on the all-white apartheid regime. However, it also found that the African National Congress; Winnie Mandela, the former wife of President Nelson Mandela; the Inkatha Freedom Party of the Zulu nation; and the Afrikaner Resistance Movement, as well as numerous prominent public and private citizens of different racial backgrounds, had been involved in various forms of terrorism and repression. The last president of the apartheid regime, F. W. de Klerk was also cited as an accessory after the fact in the **bombings** of ANC institutions, which charge he adamantly denied.

Although in theory the work of the Truth Commission was intended to clarify unsolved cases and to bring closure and healing to South Africa, many of the members of families of victims believed that the testimony of former South African military and police officials was incomplete, self-serving, and falsified, and that the work of the Commission was incomplete and flawed.

STATE CO-OPTATION. Discussion of terrorism ordinarily involves two main types: first, state terrorism either in the form of *internal repression*, use of active measures and surrogate groups outside the state's national boundaries; second, *revolutionary terrorism* by groups fighting a given regime whether in a domestic or an international arena. Both extremes ordinarily assume that the sponsoring state, or else the state being attacked, is strong relative to its antagonists. In many developing nations, however, the state may be so weak that nonstate groups can effectively usurp control over state bodies or agencies, making the penetrated state agency, in effect, a surrogate actor for the penetrating group. In such cases where the state organs are being used to perpetrate terrorism, it would be misleading to speak of state-sponsored terror since both society and the state as a whole are being attacked or usurped.

In the case of El Salvador during the 1980s, the transitional regime that seized power on 15 October 1979 tried to dissolve government-run **death squads** such as the **ORDEN** militia. Nonetheless, Salvadoran oligarchs opposed to the government's proposed land reforms enlisted the aid of military and police security personnel who maintained several death squad organizations in spite of official government policy. In the case of Northern Ireland, the Ulster Defence Regiment, an official armed forces unit, became dominated by sectarian Protestant Ulstermen, including members of the proscribed **Ulster Freedom Fighters** and **Ulster Defence Association**, who then exploited access to Ulster police files and weapons to pursue their own vendettas against the Irish Republican groups and nationalist population. In the case of the Islamic Republic of Iran, it appeared that radical **Islamic fundamentalist** factions within the Iranian government had a greater role in influencing the actions of the students holding the U.S. embassy hostages than did the president of Iran, or the Iranian interior and foreign ministries. Each of these is an example of state co-optation.

The reality of state co-optation presents U.S. policy makers with dilemmas in dealing with co-opted states. While the perpetration of internal terror or external terrorism by agencies nominally under the control of the weak state would ordinarily call for punishment of that state as the responsible party, in effect this often plays into the hands of the penetrating groups, who only gain if the state is further weakened. Failing to respond to such terrorism, however, also would have the effect of emboldening the penetrating group to continue its terrorist abuses.

STATE SPONSORS OF TERRORISM. *See* TERRORIST STATES.

STATE TERROR. Nation-states can engage in terrorism by sponsoring nonstate groups to carry out operations against enemies beyond their boundaries or else by creating their own special operations units to carry out terrorist activities as covert actions abroad. National governments can also direct terrorism against their own citizens or subject peoples to subdue political opposition, which may be called *state terror* to distinguish it from state sponsorship of terrorism outside of its borders. In its cruder forms, state terror can involve the use of **death squads**, torture, or **genocide**. In more developed and systematized forms, state terror makes extensive use of secret police and informers, some pretense of judicial procedures, and repression involving loss of employment, internal exile, or imprisonment in labor camps. The Soviet Union eventually developed the additional refinement of committing dissidents to psychiatric hospitals for indefinite "treatment."

Ordinarily such state terror has been viewed by governments of Western liberal democracies as being mainly a human rights problem and as an internal affair of the offending state. It is rarely viewed by onlookers as a threat to their national security on the order of transnational state-sponsored terrorism. Even so, public revulsion over open and notorious state terror often has compelled Western governments to join in international censure as well as diplomatic and economic sanctions against offending states, as they did in imposing sanctions against the pre-1994 South African regime for its apartheid policies.

State terror, however, has also been directed against émigrés involving state or state-sponsored actors operating outside the borders of the offending state. For example, during 1980 Libyan agents murdered at least 10 anti-Qaddafi dissidents in Great Britain and Western Europe. Later such agents also tried to hire **assassins** to kill dissidents within the United States. On 17 April 1984, during anti-Qaddafi demonstrations outside the Libyan embassy in St. James's Square, London, members of the Libyan "People's Bureau" opened fire with automatic weapons on the crowds outside, wounding 11 Libyan protestors and killing a young British policewoman. Such extraterritorial state terror not only violates the sovereignty of other nations as well as the human rights of their victims, but also threatens the national security of those nations and the rights of their citizens who could equally be **targeted** by virtue of personal or business association with targeted émigrés. *See also* DEMOCIDE; GENOCIDE.

STERN GANG. *See* LEHI.

STOCKHOLM SYNDROME. Named after a three-day hostage-holding incident in the Stockholm Kreditbank in August 1973, after which it was observed that the former hostages had developed affection and protective attitudes toward their former captors. Psychologists have also termed it *protective affiliation, traumatic bonding,* and *identification with the aggressor* and have explained it as a reaction to feelings of helplessness and total dependence on one's captors and an emotional transference that makes the captives view their own well-being as depending on the happiness and well-being of their captors whom they begin to love as well as to fear. Although this was observed in the case of the Stockholm hostages and in the case of the Iranian hostages of the Arab terrorists who occupied the Iranian embassy in London in 1980, it is a phenomenon long understood by students and practitioners of brainwashing and interrogation techniques. One of the dangers of this syndrome is that former hostages will find themselves unable or unwilling to provide police with information needed to arrest former captors or to provide testimony needed to prosecute apprehended hostage takers.

SUDANESE PEOPLE'S LIBERATION ARMY (SPLA). The SPLA is a guerrilla group comprising non-Muslim tribal peoples living in the southern parts of Sudan who oppose the policies of the central government which promoted the use of Arabic at the expense of native languages and imposed an **Islamic fundamentalist** regime upon the nation. Christians and animists, who make up about one-third of Sudan's population, have repeatedly accused the Sudanese government of deliberate discrimination and **genocidal** policies against them. They had already fought an insurgency from 1954 until 1972, at which time regional autonomy had been granted to them. Fighting resumed in 1983 when the SPLA was formed in reaction to the central government's attempt to impose Islamic law on the entire nation.

The SPLA began its career during the rule of Ja'far Nimeiry (1969-1985), a pro-Western president who began to implement Islamic law to build himself support among Islamic fundamentalists and to offset criticism of his pro-Western stance. During this time the SPLA found support from **Muammar Qaddafi**, one of Nimeiry's enemies. Under President General Bashir, the National Islamic Front, a group affiliated with the **Muslim Brotherhood**, intensified the government's Islamic fundamentalist policies. During the period from 1983-1987 the SPLA committed 11 noteworthy terrorist incidents. Seven of these involved **kidnappings** of Western foreigners, usually aid workers, technicians, or missionaries. In most cases the kidnap victims were released within a matter of a month or less. On 15 November 1983, however, the SPLA decided to hold 11 kidnapped technicians as hostages. On 2 February 1984 the SPLA attacked a barge carrying foreign technicians building a canal for the Sudanese government, killing three and wounding seven others. On 16 August 1986 the SPLA downed a domestic Sudanese air carrier with a SAM-7 missile, killing all 57 passengers and three crewmen.

Since 1990 the National Islamic Front began building its own militia, the People's Defense Force, under the supervision of Iranian **Islamic Revolutionary Guards Corps** advisors, which was then deployed against the southern rebels. In addition Sudan has retaliated against Uganda for supporting the SPLA by supporting an antigovernment group in northern Uganda known as the **Lord's Resistance Army**. Because of Sudan's involvement in supporting Islamist rebel movements within Eritrea and Ethiopia, both of these governments have allowed their territories to be used as staging areas for the SPLA and other rebel forces. Beginning in 1991 the SPLA formed an alliance with northern opposition groups in fighting the Sudanese regime.

By 1995 over one million persons had died due to famine associated with the war. Over two million people have been displaced in the government-controlled northern part of Sudan while over 650,000 have been displaced in the south with another 200,000 people having fled into neighboring countries. In July 1996 the Sudanese government lifted a ban on flights into the rebel-controlled zone in order to allow the World Food Programme to fly in a C-130 cargo plane to drop food supplies into Bahr el-Ghazal province where one-half million people faced starvation. During late 1996 Bill Richardson, a member of the U.S. House of Representatives from New Mexico, negotiated the release of three Red Cross workers held prisoner by a rebel faction led by Kerubino Kwanyin Bol, who was also at war with the dominant SPLA rebel faction led by John Garang.

On 12 January 1997 both the SPLA led by Garang and the northern opposition Ummrah group, led by the former Prime Minister Sadiq al-Mahdi ousted in 1989, coordinated attacks and threatened the hydro-electric installation at Damazin on the Blue Nile, 255 miles south of Khartoum, that supplied most of the capital's electric power. However, in late 1997 seven key rebel leaders, including Riek Machar who controlled the southern region around the town of Nasir bordering Ethiopia, signed separate peace agreements with the Sudanese government, due to negotiations carried out by the Sudanese vice president, Lieutenant General al-Zubeir Mohammad Saleh. But this was not implemented due to the latter's death on 12 February 1998. In May 1998 representatives of the Sudanese government and SPLA met in Nairobi, Kenya for peace negotiations which produced an agreement in principle to allow a referendum under international supervision in the south in two years to allow the people there to decide on the issue of self-determination. Both sides did not reach a truce, however, until 15 July 1998, when a three-month cease-fire was arranged to allow emergency food relief for the famine-stricken Bahr el-Ghazal province.

SUICIDE BOMBINGS. Suicide bombings involve the bomber being willing to sacrifice himself or herself by delivering a bomb either by carrying it on one's body or else by driving an explosives-laden vehicle to a **target** and then detonating the explosive device knowing that it will kill one's self as well. While this appears to be a tactic specifically associated with **Islamic fundamentalists**, in fact non-Muslim groups in the Middle East have also used it as well as the **Irish Republican Army** (IRA) in Northern Ireland. The motive for the suicide bomber need not be religious or **ideological** zeal: The **Syrian Social Nationalist Party** (SSNP) suicide bomber was often motivated by personal shame and the desire to redeem one's honor. while the IRA suicide bomber was typically an exposed informant whose family was threatened with death unless the mission was performed and who would otherwise face summary execution by the IRA in any case.

Suicide bombings have been associated more with Middle Eastern terrorism, both in the 1980s in Lebanon and as of 1994 in Israel and the occupied territories when **Hamas** and **Islamic Jihad in Palestine** adopted this tactic with great effect. The Arabic designation for suicide volunteers is *intiharioun*, from the Arabic word *intihar*, meaning "suicide," a term used among **Hezbollah** militiamen for persons willing to undertake suicide attacks usually as drivers of vehicle bombs. The truck bomb attacks on the U.S. embassy in Beirut (18 April 1983) and the U.S. Marine encampment at Beirut International Airport (23 October 1983) both involved *intihari* drivers, with credit for these attacks claimed by Islamic Jihad, a nom de guerre for Hezbollah.

Although *intihari* attacks have been rationalized as a form of Islamic martyrdom even Islamic clergymen supportive of Hezbollah, such as Muhammad Hussain Fadlullah, have pointed out that deliberate suicide is contrary to Islamic law, whereas bona fide martyrdom involves death that is both unavoidable and unsought. Following the withdrawal of U.S. and French multinational units from Lebanon, Hezbollah apparently switched to **kidnapping** and holding hostages as its preferred tactic for ridding Lebanon of Western influence. Following the release of Western hostages in December 1991, Hezbollah again resumed car bomb attacks with the 17 March 1992 **bombing** of the Israeli embassy in Buenos Aires and the 18 July 1994 attack on the Argentine-Israel Mutual Aid society which, however, did not involve the suicide of the bombers. On 12 April 1996 there was an attempted suicide bombing by Hezbollah in Jerusalem that went awry when the bomb prematurely detonated leaving the would-be bomber alive, so clearly Hezbollah has not completely renounced the use of this tactic.

Intihari attacks are not a monopoly of Shi'ite militias. The Syrian Social Nationalist Party has developed and deployed its own corps of *intiharioun*, while in 1987 the **Popular Front for the Liberation of Palestine-General Command** (PFLP-GC) deployed *intihari* hang glider attacks against Israeli forces in Lebanon and settlements in Galilee. The **Mujahideen-e Khalq** have also used *intiharioun* to kill government officials and proregime clergymen in Iran.

Beginning on 4 October 1994 Hamas made use of a suicide car-bomb attack on a group of Israeli soldiers but in April 1994 began to use this tactic against civilian targets as well. According to interviews of Professor Joseph Ginat with would-be Hamas suicide bombers who failed to accomplish their missions, the suicide bomber is usually an ill-educated but pious Muslim male burdened with a sense of personal sin due to use of alcohol or illicit sexual conduct who believes he cannot atone for his failings through the usual prescribed prayers, fasting, or pilgrimage. The Hamas *sheikh*, or Muslim spiritual leader, offers him through the suicide mission not only the opportunity for plenary absolution of his personal sins through his self-sacrifice but the *intihari* is also told that the personal sins of all members of his extended family will also be atoned for. Part of this preparation would involve his being led through a Muslim cemetery by his spiritual guide who would tell him that he, the bomber, no longer faced the uncertainties associated with death and dying since he would be instantly transported to paradise at the moment of his martyrdom and would bear neither the ordinary pains and fear of dying nor be subject to the torments of the *barzakh*, the transitional purgatory whose pains even pious Muslims must endure but which is waived in the case of martyrs. Professor Ginat's interviews with surviving suicide bombers are shown in the documentary films *Shaheed* and *Diary of a Terrorist*.

The most serious suicide attacks to date have been the **World Trade Center and Pentagon Attacks of 11 September 2001** in which hijackers affiliated with the **al Qa'eda** terrorist network of **Osama bin Laden** hijacked four U.S. airline passenger flights and succeeded in using three of these planes as flying bombs that they flew into the twin towers of the World Trade center and into one side of the Pentagon. The planners of these attacks understood that the full fuel tanks of these planes would make them effective incendiary bombs capable of destroying the structural integrity of the steel girders of the twin towers and so able to bring these buildings down. Suicide bombers present an unusual challenge for antiterrorism countermeasures because these ordinarily depend on deterring terrorists through a natural fear of death or other punishment whereas the suicide volunteer has already embraced death.

SUPERGRASS SYSTEM. Beginning in 1981, British authorities in Northern Ireland resorted to the general tactic of turning a captured terrorist, facing substantial charges, into a prosecution witness with immunity from prosecution for his own crimes if he would denounce, and testify in court against, several of his erstwhile comrades. Although both the Irish Republican terrorist groups and the Ulster Protestant militiamen had harsh codes of silence and enacted severe punishments, including executions, against persons regarded as willing informers, these terrorist organizations had also begun to attract scores of quasi-criminal recruits motivated more by the gains of extortion from belonging to these groups rather than by **ideology**. When arrested, such mercenary recruits could be turned much more easily than was the case with the more ideologically committed terrorists captured in the early years of the renewed Irish troubles.

This system has used trials without juries and the uncorroborated testimony of one witness to effect scores of convictions. While many of these convictions have been overturned on appeal, the tactic has sowed much distrust, mutual recriminations, and internal discord within the affected Republican and Loyalist terrorist groups and so hampered their efficiency.

SYMBIONESE LIBERATION ARMY (SLA). The SLA was a revolutionary leftist group in California that won notoriety with its **kidnapping** on 4 February 1974 of Patricia Hearst, daughter of newspaper publisher William R. Hearst, Jr. The SLA brainwashed Ms. Hearst who then, assuming the revolutionary sobriquet of "Tanya," became an active participant in their bank robberies and **bombings**. A nationwide dragnet for Ms. Hearst and the SLA led police to an SLA safe house in Los Angeles where six SLA members, including their leader Nancy Ling Perry, perished on 17 May 1974 when police tear-gas canisters caused their safe house to burn to the ground. Patricia Hearst was later arrested in September 1975 and then tried and convicted for her role in one of the group's bank robberies. She was pardoned by President Bill Clinton at the end of his second term in office.

Other members of the SLA included James Kilgore, Josephine Bortin and Martin Bortin. Josephine Bortin was in fact the sister of Kathleen Soliah, who surrendered to authorities only on 16 June 1999. According to Patty Hearst, James Kilgore had helped an SLA bank robbery in Carmichael, California in 1975. Kilgore was also a suspect in the bombing of two sheriff deputies' car at the Marin County Civic Center in 1974. In part to throw authorities off their track the SLA members began to use the name of another leftist group, the **New World Liberation Front**, with which they had no direct link. Actually very little is known about what connections, if any, the SLA had with other contemporary leftist groups.

SYRIAN SOCIAL NATIONALIST PARTY (SSNP). The SSNP was a Lebanese militia dedicated to the incorporation of Lebanon into "Greater Syria," encompassing all of Syria, Jordan, Israel, much of Iraq and Turkey, and the island of Cyprus. The SSNP began as a right-wing political party in the 1930s, modeled on the German Nazi party whose core members were largely derived from Antiochian Orthodox Christian backgrounds. Suppressed by the Lebanese government after an unsuccessful coup attempt in 1961, it eventually evolved into a militia under Syrian state sponsorship with an anti-Israeli and anti-Western agenda similar to Palestinian terrorist groups under Syrian control.

The SSNP undertook many terrorist attacks in the 1980s, including the **bombing** of the **Phalangists'** Beirut headquarters, killing President-elect Bashir Gemayel on 14 September 1982. The SSNP also specialized in car bombing attacks against Israeli **targets** in southern Lebanon. The SSNP recruited young Arab women, often pregnant out of wedlock, whom they indoctrinated to become **suicide bombers**. The Syrian state broadcasting service often aired videotaped political testaments of such bombers the day after they accomplished their mission. By 1987 the Israeli Defense Forces had come to view the SSNP suicide car bombers as much more lethal than the **Hezbollah** suicide car bombers. The SSNP is also believed to be responsible for the bombing of a TWA flight to Athens on 2 April 1986 which resulted in the deaths of only four passengers since the pilot was able to land the plane despite the damage caused by the bomb. Since the end of the 1980s the group is not known to have been active.

- T -

TAHRIR AL ISLAMI, AL. The Hizb al Tahrir al Islami (Islamic Liberation Party) was an **Islamic fundamentalist** group that developed out of the **Muslim Brotherhood**. With the suppression of the Muslim Brotherhood within Egypt following the failed **assassination** attempt upon Egyptian President Gamal Abdul Nasser in 1954, thousands of the Brothers fled Egypt for other Arab lands. In Amman the Muslim Brotherhood became a strong presence in the University of Jordan among both students and faculty. Sheikh Takieddin Nabhani, a former judge of the Islamic law court of Haifa, who settled in Nablus under Jordanian control following the 1948 war, founded the Islamic Liberation Party, which came to include many members of the Muslim Brotherhood in Jordan. This party went beyond the Muslim Brotherhood in teaching the necessity of seizing state power, eliminating rival parties, and imposing observance of Islamic law by force.

After Nasser's death in 1970 the new Egyptian president **Anwar Sadat** released those Muslim Brothers still imprisoned within Egypt and allowed exiled Egyptian members of the Brotherhood to return to

Egypt. A Jordanian of Palestinian origin named Salih Siriya formed cells of the Islamic Liberation Party in Cairo, recruiting around 140 members. On 18 April 1974 Siriya and 20 armed followers took over the Egyptian Military Technical College in the Heliopolis suburb of Cairo, killing 11 and wounding 27 people. The group apparently wanted to assassinate Sadat, who had been scheduled to visit the college, as a first step in fomenting a popular Islamic uprising. Siriya had visited Libyan leader **Muammar Qaddafi** in June 1973 and received funds to overthrow Sadat. In 1976 Siriya and his chief aid were executed for their role in this uprising.

TAKFIR. The Islamic judicial act of declaring someone, or something, to be a *kaffir*, that is, one who deliberately rejects the true faith. Under traditional Islamic law the penalty for deliberate apostasy is death. The Sunni and Shi'ite doctors of religious law reserved for themselves the right to issue religious decrees of *takfir* against those Muslims they deemed to be apostates or enemies of Islam. Such a declaration announced the religious permissibility, and even the duty of the faithful Muslim with means and opportunity, to execute the death penalty against the excommunicated person. When the head of a Muslim state is thus anathematized, the decree authorizes a coup d'état or **revolution** to remove the impious ruler.

The use of *takfir* has come into prominence twice in the recent history of terrorism. Using an interpretation of *takfir* developed by the medieval Muslim scholar Ibn Tamiyyah, **Sheikh Omar Abdul Rahman**, the religious leader of the Egyptian **Munazzamat al Jihad** group, issued a decree of *takfir* against Anwar al Sadat in 1980. Jihad activists accordingly **assassinated** Sadat on 6 October 1981. On 14 February 1989 **Ayatollah Ruhollah Khomeini** issued a decree of *takfir* against the Indian-born British author Salman Rushdie for the writing and publication of *Satanic Verses*, a novel deemed to libel the character of the Prophet Muhammad and to insult Islam. Khomeini's *takfir* was later expanded in scope to include the foreign publishers and distributors of *Satanic Verses* as well as any who gave Rushdie comfort and aid. Reading or possessing the offensive work was also proscribed and the Iranian government offered a bounty to anyone, Muslim or non-Muslim, who would enforce the decree against Rushdie. This was unusual because ordinarily decrees of *takfir* are not issued against persons or institutions that were never previously Muslim, while obeying such a decree was also neither expected nor demanded of non-Muslims.

On 29 March 1989 'Abdallah Ahdal, the rector of a mosque in Brussels, was murdered for refusing to endorse Khomeini's *takfir*. On 3 July 1991 Ettore Capriolo, the Italian translator of Rushdie's book, was stabbed in Milan. On 12 July 1991 Hitoshi Igarashi, the Japanese translator of the book, was stabbed to death in Tokyo. On 11 October 1993 William Nygnaard, the Norwegian publisher of the book, was shot three times in the back outside his home in Oslo but survived. Several incidents of **arson** against bookstores carrying the anathematized book occurred in the United States and Great Britain. Also, whereas ordinarily the decree of *takfir* would be automatically nullified by the open and sincere repentance of the excommunicated person, Khomeini specified that the *takfir* against Rushdie was irrevocable since his offense was deemed unpardonable.

TAKFIR WAL HIGRAH. The Jama'at al Muslimin (Muslim Society) is a Sunni Muslim purist and revolutionary splinter group of the **Muslim Brotherhood** that advocated total rejection of the contemporary Egyptian social and political system in favor of a fundamentalist state. The more familiar name of Takfir wal Higrah or "Atonement and Flight" (more literally, "Excommunication and Exodus") was given to it by Egyptian security organs as more descriptive of its beliefs and practices. Its leader, Shukri Ahmad Mustafa, demanded that members renounce what he regarded as deviations from pure Islam and that they try to remove themselves physically from the midst of an apostate society by living in the desert or in more traditional towns not "corrupted" by the westernization occurring under the free trade and investment policies of Anwar Sadat.

Members of this group took advantage of antigovernment food riots on 18-19 January 1977 to ransack and burn the nightclubs and casinos that had sprung up as a result of the open-door policies of Sadat. After a government crackdown on all groups critical of Anwar Sadat, whether leftist or fundamentalist, about 60 members of this group were imprisoned. Accordingly on 3 July 1977 Mustafa and some followers kidnapped a former minister of religious affairs, Sheikh Muhammad Hussayn Dhahabi, and demanded the release of their brethren. The government refused their demands. After Dhahabi's body was found on 7 July, Egyptian security forces cracked down on the society, with six people killed and 57 wounded in the fighting that ensued. Eventually about 620 members of the group were arrested, including Mustafa and four other key leaders who were tried and executed in March 1978.

The group had around 5,000 total adherents, many of whom lived in the Upper Egyptian city of Asyut, a stronghold of **Islamic fundamentalism**. While some aid came to the group from Libya, most of the group's resources came from expatriate Egyptians sympathetic to the group. In October 1981 the organization claimed responsibility for the murder of Anwar Sadat, which actually was accomplished by a different fundamentalist group, namely **Munazzamat al Jihad**.

TALIBAN. From Arabic, *Talib*, for "seeker," with the Persian/Dari *-an* plural ending, generic term for Muslim theological seminary students and also used to designate the group currently ruling most of Afghanistan. The Taliban movement began in September 1994 among the students of one Mullah Muhammad Omar of Qandahar who were dissatisfied with the arbitrary rule of the remnant **Mujahideen** factions. By 27 September 1996 the Taliban captured Kabul, the capital of Afghanistan and by mid-2000 held most of the country, although some parts were still loyal to other Afghan leaders. The Taliban are Afghani **Islamic fundamentalist** adherents of Wahhabism, an austere and puritanical branch of Sunni Islam that anathematizes any accommodation or synthesis between traditional Islamic law and more contemporary legal and political forms, and which also anathematizes Shi'ite Islam as being heretical or even apostate. Thus, unlike the Islamic rulers of Iran, the Taliban have dispensed with even the forms of a written secular-style constitution, democracy, elections, or judicial equality of the sexes.

The Taliban are connected to terrorism on two counts: They grant **sanctuary** in their territory to "Afghan" veteran fundamentalist groups, such as **Osama bin Laden**'s **al Qa'eda** group, to train and equip themselves for actions in nations outside of Afghanistan. On 20 November 1998 the Taliban announced that one of their religious courts had declared Osama bin Laden innocent of any involvement in the **East African U.S. embassies bombings**. Moreover the Taliban have steadfastly refused to obey U.S. demands to **extradite** bin Laden. Second, there is evidence of collusion between the Taliban and Pakistani security forces in promoting Muslim secessionists operating in the Indian-controlled portion of Kashmir.

Following the **World Trade Center and Pentagon Attacks of 11 September 2001**, President George W. Bush called upon the Taliban on 17 September 2001 to surrender Osama bin Laden and other members of his al Qa'eda network to U.S. authorities. Following their refusal to do so the United States launched Operation Enduring Freedom on 7 October 2001 against Taliban and al Qa'eda forces within Afghanistan. Follwoing six weeks of heavy U.S. air strikes forces of the Northern Alliance advanced and occupied Mazar-i Sharif on 9 November, Herat on 11 November, and entered Kabul by 13 November following the retreat of Taliban forces. By mid-November the Taliban were abandoning the cities and towns of Afghanistan and apparently regrouping in the mountains or else fleeing the scene.

TAMIL TIGERS. Name used by over 25 different Tamil guerrilla organizations fighting the Sinhalese-dominated government of Sri Lanka. The youth league of the Tamil United Liberation Front (TULF) political party, founded on 14 May 1972, attracted younger, more militant Tamils who founded the Tamil New Tigers as a more activist clique within the youth league. On 5 May 1976 the Tamil New Tigers reconstituted themselves separately from the TULF as the **Liberation Tigers of Tamil Eelam** (LTTE). Approximately 25 different unrelated "Tiger" organizations have appeared since the LTTE began. The LTTE and its rival Tamil Tiger groups engaged in internecine battling from May 1986 to September 1987. By April 1989 the LTTE and the remnants of three other Tiger organizations formed an umbrella group, the Eelam National Liberation Front. The LTTE and other Tamil Tiger groups had enjoyed the state sponsorship of Tamil Nadu State in India but such support ended after the Tamil Tiger groups began attacking Indian Army forces sent to Sri Lanka to restore order.

TARGETS. Terrorism is distinguished from other forms of political violence, such as conventional warfare and guerrilla warfare, in that it is largely carried out by persons other than official military personnel of a nation-state and also by the tendency of terrorists to attack civilian rather than military targets. The targeting is intended not simply to harm the immediate victims but also to capture and manipulate a target audience through which the terrorists will direct their political demands. Government buildings, military installations, and high-security facilities, such as nuclear power plants, which have armed guards, surveillance perimeters, fences, walls, barbed wire, or other special barriers, are difficult to attack or to invade and are known as "hard" targets. By contrast schools, places of worship, shopping malls, or open-air markets, that are frequented by civilians who are largely defenseless and whose premises themselves offer little protection against machine-gun fire or **bombings**, are "soft" targets attractive to terrorists.

Originally airplanes, federal courthouses, most business places, parking lots, and underground garages were soft targets and consequently become the objects of **hijackings**, hostage-barricade situations, or **bombings**. The obvious antiterrorism response is to "harden" such targets either by making them less accessible to terrorists, or else by making them less vulnerable to the effects of an attack, or else providing them with means of self-defense. Airplanes cannot be easily hardened to withstand direct bomb or missile attacks without making them too heavy to fly and so preemption by screening passengers and luggage for weapons or bombs has become standard practice in most developed nations while on-board security in the form of covert guards, such as the **U.S. Sky Marshal program**, also serve to deter hijacking.

New U.S. embassies and federal courthouses are now designed without underground garages but with parking lots separated from the main building by terraced expanses of grass which prevent vehicles from being driven up to, or into, the sides of the building. They also have smaller window spaces and Mylar coatings to reduce the effects of imploding glass shards, as well as incorporating multiple independent foundations and supports to ensure that the collapse of one part of the building, say due to a massive truck bomb or shoulder-launched rocket, would not compromise the structural integrity of the remaining building modules. In addition such buildings have screening devices at the entrances and also video cameras within and facing out of the building to note suspicious activity or allow identification of suspects in the event of a terrorist attack.

Target displacement refers to the tendency of terrorists to select alternative soft targets or different tactics in reaction to target hardening. Thus terrorists would tend to select older, "un-hardened" government offices instead of newer, hardened ones. The measures taken to prevent airplane hijackings have caused many terrorists either to attempt hijacking from airports in nations which lack security measures or else to attempt to bomb planes in flight rather than to seize the plane and its passengers and crew as hostages.

TEMPLE MOUNT OPERATION. In 1983, following the arrest of several **Gush Emunim** members plotting to **bomb** five Arab buses in Israel and the Occupied Territories, Israeli authorities learned that the group had been plotting during the previous four years to bomb the Dome of the Rock in Jerusalem with 28 precision bombs. The group believed that this Muslim shrine, which is the third holiest place in Islam after the Ka'aba in Mecca and the Mosque of the Prophet in Medina, had to be destroyed to clear the site on the Temple Mount for the construction of a Third Temple on the site of the Second Temple destroyed by the Romans in 70 A.D. This was necessary in order to facilitate the advent of the promised Messiah, who they believed would inaugurate the Jewish millennial kingdom that they believed was prophesied in scripture. Such an event would also almost have certainly triggered another Arab-Israeli war which the Gush Emunim also hoped for as they believed this would allow for the complete expulsion of Arabs and other non-Jews from the biblical Eretz Yisrael. *See also* MILLENNIALISM.

TERRA LLIURE (TL). "Free Land" was a left-wing Catalan group with the goal of reconstituting an independent Catalan homeland in Catalonia that would embrace also the Spanish provinces of Valencia and the Balaric Isles as well as the French province of Roussillon. While formed in the 1970s, it undertook a terrorist campaign in May 1981, shooting a professor of Spanish in Barcelona in the legs. That year it also exploded small **bombs** in foreign-owned banks and travel agencies in the cities of Alicante, Barcelona, Tarragona, and Valencia until December 1981 when Spanish police arrested some TL members.

On 25 July 1987, the last day to file personal income tax returns in Spain, TL bombed the Finance Ministry office in the Basque province town of Igualada. Five policemen were wounded along with the local tax commissioner and two civilians. TL has also claimed credit for the 1987 bombings in Barcelona of the U.S. consulate general and a USO club for which credit was also claimed by the **Red Army for the Liberation of Catalonia**, a radical TL splinter group. In July 1991 the group was reported to have renounced the use of terrorism.

TERRORISM. No consensus exists on the proper definition of terrorism. In part this is because "terrorism" is not simply a denotative label but also a label of reprobation such that partisans of a given party or political tendency will hesitate to apply it to those groups whom they champion, while applying it quite freely to groups of whose politics they disapprove, even when the actions being committed by the two sets of groups are substantially comparable. The other difficulty is that nearly all conventional military or insurgent forces will occasionally engage in actions, whether by design or accident, that may be plausibly described as terrorist. At what point, then, should a combatant group cease to be counted merely as a **belligerent** and begin to be counted as a terrorist group? The approach used in this dictionary has been to regard as terrorists those groups that will ordinarily attack noncombatants or nonmilitary **targets** as freely as military targets. Likewise, their choice of tactics reveals whether or not they distinguish between combatants and noncombatants. Antiaircraft artillery can be used either against warplanes or civilian planes, but using car bombs almost always entails the risk of noncombatant deaths and injuries.

To distinguish terrorism from mere criminal violence, it is not sufficient to define it as "politically motivated violence," since other forms of nonterrorist violence, such as insurgencies and mob violence, can also be politically inspired. The specific quality defining terrorism is that it *seeks deliberately to create terror in its victims for a political purpose*, whereas, other forms of political violence have as their primary object inflicting harm on objects or persons with terror being only a by-product. Terrorists cultivate fear in their victims and audiences not as an end in itself nor merely to torment their direct victims but rather to create terror in others who are the "spectators" of the terrorist event. Terrorists seek to force this "audience" to pay them attention and to respond in some manner. Therefore one definition of terrorism that has been proposed reads roughly as follows:

> Terrorism is the use of violence to create terror in others who are not the direct object of violence in order to cause them to act in certain ways. [H. H. A. Cooper, *Evaluating the Terrorist Threat: Principles of Applied Risk Assessment*, 1974]

International Terrorism—A fundamental distinction is often made between domestic, or territorial, terrorism and international terrorism: Domestic terrorism is limited to given countries or regions and is usually part of an internal insurgency or revolutionary war. International terrorism is nonterritorial in that it is not limited to any one region. An example of a domestic insurgency is found in the case of the **Farabundo Martí Liberation Front** (FMLN) in El Salvador: Following its failure to overthrow the Salvadoran government in its ill-fated "final offensive" in 1981, the FMLN retreated to the jungles and then undertook a campaign of **bombing** the economic infrastructure and murdering local officials or notables close to the government. In this case, the bombings can be viewed as a rational tactic for crippling the economic resources of the government, while killing many of the Salvadorans could be rationalized on the grounds of their being functionaries of the government. The **Argentine Anticommunist Alliance** of Argentina represents an example of a right-wing **death squad** which remained domestic in the scope of its activities.

By contrast the **Chilean Fatherland and Liberty** group, which was a right-wing **death squad**, not only engaged in domestic terrorism against leftists in Chile, but became international in scope by **assassinating** the former Chilean Foreign Minister, Orlando Letelier, outside of his home in Washington, D.C. in 1976. The campaign of bombings in England, Germany, and attempted actions in Gibralter carried out by members of the **Irish Republican Army** (IRA) in the 1970s and 1980s expanded the scope of IRA terrorism from being merely domestic to international. The English civilians or British soldiers in Germany who were killed were usually quite unconnected with Northern Ireland, and the resulting damages inflicted no direct blows on the IRA's enemies, namely the British government, Unionist politicians, or the Ulster Protestant militia groups. The object of such attacks was rather to create terror and consternation among the British public to incite them to put pressure on the British government to withdraw their troops from Northern Ireland and to allow the Irish to resolve the question of the future fate of the northern six counties on their own. Similarly many **Islamic fundamentalist** terrorist groups, such as the **al Qa'eda** group of **Osama bin Laden** have resorted to terrorism crossing international borders both in their attempts to impose their vision of Islamic rule on those Muslim nations they have targeted as well as attempts to punish nations they perceive as enemies of Islam, such as the United States and Israel.

Domestic and international terrorism often differ in that the former usually can be readily identified with some insurgent group that seeks formal recognition in the international community. In the latter case, more often the acting group is sponsored by governments that wish to maintain a "plausible deniability" of having any connection with the group, since acts of violence against noncombatant civilians in another sovereign jurisdiction are nothing less than acts of war. Another distinction is that while those responsible for acts of territorial terrorism often are seeking recognition as legitimate governments or as new nation-states, such as the Basque separatists in northern Spain or IRA members in Northern Ireland, in many cases of international terrorists the reverse is often the case, namely, that they are seeking to attack the nation-state system for tactical or **ideological** reasons.

Some key characteristics of international terrorism include the following:

1) It is a form of psychological warfare intended to create reactions on the part of its audience. It seeks out civilian victims rather than military targets since this creates greater terror in the target audience. Viewers are supposed to be forced to think, "But for God's grace there go I!" [H. H. A. Cooper, 1974]

2) It is a form of communication. Besides communicating terror, such acts are forms of **armed propaganda** that force a captive audience to listen to political demands and threats. The object is to get people to think, "Let us hear them out to see what they want," and then to get them to the point of agreeing to capitulate to certain demands. [Brian Jenkins, *International Terrorism: A New Mode of Conflict,* 1974] For instance, the continued holding of Terry Anderson and other hostages by the Lebanese **Hezbollah** group brought some of the hostages' relatives to try to bring pressure on the U.S. government to make concessions to gain their release.

3) It is also a form of criminality but not "mere criminality." It would be a mistake to equate the robberies and murders committed by terrorists with those committed by common hoodlums for the former are instrumental in serving political ends beyond the crimes themselves. On the other hand, when the political nature of the act is made clear, there is the danger of the captive audience mentally capitulating to the act of armed propaganda and accepting the terrorists' claims that they are actually freedom fighters and that their actions are justified by their allegedly noble aims.

4) International terrorism is really a form of protracted warfare being carried out for political aims, often with the sponsorship of hostile governments.

Such political warfare is a form of **low-intensity conflict** that exploits the ambivalence of the Western nation-states toward such forms of conflict, falling between the extremes of declared conventional warfare and official diplomatic peace. This warfare is very cost-effective for the sponsoring regime but very costly to the targeted countries, where businesses are forced to spend much on protecting their executives and whose citizens are frightened away from traveling abroad. Such warfare allows nations deficient in conventional military strength to use sophisticated technology to strike at their enemies easily, as was shown by the bombing of **Pan Am Flight 103** over Scotland on 21 December 1988, by a small radio bomb.

The ambivalent nature of international terrorism creates policy ambivalence on the part of its victims: If it is considered "mere criminality," then it should be treated as a police matter, requiring minimal use of force. But if it is viewed as a military matter, then maximal force ought to be used. And if it is viewed as a political matter, then attempted negotiation, compromise, and capitulation would be in order. In short, terrorism is able to thrive on the very ambiguity that shrouds its nature.

"TERRORIST'S HANDBOOK." Title of a 98-page manual published by anonymous authors using the pen name "Chaos Industries and Gunzenbombz Pyro-Technologies" and widely available on the Internet, which details construction of **bombs**, booby-traps, biological and chemical weapons and poisons, and **assassination** techniques. The proliferation of such works as this, the *Poisoner's Handbook*, and *Silent Death*, which detail how to prepare **ricin** and other lethal, natural poisons, and the older *Anarchists' Cookbook*, as well as other materials available in book or CD-ROM format, have made it possible for the "amateur" terrorist to become as skilled and lethal as his or her more "professional" counterpart.

TERRORIST STATES. The U.S. government currently lists Cuba, Iran, Iraq, Libya, North Korea, Sudan, and Syria as state sponsors of terrorism, also called "terrorist states." This list is maintained and updated pursuant to Section 6 (j) of the Export Administration Act of 1979 according to factual findings certified by the U.S. State Department each year. Testimony and evidence are reviewed to determine whether such governments are continuing to provide terrorists safe haven, travel documents, arms, training, and technical expertise and also whether such governments themselves directly engage in terrorism as tools of domestic and foreign policies. A lower level of support consists not so much of active cooperation with terrorists but rather a passive tolerance by governments in which they choose to allow terrorists to reside in, or travel through, or carry out logistical and recruitment efforts without official hindrance within their sovereign jurisdictions.

The U.S. State Department, which had listed Iran as the foremost state sponsor of terrorism in its 1993-1999 reports *Patterns of Global Terrorism*, in its 1999 report ceased designating Iran as the foremost state sponsor of terrorism. In June 1999 the U.S. Senate amended its foreign aid bill to include language designating Yugoslavia as a terrorist state, a move to which the Clinton administration objected on the grounds that such designations were the role of the U.S. State Department under the 1979 Export Administration Act. Following the 24 December 1999 **hijacking** on an Air India airliner by **Kashmiri separatists** believed to have been supported by the Pakistani government, Pakistan has come under increasing scrutiny for its ties to terrorist groups operating in Kashmir and India that also have ties to the **Taliban** regime in Afghanistan, which itself is suspected of sheltering **Osama bin Laden**.

TOKYO CONVENTION. The Convention on Offences and Certain Other Acts Committed on Board Aircraft, concluded on 14 September 1963, pertains to acts that affect in-flight safety of civilian carriers, and defines the rights and obligations of the signatory states and the pilot and crews of aircraft. The convention attempts to prevent unlawful seizure of aircraft by requiring contracting states not to give **sanctuary** or free transit to hijackers once the plane is landed in their territory and giving jurisdiction over the hijackers to the state in which the concerned aircraft is registered. *See also* AIR TRAVEL SECURITY; HIJACKING.

TOKYO SUBWAY GAS ATTACK. On 20 March 1995 members of the **Aum Shinrikyo** cult punctured plastic bags containing homemade sarin, a lethal nerve gas, which killed 12 people, injured several hundred, and produced transient symptoms in up to 5,500 others. Worse might have happened because Asahara and his followers had been preparing for an apocalyptic war which they hoped to initiate by deploying whatever **weapons of mass destruction** they could procure which they believed would lead to Asahara becoming accepted as the Messiah of a new millennium.

Aum Shinrikyo had tried without success to obtain nuclear weapons and weapons-grade sarin from poorly guarded bases of the former Soviet Red Army, and then settled on producing their own biological and chemical weapons. The sect succeeded in culturing and isolating botulinum, one of the most deadly biological poisons known, and tried on nine occasions to deploy it against various **targets**, including the Japanese Diet, the Imperial Household compound, and U.S. military bases in Japan. Following the failure of these botulinum experiments the sect produced sarin, a much simpler compound that is easier to prepare, and deployed 12 liters of the deadly liquid by vaporizing it from a trunk-mounted heater and fan in the city of Matsumoto on 27 June 1994, causing seven deaths and over 150 injuries, although as many as 600 people reported symptoms.

Shoko Asahara, leader of the cult, knew that he was being investigated by the Japanese police for the 1989 murder of Tsutsumi Sakamoto, a lawyer who had been investigating allegations of brainwashing on behalf of concerned families of members of the cult. On Asahara's orders cult members had murdered not only Sakamoto but also his wife and infant son. A siege mentality prevailed in the cult which led them to make the sarin gas attack against the national police headquarters, located in the building under which the four attacked subway lines converged. Asahara sent cult members to release the liquid sarin in four subway lines which converged underneath the building housing the national police headquarters. Accordingly followers punctured plastic bags containing sarin on the four subways on trains bound into the city from suburbs on 20 March 1995. The attack failed to produce the disruption intended in part because the sarin used was quite dilute. Nonetheless the Tokyo Subway gas attack was the first widely known use of a chemical or biological agent.

Following the subway gas attack Asahara was arrested on 16 May 1995, while found hiding in a cubbyhole in one of his sect's properties. Investigation of the cult's center on the slope of Mount Fuji revealed an elaborate three-story facility built to produce chemical and biological weapons of mass destruction. With the arrest of Asahara and 400 of his followers, who faced charges ranging from **kidnapping,** to illegal production of drugs and weapons, to murder, the Japanese government moved to ban the sect under the Anti-Subversive Law in December 1995.

TONTON MACOUTES. The "Volunteers for National Security" was a state-sponsored repressive organization created by the dictator François "Papa

Doc" Duvalier in 1957 to eliminate his enemies and quell open dissent among the people of Haiti. Its more common name, the "Tonton Macoute" is Creole, meaning "Uncle Knapsack." Originally it was a personal presidential bodyguard and became an alternative militia to counter possible coups by the Haitian military and ultimately became an instrument of mass repression.

After Jean-Claude "Baby Doc" Duvalier was deposed from the Haitian presidency in 1985, the Tonton Macoutes were officially disbanded. In reality, the organization continued to exist underground and apparently found another patron in President Henri Namphy. On 11 September 1988, soldiers and Tonton Macoute members stormed the St. John Bosco Church in Port-au-Prince, killing nine worshipers and wounding 77 and setting fire to the church. The parish priest, Jean Bertrand Aristide, was a vocal critic of the Namphy government, but the tactic backfired, as it prompted more clashes between citizens and the Tonton Macoutes leading General Prosper Avril to depose Namphy by a military coup on September 17. Yet Avril himself did not appear willing to suppress or prosecute the Tonton Macoutes, and he, too, was forced to resign on 10 March 1990. Jean-Bertrand Aristide, elected president on 16 December 1990, promised to prosecute the Tonton Macoutes but was himself ousted by a coup staged by Army officers having ties to the Tonton Macoutes on 30 September 1991.

While the label "Tonton Macoute" is no longer used, a successor organization incorporating many of the same members and methods was created by the military coup leaders which is known as FRAPH, the French acronym for the "Revolutionary Front for the Advancement and Progress of Haiti." *See* FRAPH.

TÚPAC AMARU REVOLUTIONARY MOVEMENT. The Movimiento Revolucionario Túpac Amaru (MRTA) was a Marxist urban guerrilla group that sought to create a socialist revolution within Peru following the Cuban and Nicaraguan models. It was the main rival of the **Sendero Luminoso** group within Peru from which it differed in rejecting the xenophobia and **ideological** isolationism of the latter group, stressing instead its fraternal unity with other Marxist national liberation movements and regimes. The MRTA used terrorism primarily for **"armed propaganda"** both to delegitimize the Peruvian regime and to force the U.S. diplomatic and commercial presence out of Peru.

The MRTA was formed by leftist university students, many of whom went into exile in Cuba and the Soviet Union when Peru was under military rule during the 1970s. The group therefore reflected a more Castroite and internationalist perspective than did the Sendero Luminoso. The MRTA was aided by Cuba and the former **Sandinista** government of Nicaragua and was suspected of receiving aid from Libya. The MRTA also once had contacts with the Colombian **M-19** group and is believed to have collaborated with the **Manuel Rodríguez Patriotic Front** in Chile and with the reconstituted National Liberation Army (*see* NESTOR PAZ ZAMORA COMMANDO) of Bolivia. The MRTA took its name from an earlier national, anticolonial, and revolutionary hero, namely the Inca pretender "Túpac Amaru," who led Peru's Indian peasants in an abortive anticolonial revolt two centuries ago. Although Túpac Amaru based his revolt on an appeal to Indian nativist resentment against Spaniard domination, there was little evidence that the MRTA made any systematic appeal to Indian nativism as did its rival, Sendero Luminoso.

Although formed in 1983, the MRTA became active in 1984. Of 51 confirmed MRTA terrorist actions conducted from 1984-1991, 37 involved **bombings,** four involved armed attacks using automatic weapons or light artillery, three involved car bombings, while seven involved takeovers of radio stations, news agency offices, or churches to force publication of their propaganda. At least nine of these attacks were directed at U.S. diplomatic property and persons, giving the MRTA the distinction of making the most attacks on U.S. diplomatic facilities of any group in Latin America.

On 28 September 1984 three MRTA gunmen machine-gunned the exterior of the U.S. embassy. On 9 November 1985 MRTA gunmen threw dynamite sticks at the U.S. embassy and raked it with machine-gun fire. On 4 April 1986 the MRTA made a similar attack on the Peruvian-U.S. Cultural Institute, wounding a guard, as well as attacking two Citibank offices, an IBM warehouse, and a Sears office. On 9 June 1990 the MRTA launched mortars at the U.S. ambassador's residence and, on 18 July 1990, bombed the U.S. embassy, wounding three guards. The MRTA also bombed the courtyard of the Interior Ministry on 25 July 1985 and attacked the Presidential Palace and the airplane carrying newly elected President Alberto Fujimori in November 1991.

At its peak the MRTA had 1,000 to 2,000 members but following the crackdown of the Fujimori administration over 400 of its cadres, including its founder Víctor Polay Campos, were arrested and imprisoned. Whereas they were mainly active only in Lima in the 1980s, in the 1990s they carried out activities in Cuzco, Peru, and in areas bordering Bolivia. The appearance of the MRTA in highly visible urban operations in 1984 may have moved **Sendero Luminoso** to open its campaign within the cities rather than relying solely on the rural guerrilla strategy of "encircling the cities" in order to prevent its new rival from taking center stage within Peru. The final and most dramatic action of the MRTA was the 17 December 1996 takeover of the Japanese ambassador's residence during a diplomatic reception in honor of the Japanese Emperor's birthday in which 14 MRTA members initially seized around 490 guests, including many ambassadors and high Peruvian government officials, including Carlos Giusti Acuña, a member of the Supreme Court. *See also* PERUVIAN JAPANESE EMBASSY HOSTAGE CRISIS.

TUPAMAROS. The Uruguayan Movimiento de Liberación Nacional (MLN) was a leftist guerrilla group that sought to overthrow the Uruguayan state and to drive out foreign, particularly U.S. and Brazilian, interests. The group first surfaced on 31 July 1963 with an attack on a gun club and carried out robberies and precise **bombings** against U.S. and Brazilian diplomatic vehicles and against the homes of high-ranking civilian politicians and bureaucrats. Because the group was believed to have Cuban backing, Uruguay severed diplomatic ties with Cuba in September 1964.

In 1966 the MLN embarked on a campaign of urban terrorism and took the name "Tupamaro" from that of the Peruvian Inca pretender Túpac Amaru executed by the Spaniards in 1782. From January 1968 to July 1972, the Tupamaros engaged in the bombings of institutional targets and conducted nine major bank robberies. The Tupamaros also conducted a campaign of distributing money seized from their robberies to the urban poor and of publishing financial records they had stolen supposedly documenting alleged corruption among the ruling circles of Uruguay.

Tupamaro terrorism became of international concern with the **kidnapping** on 31 July 1970 of a U.S. Agency for International Development employee, Daniel A. Mitrione, who was murdered on 9 August 1970. On 8 January 1971 British ambassador Geoffrey Jackson was abducted and held eight months in a Tupamaro "people's prison." The

Tupamaros had contacts with the Chilean **Movement of the Revolutionary Left** (MIR) and the Argentinean **People's Revolutionary Army** (ERP).

By 1972 the Tupamaros began to target members of the Uruguayan military and security forces, a move that drew a declaration of internal war by the Uruguayan government, which unleashed the military on the Tupamaros. By May 1972 the military had penetrated the Tupamaro network, uncovering an impressive infrastructure of over 200 safe houses, including a clandestine hospital complete with operating theater and a covert arms factory. By November 1972 some 2,600 members and supporters were arrested and 42 killed. The leader, Raul Sendic Antonaccio, was captured and the movement collapsed. Ironically, the Tupamaros had succeeded in destroying Uruguayan democracy since the military seized power shortly after the crackdown on the Tupamaros. The military, however, then pursued its own ruthless suppression of leftists and subversives that precluded any mass-based leftist revolution. Following the restoration of civilian rule in 1984, a general amnesty was declared in 1985. Upon his release from prison, Sendic and other surviving Tupamaros reconstituted themselves as a legal political party.

TURBAS DIVINAS, LOS. The "divine mobs" were Nicaraguan state-sponsored groups used to intimidate and suppress domestic opponents of the **Sandinista** regime in Nicaragua. These mobs consisted of Frente Sandinista de Liberación Nacional (FSLN) activists and members of the Sandinista Defense Committees, a network of blockwatch organizations. The *turbas divinas* and Defense Committees were under the control of Department F-8 for "Mass Organizations" within the General Directorate of State Security (DGSE).

During the first year following the 17 July 1979 Sandinista victory the FSLN appeared to share power with a number of non-Marxist democratic groups. As hard-line Marxist Tomás Borge Martínez consolidated FSLN control over the Interior Ministry, toleration of non-FSLN political groups ended. On 7 November 1980 organized mobs attacked an opposition rally at Nandaime led by Nicaraguan Democratic Movement leader Alfonso Robelo, and on 9 November mobs attacked the Nicaraguan Democratic Movement's (NDM) offices, destroying files and equipment and torching an NDM vehicle. When the non-FSLN paper *La Prensa* sought to publish details of the attack it was put under censorship by the Interior Ministry. Sandinista National Directorate member Daniel Ortega is reputed to have dubbed these FSLN-organized mobs the "*turbas divinas*" and, after his election as president, publicly threatened to unleash the *turbas* upon Nicaraguan opposition groups.

The *turbas divinas* destroyed the home of NDM leader Alfonso Robelo, who later left Nicaragua and joined the **contras**. In March 1981 the *turbas* began painting slogans and insults each night upon the walls of the home of Violeta Chamorro, widow of Pedro Joaquín Chamorro Cardenal, the *La Prensa* editor believed to have been murdered by right-wing Somoza supporters before the Sandinista revolution. Also in 1981 *turbas* stoned the jeep of Archbishop Miguel Obando y Bravo, a critic of the Sandinistas. On 20 July 1982 *turbas* beat up the auxiliary bishop of Managua, and in August 1982 stripped Rev. Bismarck Carballo, the Archbishop's spokesman, along with a female parishioner and paraded both of them naked in front of photographers, claiming they had been caught in adultery. In late 1982 the *turbas* attacked and vandalized a Mormon church in the San Judas neighborhood of Managua. In March 1983, during the visit of Pope John Paul II to Nicaragua, *turbas* mobbed the Pope and drowned out his public address in Managua with revolutionary and anticlerical slogans. In January 1985 *turbas* attacked the Conservative Party headquarters after the Conservatives accused the FSLN of rigging the national elections. In August 1987 the *turbas* attacked two human rights groups, the Permanent Commission on Human Rights and the January 22 Movement of Mothers of Political Prisoners.

The *turbas* generally attacked the homes and businesses of anyone suspected of being anti-Sandinista, often beating or maiming their victims as well. With the electoral defeat of the FSLN and the installation of Violeta Chamorro as Nicaragua's president on 25 February 1990, the *turbas* ceased to be a state-sponsored group and their activity largely ceased.

TURKISH PEOPLE'S LIBERATION ARMY (TPLA). The TPLA was a Soviet-sponsored Turkish leftist revolutionary group that specialized in **kidnapping** U.S. servicemen stationed at NATO bases within Turkey, **assassinations** of right-wing Turks, as well as in bank robberies and **bombings of** right-wing and U.S. **targets**. The group was founded in 1968 or shortly thereafter by leftist students from the Middle East Technical University in Ankara who underwent guerrilla training in **al Fatah** camps within Jordan and Lebanon and who also established contacts with leftist Army officers and cadets. Following the abduction of four U.S. servicemen on 4 March 1971, later released unharmed, about 18 members of the TPLA, including its leader, Deniz Gezmiş, were arrested.

Gezmiş was executed along with two comrades in 1972, but when the rest of his colleagues were released in 1974 under a general amnesty, they reactivated the organization. The TPLA members expanded their ranks by recruiting from leftist university students in Ankara and Istanbul who received training and arms from Soviet-bloc countries. By 1977 TPLA assassinations had claimed 260 lives. In 1979 around 2,000 people were killed due to **death squad** activities of the TPLA and similar groups. The military crackdown in September 1980 led to the suppression of most activities of the TPLA, which then ceased to be active.

Disagreements within the TPLA led to the splitting off in 1975 of a faction, known as Dev Yol, or the Revolutionary Road, which did not engage in terrorism or violence. In 1978 a split emerged in Dev Yol leading to the creation of Dev Sol (*see* REVOLUTIONARY PEOPLE'S LIBERATION PARTY/FRONT), or the Revolutionary Left, which acted mainly as an antirightist death squad in the environs of Ankara and is one of the few leftist terrorist groups in Turkey that survived the crackdown of 1980 and made a comeback in the late 1980s.

TURKISH PEOPLE'S LIBERATION FRONT (TPLF). The TPLF was the armed wing of the Turkish People's Liberation Party. Like the **Turkish People's Liberation Army**, with which it had no direct connection, the TPLF sought to overturn the constitutional democracy in Turkey in favor of a Marxist-Leninist state and its members also received training in **al Fatah** camps as well as covert Soviet-bloc support. On 17 May 1971 the TPLF **kidnapped** Ephraim Elrom, the Israeli consul general in Istanbul, later murdered on 22 May.

The leader of the TPLF, Mahir Çayan, escaped after briefly being imprisoned and kidnapped three NATO radar technicians on 27 March 1972, who were later murdered by the terrorists, to force Turkish officials to release another comrade still in prison. Instead the Turkish police hunted down and killed Çayan and nine of his companions in their hideout near the Black Sea. The widow of Mahir Çayan subsequently helped found the **Marxist-Leninist Armed Propaganda Unit** (MLAPU).

TPLF members later **hijacked** two Turkish airliners, once in May 1972 and again in October 1972, demanding the release of imprisoned comrades in exchange for the hostages' lives. On each occasion the

Turkish government refused their demands and the hijackers took their planes to Bulgaria where they sought political **asylum**. The TPLF continued to operate until September 1980 when it was suppressed in the overall crackdown of the Turkish military against leftist groups.

TURNER DIARIES. Novel written by William Pierce, a leader of the Neo-Nazi National Alliance, under the pen name of Andrew MacDonald, which depicts an extreme right-wing revolutionary movement against the government of the United States, which has been used by many U.S. domestic right-wing extremists as a sort of handbook of antigovernment extremist tactics. The leader of the **Order**, Robert Mathews, reportedly copied the "point system" for the killings of purported enemies of the white race from the *Turner Diaries*. The novel exults in a **white supremacist** and anti-Semitic assault on the U.S. government, which is portrayed as a virtual "Zionist Occupation Government," hostile to ordinary white, Christian, Americans. Timothy McVeigh reportedly was an avid reader of this book and sold or gave copies of it to other like-minded persons. The Southern Poverty Law Center's Klanwatch project has noted 10 major parallels between the **Oklahoma City bombing** and the terrorist **bombing** attack depicted in the *Turner Diaries*, including choice of **target** (a federal law enforcement building), type of bomb used (fuel oil and ammonium nitrate), timing of explosion (both around 9:00 a.m. when casualties would be maximized), and **ideological** motivations of the perpetrators. This suggests that Timothy McVeigh consciously modeled his attack on the Murrah Building on the attack depicted within the novel.

- U -

ULSTER DEFENCE ASSOCIATION (UDA). The UDA is a northern Irish Protestant militia founded in September 1971, committed to maintaining Protestant supremacy in the political and social life of Northern Ireland, while its ostensible purpose is to protect Protestant neighborhoods from **Irish Republican Army** (IRA) attacks. While most of its numbers and resources are devoted to defending Protestant neighborhoods, it is widely believed to support **death squad** activities involving smaller, specialized units that often assume their own names and maintain a purported independence from the UDA, such is believed to be the case with the **Ulster Freedom Fighters** (UFF), in reality merely a UDA front. The UDA enjoyed effective state support from the Ulster Defence Regiment, an official security organization dominated by sectarian Protestant **militiamen**. The relationship with the British Army was more problematic, since from September to October 1972 they had considered the British Army to be in league with their Catholic enemies. From the end of the Unionist general strike of May 1974 until 1988, they maintained an effective truce with British forces. This may explain why the UDA of all Northern Irish paramilitary groups maintained a legal status until October 1988 when both the UDA and its UFF branch were also proscribed under the Special Powers Act of 1922, following the discovery that the UDA had smuggled a large quantity of arms into Northen Ireland from South Africa. The membership of the UDA at its height in the 1970s was estimated at 30,000 but currently it numbers perhaps several hundred with a few dozen being active in the UFF branch.

The former UDA leader, Andy Tyrie, explained the UDA mission as follows: "We're a counterterrorist organization. The only way we'll get peace here is to terrorize the terrorists." The UDA financed itself partly through protection rackets, ironically the same way the IRA financed itself. The UDA was affiliated with the New Ulster Political Research Group (NUPRG) which made contingency plans for creating an independent Ulster state in the event Ulster Protestants decided to create an independent Ulster Protestant republic to forestall a feared betrayal by Westminster. In June 1981 the Ulster Loyalist Democratic Party replaced the NUPRG, and in 1988 the party again changed its name to the Ulster Democratic Party (UDP), removing Andy Tyrie from the top leadership position which was taken over by an inner council of six members. The UDA demonstrated its political power during the pro-Unionist Ulster Workers' Council general strike in 1974, directed against a British-sponsored plan to share power in Ulster with Catholics. The UDA openly joined ranks with proscribed death squads such as the **Ulster Volunteer Force**, **Red Hand Commandos**, and other illegal militias, to form an Ulster Army Council to enforce the general strike. By setting up roadblocks throughout Northern Ireland the UDA effectively shut down large sections of the country.

Beginning in mid-1980 and lasting into 1981 an **assassination** campaign was waged against republicans and nationalists in the north. John Turnley, a nationalist member of the Westminster parliament who had unseated the ultra-Unionist Ian Paisley in 1979, was shot dead in June

1980. On 16 January 1981 Bernadette Devlin McAliskey, the former Republican member of the Westminster parliament, and her husband were wounded by gunmen in their home. Later UDA men were convicted of the Turnley murder and attempted murders of the McAliskeys. Three other nationalists were also killed this way, suggesting that the UDA was behind the wave of killings. IRA supporters believed that the UDA had to have enjoyed the cover of British army patrols to have been able to penetrate the largely Catholic areas in which these murders took place.

During the period 1990-1994 the UFF stepped up its attacks on Catholic and Republicans, targeting also members of the Social Democratic Labour Party, a Catholic group seeking equal rights for Catholics but opposing the tactics of the IRA. On 5 February 1992 the UFF killed five Catholics, three more on 14 November 1992, followed by six Catholics in two days during March 1993, and finally six Catholics and one Protestant on 30 October 1993. The UDA along with the UFF joined other Protestant paramilitary groups in declaring a cease-fire on 13 October 1994 in response to the IRA cease-fire. This earned the UDP a place in the multiparty talks beginning in May 1996. However, when the UDA and UFF broke the cease-fire in December 1997 and January 1998 the UDP was expelled from the talks and only readmitted once the UFF declared a renewed cease-fire on 23 January 1998. Both the UDA and UFF reluctantly agreed to the Good Friday Accord which the UDP endorsed in April 1998.

Throughout the duration of the Northern Ireland conflict (1968-1998) the UDA has been responsible for 253 killings, which includes two killings claimed by the Loyalist Retaliation and Defence Group (LRDG) during 1991. All Protestant paramilitary groups together accounted for 989 of the 3,466 killings that occurred during this conflict.

ULSTER FREEDOM FIGHTERS (UFF). The UFF was actually nothing more than the **death squad** covertly operated by the **Ulster Defence Association** allowing the UDA "plausible deniability" for killings that it had ordered. Like its parent group, the UFF is an anti-Catholic militia formed of Ulster Protestants but marked by more open violence and rowdyism.

The UFF murdered not only **Irish Republican Army** (IRA) activists and sympathizers but also carried out random killings of Catholics not associated with anti-Unionist groups to terrorize the Roman Catholic community. In 1976 it murdered a former Sinn Fein activist, Marie Drumm, in her bed at Belfast's Mater Hospital. On 14 March 1984 it shot and wounded Sinn Fein President Gerry Adams as he was being driven through downtown Belfast. On 7 November 1986 two **bombs** planted by the UFF exploded in garbage cans on Dublin's main street causing no injuries. Two others were found and deactivated. These bombs had been planted to protest the recently concluded Anglo-Irish Agreement. On 12 February 1989 UFF members entered the home of a prominent Catholic lawyer, Pat Finucane, and killed him in the presence of his family at the dinner table. While they claimed that he had been an IRA member, this appeared to be another example of the UFF campaign of killing prominent Catholics of whatever political complexion.

ULSTER VOLUNTEER FORCE (UVF). The Ulster Volunteer Force (UVF) was a northern Irish Protestant **death squad** used to repress suspected **Irish Republican Army** (IRA) members; it had effective state support from the Ulster Defence Regiment (UDR), an official security organization dominated by sectarian Protestant militiamen. The original UVF was formed from the unification of all Ulster Protestant militias in 1913 to oppose the grant of an autonomous government to Ireland in which Protestants would have formed a minority. At that time many British officers gave the UVF covert support. Upon the partition of Ireland under the Irish Free State Act of 1922, the Royal Irish Constabulary was dissolved throughout Ireland while the Royal Ulster Constabulary (RUC) took its place in the north. Most UVF members entered the RUC at that time and continued to fight those IRA members who rejected partition. Although the UVF ceased to exist officially, the corps of its members remained within the RUC and also later entered the Ulster Special Constabulary.

A former British military policeman, Augustus Spence, declared the UVF revived in 1966 in a special newspaper advertisement on 21 May 1966. This ad declared the UVF "a military body dedicated to upholding the constitution of Ulster by force of arms if necessary" and declared war on all IRA members, threatening to kill them summarily. By the "constitution of Ulster" Spence meant Protestant supremacy in the political and social life of northern Ireland rather than any constitutional rule of law as such. The new UVF engaged in a campaign of **arsons** by firebombings of Catholic homes and businesses. The Special Powers Act (1922) banning the IRA was amended on 23 June 1966 to proscribe the UVF as well. On 26 May 1966 the UVF shot one John Scullion, who died two weeks later, for singing republican songs in public. On 25 June 1966, Augustus Spence and other UVF members shot four Catholics leaving a pub in the Shankill area, killing one of them. The UVF then carried out a **bombing** campaign in 1969, which was blamed on the IRA, that forced the moderate prime minister of North Ireland, Terence O'Neill, to resign.

The UVF was legalized again in 1973. On 31 July 1975 UVF members murdered three members of the southern Irish Miami Showcase Band outside Newry. The UVF had tried to rig the band's van with a bomb, which detonated, killing two of their own numbers as well. One of the two UVF dead happened to be a sergeant in the Ulster Defence Regiment, the successor to the Ulster Special Constabulary. The overlapping membership of the UDR and UVF and the direct material support given by UDR members to the UVF made the latter, in effect, a state-sponsored group. The UVF also had relations with the **Red Hand Commandos**, who were suspected of bombing downtown Dublin and the southern Irish town of Monaghan on 17 May 1974, killing 30 and wounding 151.

The UVF had perhaps 1,500 members at its height. In 1976 the UVF pledged to refrain from violence; in the following three years, however, 43 members were tried and convicted on charges ranging from illegal possession of arms to murder.

In 1991 the UVF joined the Combined Loyalist Military Command. In October 1994 the UVF endorsed the cease-fire declared by the Combined Loyalist Military Command and, unlike the UDA and UFF, it respected the cease-fire to the present. Several disaffected UVF members in 1996 broke away to form the **Loyalist Volunteer Force**. Throughout the duration of the Northern Ireland conflict (1968-1998) the UVF has been responsible for 448 killings which includes killings claimed by the Red Hand Commandos.

UMKHONTO WE SIZWE (MK). The Spear of the Nation (MK) was the military wing of the **African National Congress** (ANC) established by Nelson Mandela in 1961. Following the withdrawal of Portugal from Mozambique and Angola in 1975, the MK was afforded state support channeled to it through the ANC from the African national regimes established in those lands as well as Cuban military training and material support from the Soviet Union and eastern bloc. The object of MK was to destroy the South African apartheid regime through political agitation, sabotage, and terrorism.

From 1961 to 1977 the MK confined its attacks largely to sabotaging power pylons and commercial property and avoided **targeting** civilians. In 1977, in response to the South African Defense Forces killing of hundreds of blacks in South African townships, the MK started its "second campaign" in which it targeted police and military officials as well as property. In this phase, lasting until 1983, the MK conducted over 200 terrorist attacks. In 1977, the MK shot two whites in Johannesburg and embarked on more extensive **bombing** operations. On 1 June 1980 the MK bombed the three South African Coal, Gas and Oil Conversion (SASOL) plants simultaneously at midnight, one in the Orange Free State and two in Transvaal, causing $7 million in damages and wounding one guard. On 13 August 1981 MK launched several rockets against the Voortrekkerhoogte military academy near Pretoria, causing damages but only two casualties. On 21 December 1982 the MK exploded four bombs in the Koeburg nuclear plant near Capetown, which was fueled but not in operation at that time. On 20 May 1983 the MK car bombed the South Africa air force headquarters outside Pretoria in which 17 persons were killed and around 200 wounded, although virtually no damage was inflicted on the military facility itself. Attacks were also made on civilian targets, such as the 24 June 1986 bombing of Wimpy Burgers in Johannesburg, wounding 17 customers, and the bombing of the Holiday Inn-owned President Hotel the same day in which two persons were wounded.

Since 1983 the program of MK had been to terrorize white farmers, to sabotage the industrial base of South Africa, to terrorize black policemen and politicians as collaborators of the apartheid regime, and to conduct urban terrorism in the white-inhabited urban areas. As is often the case with mass-based movements, a number of terrorist incidents against whites and black collaborators also occurred for which no group has claimed credit. In the late 1980s black "football clubs" appeared, which were, in fact, youth gangs that would terrorize or kill blacks who did not support the ANC. A particularly grisly form of murder called "necklacing" was perpetrated against blacks suspected of being police informants in which an automobile tire filled with gasoline-soaked rags would be placed around the victim's neck and set afire.

With the legalization of the African National Congress and release from imprisonment of Nelson Mandela, the activities of Umkhonto we

Sizwe have been suspended. Mandela and other ANC leaders had threatened in mid-1992 to resume guerrilla warfare and terrorism if what they claimed were South African police-inspired killings of black nationalists continued. However, with the transition of power from the apartheid regime to a democratically elected government in April 1994 there was no further need for guerrilla warfare.

Beginning in 1996 the transitional government mandated an independent Truth and Reconciliation Commission to investigate allegations of terrorist actions by any and all participants in the civil conflict that led up to the end of apartheid. The 17-member commission, which was headed by Nobel Peace Prize laureate Archbishop Desmond Tutu, issued a report on 30 October 1999. Among other things this report documented the torture and execution of ANC political dissidents by its military wing in their camps in Mozambique and elsewhere and also its failure often to distinguish between military and civilian targets. *See also* SOUTH AFRICAN STATE, AND ANTISTATE, TERRORISM.

UNABOMBER. Theodore J. Kaczynski, or "Ted" Kaczynski, was the "Unabomber" responsible for 16 mailed parcel bomb attacks from 25 May 1978 to 24 April 1995 that killed three persons and maimed 23 others. These **bombings** were motivated to protect the natural world and promote a nonindustrial anarchistic world in which small autonomous groups and individuals would replace governments and other conventional social institutions. To achieve this Kaczynski believed he had to destroy industrial society by targeting key academics, computer professionals, and business executives in technology-intensive fields. His initial selection of university **targets** led the FBI to designate him as the "Unabomber."

Kaczynski's bombs were meticulously crafted and all detonator components were handmade, making tracing of them through known suppliers and outlets impossible. He also carved the initials "FC" on each bomb and used a nine-digit code name in his letters to allow authorities to authenticate messages sent in his name against possible copycatting. Apparently he also assembled and dissembled each bomb several times to ensure it would work properly and took care to avoid leaving fingerprints.

His first bombings were in the Chicago area; the Engineering Department parking lot on 25 May 1978 and the Technological Institute on 9 May 1979, both at Northwestern University in Evanston; another on 15 November 1979 detonated in the cargo hold of a plane requiring it to make an emergency landing at Dulles Airport; and another at an airline executive's home at Lake Forest, Illinois, who was injured on 10 June 1980; another bomb was safely deactivated at the University of Utah on 8 October 1981; a metal pipe bomb injured a professor of electrical engineering and computer science at the University of California in Berkeley on 2 July 1982; a parcel bomb mailed to the Fabrication Division of Boeing in Auburn, Washington was safety deactivated 8 May 1985; another bomb at the Berkeley campus maimed and partially blinded a graduate student on 15 May 1985; while another bomb exploded at Vanderbilt University in Tennessee when opened by a secretary in the computer department on 5 May 1982, seriously injuring her face.

Deaths and severe injuries caused by the Unabomber included the 11 December 1985 killing of Hugh Scrutton, a computer store owner in Sacramento, California; on 20 February 1987 a bomb wounded a computer store owner in Salt Lake City; on 22 June 1993 a bomb severely wounded a geneticist in Tiburon, California; another bomb severely injured a professor of computer science at Yale University on 24 June 1993. Parcel bombs killed Thomas Mosser, a New York City advertising executive, at his home on 10 December 1994, and also Gilbert Murray, President of the California Forestry Association, on 25 April 1995.

In June 1995 the Unabomber offered to cease his campaign of bombing if the *New York Times* and *Washington Post* would publish his roughly 30,500-word manifesto within three months. At the urging of U.S. Attorney General Janet Reno both papers did so on 19 September 1995 in an eight-page spread equivalent to about 43 letter-sized manuscript pages. The FBI hoped that the writing style and content of the manifesto, if widely circulated, would be recognized by those who knew the author who was the Unabomber. After seven months his mother and brother, David Kaczynski, contacted the FBI. Ted Kaczynski was arrested at his cabin outside Lincoln, Montana on 3 April 1993. His trial began on 12 November 1997 and on 22 January 1998, Kaczynski admitted to being the Unabomber in exchange for being spared the death penalty in favor of life imprisonment without possibility of parole. Kaczynski also faced a wrongful death suit by the family of Gilbert Murray at the time of his sentencing.

UNITA. The União Nacional para Independéncia Total de Angola (National Union for the Total Independence of Angola) is an antistate group seeking to overthrow the Marxist government of Angola that formerly received support from South Africa prior to the end of the apartheid regime in 1994. Led by Jonas Savimbi, UNITA had about 71,000 soldiers augmented by material support from South Africa and the United States who saw the support of Cuban troops and Russian advisers for the Marxist Popular Movement for the Liberation of Angola government headed by President José Eduardo dos Santos as another proxy battle in the Cold War. The civil war in Angola between anti-Marxist factions, such as UNITA and the **Cabinda Liberation Front-Cabinda Liberation Forces** (FLEC-FAC), had been ongoing from 1975 until 1994 when the UN-brokered Lusaka Accord political settlement seemed to take hold. However, in June 1998 the political settlement collapsed and UNITA resumed its attempts to overthrow the ruling government, recapturing half of the countryside and forcing 200,000 Angolans from their villages.

The cause for UNITA's resumption of fighting was due in part to instances of vindictive treatment of former UNITA fighters by government police and officials sent into the areas formerly held by UNITA. Ironically the Marxist government that formerly looked to the Soviet Union and Cuba for support against the UNITA insurgency now is relying on the United States and Western oil companies for support on the supposition that a UNITA takeover would interfere with their oil extraction interests. UNITA forces shot down an Angolan government plane near Kuito on 14 December 1998. Then, in nearby Vila Nova, on 26 December 1998 UNITA forces also shot down a C-130 carrying UN observers sent to enforce the 1994 Lusaka Accord. Fighting between UNITA and government troops in this central region of Angola had killed 200 civilians and wounded another 400. UNITA also joined forces with Cabindan rebels in attacking Angolan and foreign workers involved in oil extraction in the Cabinda enclave. Both incidents show that UNITA is now willing to attack Western foreigners present in Angola in much the same way that it previously targeted Cuban and Russian advisors of the Angolan government.

UNITED FREEDOM FRONT (UFF). The United Freedom Front (UFF) was a nonstate U.S. leftist group that engaged in terrorism for the limited purpose of protesting U.S. policy in Central America and South Africa.

Its main terrorist activity consisted of **bombings** against military and defense-related industrial **targets** in the New York metropolitan area.

On 12 May 1983 the UFF bombed the U.S. Army Reserve facility in Uniondale, New York. The following night they bombed the Naval Reserve center in Queens. The UFF accomplished its tenth major bombing by 19 March 1984 when it bombed an IBM facility near Purchase, N.Y., its third such attack on IBM. On 27 September 1984 the UFF bombed a Union Carbide office to protest the company's investments in South Africa. The UFF also had bombed facilities of Honeywell, the U.S. National Guard, and a Navy recruiting center.

Such left-wing groups as the **United Freedom Front**, **Armed Resistance Unit**, or **New World Liberation Front** tended to pick bombing targets for symbolic value and to target property rather than human life. These groups generally would use the terrorist event as "**armed propaganda**" for specific issues or causes rather than as direct military tactics to achieve revolution. Therefore, the UFF used to deposit leaflets near targets and to call news agencies to give communiqués explaining their motives and cause. Instead of mobilizing widespread discussion of their specific issue of interest, however, the net result of the UFF bombing campaign was to motivate targeted firms and similar companies to adopt costly antiterrorist security measures, such as antibomb blast walls.

The United Freedom Front was effectively ended with the arrests of its seven members from November 1984 until April 1985, who were convicted on 13 March 1985 on charges arising from the bombings conducted by the group. The similarity of the tactics and language used by such groups as the United Freedom Front, the **Sam Melville-Jonathan Jackson Unit**, and the Armed Resistance Unit have led many analysts to conclude that these were either one group or branches from a single original group.

UTA FLIGHT 772 BOMBING. On 19 September 1989 Flight 772, a DC-10 of the now-defunct French air carrier UTA, exploded in mid-flight over Niger killing all 171 people abroad. The flight had originated in Brazzaville, Congo, destined for Paris with a stop at N'Djamena airport in Chad. The DC-10 exploded on the Chad to France portion of the flight killing all aboard, most of whom were French citizens, as well as seven U.S. citizens and 49 Congolese.

On 7 May 1997 French antiterrorism investigators obtained indictments against six Libyans, one of them being Abdallah Senoussi, who was the second-ranking Libyan security official at the time of the **bombing** and who is also a brother-in-law of Libyan leader **Muammar Qaddafi.** Senoussi is believed to have ordered the bombing in retaliation for France's providing troops to Chad enabling it to resist a Libyan invasion. Libyan agents had paid a Congolese to check onto Flight UTA-772 from Brazzavile and gave him a Samsonite suitcase with three pounds of pentrite explosive and a detonator. The Congolese, who had intended to disembark in N'Djamena but was prevented from doing so, was killed with the rest of the passengers when the plane exploded above Niger.

Based on forensic evidence recovered by French antiterrorism investigators from the UTA Flight 772 wreckage spread over hundreds of square miles of desert and based also on the findings of Judge Bruguière, who was permitted by Col. Qaddafi to interrogate members of the Libyan intelligence service in July 1996, a French antiterrorism court tried and convicted in absentia Senoussi, Deputy Foreign Minister Moussa Koussa, and four other Libyans for the bombing and issued arrest warrants for them.

- V -

VIPER MILITIA. The Viper Militia was a nonstate revolutionary **white supremacist** "patriot militia" which sought to overthrow the government of the United States through attacks on federal agents and offices. Although most of the groups associated with the **militia movement** seem innocuous the Viper Militia group was actually a more activist right-wing extremist group, on the model of the Arizona Patriots and the **Order.**

On 1 July 1996 federal agents arrested 12 members of the "Viper Team of the Arizona State Militia" for conspiracy to **bomb** the Phoenix, Arizona, offices of the Bureau of Alcohol, Tobacco,and Firearms (BATF); FBI; Immigration and Naturalization Service; and Internal Revenue Service; the Phoenix Police Department headquarters; and the Arizona National Guard Center, as well as illegal possession of four automatic weapons, explosives, and other bomb-making materials. Searches of the home of the two leaders of the group, Randy L. Nelson and Dean C. Pleasant, produced grenades, blasting caps, two pistols, two machine guns, six rifles, and 11,403 rounds of ammunition.

Following a complaint to the BATF office from a hunter that armed men in camouflage suits had threatened and ordered him to leave a remote area of the Tonto National Forest, on 13 November 1995, BATF agents found a large crater similar to what would have been made by a homemade ammonium nitrate bomb. A BATF agent, Steve Ott, easily infiltrated the group and secretly videotaped sessions of the group in which they planned to bomb the federal buildings mentioned earlier, as well as the police and national guard offices. Ott later testified that Viper member Ellen Belliveau had suggested that the group **target** the families of federal agents for possible retaliation in the event group members were killed or captured while fighting the federal government. On 5 May 1996 Ellen Belliveau, an AT&T employee, volunteered to get the telephone records of federal agents while Nelson claimed he had gotten access to a computer file with the names and addresses of federal employees. A search of member Gary Bauer's home revealed three assembled bombs, a stick of dynamite, blasting caps, ammonium nitrate, and 55 gallons of nitromethane, another bomb-making ingredient.

By late December 10 of the Viper Militia members pled guilty and were given reduced sentences between two to four years imprisonment. Two pled not guilty but Charles Knight was found guilty of conspiracy and illegal possession of explosives on 8 September 1997 and sentenced to 57 months imprisonment and a $5,000 fine while on 18 November 1997 the remaining Viper Militia member, Christopher Floyd was acquitted of the explosives charge while a mistrial was declared on his conspiracy charge.

- W -

WAR CRIMES. War crimes include but are not limited to the following: 1. Violations of the laws or customs of war, such as murder, ill-treatment, or deportation to slave labor, or for any other purpose, of the civilian population of, or in, occupied territory; 2. The murder or ill-treatment of prisoners of war or persons on the high seas, and the killing of hostages, and 3. The plundering of private or public property, wanton destruction of cities, towns, villages, or other devastation not justified by military necessity.

The various Geneva Conventions of 12 August 1949 established standards for the treatment of prisoners of war. The various Hague Conventions of 1899 and 1907 defined prohibited forms of warfare and proper conduct of battle, and established general principles of "humanitarian law" for the conduct of war. The judgments of the Nuremburg tribunal established the rule of law that the international laws pertaining to warfare were applicable not simply to sovereign states but also to individuals even if those persons were acting under some legal cover as officials of a **belligerent** state or obeying its orders as its soldiers.

Generally war crimes can be viewed as a special form of **state terror** directed by the armed forces, or paramilitary forces, of a nation-state against noncombatants, whether these be civilians or prisoners of war who, although members of combatant forces of a belligerent, are under the protection of their captors and no longer pose a military threat.

WARSAW CONVENTION. Also known as the 1929 Convention for the Unification of Certain Rules Relating to Transportation by Air. This is the first international convention pertaining to protection of the air passenger's safety from all hazards associated with air travel and establishing the liability of air carriers for the safety of their passengers. Although this convention did not specifically address issues of air piracy or **bombings**, since the first known **hijacking** did not occur until February 1931, it formed the precedent for future international conventions pertaining to air security, including issues of terrorism directed at planes or passengers, and has been cited in U.S. case law (*Day v. Trans World Airlines Inc.*, 528 F.2d 31, 92d Circuit, 1975) as forming the basis for an air carrier's liability in the event of a terrorist attacks on its passengers. *See also* AIR TRAVEL SECURITY.

WEAPONS OF MASS DESTRUCTION (WMD). Also referred to as nuclear, biological, and chemical weapons (NBC), or atomic, biological, and chemical weapons (ABC), these are weapons designed to kill large numbers of **targeted** combatants or civilians. The nuclear weapons include not only fission or fusion thermonuclear strategic or tactical weapons but also "radiological" or "dirty bombs" consisting of highly radioactive isotopes or waste products made part of a conventional bomb to cause radioactive contamination or poisoning of places or persons targeted by such bombs. The biological weapons include not only bacteriological weapons such as self-reproducing lethal bacteria or viruses but also poisonous compounds that can only be obtained from living biological sources, such as botulinum and **ricin**.

Apart from the **Tokyo Subway** attack there are only two other instances in which radical or terrorist groups have used chemical or bacteriological weapons. In 1984 followers of cult leader Bhagwan Shree Rajneesh contaminated a salad bar in The Dalles, Oregon, with salmonella bacteria to prevent people from voting in an election that the cult wanted to disrupt. As a result 751 people became sick with food poisoning. In 1990 the **Liberation Tigers of Tamil Eelam** (LTTE) released containers of liquid chlorine to gas Sri Lankan army forces. While this attack succeeded in killing and immobilizing many soldiers shifting winds caused several LTTE units to suffer from the same chlorine gas. The difficulties of precision targeting and long-term goals of political legitimacy do not make WMD ideal weapons of choice for most groups.

Nonetheless public fear and ignorance about WMD allow even false WMD threats, alarms, or false claims of their use to create real public panic, incapacitate ordinary business, and can even induce psychosomatic distress among suggestible persons or crowds. On 24 April 1997 the delivery of a foul-smelling envelope with the word "anthrachs" (sic) scrawled on it not only led Washington, D.C., fire department officials to shut down the B'nai B'rith headquarters but also caused two B'nai B'rith employees to experience what they thought were the symptoms of anthrax infection. In 1997 alone the FBI investigated 68 new cases of real or fake attempts to procure or deploy WMD while in 1998 the yearly figure had reached about a hundred such cases in the United States. While most cases involved anthrax hoaxes, often directed against abortion clinics, schools, courthouses, or other government offices, the FBI regard the disruptions and emotional distress caused by these hoaxes to be a serious form of terrorism in itself. In October 2001 the first known cases of deliberate anthrax poisoning surfaced in the United States, involving four fatalities out of 17 cases of known infection. *See* ANTHRAX ATTACKS.

It should be noted that although WMD weapons present frightening scenarios of mass carnage, to date most terrorist groups have found machine guns and bombs to be much more cost-effective, lethal, and sufficiently terrorizing to serve their political agenda. Therefore in all likelihood these will remain the preferred weapons of terrorists.

WEATHERMEN/WEATHER UNDERGROUND. The Weather Underground was an **anarchistic leftist terrorist** group active from 7 October 1969 to about 1976 that was formed in the student radicalism of the late

1960s in the United States, much in the same way as the German Baader-Meinhof **Red Army Faction** (RAF), as well as several other terrorist groups drawn from middle-class university students.

The Weathermen emerged out of the Students for a Democratic Society (SDS), a student leftist antiwar group, in June 1969 during an SDS conference. Their name is taken from some Bob Dylan lyrics ("You don't need to be a weatherman to know which way the wind blows") used as the title of the position paper of the SDS leaders advocating armed revolutionary struggle. While the majority of SDS members rejected this proposal, the Weathermen core stuck to the proposal, imagining themselves the vanguard that would kindle revolution at large.

They proposed acts of **armed propaganda** aimed at pitting antiwar youth against the police and planned to incite riots in the so-called days of rage, that is, a reenactment of the demonstrations and police riot that had occurred a year earlier at the 1968 Democratic Convention in Chicago. On 7 October 1969 they **bombed** the Chicago policeman's statue in Haymarket Square. During October 8-11 about 200 or so Weathermen assembled in Grant Park and were arrested for disorderly conduct. In December 1969 the Weathermen "war council" decided to go underground and accordingly failed to appear for their trials rising from the Grant Park demonstrations, so becoming fugitives. On 6 March 1970, the Weathermen's hideout in Greenwich Village, New York, was blown up, killing three leaders due to an error one of them made while trying to assemble a bomb. Despite this mishap, the group undertook its program of armed propaganda. On 1 August 1970 they blasted the exterior of the New York branch of the Bank of Brazil with a pipe bomb. On 13 September 1970 they arranged the jail escape of Timothy Leary. On 8 October 1970 they bombed the ROTC building on the University of Washington campus, the Santa Barbara National Guard Armory, and a courthouse in San Rafael, California.

Sometime during 1970-1971 the group changed its name to the Weather Underground, partly to emphasize their voluntary decision to go underground but also because of an increasing sensitivity within the group to feminist concerns about sexism. On 1 March 1971 they bombed the U.S. Senate wing of the Capitol building. Other **targets** included the Pentagon and the State Department on 29 January 1975, the group having conducted 17 bombings to date.

An internal purge destroyed the organization sometime in 1976-1977. The decision to go underground in 1970 left the members isolated from society at large while the aboveground support network, known as the Prairie Fire Organizing Committee, faulted the underground cadre for lagging in their commitment to combating sexism and racism, which filled the vacuum in the New Left's agenda once filled by the antiwar movement. Weather Underground members then turned upon one another in internal **ideological** purges of the insufficiently "committed." Those original Weathermen leaders who were banished eventually gave themselves up to law enforcement officials: Mark Rudd in 1977, and Bernadine Dohrn and William Ayers in 1981. The ideological hard-liners formed the **May 19th Communist Coalition**, which created the **Revolutionary Armed Task Force** by merging the remnants of the Weather Underground and the **Black Liberation Army**. With the surrender of Jeffrey David Powell on 6 January 1994 the last of the six Weathermen wanted by the FBI had surfaced.

WHITE HAND. "Mano Blanca" was a state-sponsored vigilante group established in 1966 to suppress communist insurgents in Guatemala. The organization was supposedly founded by Colonel Enrique Trinadad Oliva and later led by the national police chief. It eventually turned into a right-wing **death squad** that targeted any prominent citizens suspected of harboring leftist sympathies, including trade union officials and Roman Catholic priests and prelates. The word "Mano" in the group's name originally stood for Movimiento de Acción Nacionalista Organizada.

On 17 March 1968 White Hand abducted the Archbishop of Guatemala, Monsignor Mario Casariego Acevedo, whom it held for a few days before releasing him. The organization had hoped by this action to frame leftist groups to create an antileftist backlash among church and army officials. In 1970 Colonel Carlos Arana Osorio, the counterinsurgency military commander who had destroyed two of the largest leftist guerrilla groups in the countryside, was elected president. During his presidency, White Hand, along with other right-wing groups, was permitted to conduct a terror campaign against suspected leftist elements in the cities.

WHITE PATRIOT ARMY (WPA). The WPA was a nonstate paramilitary **white supremacist** organization that sought to undertake a revolutionary "war" against the "Zionist Occupation Government" of the United States. The main leader of this organization was Frazier Glenn Miller, a former Green Beret Vietnam combat veteran, onetime member of the American Nazi Party, and leader of the Carolina Knights of the **Ku Klux Klan**, from which the WPA drew most of its members. Miller and other members, who later formed the WPA, carried out the 1979 massacre in Greensboro, North Carolina, in which they gunned down five anti-Klan demonstrators belonging to the Communist Workers Party.

In 1986 Miller and three other WPA members were arrested for conspiracy to steal military explosives to bomb the Southern Poverty Law Center of Montgomery, Alabama, an anti-Klan group that in 1985 had obtained a court order restraining Miller from paramilitary activities. The **bombing** was intended to murder Morris Dees, the director of the Center and personal nemesis of Miller. FBI investigations revealed that WPA members were also affiliated with the Carolina Klan and that three of them also were members of the **Order** from which Miller had accepted $300,000 in stolen funds. Searches of Miller's property in Missouri revealed stockpiles of contraband military arms and explosives. Miller was imprisoned for failing to obey the 1985 restraining order.

While WPA membership, and that of similar white supremacist organizations, is not known with precision due to these organizations's secretive nature, United Press International reported several marches staged by the WPA in North Carolina during 1984 each of which involved over 300 participants.

WHITE SUPREMACISM. Or white supremacy, a racist **ideology** that holds that white Caucasians are superior to nonwhite peoples, by virtue of biology, natural intelligence, or some ascriptive birthright. For many domestic U.S. right-wing groups this is either an essential tenet of the group, such as the **Ku Klux Klan**, **neo-Nazi**, or **Identity Christian** groups, or else this belief is widely held by members of a group but not necessarily part of the core ideology of the group. Those who hold white supremacist beliefs often hold anti-Semitic beliefs and exclude Jews from their definition of "white Caucasian."

While the white supremacist doctrines of North American groups tend to be joined together with Identity Christian or other fundamentalist Christian beliefs, the ideology of British and European **skinheads** and neo-Nazis is secular, agnostic, and even hostile to Christianity, which Hitler and many of his close associates viewed as an outgrowth of Judaism and therefore corrupt and non-Western. In the United States the

World Church of the Creator is a white supremacist religious group that explicitly rejects Christianity even in the Identity Christian form.

WHITE WARRIORS' UNION. The UGB, Unión de Guerreros Blancos, "White Warriors' Union," or Unión Guerrera Blanca, "White Fighting Union," was a nonstate **death squad** founded in 1976 by Roberto D'Aubuisson for the limited purpose of repressing leftist elements in Salvadoran society. Due to the involvement of the Society of Jesus and other Roman Catholic educators with **liberation theology** and espousal of leftist causes, this group was pronouncedly anti-Jesuit although it claimed itself to be loyal to the traditional values of Catholicism. In 1977 the UGB claimed credit for killing two priests in San Salvador and also **bombed** the home of a trade union leader. In 1979 the UGB killed several teachers.

Roberto D'Aubuisson was a protégé of General José Alberto Medrano, who had organized **ORDEN**, the peasant militia that evolved into a death squad that was officially abolished but not fully suppressed in November 1979. From 1979 until 1982 the UGB was only one of numerous right-wing death squads operating in El Salvador. During this period killings by death squads sometimes exceeded 800 people each month and included among their victims Archbishop Oscar Romero y Galdamez, killed on 24 March 1980. In 1982 D'Aubuisson founded and led the rightist Republican National Alliance Party (**ARENA**), itself suspected of sponsoring death squad activities. ARENA won the largest share of seats in the new Constituent Assembly in 1982. With the ascendancy of ARENA, both the remnants of the UGB and ORDEN were absorbed into D'Aubuisson's new political organization.

WORLD TRADE CENTER ATTACK OF 1993. On 26 February 1993 at 12:18 p.m. a Ryder van packed with homemade explosives detonated in the parking lot under the north tower of the World Trade Center in downtown Manhattan. The blast killed six people and injured over 1,000 more and was considered to be the worst terrorist incident to have occurred within the United States until the **Oklahoma City bombing** of 19 April 1995 which caused far more deaths. The blast crater extended through five stories of the underground parking lot. The **bomb** was estimated to have consisted of 1,000 pounds of explosives manufactured from urea, sulfuric, and nitric acid, materials later found in the possession of some of the suspects. The device was also rigged with hydrogen gas cylinders and nitroglycerin blasting caps to amplify the explosion of the resulting fireball.

Forensic analysis of remaining fragments of the vehicle bomb revealed the vehicle identification number that allowed the FBI to identify Mohammed A. Salameh as the person who rented the van who was arrested within five days of the bombing. Salameh also had rented a storage locker in New Jersey where the bomb-making materials were stored and shared an apartment with Nidal A. Ayyad, the chemical engineer who mixed the explosives in their apartment. Salameh and Ayyad shared a bank account which funded the purchase of the explosives and rental of the van. A New York taxi driver, Mahmud Abouhalima, who had helped prepare the explosives and who had bought fuel for the van, was arrested in Egypt and **extradited** to the United States. Fingerprints on military bomb-making manuals found in Salameh's apartment and records of telephone calls with Salameh led police to another suspect, Ahmad M. Ajaj, who was imprisoned at the time of the bombing.

Two other key suspects named in federal indictments, Abdul Rahman Yasin and Razmi Ahmad Yousef, had already fled the country. Yousef, who arrived from Pakistan six months before the bombing, was the actual mastermind behind the bombing who had entered the country with the specific intent of carrying out a terrorist attack on U.S. soil. On 7 February 1995 Yousef was arrested by FBI agents and State Department diplomatic security officers in Pakistan and returned to the United States the following day. On 12 November 1997 he and another associate, Ismail Eyad, were convicted for their roles in the World Trade Center bombing and sentenced to life imprisonment on 8 January 1998.

Shortly after the arrest of Salameh and Ayyad it was learned that both had regularly attended a New Jersey mosque, the Masjid as Salaam, where the resident prayer leader was **Sheikh Omar Abdul Rahman**, the blind Egyptian preacher and leader of the **Islamic Group** (IG) in Egypt who had issued the decree of **takfir** to members of the **Munazzamat al Jihad** authorizing the **assassination** of Anwar Sadat. Although he was included on a official list of suspected terrorists prohibited from entering the United States, he managed nonetheless to obtain a visa from a U.S. consulate in Sudan. Although Sheikh Abdul Rahman afterwards declared the bombing to have been contrary to Islam, such strong circumstantial evidence has linked him to the other suspects and to evidence regarding a broader conspiracy to bomb public places that he was arrested in June 1993 to await a separate trial to be held after the trial of the four main suspects in the World Trade Center case. *See* HOLLAND TUNNEL BOMB PLOT.

Not altogether separate from the question of an **Islamic fundamentalist** inspiration behind the bombing was the question of possible state or nonstate sponsorship. Sheikh Abdul Rahman, Salameh, and Ayyad all received funds from unknown sources abroad. Ahmad Ajaj and Razmi Ahmad Yousef both had guerrilla training with the Afghan **mujahideen** and possessed several false passports. At the time of his arrest Yousef was living in a hotel where his expenses were being paid by **Osama bin Laden**. None of the defendants indicated outside state support, however, when questioned by U.S. interrogators.

WORLD TRADE CENTER AND PENTAGON ATTACKS OF 11 SEPTEMBER 2001. On 11 September 2001 three teams of five-man **suicide bombers** and one four-man team **hijacked** four American domestic flights, crashing one into the World Trade Center north tower, another into the south tower, and another into the east side of the Pentagon. At 8:45 a.m. American Airlines Flight 11, from Boston to Los Angeles, crashed into the north tower of the World Trade Center and then at 9:03 a.m. United Airlines Flight 175, also a Boston to Los Angeles run, crashed into the south tower causing a massive explosion and fireball. Then at 9:43 a.m. American Airlines Flight 77, which had taken off from Dulles Airport, crashed into one side of the Pentagon causing portions of that structure to collapse and burn. The fourth flight, United Airlines Flight 93 from Newark to San Francisco, crashed at 10:00 a.m. following an apparent struggle between hijackers and the passengers. At 10:05 a.m. the south tower collapsed and at 10:29 a.m. the north tower also collapsed. The falling debris of these buildings engulfed and killed many of the first responding police and firefighters as well as thousands of civilians who had not yet been evacuated. The catastrophic collapse of these structures also caused such damage to five other buildings in the World Trade Center complex that these also collapsed afterwards.

At least 4,304 persons were killed at the World Trade Center and 125 killed at the Pentagon. Altogether all 19 hijackers and 238 passengers also perished in these attacks. Over 343 firefighters, 23 New York muncipal policeman, and 26 New York Port Authority officers are believed to have perished while attempting to evacuate the Twin Towers and the surrounding areas of the World Trade Center. This attack has been the worst mass-casualty terrorist attack ever carried out by a nonstate group.

At 9:48 a.m. the White House and Capitol buildings were evacuated and the Federal Aviation Administration ordered all aircraft in U.S. air space to land and a halt to all further civilian air traffic, a ban which remained in effect for about one week. In a national address before a joint session of the U.S. Congress on 14 September 2001, President George W. Bush declared that an effective state of war existed between the United States and the terrorist perpetrators along with any states that may have assisted them. The same day the U.S. Congress approved Senate and House of Representatives Joint Resolution No. 23, an authorization for the use of military force against suspected agents and **state sponsors** responsible for the September 11 attacks on New York and Washington, D.C. On 17 September 2001 the Bush administration identified **Osama bin Laden** and his **al Qa'eda** terrorist network as the principals responsible for these attacks and demanded that the **Taliban** regime in Afghanistan hand him over to U.S. authorities.

Following the Taliban's refusal to hand over bin Laden and other Qa'eda elements within Afghanistan, the United States launched Operation Enduring Freedom on 7 October 2001 against Taliban and al Qa'eda forces within Afghanistan. On 24 October 2001 the U.S. Congress passed the USA Patriot Act, also called the "Uniting and Strengthening America Act by Providing Appropriate Tools to Intercept and Obstruct Terrorism," which was signed into law by President George W. Bush on 25 October 2001. This law, among other things, allows officials to detain immigrants without charges, to penetrate money-laundering banks, to allow sharing of grand jury information with law enforcement and intelligence agencies, and also expanded authority to conduct wiretaps in intelligence cases. The events of 11 September 2001 have also led to measures to improve **air travel security** and the creation of the Office of Homeland Security to oversee and coordinate **homeland defense** measures.

- Z -

ZAPATISTAS. The Ejército Zapatista de Liberación Nacional (EZLN), Zapatista Army of National Liberation, which undertook an insurgency against the Mexican government in Chiapas State on 1 January 1994, has been hailed as the first "post-modern" insurgency involving the systematic use of **"netwar"** to achieve its political objectives. The name is taken from that of the revolutionary hero of southern Mexico, Emiliano Zapata.

Unlike the former leftist insurgencies, or the contemporary insurgency of the **Popular Revolutionary Army** (ERP), the EZLN did not seek a complete revolution changing the political regime in Mexico nor to secede from Mexico, but rather specific limited redress of grievances. The EZLN also did not seek foreign state sponsorship but rather moral support from nongovernmental organizations both within and outside of Mexico. Whereas previous insurgencies often viewed revolutionary violence as the only legitimate means for seeking their political goals, the EZLN has used insurgent violence primarily to attract the support of various allies in civil society who then have brought tremendous pressure on U.S. and Mexican government officials to desist from military retaliation against the EZLN in favor of dialogue and negotiation.

The "social netwar" used to apply this moral pressure consists of the coordinated actions of various groups sympathetic to the EZLN, such as advocates of the rights of indigenous peoples, environmentalists, human rights advocates, anti-NAFTA groups, as well as labor groups and left-wing groups opposed to Mexican government development policies. By adroit use of the Internet such groups have coordinated protests outside of Mexican consulates in the United States and in Canada, as well as bombarding offices of elected officials and news organizations with protests against the Mexican government and on behalf of the EZLN and its Mayan Indian allies. Finally, unlike traditional leftist insurgencies, the EZLN abandoned a rigid hierarchical structure in favor of a looser network structure in which the combatants play a larger role in forming a community consensus rather than simply obeying a central command.

The EZLN was originally made up of young intellectuals from northern Mexico involved in the Fuerzas de Liberación National (FLN) formed in reaction to the government massacre of university students at Tlatelolco in 1968. These leaders formed the General Command but most troops came from Mayan Indian villagers who had many longstanding grievances against the Mexican federal government and the Chiapas state government over the dispossession of their communal lands, which they feared would eventually be privatized to facilitate foreign investment under the North American Free Trade Agreement (NAFTA) agreement. Suspicious of outsiders, these Indians would likely have never been recruited were it not for the intervention of Samuel Ruíz, Bishop of San Cristóbal de las Casas. Both the Bishop and his diocesan clergy had embraced the cause of the Indians and the EZLN in the name of **liberation theology**. Through the mediation of these monks and priests already serving the Mayan Indian villages, the EZLN leaders, including Subcommander Marcos, believed to be Rafael Sebastián Guillén Vicente, were able gradually to recruit the Mayans to their cause.

The EZLN have had little military successes. Their initial New Year's Day occupation of five towns and the state capital of San Cristóbal de las Casas by 1,000-2,000 guerrillas was quickly routed by 12,000 federal troops. However the reaction of Mexican and international non-government groups, including the Mexican-based Coalition of Non-Governmental Organizations for Peace (CONPAZ), put tremendous pressure on the Mexican government to resolve the conflict peacefully. President Carlos Salinas de Gortari ordered a cease-fire on 12 January 1994 which the EZLN reciprocated and negotiations began through a specially created Commission for Peace and Reconciliation.

Since then negotiations proceeded unevenly with occasional breakdowns but the EZLN has on several occasions used the social netwar tactics of its allies in civil society to force the Mexican government to make concessions it would otherwise never have made. By 14 February 1995, following successful Mexican military strikes against EZLN and the capture of several of its leaders pro-EZLN public pressure brought President Ernesto Zedillo to release the captured leaders, to replace the governor of Chiapas, itself a long-standing EZLN demand, and to restore peace negotiations. On 13 January 1998 the Mexican Army began arresting those Chiapas police officers who fired on pro-Zapatista demonstrators on 12 January 1998 and by 8 April 1999 the EZLN enjoyed such national and international support that it could send 1,000 unarmed Zapatistas to reoccupy Indian villages as a form of protest without the police intervening or arresting the protestors. The EZLN further underscored its preference for relatively peaceful and more effective social netwar over guerrilla violence by Subcommander Marcos's September 1996 letter stating that the EZLN neither desired nor needed the announced support of the Popular Revolutionary Army for them.

With the election of President Vicente Fox on 2 July 2000 the new Mexican administration has been removing army troops and other federal security forces from the Chiapas region. On 28 March 2001 EZLN representatives concluded a peace accord with the Mexican government in a ceremony attended by President Fox in the lower house of the Mexican Congress in Mexico City.

ZEALOTS. Also known as the Sicarii (dagger wielders), the Zealots were first century A.D. Jewish religious nationalists in the Roman province of Judea who carried out terrorist attacks on Roman officials and Jews considered to be Roman collaborators as well as waging an open insurgency against Rome in the period from 66-70 A.D. The immediate goal of the Zealots was to purge Hellenistic cultural influences from Jewish life as well as to rid Judea of Roman domination. Their ultimate goal was actually to initiate the advent of the Messiah by forcing an apocalyptic confrontation between Rome and the Jewish nation. As Judea lacked sufficient human resources to withstand Rome's military power, the Zealots believed that by provoking such a crisis they could force God's direct intervention to save the people of Israel according to His Covenant.

The historian Josephus Flavius recorded most of the activity of the Zealots-Sicarii as having occurred in the 25 years preceding the destruction of Jerusalem by Roman forces in 70 A.D. The Gospel of Luke also mentioned one of the disciples of Jesus as being one "Simon who was called the Zealot" (Luke 6:15), while later Roman historians recorded two subsequent revolts in Judea as late as the second century that recalled the tactics of the Zealots. At least two separate groups were known as the Sicarii while another group was known as the Zealots but their common tactics and goals suggest that these various groups were either independent manifestations of a continuing **resurgence movement** in Judea or **cellular groups** emanating from the same organized conspiracy.

The tactics of the Zealots included **assassination** in broad daylight of Roman officials and members of the Temple priesthood, usually by stabbing with a dagger (*sica*) in the midst of milling crowds into which the assassin then escaped. They also took hostages for ransom and extorted protection payments from Jewish landowners. Finally, they engaged both in guerrilla warfare and in open engagements with Roman troops. The Zealots also resorted to the first recorded instances of using the tactic of massive passive resistance by staging sit-in demonstrations involving unarmed men, women, and children in the streets of Jerusalem to protest instances of Roman disregard for Jewish religious sensitivities. The Zealots timed both their assassinations and these protests to coincide with certain holy days during which Jerusalem would be packed with throngs of Jewish pilgrims. Roman officials were faced with the dilemma of backing away from confrontation, in which case more resistance to Roman authority would be encouraged, or else employing force against civilians, so providing the Zealots with more instances of Roman sacrileges with which to fuel their cause. These efforts prefigured later efforts by modern urban guerrilla groups to instigate mass uprisings by provoking authorities into indiscriminate repression in reprisal for terrorist attacks.

In spite of the success of the Zealots in provoking the mass revolt against Roman rule in Judea, ultimately Roman forces besieged and destroyed Jerusalem, including the Second Temple, and killed or enslaved the surviving Jewish population in the countryside which was sent into exile. Josephus recorded that the surviving Zealots were besieged in the fortress of Masada near the southern end of the Dead Sea. When capture of the fortress by Roman forces following a year-long siege seemed imminent the Zealots reportedly committed mass suicide rather than allowing themselves to be enslaved by the Romans.

Bibliography

Introduction

The current bibliography differs from that of the previous edition in three major respects. First, the changes of the "new world disorder" following the demise of the Soviet Union and the shocking use of weapons of mass destruction (WMD) by the bombers of the Murrah Federal Building in Oklahoma City, the World Trade Center and Pentagon, and by the Aum Shinrikyo cult in its sarin gas attack, have led to increased studies of the impact of ethnic and sectarian movements as well as of the implications of the use of WMD by terrorist or insurgent groups. This bibliography has been substantially revised to reflect these concerns without, however, unduly exaggerating their significance. Although industrial liberal democracies are vulnerable to such weapons, which indeed have a catastrophic potential, the actual probability of their use remains very low while most terrorists will continue to use the more tried and proven—and less costly—means of bombs and bullets. Therefore the section formerly called "Operational Aspects of Terrorism" has been renamed "Conventional and Nonconventional Operations" to place the increased discussion of WMD within the context of the discussion of more conventional technical aspects of terrorism and counterterrorism doctrine and tactics.

Second, the increasing public concerns over terrorism, due to the Oklahoma City bombing and the potential WMD threats, have pushed terrorism to the forefront of the national domestic and foreign political agenda. As a result in the United States alone over 40 federal executive agencies, and literally thousands of state and local governments, have become involved in varying levels of contingency planning for a wide scenario of possible terrorist threats. To reflect this increased government involvement the authors added a section devoted to "Selected U.S. Government Documents" dealing with a wide range of domestic and international concerns to the current bibliography.

Finally, the increased use of the Internet by the general public has created a proliferation of public and private information resources dealing with terrorism but it has also, as noted in the introduction, created both new venues and means for terrorist and insurgent propaganda, mobilization, and netwar actions. Therefore the final section, "Selected Internet Resources," was added to present some of the more useful Web site addresses. However, two things should be noted here. The authors decided to refrain from directly citing the Web sites of terrorist or insurgent groups themselves lest this inadvertently aid them in their work. Rather we believed it best to present Web sites useful for both the more general reader as well as counterterrorism scholars and practitioners. However, several of the links contained in "Selected Internet Resources" in fact allow interested readers to find such links on their own if they so desire.

The second thing that must be stressed is that the Internet is a fluid and rapidly changing information environment. The links presented in this bibliography may change, be disconnected, their content radically revamped, and the current Internet itself may radically change or even become obsolescent before this edition runs its course. Having made these introductory comments we can turn to discussing the bibliography further, which retains much of its previous format although the content has been greatly updated.

The literature on terrorism has burgeoned so much in the past quarter-century that a few key bibliographies and general references are necessary starting points for any systematic research of the existing literature on terrorism. The book *International Terrorism: An Annotated Bibliography and Research Guide* by Augustus R. Norton and Martin H. Greenberg covers most of the literature until 1980 fairly comprehensively with summary descriptions of key works. Amos Lakos's *Terrorism, 1980-1990: A Bibliography* is comprehensive but the volume of the literature on terrorism grew so much in that decade that few bibliographies could succeed in being annotated and comprehensive. Edward F. Mickolus's *The Literature of Terrorism: A Selectively Annotated Bibliography* treats the more seminal books and articles and can be used in conjunction with Lakos's work.

The key work for the theory and concepts of terrorism is Alex P. Schmid and Albert J. Jongman's *Political Terrorism: A New Guide to Actors, Authors, Concepts, Databases and Literature* in its revised edition of 1988. A more abbreviated yet thorough conceptual treatment of the key concepts and categories is also to be found in John R. Thackrah's *Encyclopedia of Terrorism and Political Violence*.

Fortunately a number of comprehensive databases and chronologies have been produced within the last 10 years that simplify greatly the task of researchers and students. Yonah Alexander helped to compile and organize a microforms database including the leading articles on terrorism arranged by both geographic areas and by subject matter, namely, *Terrorism: An*

International Resource File, available through University Microforms Incorporated, Ann Arbor, Michigan. Complete chronologies are also indispensable, and Edward F. Mickolus's five major chronologies spanning the periods 1968-1979, 1980-1983, 1984-1987, 1988-1991, and 1992-1995 supplement much of the material Mickolus included in his ITERATE (International Terrorism: Attributes of Terrorist Events) database. Because of their emphasis on international terrorism, however, these chronologies do not deal with purely domestic U.S. terrorism or with terrorist insurgencies that neither cross borders nor victimize foreign nationals. The RAND Corporation has also produced a series of annual terrorist chronologies that, like the ITERATE database, seek to categorize incidents geographically and by terrorist tactics.

A number of handbooks or general reference books have been produced also in the last decade that can be of help as starting points for research. For a detailed treatment of leading terrorist groups and organizations, Peter Janke's *Guerrilla and Terrorist Organisations: A World Directory and Bibliography* is both comprehensive and scholarly. A handbook that is much more ambitious in its scope is the *Almanac of Modern Terrorism* by Jay Shafritz and his colleagues, which tries to deal with leading groups, ideas, personalities, events, and technical details of weapons and tactics. Most entries in this almanac have references to more detailed sources allowing the user to gain a basic knowledge from each entry while also enabling the researcher to pursue more detailed sources if desired. Other handbooks in the public domain include the U.S. Department of Defense's *Profiles of Terrorist Groups* and the U.S. Department of State's annual report *Patterns of Global Terrorism*, which includes a basic chronology, descriptive guide to leading active terrorist groups, and analysis of terrorism by geographic region and by state sponsors. The latter report also often includes special appendices dealing in more depth with major events or controversies as well as statistical summaries using graphs and maps. One of the most ambitious recent attempts to compile a comprehensive encyclopedia of terrorism is the *Encyclopedia of World Terrorism* edited by Martha Crenshaw and John Pimlott, published in three volumes.

The political science literature contains a few journals devoted exclusively to political violence, insurgency, and terrorism. The Crane Russak publishers produced the journals *Conflict* and *Terrorism*, which were combined in 1992 as a new publication, *Studies in Conflict and Terrorism*, whose first volume (Volume 15, 1992) continues to follow the numbering of issues used in its predecessor *Terrorism*. The Frank Cass publishers produce the journals *Terrorism and Political Violence, Small Wars and Insurgencies, Low Intensity Conflict & Law Enforcement, Nationalism and Ethnic Politics*, and *European Security*, while other specialty journals include the *Journal of Conflict Studies* (formerly *Conflict Quarterly*) published by the Centre for Conflict Studies of the University of New Brunswick, Fredericton, as well as the *International Journal of Intelligence and Counterintelligence* by Intel Publications Group of Stroudsburg, Pennsylvania. The Department of the Army publishes *Military Review* which often addresses issues of terrorism and low-intensity conflict. The *TVI Report: Comprehensively Reporting Terrorism, Violence, and Insurgency Worldwide* covers matters of interest to law enforcement agencies and multinational firms as well as to academic users and is published by TVI. Occasional papers on various terrorist topics can be found in various issues of the *Adelphi Papers* of the International Institute for Strategic Studies, the *Washington Papers* of the Center for Strategic and International Studies, as well as publications of the RAND Corporation. Certain standard periodical indexes, such as the *Public Affairs Information Service* and the *ABC POLI SCI: Bibliography of Contents, Political Science and Government* will generally list most titles of occasional articles dealing with terrorism in leading political science and administrative journals.

For individuals or institutions seeking to develop a basic understanding about the realities of terrorism and the problems of dealing with it a few texts may prove especially useful. Jonathan R. White has produced a textbook *Terrorism: An Introduction*, that is suitable for college-level course in political science and criminology which covers much of the sociological theory and studies of terrorism as well as substantive treatment of major terrorist groups and movements in addition to policy issues of counterterrorism. As a general reference work Wayman Mullins's *Sourcebook on Domestic and International Terrorism: An Analysis of Issues, Organizations, Tactics, and Responses* provides much factual material on terrorist groups and their goals but also discusses the legal and diplomatic problems involved in trying to counter terrorism on the domestic and international levels. For an understanding of the development of terrorism Bruce Hoffman's *Inside Terrorism* provides an analytical historical overview of terrorism as well as a discussion of contemporary trends, such as the rise of terrorism in the name of religious causes and the growing threat of nonstate groups willing to escalate mass killings to advance their causes. Hoffman's book examines important historical cases, such as the role of Serbian intelligence in prompting the assassination of Archduke Ferdinand which sparked off World War I, as well as more obscure incidents, such as "Operation Temple Mount," a plot by Jewish extremists in Israel to destroy Muslim holy places in Jerusalem that was foiled by Israeli security forces.

In exploring the impact of terrorism upon national security and international relations Jeffrey Simon's *The Terrorist Trap: America's Experience with Terrorism* takes the unconventional position that although terrorism is strategically insignificant it has assumed an exaggerated importance and influence due to the overreaction of democratic societies to its perceived threats. Similarly, in discussing the legal issues and criminal justice strategies involved in countering terrorism Philip B. Heymann's *Terrorism and America: A Commonsense Strategy for a Democratic Society* takes the position that deterring and punishing terrorism can be sufficiently pursued through the ordinary procedures of the police and courts and does not require extraordinary powers or extra constitutional actions. Heymann supports his argument through a very careful comparative analysis of the various legal and police strategies employed not only in the United States but also in Great Britain, France, Germany, and Israel revealing how state-of-siege tactics in Israel and Northern Ireland backfired by antagonizing the minority national groups being championed by the targeted terrorist groups. Overzealous police actions in both nations in effect reinforced each national group's support for the respective terrorist organization.

For those readers concerned with the issues of information warfare Jon Arquilla and John D. Ronfeldt's *In Athena's Camp: Preparing for Conflict in the Information Age* examines not only the purported threats of cyberterrorism but also the problems of national policy makers and defense forces effectively using rapidly changing information in a complex and rapidly changing threat environment. With regards to understanding counterterrorism policy Stephen Sloan's *Beating International Terrorism: An Action Strategy for Preemption and Punishment*, which is a succinct and thorough examination of the problems of combating terrorism, has been updated in a new edition to address many of the issues of nonstate actors and threats of mass casualties that have become more salient in the post-Cold War era.

For readers specifically interested in domestic threats within the United States John George and Laird Wilcox's *American Extremists: Militias, Supremacists, Klansmen, Communists & Others* provides both an analytical overview along with detailed studies of extremist movements in the United States, spanning both left-wing and right-wing movements as well as movements that straddle the religious and political spheres. For those who have a particular concern with right-wing extremism Betty A. Dobratz and Stephanie L. Shanks-Meile's *White Power-White Pride: The White Separatist Movement in the United States*, has a detailed and fresh examination of the extremist right that avoids alarmism and moralistic condemnation and tries instead to develop a sociological explanation of right-wing movements by examining grievances of political and socioeconomic deprivation among working-class white American males.

For readers seeking to understand post-Cold War guerrilla movements in the developing nations David Ronfeldt and his coauthors' *The Zapatista Social Netwar in Mexico* not only examines in detail one of the more visible guerrilla movements in Latin America but also proposes a model of "social netwars" which may become the new model of future social and political movements throughout the developing nations.

For a historical overview of the conflict in Northern Ireland, Martin Dillon's *God and the Gun: The Church and Irish Terrorism* provides an historical overeview from 1968 until the conclusion of the Good Friday Accord along with an in-depth examination of the sectarian and communal strife underlying the conflict based on extensive interviews with IRA and Ulster Protestant militants. Dillon exposes a neglected side of the conflict, namely the division within each religious community between those secular and religious leaders who endorsed the use of terror by their respective paramilitaries and those who strongly condemned such violence. Those who seek accurate statistics and basic facts regarding the casualties of this conflict are referred to Malcolm Sutton's *Bear in Mind The Dead: An Index of Deaths from the Conflict in Ireland 1969-1993* which is being produced in a second edition updated to the end of 1998.

Several studies have focused on the growing role of Islamic fundamentalism in the conflicts on the Middle East. For a detailed case study of the rise of an important Islamic fundamentalist movement Magnus Ranstorp's *Hizb'Allah in Lebanon: The Politics of the Western Hostage Crisis* is not only pertinent to the recent history of Lebanon but also reveals the religious and political forces shaping and guiding similar groups, such as Hamas in Israel and the Islamic Group in Egypt. As one of the few Western experts who has been able to gain access to and maintain the trust of Hezbollah, Magnus Ranstorp has been able to serve as an intermediary in negotiations between Hezbollah and Israel concerning Israeli Defense Forces prisoners held in Lebanon.

For an understanding of the Aum Shinrikyo cult and other apocalyptic movements, Robert Jay Lifton's *Destroying the World to Save It: Aum*

Shinrikyo, Apocalyptic Violence and the New Global Terrorism not only provides in-depth analysis of the formation and appeal of the Aum Shinrikyo sect but also examines other cultic movements, such as the Branch Davidians and the Heavensgate UFO group. This work analyzes the millennial motivations that led such groups into contemplating the use of weapons of mass destruction or else collective suicide. Since most instances of terrorism by use of biological or chemical agents have involved such sectarian movements this work is of particular interest to those concerned about the proliferation and most likely uses of WMD by nonstate groups.

General Reference Works

Bibliographies and Dictionaries

Atkins, Stephen F. *Terrorism: A Reference Handbook*. Santa Monica, Calif.: ABC-CLIO, 1992.

Bennett, John M. *Sendero Luminoso in Context: An Annotated Bibliography*. Lanham, Md.: Scarecrow Press, 1998.

Crenshaw, Martha, and John Pimlott, eds., *Encyclopedia of World Terrorism*. Armonk, N.Y.: M. E. Sharpe, 1997.

Lakos, Amos. *Terrorism, 1980-1990: A Bibliography*. Boulder, Colo.: Westview, 1991.

Lentz, Harris M., III. *Assassinations and Executions: An Encyclopedia of Political Violence, 1865-1986*. Jefferson, N.C.: McFarland, 1988.

Mickolus, Edward F. *The Literature of Terrorism: A Selectively Annotated Bibliography*. Westport, Conn.: Greenwood Press, 1980.

Mickolus, Edward F., and Peter A. Flemming. *Terrorism, 1980-1987: A Selectively Annotated Bibliography*. Westport, Conn.: Greenwood Press, 1988.

Mullins, Wayman C. *A Sourcebook on Domestic and International Terrorism: An Analysis of Issues, Organizations, Tactics, and Responses*. 2nd ed. Springfield, Ill.: Charles C. Thomas, 1997.

Newton, Michael, and Judy Ann Newton. *Terrorism in the United States and Europe, 1800-1959: An Annotated Bibliography*, New York: Garland, 1988.

Norton, Augustus R., and Martin H. Greenberg. *International Terrorism: An Annotated Bibliography and Research Guide*. Boulder, Colo.: Westview, 1980.

Ontiveros, Suzanne Robitaille, ed. *Global Terrorism: A Historical Bibliography*. Santa Barbara, Calif.: ABC-CLIO, 1986.

Schmid, Alex P., and Albert J. Jongman. *Political Terrorism: A New Guide to Actors, Authors, Concepts, Databases and Literature*. Rev. ed. New Brunswick, N.J.: Transaction Books, 1988.

Sifakis, Carl. *Encyclopedia of Assassinations*. New York: Facts on File, 1991.

Smith, Myron J. *The Secret Wars: A Guide to Sources in English.* 3 vols. Santa Barbara, Calif.: ABC-CLIO, 1980-1981.

Thackrah, John Richard. *Encyclopedia of Terrorism and Political Violence.* New York: Routledge & Kegan Paul, 1987.

Directories and Yearbooks

Alexander, Yonah, and A. H. Foxman, eds. *The 1988-89 Annual on Terrorism.* Zoetermeer, The Natherlands: Martinus Nijhoff, 1990.

Janke, Peter. *Guerrilla and Terrorist Organisations: A World Directory and Bibliography.* New York: Macmillan, 1983.

Schechterman, Bernard, and Martin Slann, eds. *Violence and Terrorism.* (Annual editions since 1991/1992). Sluice Dock, Guilford, Conn.: Dushkin.

Shafritz, Jay M., E. F. Gibbons, Jr., and Gregory E. J. Scott., *Almanac of Modern Terrorism.* New York: Facts On File, 1991.

Chronologies and Databases

Alexander, Yonah ed., *Terrorism: An International Resource File, 1986,* Ann Arbor, Mich.: University Microforms Incorporated, 1987.

_____. *Terrorism: An International Resource File, 1987,* Ann Arbor, Mich.: University Microforms Incorporated, 1988.

_____. *Terrorism: An International Resource File, 1988,* Ann Arbor, Mich. University Microforms Incorporated, 1989.

Gardela, Karen, and Bruce Hoffman. RAND/R-3890-RC, *The RAND Chronology of International Terrorism for 1986.* Santa Monica, Calif.: RAND, 1990.

_____. RAND/R-4006-RC, *The RAND Chronology of International Terrorism for 1987.* Santa Monica, Calif.: RAND, 1991.

Gordon, Avishag. "The Spread of Terrorism Publication: A Database Analysis." *Terrorism and Political Violence* 10, no. 4 (Winter 1998): 190-193.

Hoffman, Bruce, and David Claridge. "The RAND-St. Andrews Chronology of International Terrorism and Noteworthy Domestic Incidents, 1996." *Terrorism and Political Violence* 10, no. 2 (Summer 1998): 135-180.

Hoffman, Bruce, and Donna Kim Hoffman. "The RAND-St. Andrews Chronology of International Terrorism, 1994." *Terrorism and Political Violence* 7, no. 4 (Winter 1995): 181-229, also available as RAND Reprint RAND/RP-562-1.

_____. "The RAND-St. Andrews Chronology of International Terrorism, 1995." *Terrorism and Political Violence* 8, no. 3 (Autumn 1996): 87-127.

Mickolus, Edward F. "Chronology of Transnational Terrorist Attacks Upon American Business People, 1968-1976." *Terrorism* 1 (1978): 217-235.

Mickolus, Edward F. *Codebook: ITERATE (International Terrorist: Attributes of Terrorist Events)*. Ann Arbor: Inter-University Consortium for Political and Social Research, University of Michigan Press, 1976.

Mickolus, Edward F. *Terrorism, 1988-1991*. Westport, Conn.: Greenwood, 1993.

Mickolus, Edward F. *Transnational Terrorism: A Chronology of Events, 1968-1979*. Westport, Conn.: Greenwood, 1980.

Mickolus, Edward F., and Peter Flemming. *International Terrorism in the 1980s: A Chronology of Events, Volume II, 1984-1987*. Ames: Iowa State University Press, 1989.

Mickolus, Edward F., Todd Sandler, and Jean M. Murdock. *International Terrorism in the 1980s: A Chronology of Events, Volume I, 1980-1983*. Ames: Iowa State University Press, 1989.

Mickolus, Edward F., and Susan L. Simmons. *Terrorism, 1992-1995: A Chronology of Events and a Selectively Annotated Bibliography*. Westport, Conn.: Greenwood, 1997.

Rummel, Rudolph J. *Statistics of Democide: Genocide and Mass Murder Since 1900*. Charlottesville, Va.: Center for National Security Law, School of Law, University of Virginia, and Transaction Publishers, Rutgers University, 1997.

Schmid, A. P., and A. J. Jongman. "Violent Conflicts and Human Rights Violations in the Mid-1990s." *Terrorism and Political Violence* 9, no. 4 (Winter 1997): 166-192.

General Descriptive and Theoretical Works

Adams, James. *The Financing of Terror.* London: New English Library, 1986.

Alexander, Yonah, ed. *International Terrorism: National, Regional and Global Perspectives.* New York: Praeger, 1976.

Alexander, Yonah, and Seymour M. Finger, eds. *Terrorism: Interdisciplinary Perspectives.* New York: John Jay, 1977.

Alexander, Yonah, and Robert A. Kilmarx, eds. *Political Terrorism and Business: The Threat and Response.* New York: Praeger, 1979.

Alexander, Yonah, and Dennis Pluchinsky, eds. *Europe's Red Terrorists: The Fighting Communist Organizations.* London: Frank Cass, 1992.

Allison, Graham T., Owen R. Coté, Jr., Richard A. Falkenrath, and Steven E. Miller. *Avoiding Nuclear Anarchy: Containing the Threat of Loose Russian Nuclear Weapons and Fissile Material.* Cambridge, Mass.: MIT Press, 1996.

Amos, John W., II., and Russel H. S. Stolfi. "Controlling International Terrorism: Alternatives Palatable and Unpalatable," *Annals of the American Academy of Political and Social Science* 463 (September 1982): 69-83.

Bell, J. Bowyer. "Transnational Terror and World Order," *South Atlantic Quarterly* 74, no. 4 (1975): 404-417.

_____. *The Dynamics of the Armed Struggle.* London: Frank Cass, 1998.

Blaufarb, Douglas S. "Terrorist Trends and Ties," *Problems of Communism* 31, no. 3 (1982): 73-77.

Brainerd, Gideon H., Jr. "Terrorism: The Theory of Differential Effects." *Conflict* 5, no. 3 (1984): 233-244.

Burton, Anthony M. *Urban Terrorism: Theory, Practice and Response.* New York: The Free Press, 1975.

Byman, Daniel. "The Logic of Ethnic Terrorism." *Studies in Conflict and Terrorism* 21, no. 2 (April-June 1998): 149-169.

Campbell, Bruce B., and Arthur D. Brenner, eds. *Death Squads in Global Perspective.* New York: St. Martin's Press, 2000.

Chapman, Robert D. "State Terrorism." *Conflict: An International Journal for Conflict and Policy Studies* 3, no. 4 (1982): 283-298.

Clawson, Patrick. "Terrorism in Decline?" *Orbis* 33, no. 3 (1989): 263-276.

Cline, Ray, and Yonah Alexander. *Terrorism as State-Sponsored Covert*

Warfare. Fairfax, Va.: Herobook, 1986.

Clutterbuck, Richard. *Guerrillas and Terrorists.* London: Faber and Faber, 1977.

_____. *Kidnap and Ransom: The Response.* London: Faber and Faber, 1978.

Cotter, John M. "Sounds of Hate: White Power Rock and Roll and the Neo-Nazi Skinhead Subculture." *Terrorism and Political Violence* 11, no. 2 (Summer 1999): 111-140.

Crenshaw, Martha. "The Causes of Terrorism." *Comparative Politics* 13, no. 4 (1981): 379-400.

_____. "An Organizational Approach to the Analysis of Political Terrorism." *Orbis* 29, no. 3 (1985): 465-489.

_____. "Current Research on Terrorism: The Academic Perspective." *Studies in Conflict and Terrorism* 15, no. 1 (1992): 1-12.

_____, ed. *Terrorism in Context.* University Park, Penn.: Pennsylvania State University Press, 1995.

Dobson, Christopher. *War Without End: The Terrorists, An Intelligence Dossier.* London: Harrap, 1986.

Dobson, Christopher, and Ronald Payne. *The Carlos Complex: A Study in Terror.* New York: G. P. Putnam's Sons, 1977.

Dobson, Christopher, and Ronald Payne. *The Terrorists, Their Weapons, Leaders and Tactics.* New York: Facts on File, 1982.

Duvall, Raymond, and Michael Stohl. *The Politics of Terrorism,* 3rd ed. New York: Marcel Dekker, 1988.

Emerson, Steven. *Secret Warriors.* New York: Putnams, 1993.

Falk, Richard. *Revolutionaries and Functionaries: The Dual Face of Terrorism.* New York: E. P. Dutton, 1988.

Finger, Seymour Maxwell. "The United Nations and International Terrorism." *Jerusalem Journal of International Relations* 10, no. 1 (1988): 12-43.

Fishel, John T. "Little Wars, Small Wars, LIC, OOTW, the GAP, and Things That Go Bump in the Night." *Low Intensity Conflict & Law Enforcement* 4, no. 3 (1995): 372-398.

Ford, Franklin L. *Political Murder: From Tyrannicide to Terrorism.* Cambridge, Mass.: Harvard University Press, 1985.

Freedman, Lawrence Zelic, et al. *Terrorism and International Order.* London: Routledge and Kegan Paul, 1987.

Freedman, Lawrence Zelic, and Yonah Alexander, eds. *Perspectives on Terrorism.* Wilmington, Del.: Scholarly Resources Inc., 1983.

Frey, R. G. and Morris, Christopher W. Morris, eds. *Violence, Terrorism, and*

Justice. Cambridge, Mass.: Cambridge University Press, 1991.

Friedlander, Robert A. *Terrorism: Documents of International and Local Control*, 5 vols. Dobbs Ferry, N.Y.: Oceana Publications, 1979.

George, Alexander, ed. *Western State Terrorism.* New York: Routledge, Chapman and Hall, 1991.

Grosscup, Beau. *The Newest Explosions of Terrorism: Latest Sites of Terrorism in the 1990s and Beyond.* Far Hills, N.J.: New Horizon, 1998.

Guelke, Adrian. *The Age of Terrorism and the International Political System.* New York: St. Martin's, 1998.

Gutteridge, William, ed. *Contemporary Terrorism.* New York: Facts on File, 1986.

Hanle, Donald J. *Terrorism: The Newest Face of Warfare.* Pergamon-Brassey Terrorism Library, Vol. 1, Washington, D.C.: Pergamon, 1989.

Harmon, Christopher C. *Terrorism Today.* London: Frank Cass, 2000.

Heymann, Philip B. *Terrorism and America: A Commonsense Strategy For a Democratic Society.* Cambridge, Mass.: MIT Press, 1998.

Hof, Frederic C. "The Beirut Bombing of October 1983: An Act of Terrorism?" *Parameters: Journal of the US Army War College* 15, no. 2 (1985): 69-74.

Hoffman, Bruce. "Current Research on Terrorism and Low-Intensity Conflict." *Studies in Conflict and Terrorism* 15, no. 1 (1992): 25-38.

_____. "Why Terrorists Don't Claim Credit." *Terrorism and Political Violence* 9, no. 1 (Spring 1997): 1-6.

_____. *Inside Terrorism.* New York: Columbia University Press, 1998.

Holden-Rhodes, J.F., and Peter A. Lupsha. "Horsemen of the Apocalypse: Gray Area Phenomena and the New World Disorder." *Low Intensity Conflict & Law Enforcement* 2, no. 2 (1993): 212-226.

Hunter, Shireen. "Terrorism: A Balance Sheet." *Washington Quarterly* 12, no. 3 (1989): 17-32.

Jenkins, Brian M. "New Modes of Conflict." *Orbis* 28, no. 1 (Spring 1984): 5-16.

_____. "Will Terrorists Go Nuclear?" *Orbis* 29, no. 3 (1985): 507-516.

_____. "Defense Against Terrorism." *Political Science Quarterly* 101, no. 5 (1986): 773-786.

_____. "The Future Course of International Terrorism," in Paul Wilkinson, ed. *Contemporary Research on Terrorism.* Aberdeen, Scotland: Aberdeen University Press, 1987. pp. 581-585.

Jenkins, Philip. "Whose Terrorists? Libya and State Criminality." *Contemporary Crises* 12, no. 1 (1987): 5-24.

Kaplan, Jeffrey. "'Leaderless Resistance'." *Terrorism and Political Violence* 9, no. 3 (Autumn 1997): 80-95.

Kirk, Richard M. "Political Terrorism and the Size of Government: A Positive Institutional Analysis of Violent Political Activity." *Public Choice* 40, no. 1 (1983): 41-52.

Kupperman, Robert H. "Terror, the Strategic Tool: Response and Control," *Annals of the American Academy of Political and Social Science* 463 (September 1982): 24-38.

Kurz, Anat, ed. *Contemporary Trends in World Terrorism*. New York: Praeger, 1987.

Laqueur, Walter. "The Origins of Guerrilla Doctrine." *Journal of Contemporary History* 10 (July 1975).

_____. "Reflections on Terrorism." *Foreign Affairs* 65 (Fall 1986): 86-100.

_____. *The Age of Terrorism*. Boston: Little, Brown and Company, 1987.

_____. "Postmodern Terrorism." *Foreign Affairs* 75, no. 5 (September-October 1996): 24-35.

_____. "The New Face of Terrorism." *Washington Quarterly* 21, no. 4 (Autumn 1998): 169-178.

Laqueur, Walter, and Yonah Alexander, eds. *The Terrorism Reader: A Historical Anthology*. New York: New American Library, 1987.

Leeman, Richard W. "Terrorism as Rhetoric: An Argument of Values." *Journal of Political Science* 14, nos. 1-2 (1986): 33-42.

Lesser, Ian, Bruce Hoffman, John Arquilla, David Ronfeldt, and Michele Zanini. *Countering the New Terrorism*. Santa Monica, Calif.: RAND, 1999.

Levitt, Geoffrey M. *Democracies Against Terror.* New York: Praeger, 1988.

Li, Richard P. Y., and William R. Thompson. "The Coup Contagion Hypothesis." *Journal of Conflict Resolution* 19 (March 1975): 63-88.

Livingston, Neil C. "States in Opposition: The War Against Terrorism." *Conflict: An International Journal for Conflict and Policy Studies* 3, nos. 2-3 (1981): 83-142.

_____. *The War Against Terrorism*. Lexington, Mass.: Lexington Books, 1982.

Livingston, Susan Morrisey. "Terrorism: 'The Original Cheap Shot': An Interview with Ambassador Diego Asencio." *World Affairs* 146, no. 1 (Summer 1983): 42-53.

_____. "Terrorist Wrongs Versus Human Rights: An Interview with Assistant Secretary of State Elliott Abrams." *World Affairs* 146, no. 1 (Summer 1983): 69-78.

Long, David E. *The Anatomy of Terrorism*. New York: The Free Press, 1990.

Manwaring, Max G. *Gray Area Phenomena: Confronting the New World Disorder*. Boulder, Colo.: Westview, 1993.

Manwaring, Max G., and Wm. J. Olsen. *Managing Contemporary Conflict: Pillars of Success*. Boulder, Colo.: Westview, 1996.

Maranto, Robert. "The Rational Terrorist: Toward a New Theory of Terrorism." *Journal of Political Science* 14, nos. 1-2 (1986): 16-24.

McForan, Desmond. *The World Held Hostage: The War Waged by International Terrorism*. London: Oak-tree Books, 1986.

Merari, Ariel. "Classification of Terrorist Groups." *Terrorism* 1 (1978): 331-346.

Merkl, Peter H., ed. *Political Violence and Terror: Motifs and Motivations*. Berkeley: University of California Press, 1986.

Merkl, Peter H., and Leonard Weinberg, eds. *The Revival of Right-Wing Extremism in the Nineties*, Portland, Ore.: Frank Cass Publishers, 1997.

Mickolus, Edward F. "Statistical Approaches to the Study of Terrorism," in Alexander, Yonah, and Finger, Seymour M., eds. *Terrorism: Interdisciplinary Perspectives*. New York: John Jay, 1977. pp. 209-269.

_____. "Comment-Terrorists, Governments, and Numbers: Counting Things Versus Things That Count." *Journal of Conflict Resolution* 31, no. 1 (1987): 54-62.

Miller, Abraham H. "The Evolution of Terrorism." *Conflict Quarterly* 5, no. 4 (Fall 1985): 5-16.

Miller, David. "The Use and Abuse of Political Violence." *Political Studies* 32, no. 3 (1984): 401-419.

Miller, Reuben. "Acts of International Terrorism: Governments' Responses and Policies." *Comparative Political Studies* 19, no. 3 (1986): 385-414.

Monaghan, Rachel. "Animal Rights and Violent Protest." *Terrorism and Political Violence* 9, no. 4 (Winter 1997): 106-116.

Mozaffari, Mehdi. "The New Era of Terrorism: Approaches and Typologies." *Cooperation and Conflict* 23, no. 4 (1988): 179-196.

Murray, John, and Richard H. Ward, eds. *Extremist Groups*. Chicago: University of Illinois Press, 1997.

Newman, Graeme R., and Michael J. Lynch. "From Feuding to Terrorism: The Ideology of Vengeance." *Contemporary Crises* 11, no. 3 (1987): 223-242.

Norton, Augustus R., and Martin H. Greenberg, eds. *Studies in Nuclear Terrorism*. Boston: G. K. Hall, 1979.

Oakley, Robert. "International Terrorism." *Foreign Affairs* 65, no. 3 (1987): 611-629.

Ochberg, Frank M., and David A. Soskis. *Victims of Terrorism.* Boulder, Colo.: Westview, 1982.

O'Neill, Bard E. *Insurgency and Terrorism: Inside Modern Revolutionary Warfare.* New York: Pergamon, 1990.

Onwudiwe, Ihekwoaba D. *The Globalization of Terrorism.* College Park: University of Maryland Press, 2000.

O'Sullivan, Noel, ed. *Terrorism, Ideology and Revolution.* Brighton, U.K.: Wheatsheaf Books, 1986.

Pierre, Andrew J. "The Politics of International Terrorism." *Orbis* 19, no. 4 (1976): 1251-1269.

Pluchinsky, Dennis. "Terrorist Documentation." *Terrorism* 14, no. 4 (1991): 241-252.

Pluchinsky, Dennis A. "Academic Research on European Terrorist Developments: Pleas from a Government Terrorism Analyst." *Studies in Conflict and Terrorism* 15, no. 1 (1992): 13-24.

Poland, James M. *Understanding Terrorism: Groups, Strategies, and Responses.* Englewood Cliffs, N.J.: Prentice Hall, 1988.

Rapoport, David C., ed. *Inside Terrorist Organizations.* New York: Columbia University Press, 1988.

Rapoport, David C., and Yonah Alexander, eds. *The Morality of Terrorism: Religious and Secular Justifications.* New York: Pergamon, 1982.

Reich, Walter, ed. *Origins of Terrorism: Psychologies, Ideologies, Theologies, States of Mind.* Washington, D.C.: Woodrow Wilson Center, 1998. 488 p, revised edition with new introduction by Walter Laqueur.

Reeve, Simon. *The New Jackals: Ramzi Yousef, Osama bin Laden, and the Future of Terrorism.* Boston, Mass.: Northeastern University Press, 1999.

Ross, Jeffrey Ian, and R. Reuben Miller. "The Effects of Oppositional Political Terrorism: Five Actor-Based Models." *Low Intensity Conflict & Law Enforcement* 6, no. 3 (1997): 76-107.

Rubenstein, Richard. *Alchemists of Revolution: Terrorism in the Modern World.* New York: Basic Books, 1987.

Rummel, Rudolph J. *Understanding Conflict and War.* Beverly Hills, Calif.: Sage [Vol. 1, 1975; Vol. 2, 1976; Vol. 3, 1977; Vol. 4, 1979; and Vol. 5, 1981].

Sandler, Todd, John T. Tschirhart, and Jon Cauley. "A Theoretical Analysis of Transnational Terrorism." *American Political Science Review* 77, no. 1 (1983): 36-54.

Schlagheck, Donna. *International Terrorism: An Introduction to the Concepts and Actors.* Lexington, Mass.: Lexington Books, 1988.

Schmid, Alex P., Jongman, Albert J., et al. *Violence as Communication: Insurgent Terrorism and the Western News Media.* London and Beverly Hills: Sage, 1982.

Segaller, Stephan. *Invisible Armies: Terrorism into the 1990s.* London: Sphere, 1987.

Shain, Yossi. "The War of Governments Against Their Opposition in Exile." *Government and Opposition* 24, no. 3 (1989): 341-356.

Sick, Gary. "Terrorism: Its Political Uses and Abuses." *SAIS Review* 7, no. 1 (1987): 11-26.

Simon, Jeffrey D. *The Terrorist Trap: America's Experience with Terrorism.* Bloomington: Indiana University Press, 1994.

Slann, Martin and Bernard Schechtermann, eds. *Multidimensional Terrorism.* Boulder, Colo.: Lynne Rienner, 1987.

Sobel, Lester A., ed. *Political Terrorism, 1975-1978.* 2 vols. New York: Facts on File, 1978.

Sproat, Peter Alan. "Can the State Be Terrorist?" *Terrorism* 14, no. 1 (1991): 19-30.

Sterling, Claire. *The Terror Network: The Secret War of International Terrorism.* New York: Holt, Rinehart, and Winston, 1981.

Stohl, Michael. "National Interests and State Terrorism in International Affairs." *Political Science* 36, no. 1 (1984): 37-52.

Stohl, Michael. *Terrible Beyond Endurance? The Foreign Policy of State Terrorism.* New York: Greenwood, 1988.

Taylor, Bron. "Religion, Violence, and Radical Environmentalism: From Earth First! to the Unabomber to the Earth Liberation Front." *Terrorism and Political Violence* 10, no. 4 (Winter 1998): 1-42.

Taylor, Max, and John Horgan, eds. *The Future of Terrorism.* London: Frank Cass, 2000.

Tucker, Jonathan B., ed. *Toxic Terror: Assessing Terrorist Use of Chemical and Biological Weapons.* Cambridge, Mass.: MIT Press, 2000.

Tugwell, Maurice A. "Guilt Transfer," in Rapoport, David C., and Yonah Alexander, eds. *The Morality of Terrorism: Religious and Secular Justifications.* New York: Pergamon, 1982. pp. 275-289.

Vought, Donald B. "Century Twenty-One: An Age of Terror and Violence." *Low Intensity Conflict & Law Enforcement* 2, no. 1 (1993): 153-169.

Wallack, Michael. "Terrorism and 'Compellence'," *International Perspec-*

tives, (November-December 1987): 13-16.

Weinberg, Leonard and Paul Davis. *Introduction to Political Terrorism.* New York: McGraw-Hill, 1989.

White, Jonathan R. *Terrorism: An Introduction.* Wadsworth Contemporary Issues in Crime and Justice Series. Belmont, Calif.: Wadsworth, 2001.

Wilkinson, Paul. *Terrorism and the Liberal State.* New York: John Wiley and Sons, 1978.

_____. "The Future of Terrorism." *Futures* 20, no. 5 (1988): 493-505.

_____, ed. *British Perspectives on Terrorism.* London: George, Allen & Unwin, 1991.

Wilkinson, Paul, and Alasdair M. Stewart, eds. *Contemporary Research on Terrorism.* Aberdeen, Scotland: Aberdeen University Press, 1987.

Windsor, Philip. "Terrorism and International Order." *Atlantic Community Quarterly* 25, no. 2 (1987): 201-209.

Conventional and Nonconventional Operations

Arquilla, John, and David Ronfeldt. *The Advent of Netwar.* Santa Monica, Calif.: RAND, MR-789-OSD, 1996.

_____ and _____. *In Athena's Camp: Preparing for Conflict in the Information Age.* Santa Monica, Calif.: RAND, MR-880-OSD/RC, 1997.

_____ and _____. "The Advent of Netwar: Analytical Background." *Studies in Conflict and Terrorism* 22, no. 3 (July-September 1999): 193-206.

Badolato, Edward V. "Environmental Terrorism: A Case Study." *Terrorism* 14, no. 4 (1991): 237-240.

Beres, Louis René. "Preventing the Ultimate Nightmare: Nuclear Terrorism Against the United States." *International Journal of Intelligence and Counterintelligence* 10, no. 3 (Fall 1997): 333-342.

Bunker, Robert J. "Information Operations and the Conduct of Land Warfare." *Military Review* 78, no. 5 (September-November 1998): 4-17.

Cameron, Gavin. "Multi-track Microproliferation: Lessons from Aum Shinrikyo and Al Qaida." *Studies in Conflict and Terrorism* 22, no. 4 (October-December 1999): 277-310.

Campbell, James K. "Excerpts from Research Study: 'Weapons of Mass Destruction and Terrorism: Proliferation by Non-State Actors'." *Terror-*

ism and Political Violence 9, no. 2 (Summer 1997): 24-20.

Cetron, Marvin J., and Owen Davies. "The Future Face of Terrorism." *The Futurist* 28 (Nov./Dec. 1994): 10-15.

Cillufo, Frank J., and Curt H. Gergely. "Information Warfare and Strategic Terrorism." *Terrorism and Political Violence* 9, no. 1 (Spring 1997): 84-94.

Cimbala, Stephen J. "Information Warfare and Nuclear Conflict Termination." *European Security* 7, no. 4 (1998): 69-90.

Demarest, Geoffrey. "Geopolitics and Urban Armed Conflict: The Potential Challenge to US Army Operations." *Small Wars and Insurgencies* 6, no. 1 (Spring 1995): 44-67.

Devost, Matthew G., Brian K. Houghton, and Neal Allen Pollard. "Information Terrorism: Political Violence in the Information Age." *Terrorism and Political Violence* 9, no. 1 (Spring 1997): 72-83

Diehl, Paul F. "Avoiding Another Beirut Disaster for the Employment of U.S. Troops in Peacekeeping Roles." *Conflict* 8, no. 4 (1988): 261-270.

Dobson, Christopher, and Ronald Payne. *The Terrorists, Their Weapons, Leaders and Tactics*. New York: Facts on File, 1982.

Falkenrath, Richard A., Robert D. Newman, and Bradley A. Thayer. *America's Achilles' Heel: Nuclear, Biological, and Chemical Terrorism and Covert Attack*. Cambridge, Mass.: The MIT Press, 1998.

Gotowicki, Stephen H. "Confronting Terrorism: New War Form or Mission Impossible?" *Military Review* 77, no. 3 (May-June 1997): 61-66.

Hoffman, Bruce. *Responding to Terrorism Across the Technological Spectrum*. Santa Monica, Calif.: RAND, P-7874, 1994.

Holden, Robert T. "The Contagiousness of Aircraft Hijacking." *American Journal of Sociology* 91, no. 4 (1986): 874-904.

Jenkins, Brian M. "Defense Against Terrorism," *Political Science Quarterly* 101, no. 5 (1986): 773-786.

Laqueur, Walter. "Terrorism Via the Internet: Views of W. Laqueur." *The Futurist* 31 (March-April 1997): 64-65.

Livingston, Neil C. "Fighting Terrorism: The Private Sector." *Conflict: An International Journal for Conflict and Policy Studies* 3, nos. 2-3 (1982): 177-222.

_____. "Death Squads." *World Affairs* 146 (Winter 1984): 42-53.

Madsen, Wayne. "Intelligence Agency Threats to Computer Security." *International Journal of Intelligence and Counterintelligence* 6, no. 4 (Winter 1993): 413-488.

Manwaring, Max G., Edwin G. Corr. "The 'Almost Obvious' Lessons of Peace Operations." *Small Wars and Insurgencies* 9, no. 1 (Spring 1998): 192-199.

McGeorge, Harvey J., II. "Kinetics of Terrorism." *World Affairs* 146, no. 1 (1983): 23-41.

McMahon, K. Scott. "Unconventional Nuclear, Biological, and Chemical Weapons Delivery Methods: Whither the 'Smuggled Bomb.'" *Comparative Strategy* 15 (April-June 1996): 123-134.

Muir, Angus M. "Terrorism and Weapons of Mass Destruction: The Case of Aum Shinrikyo." *Studies in Conflict and Terrorism* 22, no. 1 (January-March 1999): 79-91.

Netwar Topic, Special Issue: Netwar Across the Spectrum of Conflict, *Studies in Conflict and Terrorism* 22, no. 3 (July-September 1999): 189-276.

Patrick, William C., III, "Biological Terrorism and Aerosol Dissemination." *Politics and the Life Sciences* 15 (September 1996): 208-210.

Ronfeldt, David. "Netwar Across the Spectrum of Conflict: An Introductory Comment." *Studies in Conflict and Terrorism* 22, no. 3 (July-September 1999): 189-192.

Rose, Gideon. "It Could Happen Here: Facing The New Terrorism: Review Article." *Foreign Affairs* 78, no. 2 (March-April 1999): 131-137.

Sam Nunn Policy Forum. *Terrorism, Weapons of Mass Destruction, and U.S. Security*. Athens, Ga.: Sam Nunn Policy Forum, 1997.

Sandler, Todd, and John L. Scott. "Terrorist Success in Hostage-Taking Incidents: An Empirical Study." *Journal of Conflict Resolution* 31, no. 1 (1987): 35-53.

Schweitzer, Glenn E., and Carole Dorsch. "Superterrorism: Searching for Long-Term Solutions." *The Futurist* 33, no. 6 (June-July 1999): 40-45.

Simon, Jeffrey D. *Terrorists and the Potential Use of Biological Weapons: A Discussion of Possibilities.* R-3771-AFMIC. Santa Monica, Calif.: RAND, 1989.

Sloan, Stephen. "International Terrorism: Academic Quest, Operational Art and Policy Implications." *Journal of International Affairs* 32 (Spring/Summer 1978): 1-5.

_____. *Simulating Terrorism*. Norman: University of Oklahoma Press, 1981.

Snitch, Thomas H. "Terrorism and International Assassinations: A Transnational Assessment, 1968-1980." *Annals of the American Academy of Political and Social Science* 463 (September 1982): 54-68.

Sprinzak, Ehud. "The Great Superterrorism Scare." *Foreign Policy* 112 (Fall

1998): 110-124.

Whine, Michael. "Cyberspace—A New Medium for Communication, Command, and Control by Extremists." *Studies in Conflict and Terrorism* 22, no. 3 (July-September 1999): 231-246.

Wilkinson, Paul. "The Role of the Military in Combatting Terrorism." *Terrorism and Political Violence* 8, no. 3 (Autumn 1996): 1-11.

_____. *Technology and Terrorism.* London: Frank Cass, 1993.

Wolf, John B. "Organization and Management Practices of Urban Terrorist Groups." *Terrorism* 1, no. 2 (1978): 169-186.

Zawodny, J. K. "Infrastructures of Terrorist Organizations," in Freedman, Lawrence Zelic and Yonah Alexander, eds. *Perspectives on Terrorism.* Wilmington, Del.: Scholarly Resources Inc., 1983.

Zilinskas, Raymond A. "Aum Shinrikyo's Chemical/Biological Terrorism as a Paradigm?" *Politics and the Life Sciences* 15 (September 1996): 237-239.

International and Domestic Legal Issues

Abramovsky, Abraham. "Multilateral Conventions for the Suppression of Unlawful Seizure and Interference with Aircraft." *Columbia Journal of Transnational Law* 14, nos. 1-3 (1975): (1) 381-405, (2) 268-300, and (3) 451-484.

Almond, Harry H. Jr. "The Legal Regulation of International Terrorism." *Conflict: An International Journal for Conflict and Policy Studies* 3, nos. 2-3 (1982): 143-166.

Bassiouni, M. Cherif, ed. *International Terrorism and Political Crimes: Proceedings of the Third Conference on Terrorism and Political Crimes,* Syracuse, Italy. Springfield, Ill.: Charles C. Thomas, 1974.

Borkowski, George M. "Use of Force: Interception of Aircraft." *Harvard International Law Review* 27, no. 2 (1986): 761 et seq.

Braungart, Richard G., and Margaret M. Braungart. "International Terrorism: Background and Response." *Journal of Political and Military Sociology* 9, no. 2 (1981): 263-288.

Caras, James. "Economic Sanctions: United States Sanctions Against Libya." *Harvard International Law Review* 27, no. 2 (1986): 672-678.

Carr, Caleb. "Terrorism as Warfare: The Lessons of Military History." *World*

Policy Journal 13 (Winter 1996-1997): 1-12.

Cassese, Antonio. *Terrorism, Politics, and Law: The Achille Lauro Affair.* London: Basil Blackwell, 1989.

Chamberlain, Kevin. "Collective Suspension of Air Services with States Which Harbour Hijackers." *International and Comparative Law Quarterly* 32, no. 3 (1983): 616-632.

Charters, David A., ed. *The Deadly Sin of Terrorism: Its Effect on Democracy and Civil Liberty in Six Countries.* Westport, Conn.: Greenwood, 1994.

Chinkin, Christine. "The Foreign Affairs Powers of the U.S. President and the Iranian Hostages Agreement: *Dames and Moore v. Regan.*" *International and Comparative Law Quarterly* 32, no. 3 (July 1983): 600-615.

Claburn, Jeffrey. "Public Constraints on Assassination as an Instrument of U.S. Foreign Policy." *International Journal of Intelligence and Counterintelligence* 7, no. 1 (Spring 1994): 97-110.

Deutch, John M. "Terrorism." *Foreign Policy* 108 (Fall 1997): 10-22.

Donelan, Michael. "Terrorism: Who Is a Legitimate Target?" *Review of International Studies* 13, no. 3 (1987): 229-234.

Dowling, Kathryn. "Civil Rights, Human Rights, and Terrorism in Northern Ireland." *Journal of Intergroup Relations* 7, no. 4 (1979-80): 3-23.

Enders, Walter, and Todd Sandler. "Transnational Terrorism in the Post-Cold War Era." *International Studies Quarterly* 43, no. 1 (March 1999): 145-167.

Evans, Alona E., and John F. Murphy. *Legal Aspects of International Terrorism.* Lexington, Mass: Lexington Books, 1978.

Feith, Douglas J. "The Law of War: The Terrorists Are Rolled Back." *Atlantic Community Quarterly* 25, no. 2 (1987): 210-212.

Frey, Bruno S. "Fighting Political Terrorism by Refusing Recognition." *Journal of Public Policy* 7, no. 2 (1987): 179-188.

Gilbert, Geoffrey S. "Terrorism and the Political Offense Exemption Reappraised." *International and Comparative Law Quarterly* 34, no. 4 (1985): 695-723.

Halberstam, Malvina. "Terrorism on the High Seas: The *Achille Lauro,* Piracy, and IMO Convention on Maritime Safety." *American Journal of International Law* 82, no. 2 (1988): 269-310.

Hoffman, Bruce. "The Confluence of International and Domestic Trends in Terrorism." *Terrorism and Political Violence* 9, no. 2 (Summer 1997): 1-15.

Jacobs, James B., and Kimberly Potter. *Hate Crimes: Criminal Law and Identity Politics.* New York: Oxford University Press, 1998.

Kuber, Douglas. "A Sewing Lesson in Political Offense Determinations: Stitching-Up the International Terrorist's Loophole." *Hastings International and Comparative Law Review* 10, no. 2 (1987): 499-524.

McCauley, Clark. *Terrorism Research and Public Policy.* London: Frank Cass, 1991.

Murphy, John F. *State Support of International Terrorism: Legal, Political, and Economic Dimensions.* Boulder, Colo.: Westview, 1989.

_____. "The Need for International Cooperation in Combatting Terrorism,. *Terrorism* 13, no. 6 (1990): 381-396.

O'Brien, Sean P. "Foreign Policy Crises and the Resort to Terrorism: A Time-Series Analysis of Conflict Linkages." *Journal of Conflict Resolution* 40 (June 1996): 320-335.

Paasche, Franz W. "The Use of Force in Combatting Terrorism." *Columbia Journal of Transnational Law* 25, no. 2 (1987): 377-402.

Paust, Jordan J. "Terrorism and 'Terrorism-Specific' Statutes." *Terrorism* 7, no. 2 (1984): 233-239.

_____. "The Link Between Human Rights and Terrorism and Its Implications for the Law of State Responsibility." *Hastings International and Comparative Law Review* 11, no. 1 (1987): 41-54.

Porter, Jack Nusan, ed. *Genocide and Human Rights.* Washington, D.C.: University Press of America, 1982.

Rajput, R. S. "International Conventions on Aerial Hijacking: An Approach to Combat Terrorism." *Indian Journal of Political Science* 51, no. 1 (1990): 98-125.

Rubin, Alfred P. "Current Legal Approaches to International Terrorism." *Terrorism* 13, nos. 4-5 (1990): 277-298.

Rubner, Michael. "Antiterrorism and the Withering Away of the 1973 War Powers Resolution." *Political Science Quarterly* 102, no. 2 (1987): 193-216.

Schachter, Oscar. "Self-Help in International Law: U.S. Action in the Iranian Hostage Crisis." *Journal of International Studies* 37, no. 2 (1984): 231-246.

Schuetz, G. Gregory. "Apprehending Terrorists Overseas under United States and International Law: A Case Study of the Fawaz Younis Arrest." *Harvard International Law Journal* 29, no. 2 (1988): 499-532.

Shultz, Richard H., and J. Marlow Schmauder, "Emerging Regional Conflicts and U.S. Interests: Challenges and Responses in the 1990s." *Studies in Conflict and Terrorism* 17, no. 1 (January-March 1994): 1-22.

Smith, Brent L. "Antiterrorism Legislation in the United States: Problems and Implications." *Terrorism* 7, no. 2 (1984): 213-31.

Sofaer, Abraham D. "Terrorism and the Law." *Foreign Affairs* 64, no. 5 (1986): 901-923.

Stein, Ted L. "Contempt, Crisis, and the Court: The World Court and the Hostage Rescue Attempt." *American Journal of International Law* 76, no. 3 (1982): 499-531.

Temple, Caleb L. "Terrorism and International Law: Two Barriers to Consensus." *Conflict* 10, no. 3 (1990): 215-226.

Warbrick, Colin. "The Prevention of Terrorism (Temporary Provisions) Act 1976 and the European Convention on Human Rights: The McVeigh Case." *International and Comparative Law Quarterly* 32, no. 3 (July 1983): 757 et seq.

Police and Law-Enforcement Issues

Baker, Stewart A. "Should Spies Be Cops?" *Foreign Policy* 97 (Winter 1994-1995): 36-52.

Bodrero, D. Douglas. "Confronting Terrorism on the State and Local Level." *FBI Law Enforcement Bulletin* 68 (March 1999): 11-18.

Bolz, Frank, Jr., Kenneth J. Dudonis, and David P. Schulz. *The Counter-Terrorism Handbook: Tactics, Procedures, and Techniques.* Elsevier Series in Practical Aspects of Criminal and Forensic Investigations, No. 16. New York: Elsevier Science, 1990.

Boyce, Daniel. "Narco-Terrorism." *FBI Law Enforcement Bulletin* 56, no. 11 (October 1987): 24-27.

Brock, David. "The World of Narcoterrorism." *American Spectator* 22 (June 1989): 24-28.

Clutterbuck, Richard. "Air Piracy: A Gleam of Hope for the World." *Army Quarterly and Defence Journal* 104, no. 4 (1974): 402-408.

Cotler, Irwin. "Towards a Counter-Terrorism Law and Policy." *Terrorism and Political Violence* 10, no. 2 (Summer 1998): 1-14.

Courter, Jim. "Protecting Our Citizens." *Policy Review* 36 (Spring 1986): 10-17.

Crenshaw, William A. "Civil Aviation: Target for Terrorism." *Annals of the*

American Academy of Political and Social Science 498 (July 1988): 60-69.

Freeh, Louis J. "Responding to Terrorism." *FBI Law Enforcement Bulletin* 68 (March 1999): 1-2.

Fuller, T. C. "Bomb Threat: A Primer For the First Responder." *FBI Law Enforcement Bulletin* 68 (March 1999): 28-31.

Gates, Daryl F. "The Role of Analysis in Combating Modern Terrorism: The Los Angeles Police Department Anti-Terrorist Division." *FBI Law Enforcement Bulletin* 58 (June 1989): 1-5.

Gregory, F. E. C. "Police Cooperation and Integration in the European Community: Proposals, Problems and Prospects." *Terrorism* 14, no. 3 (1991): 145-156.

Harris, John W., Jr.. "Domestic Terrorism in the 1980's." *FBI Law Enforcement Bulletin* 56, no. 11 (October 1987): 5-13.

Herrera, Hector A. "Kidnapping Policy During the Drug War Era: Ethical and Legal Implications." *Low Intensity Conflict & Law Enforcement* 5, no. 3 (1996): 484 et seq.

Horchem, Hans J. "Terrorism and Government Response: The German Response." *Jerusalem Journal of International Relations* 4, no. 3 (1980): 43-55.

Hughes, Martin. "Terror and Negotiation." *Terrorism and Political Violence,* 2, no. 1 (Spring 1990): 73-82.

Hulnick, Arthur S. "Intelligence and Law Enforcement: The 'Spies Are Not Cops' Problem." *International Journal of Intelligence and Counterintelligence* 10, no. 3 (Fall 1997): 269-286.

Jenkins, Brian M. "Aviation Security in the United States." *Terrorism and Political Violence* 10, no. 3 (Autumn 1998): 101-111.

Landes, William M. "An Economic Study of U.S. Aircraft Hijacking, 1961-1976." *Journal of Law and Economics* 21, no. 1 (1978): 1-31.

Lewis, John F., Jr. "Fighting Terrorism in the 21st Century." *FBI Law Enforcement Bulletin* 68 (March 1999): 3-10.

Martell, D. F. "FBI's Expanding Role in International Terrorism Investigations." *FBI Law Enforcement Bulletin* 56, no. 11 (October 1987): 28-32.

Martin, Robert A. "The Joint Terrorism Task Force: A Concept That Works." *FBI Law Enforcement Bulletin* 68 (March 1999): 23-27.

Nelson, Kurt. "Mass Transit: Target of Terror." *FBI Law Enforcement Bulletin* 68 (January 1999): 19-24.

Pizer, Harry, and Stephen Sloan. *Corporate Aviation Security: The Next*

Frontier in Aerospace Operations. Norman: University of Oklahoma Press, 1992.

Pockrass, Robert M. "Building a Civil Police Counter-Terrorist Team" *Conflict* 8, no. 4 (1988): 327-332.

Pomerantz, Steve L. "The FBI and Terrorism." *FBI Law Enforcement Bulletin* 56, no. 11 (October 1987): 14-17.

Rosenau, William. "Facing the Unpalatable: The US Military and Law Enforcement in Operations Other Than War." *Low Intensity Conflict & Law Enforcement* 4, no. 2 (1995): 187-202.

Schwender, Craig S. "The Geneva Conventions Protocols and the Terrorist Threat." *Military Review* 75, no. 1 (February 1995): 31-37.

Sessions, William S. "The FBI's Mission in Countering Terrorism." *Terrorism* 13, no. 1 (1990): 1-6.

Smith, Brent L., and Kathryn D. Morgan. "Terrorists Right and Left: Empirical Issues in Profiling American Terrorists." *Studies in Conflict and Terrorism* 17, no. 1 (January-March 1994): 39-57.

St. John, Peter. *Air Piracy, Airport Security, and International Terrorism: Winning the War Against Hijackers.* New York: Quorum Books, 1991.

_____. "The Politics of Aviation Terrorism." *Terrorism and Political Violence* 10, no. 3 (Autumn 1998): 27-49.

Stone, J. L., Jr. "Irish Terrorism Investigations." *FBI Law Enforcement Bulletin* 56, no. 11 (October 1987): 18-23.

Turner, Michael A. "CIA-FBI Non-Cooperation: Cultural Trait or Bureaucratic Inertia?" *International Journal of Intelligence and Counterintelligence* 8, no. 3 (Fall 1995): 259-274.

Vincent, Billie H. "Aviation Security and Terrorism." *Terrorism* 13, no. 6 (1990): 397-440.

Wilkinson, Paul, and Brian Jenkins, eds. Special Issue on Aviation Terrorism and Security, *Terrorism and Political Violence* 10, no. 3 (Autumn 1998):v.-171.

Wilkinson, Paul, and Brian Jenkins, eds. *Aviation Terrorism and Security.* London: Frank Cass, 1999.

Wolf, John B. "Analytical Framework for the Study and Control of Agitational Terrorism." *Police Journal* (England) 49 (July-September 1976): 165-171.

Wright, Stuart A. "Anatomy of a Government Massacre: Abuses of Hostage-Barricade Protocols During the Waco Standoff." *Terrorism and Political Violence* 11, no. 2 (Summer 1999): 39-68.

National Security and Counterterrorism

Alexander, Yonah. "Special Report: Technology Against Terrorism, The Federal Effort." *Terrorism* 14, no. 2 (1991): 111 et seq.

Alexander, Yonah. "Will Terrorists Use Chemical Weapons?" *JINSA Security Affairs* (June-July 1990).

Amit, Meir. "Diminishing the Threat Against Terrorism: Intelligence and the War Against Terrorism." *IDF Journal* (Fall 1989).

Behm, Allan J., and Michael J. Palmer. "Coordinating Counterterrorism: A Strategic Approach to a Changing Threat." *Terrorism* 14, no. 3 (1991): 171-194.

Berkowitz, Bruce D., and Allan E. Goodman. "The Logic of Covert Action." *National Interest* 51 (Spring 1998): 38-46.

Bernstein, Alvin H. "Iran's Low-Intensity War Against the United States." *Orbis* 30, no. 1 (1986): 149-167.

Bodansky, Yossef. *Target America: Terrorism in the U.S. Today.* New York: Shapolsky, 1993.

Bremer, L. Paul, III. "Continuing the Fight Against Terrorism." *Terrorism* 12, no. 2 (1989): 81-88.

Brenchley, Frank. "Diplomatic Immunities and State-Sponsored Terrorism." *Conflict Studies* 164 (1984).

_____. "Living With Terrorism: The Problem of Air Piracy." *Conflict Studies* 184 (1986).

Burgess, William H. III. "Iranian Special Operations in the Iran-Iraq War: Implications for the United States." *Conflict*, 8, no. 1 (1988): 22-40.

Bush, George H. "Prelude to Retaliation: Building a Governmental Consensus on Terrorism." *SAIS Review* 7, no. 1 (1987): 1-10.

Celmer, Marc A. *Terrorism, U.S. Strategy, and Reagan Policies.* Westport, Conn.: Greenwood. 1987.

Clutterbuck, Richard. *Kidnap, Hijack and Extortion: The Response.* London: Macmillan, 1987.

_____. *Terrorism and Guerrilla Warfare: Forecasts and Remedies.* London: Routledge, Chapman and Hall, 1990.

Corr, Edwin G., and Stephen Sloan, eds., *Low Intensity Conflict: Old Threats in a New World.* Boulder, Colo.: Westview, 1992.

Crabtree, Richard D. "U.S. Policy for Countering Terrorism: The Intelligence Dimension." *Conflict Quarterly* 6, no. 1 (Winter 1986).

Crenshaw, William A. "Civil Aviation: Target for Terrorism." *Annals of the American Academy of Political and Social Science* 498 (July 1988): 60-69.

DiLaura, Arnold E. "Preventing Terrorism: An Analysis of National Strategy." *SAIS Review* 7, no. 1 (1987): 27-38.

Eppright, Charles T. "'Counterterrorism' and Conventional Military Force: The Relationship Between Political Effect and Utility." *Studies in Conflict and Terrorism* 20, no. 4 (October-December 1997): 333-344.

Foxell, Joseph W. Jr. "The Debate on the Potential for Mass-Casualty Terrorism: The Challenge to US Security." *Terrorism and Political Violence* 11, no. 1 (Spring 1999): 94-109.

Gal-Or, Noemi, ed. *Tolerating Terrorism in the West: An International Survey*. London: Routledge, Chapman and Hall, 1991.

Ganor, Boaz. *Countering State-Sponsored Terrorism*. Herzliya, Israel: International Policy Institute for Counter-Terrorism, 1993.

Goldman, John Richard. "Terrorism and the Role of Security Strategies." *Journal of Political Science* 14, nos. 1-2 (1986): 1-9.

Green, L. C. "Terrorism and Its Response." *Terrorism* 8 (1985): 33-77.

Hastedt, Glenn. "Intelligence Failure and Terrorism: The Attack on the Marines in Beirut." *Conflict Quarterly* 8, no. 2, (Spring 1988): 7-22.

Hewitt, Christopher. *The Effectiveness of Anti-Terrorism Policies*. Lanham, Md: University Press of America, 1984.

Hicks and Associates, Inc., *Current and Projected US Strategy and Policy for Combating Terrorism*. Report Prepared for Raytheon Systems Company, 1998.

Hoffman, Bruce. "The Role of Foreign Policy, Intelligence, and Law Enforcement in the Prevention of Transnational Terrorism." *Low Intensity Conflict & Law Enforcement* 4, no. 1 (1995): 56-71.

Hudson, Rex A. "Dealing with International Hostage-Taking: Alternatives to Reactive Counterterrorist Assaults." *Terrorism* 12, no. 3 (1989): 321 et seq.

Jenkins, Brian M. "A U.S. Strategy for Combatting Terrorism." *Conflict: An International Journal for Conflict and Policy Studies* 3, nos. 2-3 (1981): 167-176.

_____. RAND/R-3302-AF, *International Terrorism: The Other World War*. Santa Monica, Calif.: Rand, 1985.

Johns, Milton C. "The Reagan Administration's Response to State-Sponsored Terrorism." *Conflict* 8, no. 4 (1988): 241-260.

Jones, William F. W. "Terrorism and Electrical Energy Interruption: The

Role of The Federal Emergency Management Agency." *Terrorism* 13, no. 6 (1990): 441-446.

Kerr, Donald M. "Coping With Terrorism." *Terrorism* 8 (1985): 113-126.

Klare, Michael T., and Peter Kornblush, eds. *Low Intensity Warfare: Counterinsurgency, Proinsurgency, and Antiterrorism in the Eighties.* New York: Pantheon, 1988.

Kumamoto, Robert. "Diplomacy from Below: International Terrorism and American Foreign Relations, 1945-1962." *Terrorism* 14, no. 1 (1991): 31-48.

Larsen, David L. "The American Response to the Iranian Hostage Crisis: 444 Days of Decision." *International Social Science Review* 57, nos. 3-4 (1982): 195-209.

Lee, Dwight R., and Todd Sandler. "On The Optimal Retaliation against Terrorists: The Paid-Rider Option." *Public Choice* 6, no. 2 (1989): 141-152.

Leventhal, Paul L., and Milton M. Hoenig. "The Hidden Danger: Risks of Nuclear Terrorism." *Terrorism* 10, no. 1 (1987): 1-22.

Livingston, Neil C. "Fighting Terrorism: The Private Sector." *Conflict: An International Journal for Conflict and Policy Studies* 3, nos. 2-3 (1982): 177-222.

MacWilson, Alastair C. *Hostage-Taking Terrorism: Incident-Response Strategy.* New York: St. Martin's Press, 1992.

Martin, David, and John Walcott. *Best Laid Plans: The Inside Story of America's War Against Terrorism.* New York: Harper & Row, 1988.

McCrea, Brett A. "US Counter-Terrorist Policy: A Proposed Strategy for a Non-Traditional Threat." *Low Intensity Conflict & Law Enforcement* 3, no. 3 (1994): 493-508.

McGeorge, Harvey J., II. "Plan Carefully, Rehearse Thoroughly, Execute Violently: The Tactical Response to Hostage Situations," *World Affairs,* 146, 1 (1983): 59-68.

———. "Kinetics of Terrorism." *World Affairs* 146, no. 1 (Summer 1983): 23-41.

Miller, Abraham H., and Nicholas A. Damask. "The Dual Myths of 'Narco-Terrorism': How Myths Drive Policy." *Terrorism and Political Violence* 8, no. 1 (Spring 1996): 132-166.

Mullins, Wayman C. "Stopping Terrorism: The Problems Posed by the Organizational Infrastructure of Terrorist Organizations." *Journal of Contemporary Criminal Justice* (December 1988).

Netanyahu, Benjamin, ed. *Terrorism: How the West Can Win.* New York:

Farrar, Strauss, Giroux, 1986.

Ofri, Arie. "Intelligence and Counterterrorism." *Orbis* 28, no. 1 (1984): 41-52.

O'Neill, Bard E. *Insurgency and Terrorism: Inside Modern Revolutionary Warfare.* New York: Pergamon, 1990.

Oots, Kent L. "Bargaining with Terrorists: Organizational Considerations." *Terrorism* 13, no. 2 (1990): 145-158.

Post, Jerrold M. "Rewarding Fire with Fire: Effects of Retaliation on Terrorist Group Dynamics." *Terrorism* 10, no. 1 (Winter 1987): 23-36.

_____. "Prospects for Nuclear Terrorism: Psychological Motivations and Constraints." *Conflict Quarterly* 7, no. 3 (Summer 1987): 47-58.

Prince, James. "Is There a Role for Intelligence in Combatting Terrorism?" *Conflict* 9, no. 3 (1989): 301-318.

Prunckun, Henry W., Jr., and Philip B. Mohr, "Military Deterrence of International Terrorism: An Evaluation of Operation El Dorado Canyon." *Studies in Conflict and Terrorism* 20, no. 3 (July-September 1997): 267-280.

Raufer, Xavier, "Gray Areas: A New Security Threat." *Political Warfare: Intelligence, Activities, Measures and Intelligence Report* 20 (Spring 1992): 1.

Revell, Oliver B. "Structure of Counterterrorism Planning and Operations in the United States." *Terrorism* 14, no. 3 (1991): 135-144.

Rubin, Barry, ed. *The Politics of Counterterrorism: The Ordeal of Democratic States.* Washington, D.C.: Johns Hopkins Foreign Policy Institute, 1990.

_____, ed. *Terrorism and Politics.* New York: St. Martin's Press, 1991.

Schmid, Alex P., and Ronald D. Crelinsten, eds. *Western Response to Terrorism.* London: Frank Cass, 1998.

Schultz, Richard H., and Stephen Sloan, eds. *Responding to the Terrorist Threat: Security and Crisis Management.* New York: Pergamon, 1980.

Shafer, D. Michael. "The Unlearned Lessons of Counterinsurgency." *Political Science Quarterly* 103, no. 1 (1988): 57-80.

Simon, Jeffrey D. RAND/R-3423-RC, *Misperceiving the Terrorist Threat.* Santa Monica, Calif.: RAND, 1987. 17 p.

_____. RAND/R-3840-C3I, *U.S. Countermeasures Against International Terrorism.* Santa Monica, Calif.: RAND, 1990.

Sloan, Stephen. "In Search of a Counterterrorism Doctrine." *Military Review* 66, no. 1 (June 1986): 44-48.

_____. "U.S. Anti-Terrorism Policies: Lessons to be Learned to Meet an

Enduring and Changing Threat." *Terrorism and Political Violence* 5, no. 1 (Spring 1993): 106-131.

_____. *Beating International Terrorism: An Action Strategy for Preemption and Punishment.* New edition with expanded introduction, Maxwell Air Force Base, Al.: Air University Press, April 2000.

_____. "Non-Territorial Terrorism: An Empirical Approach to Policy Formation." *Conflict: An International Journal for Conflict and Policy* 1 (1978): 131-144.

Smith, G. Davidson. *Combatting Terrorism.* London: Routledge, Chapman and Hall, 1990.

Soule, John W. "Problems in Applying Counterterrorism to Prevent Terrorism: Two Decades of Violence in Northern Ireland Reconsidered." *Terrorism* 12, no. 1 (1989): 31-46.

St. John, Peter. "Analysis and Response of a Decade of Terrorism." *International Perspectives* (September-October, 1981): 2-5.

Stoffa, Adam Paul. "Special Forces, Counterterrorism, and the Law of Armed Conflict." *Studies in Conflict and Terrorism* 18, no. 1 (January-March 1995): 47-66.

Stohl, Michael. "National Interests and State Terrorism in International Affairs." *Political Science* 36, no. 1 (1984): 37-52.

Thompson, Leroy. *The Rescuers: The World's Top Anti-Terrorist Units.* Trowbridge, Wiltshire: David and Charles, 1986.

Wagner-Pacifici, Robin. "Negotiation in the Aldo Moro Affair: The Suppressed Alternative in a Case of Symbolic Politics." *Politics and Society* 12, no. 4 (1983): 487-517.

Waugh, William L., Jr. *Terrorism and Emergency Management: Policy and Administration.* New York: Marcel Dekker, 1990.

Wilcox, Philip C., Jr. "The Western Alliance and the Challenge of Combatting Terrorism." *Terrorism and Political Violence* 9, no. 4 (Winter 1997): 1-7.

Wolf, John B. "Terrorist Manipulation of the Democratic Process." *Police Journal* (England) 48 (April-June 1975): 102-112.

Wright, Jeffrey W. "Terrorism: A Mode of Warfare." *Military Review* 64, no. 10 (1984): 35-45.

Zamir, Meir. "Iran: Consequences of the Abortive Attempt to Rescue the American Hostages." *Conflict* 3, no. 1 (1983): 55-77.

Terrorism and the Mass Media

Alexander, Yonah. "Terrorism, the Media and the Police." *Journal of International Affairs* 32, no. 1 (1978): 101-113.

Anderson, Terry. "Terrorism and Censorship: The Media in Chains." *Journal of International Affairs* 47 (Summer 1993): 127-136.

Bassiouni, M. Cherif. "Media Coverage of Terrorism: The Law and the Public." *Journal of Communication* 32, no. 2 (1982): 128-143.

Bremer, L. Paul, III. "Terrorism, the Media, and the Government." *Parameters: U.S. Army War College Quarterly* 18, no. 1 (1988): 52-59.

Clutterbuck, Richard. *The Media and Political Violence*. London: Macmillan, 1987.

Crelinsten, Ronald D. "Images of Terrorism in the Media." *Terrorism* 12, (1989): 167-198.

_____. "Television and Terrorism: Implications for Crisis Management and Policy-Making." *Terrorism and Political Violence* 9, no. 4 (Winter 1997): 8-32.

Dowling, Ralph E. "Terrorist Motivation: Media Coverage or Human Social Action?" *Conflict Quarterly* 9, no. 3 (Summer 1989): 41-53.

Farnen, Russell F. "Terrorism and the Mass Media: A Systemic Analysis of a Symbiotic Process." *Terrorism* 13, no. 2 (1990): 99-144.

Kelly, Michael J., and Mitchell, Thomas H., "Transnational Terrorism and the Western Elite Press." *Political Communication and Persuasion* 1. no. 3 (1981): 289-290.

Kingston, Shane. "Terrorism, the Media, and the Northern Ireland Conflict." *Studies in Conflict and Terrorism* 18, no. 3 (July-September 1995): 203-231.

Lumley, Bob, and Philip Schlesinger. "The Press, the State and Its Enemies: The Italian Case." *Sociological Review* (United Kingdom) 30, no. 4 (1982): 603-626.

Miller, Abraham H. "How the CIA Fell Victim to Myth Posing as Journalism." *International Journal of Intelligence and Counterintelligence* 10, no. 3 (Fall 1997): 257-268.

_____, ed. *Terrorism: The Media and the Law*. New York: Transnational, 1982.

Nacos, Brigitte, David P. Fan, and John T. Young. "Terrorism and the Print Media: The 1985 TWA Hostage Crisis." *Terrorism* 12, no. 2 (1989):

107-116.

Picard, Robert G. "The Maturation of Communication and Terrorism Studies (review article),. *Journal of Communication* 44 (Winter 1994): 122-127.

Picard, Robert G., and Rhonda S. Sheets. "Terrorism and the News Media: A Research Bibliography, Part III." *Political Communication and Persuasion* 4, no. 3 (1987): 217 et seq.

_____ and _____. "Terrorism and the News Media: A Research Bibliography, Part IV." *Political Communication and Persuasion* 4, no. 4 (1987): 325 et seq.

Rapoport, David C. "The Media and Terrorism: Implications of the Unabomber Case." *Terrorism and Political Violence* 8, no. 1 (Spring 1996): vii et seq.

Schmid, Alex P., and de Graaf, Janny, *Violence As Communication: Insurgent Terrorism and the Western News Media*. London and Beverly Hills, Calif.: Sage, 1982.

Tugwell, Maurice A. "Terrorism and Propaganda: Problem and Response." *Conflict Quarterly* 6, no. 2 (1986): 5-15.

Weimann, Gabriel. "Conceptualizing the Effects of Mass-Mediated Terrorism," *Political Communication and Persuasion*, 4, 3 (1987): 213-216.

Sociological Studies

Amir, Marianne, Zeev Kaplan, and Moshe Kotler. "Type of Trauma, Severity of Posttraumatic Stress Disorder Core Symptoms, and Associated Features." *Journal of General Psychology* 123 (October 1996): 341-351.

Barkun, Michael. *Religion and the Racist Right: The Origins of the Christian Identity Movement,* Chapel Hill: University of North Carolina Press, 1996.

_____, ed. *Millennialism and Violence*. London: Frank Cass, 1996.

Beeman, William O. "Terrorism: Community Based or State Supported." *American-Arab Affairs* 16 (Spring 1986): 1-8.

Bjørgo, Tore, ed. *Terror from the Extreme Right*. London: Frank Cass, 1995.

Crenshaw, Martha. "The Logic of Terrorism: Terrorist Behavior as a Product of Strategic Choice," in Walter Reich, ed. *Origins of Terrorism: Psy-*

chologies, Ideologies, Theologies, States of Mind. Cambridge, Mass.: Cambridge University Press, 1990. pp. 7-24.

Davis, Paul B. "American Experiences and the Contemporary Perception of Terrorism." *Small Wars and Insurgencies* 7, no. 2 (Autumn 1996): 220-242.

Elliott, Deni. "Family Ties: A Case Study of Coverage of Families and Friends During the Hijacking of TWA 847." *Political Communication and Persuasion* 5, no. 1 (1988): 67-76.

Ferracuti, Franco. "A Sociopsychiatric Interpretation of Terrorism." *Annals of the American Academy of Political and Social Science* 463 (September 1982): 129-140.

Georges-Abeyie, Daniel E. "Women as Terrorists," in Lawrence Freedman and Yonah Alexander, eds., *Perspective in Terrorism,* Wilmington, Del.: Scholarly Resources, 1983: 71-84.

_____. "Political Criminogenesis of Democracy in the Criminal Settler-State: Terror, Terrorism, and Guerrilla Warfare." *Terrorism* 14, no. 1 (1991): 145-156.

Ginges, Jeremy. "Deterring the Terrorist: A Psychological Evaluation of Different Strategies for Deterring Terrorism." *Terrorism and Political Violence* 9, no. 1 (Spring 1997): 170-185.

Hewitt, Christopher. "Terrorism and Public Opinion: A Five Country Comparison." *Terrorism and Political Violence* 2, no. 2 (Summer 1990): 145-170.

Hoffman, Bruce. "'Holy Terror': The Implications of Terrorism Motivated by a Religious Imperative: Islamic, Jewish, White Supremacist and Sikh Terrorists." *Studies in Conflict and Terrorism* 18, no. 4 (October-December 1995): 271-284.

Holden, Robert T. "The Contagiousness of Aircraft Hijacking." *American Journal of Sociology* 91, no. 4 (1986): 874-904.

Mason, T. David. "Nonelite Response to State-Sanctioned Terror." *Western Political Quarterly* 42, no. 4 (1989): 467-492.

Merkl, Peter H., and Leonard Weinberg, eds. *The Revival of Right Wing Extremism in the Nineties.* London: Frank Cass, 1996.

Oots, Kent Layne. "Organizational Perspectives on the Formation and Disintegration of Terrorist Groups." *Terrorism* 12, no. 3 (1989): 139-152.

Oots, Kent Layne, and Thomas C. Wiegele, "Terrorist and Victim: Psychiatric and Physiological Approaches from a Social Science Perspective." *Terrorism: An International Journal* 8, no. 1 (Winter 1985): 1-32.

Ranstorp, Magnus. "Terrorism in the Name of Religion." *Journal of Inter-*

national Affairs 50 (Summer 1996): 41-62.

Rapoport, David C. "Fear and Trembling in Three Religious Traditions." *American Political Science Review* 78, no. 3 (1984): 658-678.

_____. "Why Does Religious Messianism Produce Terror?" in Paul Wilkinson, ed. *Contemporary Research on Terrorism.* Aberdeen, Scotland: Aberdeen University Press, 1987. pp. 72-88.

_____. "Messianic Sanctions for Terror." *Comparative Politics* 20, no. 2 (1988): 195-214.

_____. "Sacred Terror: A Contemporary Example from Islam," in Walter Reich, ed. *Origins of Terrorism: Psychologies, Ideologies, Theologies, States of Mind.* Cambridge, Mass.: Cambridge University Press, 1990. pp. 103-130.

Sterntz, T. "A Terrorist Organizational Profile: A Psychological Role Model," In Yonah Alexander and John M. Gleason, eds., *Behavioral and Quantitative Perspectives on Terrorism.* New York: Pergamon, 1981.

Tabor, James D., and Eugene Gallagher, *Why Waco? Cults and the Battle for Religious Freedom in America.* Berkeley: University of California Press, 1995.

Tugwell, Maurice A. "Terrorism and Propaganda: Problem and Response." *Conflict Quarterly* 6, no. 2 (1986): 5-15.

Turk, Austin T. "Social Dynamics of Terrorism." *Annals of the American Academy of Political and Social Science* 463 (September 1982): 119-128.

Wasmund, Klaus. "The Political Socialization of Terrorist Groups in West Germany." *Journal of Political and Military Sociology* 11, no. 2 (1983): 223-239.

Weinberg, Leonard, ed. *Political Parties and Terrorist Groups.* London: Frank Cass, 1992.

Terrorism by Region

North America (Canada and the United States)

Aho, James A. *The Politics of Righteousness: Idaho Christian Patriotism.* Seattle: University of Washington Press, 1990.

Anti-Defamation League of B'nai B'rith. *Extremism on the Right.* New York: Anti-Defamation League of B'nai B'rith, 1983.

_____. Civil Rights Division. "Neo-Nazi Skinheads: A 1990 Status Report," *Terrorism,* 13, 3 (1990): 243-275.

_____. *ADL Special Report: The Militia Movement in America.* New York: Anti-Defamation League of B'nai B'rith, 1995.

Arostegui, Martin C. "Terrorism in the United States." *Clandestine Tactics and Technology: Group and Area Studies* 9, no. 2 (n.d.): 4.

Bell, Robert G. "The U.S. Response to Terrorism Against Civil Aviation." *Orbis* 19, no. 4 (1976): 1326-1343.

Center for Democratic Renewal. *Aryan Nations Far-Right Underground Movement.* Atlanta, Ga.: Center for Democratic Renewal, 1986.

Charters, David A. "The Amateur Revolutionaries: A Reassessment of the FLQ." *Terrorism and Political Violence* 9, no. 1 (Spring 1997): 133-169.

Clawson, Patrick. "Coping with Terrorism in the United States." *Orbis* 33, no. 3 (1989): 341-357.

Coates, James. *Armed and Dangerous: The Rise of the Survivalist Right.* New York: Hill and Wang, 1987.

Collins, J. G. "Terrorism and Animal Rights." *Science* 6 (1990): 4-5.

Corcoran, James. *Bitter Harvest: The Birth of Paramilitary Terrorism in the Heartland.* New York: Penguin, 1995.

Dees, Morris, with James Corcoran. *Gathering Storm: America's Militia Threat.* New York: HarperCollins, 1996.

Dennis, Stuart. "The Weathermen." *Government and Opposition* (United Kingdom) 9, no. 4 (1974): 430-459.

Dobratz, Betty A., and Stephanie L. Shanks-Meile. *White Power-White Pride: The White Separatist Movement in the United States.* New York: Twayne, 1997.

Dolgin, Janet L. *Jewish Identity and the JDL.* Princeton, N.J.: Princeton University Press, 1977.

Eagan, Sean P. "From Spikes to Bombs: The Rise of Eco-Terrorism." *Studies in Conflict and Terrorism* 19, no. 1 (January-March 1996): 1-18.

Flynn, Kevin, and Gary Gerhardt. *The Silent Brotherhood: Inside America's Racist Underground.* New York: The Free Press, 1989.

George, John, and Laird Wilcox. *American Extremists: Militias, Supremacists, Klansmen, Communists & Others.* Buffalo, N.Y.: Prometheus, 1996.

Gleason, John M. "A Poisson Model of Incidents of International Terrorism in the United States." *Terrorism* 4, nos. 1-4 (1980): 259-265.

Haider-Markel, Donald F., and Sean P. O'Brien. "Creating a 'Well-Regulated Militia': Policy Responses to Paramilitary Groups in the American States." *Political Research Quarterly* 50, no. 3 (September 1997): 531-565.

Harris, J. W., Jr. "Domestic Terrorism in the 1980s." *FBI Law Enforcement Bulletin* 56 (1987): 5-13.

Hoffman, Bruce. RAND/R-3351, *Terrorism in the United States and the Potential Threat to Nuclear Facilities.* Santa Monica, Calif.: RAND, 1986.

_____. RAND/R-3618, *Recent Trends and Future Prospects of Terrorism in the United States.* Santa Monica, Calif.: RAND, May 1988.

Holt, Simma. *Terrorism in the Name of God.* Toronto: McClelland and Stewart, 1964.

LaPonce, Jean, and William Safran, eds. "Special Issue: Ethnicity and Citizenship: The Canadian Case." *Nationalism and Ethnic Politics* 1, no. 3 (Autumn 1995).

Monroe, Charles P. "Addressing Terrorism in the United States." *Annals of the American Academy of Political and Social Science* 463 (September 1982): 141-148.

Monti, Daniel J. "The Relation Between Terrorism and Domestic Civil Disorders." *Terrorism* 4, nos. 1-4 (1980): 123-141.

Mullins, Wayman C. *Terrorist Organizations in the United States.* Springfield, Ill.: Charles C. Thomas, 1988.

New York State Policy Group on Terrorism. "Report on the Brinks Incident," *Terrorism* 9 (1987): 169-206.

Nice, David C. "Abortion Clinic Bombings as Political Violence." *American Journal of Political Science* 32 (February 1988): 178-195.

Ross, Jeffrey Ian. "Attributes of Domestic Political Terrorism in Canada." *Terrorism* 11 (1988): 213-233.

_____. "The Rise and Fall of Quebecois Separatist Terrorism: A Qualitative Application of Factors from Two Models." *Studies in Conflict and Terrorism* 18, no. 4 (October-December 1995): 285-97.

Ross, Jeffrey Ian, and Ted Robert Gurr. "Why Terrorism Subsides: A Comparative Study of Canada and the United States." *Comparative Politics* 21, no. 4 (1989): 405-426.

Stanton, Bill. *Klanwatch: Bringing the Ku Klux Klan to Justice.* New York: Grove Weidenfeld, 1991.

Stern, Kenneth. *A Force Upon the Plain: The American Militia Movement and the Politics of Hate.* New York: Simon and Schuster, 1994.

Stickney, Brandon. *"All-American Monster": The Unauthorized Biography of Timothy McVeigh.* New York: Prometheus, 1996.

Suall, Irwin, and David Lowe. "The Hate Movement Today: A Chronicle of Violence and Disarray." *Terrorism* 10, 4 (1987): 345-364.

Walter, Jess. *Every Knee Shall Bow : The Truth and Tragedy of Ruby Ridge and the Randy Weaver Family.* New York: HarperCollins, 1995.

Wilcox, Michele, and John Lynxwiler. "Abortion Clinic Violence as Terrorism." *Conflict* 8 (Summer 1988): 5-26.

Woodcock, George, and Ivan Avakumovic. *The Doukhobors.* Toronto: McClelland and Stewart, 1977.

Yerbury, J. C. "The 'Sons of Freedom' Doukhobors and the Canadian State." *Canadian Ethnic Studies* 16, No. 2 (1984): 47-70.

Young, Robert. "'Monkeywrenching' and the Processes of Democracy." *Environmental Politics* 4 (Winter 1995): 199-214.

Central and South America

Adams, James. "The Narc-Farc Connection," in *The Financing of Terror*, ed. James Adams. Sevenoaks, Kent: New English Library, 1986: 215-234.

Andreas, Peter, and Coletta Youngers. "'Busting' The Andean Cocaine Industry: America's Counterproductive War on Drugs." *World Policy Journal* 6, no. 3 (1989): 529-562.

Armony, Ariel C. "Argentina and the Origin of Nicaragua's Contras." *Low Intensity Conflict & Law Enforcement* 2, no. 3 (1993): 434-459.

Asencio, Diego, Nancy Asencio, and Ron Tobias. *Our Man Is Inside.* Boston: Little and Brown, 1983.

Bagley, Bruce Michael. "Colombia and the War on Drugs." *Foreign Affairs* 67, no. 1 (1988): 70-92.

Baratta, Robert Thomas. "Political Violence in Ecuador and the AVC." *Terrorism* 10, no. 3 (1987). 165-174.

Black, George. *Garrison Guatemala.* New York: Monthly Review, 1984.

Blake, Samuel W. "Totalitarianism in Sandinista Nicaragua." *Studies in Conflict and Terrorism* 15, no. 3 (1992): 201-224.

Booth, John A. "Guatemalan Nightmare: Levels of Political Violence." *Journal of Interamerican Studies and World Affairs* 22, no. 2 (1980): 195-

225.

Browning, David. "Conflicts in El Salvador." *Conflict Studies* 168 (1984).

Buckman, Robert T. "The Cali Cartel: An Undefeated Enemy." *Low Intensity Conflict & Law Enforcement* 3, no. 3 (1994): 430-452.

Corr, Edwin G., and Courtney E. Prisk. "El Salvador: The FMLN Insurgency and the Prospects for Democracy and Peace," in Edwin G. Corr and Stephen Sloan eds., *Low Intensity Conflict: Old Threats in a New World*. Boulder, Colo.: Westview, 1992. pp. 223-253.

Demarest, Geoffrey B. "Redefining the School of the Americas." *Military Review* 74, no. 10 (October 1994): 43-51.

Dickey, Christopher. "Behind the Death Squads: Who They Are, How They Work, and Why No One Can Stop Them." *The New Republic* 189, (December 26, 1983): 16-21.

Falcoff, Mark. *Modern Chile: 1970-1989: A Critical History*. New Brunswick, N.J.: Transaction, 1989.

Filippone, Robert. "The Medellin Cartel: Why We Can't Win the Drug War." *Studies in Conflict and Terrorism* 17, no. 4 (October-December 1994): 323-344.

Fishel, John T. "Coca, Cocaine, Sicarios, and Senderistas." *Low Intensity Conflict & Law Enforcement* 3, no. 1 (1994): 31-45.

Fontaine, Roger W. *Terrorism: The Cuban Connections*. New York: Crane Russak, 1988.

Frankland, Erich G. "Under the Gun in El Salvador: The Evolving Relationship Between the Military and Democracy." *Low Intensity Conflict & Law Enforcement* 3, no. 1 (1994): 104-135.

Garabedian, John H. "A Narrative Account of the Capture of Abimael Guzman Based on Press Reporting." *Low Intensity Conflict & Law Enforcement* 2, no. 2 (1993): 370 et seq.

Gillespie, Richard. *Soldiers of Peron: Argentina's Montoneros*. Oxford; Clarendon Press, 1982.

Guevara, Ernesto Che. *Guerrilla Warfare*. [1960] Translated by J. P. Morray. Lincoln: University of Nebraska Press, 1985.

Halperin, Ernst. *Terrorism in Latin America*. The Washington Papers, No. 33. Beverly Hills, Calif.: Sage, 1976.

Ierardi, Anthony R., and E. Casey Wardynski. "The Zapatista Rebellion in Chiapas." *Military Review* 74, no. 10 (October 1994): 64-75.

Janke, Peter. "Terrorism in Argentina." *Journal of the Royal United Services Institute for Defence Studies* (United Kingdom) 119, no. 3 (1974): 43-48.

Johnson, Kenneth F. "On the Guatemalan Political Violence." *Politics and Society* 4, no. 1 (1973): 55-82.

Klette, Immanuel J. "U.S. Assistance to Venezuela and Chile in Combatting Insurgency, 1963-1964: Two Cases." *Conflict* 3, no. 4 (1982): 227-244.

Krigsman, Henry Axel, Jr. "Che's Bolivian Expedition: A Case of Revolutionary Failure." *Low Intensity Conflict & Law Enforcement* 6, no. 1 (1997): 53-76.

Lefever, Ernest W. "Murder in Montevideo: The AID/Mitrione Story." *Freedom At Issue* 21 (1973): 14-16.

Livingston, Neil C. "Death Squads." *World Affairs* 146, no. 3 (1983-1984): 239-248.

Livingston, Susan Morrisey. "Terrorism: 'The Original Cheap Shot': An Interview with Ambassador Diego Asencio." *World Affairs* 146, 1 (1983): 42-53.

Manwaring, Max G. "National Security Implications of Drug Trafficking for the USA and Colombia." *Small Wars and Insurgencies* 5, no. 3 (Winter 1994): 379-408.

_____. "Latin American Security and Civil-Military Relations in the New World Disorder." *Low Intensity Conflict & Law Enforcement* 4, no. 1 (1995): 29-43.

Marchak, Patricia. *God's Assassins: State Terrorism in Argentina in the 1970s.* Montreal: McGill-Queen's University, 1999.

Marighella, Carlos. *Manual of the Urban Guerrilla,* translated by Gene Z. Hanrahan. Chapel Hill, N.C.: Documentary, 1985.

Mason, T. David, and Dale A. Krane. "The Political Economy of Death Squads: Toward a Theory of the Impact of State-Sanctioned Terror." *International Studies Quarterly* 33, no. 2 (1989): 175-198.

Maullin, Richard L. *Soldiers, Guerrillas, and Politics in Colombia.* Lexington, Mass.: Lexington, 1973.

McCormick, Gordon H. *The Shining Path and the Future of Peru,* RAND/R-3781-DOS/OSD. Santa Monica, Calif.: RAND, 1990.

Nolan, David. *The Ideology of the Sandinistas and the Nicaraguan Revolution.* Coral Gables: Institute of Interamerican Studies, University of Florida Press, 1984.

d'Oliveira, Sergio L. "Uruguay and the Tupamaro Myth." *Military Review* 53, no. 4 (1973): 25-36.

Palmer, David Scott. "Rebellion in Rural Peru: The Origins and Evolution of Sendero Luminoso." *Comparative Politics* 18, no. 2 (January 1986):

558   Bibliography

127-146.

_____. "Latin America in the 1990s: New Opportunities and New Challenges." *Small Wars and Insurgencies* 7, no. 1 (Spring 1996): 65-78.

Pardo-Maurer, Rogelio. *The Contras, 1980-1989: A Special Kind of Politics.* The Washington Papers, No. 147. New York: Praeger, 1990.

Petras, James. "The Anatomy of State Terror: Chile, El Salvador, and Brazil." *Science and Society* 51, 3no. (1987): 314-338.

Phillips, Dion E. "Terrorism and Security in the Caribbean: The 1976 Air Cubana Disaster Off Barbados." *Terrorism* 14, no. 4 (1991): 209-220.

Pinheiro, Alvaro de Souza. "Guerrillas in the Brazilian Amazon." *Military Review* 76, no. 2 (March-April 1996): 38-55.

Porzecanski, Arturo L. *Uruguay's Tupamaros: The Urban Guerrilla.* New York: Praeger, 1973.

Radu, Michael S. "Terror, Terrorism, and Insurgency in Latin America." *Orbis* 28, no. 1 (Spring 1984): 27-40.

Ramsey, Russell W. "The Urban Guerrilla in Latin America: A Select Bibliography." *Latin American Research Review* 8, no. 1, (1973): 3-44.

Rensselaer, Lee, III. "Dimensions of the South American Cocaine Industry." *Journal of InterAmerican Studies and World Affairs* 30 (Summer/Fall 1988): 87-104.

Ronfeldt, David, John Arquilla, Graham E. Fuller, and Melissa Fuller. *The Zapatista Social Netwar in Mexico.* Santa Monica, Calif.: RAND, 1998.

Rosenau, William. "Is the Shining Path the 'New Khmer Rouge'?" *Studies in Conflict and Terrorism* 17, no. 4 (October 1994): 305-322.

Russell, Charles A., James A. Miller, and Robert E. Hildner. "The Urban Guerrilla in Latin America: A Select Bibliography." *Latin American Research Review* 9, no. 1, (1974): 37-80.

Sater, William. *The Revolutionary Left and Terrorist Violence in Chile,* RAND/ N-2490-AF. Santa Monica, Calif.: RAND, 1986.

Sereseres, Caesar. "Guatemala: A Country Response Without Outside Help," in Edwin G. Corr and Stephen Sloan, eds. *Low Intensity Conflict: Old Threats in a New World.* Boulder, Colo.: Westview, 1992. pp. 101-123.

Simpson, John, and Jana Bennett. *The Disappeared and the Mothers of the Plaza: The Story of the 11,000 Argentinians Who Vanished.* New York: St. Martin's Press, 1985.

Steinitz, Mark S. "Insurgents, Terrorists, and the Drug Trade." *Washington Quarterly* 8, no. 4 (1985): 141-153.

Tarazona-Sevillano, Gabriela, with John B. Reuter. *Sendero Luminoso and the Threat of Narcoterrorism.* The Washington Papers, No. 144. New

York: Praeger, 1990.

Taylor, Robert W., and Harry E. Vanden. "Defining Terrorism in El Salvador: 'La Matanza'." *Annals of the American Academy of Political and Social Science* 463 (September 1982): 106-118.

Turbville, Graham H. "Mexico's Other Insurgents." *Military Review* 77, no. 3 (May-June 1997): 81-90.

Turner, Robert F. "The CIA's Nicaragua 'Murder Manual': A Sandinista 'Dirty Trick?'." *International Journal of Intelligence and Counterintelligence* 9, no. 1 (Spring 1996): 33-42.

Wardlaw, Grant. "Linkages Between the Illegal Drugs Traffic and Terrorism." *Conflict Quarterly* 8, no. 3 (Summer 1988).

British Isles and Europe

Alexander, Yonah and Alan O'Day, eds. *Terrorism in Ireland.* New York: St. Martin's, 1984.

Alexander, Yonah, and Dennis A. Pluchinsky, eds. *European Terrorism: Today and Tomorrow.* Brassey's Terrorism Library. Washington, D.C.: Brassey's, 1992.

_____ and _____, eds. *Europe's Red Terrorists: The Fighting Communist Organizations.* London: Frank Cass, 1992.

Anderson, James H. "The Neo-Nazi Menace in Germany." *Studies in Conflict and Terrorism* 18, no. 1 (January-March 1995): 39-46.

Aston, Clive C. "Political Hostage Taking in Western Europe." *Conflict Studies* 157 (1984).

Bahry, Donna, and Brian D. Silver. "Intimidation and the Symbolic Uses of Terror in the USSR." *American Political Science Review* 81, no. 4 (1987): 1065-1098.

Baldy, Tom F. *Battle for Ulster.* Washington, D.C.: National Defense University, 1987.

Bell, J. Bowyer. "The Escalation of Insurgency: The Provisional Irish Republican Army's Experience, 1969-71." *Review of Politics* 35, no. 3 (1973): 398-411.

_____. "Dragonworld (II): Deception, Tradecraft, and the Provisional IRA." *International Journal of Intelligence and Counterintelligence* 8, no. 1 (Spring 1995): 21-50.

_____. "The Irish Republican Army Enters an Endgame: An Overview." *Studies in Conflict and Terrorism* 18, no. 3 (July-September 1995): 153-174.

_____. "Ireland: The Long End Game," *Studies in Conflict and Terrorism.* 21, no. 1 (January-March 1998): 5-28.

_____. *The IRA 1968-2000.* London: Frank Cass, 2000.

Billig, Michael, and Raymond Cochrane. "The National Front and Youth." *Patterns of Prejudice* 15, no. 4 (1981): 3-15.

Birch, Julian. "Ethnic Cleansing in the Caucasus." *Nationalism and Ethnic Politics* 1, no. 4 (Winter 1995).

Blagg, James A. "European Terrorism: Down, But Not Out." *Military Review* 75, no. 1 (February 1995): 15-19.

Bruce, Steve. "Paramilitaries, Peace, and Politics: Ulster Loyalists and the 1994 Truce." *Studies in Conflict and Terrorism* 18, no. 3 (July-September 1995): 187-202.

Catanzaro, Raimondo. *The Red Brigades and Left-Wing Terrorism in Italy.* New York: St. Martin's, 1991.

Clutterbuck, Richard. "Terrorism and the Security Forces in Europe." *Army Quarterly and Defence Journal* 111, no. 1 (1981): 12-29.

Collins, J. G. "Terrorism and Animal Rights." *Science* 249, no. 4967 (1990): 345.

Corsun, Andrew. "Group Profile: The Revolutionary Organization 17 November in Greece." *Terrorism* 14, no. 2 (1991): 77-104.

Davis, Thomas C. "Patterns of Identity: Basques and the Basque Nation." *Nationalism and Ethnic Politics* 3, no. 1 (Spring 1997).

Dillon, Martin, *God and the Gun: The Church and Irish Terrorism.* London: Routledge, 1998.

Drake, Richard. *The Revolutionary Mystique and Terrorism in Contemporary Italy.* Bloomington: Indiana University, 1989.

Dunn, Seamus, and Valerie Morgan. "Protestant Alienation in Northern Ireland." *Studies in Conflict and Terrorism* 18, no. 3 (July-September 1995): 175-185.

Enders, Walter, and Todd Sandler. "Causality Between Transnational Terrorism and Tourism: The Case of Spain." *Terrorism* 14, no. 1 (1991): 49-58.

_____ and _____. "Terrorism and Foreign Direct Investment in Spain and Greece,. *Kyklos* 49, no. 3 (1996): 331-352.

Evans, Ernest, "The U.S. Peace Initiative in Northern Ireland: A Comparative Analysis." *European Security* 7, no. 2 (1998): 63-77.

Great Britain. Parliament. "Report of the Commission of Inquiry into Police Interrogation Procedures in Northern Ireland." (Mr. Justice Bennett). Cmnd. 7477. London: H.M.S.O., 1979.

Great Britain. Parliament. "Report of the Commission to Consider Legal Procedures to Deal with Terrorist Actions in Northern Ireland." (Lord Diplock). Cmnd. 5185. London: H.M.S.O. , 1972.

Gregory, F. E. C. "Police Cooperation and Integration in the European Community: Proposals, Problems and Prospects." *Terrorism* 14, no. 3 (1991): 145-156.

Henze, Paul. *The Plot to Kill the Pope*. New York: Charles Scribner's Sons, 1985.

Hoffman, Bruce. "Right-Wing Terrorism in Europe." *Orbis* 28, no. 1 (Spring 1984): 16-26.

_____. "Is Europe Soft on Terrorism?" *Foreign Policy* 115 (Summer 1999): 62-76 .

Horchem, Hans J. "Terrorism in West Germany." *Conflict Studies* 186 (April 1986): 1-20.

Horgan, John, and Max Taylor. "The Provisional Irish Republican Army: Command and Functional Structure." *Terrorism and Political Violence* 9, no. 3 (Autumn 1997): 1-32.

Jamieson, Alison. "Political Kidnapping in Italy." *Conflict* 8, no. 1 (1988): 41-48.

_____. *The Heart Attacked: Terrorism and Conflict in the Italian State*. London: Marion Boyars, 1989.

Jenkins, Philip. "The Assassination of Olof Palme: Evidence and Ideology." *Contemporary Crises* 13, no. 1 (1989): 15-33.

Kelley, Kevin J. *The Longest War: Northern Ireland and the IRA*. Westport, Conn.: Lawrence Hill, 1988.

Khatami, Siamak. "Between Class and Nation: Ideology and Radical Basque Ethnonationalism." *Studies in Conflict and Terrorism* 20, no. 4 (October-December 1997): 395-418.

Lamb, Christina. "ETA's Latest Atrocity Threw All Spain into Anguish. Even in the Heart of the Basque Region There are Signs of a Yearning for Peace." *New Statesman* (London) 126 (July 25, 1997): 15.

Lee, Alfred McClung. *Terrorism in Northern Ireland*. Bayside, N.Y.: General Hall, 1988.

Lee, Martin A. "Hitler's Offspring." *The Progressive* March 1993: 28-31.

Lloyd, John. "Interview with David Trimble." *New Statesman* (London) 27, No. 4400 (August 28, 1998): 10-11.

Meade, Robert C., Jr. *Red Brigades: The Story of Italian Terrorism*. New York: St. Martin's, 1990.

Merkl, Peter H. "Rollerball or Neo-Nazi Violence," in Peter H. Merkl ed. *Political Violence and Terror: Motifs and Motivations*. Berkeley: University of California Press, 1986. pp. 229-255.

Moss, David. "The Kidnapping and Murder of Aldo Moro." *European Journal of Sociology* (United Kingdom) 22, no. 2 (1981): 265-295.

Moxon-Brown, Edward P. "The Water and the Fish: Public Opinion and the Provisional IRA in Northern Ireland." *Terrorism* 5, nos. 1-2 (1981): 41-72.

_____. "Alienation: The Case of the Catholics in Northern Ireland." *Journal of Political Science* 14, nos. 1-2 (1986): 74 et seq.

_____. "Spain and the ETA: The Bid for Basque Autonomy." *Conflict Studies* 201 (1987).

Neuman, Saul, and Scott Piroth. "Terror and Tolerance: The Use of Ballots, Bombs, and Bullets by Ethnoregional Movements in Advanced Industrial Democracies." *Nationalism and Ethnic Politics* 2, no. 3 (Autumn 1996).

O'Ballance, Edgar. "IRA Leadership Problems." *Terrorism* 5, nos. 1-2 (1981): 73-82.

Pisano, Vittorfranco S. "Genesis, Rise, and Decline of Italian Terrorism." *Conflict* 10, no. 3 (1990): 227-238.

Pluchinsky, Dennis. "Middle Eastern Terrorist Activity in Western Europe: A Diagnosis and Prognosis." *Conflict Quarterly* 6, no. 3 (Summer 1986): 40-52.

_____. "Germany's Red Army Faction: An Obituary." *Studies in Conflict and Terrorism* 16, no. 2 (April-June 1993): 135-157.

_____. "Terrorism in the Former Soviet Union: A Primer, a Puzzle, a Prognosis." *Studies in Conflict and Terrorism* 21, no. 2 (April-June 1998): 119-147.

Raufer, Xavier. "The Red Brigades: Farewell to Arms." *Studies in Conflict and Terrorism* 16, no. 4 (October-December 1993): 241-262.

Reinares, Fernando. "Nationalism and Violence in Basque Politics." *Conflict* 8, nos. 2-3 (1988): 141-155.

Robertson, Ken. "Terrorism: Europe Without Borders." *Terrorism* 14, nos. 2 (1991): 105-110.

Robertson, Myles. "Internal Security: Terrorism, Government, Business, and the European Trends." *Low Intensity Conflict & Law Enforcement* 4, no. 1 (1995): 89-105.

Salvioni, Daniela, and Anders Stephanson. "Reflections on the Red Brigades." *Orbis* 29, no. 3 (1985): 489-506.

Scherer, John L. "The Plot to Kill the Pope." *Terrorism* 7 (1985): 351-366.

Schiller, David T. "Germany's Other Terrorists." *Terrorism* 9 (1987): 87-99.

Silke, Andrew. "In Defense of the Realm: Financing Loyalist Terrorism in Northern Ireland—Part One: Extortion and Blackmail." *Studies in Conflict and Terrorism* 21, no. 4 (October-December 1998): 331-361.

Smith, G. Davidson. "Political Violence in Animal Liberation." *Contemporary Review* 247, no. 1434 (1985): 26-31.

Solomon, Gerald B. H., and Robert M. Jenkins. "The Impact of EC 1992 on Terrorism and Drug Trafficking in Europe: U.S. Concerns." *Terrorism* 13, no. 1 (1990): 15-22.

Sterling, Claire. "Italian Terrorists: Life and Death in a Violent Generation." *Encounter* (United Kingdom) 57, no. 1 (1981): 18-31.

Sutton, Malcolm. *Bear in Mind The Dead: An Index of Deaths from the Conflict in Ireland 1969-1993.* Belfast: Beyond the Pale Publications, 1994.

Taylor, Peter. *Behind the Mask: The IRA and Sinn Fein.* New York: TV Books, 1997.

Tugwell, Maurice A. "Politics and Propaganda of the Provisional IRA." *Terrorism* 5, nos. 1-2 (1981): 13-40.

Turbville, Graham H., Jr. "The Chechen Ethno-Religious Conflict, Terrorism, and Crime." *Military Review* 74, no. 3 (March 1994): 19-22.

Weinberg, Leonard, and William Lee Eubank. "Change and Continuity in the Recruitment of Italian Political Terrorists." *Journal of Political Science* 14, nos. 1-2 (1986): 43-57.

White, Timothy J. "The Law, the State, and Republicanism in Ireland." *Journal of Social, Political and Economic Studies* 22 (Winter 1997): 417-432.

Wright, Joanne. *Terrorist Propaganda: The Red Army Faction and the Provisional IRA, 1968-86.* New York: St. Martin's, 1990.

Middle East (North Africa and Southwest Asia)

Abrahamian, Ervand. *The Iranian Mojahedin.* New Haven, Conn.: Yale University Press, 1989.

564   Bibliography

Ajami, Fouad. *The Vanished Imam: Musa al Sadr and the Shi'a of Lebanon.* Ithaca, N.Y.: Cornell University Press, 1986.

Akhavi, Shahrough. "Post-Khomeini Iran: Global and Regional Implications." *SAIS Review,* 10, 1no. (1990): 149-162.

Alexander, Yonah. "Middle Eastern Fundamentalism and Terrorism: Interdisciplinary Perspectives." *Terrorism,* 11, no. 5 (1988): 345.

Ali, Yasser Hammad al-Hassan. "Killing Collaborators: A Hamas How-To." [Videotape Transcript] *Harper's Magazine* May 1993: 10-13.

Alianak, Sonia L. "Religion, Politics, and Assassination in the Middle East: the Messianic Model following Rapoport's Model of 'Holy Terror'." *World Affairs* (Washington, D.C.), 160 (Winter 1998): 163-175.

Anderson, Sean K. "Iranian State-Sponsored Terrorism,. *Conflict Quarterly* 11, no. 4 (1991): 19-34.

_____. "Warnings Versus Alarms: Terrorist Threat Analysis Applied to the Iranian State-Run Media." *Studies in Conflict and Terrorism* 21 (Fall 1998): 277-303.

Anti-Defamation League of B'nai B'rith. *ADL Special Background Report: Hamas, Islamic Jihad, and the Muslim Brotherhood: Islamic Extremists and the Terrorist Threat to America.* New York: ADL, 1993.

Asaf, Hussain. *Political Terrorism and the State in the Middle East.* London: Mansell, 1985.

Bahgat, Gawdat. "Iran and Terrorism: The Transatlantic Responses,. *Studies in Conflict and Terrorism* 22, no. 2 (April-June 1999): 141-152.

Beres, Louis René. "The Iranian Threat to Israel: Capabilities and Intentions." *International Journal of Intelligence and Counterintelligence* 9, no. 1 (Spring 1996): 51-62.

_____. "Israel, the 'Peace Process,' and Nuclear Terrorism: Recognizing the Linkages." *Studies in Conflict and Terrorism* 21, no. 1 (January-March 1998): 59-86.

Bernstein, Alvin H. "Iran's Low-Intensity War Against the United States." *Orbis* 30, no. 1 (1986): 149-167.

Bouchat, Clarence J. "A Fundamentalist Islamic Threat to the West." *Studies in Conflict and Terrorism* 19, no. 4 (October-December 1996): 339-352.

Brown, James. "The Turkish Imbroglio: Its Kurds." *Annals of the American Academy of Political and Social Science* 541 (September 1995): 116-129.

Brynen, Rex. *Sanctuary and Survival: The PLO Lesson in Lebanon.* Boulder, Colo.: Westview, 1990.

Burgess, William H., III. "Iranian Special Operations in the Iran-Iraq War: Implications for the United States." *Conflict* 8, no. 1 (1988): 22-40.

Button, Stephen H. "Turkey Struggles with Kurdish Separatism." *Military Review* 75, no. 1 (February 1995): 70-83.

Chasidi, Richard J. *Serenade of Suffering: A Portrait of Middle East Suffering, 1968-1993.* Lanham, Md.: Lexington, 1999.

Cline, Lawrence E. "Egyptian and Algerian Insurgencies: A Comparison." *Small Wars and Insurgencies* 9, no. 2 (Autumn 1998): 114-133.

Cobban, Helena. "Relationships Between Palestinians Inside and Outside." *American-Arab Affairs*, 31 (Winter 1989-90): 38-41.

Criss, Nur Bilge. "The Nature of PKK Terrorism in Turkey." *Studies in Conflict and Terrorism* 18, no. 1 (January-March 1995): 17-37.

Cubert, Harold M. *The PFLP's Changing Role in the Middle East.* London: Frank Cass, 1997.

Deeb, Marius. *Militant Islamic Movements in Lebanon: Origins, Social Basis, and Ideology.* Washington, D.C.: Center for Contemporary Arab Studies, Georgetown University, 1986. (Occasional Papers Series).

Don-Yehiya, Eliezer. "Jewish Messianism, Religious Zionism, and Israeli Politics: The Impact and Origins of Gush Emunim." *Middle Eastern Studies* 23, no. 2 (1987): 215-234.

Duran, Khaled. "The Second Battle of Algiers." *Orbis* 33, no. 3 (1989): 403-422.

Emerson, Steven and Brian Duffy. *The Fall of Pan Am 103: Inside the Lockerbie Investigation.* New York: G.P. Putnam's Sons, 1990.

Ferdows, Amir H. "Khomaini and Fadayan's Society and Politics." *International Journal of Middle East Studies* 15, no. 2 (May 1983): 241-258.

Fisk, Robert. *Pity the Nation:: The Abduction of Lebanon.* New York: Simon and Schuster, 1990.

Frankland, Erich G. "A New Nationalism for a New World Order? The Kurds,. *Small Wars and Insurgencies* 6, no. 2 (Autumn 1995): 183-208.

Frisch, Hillel. "The PLO and the Arabs in Israel, 1967-93: Politicization or Radicalization?" *Nationalism and Ethnic Politics* 2, no. 3 (Autumn 1996).

Garfincle, Adam M. "Sources of the Al-Fatah Mutiny." *Orbis* 27, no. 3 (1983): 603-640.

Gawrych, George W. "Jihad in the 20th Century." *Military Review* 75, no. 5 (October 1995): 33-39.

Goldberg, Giora. "Haganah, Irgun and 'Stern': Who Did What?" *Jerusalem Quarterly* 25 (1982): 116-120.

Green, Jerrold D. "Countermobilization as a Revolutionary Form." *Comparative Politics* 16, no. 2 (1984): 153-170.

Gunter, Michael. "Cycles of Terrorism: The Question of Contemporary Turkish Counterterror and Harassment Against the Armenians." *Journal of Political Science* 14, nos. 1-2 (1986): 58-73.

_____. "Contemporary Armenian Terrorism." *Terrorism* 8 (1986): 213-253.

_____. *The Kurds in Turkey: A Political Dilemma,* Boulder, Colo.: Westview, 1990.

Gutteridge, William ed. "Libya: Still a Threat to Western Interests?" *Conflict Studies* 160 (1984).

Hajjar, Sami. "Political Violence in Islam: Fundamentalism and Jihad." *Small Wars and Insurgencies* 6, no. 3 (Winter 1995): 328-356.

Hamden, Raymond H. "The Psychological Aspects of IsTishShad: Suicide or Sacrifice?" Paper presented before the U.S. Senate Anti-Terrorism Caucus on 26 March 1986, from Yonah Alexander, ed., *Terrorism: An International Resource File, 1986,* Microfiche Collection No. T-354.

al Hassan, Khaled. "The PLO and the Intifada." *American-Arab Affairs* 31 (Winter 1989-1990): 42-48.

Hof, Frederic C. "The Beirut Bombing of October 1983: An Act of Terrorism?" *Parameters: Journal of the US Army War College* 15, no. 2 (1985): 69-74.

Hoffman, Bruce. Rand/P-7116 *Shi'a Terrorism: The Conflict in Lebanon and the Hijacking of TWA Flight 847.* Santa Monica:, Calif. RAND, 1985.

_____. RAND/R-3783-USDP, *Recent Trends and Future Prospects of Iranian Sponsored International Terrorism.* Santa Monica, Calif.: RAND, 1990.

Hunter, F. Robert. *The Palestinian Intifada: A War by Other Means.* Berkeley: University of California Press, 1991.

Hunter, Shireen. "Islamic Fundamentalism: What It Really Is and Why It Frightens the West." *SAIS Review* 6, no. 1 (1986): 189-200.

Hyland, Francis P. *Armenian Terrorism: The Past, the Present, the Prospects.* Boulder, Colo.: Westview, 1991.

Israeli, Raphael. "The Charter of Allah: The Platform of the Islamic Resistance Movement," in Yonah Alexander and A. H. Foxman, eds. *The 1988-89 Annual on Terrorism.*Zoetermeer: Martinus Nijhoff, 1990. pp. 99-134.

Jansen, Johannes J. G. *The Neglected Duty: The Creed of Sadat's Assassins and Islamic Resurgence in the Middle East.* New York: Macmillan,

1986.

Jenkins, Philip. "Whose Terrorists? Libya and State Criminality." *Contemporary Crises* 12, no. 1 (1987): 5-24.

Kash, Douglas. "Libyan Involvement and Legal Obligations in Connection with the Bombing of Pan Am Flight 103." *Studies in Conflict and Terrorism* 17, no. 1 (January-March 1994): 23-38.

Katzman, Kenneth. *The Warriors of Islam: Iran's Revolutionary Guard.* Boulder, Colo.: Westview, 1993.

Khalidi, Rashid. *Under Siege: PLO Decision-Making During the 1982 War.* New York: Columbia University, 1986.

Kibble, David G. "Understanding Islamic Fundamentalism." *Military Review* 75, no. 5 (October 1995): 40-45.

_____. "The Threat of Militant Islam," *Studies in Conflict and Terrorism.* 19, no. 4 (October-December 1996): 353-364.

Klein, Menachem. "Competing Brothers: The Web of Hamas-PLO Relations." *Terrorism and Political Violence* 8, no. 2 (Summer 1996): 111-132.

Kostiner, Joseph. "The Rise and Fall of Militant Opposition Movements in the Arabian Peninsula," in Anat Kurz, ed., *Contemporary Trends in World Terrorism.* New York: Praeger, 1987. pp. 43-52.

Kramer, Martin. "The Structure of Shi'ite Terrorism," in Anat Kurz, ed., *Contemporary Trends in World Terrorism.* New York: Praeger, 1987. pp. 43-52.

_____. "The Moral Logic of Hizballah," in Walter Reich, ed. *Origins of Terrorism: Psychologies, Ideologies, Theologies, States of Mind.* Cambridge, Mass.: Cambridge University Press, 1990. pp. 131-157.

Kuriyama, Yoshihiro. "Terrorism at Tel Aviv Airport and A 'New Left' Group in Japan." *Asian Survey* 13, no. 3 (1973): 336-346.

Kurz, Anat, and Ariel Merari. *ASALA: Irrational Terror or Political Tool?* Boulder, Colo.: Westview, 1985.

Kushner, Harvey W. "Suicide Bombers: Business as Usual." *Studies in Conflict and Terrorism* 19, no. 4 (October-December 1996): 329-337.

Le Vine, Victor T., and Barbara L. Salert. "Does a Coercive Official Response Deter Terrorism? The Case of the PLO." *Terrorism and Political Violence* 8, no. 1 (Spring 1996): 22-49.

Lewis, Bernard. "License to Kill: Usama bin Ladin's Declaration of Jihad." *Foreign Affairs* 77, no. 6 (November-December 1998): 14-19.

Litvak, Meir. "Palestinian Nationalism and Islam: The Case of Hamas." *Nationalism and Ethnic Politics* 2, no. 4 (Winter 1996).

Lustick, Ian S. "Israel's Dangerous Fundamentalists." *Foreign Policy* 68 (Fall 1987): 118-139.

Media Analysis Center. "The Covenant of the Islamic Resistance Movement (Hamas)." Jerusalem: Media Analysis Center, 1988. 12 p. (Mideast Backgrounds, 251.) Also in Yonah Alexander ed., *Terrorism: An International Resource File*, 1988, microfiche T-831.

Merari, Ariel. "The Readiness to Kill and Die: Suicidal Terrorism in the Middle East," in W. Reich, ed. *Origins of Terrorism*. Cambridge, Mass.: Cambridge University Press, 1990. pp. 192-210.

Metz, Steven. "The Ideology of Terrorist Foreign Policies in Libya and South Africa." *Conflict* 7, no. 4 (1987): 379-402.

Muslih, Muhammad Y. "Moderates and Rejectionists Within the Palestine Liberation Organization." *Middle East Journal* 2 (1976): 127-140.

Norton, Augustus R. *Amal and the Shi'a: Struggle for the Soul of Lebanon*. Austin: University of Texas Press, 1987.

Norton, Graham. "The Terrorist and the Traveller: A Gulf Aftermath Assessment." *World Today* 47, no. 5 (1991): 80-82.

O'Neill, Bard E. "Towards A Typology of Political Terrorism: The Palestinian Resistance Movement." *Journal of International Affairs* 32, no. 1 (1978): 17-42.

Orlow, Dietrich. "Political Violence in Pre-Coup Turkey." *Terrorism* 6, no. 1 (1982): 53-71.

Peleg, Samuel. "They Shoot Prime Ministers Too, Don't They? Religious Violence in Israel: Premises, Dynamics, and Prospects." *Studies in Conflict and Terrorism* 20, no. 3 (July-September 1997): 227-247.

Peretz, Don. "Intifadeh: The Palestinian Uprising." *Foreign Affairs* 66 (Summer 1988): 964-980.

Pipes, Daniel. "The Scourge of Suicide Terrorism." *The National Interest* 4 (Summer 1986): 95-99.

_____. "Why Asad's Terror Works and Qadhdhafi's Does Not." *Orbis* 33, no. 4 (1989): 501-508.

Pluchinsky, Dennis. "Middle Eastern Terrorist Activity in Western Europe: A Diagnosis and Prognosis." *Conflict Quarterly* 6, no. 3 (Summer 1986): 40-52.

Quester, George. "Some Explanations for State-Supported Terrorism in the Middle East," in Michael Stohl and George A. Lopez, eds. *Terrible Beyond Endurance?: The Foreign Policy of State Terrorism*. New York: Greenwood Press, 1988. pp. 223-246.

Ranstorp, Magnus. *Hizb'Allah in Lebanon: The Politics of the Western*

Hostage Crisis. New York: St. Martin's, 1997.

_____. "Interpreting the Broader Context and Meaning of Bin-Laden's Fatwa." *Studies in Conflict and Terrorism* 21, no. 4 (October-December 1998): 321-330.

Rapoport, David C. "Fear and Trembling in Three Religious Traditions." *American Political Science Review* 78, no. 3 (1984): 658-678.

_____. "Messianic Sanctions for Terror." *Comparative Politics* 20, no. 2 (1988): 195-214.

_____. "Sacred Terror: A Contemporary Example From Islam," in Walter Reich, ed. *Origins of Terrorism: Psychologies, Ideologies, Theologies, States of Mind.* Cambridge, Mass.: Cambridge University Press, 1990. pp. 103-30.

Renzi, A.E. "Arafat and the PLO: Government or Gangsters?" *Low Intensity Conflict & Law Enforcement* 5, no. 2 (1996): 194-205.

Rubin, Barry. "The Political Uses of Terrorism in the Middle East," in Barry Rubin, ed. *The Politics of Terrorism: Terror as a State and Revolutionary Strategy.* Lanham, Md.: University Press of America, 1989. pp. 27-66.

_____. *Revolution Until Victory? The Politics and History of the PLO.* Cambridge, Mass.: Harvard University Press, 1994.

Satloff, Robert. "Islam in the Palestinian Uprising." *Orbis* 33, no. 3 (1989): 389-402.

Schahgaldian, Nikola. RAND/R-3473, *The Iranian Military Under The Islamic Republic.* Santa Monica, Calif.: RAND, March 1987.

_____. RAND/R-3788-USDP, *The Clerical Establishment in Iran.* Santa Monica, Calif.: RAND, 1989. 140 p.

Schbley, Ayla H. "Resurgent Religious Terrorism: A Study of Some of the Lebanese Shi'a and Contemporary Terrorism." *Terrorism* 12, no. 4 (1989): 213-248.

_____. "Religious Terrorists: What They Aren't Going to Tell Us." *Terrorism* 13, no. 3 (1990): 237-242.

Schechterman, Bernard, and Bradford R. McGuinn. "Linkages Between Sunni and Shi'i Radical Fundamentalist Organizations: A New Variable in Recent Middle Eastern Politics?" *The Political Chronicle* 1, no. 1 (1989).

Schweitzer, Yoram. "Terrorism: A Weapon in the Shi'ite Arsenal," in Anat Kurz, ed., *Contemporary Trends in World Terrorism.* New York: Praeger, 1987. pp. 43-52.

Seale, Patrick. *Abu Nidal: A Gun for Hire.* New York: Random House, 1992.

Shadid, Mohammad K. "The Muslim Brotherhood Movement in the West Bank and Gaza." *Third World Quarterly* April 1988.

Shapira, Shimon. "The Origins of Hizballah." *The Jerusalem Quarterly* 46 (Spring 1988): 115-130.

Sick, Gary. "Iran's Quest for Superpower Status." *Foreign Affairs* 65, no. 4 (1987): 697-715.

Sivan, Emmanuel. "Sunni Radicalism in the Middle East." *International Journal of Middle East Studies* 21, no. 1 (1989): 1-30.

St. John, Peter. "Algeria: A Case Study of Insurgency in the New World Order." *Small Wars and Insurgencies* 7, no. 2 (Autumn 1996): 196-219.

St. John, Ronald Bruce. "Terrorism and Libyan Foreign Policy, 1981-1986." *World Today* 42, no. 7 (July 1984): 111-114.

Taheri, Amir. *The Spirit of Allah: Khomeini and the Islamic Revolution.* Bethesda, Md.: Adler and Adler, 1986.

_____. *Holy Terror: Inside the World of Islamic Terrorism,* Bethesda, Md.: Adler and Adler, 1987.

_____. *Nest of Spies: America's Journey to Disaster in Iran.* New York: Pantheon, 1988.

Terrill, W. Andrew. "Saddam's Failed Counterstrike: Terrorism and the Gulf War." *Studies in Conflict and Terrorism* 16, no. 3 (July-September 1993): 219-232.

Wallach, Janet, and John Wallach. *Arafat: In the Eyes of the Beholder* New York: Lyle Stuart/Carol, 1990.

Wege, Carl Anthony. "The Abu Nidal Organization." *Terrorism* 14, no. 1 (1991): 59 et seq.

_____. "Hizbullah Organization." *Studies in Conflict and Terrorism* 17, no. 2 (April-June 1994): 151-164.

_____. "Iranian Intelligence Organizations." *International Journal of Intelligence and Counterintelligence* 10, no. 3 (Fall 1997): 287-298.

Wright, Robin. *Sacred Rage: The Wrath of Militant Islam.* New York: Simon & Schuster, 1986.

_____. "The Islamic Resurgence: A New Phase?" *Current History* 87, no. 526 (1988): 53-56, 85-86.

_____. *In the Name of God: The Khomeini Decade.* New York: Simon & Schuster, 1989.

_____. "Islam's New Political Face." *Current History* 90, no. 552 (1991): 25-28.

Yishai, Yael. "The Jewish Terror Organization: Past or Future Danger?" *Conflict* 6, no. 4 (1986): 306-332.

Zanini, Michele. "Middle Eastern Terrorism and Netwar." *Studies in Conflict and Terrorism* 22, no. 3 (July-September 1999): 247-257.

Southern and Eastern Asia and Pacific

Akbar, M. J. *India: The Siege Within: Challenges to a Nation's Unity.* Bungay, Suffolk: Penguin, 1985.

Austen, Dennis, and Anirudha Gupta. "Lions and Tigers: The Crisis in Sri Lanka." *Conflict Studies* 211 (1988): 1-19.

Bermudez, Joseph S., Jr. *Terrorism: The North Korean Connection.* New York: Crane Russak, 1990.

Bose, Ajoy. "Blast from the Past: The Assassination of Punjab's Chief Minister Resurrects the Spectre of Sikh-Separatist Terrorism and Puts Prime Minister Rao on the Defensive." *Far Eastern Economic Review* 158 (September 14, 1995): 16-17.

Chalk, Peter. "Political Terrorism in South-East Asia." *Terrorism and Political Violence* 10, no. 2 (Summer 1998): 118-134.

Dale, Stephen Frederic. "Religious Suicide in Islamic Asia: Anticolonial Terrorism in India, Indonesia, and the Philippines." *Journal of Conflict Resolution* 32, no. 1 (1988): 37-60.

Farrell, William R. *Blood and Rage: The Story of the Japanese Red Army.* Lexington, Mass.: Lexington, 1990.

George, T. J. S. *Revolt in Mindanao: The Rise of Islam in Philippine Politics.* Kuala Lumpur: Oxford University Press, 1980.

Grewal, J. S. *The New Cambridge History of India* (II.3) *The Sikhs of the Punjab.* Cambridge, Mass.: Cambridge University Press, 1990.

Holtzappel, Coen. "The 30 September Movement: A Political Movement of the Armed Forces or an Intelligence Operation?" *Journal of Contemporary Asia* (Sweden) 9, no. 2 (1979): 216-240.

Jeffrey, Robin. *What's Happening to India? Punjab, Ethnic Conflict, Mrs. Gandhi's Death and the Test for Federalism.* New York: Holmes and Meier, 1986.

Joshi, Manoj. "On the Razor's Edge: The Liberation Tigers of Tamil Eelam." *Studies in Conflict and Terrorism* 19, no. 1 (January-March 1996): 19-42.

Kaplan, David E., and Andrew Marshall. *The Cult at the End of the World: The Incredible Story of Aum.* London: Hutchinson, 1996.

Kim, Jae Taik. "North Korean Terrorism: Trends, Characteristics and Deterrence." *Terrorism* 11 (1988): 309-322.

Kuriyama, Yoshihiro. "Terrorism at Tel Aviv Airport and A 'New Left' Group in Japan." *Asian Survey* 13, no. 3 (1973): 336-346.

Lifton, Robert Jay. *Destroying the World to Save It: Aum Shinrikyo, Apocalyptic Violence and the New Global Terrorism.* New York: H. Holt, 1999.

Metraux, Daniel A. "Religious Terrorism in Japan: The Fatal Appeal of Aum Shinrikyo." *Asian Survey* 35 (December 1995): 1140-1154.

Nagarajan, K. V. "Troubled Paradise: Ethnic Conflict in Sri Lanka." *Conflict* 6, no. 4 (1986): 333-354.

Nandi, Proshanta K. "Socio-Political Context of Sikh Militancy in India." *Journal of Asian and African Studies* 31 (December 1996): 178-190.

Noble, Pela Garner. "The Philippines: Autonomy for the Muslims," in John L. Esposito, ed., *Islam in Asia: Religion, Politics and Society.* New York: Oxford University Press, 1987.

Oberst, Robert C. "Sri Lanka's Tamil Tigers." *Conflict* 8, nos. 2-3 (1988): 185-202.

Rashid, Ahmed. "Playing Dirty: Taliban Try to Starve Hazaras into Submission." *Far Eastern Economic Review.* 160 (November 27, 1997): 26-28.

Reddy, N. Subba. "Crisis of Confidence among the Tribal People and the Naxalite Movement in Srikakulam District." *Human Organization* 36, no. 2 (1977): 142-149.

Schultz, Richard. "The Limits of Terrorism in Insurgency Warfare: The Case of the Viet Cong." *Polity* 11, no. 1 (1978): 67-91.

Smith, Charles. "Ignorance Isn't Bliss: After Gas Attack, Intelligence-Gathering Questioned." *Far Eastern Economic Review* 158 (June 8, 1995): 22.

Steinhoff, Patricia G. "Portrait of a Terrorist: An Interview with Kozo Okamoto." *Asian Survey* 16, no. 9 (1976): 830-845.

Tanham, George K. RAND/N-3040-USDP, *New Caledonia: The Fragile Peace.* Santa Monica, Calif.: RAND, June 1990.

Unnithan, N. Prabha. "Explaining Collective Violence in India: Social Cleavages and Their Consequences." *Studies in Conflict and Terrorism* 18, no. 2 (April-June 1995): 93-110.

Watanabe, Manabu. "Religion and Violence in Japan Today: A Chronological and Doctrinal Analysis of Aum Shinrikyo." *Terrorism and Political Violence* 10, no. 4 (Winter 1998): 80-100.

Weatherbee, Donald E. "Communist Revolutionary Violence in the ASEAN States." *Asian Affairs: An American Review* 10, no. 3 (1983): 1-17.

Wickramanayake, D. "Harijan Terror in India." *Plural Societies* (Netherlands) 6, no. 3 (1975): 17-20.

Wijesekera, Daya. "The Liberation Tigers of Tamil Eelam: The Asian Mafia." *Low Intensity Conflict & Law Enforcement* 2, no. 2 (1993): 308-317.

_____. "The Cult of Suicide and the Liberation Tigers of Tamil Eelam." *Low Intensity Conflict & Law Enforcement* 5, no. 1 (1996): 18-28.

Yaeger, Carl H. "Sikh Terrorism in the Struggle for Khalistan." *Terrorism* 14, 4 (1991): 221-232.

Zasloff, Joseph J. "Materials on Massacre of Korean Officials in Rangoon." *Korea and World Affairs* (South Korea) 7, no. 4 (1983): 735-764.

Sub-Saharan Africa

Alao, Abiodun. "A Comparative Evaluation of the Armed Struggle in Namibia, South Africa and Zimbabwe." *Terrorism and Political Violence* 8, no. 4 (Winter 1996): 58-77.

Alden, Chris. "Political Violence in Mozambique,. *Terrorism and Political Violence* 8, no. 4 (Winter 1996): 40-57.

Arnold, S. L. "Somalia: An Operation Other Than War." *Military Review* 73, 12 (December 1993): 26-35.

Clifford-Vaughan, F. M. "Terrorism and Insurgency in South Africa." *Journal of Social, Political and Economic Studies* 12, no. 2 (1987): 259-276.

Frankland, Erich G., and Tammy Noble. "A Case of National Liberation with Feminist Undertones: The Secession of Eritrea." *Small Wars and Insurgencies* 7, no. 3 (Winter 1996): 401-424.

Friedland, Elaine A. "South Africa and Instability in Southern Africa." *Annals of the American Academy of Political and Social Science* 463 (September 1982): 95-105.

Gutteridge, William, and J. E. Spence. "Violence in Southern Africa." *Terrorism and Political Violence* 8, no. 4 (Winter 1996): 1-10.

_____ and _____. *Violence in Southern Africa*. Portland, Oreg.: Frank Cass, 1997.

Hills, A. E. "Low Intensity Conflict and Law Enforcement in Sub-Saharan Africa." *Low Intensity Conflict & Law Enforcement* 5, no. 1 (1996): 1-17.

Hills, Alice. "Warlords, Militia and Conflict in Contemporary Africa: A Re-Examination of Terms." *Small Wars and Insurgencies* 8, no. 1 (Spring 1997): 35-51.

Johnston, Alexander. "Politics and Violence in KwaZulz-Natal." *Terrorism and Political Violence* 8, no. 4 (Winter 1996): 78-107.

Metz, Steven. "The Ideology of Terrorist Foreign Policies in Libya and South Africa." *Conflict* 7, no. 4 (1987): 379-402.

Nimer, Benjamin. "Terrorism and Southern Africa." *Terrorism* 13, no. 6 (1990): 447-454.

Rich, Raul. "Insurgency, Terrorism and the Apartheid System in South Africa." *Political Studies* (United Kingdom) 32, no. 1 (1984): 68-85.

Selected U.S. Government Documents

International Terrorism

U.S. Congress, House Committee on International Relations, Subcommittee on International Operations and Human Rights. *Attempts by Rogue Regimes to Influence U.S. Policy:* Hearing before the Subcommittee on International Operations and Human Rights of the Committee on International Relations, House of Representatives, One Hundred Fourth Congress, second session, March 19, 1996. Washington, D.C.: U.S. G.P.O, 1996. Y 4.IN 8/16: R 26

U.S. Congress, House Committee on the Judiciary, Subcommittee on Crime. *Extraterritorial Jurisdiction over Terrorist Acts Abroad:* Hearings before the Subcommittee on Crime of the Committee on the Judiciary, House of Representatives, One Hundred First Congress, first session, May 31, June 13, and July 13, 1989. Washington, D.C.: U.S. G.P.O.,

1990. Y 4.J 89/1: 101-67

U.S. Congress, House of Representatives, House Permanent Select Committee on Intelligence. *Resolution of Inquiry Concerning Terrorist Bombings in Beirut, Lebanon*, by U.S. House of Representatives, 99th Congress, 1st session. Washington, D.C.: U.S. G.P.O., 1985. Y 1.1/8: 99-171

U.S. Congress, House Committee on International Relations, Subcommittee on Africa. *Terrorism in Algeria: Its Effect on the Country's Political Scenario, on Regional Stability, and on Global Security:* Hearing before the Subcommittee on Africa of the Committee on International Relations, House of Representatives, One Hundred Fourth Congress, first session, October 11, 1995. Washington, D.C.: U.S. G.P.O., 1996. Y 4.IN 8/16: AL 3

U.S. Congress, House Committee on International Relations, House of Representatives, One Hundred Fourth Congress, first session, September 28, 1995. *Terrorism in Latin America: The AMIA Bombing in Argentina.* Washington, D.C.: U.S. G.P.O., Y 4.IN 8/16:L 34

U.S. Congress, House Committee on National Security. *Terrorist Attack Against United States Military Forces in Dhahran, Saudi Arabia*: Hearing held September 18,1996 by Committee on National Security, House of Representatives, One Hundred Fourth Congress, second session. Washington, D.C.: U.S. G.P.O., 1997. Y 4.SE 2/1 A: 995-96/ 43

U.S. Congress, Senate Committee on Foreign Relations. *International Terrorism, Insurgency, and Drug Trafficking: Present Trends in Terrorist Activity*: joint hearings before the Committee on Foreign Relations and the Committee on the Judiciary, United States Senate, Ninety-ninth Congress, first session, May 13, 14, and 15, 1985. Washington, D.C.: U.S. G.P.O., 1986. Y 4.F 76/2: S.hrg.99-372

U.S. Congress, Senate Committee on Foreign Relations, Subcommittee on African Affairs, One Hundred Fifth Congress, first session, September 25, 1997. *Religious Persecution in Sudan*: Hearing before the Subcommittee on African Affairs of the Committee on Foreign Relations, United States Senate. Washington, D.C.: U.S. G.P.O, 1997. Y 4.F 76/ 2:S.HRG.105-280

Congressional Research Service. *International Terrorism: A Compilation of Major Laws, Treaties, Agreements, and Executive Documents.* Washington, D.C.: U.S. Government Printing Office, July 1991.

U.S. Department of State. *The Hawari Group.* Washington, D.C.: U.S. Department of State, Office of the Ambassador-at-Large for Counter-Terrorism, October 31, 1988, 3 p. Also in Yonah Alexander ed., *Terrorism: An International Resource File*, microfiche T-786.

U.S. Department of State, Bureau of Public Affairs, Office of Public Communication, Editorial Division. *International Terrorism: U.S. Policy on Taking Americans Hostage.* Public information series. 1986 S 1.71/ 5: In 8

U.S. Department of State, Coordinator of Public Diplomacy for Latin America and the Caribbean. *Inside the Sandinista Regime: A Special Investigator's Perspective.* Washington, D.C.: Government Printing Office, 1986.

U.S. Department of State, Coordinator of Public Diplomacy for Latin America and the Caribbean. *"The 72-Hour Document": The Sandinista Blueprint For Constructing Communism in Nicaragua.* Washington, D.C.: Government Printing Office, 1986.

U.S. President, William J. Clinton. *Declaration of a National Emergency with Respect to the Middle East Peace Process:* Message from the President of the United States transmitting his declaration of a national emergency with respect to the grave acts of violence committed by foreign terrorists that threaten to disrupt the Middle East peace process, pursuant to 50 U.S.C. 1703(b). House document referred to the Committee on International Relations, 104th Congress, 1st session; 104-23. Washington, D.C.: U.S. G.P.O., 1993. Y 1.1/7: 104-23

U.S. President, Ronald Reagan. *The New Network of Terrorist States.* United States Department of State, Bureau of Public Affairs. Current policy no. 721. S 1.71/4: 721

Domestic Terrorism

U.S. Congress, House Committee on the Judiciary, Subcommittee on Crime and Criminal Justice. *Clinic Blockades*: Hearing before the Subcommittee on Crime and Criminal Justice of the Committee on the Judiciary, One Hundred Second Congress, second session, May 6, 1992. Washington, D.C.: U.S. G.P.O., 1993. Y 4.J 89/1: 102/79

U.S. Congress, House Committee on the Judiciary, Subcommittee on Civil and Constitutional Rights. *Domestic Security Measures Relating to Terrorism:* Hearings before the Subcommittee on Civil and Constitutional Rights of the Committee on the Judiciary, House of Representatives, Ninety-eighth Congress, second session, February 8 and 9, 1984. Washington, D.C.: U.S. G.P.O., 1984. Y 4.J 89/1: 98/51

U.S. Congress, House Committee on the Judiciary, Subcommittee on Civil and Constitutional Rights. *Federal Capabilities in Crisis Management and Terrorism:* Hearings before the Subcommittee on Civil and Constitutional Rights of the Committee on the Judiciary, House of Representatives, Ninety-fifth Congress, second session, hearings held Aug. 16–Oct. 4, 1978. Washington, D.C.: U.S. G.P.O., 1978. Y 4.J 89/1: 95/77

U.S. Congress, House Committee on Post Office and Civil Service. Subcommittee on Postal Operations and Services. *The Use of Mail to Send Bombs:* Hearing before the Subcommittee on Postal Operations and Services of the Committee on Post Office and Civil Service, House of Representatives, One Hundred Third Congress, second session, March 22, 1993. Washington, D.C.: U.S. G.P.O., 1994. Y 4.P 84/10: 103-38

U.S. Congress, House Committee on Transportation and Infrastructure, Subcommittee on Public Buildings and Economic Development. *Federal Building Security:* Hearing before the Subcommittee on Public Buildings and Economic Development of the Committee on Transportation and Infrastructure, House of Representatives, One Hundred Fourth Congress, second session, April 4–May 24, 1996. Washington: U.S. G.P.O., 1997. Y 4.T 68/2: 104-70

U.S. Congress, Senate Committee on the Judiciary, Subcommittee on Terrorism, Technology, and Government Information. *The Federal Raid on Ruby Ridge, Idaho*: Hearings before the Subcommittee on Terrorism, Technology, and Government Information of the Committee on the Judiciary, United States Senate, One Hundred Fourth Congress, first session. Sept. 6-8, 12, 14-15, 19-22, 26; and Oct. 13, 18-19, 1995. Washington, D.C.: U.S. G.P.O., 1997. Y 4.J 89/2:S. HRG.104-799.

U.S. Congress, Senate Committee on the Judiciary, Subcommittee on Terrorism, Technology, and Government Information. *The Militia Movement in the United States:* Hearing before the Subcommittee on Terrorism, Technology, and Government Information of the Committee on the Judiciary, United States Senate, One Hundred Fourth Congress, first session, June 15, 1995. Washington, D.C.: U.S. G.P.O.: 1997. Y 4.J 89/2:S. HRG.104-804

U.S. Congress, Senate Committee on Appropriations, Subcommittee on Commerce, Justice, State, the Judiciary, and Related Agencies. *Supple-*

mental Appropriations Relating to the Oklahoma City Bombing for Fiscal Year 1995: Hearing before a subcommittee of the Committee on Appropriations, United States Senate, One Hundred Fourth Congress, first session: special hearing. Washington, D.C.: U.S. G.P.O., 1996. Y 4.AP 6/2: S.HRG.104-304

U.S. Congress, Senate Committee on the Judiciary, Subcommittee on Immigration and Refugee Affairs. *Terrorism, Asylum Issues, and U.S. Immigration Policy:* Hearing before the Subcommittee on Juvenile Justice of the Committee on the Judiciary, United States Senate, One Hundred Third Congress, first session, on S. 667: An Amendment to the Immigration and Nationality Act to Improve Procedures for the Exclusion of Aliens to Enter the United States by Fraud, May 28, 1993. Washington, D.C.: U.S. G.P.O.:1994. Y 4.J 89/2:S.HRG.103-595

U.S. Congress, Senate Committee on the Judiciary, Subcommittee on Government Operations, Technology, and Terrorism: *The Weather Underground,* Report of the Subcommittee to Investigate the Administration of the Internal Security Act and Other Internal Security Laws: Ninety-fourth Congress, first session. Washington, D.C.: U.S. G.P.O., 1975. Y 4.J 89/2:S.W37

U.S. Department of Justice, Law Assistance Administration. *Disorders and Terrorism:* Report of the Task Force on Disorders and Terrorism. Washington, D.C.: Government Printing Office, 1976.

U.S. Department of Justice, United States Marshals Service. *Vulnerability Assessment of Federal Facilities.* Washington, D.C.: The Service, 1995. J 25.2: V 97

Weapons of Mass Destruction

Libicki, Martin C. *The Next Enemy.* Washington, D.C.: National Defense University, Institute for National Strategic Studies, 1995. D 5.417: 35

Motley, James B. *US Strategy to Counter Domestic Political Terrorism.* Washington, D.C.: National Defense University; Superintendent of Documents, U.S. G.P.O., distributor, 1983. D 5.409: 83-2

Seminar on Responding to the Consequences of Chemical and Biological Terrorism. *Proceedings of the Seminar on Responding to the Consequences of Chemical and Biological Terrorism: July 11-14, 1995,* conducted at the Uniformed Services University of the Health Sciences, 4301 Jones Bridge Road, Bethesda, Md., sponsored by the U.S. Public Health Service, Office of Emergency Preparedness. Bethesda, Md.: The Office, 1996. HE 20.2: C 42/2

U.S. Congress, House Committee on Interior and Insular Affairs, Subcommittee on General Oversight and Investigations. *Threat of Sabotage and Terrorism to Commercial Nuclear Powerplants:* Oversight hearing before the Subcommittee on General Oversight and Investigations of the Committee on Interior and Insular Affairs, House of Representatives, One Hundredth Congress, second session, hearing held in Washington, D.C., March 9, 1988. Washington, D.C.: U.S. G.P.O., 1988. Y 4.In 8/14: 100-43

U.S. Congress, House Committee on National Security, Subcommittee on Military Research and Development. *The Federal Response to Domestic Terrorism Involving Weapons of Mass Destruction and the Status of the Department of Defense Support Program:* Hearing before the Military Research and Development Subcommittee of the Committee on National Security, House of Representatives, One Hundred Fifth Congress, first session: hearing held, November 4, 1997. Washington, D.C.: U.S. G.P.O., 1998. Y 4.SE 2/1 A:997-98/21

U.S. Congress, Senate Committee on Foreign Relations, Subcommittee on European Affairs. *Loose Nukes, Nuclear Smuggling, and the Fissile-Material Problem in Russia and the Newly Independent States:* Hearings before the Subcommittee on European Affairs of the Committee on Foreign Relations, United States Senate, One Hundred Fourth Congress, first session, Aug. 22-23, 1995. Washington, D.C.: U.S. G.P.O., 1995. Y 4.F 76/2: S.HRG.104-253

U.S. Public Law 101-298. *Biological Weapons Anti-Terrorism Act of 1989:* An Act to Implement the Convention on the Prohibition of the Development, Production, and Stockpiling of Bacteriological (Biological) and Toxin Weapons and Their Destruction, by Prohibiting Certain Conduct Relating to Biological Weapons, and for Other Purposes. Washington, D.C.: U.S. G.P.O., 1990. AE 2.110: 101-298

U.S. General Accounting Office. *Domestic Terrorism: Prevention Efforts in Selected Federal Courts and Mass Transit Systems:* Report to the chairman, Subcommittee on Civil and Constitutional Rights, Committee on the Judiciary, House of Representatives by the United States General Accounting Office. Washington, D.C.: The Office, 1988. GA 1.13: PEMD-88- 22

State-Sponsored Terrorism

Erickson, Richard J. *Legitimate Use of Military Force Against State-Sponsored International Terrorism.* Maxwell Air Force Base, Ala.: Air University; Washington, D.C.: U.S. G.P.O., 1989. D 301.26/6: T 27/3

U.S. Congress, House Committee on Foreign Affairs, Subcommittee on International Security, International Organizations, and Human Rights. *U.S. Security Policy Toward Rogue Regimes:* Hearings before the Subcommittee on International Security, International Organizations, and Human Rights of the Committee on Foreign Affairs, House of Representatives, One Hundred Third Congress, first session, July 28 and September 14, 1993. Washington, D.C.: U.S. G.P.O., 1994. Y 4.F 76/1: SE 2/23

U.S. Congress, House Committee on Foreign Affairs, Subcommittee on Human Rights and International Organizations. Political Killings by Governments of Their Citizens: Hearings before the Subcommittee on Human Rights and International Organizations of the Committee on Foreign Affairs, House of Representatives, Ninety-eighth Congress, first session, November 16 and 17, 1983. Washington, D.C.: U.S. G.P.O., 1984. Y 4.F 76/1: P 75/9

U.S. Congress, Senate Committee on Armed Services. *State-Sponsored Terrorism:* Hearing before the Committee on Armed Services, United States Senate, Ninety-ninth Congress, second session, January 28, 1986. Washington, D.C.: U.S. G.P.O., 1986. Y 4.Ar 5/3: S.hrg.99-795

U.S. Congressional Research Service. *State-Sponsored Terrorism*: Report prepared for the Subcommittee on Security and Terrorism for the use of the Committee on the Judiciary, United States Senate, 99th Congress, 1st session. Washington, D.C.: U.S. G.P.O., 1985. Y 4.J 89/2: S.prt.99-56

Counterterrorism

Boston, Guy D. *Terrorism: A Selected Bibliography,* by Guy D. Boston, Marvin Marcus, Robert J. Wheaton. Washington, D.C.: U.S. Department of Justice, Law Enforcement Assistance Administration, National

Institute of Law Enforcement and Criminal Justice, National Criminal Justice Reference Service: U.S. G.P.O., 1976. J 1.20/2: T 27

Bremer, Paul L., 3rd. *Counterterrorism, Strategy and Tactics.* Washington, D.C. : U.S. Dept. of State, Bureau of Public Affairs, Office of Public Communication, Editorial Division, 1987. TD 8.2: C 27

Fultz, Keith O. *Aviation Security: Urgent Issues Need to be Addressed: Statement of Keith O. Fultz, Assistant Comptroller General, Resources, Community, and Economic Development Division, before the Subcommittee on Aviation, Committee on Transportation and Infrastructure, House of Representatives on behalf of United States General Accounting Office on September 11, 1996. Washington, D.C. : The Office, Gaithersburg, Md. (P.O. Box 6015, Gaithersburg 20884-6015) 1996. GA 1.5/2: T-RCED/ NSIAD-96- 251 [microform]

General Accounting Office. *Combatting Terrorism: Federal Agencies' Efforts to Implement National Policy and Strategy.* General Accounting Office, GAO/NSIAD-97-254. Washington, D.C.: September, 1997.

International Assembly on Emergency Medical Services (1st, 1982: Baltimore, Md.). *Mass Casualties, A Lessons Learned Approach: Accidents, Civil Disorders, Natural Disasters, Terrorism,* by R. Adams Cowley, editor, associate editors, Sol Edelstein, Martin Silverstein. Washington, D.C.: U.S. Dept. of Transportation, National Highway Traffic Safety Administration, 1982. DOT HS 806 302

Sloan, Stephen. *Beating International Terrorism: An Action Strategy for Preemption and Punishment.* Maxwell A.F.B., Ala.: Air University Press; Washington, D.C.: U.S. G.P.O., 1986. D 301.26/6:T 27/2

U.S. Congress. "Act for the Prevention and Punishment of the Crime of Hostage Taking and Aircraft Sabotage," *International Legal Materials,* 24, 6 (1985): 1551-1552.

U.S. Department of Justice, Office of Justice Programs, National Institute of Justice. *State and Local Responses to Terrorism.* Washington, D.C.: U.S. Department of Justice, Office of Justice Programs, National Institute of Justice, 1995. J 28.32: T 27

U.S. Department of State, Bureau of Diplomatic Security. *Rewards Program for Terrorism Information.* Washington, D.C.: U.S. Dept. of State, Bureau of Diplomatic Security, 1993. S 1.2: R 32

U.S. Vice President's Task Force on Combatting Terrorism. (VP's Commission Report). *Public Report of the Vice President's Task Force on Combatting Terrorism.* Washington, D.C.: The Task Force, U.S. G.P.O., 1986. PrVp 40.2: T 27

Victims of Terrorism

U.S. Congress, House Committee on the Judiciary. *Amendment to Make a Technical Correction to Title 28, United States Code, Relating to Jurisdiction for Lawsuits Against Terrorist States:* Report (to accompany H.R. 1225, including cost estimate of the Congressional Budget Office), Report of 105th Congress, 1st session, House of Representatives; 105-48. Washington, D.C.: U.S. G.P.O., 1997. Y 1.1/8: 105-48

U.S. Congress. House Committee on Post Office and Civil Service. *Victims of Terrorism Compensation Act:* Report to accompany H.R. 2851, referred jointly to the Committee on Foreign Affairs and the Committee on Post Office and Civil Service including cost estimate of the Congressional Budget Office, 99th Congress, 1st session, House of Representatives; 99-201, parts 1-2. Washington, D.C.: U.S. G.P.O., 1985. Y 1.1/8: 99-201/ pt.1-2

U.S. Congress, Senate Committee on Foreign Relations. *International Convention Against the Taking of Hostages,* Report (to accompany Ex. N, 96-2). Washington, D.C. : U.S. G.P.O., 1981. Y 1.1/6: 97-17

U.S. President William J. Clinton. *Requests for Emergency Fiscal Year 1995 Supplemental Appropriations: Communication from the President of the United States Transmitting His Request to Make Available Emergency Appropriations Totaling $142 Million to Address Urgent Needs Arising from the Bombing of the Alfred P. Murrah Federal Building in Oklahoma City:* Balanced Budget and Emergency Deficit Control Act of 1985, as amended, pursuant to 31 U.S.C. 1107. Washington, D.C.: U.S. G.P.O., 1995. Y 1.1/7: 104-62

U.S. Public Law 104-132. *Antiterrorism and Effective Death Penalty Act of 1996: An Act to Deter Terrorism, Provide Justice for Victims, Provide for an Effective Death Penalty, and for other Purposes.* Washington, D.C.: U.S. G.P.O., 1996. AE 2.110: 104-132

Terrorist Profiles

U.S. Department of Defense. *Terrorist Group Profiles.* Washington, D.C.

[Dept. of Defense]: U.S. G.P.O., 1988: D 1.2: T 27

U.S. Department of State. *Patterns of Global Terrorism,* U.S. Government Printing Office, published annually and ontains an appendix with profiles of currently active international terrorist groups.

Selected Internet Resources

Public Internet Web Sites

Air University, Maxwell Air Force Base, "Terrorist and Insurgent Organizations", containing bibliographies and periodicals citations on all major terrorist or insurgent groups. <http://www.au.af.mil/au/aul/bibs/tergps/tg98tc.htm> [Accessed 13 November 2001].

U.S. Department of Defense, Countering Terrorism and Protecting Our Forces Homepage. Information about the Department of Defense's efforts to fight terrorism at home and abroad.<http://www.defenselink.mil/other_info/terrorism.html> [Accessed 13 November 2001].

Domestic Preparedness Homepage: Enhancing the Capabilities of Federal, State, and Local Emergency Responders. Site maintained by interagency task-force comprising FBI, Department of Defense, Department of Energy, Environmental Protection Agency, FBI, Federal Emergency Management Agency, and the Public Health Service, as well as state and local partners to enable first-responders and communities to deal with conventional and unconventional terrorist threats and attacks. <http://dp.sbccom.army.mil/> [Accessed 13 November 2001].due to the transition of the Domestic Preparedness program to DOJ. For current information on similar products and services, please visit the Homeland Defense website at <http://hld.sbccom.army.mil/> [Accessed 13 November 2001].

Federal Emergency Management Agency: Backgrounder and Fact Sheet on Terrorism. <http://www.fema.gov/old97/terror.html>[Accessed 13 November 2001]..

U.S. Department of Justice, Federal Bureau of Investigation (FBI) Homepage. <http://www.fbi.gov/> [Accessed 13 November 2001].

U.S. Department of Justice, Federal Bureau of Investigation (FBI) "Terrorism in the United States Report" for 1995. <http://www.fbi.gov/publications/terror/terroris.htm> [Accessed 13 November 2001].

U.S. Department of Justice, FBI Library, containing 1995, 1996, and 1997 Reports of "Terrorism in the United States". (PDF Format) <http://www.fbi.gov/publications/terror/terroris.htm> [Accessed 13 November 2001].

Naval Postgraduate School, Dudley Knox Library, Terrorist Group Profiles <http://web.nps.navy.mil/~library/tgp/tgpmain.htm> [Accessed 13 November 2001].

U.S. Department of State, Bureau of Diplomatic Security: Counter-Terrorism Rewards Program, "HEROES" Homepage. <http://www.dssrewards.net/english/background.html> [Accessed 13 November 2001]

U.S. Department of State: Office of the Co-Ordinator for Counter-terrorism. Official statements, fact sheets and speeches. <http://www.state.gov/www/global/terrorism/index.html> [Accessed 13 November 2001].

U.S. Department of State: "Patterns of Global Terrorism" Reports (Reports of April 1993 to April 1998 inclusive). <http://www.state.gov/www/global/terrorism/annual_reports.html> [Accessed 13 November 2001].

U.S. Department of State, Foreign Terrorist Organizations, Designations by Secretary of State Madeleine K. Albright, Office of the Coordinator for Counterterrorism, Oct. 8, 1999. <http://www.state.gov/www/global/terrorism/fto_1999.html> [Accessed 13 November 2001].

Private Internet Web Sites

Anti-Defamation League On-Line. <http://www.adl.org/default.htm> [Accessed 13 November 2001].

B'nai B'rith Anti-Defamation League Archived Press Releases on Militias. <http://www.adl.org/PresRele/Militi_71/CD_71.asp> [Accessed 13 November 2001].

CAIN Web Service. Conflict Archive on the Internet: The Northern Ireland Conflict (1968 to the Present). <http://cain.ulst.ac.uk/index.html>. One of the most detailed sources of information on the North Ireland conflict [Accessed 13 November 2001].

CAIN Web Service. Malcolm Sutton: An Index of Deaths from the Conflict in Ireland. <http://cain.ulst.ac.uk/sutton/book/ index.html>. Comprehensive statistics on deaths in Northern Ireland conflict. [Accessed 13 November 2001].

Center for Democracy and Technology. CDT's Counter-Terrorism Issues Page. <http://www.cdt.org/policy/terrorism/> [Accessed 13 November 2001].

Defence and Security Review. <http://www.pollux.com/dsr97/> [Accessed 13 November 2001].

Dossier: Intelligencia Terrorismo: Pagina Actualizada Semanalmente y Publicada Desde Concepción, Chile <http://www.geocities.com/cebp12232214/>. Spanish-language weekly report maintained by Carlos Eduardo Basso Prieto on terrorist groups active in Central and Latin America. [Last Accessed 17 January 2001]

Freedom, Democracy, Peace: Power, Democide, and War HOME PAGE of R. J. Rummel <http://www.hawaii.edu/powerkills/>. Excellent resource for information on state terror, genocide, and social science literature related to terrorism studies. [Accessed 13 November 2001].

International Association for Counter-Terrorism and Security Professionals. <http://www.cdt.org/policy/terrorism/>. {Accessed 13 November 2001].

Jane's Intelligence Watch Report, Terrorism Watch Report. (Certain sections of this site are available only on a subscription basis.) <http://intelweb.janes.com/>. [Accessed 13 November 2001].

Jane's Intelligence Watch Report, Terrorist and Insurgency Groups. <http://intelweb.janes.com/resource/Groups_table.htm>. Access limited to registered users. [Accessed 13 November 2001].

The Militia Watchdog Page. Monitors "far-right extremism" in the United States. <http://www.militia-watchdog.org/>. [Accessed 13 November 2001].

RAND Corporation Homepage. <http://www.rand.org/>. [Accessed 13 November 2001].

RAND Corporation. Select publications related to terrorism. <http://www.rand.org/publications/>. [Accessed 13 November 2001].

Southern Poverty Law Center, Homepage. <http://www.splcenter.org/splc.html>. [Accessed 13 November 2001].

Southern Poverty Law Center, Intelligence Project on Militias. <http://www.splcenter.org/intelligenceproject/ip-index.html>. [Accessed 13

November 2001].

Southern Poverty Law Center, "Active Hate Groups in the U.S." <http://
www.splcenter.org/cgi-bin/goframe.pl?dirname=/
intelligenceproject&pagename=ip-2.html>. [Accessed 13 November
2001].

The Terrorism Research Center: Next-Generation Terrorism Analysis. <http:/
/www.terrorism.com/index.shtml>. [Accessed 13 November 2001].

Terrorists, Freedom Fighters, Crusaders, Propagandists, and Mercenaries
on the Net. <http://www.cromwell-intl.com/security/netusers.html>.
[Accessed 13 November 2001].

This is Baader-Meinhof: Germany in the Post-War Decade of Terror, 1968-
1977. <http://www.baader-meinhof.com/index.htm>. Site by Richard
Huffman covering in-depth the activities of various West German leftist terrorist groups focusing on the Red Army Faction but covering
many other similar organizations as well. [Accessed 13 November
2001].

Virtual World of Intelligence. Site concerned with "Conspiracies, Most
Wanted, Intelligence Agencies, Internet Crime, Law Enforcement, Military, Terrorists Activities" and other topics.<http://
www.virtualfreesites.com/covert.militias.html>. [Accessed 13 November 2001].

On-Line Linkage: All of the above links can be accessed at the author's
<http://www.isu.edu/~andesean/TERRORLINKS.htm> homepage site.
[Accessed 13 November 2001].

About the Authors

Stephen Sloan (B.A., Washington Square College of New York University; M.A. and Ph.D., Graduate School of Arts and Sciences at New York University) is Professor of Political Science at the University of Oklahoma. Dr. Sloan's interest in the study of terrorism is part of his long-term commitment to the study of political violence. His fieldwork in the Republic of Indonesia, coinciding with the abortive coup d'état of 1965 in which over 100,000 people were killed, led to the publication of his first book, *A Study in Political Violence: The Indonesian Experience* (Rand McNally, 1971). Since 1966 Dr. Sloan has pioneered the development of simulations of terrorist incidents to assist domestic and foreign law-enforcement departments, as well as the U.S. Army and U.S. Air Force, in developing counterterrorist operational skills. His policy and field training led to publication of a second book, *Simulating Terrorism* (University of Oklahoma Press, 1980). Dr. Sloan also has been deeply involved in formulating counterterrorism doctrine for the military, as well as contributing to an evaluation of U.S. policies toward terrorism. In 1986 he served as an expert contributor to the Vice President's Task Force on Combating Terrorism. Dr. Sloan's latest books include: *Low-Intensity Conflict: Old Threats in a New World*, coedited with Edwin G. Corr (Westview, 1992), and *Corporate Aviation Security: The Next Frontier in Aerospace Operations*, coauthored with Harry Pizer (University of Oklahoma Press, 1992). Dr. Sloan is also the first visiting fellow of the Oklahoma National Memorial Institute for the Prevention of Terrorism.

Sean K. Anderson (B.A., Western Washington University; M.A. and Ph.D., University of Oklahoma) is Associate Professor of Political Science at Idaho State University. From 1980 to 1982, Dr. Anderson worked as chief editor in the International Department of the Pars News Agency (now the Islamic Republic News Agency) in Tehran, Iran. In April 1990 he presented a paper, "Iranian State Sponsorship of Terrorism," at the third annual Counter-Terror Study Centre conference held at Winnipeg, Manitoba, which was later revised and published in *Conflict Quarterly*, Volume 11, Number 4 (Fall 1991). He also wrote "Warnings Versus Alarms: Terrorist Threat Analysis

587

Applied to the Iranian State-Run Media," published in *Studies in Conflict and Terrorism*, 21 (Fall 1998): 277-303. Dr. Anderson also works with state and local emergency planning and disaster relief agencies and also participated in the April 2000 inaugural conference of the Oklahoma City Memorial Institute for the Prevention of Terrorism.